Early Modern Natural Law in East-Central Europe

Early Modern Natural Law

VOLUME 5

The titles published in this series are listed at *brill.com/emnl*

Early Modern Natural Law in East-Central Europe

Edited by

Gábor Gángó

BRILL

LEIDEN | BOSTON

Cover illustrations: Portrait of Łukasz Opaliński, by Stanisław Kostecki (c. 1640), Wikimedia Commons; Portrait of Carl Anton Martini, Institute of Public Law, University of Innsbruck.

The Library of Congress Cataloging-in-Publication Data is available online at https://catalog.loc.gov
LC record available at https://lccn.loc.gov/2023003856

Typeface for the Latin, Greek, and Cyrillic scripts: "Brill". See and download: brill.com/brill-typeface.

ISSN 2589-5982
ISBN 978-90-04-54582-3 (hardback)
ISBN 978-90-04-54584-7 (e-book)

Printed by Printforce, the Netherlands

Contents

PART 3
Hungary and Transylvania

PART 4
Russia

Preface

Approaches to Natural Law in East-Central Europe

Gábor Gángó and Knud Haakonssen

The present volume has its origins in an international conference on 'Natural law in Eastern Europe' and is a contribution to the network on Natural Law 1625–1850.[1] The Network is devoted to inter-disciplinary research on early modern natural law considered as an intellectual culture anchored in educational institutions but with wide-ranging intellectual, political and social significance.[2] Without ignoring the common idea of natural law as a chapter in the doctrinal history of philosophy or legal and political theory, this approach identifies natural law not in terms of universal ideas but instead by means of its institutional, educational, literary, and linguistic manifestations in widely different locales. By the same token, it suspends common ideas of development and progress and adopts an episodic approach to the subject.[3] With this programme the network seeks to supplement more traditional lines of scholarship on natural law, of which there is an extensive amount in various specialist disciplines as far as North-Western Europe, especially Germany, is concerned. In contrast, the Eastern European region has been rather underexplored territory, but the wide brief adopted by the Network has made it obvious to address the question of natural law east of the Empire and in its borderlands. Many systematic, historical, and interdisciplinary questions have not hitherto been

1 Max Weber Centre for Advanced Cultural and Social Studies, University of Erfurt, 21–23 November 2019. The conference was generously supported by the German Research Foundation (DFG) and by Erfurt University.

2 For a presentation of the Network and its general methodology, see Frank Grunert, Knud Haakonssen, and Diethelm Klippel, 'Natural Law 1625–1850. An International Research Network,' *Aufklärung*, 30 (2018): 267–276.

3 For some samples in a fast-growing literature, see Gábor Gángó, 'Johann Christian von Boineburg, Samuel Pufendorf, and the Foundation Myth of Modern Natural Law,' *History of European Ideas*, 48 (2022) https://www.tandfonline.com/doi/abs/10.1080/01916599.2022.2099044 (accessed on 17 November 2022). Knud Haakonssen and Ian Hunter, ed., *The Cambridge Companion to Pufendorf* (Cambridge: Cambridge University Press, 2023); Ian Hunter, *Rival Enlightenments: Civil and Metaphysical Philosophy in Early Modern Germany* (Cambridge: Cambridge University Press, 2001); Ian Hunter, 'The Law of Nature and Nations,' in *The Routledge Companion to Eighteenth Century Philosophy*, ed. Aaron Garrett (Abingdon, Oxon, 2014), 559–592; Felix Waldmann, 'Natural Law and the Chair of Ethics in the University of Naples, 1703–1769,' *Modern Intellectual History*, 19 (2022): 54–80.

asked, let alone answered. Which works and tenets of modern natural law reached East-Central Europe, and how? How was it received, what influence did it have? And how did theorists and users of natural law in Eastern Europe enrich the pan-European discourse?

Given that natural law was anything but a unitary theoretical structure, the papers here are devoted to the particular manifestations of natural law in multiple, often overlapping but also contrasting contexts. On the one hand the socio-political characteristics of individual nations in the region are invoked, on the other due consideration is given to over-arching political structures in the region. Within the three state formations – Russia, Poland-Lithuania, and the Habsburg Empire – a social, political, and religious multiplicity co-existed with spatially overlapping and synchronous, though distinct interpretive communities. With regard to the reception of natural law in these different interpretive communities, parallel and rivalling phenomena could be detected and the interconnectedness of these belong to the primary fields of interest in the present volume.

Including East-Central Europe in the geographical spectrum for early modern natural law opened up hitherto underexplored fields of investigation. The present volume presents, for the first time, more or less detailed historical and interpretative accounts of the instruction in natural law in East European cities such as Saint Petersburg, Vilnius, Warsaw, Cracow, Elbląg, Toruń, Gdańsk, Prague, Vienna, Sárospatak, Debrecen, and Cluj. These accounts are embedded in the context of religious and political debates of the region. Details of the already established reception of Hugo Grotius by Polish Socinians, the use of Samuel Pufendorf's manuals in Lutheran towns of Royal Prussia, or the reception of natural law by Unitarians in Transylvania highlight the potential of seeing natural jurisprudence as an integral part of political and religious counter-cultures in East-Central Europe. The volume pays special attention to the tension between ideas of the state and its legislation, administration, and policies, on the one hand, and identitarian discourses of religious or national groups, on the other; both the perspective from above and that from below made use of certain elements of modern natural law.

The first thematic bloc of the volume deals with Poland-Lithuania. The four contributions make it clear that both in its Roman Catholic and its Lutheran form natural law was instrumental in the development of critical positions towards the existing political system of the Polish-Lithuanian noble republic. In 'Natural law in Polish and Lithuanian sources: a comparative perspective,' Steffen Huber reconstructs the humanist-Aristotelian Catholic natural law tradition in Vilnius, Warsaw and Cracow. The paper points out the context of practical philosophy in the Jesuit school network, centred at the University of

Vilnius, and it presents a number of hitherto under-explored archive materials. On the basis of these sources, Huber outlines the main characteristics of Polish-Lithuanian (academic) natural law as a set of rather unsystematic elements embracing naturalism, contractarianism, and cultural pluralism.

In 'The influence of natural law on the discourse of toleration in seventeenth-century Poland-Lithuania,' Karin Friedrich explores Grotius's views of Polish religious policies together with his impact on Polish political thought and legislation. Friedrich concludes that Grotius's idea of sociability suited the civic humanism and the republican model of the Commonwealth more than Lipsius's *respublica Christiana*. She also shows how the views of Grotius as a religious thinker reverberated in some system-critical circles of radical Protestants in seventeenth-century Poland.

Anna Grześkowiak-Krwawicz contributes a comprehensive intellectual profile of the Polish political system in order to understand the context in which natural law arguments for modernisation and Europeanisation of the political culture were embedded. In 'Why was the political discourse of the Polish-Lithuanian nobility so weakly influenced by natural law?,' she argues that Polish discourses did not adopt natural law as the basis for theories of the state and authority. Instead, Polish intellectuals in the early modernity turned to these ideas only when they became relevant to human rights and thus struck a chord with the growing need to account not only for political society but for the entire social community.

Gábor Gángó's paper, 'Ernst König and the teaching of natural law at the academic gymnasia of Royal Prussia,' shows that the rector of the academic gymnasia in Toruń and Elbląg, Ernst König, not only introduced the teaching of natural law in these institutions, but his efforts exerted a lasting impact on the instruction in natural jurisprudence in all three gymnasia of Royal Prussia, including the Athenaeum in Gdańsk. The works of König's most important author, Samuel Pufendorf, served varying functions according to the rector's changing didactic goals. His principal objective was to transform the teaching of political science by means of Pufendorf rather than to introduce modern science and philosophy into the curricula of the Lutheran gymnasia.

In the section on the Austrian Empire, Martin P. Schennach analyses a number of scholarly works of jurisprudence with natural law references in Austria in the late eighteenth century. These were works that paved the way for, or reflected public law in the composite state of the Habsburgs. As his 'Natural law in Austrian and Hungarian science of public law in the second half of the eighteenth century: a comparison' shows, Austrian and Hungarian *Staatsrechtslehre* had similar roots in *Reichspublizistik* and *Territorialstaatsrecht*. Nevertheless, natural law and *Allgemeines Staatsrecht* played different roles in Austrian and Hungarian public law. Whereas natural law was avoided by Austrian writers, evidently afraid of its emancipatory potential, Hungarian scholars had no fear of listing natural law among the sources of Hungarian 'ius publicum.'

Ivo Cerman focuses on the role natural law played in academic teaching in Bohemia. His 'The chair of natural law in Prague 1748–1775,' based on extensive archival research, provides a chronological reconstruction of scholarly treatises, lectures, and dissertations at and around the University of Prague. On the basis of the works and teaching activity of Nikolaus Ignaz Koenigsmann, Josef Anton Schuster, and Johann Franz Lothar Schrodt, Cerman outlines the general characteristics of the Bohemian version of natural law, both private and public, in a Catholic context.

The papers of the third bloc of this volume focus on Hungary and Transylvania. Borbála Lovas's paper, 'The dream of freedom, peace and order: Natural and divine law in the works of a Unitarian bishop from sixteenth-century Transylvania,' outlines György Enyedi's intellectual portrait and highlights biblical and literary aspects of his sermons. Lovas presents the reception of Enyedi's *Explicationes Locorum Veteris et Novi Testamenti* (1598) by and in circles around Hugo Grotius, John Locke, or Sir Isaac Newton and shows how some political thoughts in his sermons anticipated a constellation in which the theses of modern natural law were received by the Unitarian Church in Transylvania in the seventeenth and eighteenth centuries.

Péter Balázs and Gábor Gángó suggest that political culture in early modern Hungary and Transylvania was more complex in terms of language and tradition than commonly thought. Research into the reception of classical republicanism and ancient constitutionalism should be complemented by systematic exploration of the impact of natural law. Their paper 'Protestant schooling and natural law in Transylvania and Hungary' gives a comprehensive account on the reception of natural law in Unitarian and Reformed Protestant institutions. The survey is based on Balázs's basic research concerning the Reformed Protestant and the Unitarian College in Cluj and Gángó's archival research in Sárospatak and Debrecen. These institutions were by far the most significant places for the dissemination of the tenets of modern natural law.

To complement the picture with portraits of prominent intellectuals, this section contains two studies, one that present the life and works of the Chancellor of Transylvania and a pupil of Pufendorf, Miklós Bethlen; and one that introduces the Protestant minister Miklós Apáti, a friend of the Cartesian Pierre Poiret. The author of both contributions, József Simon addresses the question of how natural law proved inspiring in Miklós Bethlen's *Autobiography* (1701), especially in its voluminous philosophical Preface as well as in

Miklós Apáti's *Vita triumphans civilis* (Amsterdam 1688), a moral and philosophical guide for the Protestant community in Hungary. In a close reading 'Political psychology and natural law in Miklós Bethlen's Preface to his *Autobiography* (1708)' Simon suggests that Bethlen through attendance at Pufendorf's lectures in Heidelberg in 1661 had been inspired to a socio-psychological theory of 'civic' or 'moral qualities.' As Simon argues, Bethlen did not accept the theory of natural law as an ultimate explanation of human social community. However, Bethlen's themes (public communication, reputation, honour, shame, and ambition as political passions) are situated within the theoretical language created by modern natural law. As to Apáti's work, Simon establishes the parallels between *Vita triumphans civilis* and Antoine Le Grand's *Institutio philosophiae* in his study 'Moral indifference and hypothetical moral necessity in Miklós Apáti's *Vita triumphans civilis* (1688),' with special attention to their theory of free will and moral obligation.

In the section on Russia, Ivo Cerman revisits an enigmatic figure in the history of natural law, Frédéric-Henri Strube de Piermont, a participant in various endeavours to give the legal system in Russia a natural law foundation. In 'Strube de Piermont: The passionate natural law in Russia' Cerman situates Strube's story against the backdrop of the broader history of the reception of natural law in Russia. The turn towards the passionate side of human nature as a foundation for natural law was a European phenomenon, often based upon a dubious interpretation of Christian Thomasius, who also taught Strube. In his time this German émigré was an influential author whose *Recherche nouvelle de l'origine et des fondemens du droit de la nature* (1740) as well as *Ebauche des loix naturelles* (1744) fitted into this broader development in European natural law theory.

The studies assembled here will undoubtedly give rise to several general conclusions, but we would make the following observations. In the Eastern part of the European continent the institutions were generally characterised by a sharper profile than their professors, and the confessional differences provide more fundamental dividing lines than the state or national borders. Communication and knowledge transfer seem to have taken place only within national *and* confessional borders. Apart from indirect polemics, there was no inter-confessional communication, while scholarly exchange across national borders existed only with Western university centres. Accordingly, the dissemination of locally created knowledge of natural law in East-Central Europe was confined to regional contexts. In connection with communication, it is also important to note that in the absence of printing machines, manuscript books and hand-written lecture texts had to be relied upon, and they were widely used.

It is notable that the reception of modern, post-Grotian natural law in East-Central Europe saw a confessionalisation of these ideas, a subject that invites closer comparison with similar developments in the West. It is clear that neither a moral consensus disconnected from theology, nor an inter-confessional common denominator was formulated on a natural law basis. The propagation of Protestant natural law was congruent with the propagation of religious Reformation. While important branches of natural law in Germany at least in principle aimed at a theoretical foundation for peaceful co-existence of the confessions as provided for in the major peace treaties, in the East natural law was uniformly a theoretical instrument in support of the antagonistic positions in religious politics. A few exceptions apart, Protestant students brought home natural law as a concise, ready-for-use curriculum rather than an open intellectual enterprise. Schoolbooks, compendia, natural law catechisms form the majority of natural law books in the school libraries.

The development of Catholic natural law seems fundamentally different from the parallel phenomena in Germany. In Germany the instruction of natural law at the Catholic universities while clearly critical of the Protestant ideas, especially those of Pufendorf and Thomasius, nevertheless absorbed a number of compatible elements from the Protestant tradition. But in East-Central Europe Catholic natural law kept its distance. Before the partition of Poland, Catholic natural law there took a sharply polemical stance towards Pufendorf. Particular to Polish-Lithuanian political discourse was a humanist-Aristotelian natural law inspired by the teaching of Francisco Suárez at the University of Ingolstadt which was received at the University of Vilnius. As for the Habsburg lands, after 1777 the Imperial Court imposed the Catholic natural law of Carl Anton Martini as a unified theory of the Empire (*Gesamtstaatsidee*). Thanks to its monopolized curricula in Catholic educational institutions, this theory of the Austrian state was propagated from the chairs of natural law to the Empire as a whole. Catholic natural law was placed in the service of political absolutism.

There was a fundamental difference between Protestant and Catholic natural law in the dissemination of the tenets of natural law which in the former case was a from-below process in the Protestant confessions, while a from-above one in the case of the Catholic Church. The objective of the former was to promote the equal status of citizens in private law and to secure religious tolerance within the framework of absolute state power. The ambition of Catholic natural law teaching was to offer a justice-based, synallagmatic legal theory of the relation between the absolute state and the citizen instead of the idea of political authority based upon power or on the right of conquest. Especially after the Turkish wars, Protestant emphasis was on security against state violence and intolerance, while Catholic natural law was a means for the government itself to establish religious and social peace.

Protestant and Catholic natural law had a common denominator in the form of their wider intellectual impact. They both contributed to the processes of what is commonly understood as enlightenment the region, i.e., to an emphasis on the importance of rational and coherent argument in morals, politics and theology and to the application of moral philosophical principles to social theory and legal codification. They facilitated the introduction of a new political and juridical discourse that was supranational and used a terminology compatible with that of the West. Through the education of the political class and the ecclesiastical intelligentsia, these achievements became part of the wider political culture, even if natural law did not have the impact on legal reform and the conduct of politics that it had in several areas in the West. This confessionally embedded natural-law Enlightenment, focusing on private law and social theory, was arguably more significant, at least in its consequences, than the commonly explored and celebrated elements of East European Enlightenment that were inspired by such figures of the Francophone Enlightenment as Voltaire, Helvétius, and Rousseau: the derision of religion and the clergy as well as the critique of refined civilization and luxury.

Natural law was transmitted to East-Central Europe as a large, broadening set of doctrines from Pufendorf to Thomasius, Wolff, and Heineccius, developed with Grotius as a common but contested point of reference. The ideas came in the form of these thinkers' own treatises but first of all in textbooks and compendia written by their commentators. These natural law doctrines harboured deep theoretical differences, and they were adapted for use in a wide variety of locales. Nevertheless, they did reflect the relatively stable Westphalian political and social system that most of them were aimed at shoring up in their different places and times during the long period from the 1660s to the 1789 French Revolution (though they continued to have significant influence also in the post-Revolutionary period). This relative stability becomes manifest in comparison with the fundamental changes that the East-Central European region underwent in this period: an increasingly intolerant Poland-Lithuania from the Swedish wars, through the Great Northern War, to its successive partitions; the Czech lands, Hungary, Transylvania and the composite state formation they belonged to, the Habsburg Empire as a whole, from the Turkish and religious wars on its South-Eastern confines, through a series of wars threatening its very existence, to the consolidation of its ruler dynasty, its borders, and its administration. From this follows that the function of natural law as a social theory changed a lot with relation to the changing political circumstances.

To this purpose the natural law ideas that the professors of natural law in East-Central Europe had adopted from the West were well suited. Like their colleagues in the West, they adopted the theory with the help of cases and examples taken from their national legal and political traditions and applied it to the reality of their respective communities. Modern natural law had a flexibility that enabled them to select, compile and organise the tenets they needed. This was also the case in the West, but the greater complexity and deeper conflicts in the East meant that natural law here lost its coherent character and became an applied social theory and a practical guide to morality sooner and more obviously than in the West.

The adoption of modern natural law was enabled, most of all, by intellectual and confessional links to the West. Its vehicle was the confessional affiliations that we discussed above, not the intellectual exchange of the *respublica litteraria*. It was the changes in the economic, political, and social circumstances that necessitated the adaptation of a suitable vocabulary of human sciences and political discourse. For many professors, the humanist-Aristotelian vocabulary no longer seemed adaptable to social reality, and this led to a precarious balance between the system-critical and the system-supportive sides of natural law (most of all in its Pufendorfian variant) when it was used in the East-Central European political systems. It was this tension that generally resulted in the previously mentioned emphasis on private law and the neglect of elements such as public law, political contract theory, and especially the anthropology of basic rights (first of all, the right to preservation of life). Instead, the focus of the academic courses was on private contracts and legal relations within communities: marriage, family, social relations, and not least freedom of conscience and religious politics. These cautiously critical attitudes were especially noticeable towards the religious policies by the Habsburg Court in Hungary or the Catholic political elite in Poland.

The conflict between the old humanist-Aristotelian curriculum and the new natural law in East-Central Europe led to temporary compromises in some places but in most to the eventual victory of the old curriculum. This was the case in Toruń and Elbląg as well as in Sárospatak. And if natural law had difficulties retaining a lasting role in the educational system, it is not surprising that its impact on political discourse was rather limited. The humanist curriculum was deeply anchored in the politics of Poland and Hungary. The republican political ethos and civic virtue ethics in a Ciceronian vein survived the challenge of natural law with long repercussions for politics in theory and practice in East-Central Europe.

Acknowledgement

The editor wishes to express his sincere gratitude to Knud Haakonssen for initiating investigations on East European natural law traditions at the Research Centre for Early Modern natural law, Max Weber Centre for Advanced Cultural and Social Studies of the University of Erfurt. The editor also thanks Professor Haakonssen for wide-ranging professional, linguistic, and logistic support as a series editor during the editing process of this volume.

Notes on Contributors

Péter Balázs

studied history and French studies at the University of Szeged, Hungary. He obtained his Ph.D. (2004) in philosophy in *co-tutelle* at the Université Paris I / the University of Szeged on the political and moral philosophy of the marquis d'Argenson. He is Associate Professor at the Modern History Department of the University of Szeged and author of a book devoted to the Hungarian Enlightenment and a number of studies written on the European Enlightenment and the historiography of the French revolution, published in Hungarian and international periodicals, such as *Le Dix-huitième Siècle* and *La Lettre Clandestine*.

Ivo Cerman

is a Czech historian who specializes on the history of ethics, natural law and aristocratic education in the eighteenth century. His background comes from the Universities of Prague and Tübingen. His publications include *Habsburgischer Adel und Aufklärung* (Stuttgart: Franz Steiner Verlag, 2010); *The Enlightenment in Bohemia: Religion, morality and multiculturalism* (Oxford: Voltaire Foundation, 2011) and *Casanova: Enlightenment Philosopher* (Oxford: Voltaire Foundation, 2016). He is lecturer in modern history at the University of South Bohemia.

Karin Friedrich

is Professor of Early Modern European History at the University of Aberdeen. After a Ph.D. from Georgetown University she held a post at the School of Slavonic and East European Studies, UCL. Her research focuses on the German-Polish borderlands in the context of early modern Europe, citizenship, religious and political identities, and the constitution of early modern commonwealths. Her books include, among others, the prize-winning *The Other Prussia. Poland, Prussia and Liberty, 1569–1772* (Cambridge University Press, 2000/2006, translated into Polish), and *Brandenburg-Prussia, 1466–1806. The Rise of a Composite State* (Palgrave, 2011). She is currently finalising a political biography of Bogusław Radziwiłł (1620–1669).

Gábor Gángó

studied history, literary studies (Ph.D. 1997), and philosophy (Ph.D. 2004) at ELTE Budapest University. He has been working at various universities, including the University of Vienna (Visiting Professor, 2000–2001), Pázmány Péter

Catholic University Budapest (Full Professor, 2011–2022), and the University of Padua (Research Fellow, 2021–2023). He is scientific advisor at the Institute of Philosophy of the Research Centre for the Humanities, Budapest, and Associated Fellow at the Max Weber Centre for Advanced Cultural and Social Studies, Erfurt University. His historical and philosophical interest in East-Central Europe ranges from the intellectual history of the Early Modernity and the nineteenth-century Habsburg Empire to variations of twentieth-century cultural modernism.

Anna Grześkowiak-Krwawicz
Professor, (Ph.D. 1986, Polish Academy of Sciences, Institute of History) is head of the Enlightenment Literature Department, Institute of Literary Research, Polish Academy of Sciences since 2007, professor since 2013. She was president of the Polish Society for Eighteenth-Century Studies (2002–2022). Her main interests encompass the political ideas and discourse in the Polish-Lithuanian Commonwealth in the sixteenth–eighteenth centuries, and the culture of the Enlightenment. Her most important books in English are *Queen Liberty: The concept of freedom in the Polish-Lithuanian Commonwealth* (Brill 2012) and *The Political Discourse of the Polish-Lithuanian Commonwealth: Concepts and Ideas* (Routledge 2021).

Knud Haakonssen
has taught philosophy and intellectual history in Australia, the US, the UK, Germany and Denmark. He has studied the diaspora of modern natural law, its adaptation as moral philosophy, and its academic institutionalisation in various contexts: *Natural Law and Moral Philosophy* (Cambridge UP 1996), *Reid on Practical Ethics* (Edinburgh UP 2007), (co-ed.) *Ludvig Holberg (1684–1754). Learning and Literature in the Nordic Enlightenment* (Routledge 2017), (co-ed.) *Cambridge Companion to Pufendorf* (Cambridge UP 2022), (co-ed.) Francis Hutcheson, *System of Moral Philosophy* (Liberty Fund 2023), (ed.) Pufendorf, *The Law of Nature and Nations* (Liberty Fund forthcoming). Also (ed.) *Cambridge History of Eighteenth-Century Philosophy* (Cambridge UP 2006), (ed.) *Cambridge Companion to Adam Smith* (Cambridge UP 2006).

Steffen Huber
is head of the Department of Polish Philosophy at the Institute of Philosophy, Jagiellonian University, Cracow. His publications concern early modern philosophy, e.g. a monograph on the Polish philosopher Andrzej Frycz Modrzewski and a German language introduction to the history of social philosophy in Poland (both 2014). He translated philosophical and literary works from Pol-

ish into German. Presently, he works on an edition of manuscript sources from the seventeenth century. Last English language publication: 'The Philosopher's Refusal of Action. Andrzej Frycz Modrzewski (1503–1572),' in: *Penser et agir à la Renaissance. Thought and action in the Renaissance*, ed. Philippe Desan and Véronique Ferrer (Genève 2020).

Borbála Lovas
studied at ELTE University, Budapest, and received her Ph.D. in European and Hungarian Renaissance Studies. She is assistant professor at the Department of Old Hungarian Literature, ELTE University, and principal investigator of the research group History of Early Modern Unitarian Sermon Literature in Transylvania and Hungary. Her research interests include sixteenth–seventeenth-century vernacular sermons, biblical and love stories, manuscript culture, and the printing history of works by Hungarian authors. Her latest paper in English, 'The Posthumous Reception of an Antitrinitarian Bishop at Home and Abroad: The Afterlife of György Enyedi's *Explicationes*,' was published in the volume *Print Culture at the Crossroads: The Book and Central Europe*, ed. by. Elizabeth Dillenburg, Howard Louthan, and Drew B. Thomas (Brill 2021).

Martin P. Schennach
(Prof. Dr. Dr., MAS) is professor for legal history at the University of Innsbruck (since 2012). He studied history and law in Innsbruck and Vienna (both completed with a Ph.D.). Post-graduate studies in Vienna ('Master of advanced studies for historical and archival science'), member of the *Institut für Österreichische Geschichtsforschung* in Vienna; habilitation for 'legal history' (2008) and 'Austrian history' (2011). His main areas of research include history of legislation and codification, constitutional history (especially state-building in early modern times, assemblies of the Imperial estates, early constitutionalism), historical implementation of the law, history of criminal law, research on revolts in early modern times, history of science (especially the history of public law in Austria).

József Simon
studied philosophy and Hungarian literature at the Universities of Szeged, Hungary, and Göttingen, Germany. He is Associate Professor at the Department of Philosophy of Szeged University and a Research Fellow at the Institute of Philosophy of the Research Centre for the Humanities in Budapest, Hungary. He has widely published in the English, German, and Hungarian

languages on early modern history of philosophy, including his monograph *Die Religionsphilosophie Christian Franckens 1552–1610?: Atheismus und radikale Reformation im Frühneuzeitlichen Ostmitteleuropa* (Wiesbaden: Harrassowitz, 2008).

PART 1

Poland-Lithuania

CHAPTER 1

Natural Law in Polish and Lithuanian Sources: A Comparative Perspective

Steffen Huber

1 Introduction

For centuries Polish and Lithuanian philosophers used the notion of natural law. Given the unique form of government of their republic, did they elaborate a specific understanding of natural law?

The very beginning and the very end of the Polish-Lithuanian union brought about works which are generally viewed as natural law philosophy. Shortly after 1400, Paulus Vladimiri, Francesco Zabarella and Stanislaus de Scarbimiria, while representing the interests of Jogaila (Jagiełło) on the European scene and especially at the Council of Constance, created a normative vision of politics on the basis of *ius naturae* and *ius gentium*.[1] The authors of the 1791 constitution applied the enlightened theory of separation of powers (Montesquieu).[2] Around 1800, Hieronim Stroynowski and Joachim Chreptowicz followed the French Physiocrats.[3] Feliks Słotwiński and Adam Jerzy Czartoryski incorporated Kantian moral philosophy in their understanding of natural law.[4]

As for the intervening period and especially the seventeenth century, there is no discernible *opinio communis* among historians. Unlike in Western

1 Paulus Vladimiri, 'Tractatus de Potestate Papae et Imperatoris Respectu Infidelium,' in *Starodawne Prawa Polskiego Pomniki*, ed. Michał Bobrzynski, vol. 1 (Kraków: Sumptibus Academiae Litterarum, 1878), 159–194; Thomas Wünsch, 'Kirchenreform und Konziliarismus in Polen. Europäischer Kontext und eigenständige Entwicklung,' *Acta Mediaevalia Lublin* 12 (1999): 159–173.

2 *New Constitution of the Government of Poland, Established by the Revolution, the Third of May, 1791* (London: J. Debrett, 1791).

3 Hieronim Stroynowski, *Nauka prawa przyrodzonego, politycznego, ekonomiki polityczney i prawa narodów* (Wilno [Vilnius]: w Drukarni Królewskiey przy Akademii, 1785). Joachim Litawor Chreptowicz, *O prawie natury pismo oryginalne jednego z współziomków* (Warszawa: w Drukarni Gazety Warszawskiey, 1814).

4 Feliks Słotwiński, *Prawo natury prywatne* (Kraków: w Drukarni u Stanisława Gieszkowskiego, 1825). Toulouzan (= Adam Jerzy Czartoryski), *Essai sur la diplomatie ou manuscrit d'un philhellène* (Paris and Marseille: Firmin Didot Frères, 1830).

 | DOI:10.1163/9789004545847_002

Europe, natural law in our region has not yet become a subject of comprehensive research. It is difficult to say whether it was an essential or rather a decorative element of early modern Polish and Lithuanian thought. Thus, it is worthwhile comparing features of Western and Eastern European natural law and having a closer look on selected sources.

2 A West-East Perspective

2.1 *The West*

Over the last decades, more research has been carried out on the history of natural law thought in Western than in Eastern Europe. But even in the West there is no fixed canon and we certainly cannot expect such a thing to be found for the Eastern part of the continent. What concept, then, could be of use at the beginning of our analysis? A popular approximation runs as follows: The pre-modern versions of natural law stemmed from Scholastics, mainly Aquinas and his followers throughout the centuries. Renaissance humanism and Protestant ideas of the sixteenth century (Luther, Melanchthon, Calvin, Zwingli, Sozzini). The second school of Salamanca (Suárez, Soto) often appears as a phenomenon of transition, while Grotius is unanimously viewed as the father of modern natural law, followed by competing naturalists (Hobbes, Pufendorf, Thomasius) and metaphysicians (Alberti, Leibniz, Wolff) as well as influential commentators (Barbeyrac), eclectic authors (de Vattel) and unique heirs (Rousseau). Kant's critical philosophy tends to stand for a synthesis effectively solving the contradictions between 'Epicurean,' 'Aristotelian' and 'Platonist' approaches and, thus, for the perspective vanishing point of early modern natural law. Conceptually, natural law integrates metaphysics and its critique, ethical and political theory, and juridical thought aiming at the definition of the fundaments and principles of social normativity in an enlightened and prevailingly absolutist manner.

If such an understanding was to be directly applied to the Polish and Lithuanian discourse, it would not leave much place for a regional natural law tradition. Luckily, this canon is all but set in stone. The continuity of natural law and its differentiation into 'pre-modern' and 'modern' phases remains a challenge.[5] Knud Haakonssen observes that natural law as 'an academic dis-

5 Jean-Francois Courtine, 'Vitoria, Suárez et la naissance du droit naturel moderne,' in *Histoire de la philosophie politique*, ed. Alain Renaut (Paris: Calmann-Lévy, 1999), vol. 2, 127–181; Merio Scattola, *Das Naturrecht vor dem Naturrecht: Zur Geschichte des 'ius naturae' im 16. Jahrhundert* (Tübingen: Niemeyer, 1999).

cipline institutionalized for political reasons [...] harboured fundamentally different philosophies.' However, the 'lack of doctrinal coherence' is 'obscured by the fact that natural law of all sorts shared a distinctive idiom.'[6] In a similar perspective, Ian Hunter stresses that 'the central topos of natural law – the idea of a law that is natural in the double sense of being embedded in human nature and accessed through natural reason – did not delineate a common intellectual object.' He therefore criticizes 'a good deal of recent scholarship' for tending to 'over-unif[y the] discursive forms and over-simplif[y] their historical contexts and forms of development.'[7] The latter remark refers to eighteenth-century Western Europe but can be extended to other periods and regions. From the point of view of medieval studies, Dieter Schwab points out the necessity of acknowledging the philosophical character of natural law which is not a specifically juridical term. It does not refer exclusively to the public or social order. Primarilly, it refers rather to a natural order of being in the widest sense, including natural ethics. Following the model of Roman law, terms such as 'ius naturale' or 'lex naturalis' are not only predominantly used as synonyms but can be defined in a broader perspective obtaining even the natural instinct of the animals to which group, by a certain part of his essence, man belongs.[8]

Natural law meandered back and forth between metaphysics and naturalism, religion and secularism. As Hunter observed in the *Institutiones* of Thomasius, the religious doctrine could be even an instrument of secularizing natural law.[9] This is also the case in many East European contexts.

Finally, it should be remembered that the systematization of natural law started with Samuel Pufendorf.[10] From an East European perspective, this heritage proves problematic. Like Hobbes and Thomasius, Pufendorf had a very weak contemporary reception in East-Central Europe. In his historiographic approach Pufendorf tended to ignore the pre-Grotian, Renaissance humanist, and early Jesuit models which influenced the Eastern European tradition.

6 Knud Haakonssen, 'Early Modern Natural Law Theories,' in *The Cambridge Companion to Natural Law Jurisprudence*, ed. George Duke and Robert P. George (Cambridge: Cambridge University Press, 2017), 78–79.

7 Ian Hunter, 'The Law of Nature and Nations,' in *The Law of Nature and Nations*, ed. by Aaron Garrett (London: Routledge, 2014), 559sqq.

8 Dieter Schwab, 'Der Staat im Naturrecht der Scholastik,' in *Naturrecht und Staat. Politische Funktionen des europäischen Naturrechts (17.–19. Jahrhundert)*, ed. Diethelm Klippel (München: Oldenbourg Verlag, 2006), 1–2.

9 Haakonssen, 'Early Modern Natural Law Theories,' 90; Ian Hunter, *Rival Enlightenments: Civil and Metaphysical Philosophy in Early Modern Germany* (Cambridge: Cambridge University Press, 2001), 62, 111; Hunter, 'The Law of Nature and Nations,' 570.

10 Haakonssen, 'Early Modern Natural Law Theories,' 78.

Most importantly, Hobbes, Pufendorf and Thomasius answered to specific political situations existing after the English Civil War and the Thirty Years' War. Hunter describes this as a series of 'attempts by political and natural jurists to render the state independent of the fratricidal moral communities that had plunged Europe into religious civil war.' The outcome was what Brückner called the 'instrumental fracturing of the "life-world."'[11] However, this is just one version of modernity remaining bound to contingent circumstances. It ought not to be applied to other regional contexts without reflection.

2.2 *Poland-Lithuania*

Until the early eighteenth century, there was more continuity in Poland and Lithuania than in Western Europe. Natural law remained rooted in medieval and, especially, Renaissance thought. It drew rather on Suárez and Grotius than on Hobbes and Pufendorf, remaining open for metaphysics and reluctant to accept naturalism. However, this observation must not lead to the conclusion that modernity was rejected or 'belated.' Rather it points to the necessity of considering the political system of the Polish-Lithuanian union and its specific chronology.

First established in the late fourteenth century, the union always faced threats to its internal and external relations. Its juridical definitions barely hid the tension between a temporal personal union of two separate entities and an incorporation of Lithuania as a province into the Crown of Poland. In the earliest document, the Act of Krėva/Krewo (1386), the Grand Duke of Lithuania and future King of Poland Jogaila/Jagiełło 'promised to permanently connect his lands of Lithuania and Ruthenia to the crown of the Kingdom of Poland.'[12] The formula of '*perpetuo applicare*' was a matter of controversy until the end of the union in 1795. While building their respective national narratives in the nineteenth and twentieth centuries, Polish and Lithuanian historians held numerous disputes on the issue. Only recently, a Polish-Lithuanian dialogue on historiography opens common interpretational vistas.[13]

---

11 Hunter, *Rival Enlightenments*, 68.

12 Stanisław Kutrzeba and Władysław Semkowicz, eds., *Akta unii Polski z Litwą 1385–1791* (Kraków: nakład Polskiej Akademii Umiejętności, 1932), 2 (nr. 1): 'promittit terras suas Litvaniae et Rusiae coronae regni Poloniae perpetuo applicare.'

13 Jūratė Kiaupienė and Andrzej Zakrzewski, 'Unie polsko-litewskie – próba nowego spojrzenia,' in *Lex est Rex in Polonia et Lithuania. Tradycje prawno-ustrojowe Rzeczypospolitej – doświadczenie i dziedzictwo*, ed. Adam Jankiewicz (Warszawa: Biuro Trybunału Konstytucyjnego, 2008), 65–82; Andrzej Rachuba, Jūratė Kiaupienė, and Zigmuntas Kiaupa, *Historia Litwy: Dwugłos Polsko-Litewski* (Warszawa: DiG, 2008), 273–280; Jūratė

Given the strength of Eastern Christendom in the vast Ruthenian territories and the durable pagan enclaves in Samogitia, Lithuania was a state of immense cultural diversity. It was necessary, thus, to coin an integrative formula of the union and communicate it to the broader European public. How could a more or less pagan state that fought against the Teutonic Order demand acceptance from the Church? This problem was solved during the Council of Constance (1414–18) through a semi-official *ius gentium* doctrine based on the Padua school of Roman law. Polish historians sometimes called it pleonastically the first Polish school of natural law, law of nations or international law.[14] Its point was a universalist, confessionally indifferent but still clearly theological anthropology leading to what modern international law describes as the right to collective self-determination.

Instead of conceptually anticipating modern natural law, this *ius gentium* mirrored the practical needs of a new political entity around 1400. It marks the very beginning of academic life in a region that had not participated in medieval Scholasticism. It combined metaphysical and naturalist perspectives. And, as the Belarusian historian N.A. Kutuzava rightly observed, it concerned both the external relations between states and the internal relations of people(s) within their state: in other words, the right to collective self-determination both as an international and a civic norm.[15] Needless to say, the

Kiaupienė and Lidia Korczak, eds., *1413 m. Horodlės aktai (dokumentai ir tyrinėjimai) / Akty horodelskie z 1413 roku (dokumenty i studia)* (Vilnius and Kraków: Lietuvos istorijos institutas leidykla, 2013). For the nature of the union and the wider context cf. Robert Frost, *The Oxford History of Poland-Lithuania. Vol. 1: The Making of the Polish-Lithuanian Union, 1385–1569* (Oxford: Oxford University Press, 2015) and vol. 2 (forthcoming).

14 Ludwik Ehrlich, ed., *Polski wykład prawa wojny XV wieku* (Warszawa: Wydawnictwo prawnicze, 1955); Stanislaus F. Belch, *Paulus Vladimiri and his doctrine concerning international law and politics* (Den Haag and Paris: Mouton & Co., 1965). For further literature cf. Steffen Huber, *Einführung in die Geschichte der polnischen Sozialphilosophie* (Wiesbaden: Harrassowitz, 2014), 67–71.

15 N.A. Kutuzava, 'Брэсцкая унія як сацыякультурны феномен: сацыяльна-палітычныя праблемы,' in *Гісторыя філасофскай і грамадска-палітычнай думкі Беларусі*, ed. by V.B. Evaroiski (Minsk: Belaruskaja navuka, 2013), 255–278, here: 277. The process of legislation not only between and within states, but also between and within estates, cities, national, religious, and professional communities has been recently discussed with reference to Lithuania's modern constitutionalism by Jevgenij Machovenko, Lina Griškevič, 'Bendravalstybinės LDK privilegijos kaip Lietuvos konstituciniai aktai,' *Teisė* 93 (2014): 46–66, e.g. the Act of Horodlė (1413) as both a privilege covering the whole society of the Great Duchy of Lithuania ('bendravalstybinė LDK privilegija') and a normative international treaty between Lithuania and Poland ('tarpvalstybinė norminė sutartis,' 58). Machovenko's and Griškevič's approach has been followed by the contributors to: Lina Griškevič et al., eds., *Lietuvos konstitucionalizmo istorija* (Vilnius: Vilniaus universiteto lei-

civic dimension referred to families, towns, and regions, ethnic and religious communities rather than individuals. This explains the ambiguity of Polish and Lithuanian natural law thought throughout the four centuries following the Act of Krėva/Krewo: its 'pro-modern' openness for transconfessional and multicultural approaches and its 'pre-modern' collective and metaphysical patterns.

When modern natural law started to emerge in Western Europe, Poland and Lithuania were two noble republics bound together in the 'Republic of Two Nations' or the 'Commonwealth' (*Rzeczpospolita* as the Polish translation of *res publica*). Formally founded in 1569, it passed a stable period until the mid-seventeenth century and remained an important player in East European politics until the beginning of the eighteenth century. While France after the St. Bartholomew's Day massacre (1572) became an absolute monarchy, Poland-Lithuania accepted religious pluralism and was proud of its most unique republican feature, the free election of the king. While the Western part of Central Europe was struggling for religious and territorial domination in the Thirty Years' War, the Republic of Two Nations expanded economically and militarily, in some incidents around 1610 even trying to dominate Moscow. Starting with the Khmelnitsky uprising in 1648, it was hit by a series of devastating wars in the mid-seventeenth century. First, the South-Eastern region around Kyiv fell away. During the 1650s and 1660s, the two nations found themselves at war with Russia and Sweden, losing much territory in the East of Lithuania and, more importantly, a great part of their economic force in the remaining territories. However, the crisis of the mid-seventeenth century did not undermine the form of the political system nor did it eliminate the still considerable military resources that were essentially based on direct civic engagement.

Throughout the seventeenth century, a self-confident elite was able to lead a frank and critical dialogue not only with Suárez and Grotius but even with Bodin. However, the works of Hobbes, Pufendorf and Thomasius did not meet with a systematic reception. Their drawing on hereditary monarchy, central administration, state control over religion and education, standing armies, permanent taxes, stringent codification of law and, generally, unification of the territorial state aroused the fears of a republican political class.

---

dykla, 2016). Of course, this multi-layer understanding of legislation changed in various aspects during the centuries. However, it lasted until the end of the Polish-Lithuanian Commonwealth (1795) and still remains alive in the legal cultures of Lithuania and Poland.

With the Great Northern War (1700–21) and the rivalry until 1736 between the Saxon Kings August II and August III on the one hand, and Stanisław Leszczyński on the other, it became clear that the Commonwealth had found itself in an existential crisis. Popular pamphlet literature and school philosophy stressed the need to undertake extraordinary efforts.[16] The old strategy of merging competing narratives in the model of the *res publica mixta* was replaced by more unequivocal views. Reformist and conservative visions of natural law did no longer seem compatible. The hermeneutic methods elaborated by Renaissance thinkers as well as the theories of Suárez and Grotius were forgotten. As mentioned above, the stage of Hobbes, Pufendorf and Thomasius was skipped. De Vattel and especially Montesquieu, over time also Rousseau and Kant, became the new references. Poland-Lithuania reached the point from which Western natural law had started after the devastating wars of the seventeenth century: an existential crisis inspiring readiness for fundamental reforms. Natural law became a means of radical criticism and systematic construction, as in the Western discourse. However, the weakness of Poland-Lithuania and the growing dominance of its neighbours, especially Russia, Prussia and Austria, finally prevented those reforms from saving the republic.

It should be borne in mind that Poland and Lithuania were distinct political entities and followed different paths especially in the field of law. Poland started to develop its law in a in organized manner under King Casimir III the Great in the fourteenth century. When the personal union with Lithuania was being settled, Cracow became the only academic centre of both countries for about 200 years. Its university bloomed until the early sixteenth century, followed by the royal court as a patron of science and arts. Later on, the considerable domains (*dwory*) of many noble families became the fundament of a new, uncentralized, republican culture. Between 1520 and 1560, the so-called execution movement demanded a modernization of Polish law. In its first years, this bottom-up movement of the emerging new republican political class followed humanist patterns. However, after 1540 it successfully obstructed the royal court's efforts to codify Polish law. Proud of its own, essentially oral tradition of law (*prawo ziemskie*), the nobility viewed the natural law thought of the humanists and philosophers as a threat to their republic. Therefore, in Poland the systematization, unification and codification of law became stuck in the mid-sixteenth century.

---

16 Anna Grześkowiak-Krwawicz, *Regina Libertas. Wolność w polskiej myśli politycznej XVIII wieku* (Gdańsk: Wydawnictwo słowo/obraz terytoria, 2006).

In this very period, Lithuania started its rapid ascent based on imported patterns of Western Renaissance culture. The most impressive documents of this process are the three Lithuanian Statutes of 1529, 1566 and 1588 which brought a comprehensive codification and harmonization of the regional law systems. Their particular focus was on Ruthenian law, i.e. the heretofore predominantly oral tradition of the Eastern Christian population. The Lithuanian Statutes influenced the legal culture in Poland and other countries of the region, including Russia. Moreover, Lithuania differed from Poland also in social and political terms. Originally less focused on the nobilty, the political system was dominated by a small number of aristocratic families and based on a stronger central power. During the seventeenth century, the Polish model of noble freedom had a growing impact on the Lithuanian society. However, Lithuania always preserved its own identity and, when it came to law, had a solid basis to feel a sense of superiority towards Poland.

3 Natural Law Discourses in Poland-Lithuania

3.1 *The Humanists of the Sixteenth Century*

In sixteenth-century Poland and Lithuania, the 'natural law before natural law' (Merio Scattola) was represented by the philosopher Andreas Fricius Modrevius (Andrzej Frycz Modrzewski, 1503–1572[17]) and, to a lesser extent, the Spanish-born lawyer Roisius (Pedro Ruiz de Moros, 1505–1571). Modrzewski was the author of the most comprehensive philosophical theory of power of the Polish Renaissance.[18] A follower of Erasmus and Melanchthon, he felt also attracted by the Augustinian ideas of Luther and Calvin. His approach was a hermeneutic one. Law appeared as the primary means of politics which, conceived in a broad anthropological and ethical perspective, reacts to the intrinsic evil of human nature (St. Paul, Melanchthon). On the one hand, Modrzewski held that law-making is a task for specialists. On the other hand, he stressed the need for anthropological and ethical knowledge in a broad philosophical perspective including metaphysics. Both aspects are combined

17 As to the name form, the praxis in the scholarship is far from being uniform. Andrzej Piotr Modrzewski opted for a Latin pen name 'Andreas Fricius Modrevius,' which was 're-Polonised' as 'Andrzej Frycz Modrzewski.' As in the case of Classical Latin authors, he was usually referred to as 'Fricius (Modrevius).' In this volume, we mention proper names, individuals or geographical entities, in their recent national form. On this basis, we have preferred the name form 'Modrzewski' (editor).

18 Andrzej Frycz Modrzewski, *Commentariorum de republica emendanda libri quinque* (Basileae: Oporinus, 1554).

in the hermeneutic process of writing legal provisions, court judgements and, which is especially stressed by Modrzewski, comprehensive court opinions. Only the philosophically mature *ius scriptum* guarantees a sound psychological distance to conflicts and especially to the dramatic, moving, upsetting, horrible aspects discussed in criminal cases. By drawing on the Stoic understanding of true justice as punishing with delay, Modrzewski developed an alternative to the oral tradition and practice of the Polish nobility.[19] In this proto-modern setting, the maxims of natural law mark the aporetic moment of questioning traditional and seemingly self-evident rules. Natural law makes the evil of existing law visible and thus helps to render law more rational. With these views and his approach to religion, Modrzewski remained an esteemed intellectual without political influence.[20]

Roisius suffered the same fate while holding the chair of Roman Law at the University of Cracow between 1540 and 1550. However, when he found his way to reform-oriented political circles of Vilnius, his career took off. He became engaged in the redaction of the Second Lithuanian Statute and published numerous works, among them the widely known *Decisiones*.[21] Like

---

19 Modrzewski, *Commentariorum de republica emendanda libri quinque*, libri I (De moribus), II (De legibus).

20 Wladislaus Maliniak, *Andreas Fricius Modrevius. Ein Beitrag zur Geschichte der Staats- und Völkerrechtstheorien* (Wien: A. Hölder, 1913); Waldemar Voisé, *Frycza Modrzewskiego nauka o państwie i prawie* (Warszawa: Książka i Wiedza, 1956); Alodia Kawecka-Gryczowa, *Andrzej Frycz Modrzewski: Bibliografia* (Wrocław: Ossolineum, 1962); Aleksander Łuczak, *Die Staats- und Rechtslehre des polnischen Renaissancedenkers Andrzej Frycz Modrzewski* (Zürich: Juris, 1966); Tadeusz Bieńkowski, ed., *Andrzej Frycz Modrzewski i problemy kultury polskiego Odrodzenia* (Wrocław: Ossolineum, 1974); Waldemar Voisé, 'Deux républiques opposées: Fricius et Bodin,' *Czasopismo Prawno-Historyczne* 29 (1977/2): 55–63; Steffen Huber, *Polifonia tradycji. Filozofia praktyczna i teoretyczna Andrzeja Frycza Modrzewskiego* (Warszawa: Sub Lupa, 2014); Steffen Huber, 'The Philosopher's Refusal of Action: Andreas Fricius Modrevius (1503–1572),' in *Penser et agir à la Renaissance*, ed. Philippe Desan, Véronique Ferrer (Genève: Droz 2020), 529–551.

21 Petrus Roisius, *Decisiones*, 1st ed. (Cracoviae: Matthaeus Siebeneycher, 1563); 2nd ed. (Francoforti: Feyerabend, 1570, quotations from this edition); 3rd ed. (Venetiis: apud Bartholomaeum Rubinum, 1572). Tomasz Fijałkowski, 'Piotr Rojzjusz – polski romanista XVI wieku. Zarys problematyki,' in *Z dziejów polskiej kultury umysłowej w XVI i XVII wieku*, ed. Waldemar Voisé (Wrocław: Ossolineum, 1976), 7–76; Andrzej Kremer, 'Pedro Ruiz de Moros: hiszpański profesor prawa rzymskiego Akademii Krakowskiej w XVI wieku,' in *Vetera novis augere: studia i prace dedykowane Profesorowi Wacławowi Uruszczakowi*, ed. Stanisław Grodziski, Dorota Malec, and Anna Karabowicz (Kraków: WUJ, 2010), 479–490; Marzena Dyjakowska, 'Decisiones Lituanicae Piotra Rojzjusza – przykład renesansowego źródła poznania stosowania prawa rzymskiego przed sądem asesorskim w Wilnie. Problemy badawcze i translatorskie,' *Krakowskie Studia z Historii Państwa i Prawa* 13 (2020/1): 1–15.

Modrzewski, but with less interest in general hermeneutics, he treats natural law as an instrument of criticism and key to legislation:

> What has been introduced as a custom and remains contrary to natural law, should be called usurpation and corruption rather than customary law. [...] No one should be proud of the fact that some rule is very old if it is against natural and divine law.[22]

Rules are now clearly defined and compared to each other literally. If natural law, law of nations and divine law claim the waters of the ocean to be free for everyone, custom cannot prohibit fishing or shipping.[23] Divine law not only demands that 'thou shalt not kill' but also defines the exceptions resulting from the right to self-defense which, for its part, is precisely defined by divine and natural law.[24] Moral principles are being turned into first premises of juridical syllogisms. However, the syllogisms are reshaping only a part of the various laws of Poland-Lithuania. Divine or natural law is binding for the legislator when it comes to morality, as Roisius shows in the context of the biblical prohibition of interest rates:

> If something like this [i.e. the right to levy interest] was to be established against divine law, there would arise a right to sin. The legislator is required to act against this as he is supposed to correct sin through positive law and not to tolerate it.[25]

Divine and natural law defines the direction in which positive law ought to develop society's morality. But divine and natural law affects positive law only

---

22 Roisius, *Decisiones*, 174 (Pos. 169): 'Enimvero si quid, quod iuri naturali repugnat, introductum moribus est, it, ut modo dicebam, usurpatio aut corruptela potius appellari, quam consuetudo debet [...]. Ne quisquam sibi temporis longinquitate blandiatur in iis, quae iuri naturali atque divino adversantur'; 191 (Pos. 342): 'Quod contra ius divinum mores introduxerunt, aequè, atque quod leges, nullas habere vires unquam potuit. Nam cum eadem sit scripti quae non scripti iuris authoritas [...], ut est saepe dictum, quod lege non licet, consuetudine licere non debet, legem autem Dei propter summam conditoris authoritatem nulla humana lege abrogari posse. [...] Non potest esse denique tam antiqua consuetudo [...], quae divinam legem antecesserit, nec si antecessiset, eo magis valere dici potest: Lex enim et antecedentem et insequentem consuetudinem tollit.'

23 Roisius, *Decisiones*, 174 (Pos. 168).

24 Roisius, *Decisiones*, 78 (Pos. 445–446); 80 (Pos. 470sqq.).

25 Roisius, *Decisiones*, 176 (Pos. 191): 'Si quid in hoc genere quaestus contra ius divinum constitueretur, peccandi fieret potestas, cui obviam ire legislator debet, cuius partes sunt lata lege peccata corrigere, non indulgere.'

through morality. It does not affect the morally indifferent contents of positive law nor the latter's formal structure. Finally, divine and natural law is not the only source of normativity. One of Roisius's arguments against the customs and the customary law of the Polish nobility is *ex iure positivo*: 'The Polish people (*populus Polonus*) are not entitled to take legislative initiative without the King and the senate. Thus they were never formally allowed to introduce a new custom.'[26] Even in the horizon of philosophical law, constitutional law remains irreducibly positive law. Thus, although prefering the monarchical model of power, Roisius describes the republican order of Poland-Lithuania with objectivity and accepts it as it is.

For both Modrzewski and Roisius natural law is not system-building. It is unable to thoroughly construct a corpus of positive law. It is not a sufficient material source. It uses religious exemplifications and sometimes, especially in Roisius, remains dependent on biblical content. Nevertheless, the works of Modrzewski and Roisius document that natural law was connected to legislation both in a philosophical and juridical perspective already before the foundation of the Commonwealth (1569) and the first free election of the monarch (1573). Moreover, these works unveil the tensions between the humanist pro-reform understanding of natural law and the social roots of the rising republican system as well as between the naturalist and confessionalist interpretations of natural law. They help explain why Polish-Lithuanian natural law necessarily needed to be built on a Renaissance basis which remained intact at least until the mid-seventeenth century. The humanist anthropology and the multicultural perspectivism are intervowen with the Ancient and Renaissance models of the *res publica mixta*. Although very critical with regard to the mythology of the republican nobility, Modrzewski and Roisius confirmed on an academic level the model of the Renaissance republic which in Europe used to be associated with Venice.

3.2 *Selected Sources from Vilnius, Seventeenth Century*

In the following, four selected sources from the seventeenth century will be discussed. All of them are connected to the University of Vilnius. The anonymous course of *Philosophia practica* taught in Ingolstadt in 1612[27] and the treatise *De politica hominum societate* published by Aron Aleksander Olizarowski

---

26 Roisius, *Decisiones*, 178 (Pos. 211): 'Adde populum Polonum condendae legis authoritatem non habere, sed simul cum Rege et senatu. Ergo convenienter nec consuetudinem potuit introducere.'

27 *Philosophia practica* (Ingolstadt, 1612), Manuscript F9-8, Wroblewski Library of the Lithuanian Academy of Sciences.

(Aaron Alexander Olizarovius) in Gdańsk in 1651[28] represent the most creative period of this University which ended abruptly in 1655 due to the Russian and Cossack occupation of the Lithuanian capital. The *Praelectiones politicae* held by Zacharias Modzelewski in 1690[29] and by Christophorus Puciłowski in the following year[30] represent the recovery phase which had started in the 1660s and ended in the early eighteenth century.

3.2.1 Anonymous 1612

In 1612, an unidentified scholar stemming from Lithuania or Poland taught courses of logics and practical philosophy at the Jesuit dominated University of Ingolstadt, Bavaria, possibly to a Lithuanian audience.[31] The manuscripts of both courses, written in an extraordinarily careful manner reminiscent of printed books, may have been used later on by professors of the University of Vilnius.

In the 1612 manuscript, practical philosophy is based on an Aristotelian model and, at the same time, on the analytical method of Bartholomäus Keckermann (1572–1609). The manuscript documents the crucial role the University of Ingolstadt played in transferring early modern thought between the Catholic and Protestant worlds and between Southern Europe (Spain) and the Baltic region. Natural law appears as a secondary but nonetheless system relevant category helping to root practical philosophy in a partly naturalist paradigm. According to the author, law is basically divided into civil (*ius civile*) and domestic (*ius domesticum*).[32] The first concerns the society established between free people in order to provide them with a sufficient number of things necessary for life. The latter refers to the house or family; it organizes the relations between parents and children, free family members and servants, as well as husband and wife. Remarkably in this Aristotelian context, it is rather domestic than civil law that leads to a good life. Even more exceptionally, natural law is not situated above civil and domestic law as their superior source of normativity. Instead, alongside positive law (*ius positivum*)

---

28 Aaron Alexander Olizarovius, *De Politica Hominum Societate Libri Tres* (Dantisci: Sumptibus Georgii Forsteri, 1651).

29 Zacharias Modzelewski, *Praelectiones politicae anni 1690* (Vilnius, 1691), fol. 1–18v, Manuscript F3-1390, Library of the University of Vilnius.

30 Christophorus Puciłowski, *Praelectiones politicae anni 1691* (Vilnius, 1691), fol. 94–127, Manuscript F3-1390, Library of the University of Vilnius.

31 *Logica* (Ingolstadt, 1612), Manuscript F3-2170, Library of the University of Vilnius; *Philosophia practica*. Cf. Romanas Plečkaitis, *Lietuvos filosofijos istorija*. Vol. 1: *Viduramžiai – renesansas – naujieji amžiai* (Vilnius: Kultūros, filosofijos ir meno institutas, 2004), 44.

32 *Philosophia practica*, fol. 49v–50r.

it forms a subcategory of civil law. Its definition is twofold. First, in a naturalist sense, it is 'that which nature has given to all humans deep inside them' which evokes Ulpian's formula of 'that which nature has taught all animals.'[33] However, the Ingolstadt author refers it exclusively to 'all humans.' Second, in a moderately anti-naturalist sense, natural law 'has its origin and authority directly from God, and God by nature has given this authority to all minds deep inside them.'[34] Thus, God is irreducible but appears somewhat *remotus*, practically indistinguishable from nature as far as the content of natural law is concerned.

This construction seems to facilitate a Platonist interpretation of natural law as a collection of innate ideas. However, the content of natural law does not imply a strong ontological transcendence. Not only is it situated at the same level as positive (written) law. But the latter has an autonomous, ontologically immanent instance of moral justice, *aequitas*, which means the 'moderation and benevolent interpretation' of the abstract rules of written law by taking into consideration the circumstances of place, time, and persons.[35] Thus, natural law is not a medium layer in a spheric hierarchy, beneath eternal law and divine law, above law of nations and civil law. Rather it merges with both eternal (divine) law and law of nations, as the three rules defined by our author show. The first precept of natural law is the right to self-defense (*se ipsum defendere*), the second prohibits violence against envoys (*legatos non violare*, a classic *ius gentium* rule) and the third demands respect for elders (*parentes honorare*, a classic *ius divinum* principle).[36]

The whole of this eclectic philosophical law confirms the rules of positive and domestic law. For example, the subordination of wives to their husbands and the prohibition of interest rates are presented as commands of domestic law which are consistent with natural law. Of course, both precepts traditionally belong to eternal or divine law which, as we saw, has become indistinguishable from natural law. Our author also presents principles of political and social life as rules of civil law which are consistent with natural law. In

33 *Philosophia practica*, fol. 50r.: 'quod natura omnibus hominibus indidit.'

34 *Philosophia practica*, fol. 50r.: 'iuris naturalis proprium est originem suam et auctoritatem habere immediate a Deo quam Deus mentibus indidit a natura.'

35 *Philosophia practica*, fol. 50r.–v.: 'Cum moderatione consideratum definitur ius positivum quod generalissimas causas et regulas ac leges scriptas accomodat locus, tempus et personas, hoc ius alias definitur uno verbo aequitas, quae non est contraria iustitiae, sed potius cum illa nectitur, nec est ius naturale, sed positivam quia illa est iuris moderatio et benigna interpraetatio.'

36 *Philosophia practica*, fol. 50r. Cf. *Logica*, fol. 221v.: the presumably same author calls 'legatos non violare' a ius gentium rule and emphasises that breaking it delivers a 'causa belli.'

this context, his argumentation is moderately reformist. In politics, natural law entitles citizens to control the legitimacy of civic authorities.

In social life, natural law helps to clarify and smooth potentially conflictual relations between different groups. Peasants who form the lowest class are not mere working instruments but human beings in the fullest sense of the word. Created by God in His image, they do not deserve to live in slavery: 'without any difference, every human being should be free and, as a consequence, a citizen.'[37] Foreigners generally need to be accepted on behalf of natural and divine law but they should be hard-working and law-abiding. In these two points, the author formally presents arguments *pro* and *contra*, showing that the more egalitarian and less xenophobic arguments fit better with natural and divine law. However, in two points concerning ethnic and religious minorities, he proceeds in a different manner. In the case of Romani people (*zygari*) he presents only the xenophobic arguments, leaving them uncommented. As for the Jews, he seems to give priority to a series of biblical arguments in favour of accepting them as the chosen nation from which Jesus was born. However, their description as pious, cultivated and innocuous neighbours is followed by a number of antisemitic motifs 'brought forward by the opponents.' Remarkably, in these two points natural law is not mentioned.[38]

In sum, natural law does not form an overarching principle or superior source of strong normativity. Its weakly elaborated rules do not allow for syllogistic inference. Instead of delivering an Archimedean point for the reform of positive law, it remains a subsidiary tool of restricted range. Nevertheless, natural law is irreducible and meaningful. Much like the law of nations described by Kutuzava (see above), it helps to balance the relations between the manifold communities of the republic by integrating a naturalist approach with a holistic metaphysic and a cross-confessional religiosity. Most importantly, it enhances the intensive dialogue with Western thought. The main authorities quoted in this text, Bartholomäus Keckermann but also Jean Bodin and Gregorius Tholosanus, open up an alternative to the humanist tradition of the sixteenth century embodied by Andrzej Frycz Modrzewski and Petrus Roisius. While in the sixteenth century the dialogue with the West had been focused on anthropology, ethics and metaphysics, now it referred from a comparative East-West perspective to the political system as a philosophical problem.

Finally, the 1612 manuscript documents a new beginning in academic jurisprudence and political philosophy in Poland-Lithuania. The University of

37 *Philosophia practica*, fol. 131r.: 'Omnis homo sine discrimine debet esse liber et per consequens civis.'

38 *Philosophia practica*, fol. 131v.–133v., cf. fol. 126r.

Vilnius was formally founded in 1578 on the basis of the local Jesuit Academy. However, because the older University of Cracow defended its relevant monopoly, it was denied a law faculty until the mid-seventeenth century (see below). During this period, the Jesuit University of Ingolstadt became a strategic place for Vilnius lawyers. A remarkable number of Polish and Lithuanian students, many from influential families, registered in Ingolstadt.[39] Thus, the Ingolstadt manuscript stands for the participation of the University of Vilnius in the discourse which transfigured Iberian Jesuit thought into trans-confessional natural law.

3.2.2 Olizarowski 1651

Olizarowski's treatise is the most prominent and comprehensive source discussed here. Translated into Lithuanian and well edited, it is still awaiting a Polish language edition.[40] Aron Aleksander Olizarowski (1610–1659) studied philosophy, medicine, and law at Polish Jesuit academies, Padua, Graz, and Ingolstadt. In 1641, the King of Poland and Grand Duke of Lithuania Władysław IV finally granted the University of Vilnius the privilege of founding a faculty of law. Olizarowski was involved in employing two Ingolstadt lawyers at the new faculty and, after finishing his juridical studies in Ingolstadt, was appointed professor of canon law in Vilnius in 1646.[41] He published *Quaestiones Politicae in Utramque Partem Disputatae* (Ingolstadt, 1643) and *De politica hominum societate* (Gdańsk, 1651).[42] The latter treatise, his *opus magnum*, attracted some attention because of the author's resolute defence of the peasants. In this context, Olizarowski used an original construction of natural law, finally arriving at an eclectic pro-modern vision of the Polish-Lithuanian republic.

---

39 *Annales Ingolstadiensis Academiae*, vol. 2: 1572–1672 (Ingolstadt: Krüll, 1782), passim.

40 Aron Aleksander Olizarowski, *De politica hominum societate / Apie politinę žmonių sąjungą*, trans. Jolita Sarcevičienė (Vilnius: Aidai, 2003).

41 Stanisław Kot, *Aron Aleksander Olizarowski* (Wilno [Vilnius]: Józef Zawadzki, 1929); Eugenjusz Jarra, 'Aron Aleksander Olizarowski jako filozof prawa,' in *Księga Pamiątkowa celem uczczenia 350-ej rocznicy założenia Uniwersytetu Stefana Batorego w Wilnie* (Warszawa: Uniwersytet Warszawski, 1931), 33–72; Piotr Niczyporuk, 'Aaron Aleksander Olizarowski profesorem prawa Akademii Wileńskiej,' *Miscellanea Historico-Iuridica* 14 (2015/2): 181–206; Piotr Niczyporuk, 'Assertiones ex jurisprudentia Aarona Aleksandra Olizarowskiego – rozprawa, która nigdy nie powstała,' in *Ustrój państwa, myśl polityczno-prawna, współczesne systemy rządów. Prace ofiarowane Profesorowi Adamowi Jamrozowi z okazji Jego jubileuszu*, ed. Stanisław Bożyk and Artur Olechno (Białystok: Temida, 2018), 705–714; Piotr Niczyporuk, 'Pubilkacje romanistyczne w Akademii Wileńskiej w latach 1644–1655,' *Z dziejów prawa* 12 (2019): 163–184.

42 Aron Aleksander Olizarowski, *Quaestiones Politicae in Utramque Partem Disputatae* (Ingolstadii: Typis Gregorii Haenlini, 1643); Olizarowski, *De Politica Hominum Societate Libri Tres*.

The treatise, about 360 printed pages, starts with a *Prooemium* and six *Questiones prooemiales* concerning the aim of human life (happiness) and the structure of practical philosophy (ethics, economy, politics). The three books that follow are titled *De domo, De civitate,* and *De republica.* The first book, *De domo,* which accounts for half of the whole treatise (180 pages), discusses marriage, parenting, and education as well as the organization of work. In this context Olizarowski raises the issue of servitude including its politically trickiest aspect, the liberty of peasants. The second book, *De civitate,* of almost a hundred pages, adopts a particular Lithuanian-Polish perspective: there is no single *civitas* but an unlimited number of heterogeneous societies (*civitates*) in towns and rural areas which form the *res publica.* Against this backdrop, Olizarowski delivers a normative view of the estate order, in particular the nobility, combined with severe criticism of the nobility's self-image. The third book, *De republica,* brings forward a normative theory of government forms. Democracy and aristocracy appear to be intrinsically bad and supportable only as historic pre-forms of the monarchy. The latter, notwithstanding the threat of degenerating into tyranny, is the best possible outcome of the historic path leading from kinship and local communities to a true political society (*societas politica*). With reference to Jean Bodin, Olizarowski criticizes the so far unquestioned Polish and Lithuanian tradition of *res publica mixta.* He challenges the republican tradition of the free election of the King of Poland and Grand Duke of Lithuania, openly arguing in favour of the *electio vivente rege* and a dynasty of the throne as well as the endowment of the king with extensive rights concerning taxation. Thus, he depreciates fundamental privileges of the nobility.[43]

How were these views to be combined with the republican doctrine of the rule of law (*in Polonia lex est rex*)? How was the Western idea of the central state to be merged with the confederal Polish-Lithuanian model? And how were the nobility to be persuaded to adopt a more egalitarian model of society? The core of Olizarowski's method is juridical and humanist hermeneutics. He integrates the following heterogeneous elements: a naturalist reinterpretation of Aristotle's practical philosophy, casuistry, normativity of natural law,

43 Olizarowski, *De Politica Hominum Societate Libri Tres,* liber III, caput IX, 313–329. Cf. Stanisław Pyszka, 'Il diritto alla liberta personale ed alla cittadinanza di contadini Polacchi a Lituani in Aron Aleksander Olizarowski (1610–1659),' *Forum Philosophicum* 7 (2002): 205–237; Michał Sczaniecki, 'Jean Bodin et Pologne,' *Czasopismo Prawno-Historyczne* 29 (1977/2): 39–53; Paweł Rybicki, 'Z dziejów polskiego arystotelizmu: "De Politica Hominum Societate" Arona Aleksandra Olizarowskiego,' *Studia i Materiały z Dziejów Nauki Polskiej* 7 (1959): 83–136.

and contractualism. The outcome is an eclectic pro-monarchic vision of the republic.

Olizarowski's Aristotelianism differs considerably from the simplistic holism of many Jesuits, especially when it comes to the division of practical philosophy into ethics, economy, and politics. As a rule, ethics deliver the normative basis for economy and politics. Olizarowski instead holds that politics should follow economy. According to him, both economy and politics concern men in their grammatical plurality (*homines*) while ethics concerns man in his grammatical singularity (*homo*). Economy as the theory of small social entities and local societies delivers the normative patterns for politics as the theory of complex societies such as the republic. Ethics, when speaking of 'man,' regards the individual. When it tries to transcend the individual horizon, it arrives only at the abstract concept of the human species as created by God. Either way, ethics is unable to understand the social reality. It remains relevant for monks and, more specifically, hermits who have left the real society behind themselves to go into the desert and speak to God. Any political engagement of ethicists, i.e. monks and hermits, harms the republic, and thus the hermit needs to be 'anti-political' (*monachus antipoliticus*).[44] However, law is still understood in the light of a Christian intellectual culture and in a perspective merging Thomas Aquinas and Cicero. This is a recourse to Renaissance thought. Despite all his criticism of the instrumentalization of religion for politics and vice versa, Olizarowski stands far away from Hobbes, Pufendorf and Thomasius. He has no secularization experience whatsoever to draw on. Meanwhile, as Hunter portrays them, Pufendorf and Thomasius try to 'reconstruct natural law from within, seeking to give it a form that would reflect the secularization of civil governance that had taken place in the political-jurisprudential sphere' so that 'ethics would be subordinate to the end of social peace and to the laws of the only institution capable of attaining this end, the sovereign territorial state.'[45] For Olizarowski, this is simply beyond imagination.

Moreover, Olizarowski retains law in the horizon of an inherited social practice which needs correction and amendment out of itself. This excludes radical

44 Olizarowski, *De Politica Hominum Societate Libri Tres*, quaestio prooemialis IV, § 2 (without pagination). The 'monachus' refers to ethics as 'monastica' (from the Greek μοναστική). 'Monastically' understood, man is a monad (μόνας), that is to say, a being deprived of relation. This argument is not rooted in any traditional interpretation of Aristotle. With its allusions to the Greek language it seems to be directed against the so-called 'Greeks,' i.e. the Eastern Christian population of Lithuania.

45 Hunter, *Rival Enlightenments*, 127.

theoretization in the sense of seventeenth-century philosophy and, especially, the Cartesian moment described by Scattola as constitutive for the Western version of modernity:

> The compelling power of modern natural law consists in a truly internal constraint […]. Natural law is constructed within the individual, in a small personal world, which is completely and perfectly isolated from the outside. The subject of natural right could be alone […]. He needs other human beings only as objects of his rights and duties and as a necessary environment made of equal men; but he does not need them as source of right.[46]

In Olizarowski, the source of right is not subjectivity as opposed to objectivity but inter-subjectivity based on a common, if unpredictably changing, experience of objectivity.

This is more than an argument *ex grammatica arte*: sacred loneliness and social order are shown as two distinct layers of human nature. They are equally constitutive but clearly disjunctive. In the historical context, this is a relevant political argument, too. In the mid-seventeenth century vast territories including the cultural strongholds of Polotsk and Kyiv fell away from the Commonwealth due to the conquest by Muscovite armies, while the emancipation movements of the Ruthenian population grew stronger. In this process, the political version of hesychasm (from the Greek ἡσυχία: stillness, quiet) encouraged especially the plebeian classes to accept the monastic community as a model of civic life. Against this backdrop, the above-mentioned figure of the anti-political hermit (*monachus antipoliticus*) appears as a warning of the ongoing disintegration of the Commonwealth.

Finally, Olizarowski builds a dualist model of a worldly (but not secularized) republic and an internalised cross-confessional religious belief in a *Deus remotus*. He does not intend to ban ethical principles from politics. Instead of formally ascribing them to ethics, he places them in an economic context which sensitizes the reader to the ever-changing social roles and renders natural law more empirical and naturalist. Economic practice, understood as both normative and historically changing, becomes the source of knowledge on natural law.

---

46 Merio Scattola, 'Before and after Natural Law. Models of Natural Law in Ancient and Modern Times,' in *Early Modern Natural Law Theories. Contexts and Strategies in the Early Enlightenment*, ed. Timothy J. Hochstrasser and Peter Schröder (Dordrecht: Kluwer Academic, 2003), 14–15.

Olizarowski conceives natural law with double reference to Ulpian's formula '*quod natura omnia animalia docuit*' and the Ciceronian '*utilitas*.'[47] Thus, natural law was not merely to encourage people to reproduce, but to build a truly human society. This concerns, first, life in the cycles of generations: the relation between female and male (mutual attraction, sexuality, marriage in its psychological, social and legal aspects), parenting young children (physiological needs, different roles of mother, father and other family members, school) and older children (different education for girls and boys, school, arts and sciences, civic education).[48] Second, economy entails the world of work and property (earning and spending money for the family, making contracts with other free men, slavery and liberty).[49] Thus, the normativity of natural law is rooted in the immutable structure of the generational cycle but also in the economic work which inevitably becomes political.

On its way to political theory, natural law goes through casuistry. Olizarowski pays much attention to the following *casus*: A peasant owns a beehive that is situated in a forest owned by a nobleman. Who rightfully owns the honey in the beehive? What practical means are at the disposal of both the peasant and the nobleman to assert their claims? Which of those means are morally and legally correct and which are not? In his answer, Olizarowski draws a line from the ownership of honey to the more general problem of the relation between the peasantry and the nobility. As this concerns the distribution of economic profit and loss, it can be described in terms of Roman private law as a *societas* which in Olizarowski becomes the basic model of *societas politica*. A political society develops as positively or negatively as its economic structures allow. A society that *de facto* distributes all profits to the nobleman and all losses to the peasant is deeply rotten. In the Latin tradition it is called a leonine contract (*societas leonina*). The seemingly particular problem turns out to be systemically relevant and, moreover, emblematic of the economic and political situation of the Polish-Lithuanian Commonwealth. By damaging economic life, it prevents the society (*societas*) from becoming a true political society (*societas politica*). Thus, only a deep economic and political reform that improves the situation of the plebeian classes could save the republic.[50]

This outcome of Olizarowski's economic analysis should be understood against the backdrop of the above discussed 'economization' of politics. The

---

47 Olizarowski, *De Politica Hominum Societate Libri Tres*, quaestio prooemialis v (without pagination).

48 Olizarowski, *De Politica Hominum Societate Libri Tres*, liber I, capita I–X, 1–143.

49 Olizarowski, *De Politica Hominum Societate Libri Tres*, liber I, caput IX, 143–180.

50 Olizarowski, *De Politica Hominum Societate Libri Tres*, liber I, caput IX, 143–180.

author does not intend to establish an amoral or anti-moralistic model of politics. On the contrary, he strengthens the normativity of natural law in its 'economic' version. Natural law as the traditional vehicle of the critique on social injustice finally becomes independent on religious arguments.

With this clear vision, Olizarowski goes beyond the Renaissance hermeneutics. He makes a step towards mercantilism and contractualism. He uses Bodin's arguments in the effort to strengthen the monarchic element of the republic. However, he remains on the ground of Renaissance thought and the republican tradition when it comes to law. Authorities (*magistratus*, p. 244) must obey the positive law and the decisions of the ruler. The ruler must follow law, both positive and natural, otherwise he becomes a tyrant (p. 305). A diffusive normativity inheres in natural law, philosophical rather than strictly juridical, far away from a thorough deducibility. Carefully, without overstraining his readers, Olizarowski binds the Polish-Lithuanian discourse closer to the West.

3.2.3 Modzelewski 1690, Puciłowski 1691

After the wars of the 1650s and 1660s, the Jesuits unsuccessfully tried to re-establish the former excellent status of the University of Vilnius. In 1677 they founded a chair of political philosophy which for many years taught *Praelectiones politicae*. These lectures document the intellectual ambience of the Vilnius University around 1690 and help to understand the framework conditions for natural law thought in Poland-Lithuania.[51] One of the sources kept in the library of the University of Vilnius presents large sections of two courses taught in 1690 and 1691.[52] The first one was conceived by Zacharias Modzelewski (1648–1710) whose career path through the University of Vilnius and the Jesuit schools of Warsaw and several provincial towns allows to view him as a typical Jesuit professor. His *Praelectiones* are extraordinarilly detailed and philosophically well balanced. The second course was held by Christophorus Puciłowski, a professor inclined to argue in a more confessionalist than philosophical manner.

Zacharias Modzelewski starts by describing the Polish-Lithuanian custom of choosing, enthroning and dethroning the king. The procedure includes two controversial instruments of noble democracy. These are, first, the 'confederation' (*confederatio*), an extensive bottom-up political initiative, in many cases

---

51 Cf. also Andrea Mariani, 'The contribution of the Society of Jesus to the political culture of Lithuanian elites,' *Open Political Science* 2019; 2: 153–173, here: 170.

52 Modzelewski, *Praelectiones politicae anni 1690*; Puciłowski, *Praelectiones politicae anni 1691*.

armed, able to dispense well defined legal instruments directed 'against any disturber of the public peace.'[53] Second, is the 'covenant' (*pacta conventa*), containing the 'fundamental laws of the kingdom based on oldest custom' which needed to be signed by future kings before taking office.[54] Like many Jesuits, Modzelewski tended towards a more absolutist vision of monarchy. Nonetheless, he unambiguously acknowledges both instruments as fundamental elements of the political order of the Polish-Lithuanian republic. In his view, the monarchy appears to be a mutual compromise between the ruler and his subjects. If the King terminates, *de iure* or *de facto*, the compromise, he could be legally dethroned.

When it comes to the critical issue of whether the ruler is to be restricted by law or not, Modzelewski uses a scholastic distinction. If the *princeps legibus solutus* means a ruler free to develop the law in any direction whatsover, this cannot not be accepted. According to Modzelewski, the head of the political body needs to be 'forced by its remaining parts, i.e. by the king's subjects, to be conformant with them.'[55] This excludes the vision of the king as a higher rational principle which freely rules over lower corporal units or, as Modzelewski puts it, through a general *vis directiva*. On the other hand, Modzelewski readily accepts an absolute power that enforces law: *vis coactiva seu punitiva*. Such a capacity is necessary for the superior power in any political system. By definition, the monarch cannot be forced or punished by anybody else. Logically, no one can be forced or punished by himself. Thus, in this specific sense, the monarch of a republic needs to be *legibus solutus*. But nevertheless the ruler's authority depends on law and grows with the authority of the law.[56] True political power always aims to submit itself to law.[57] Modzelewski reconciles the absolute monarchy with the principle '*in Polonia*

53 Modzelewski, *Praelectiones politicae anni 1690*, fol. 84r.: 'convocatio generalis et confederatio contra quosvis pacis publica perturbatores.'

54 Modzelewski, *Praelectiones politicae anni 1690*, fol. 84v–85r.: 'ordines de pactis conventis, ut legibus Regni fundamentalibus sunt soliciti ut factum est in ultimis duabus electionibus alioque vetusto more, pacta conventa ante electionem scribi solebant. Porro ad pacta haec conscribenda, non pauci ex singulis tribus gentibus designantur, a quibus conscripta in Senatus universi, nunciorumque omnium praesentia a Mareschalis Ordinis equestris leguntur, ac ab omnibus examinantur.'

55 Modzelewski, *Praelectiones politicae anni 1690*, fol. 89v.: 'princeps tanquam caput caeteris membris (id est subditis suis) tenetur sese conformare.'

56 Modzelewski, *Praelectiones politicae anni 1690*, fol. 89v.: 'de authoritate iuris nostra pendet authoritas.'

57 Modzelewski, *Praelectiones politicae anni 1690*, fol. 89v.: 'maius imperium est submittere legibus principatum.'

lex est rex.' As we saw, he does so by means of a distinction which would not necessarilly convince republican citizens.

How, then, should law be made? According to Modzelewski, this depends on the form of government and, more specifically, on the king's method of acquiring power. The basic distinction is between the forceful acquisition of power by the future king and the free election of the king by his subjects. The first option is a scenario of civil war ending with the imposition of laws upon subjects who do not accept either the laws or the king. The second option contains two sub-options. First, when freely choosing a ruler, the *populus* might decide to transfer all of its power to him (*omnem suam potestatem*). In this case, no further consent of the subjects will be needed for the ruler to freely make law. Second, the *populus* might retain a certain field of legislation for itself. Then, relevant law needs to be accepted by the subjects.[58] The latter is the case of Poland-Lithuania.

Modzelewski's distinctions are remarkable for several reasons. Instead of the usual Aristotelian-Polybian terminology of forms of government he prefers Macchiavelli's distinction between new and old power. Unlike in a purely republican discourse, Modzelewski describes the formal election of a hereditary ruler as a specific version of the free election, as power rooted in history, custom and law. Although acquiring the plenitude of power, such a ruler clearly differs from a tyrant and from purely absolute rulers. The latter can be found in archaic families as well as in contemporary states of the Turks and Muscovites where 'one holds perpetual power on everything and does not need to obey any councils nor give an account of the reasons behind his way of administering.'[59] In a moderate absolute monarchy, much like in a republican monarchy, law forms the definite, secure and long-term conditions of social life. The ruler is limiting himself and limited by his subjects to the role of an interpreter and corrector of law.[60] In sum, Modzelewski is undoubtedly

58 Modzelewski, *Praelectiones politicae anni 1690*, fol. 90rv: 'vel populus Regem eligens ei omnem suam contulit potestatem, vel ius retinuit, ne leges ferri possint sine suo consensu? Si prius, Rex potest ferre Legem invito magis populo. Si posterius? Non potest.'

59 Modzelewski, *Praelectiones politicae anni 1690*, fol. 68v.–69r.: 'denique Plenum ac Absolutum regnum est, in quo unus omnium rerum perpetuam habet potestatem, nec ullius consiliis obedire, aut cuiquam rationem admistrationis reddere tenetur. Similis est haec species regni Imperio oeconomico, in quo Pater familias rerum omnium potestatem habet et omnia ad familiae administrat utilitatem. [...] Talis quoque nunc monarchia est in Turcia et Moschovia.'

60 Modzelewski, *Praelectiones politicae anni 1690*, fol. 72v.: 'utrisque Regi seu hominibus et legibus imperium esse concedendum. Legibus quidem in iis rebus et negotiis, in quibus manifeste et certo aliquid definiunt ac statuunt. Regi vero sine hominibus in iis negotiis,

attracted by Western enlightened absolutism, as is shown by his attachment to Bodin and Lipsius. At the same time, he stands for the republican values of Poland-Lithuania. In a context like this, natural law merges with republican custom in the effort of limiting the absolute power to the *vis coactiva seu punitiva* and preventing it from becoming a *vis directiva*.

The second lecturer, Christophorus Puciłowski, integrates a wide range of humanist topoi and political myths of the nobility (Sarmatism). Although arguing in a mostly religious, fideistic and providentialist manner, he makes a naturalist point on natural law. Catholic religion is the main fundament of the state and any mixture or confusion of confessions destroys the 'unity of souls.'[61] There are a number of instruments for the conservation of religious faith: punishment of crimes and sins, distribution of offices, dogmatic discipline, and cooperation of religious and worldly authorities including common control over the academic world.[62]

Against this backdrop, an inexperienced audience can easily ignore an essential differentiation concerning the term 'faith' (*fides*). Puciłowski first distinguishes and then implicitly merges two meanings: that of religious faith and that of non-religious faithfulness (good faith, social confidence or trust). While the first meaning is theological, the latter is philosophical, close to Stoicism and Roman law as understood by Renaissance humanism. Doubtlessly, the author wants the following simplistic interpretation to be heard: Catholicism is the only true religious faith and thus the only source of faithful relations between citizens. However, further arguments lead to a different view. Puciłowski views the core of the specifically Catholic faith in its attitude towards enemies. Here, indeed, religious faith is the source of non-religious faithfulness: 'only the Catholic religion teaches to keep faith even with enemies.'[63] As a result, Catholics 'do not dare to violate a promise (*fides*) they gave to their enemy and confirmed by oath.'[64] But this Catholic attitude

---

in quibus leges deficiunt, et nihil certo potuerunt determinare: quia Rex prudens potest particularia diiudicare, atque hoc modo legibus accommodare; cum Rex sit legis interpres et corrector.'

61 Puciłowski, *Praelectiones politicae anni 1691*, fol. 102r.–v.: 'religio est principale fundamentum conservans Rem publicam. Ratio quia per religionem Res publica unitur cum DEO tanquam cum capite suo, parente et conservatore. […] [U]na debet esse Religio in Respublica. Ratio quia promiscua confusaque Rei publicae Religio tollit unitatem animorum, sine qua ipsa stare non potest.'

62 Puciłowski, *Praelectiones politicae anni 1691*, fol. 111r. sqq.

63 Puciłowski, *Praelectiones politicae anni 1691*, fol. 108: 'religio catholica sola docet fidem servare etiam hostibus.'

64 Puciłowski, *Praelectiones politicae anni 1691*, fol. 108: 'non audet violare fidem magis hosti datam, et iuramento confirmatam.'

has two different roots, one inherent to all human nature as such (if somewhat better understandable through Catholic doctrine) and the other specifically Catholic. The first one is explained with reference to St. Augustine: breaking a promise means breaking natural law, and once natural law is broken, 'there will not be either religion nor law of nations nor commerce nor agreements with enemies. Then, it will be over with contracts, alliances and promises.'[65] The logical sequence is important: natural law forms the fundament for religion, not the other way around. Alongside a contract-based social practice, good religious life turns out to be dependent on the real functioning of natural law. It is only logical that even the pagans are aware that 'only due to the love of honesty and credibility faith grows and strengthens.'[66] This is a universalist, trans-confessional, and naturalist point.

The specifically Catholic aspect is that God severely punishes those Catholics who, by not keeping their promises, 'break the faith' (*violare fidem*). For example, the Polish King Władysław III (born 1424, enthroned 1440) defeated the Turks and solemnly signed with them a 'non unjust' peace contract for ten years. However, on the advice of the pontifical legate he resumed the fight. This time he lost and was beheaded by the Turks in 1444.[67] With this topos Puciłowski once more merges two different narratives. First is the specific interpretation of natural law as it was known in Poland and Lithuania since the times of Paulus Vladimiri (see above) and Renaissance humanism. It claimed the unconditional legal force of contracts between partners who belong to different cultures and religions. This tradition stressed the importance of the internal motivation of the partners instead of an external natural or supra-natural authority which would force them to keep their promises. The theological background is Pelagian and rationalist, conceiving natural law as the natural presence of God's law in man. In this context, the supranatural intervention of God as a decisive political factor would appear as a concession to a voluntarist theology and, thus, as the antithesis of a rational natural law. The second narrative evoked by Puciłowski is the Sarmatian tradition which rejected the rationalist universalism of the Renaissance humanists. It

65 Puciłowski, *Praelectiones politicae anni 1691*, fol. 108: 'Fides, inquit, quando promittitur magis hostibus est servanda, contra quos bellum geritur, tolle fidem, naturae legem tolles, nulla erit Religio nulla gentium iura, nulla commertia, nullae cum hostibus conventiones, actum erit de pactis, federibus, promissionibus.' – The phrase 'actum erit' seems to mean basically 'it will be over' but can also be read as alluding to the Roman law formula 'id quod actum est' ('that which had been agreed on,' i.e. 'the original, true and sincere intention which after some confusion needs to be defined with more clearness').

66 Puciłowski, *Praelectiones politicae anni 1691*, fol. 108v.

67 Puciłowski, *Praelectiones politicae anni 1691*, fol. 108v–109.

cultivated a mystical providentialism claiming that God directly participates in the political life of the Sarmats, his chosen nation. The Sarmatian God was the emotional counter-draft to the humanist and rationalist concept of the *Deus remotus*. Puciłowski tries to make the audience forget the unbridgable differences between these traditions. From the point of view of the Western discourse after Hobbes and Pufendorf, Puciłowski's argumentation is as far from modern natural law as it can be. However, Puciłowski accepts the locally available forms of modernity and naturalism. While embedding them in a baroque imagery he does not lose sight of the pre-modern natural law. Finally, he limits confessionalism and monarchism by describing in an eclectic manner the practice of a multicultural society and a republican state.

Both Modzelewski and Puciłowski belonged to a generation that was proud of Poland-Lithuania's political system and barely saw the need for reforms. In the late seventeenth century, Poland-Lithuania was still a relatively well governed federation that achieved political and military successes. But it was not prepared for the changing political situation around 1700.

3.3 *Outlook: The Eighteenth Century*

The early eighteenth century brought an intensive direct reception of Western natural law. The first political milieu to produce a truly eighteenth-century political theory was that of the opponent of both Saxon kings, Stanisław Leszczyński, who was elected King of Poland and Grand Duke of Lithuania in the years 1704–09 (an interruption to the reign of August II) and 1733–36 (parallel to August III). Leszczyński led his struggle for the throne on behalf of the republican tradition of the nobility. At the same time, he strove for the modernization of the political system. In his political camp, Stanisław Dunin-Karwicki (1640–1725) argued for a pure republic as a counter-project to the Saxon vision of an absolute monarchy.[68] Another writing, the anonymous treatise *A Free Voice Ensuring Freedom* which used to be formally ascribed to Leszczyński himself, sketches out a new balance between the monarchical and the republican elements.[69] The author demands a standing army, regular

68 Stanisław Dunin-Karwicki, 'Exorbitantiae we wszystkich trzech stanach Rzeczypospolitey krótko zebrane' (Warszawa, 1705), Manuscript 6672 I, Biblioteka Narodowa, Warszawa; Latin version: Stanisław Dunin-Karwicki, 'De corrigendis defectibus in statu Reipublicae Polonae' (1708), Manuscript 975/I, Ossolineum Wrocław; Stanisław Dunin-Karwicki, *De ordinanda republica seu de corrigendis defectibus in statu Reipublicae Polonae*, Reprint of the printed edition of 1746 (Kraków: Typis officinae ephemeridum 'Czas,' 1871).

69 Stanisław Leszczyński, *Głos wolny, wolność ubezpieczający* (Kraków: Wydawnictwo Biblioteki Polskiej, 1858).

collection of taxes, and active stimulation of the economy. These two works, written during an existential crisis of the Commonwealth, document the new readiness of a large part of the noble citizenship to undertake bold reforms. At the same time, they mark the end of the Renaissance paradigm.

The new discourse was focused on the problematic institution of the *liberum veto*, i.e. the blocking of legislation by a small group or even a single member of parliament.[70] The *liberum veto* was not only a hindrance for internal politics but also a deadly weapon in the hands of Poland-Lithuania's neighbours. The first author to connect the critique on the *liberum veto* with a natural law perspective was Stanisław Konarski (1700–1773), the most advanced political writer of the middle of the eighteenth century. His comprehensive treatise *On the effective proceeding of councils or On the maintaining of the ordinary Sejms* was written during the first half of the reign of King August III (1733–63) when Konarski was a follower of Leszczyński. Once it was printed on the cusp of the reign of Stanisław August Poniatowski (1764–95), it practically silenced the supporters of the *liberum veto*.[71] As a specialist in the history of law, Konarski unmasked the phantasmagoric mythology behind the *liberum veto*. In Konarski's own vision, the law of nature appears as the essence of the postlapsarian nature of man. The limited epistemic faculties, the strong affects, and especially the selfishness of human beings require a new model of civic unity. Moreover, there are irreducible differences in temperament, education, belief and judgement throughout the society. A parliamentary practice based on the technique of unanimous voting demands God to constantly perform miracles. It is more realistic to switch to majority voting. From a purely anthropological and metaphysical point of view, Konarski's argumentation was a recourse to Renaissance Stoicism. However, his extremely detailed description of a possible new practice in a desperate political situation marks a conceptual breakthrough.[72] Konarski successfully separated the political discourse from religious tradition and finally drew the vision of a new republic away from the Renaissance model. Natural law was not viewed any more as a mere regulative idea for a mixed republic. Conceived in a up-to-date Western manner, it became an autonomous, superior and normative source of law. In the second half of the eighteenth century, this breakthrough was intellectually achieved with reference to Montesquieu by the authors of the 1791 Constitu-

70 Grześkowiak-Krwawicz, *Regina Libertas*, 143sqq. and passim.

71 Stanisław Hieronim Konarski, *O skutecznym rad sposobie, albo, O utrzymywaniu ordynaryinych seymow* (Warszawa: Drukarnia J.K. Mci y Rzpltey u XX Scholarum Piarum, 1760).

72 Grześkowiak-Krwawicz, *Regina Libertas*, 223sqq. and passim.

tion, with reference to Vattel by the Physiocrats Stroynowski and Chreptowicz and, finally, with reference to Kant by the last generation of Enlighteners, i.e. Słotwiński and Czartoryski.

4 Summary

Did the Polish-Lithuanian Commonwealth elaborate a specific understanding of natural law? The answer is not obvious. Unlike in the West, natural law did not become a significant juridical category in the seventeenth century. It remained in the academic field of ethics and anthropology, partly also theology, from where it discreetly radiated to the public discourse. The pluralism of law systems, the strong civil society, the weak state institutions, the unbalanced estate order and the mistrust of the political class towards modern governance prevented natural law from becoming a system of principles sufficient for the deduction of the rules of positive law. Remarkably, the juridical culture in today's Poland is generally viewed as natural law. But this is the outcome of later historical periods.

However, the answer is more positive if we refrain from the aspect of deducibility. Natural law played an important role in the Polish-Lithuanian discourse due to its capability to mediate and arbitrate between three conflicting features of the republic. These were, first, the republican form of government, mostly defined as a mixed republic and, starting from the early eighteenth century, also as a pure republic (however, always with a monarch). Second, this republic was dominated by the nobility while other estates, classes and social groups were strongly disadvantaged. Third, a strong autonomy of numerous ethnic, linguistic and religious groups competed with what early modern theories conceive as the sovereignty of the state.

The first aspect, the republican government, was connected to natural law through natural rationality, usually understood in an Aristotelian (*animal rationale*) and Ciceronian (*recta ratio*) sense. The republic appeared as a structure which, if well equilibrated, mirrors the natural order. However, the natural order could hardly be conceived as defined once and for all. Before the eighteenth century, Polish and Lithuanian philosophers did not become interested in the problem of nature as the external world (*natura rerum* or *natura naturata*). Their perspective was anthropological, ethical, economic, and political. Nature remained the nature of man. The discussion was about its dependence on, or independence of, divine nature and about harmonizing the republic's shape with the given understanding of human nature. The republic was not viewed as a modern state, be it a city or territorial state, but as the confederation of two monarchies, Poland and Lithuania. In such a setting, natural law remained bound to an understanding of human nature in a multi-cultural, multi-confessional and multi-state territorial republic.

The second aspect concerns the universalism of natural law. Natural law is about man as such, his natural rationality and sociability on which politics is founded. In this regard, it was regularly used to criticize the dominance of the nobility and demand more egalitarian structures. The nobility itself did not elaborate a natural law doctrine. In the sixteenth century, natural law was embraced by intellectuals affiliated with the royal court through European humanist networks. These intellectuals left a lasting mark: a moderate but evident social egalitarianism.

Third, the republic consisted not only of its above mentioned official geographical parts and estates but also of a high number of self-governed entities: towns and minorities. Many of them used their own law. In the beginnings of the Polish-Lithuanian natural law discourse, this pluralism was viewed as a major obstacle to the coherence of the republic. Renaissance authors who argued for the unification of law on the basis of Roman law viewed natural law only as a subsidiary source of normativity and a catalyst helping to bring about civic unity with respect for the differing cultures. This paradigm prevented the reception of Western concepts of natural law during the seventeenth century and remained in place until the early eighteenth century.

Thus, the Polish-Lithuanian approach to natural law, with its predominant roots in Renaissance humanism, did not meet the criteria of systematic natural law of the seventeenth century. However, it was anything but an unspecific rejection of the harbingers of modernity. It pragmatically embraced naturalism, contractualism and cultural pluralism, sometimes even earlier than this happened in the Western discourse. From a philosophical point of view, Scattola seems to have captured this variety in a nutshell when describing the Aristotelian *phronesis* as one of the roots of the 'natural law before natural law': it is prudent practice and practical prudence which, essentially, will never become a theory.[73]

Acknowledgement

The linguistic proofreading was supported by the Max Weber Centre for Advanced Cultural and Social Studies of the University of Erfurt.

73 Scattola, *Das Naturrecht vor dem Naturrecht*, 19.

Bibliography

Primary Sources

Annales Ingolstadiensis Academiae, vol. 2: 1572–1672, Ingolstadt: Krüll, 1782.

Chreptowicz, Joachim Litawor, *O prawie natury pismo oryginalne jednego z współziomków*, Warszawa: w Drukarni Gazety Warszawskiey, 1814.

Czartoryski, Adam Jerzy, *Essai sur la diplomatie ou manuscrit d'un philhellène*, Paris and Marseille: Firmin Didot Frères, 1830.

Dunin-Karwicki, Stanisław, 'De corrigendis defectibus in statu Reipublicae Polonae' (1708), Manuscript 975/I, Ossolineum Wrocław.

Dunin-Karwicki, Stanisław, *De ordinanda republica seu de corrigendis defectibus in statu Reipublicae Polonae*, Reprint of the printed edition of 1746, Kraków: Typis officinae ephemeridum 'Czas,' 1871.

Dunin-Karwicki, Stanisław, 'Exorbitantiae we wszystkich trzech stanach Rzeczypospolitey krótko zebrane' (Warszawa, 1705), Manuscript 6672 I, Biblioteka Narodowa, Warszawa.

Konarski, Stanisław Hieronim, *O skutecznym rad sposobie, albo, O utrzymywaniu ordynaryinych seymow, etc.*, Warszawa: Drukarnia J.K. Mci y Rzpltey u XX Scholarum Piarum, 1760.

Kutrzeba, Stanisław and Władysław Semkowicz, eds., *Akta unii Polski z Litwą 1385–1791*, Kraków: nakład Polskiej Akademii Umiejętności, 1932.

Leszczyński, Stanisław, *Głos wolny, wolność ubezpieczający*. Kraków: Wydawnictwo Biblioteki Polskiej, 1858.

Logica (Ingolstadt, 1612), Manuscript F3-2170, Library of the University of Vilnius.

Modrzewski, Andrzej Frycz, *Commentariorum de republica emendanda libri quinque*, Basileae: Oporinus, 1554.

Modzelewski, Zacharias, *Praelectiones politicae anni 1690* (Vilnius, 1691), fol. 1–18v, Manuscript F3-1390, Library of the University of Vilnius.

New Constitution of the Government of Poland, Established by the Revolution, the Third of May, 1791, London: J. Debrett, 1791.

Niczyporuk, Piotr, 'Pubilkacje romanistyczne w Akademii Wileńskiej w latach 1644–1655,' *Z dziejów prawa* 12 (2019): 163–184.

Olizarowski, Aron Aleksander, *De politica hominum societate / Apie politinę žmonių sąjungą*, trans. Jolita Sarcevičienė, Vilnius: Aidai, 2003.

Olizarowski, Aron Aleksander, *De politica hominum societate libri tres*, Dantisci: Sumptibus Georgii Forsteri, 1651.

Olizarowski, Aron Aleksander, *Quaestiones politicae in utramque partem disputatae*, Ingolstadii: Typis Gregorii Haenlini, 1643.

Philosophia practica (Ingolstadt, 1612), Manuscript F9-8, Wroblewski Library of the Lithuanian Academy of Sciences.

Puciłowski, Christophorus, *Praelectiones politicae anni 1691* (Vilnius, 1691), fol. 94–127, Manuscript F3-1390, Library of the University of Vilnius.

Roisius, Petrus, *Decisiones*, 1st ed., Cracoviae: Matthaeus Siebeneycher, 1563.

Roisius, Petrus, *Decisiones*, 2nd ed., Francoforti: Feyerabend, 1570.

Roisius, Petrus, *Decisiones*, 3rd ed., Venetiis: apud Bartholomaeum Rubinum, 1572.

Słotwiński, Felix, *Prawo natury prywatne*, Kraków: w Drukarni u Stanisława Gieszkowskiego, 1825.

Stroynowski, Hieronim, *Nauka prawa przyrodzonego, politycznego, ekonomiki polityczney i prawa narodów*, Wilno [Vilnius]: w Drukarni Królewskiey przy Akademii, 1785.

Vladimiri, Paulus, 'Tractatus de Potestate Papae et Imperatoris Respectu Infidelium,' in *Starodawne Prawa Polskiego Pomniki*, ed. Michał Bobrzynski, vol. 1, 159–194, Kraków: Sumptibus Academiae Litterarum, 1878.

Secondary Sources

Belch, Stanislaus F., *Paulus Vladimiri and his doctrine concerning international law and politics*, Den Haag and Paris: Mouton & Co., 1965.

Bieńkowski, Tadeusz, ed., *Andrzej Frycz Modrzewski i problemy kultury polskiego Odrodzenia*, Wrocław: Ossolineum, 1974.

Courtine, Jean-Francois, 'Vitoria, Suárez et la naissance du droit naturel moderne,' in *Histoire de la philosophie politique*, ed. Alain Renaut, vol. 2, 127–181, Paris: Calmann-Lévy, 1999.

Dyjakowska, Marzena, 'Decisiones Lituanicae Piotra Rojzjusza – przykład renesansowego źródła poznania stosowania prawa rzymskiego przed sądem asesorskim w Wilnie. Problemy badawcze i translatorskie,' *Krakowskie Studia z Historii Państwa i Prawa* 13 (2020/1): 1–15.

Ehrlich, Ludwik, ed., *Polski wykład prawa wojny XV wieku*, Warszawa: Wydawnictwo prawnicze, 1955.

Fijałkowski, Tomasz, 'Piotr Rojzjusz – polski romanista XVI wieku. Zarys problematyki,' in *Z dziejów polskiej kultury umysłowej w XVI i XVII wieku*, ed. Waldemar Voisé, 7–76, Wrocław: Ossolineum, 1976.

Frost, Robert, *The Oxford History of Poland-Lithuania. Vol. 1: The Making of the Polish-Lithuanian Union, 1385–1569*, Oxford: Oxford University Press, 2015.

Griškevič, Lina, et al., eds., *Lietuvos konstitucionalizmo istorija*, Vilnius: Vilniaus universiteto leidykla, 2016.

Grześkowiak-Krwawicz, Anna, *Regina Libertas. Wolność w polskiej myśli politycznej XVIII wieku*, Gdańsk: Wydawnictwo słowo/obraz terytoria, 2006.

Haakonssen, Knud, 'Early Modern Natural Law Theories,' in *The Cambridge Companion to Natural Law Jurisprudence*, ed. by George Duke and Robert P. George, 76–102, Cambridge: Cambridge University Press, 2017.

Haakonssen, Knud. *Natural Law and Moral Philosophy: From Grotius to the Scottish Enlightenment*. Cambridge: Cambridge Univerity Press, 1996.

Huber, Steffen, *Einführung in die Geschichte der polnischen Sozialphilosophie*, Wiesbaden: Harrassowitz, 2014.

Huber, Steffen, *Polifonia tradycji. Filozofia praktyczna i teoretyczna Andrzeja Frycza Modrzewskiego*, Warszawa: Sub Lupa, 2014.

Huber, Steffen, 'The Philosopher's Refusal of Action: Andreas Fricius Modrevius (1503–1572),' in *Penser et agir à la Renaissance*, ed. Philippe Desan and Véronique Ferrer, 529–551, Genève: Droz, 2020.

Hunter, Ian, *Rival Enlightenments: Civil and Metaphysical Philosophy in Early Modern Germany*, Cambridge: Cambridge University Press, 2001.

Hunter, Ian, 'The Law of Nature and Nations,' in *The Law of Nature and Nations*, ed. by Aaron Garrett, 559–592, London: Routledge, 2014.

Jarra, Eugenjusz, 'Aron Aleksander Olizarowski jako filozof prawa,' in *Księga Pamiątkowa celem uczczenia 350-ej rocznicy założenia Uniwersytetu Stefana Batorego w Wilnie*, 33–72, Warszawa: Uniwersytet Warszawski, 1931.

Kawecka-Gryczowa, Alodia, *Andrzej Frycz Modrzewski: bibliografia*, Wrocław: Ossolineum, 1962.

Kiaupienė, Jūratė and Lidia Korczak, eds., *1413 m. Horodlės aktai (dokumentai ir tyrinėjimai) / Akty horodelskie z 1413 roku (dokumenty i studia)*, Vilnius and Kraków: Lietuvos istorijos institutas leidykla, 2013.

Kiaupienė, Jūratė and Andrzej Zakrzewski, 'Unie polsko-litewskie – próba nowego spojrzenia,' in *Lex est Rex in Polonia et Lithuania. Tradycje prawno-ustrojowe Rzeczypospolitej – doświadczenie i dziedzictwo*, ed. Adam Jankiewicz, 65–82, Warszawa: Biuro Trybunału Konstytucyjnego, 2008.

Kot, Stanisław, *Aron Aleksander Olizarowski*, Wilno (Vilnius): Józef Zawadzki, 1929.

Kremer, Andrzej, 'Pedro Ruiz de Moros: hiszpański profesor prawa rzymskiego Akademii Krakowskiej w XVI wieku,' in *Vetera novis augere: studia i prace dedykowane Profesorowi Wacławowi Uruszczakowi*, ed. Stanisław Grodziski, Dorota Malec, and Anna Karabowicz, 479–490, Kraków: WUJ, 2010.

Kutuzava, N. A., 'Брэсцкая унія як сацыякультурны феномен: сацыяльна-палітычныя праблемы,' in *Гісторыя філасофскай і грамадска-палітычнай думкі Беларусі*, ed. V.B. Evaroiski, 255–278, Minsk: Belaruskaja navuka, 2013.

Łuczak, Aleksander, *Die Staats- und Rechtslehre des polnischen Renaissancedenkers Andrzej Frycz Modrzewski*, Zürich: Juris, 1966.

Machovenko, Jevgenij and Lina Griškevič, 'Bendravalstybinės LDK privilegijos kaip Lietuvos konstituciniai aktai,' *Teisė* 93 (2014): 46–66.

Maliniak, Wladislaus, *Andreas Fricius Modrevius. Ein Beitrag zur Geschichte der Staats- und Völkerrechtstheorien*, Wien: A. Hölder, 1913.

Mariani, Andrea, 'The contribution of the Society of Jesus to the political culture of Lithuanian elites,' *Open Political Science* 2019; 2: 153–173.

Niczyporuk, Piotr, 'Aaron Aleksander Olizarowski profesorem prawa Akademii Wileńskiej,' *Miscellanea Historico-Iuridica* 14 (2015/2): 181–206.

Niczyporuk, Piotr, 'Assertiones ex jurisprudentia Aarona Aleksandra Olizarowskiego – rozprawa, która nigdy nie powstała,' in *Ustrój państwa, myśl polityczno-prawna, współczesne systemy rządów. Prace ofiarowane Profesorowi Adamowi Jamrozowi z okazji Jego jubileuszu*, ed. Stanisław Bożyk and Artur Olechno, 705–714, Białystok: Temida, 2018.

Niczyporuk, Piotr, 'Pubilkacje romanistyczne w Akademii Wileńskiej w latach 1644–1655,' *Z dziejów prawa* 12 (2019): 163–184.

Plečkaitis, Romanas, *Lietuvos filosofijos istorija.* Vol. 1: *Viduramžiai – renesansas – naujieji amžiai*, Vilnius: Kultūros, filosofijos ir meno institutas, 2004.

Pyszka, Stanisław, 'Il dritto alla liberta personale ed alla cittadinanza di contadini Polacchi a Lituani in Aron Aleksander Olizarowski (1610–1659),' *Forum Philosophicum* 7 (2002): 205–237.

Rachuba, Andrzej, Jūratė Kiaupienė and Zigmuntas Kiaupa, *Historia Litwy: Dwugłos Polsko-Litewski*, Warszawa: DiG, 2008.

Rybicki, Paweł, 'Z dziejów polskiego arystotelizmu: "De Politica Hominum Societate" Arona Aleksandra Olizarowskiego,' *Studia i Materiały z Dziejów Nauki Polskiej* 7 (1959): 83–136.

Scattola, Merio, 'Before and after Natural Law. Models of Natural Law in Ancient and Modern Times,' in *Early Modern Natural Law Theories. Contexts and Strategies in the Early Enlightenment*, ed. Timothy J. Hochstrasser and Peter Schröder, 1–30, Dordrecht: Kluwer Academic, 2003.

Scattola, Merio, *Das Naturrecht vor dem Naturrecht: Zur Geschichte des 'ius naturae' im 16. Jahrhundert*, Tübingen: Niemeyer, 1999.

Schwab, Dieter, 'Der Staat im Naturrecht der Scholastik,' in *Naturrecht und Staat. Politische Funktionen des europäischen Naturrechts (17.–19. Jahrhundert)*, ed. Diethelm Klippel, 1–18, München: Oldenbourg Verlag, 2006.

Sczaniecki, Michał, 'Jean Bodin et Pologne,' *Czasopismo Prawno-Historyczne* 29 (1977/2): 39–53.

Voisé, Waldemar, 'Deux républiques opposées: Fricius et Bodin,' *Czasopismo Prawno-Historyczne* 29 (1977/2): 55–63.

Voisé, Waldemar, *Frycza Modrzewskiego nauka o państwie i prawie*, Warszawa: Książka i Wiedza, 1956.

Wünsch, Thomas, 'Kirchenreform und Konziliarismus in Polen. Europäischer Kontext und eigenständige Entwicklung,' *Acta Mediaevalia Lublin* 12 (1999): 159–173.

CHAPTER 2

The Influence of Natural Law on the Discourse of Toleration in Seventeenth-Century Poland-Lithuania

Karin Friedrich

1 Introduction

As Hugo Grotius said, 'the wish to legislate on religion is not Polish.'[1] In contrast to the many early modern European states plagued by religious warfare, Poland-Lithuania gained an almost legendary reputation of religious toleration, as a 'state without stakes.'[2] This image is not entirely wrong. Orthodox Ruthenians dominated in Piast Poland's south-eastern borderlands, and pagans survived in Lithuania, after the 1385 Treaty of Krėva/Krewo created a union between the crown of Poland and the Grand Duchy of Lithuania under the Jagiellonian dynasty. King Władysław Jagiełło used Hussite troops in the wars against the Teutonic Knights. Religious diversity had been a reality of everyday life long before the Reformation in Wittenberg or Geneva. At the Council of Constance in July 1416, Paulus Vladimiri (c.1370–1435), rector of the Jagiellonian university in Cracow, called out the Teutonic Knights' attacks against the pagans on the Baltic coast an injustice and incompatible with divine and natural law. He did so in the spirit of his university's conciliarist tradition. By defending the right of pagans, infidels and Jews to their life and property, he anticipated the natural law arguments that followers of the School of Salamanca later used in defence of the natives in the Spanish colonies in the Americas.[3] He was well aware of the statute of Kalisz, issued by Duke Bolesław

1 For the quote from *Hugonis Grotii Epistolae ad Israelem Jaski* (Dantisci: Rhetius, 1670), see Stanisław Kot, 'Hugo Grotius a Polska,' in Stanisław Kot, *Polska złotego wieku a Europa. Studia i szkice*, ed. Henryk Barycz (Warszawa: PIW, 1987), 597. I would like to thank Gábor Gángó for his feedback on this chapter.

2 Typically, Janusz Tazbir, *A State Without Stakes: Religious Toleration in Reformation Poland-Lithuania* (New York: Kościuszko Foundation, 1973).

3 Paweł Włodkowicz, 'Traktat o władzy papieża i cesarza w stosunku do pogan,' in *700 lat myśli polskiej. Filozofia i myśl społeczna XVII wieku*, ed. Jan Domański (Warszawa: PWN, 1978), 184–203. See also Thomas Wünsch, *Konziliarismus in Polen: Personen, Politik und Programme*

 | DOI:10.1163/9789004545847_003

the Pious in 1264, which had established separate tribunals for criminal matters involving Christians and Jews; it was ratified several times by successive kings well into the sixteenth century. In consequence, Poland became a magnet for Jews and religious groups expelled from other parts of Europe.

In 1592, the Lutheran historian and deputy to the Polish Diet (Sejm), Swiętosław Orzelski (1549–1598), wrote approvingly: 'There is nothing new about the large number of religions in Poland. Next to the Greek religion, pagans and Jews have been known for a long time, and many other non-Roman Catholics have lived here for centuries.'[4] More critically, Stanisław Hozjusz (Hosius, 1504–1579), the bishop of Warmia, warned that the Pope suspected that Poland-Lithuania had become an 'asylum hereticorum,' a state of affairs that in his opinion needed urgent redress.[5] Yet alarmed by the spectacle of violent warfare between religious factions in sixteenth-century France and the Netherlands, the Inquisition in Spain and Italy, and the conflicts in the German lands of the Empire, a majority of voices in sixteenth-century Poland agreed that prosperity and peace depended on finding pragmatic solutions to religious struggle. For the Renaissance and Reformation periods, scholars such as Howard Louthan, Paul Knoll, Maciej Ptaszyński and Natalia Nowakowska have therefore consistently traced the influence on the Polish kingdom of irenical ideas from Erasmus to Melanchthon.[6]

Religious peace demands a minimum of religious toleration when living side-by-side: the 'absence of coordinated destruction combined with the continued presence of religious diversity.'[7] While making use of this working definition, it is not my intention to add ever more detail to an analysis of

---

aus Polen zur Verfassungsfrage der Kirche in der Zeit der mittelalterlichen Reformkonzilien (Paderborn: F. Schöningh, 1998).

4 Swiętosław Orzelski, *Bezkrólewia ksiąg ośmioro*, ed. Edward Kuntze (Kraków: Nakładem Polskiej Akademii Umiejętności, 1917), 339 [all quotes from Polish are translated by the author, K.F.].

5 Ambroise Jobert, *De Luther à Mohila: la Pologne pendant la crise de la chrétienté 1517–1648* (Paris: Collection historique de l'Institut d'Etudes Slaves, 1974), 110–111.

6 Howard Louthan, 'A Model for Christendom? Erasmus, Poland and the Reformation,' *Church History* 83 (March 2014): 18–37; Maciej Ptaszyński, *Reformacja w Polsce a dziedzictwo Erazma z Rotterdamu* (Warszawa: Wydawnictwo Uniwersytetu Warszawskiego, 2018); Paul Knoll, 'Religious Toleration in Sixteenth-Century Poland. Political Realities and Social Constraints,' in *Diversity and Dissent. Negotiating Religious Difference in Central Europe, 1500–1800*, ed. Howard Louthan, Gary Cohen, and Franz A.J. Szabo (New York and Oxford: Berghahn, 2011), 30–52; Natalia Nowakowska, *King Sigismund of Poland and Martin Luther: The Reformation before Confessionalization* (Oxford: Oxford University Press, 2018).

7 Wayne T. Te Brake, *Religious War and Religious Peace in Early Modern Europe* (Cambridge: Cambridge University Press, 2017), 17.

the extent, practice and limits of 'toleration' in Poland-Lithuania – a task well accomplished over recent decades by a growing historiography.[8] My aim is rather to explore elements of natural law theory that determined the discussion about toleration in Poland-Lithuania, from the Confederation of Warsaw in 1573 to the beginning of the Second Northern War (1655–60), when the liberties of non-Roman-Catholics in the Commonwealth significantly declined. Poland-Lithuania continued its dialogue with the late humanist European republic of letters and international Calvinism during the first decades of the seventeenth century, where the works of Hugo Grotius (1583–1645) attracted lively attention. In the context of the 300th anniversary of the publication of Grotius's magnum opus, *De Jure belli ac pacis* (1625), Stanisław Kot was one of the first to shed light on Grotius's relationship with Poland-Lithuania and the considerable number of Poles who entered his scholarly and diplomatic networks, particularly during his lengthy stays in Paris (1598–1599, 1621–1631 and 1634–1645).[9] Based on Grotius's extensive correspondence during his exile, Kot traced the Dutchman's engagement with conflicting religious doctrines across political borders, cultures and constitutions. Grotius's understanding

8 For example, Kazimierz Bem, *Calvinism in the Polish-Lithuanian Commonwealth, 1548–1648: The Churches and the Faithful* (Leiden, Boston: Brill, 2020); Tomasz Kempa, *Konflikty wyznaniowe w Wilnie od początku reformacji do końca XVII wieku* (Toruń: Wydawnictwo Naukowe Uniwersytetu Mikołaja Kopernika, 2016); Dariusz Chemperek, ed., *Ewangelicyzm Reformowany w pierwszej Rzeczypospolitej: Dialog z Europą i wybory aksjologiczne w świetle literatury i piśmiennictwa XVI–XVII wieku* (Warszawa: Wydawnictwo Uniwersytetu Warszawskiego, 2015); David Frick, *Kith, Kin, and Neighbors: Communities and Confessions in Seventeenth-Century Wilno* (Ithaca and London: Cornell University Press, 2013); Sławomir Kościelak, *Katolicy w protestanckim Gdańsku od drugiej połowy XVI do końca XVIII wieku* (Gdańsk: Wydawnictwo Uniwersytetu Gdańskiego 2012); Kęstutis Daugirdas, 'Rezeption der Theologie Calvins im Großfürstentum Litauen und Königreich Polen,' in *Calvin und Calvinismus. Europäische Perspektiven*, ed. Irene Dingel and Hermann Selderhuis (Göttingen: Vandenhoeck & Ruprecht, 2011), 155–220; Wojciech Kriegseisen, *Stosunki wyznaniowe w relacjach państwo-kościół między reformacją a oświeceniem: Rzesza Niemiecka, Niderlandy Północne, Rzeczpospolita polsko-litewska* (Warszawa: Semper, 2010); Yvonne Kleinmann et al., ed. *Kommunikation durch symbolische Akte. Religiöse Heterogenität und politische Herrschaft in Polen-Litauen* (Stuttgart: Steiner, 2010); Tomasz Kempa, *Wobec kontrreformacji: protestanci i prawosławni w obronie swobód wyznaniowych w Rzeczypospolitej w końcu XVI i w pierwszej połowie XVII wieku* (Toruń: Adam Marszałek, 2007); Liudmila V. Charipova, *Latin Books and the Eastern Orthodox Clerical Elite in Kiev, 1632–1780* (Manchester and New York: Manchester University Press, 2006); Adam Kaźmierczyk, Andrzej Link-Lenczowski, and Mariusz Markiewicz, ed., *Rzeczpospolita wielu wyznań. Materiały z międzynarodowej konferencji. Kraków 18–20 listopada 2002* (Kraków: Księgarnia Akademicka, 2004); Michael G. Müller, *Zweite Reformation und städtische Autonomie im Königlichen Preußen. Danzig, Elbing und Thorn in der Epoche der Konfessionalisierung 1557–1660* (Berlin: Akademie Verlag, 1997).

9 Kot, 'Hugo Grotius a Polska,' 581, 587.

of constitutional monarchy and his emphasis on sociability and reason also suited the moderate 'constitutionalists' among the Polish politicians of the mid-seventeenth century, such as Łukasz Opaliński (1612–1666) and Szymon Starowolski S.J. (1588–1656) – both contemporaries of Grotius. While historians have recognised the works by Niccolò Machiavelli (1469–1527), Jean Bodin (1530–1596), Justus Lipsius (1547–1606), and Francisco Suárez (1548–1617) as important 'Western influences' on early modern Polish political thought,[10] natural law thinking has – with the exception of the Academic Gymnasia in Royal Prussia[11] – rarely been associated with the Commonwealth's early modern political culture. In fact, there are some good arguments why a significant natural law tradition in Poland-Lithuania has not been identified as such.[12] Even less frequently have historians of ideas tried to find what inspirations Western natural law theory might have drawn from Poland-Lithuania's multi-religious experience. Before Grotius's influence on European natural law thinking was cemented in the later seventeenth century, particularly in

10 For example, Robert Frost, 'Medicinal Herbs and Poison Plants: Reading Machiavelli in the Polish-Lithuanian Commonwealth, 1560–1700,' in *Unie międzypaństwowe, parlamentaryzm, samorządność*, ed. Wacław Uruszczak et al. (Warszawa: Wydawnictwo Sejmowe, 2020), 28–53; Maria O. Pryshlak, *Państwo w filozofii politycznej Łukasza Opalińskiego*, transl. Grzegorz Chomicki (Kraków: Historia Iagiellonica, 2000); Joanna Orzeł, 'Rzeczpospolita Obojga Narodów w pismach Jeana Bodina,' in *Kontakty, tradycje i stosunki polsko-francuskie od XVI do początków XX wieku. Zbiór studiów*, ed. Joanna Orzeł and Mariusz Mróz (Toruń: Wydawnictwo Adam Marszałek, 2012), 44–56. For good summaries of the influence of European political ideas on Poland, see Dorota Pietrzyk-Reeves, *Polish Republican Discourse in the Sixteenth Century* (Cambridge: Cambridge University Press, 2020) and Benedict Wagner-Rundell, *Common Wealth, Common Good. The Politics of Virtue in Early Modern Poland-Lithuania* (Oxford: Oxford University Press, 2015). On Suárez, see Henryk Olszewski, *Historia doktryn politycznych i prawnych* (Warszawa: PWN, 1982), esp. 134–136, and Stanisław Obirek S.J., *Jezuici w Rzeczypospolitej obojga narodów w latach 1564–1668. Działalność religijna, społeczno-kulturalna i polityczna* (Kraków: Wydział Filozoficzny Towarzystwa Jezusowego, 1996), esp. 141–142.

11 For a good summary of these works, see Kazimierz Maliszewski, 'Najnowsze zbiorowe dzieło z historii Gdańskiego Gimnazjum Akademickiego w dobie Rzeczypospolitej,' *Zapiski Historyczne* 78 (2013/3): 175–186. See also Tadeusz Bieńkowski, 'Nauczanie filozofii w Gdańsku w XVI–XVII wieku,' in *Nauczanie filozofii w Polsce w XV–XVIII wieku*, ed. Lech Szczucki (Wrocław et al.: Zakład Narodowy im. Ossolińskich, 1978), 157–165, and Stanisław Pyszka S.J., *Nauczanie filozofii moralnej w uniwersytetach i gimnazjach akademickich w Polsce i na Litwie od XV do XVII wieku w świetle podręczników wykładowych* (Kraków: Wydawnictwo WAM, 2011), on Gdańsk, esp. 61–69. See also Gábor Gángó's study in this volume.

12 See the contributions by Anna Grześkowiak-Krwawicz and Steffen Huber in this volume. Huber summarizes the state of art on the topic, and stresses the difficulties of categorizing early modern philosophical approaches to natural law.

Protestant legal and political thinking through the work of Samuel Pufendorf (1632–1694) and Jean Barbeyrac (1674–1744) who dismissed Grotius's concept of a 'voluntary law of nations' but stressed his role in formulating a secular law of nature, the Dutchman's role as an irencial biblical scholar and historian found great appreciation among his contemporaries in Poland-Lithuania.[13] West European historiography has largely overlooked the reception of Grotian ideas which were directly informed by the example of Polish toleration. With the political decline of the Polish-Lithuanian Commonwealth during the eighteenth century, the awareness of the influence of East-Central European religious pluralism on Grotius's ideas on toleration and sociability waned. Grotius's dialogue with Polish and Lithuanian Catholics, Calvinists and even Antitrinitarians, however, will require greater attention in the future.

2 Toleration and the Confederation of Warsaw (1573)

While practical toleration is best measured by the success of peaceful religious coexistence, specific political and legal actions prepared the way for the conditions of toleration in the Commonwealth. Following the 1570 Consensus of Sandomierz, an agreement between the dominant Protestant groups in the Commonwealth, the Interregnum Sejm of 1573 formed the Confederation of Warsaw. It was an electoral pact that laid down the mutual toleration of all 'dissidentes in religione': Catholics, Orthodox, Lutherans, Calvinist-Reformed and Bohemian Brethren, excluding, however, Antitrinitarian groups (Arians, Socinians or Polish Brethren). The Confederation's 'agreement to disagree' in doctrinal matters of religion and to uphold each other's right to exercise their chosen religion became part of the *pacta conventa*,[14] to which all future Polish

13 Simone Zurbuchen, ed., *The Law of Nations and Natural Law 1625–1800* (Leiden: Brill, 2019), see especially the Introduction by Simone Zurbuchen, 1–9, and the chapter by Frank Grunert, 'The Law of Nations in German historia literaria and Encyclopaedias in the Eighteenth Century,' 89–105, and passim, e.g. 21, 92, 135. See also Merio Scattola, *Das Naturrecht vor dem Naturrecht. Zur Geschichte des 'ius naturae' im 16. Jahrhundert* (Tübingen: Max Niemeyer, 1999), 215–217.

14 *Confoederatio Generalis Warsaviensis 1573*, in *Volumina Legum II* [Saint Petersburg: s.l. 1859] ed. Jozafat Ohryzki (repr. Warszawa: Wydawnictwo Artystyczne i Filmowe, 1980), 124–125 (§ 841). The articles of the Warsaw Confederation were first presented to Henri of Valois as part of the Articuli Henriciani after his election in 1573. See Dariusz Makiłła, *Artykuły henrykowskie (1573–1576)* (Warszawa: Vizja Press, 2012). Among the large literature on the Consensus and the Confederation of Warsaw, see Oskar Halecki, *Zgoda*

kings were bound to swear an oath upon their election. This act came as close to making toleration part of the kingdom's laws as was possible in the Polish monarchy, which did not have a codified legal system.

The Lithuanian Council went further. It incorporated the text of the Confederation into the Lithuanian Statute, a separate law codex for the Grand Duchy of Lithuania, which saw its third revision in 1588.[15] Protestant and Orthodox nobles could henceforth claim equal rights with Catholics in being appointed to offices, to exercise their religion in peace, patronize their subjects, schools and churches, and find defence in the law courts of the Grand Duchy. In reality, conflict flared up during the 1590s, when the number of attacks by Jesuit students and Catholic crowds on Protestant institutions increased, particularly in cities and noble-owned parishes, while tribunal decisions were increasingly directed by Catholics.[16] The Calvinist church in Vilnius/Wilno was repeatedly destroyed in 1591, 1611 and 1640, despite the legal protection the Lithuanian Statute should have accorded.[17] In Poland-Lithuania, the Antitrinitarian Academy at Raków was closed down in 1638, and the church of the Bohemian Brethren in Leszno went up in flames in 1656.

Despite these violations, the Warsaw Confederation attracted the attention of European political and legal thinkers. In contrast to the Consensus of Sandomierz, which was as much an attempt to formulate a shared Protestant theological position against the Tridentine decrees as it was a statement against

---

Sandomierska 1570 r. Jej geneza i znaczenie w dziejach reformacyi Polskiej za Zygmunta Augusta (Warszawa: Anczyca i spółki, 1915); Karin Friedrich, 'Die Reformation,' in *Polen in der europäischen Geschichte. Ein Handbuch in Vier Bänden*, general ed. Michael G. Müller, vol. ed. Hans-Jürgen Bömelburg, vol. II: Die Frühe Neuzeit (Stuttgart: Hiersemann, 2011), 123–143; Alfons Brüning, *Unio non est unitas: Polen-Litauens Weg im konfessionellen Zeitalter (1569–1648)* (Wiesbaden: Harrassowitz, 2008); Jolanta Dworzaczkowa, *Bracia Czescy w Wielkopolsce w XVI i XVII wieku* (Warszawa: Semper, 1997); Mirosław Korołko, *Klejnot wolnego sumienia: Polemika wokół konfedercji warszawskiej w latach 1573–1658* (Warszawa: Instytut Wydawniczy PAX, 1974).

15 *Statut Wielkiego Xięstwa Litewskiego naprzód za Naiaśnieyszego Hospodara Króla Jegomości Zygmunta III w Krakowie w roku 1588. Drugi raz w Wilnie 1619 roku.* [...] *Teraz zaś piąty raz ze szczęśliwie panuiącego Naiaśnieyszego Króla Jegomości Augusta Trzeciego przedrukowany* (Wilno: Drukarnia S.J., 1744), 62–65.

16 Specific examples are given in Marek Wajsblum, *Ex regestro arianismi. Szkice z dziejów upadku protestantyzmu w Małopolsce* (Kraków: Nakł. Towarzystwa Badań nad dziejów Reformacji w Polsce, 1937). See also Henryk Wisner, *Rozróżnieni w wierze. Szkice z dziejów Rzeczypospolitej schyłku XVI i połowy XVII wieku* (Warszawa: Książka i Wiedza, 1982), 82–109.

17 Kempa, *Konflikty wyznaniowe w Wilnie*, 299–339, 402–439.

Antitrinitarianism,[18] the Confederation of 1573 saw itself in the tradition of a wider reform movement demanding an 'executio legum et bonum,' which had been directed against inefficient royal jurisdiction, office accumulation and the alienation of royal lands by influential magnates.[19] During the 1550s and 1560s, the Polish nobility had also aimed its anger against the influence of an overbearing ecclesiastical jurisdiction. There were parallels with the Holy Roman Empire where since the 1495 imperial reforms the estates had fought for a regular summoning of the Imperial Diet, protection from the tithe, and for a strengthening of the Imperial Chamber Tribunal (*Reichskammergericht*). The Peace of Augsburg of 1555, which followed the wars of the Schmalkaldic League – an alliance of Protestant princes in their battle against the Emperor and his Catholic supporters – granted the territorial rulers in the Empire the power to implement their religion on their subjects (*cuius regio, eius religio*).[20] Similarly, the Confederation of Warsaw guaranteed that secular and ecclesiastical lords could determine their subjects' religion through their rights of patronage and jurisdiction.[21] Particularly after the union of 1569, when ever more Catholic landowners assumed power over Orthodox subjects in Ukraine, and Calvinist magnates in Lithuania were in charge over confessionally-mixed landed populations, toleration frequently continued in practice. It was rarely reflected in a natural law discourse. Only occasionally, natural law principles shone through political arguments in the debate about toleration, as in 1566, when Hieronim Ossoliński, castellan of Sandomierz and one of the Calvinist members of the executionist movement, warned against ecclesiastical jurisdictions over civic matters: 'The *lex naturae* tells you not to do to others what you do not want others do to you.'[22] Here the Calvinists found common ground with the scholastic tradition of natural law in a variation on Suárez's voluntarism, which stresses the morality of God's will and makes actions either just and

18 Michael G. Müller, 'Der Consensus Sandomiriensis – Geschichte eines Scheiterns? Zur Diskussion über Protestantismus und protestantische Konfessionalisierung in Polen-Litauen,' in *Konfessionelle Pluralität als Herausforderung. Koexistenz und Konflikt in Spätmittelalter und Früher Neuzeit*, ed. Joachim Bahlcke et al. (Leipzig: Leipziger Universitätverlag, 2006), 397–407.

19 Anna Sucheni-Grabowska, *Spory królów ze szlachtą w złotym wieku: Wokół egzekucji praw* (Kraków: Krajowa Agencja Wydawnicza, 1988).

20 For such a comparison see Damien Tricoire, 'Beyond fundamentalism and tolerance narratives: Catholic representation of political-religious order and policy-making in the Holy Roman Empire and Poland-Lithuania,' in *Frühneuzeitliche Reiche in Europa*, ed. Tomasz Gromelski et al. (Wiesbaden: Harrassowitz, 2016), 223–235.

21 *Volumina Legum*, II, 124.

22 Cited in Stanisław Grzybowski, *Teoria reprezentacji w Polsce epoki Odrodzenia* (Warszawa: PWN, 1959), 269–270.

moral (willed by God) or unjust and immoral (forbidden by God). On the same natural law basis, Protestants argued for the free choice of religion, while many Catholic writers saw such liberty as an expression of the vice of self-interest, causing injury to the fabric of a virtuous republic.[23]

The Polish legal discourse also alighted on the *ius commune* which Stanisław Grzybowski identified as a law encompassing all people in the *res publica* and as part of a Polish concept of natural law.[24] From the scholastic perspective, the source of law was always divine and universal. In contrast, the *ius commune* was clearly of human origin, but like natural law it applied to all human beings and was neither a privilege, nor linked to a particular estate (noble or urban), nor was it part of any other particular law, such as canon law or customary law. Good customs could decay over time and customary law could corrupt. As critics pointed out, customary Polish legal practice punished nobles less severely than commoners for the same crime, which violated natural law.[25] Jakub Przyłuski, in his 1533 summary of Polish legal statutes had fiercely opposed such laws as 'constituted against right reason.'[26] This legal practice also stood in stark contrast to Paulus Vladimiri's position, that natural law applied to all human beings, even to pagans. In the late sixteenth century, however, Paulus Vladimiri had fallen out of fashion. Instead, the 'process of confederation,' the ultimately unsuccessful attempt to implement the agreement of 1573, was closely bound up with the defence of privileges and immunities for the nobility by the nobility. Exceptionally, the major cities of Royal Prussia had gained the freedom of religious exercise for the Augsburg Confession from the king in 1557, and the Sejm of 1606 discussed a project aimed at expanding toleration to all subjects. The latter was never implemented.[27] The demand for religious toleration increasingly turned into a secular argument, and for the time being, this helped glossing over theological differences between the citizens who tried to avoid disagreements over matters that Luther had already identified as *adiaphora*.[28] The formula of 'lex est rex,' popular among the nobles in the Sejm, indicated the civic nature of law, pro-

23 Pietrzyk-Reeves, *Polish Republican Discourse*, 172.

24 Grzybowski, *Teoria reprezentacji*, 248.

25 Grzybowski, *Teoria reprezentacji*, 265–267.

26 Jakub Przyłuski, *Leges Seu Statuta Ac Privilegia Regni Poloniae Omnia* (s.l., 1553), quoted in Grzybowski, *Teoria reprezentacji*, 268.

27 Biblioteka PAN w Kórniku rkps 325, Fol. 579, cited in Henryk Wisner, *Najjaśniejsza Rzeczpospolita. Szkice z dziejów Polski szlacheckiej XVI–XVII wieku* (Warszawa: PIW, 1978), 150.

28 Andrew Spicer, 'Luther, Adiaphora and the material culture of worship,' *Studies in Church History* 56 (2020): 246–272.

tected by the virtues ascribed to nobility.[29] If in Polish discourse on toleration the source of religious freedom was meant to be the law, it was positive law, agreed by – and applied to – the noble citizens of the republic. Toleration was understood to be a privilege of citizenship.

Such pragmatism was justified in face of the decisions of the Tridentine Council by which the Catholic Church had regained the initiative after the Reformation. Political and legal thinkers from all denominations focused on the problems that a coercive restoration of unity under the church of Rome might trigger in the multi-national and multi-religious Commonwealth. Andrzej Frycz Modrzewski (1503–1572) was a pupil of Melanchthon who brought Erasmus's library to Poland-Lithuania and attended the council of the Protestant Schmalkaldic League against the Emperor. He knew, therefore, what was at stake in the religious debates in the Empire, leading up to the 1555 Peace of Augsburg. In his main opus, *De Republica emendanda* of 1551, Modrzewski recommended respect for religious dissenters. Faith must be free from coercion, as 'the human spirit is so free that it feels and thinks freely even under torture and does not agree with what the torturer wants it to think.'[30] Although he formally never joined a Protestant denomination, he idealised the unity of the early Christian church. In 1558, he reminisced proudly that Lutheran books 'were brought to us from Germany' in barrels,[31] and towards the end of his life he sympathized with the Antitrinitarian movement. Amidst religious ambiguity and dissimulation – widespread among the early reformers[32] – many of his Protestant contemporaries embraced his Humanist irenicism. Due to the relatively late arrival of the Reformation in Poland-Lithuania[33] and a considerable degree of indifference by the

---

29 Formulated by Lew Sapieha in his preface to the Lithuanian Statute of 1588. See Juliusz Bardach, 'Elity Wielkiego Księstwa Litewskiego a Polski przekład *De Respublica Emendanda* Andrzeja Frycza Modrzewskiego,' in *Kultura staropolska – kultura europejska. Prace ofiarowane Januszowi Tazbirowi w siedemdziesiątą rocznicę urodzin* (Warszawa: Semper, 1997), 307–314, here 313–314.

30 Andrzej Frycz Modrzewski, *Dzieła wszystkie.* Tom I: *O poprawie Rzeczypospolitej* (Warszawa: PIW, 1953).

31 Maciej Ptaszyński, 'The Polish-Lithuanian Commonwealth,' in *A Companion to the Reformation in Central Europe*, ed. Howard Louthan and Graeme Murdock (Leiden: Brill, 2015), 45.

32 Barbara Stollberg-Rilinger, 'Einleitung,' in *Konfessionelle Ambiguität. Uneindeutigkeit und Verstellung als religiöse Praxis in der Frühen Neuzeit*, ed. Andreas Pietsch and Barbara Stollberg-Rilinger (Gütersloh: Gütersloher Verlagshaus, 2013), 9–26.

33 After a fierce but short period of oppression in 1525, Sigismund the Old failed to squash the Reformation in Gdańsk; Sławomir Kościelak, 'Dzieje wyznaniowe w Prusach Królewskich w XVI–XVIII w.,' in *Prusy Królewskie. Społeczeństwo, kultura, gospodarka, 1454–1772*, ed. Edmund Kizik (Gdańsk: Muzeum Narodowe, 2012), 213.

monarchs towards doctrinal conflict before the 1570s,[34] Modrzewski found a greater reception abroad than in his own country. He was 're-discovered' by a nostalgic Polish Protestant literature in the seventeenth century which across the Commonwealth fought for the survival of its Reformed churches and a return to the principles of 1573.[35] In retrospect, Modrzewski influenced the emerging image that Poland-Lithuania represented an exceptional – but endangered – model of pragmatic toleration in a Europe deeply conflicted by religious strife.[36] Little wonder then, that Grotius included Modrzewski in a 'library of irenical books' which he constructed together with the Huguenot Jan Hotman de Villiers in Paris during the 1630s. Having abandoned the idea of reuniting Christianity but aiming at practical measures to enable peaceful coexistence, Hotman and Grotius built their library as a resource for moderate religious inspiration, excluding more radical positions such as Anabaptist and Antitrinitarian thought.[37] As part of this programme, Grotius recommended *De Republica emendanda* to other Flemish writers.[38]

3 Hugo Grotius and Poland-Lithuania

The Confederation of Warsaw reminded Grotius of the Pacification of Ghent which in 1576 aimed to unite the seventeen Dutch provinces against the Spanish Habsburgs and appealed to each province to exercise toleration towards its religious minorities. Similarly, the 1579 Union of Utrecht put greater emphasis on individual freedom of conscience to prevent religious persecution in the Netherlands.[39] Yet in Grotius's own time, it had become clear that more or less

34 Nowakowska, *King Sigismund of Poland*, 135–141.

35 Maciej Ptaszyński, 'Religiöse Toleranz oder politischer Frieden? Verhandlungen über den Religionsfrieden in Polen-Litauen im 16. und 17. Jahrhundert,' in *Unversöhnte Verschiedenheit. Verfahren zur Bewältigung religiös-konfessioneller Differenz in der europäischen Neuzeit*, ed. Johannes Paulmann, Matthias Schnettger, and Thomas Weller (Göttingen: Vandenhoeck & Ruprecht, 2016), 162.

36 Michael G. Müller, '"Nicht für die Religion selbst ist die Conföderation inter dissidentes eingerichtet…." Bekenntnispolitik und Respublica-Verständnis in Polen-Litauen,' in *Aspekte der politischen Kommunikation*, ed. Luise Schorn-Schütte, Beiheft *Historische Zeitschrift* 39 (2004): 312.

37 Mona Garloff, 'Irenik als gelehrte Praxis. Religionspolitische Friedensprojekte im Zeitalter der europäischen Konfessionskonflikte,' *Daphnis* 45 (2017): 13–36, here 33. Incorporating Stoic ideas and a discourse of mutual concord, Grotius called the project 'Via ad pacem ecclesiasticam.'

38 Kot, 'Grotius a Polska,' 602–603.

39 Martin van Gelderen, *The Political Thought of the Dutch Revolt 1555–1590* (Cambridge: Cambridge Univerity Press, 1992), 52.

voluntary 'agreements to disagree' gave no guarantee of toleration. The Dutch philosopher expressed his concern over the news of the attack on the Calvinist church in Vilnius in 1639 by a mob of students from the Jesuit college and condemned religiously motivated protests in Ruthenia: 'Why would people [in Poland], where public law instructs people not to impede how others worship God according to their beliefs, get into a fight with each other over the toleration of the Greek Orthodox?'[40] After the removal of the Vilnius Calvinist community beyond the city walls in 1640, Grotius addressed Israel Jaski, his correspondent in Gdańsk, showing great disappointment over the disregard for the former toleration agreement: 'It hurts me much what you write about Vilnius, because all conflict caused by religious hatred saddens me, and this is something that is so much directed against the constitution of your kingdom.'[41]

Grotius had survived his own experience with religious persecution. Closely associated with the Remonstrants (or Arminians) in the Dutch Republic during their struggle with the strictly Calvinist Gomarists in 1614–18, Grotius supported Johan van Oldenbarnevelt (1547–1619), the Dutch statesman who argued in favour of a national synod under a civil government, until both fell out with Maurice of Nassau in 1618. The conflict led to Oldenbarnevelt's execution and to Grotius's imprisonment and subsequent exile. In contrast, in the Polish-Lithuanian Commonwealth of free citizens who strongly believed in self-government, and where regular compromise was necessary to oil the machinery of the commonweal, Grotius's Arminianism, his irenicisim, and his definition of natural right were guaranteed a positive reception. The strict version of Calvinist predestination and social control, represented by the Genevan church, was not popular in the Commonwealth where, post-1595, the Heidelberg Catechism had become the official religious doctrine of the Reformed evangelical churches in Lesser Poland and Lithuania.[42]

For inspiration and arguments, Grotius could look to the writings of the influential Calvinist theologian in Lithuania, Andreas Volanus or Andrzej Wolan (1531–1610). As royal secretary and diplomat, Wolan was an authoritative figure who made his name through measured theological disputations

---

40 *Hugonis Grotii Epistolae ad Israelem Jaski* (Dantisci: Rhetius, 1670), 75–76, cited in Kot, 'Grotius a Polska,' 597.

41 *Epistolae Grotii*, 75–76, als cited in Kot, 'Grotius a Polska,' 597, who adds a quote that does not follow the above citation in the same letter in the original: 'Perhaps you would be happier if the Turks still threatened you with war, as you would be forced to keep greater internal harmony and obeyed the force of the law which would uphold it.'

42 Bem, *Calvinism*, 76 and 148.

aimed against both the post-Tridentine Catholic as well as the newly emerging Antitrinitarian doctrines. In contrast to Piotr Skarga (1536–1612), who backed a strong monarchy with confessionalizing powers to eradicate dissent in Poland-Lithuania, Wolan addressed his treatise to his Lithuanian patron, Mikołaj Radziwiłł 'Rudy' (1512–1584). Rudy had fiercely resisted the union between Poland and Lithuania, but when he could not prevent it, he established himself as a powerful protector of the Protestants in the Commonwealth.[43] In 1573, shortly before the free election of Henri of Valois, Wolan held a 'Speech to the Senate of Poland and the Grand Duchy of Lithuania on how to institute a good ruler' in which he stressed that in the newly-formed Commonwealth the king was kept in check by the law, had to lead by moral example, and was guided and controlled by the senators who should not be afraid to limit a ruler's tendency to act wantonly: 'effreni Principis libidini obsistat, sanisque consiliis omnes eius cupiditates coerceat.'[44]

Wolan's work is usually not cited in connection with natural law teaching, but if we follow Merio Scattola's idea of a 'natural law before natural law,' Wolan's borrowing from Aristotelian and Ciceronian moral teaching shows that there was receptiveness for natural law notions in Poland-Lithuania at the turn of the seventeenth century among all confessions: 'Law is nothing else but good understanding [...] which teaches what is right and censures actions that lead to the opposite.' Nothing better helps freedom and peace than 'right reason' and 'rectum mentis iudicium.'[45] According to Wolan, opposing a capricious or tyrannical king was not the task of the unruly nobility (*szlachta*), but of the 'optimates' of the realm to secure the preservation of legality and the defence of the borders of the commonwealth.[46] The task of senators was also to prevent the king from acting against dissidents in alliance with the Catholic *szlachta*. Although the electoral capitulations of the *pacta conventa* limited monarchical powers, it was a promise that could only work as long as a majority of the citizens was willing to enforce them.

Yet the Confederation of Warsaw had not been signed by the Polish Catholic hierarchy who, with the exception of one bishop, had never accepted it and

---

43 Marceli Kosman, 'Rola Radziwiłłów w ruchu Kalwińskim na Litwie,' *Miscellanea Historico-Archivistica* 3 (1989): 122–139, here 133.

44 Andrzej Wolan, *Oratio ad Senatum Regni Poloniae Magnique Ducatus Lituaniae quo boni Principis in Republica constituendi modus ostenditur* (s.l. [Kraków], 1573), A3v.

45 Andrzej Wolan, *De Libertate Politica sive civile*, ed. Maciej Eder and Roman Mazurkiewicz, ed. acad. Wacław Uruszczak (Warszawa: Neriton, 2010), 101–103.

46 Wolan, *De Libertate*, 113–114, warning of 'licentia.' He condemned, however, the inequality in the application of law, as had Modrzewski, esp. after homicide of non-nobles (ch. x, 148–164).

at the synod of Piotrków in 1577 swiftly condemned it as 'against God, contrary to, and calamitous for, the peace and unity of the Christian faith.'[47] The bishops sang from the same hymn sheet as Justus Lipsius who argued that the defence and unity of a body politic was best served by one official religion to which all subjects and citizens had to adhere. This idea was gaining a firm foothold among territorial rulers across Europe. They could look towards the Holy Roman Empire, where a member of the Imperial Aulic Council, Andreas Erstenberger [alias Franciscus Burckard, d. 1592], in a work dedicated to Ernst of Bavaria in 1586, combined Lipsius's teaching with a strong argument against *licentia credendi*, that 'would leave individual conscience free in matters of faith.' Real freedom, Erstenberger contended, was entirely conditioned by obedience to God and natural law. This was only possible inside the church, and anyone outside it, using free conscience, could easily be prone to error. Conscience provided the ability to make moral judgement, but being human, it could easily fail. Christians had to accept that a moral *res publica* could only securely flourish within the church of Rome, and not among heretics who resisted authority and ecclesiastical institutions. Evoking the power of natural law, he argued that religious unity within the Roman church was a condition for peace in the community and its body politic.[48]

The natural law ideas of Lipsius, who declared church unity a matter of 'reason of state,' were well received by the rising Jesuit Order in Poland-Lithuania, who followed Francisco Suárez's voluntarist teachings of natural law as expression of God's will.[49] One of them was the Jesuit court preacher and royalist Piotr Skarga, who combined his high regard for law (positive and natural), with his definition of the Commonwealth as the bulwark of Christianity against the heathen: 'so that this Catholic kingdom in Europe shall not be spoiled, in which the Church has strong roots and the praise for the true God [...] which is the wall against the pagan Turks and Tatars. Whoever spoils its wholeness and unity will be killed by his mother.'[50] For Skarga, obedience to divine and natural law was the only way to rescue the Commonwealth from

47 Wisner, *Rozróżnieni w wierze*, 35.

48 Andreas Erstenberger, *De autonomia, das ist von der Freystellung mehrerley Religion und Glauben* (Munich: Adam Berg, 1586), cited in Robert v. Friedeburg and Michael J. Seidler, 'The Holy Roman Empire of the German Nation,' in *European Political Thought 1450–1700. Religion, Law and Philosophy*, ed. Howell A. Lloyd et al. (New Haven, Conn.: Yale University Press, 2007), 142.

49 Cited in Quentin Skinner, *The Foundations of Modern Political Thought*, vol. II (Cambridge: Cambridge University Press, 1978), 144–145.

50 Stanisław Obirek S.J., *Wizja kościoła i państwa w kazaniach ks. Piotra Skargi S.J.* (Kraków: Wydawnictwo WAM, 1994), 177–178.

division, while 'heretics' infected the republic with the illness of turbulence.[51] The dissidents' claim that a free republic had to guarantee individual freedom of conscience was for Skarga a call for anarchy and triggered accusations of heresy. Yet Skarga knew well that subordination to an all-powerful Catholic monarch was anathema to Poland-Lithuania's constitutionalists, amongst them many Catholic republicans who shared his call for unity under the Roman church. His attack therefore was couched in republican terms and stressed the role of natural law as a limiting principle, which prevented *absolutum dominium* – a concept in Poland-Lithuania always used synonymously with tyranny.[52]

As Grotius was seeking to establish a lasting peace arrangement which could help to create political and social unity and revive Dutch trade, he sympathized with Lipsius's idea that religion could act as *vinculum societatis*. He was also aware of the dangers of tyranny, both religious and secular; hence, he strongly criticized historic examples of religious coercion, such as the Anabaptist kingdom of Münster, which in the 1530s had led to a theocratic rule of terror over the city's inhabitants.[53] On the other hand, his understanding of toleration had clearly set limits. Had he lived longer, Grotius might have supported Polish legislation in the Sejm of 1652 and 1658 against the Antitrinitarians, whose refusal to wear arms, accept civic office and whose denial of Christ's deity he criticized in his treatise *De satisfactione Christi* (1617).[54] Lipsius's Stoicism could be put to good use by moderate Catholics as well as Protestants: thus, Skarga, Modrzewski and Grotius shared common ground in their support for strong government limited by moral laws.

4 Circa Sacra

The work most relevant to the question of church-state relations is Grotius's *Of the Authority of the Highest Powers about Sacred Things* (*De imperio summarum potestatum circa sacra*), which denies that a man could serve two mas-

51 Piotr Skarga, *Upominanie do ewangelików y do wszystkich społem Niekatolików* [...] (Kraków: Architypographia Lazarzowa, 1592), reprinted in Korołko, *Klejnot wolnego sumienia*, 183.

52 Pietrzyk-Reeves, *Polish Republican Discourse*, 220–221.

53 Bas de Gaay Fortman, 'Between Principles and Practice: Grotius's commitment to religious peace in a contemporary context,' *Grotiana* 34 (2013): 25–40, here 29.

54 Hans W. Blom, 'Grotius and Socinianism,' in *Socinianism and Arminianism. Antitrinitarians, Calvinists, and cultural exchange in seventeenth-century Europe*, ed. Martin Mulsow and Jan Rohls (Leiden: Brill, 2005), 121–147.

ters. Suspicious of church interference in the Commonwealth and religiously-motivated factionalism, Grotius recommended political remedies: 'the person or assembly, not just a king, but sometimes an aristocratic council in a republic, the estates or any other body that has supreme power, must be one, not in nature but in counsel.'[55] Grotius's insistence on political unity which he set out in his early work *De Republica Emendanda* of 1601 – note the similarity of title with Modrzewski's opus – remained a central element of his thought and was informed by the Polish experience. In his conception of an aristocratic republic, Grotius drew parallels between the council of grandees – the senate in Poland-Lithuania – with the Hebrew Sanhedrin, which guaranteed the unity of the republic.[56] As in the writings of Polish constitutionalist thought, the senate played a central role for Grotius. It checked the tyranny of the ruler or the 'mob,' the popular element. Likewise, Łukasz Opaliński singled out the senators as the republic's most trusted guardians. They were to negotiate the balance between the *szlachta* and the king, who himself was subject to laws, man-made and natural: 'In the Commonwealth, where the state is not the hereditary property of one, but a society linked to laws and the common fatherland of its citizens, all are concerned for the common good.'[57] Opaliński followed not only Lipsius's Neo-Stoic catalogue of virtues as inspiration for good government, but also Grotius's negative opinion about the 'rude multitude' in the chamber of *szlachta* deputies, devoid of reason and morality. Constitutionalist thought, from Wolan to Opaliński, bridged the confessional divide. The right of the individual to free conscience could not override the concern for the common good. Knud Haakonssen has characterized this concern as a typical element of natural law theory: the common social world had to 'arise from accommodation of some sort among competing claims.'[58] Toleration à la polonaise was the perfect answer to that endeavour.

Another element of Grotius's idea of toleration was his focus on contract law, which regulated the competition between self-interests and common

55 Hugo Grotius, *Of the Authority of the Highest Powers about Sacred Things. Or, The right of the state in the Church. Wherein are contained many judicious discourses, pertinent to our times, and of speciall use for the order and peace of all Christian churches* (London: T.W. for Joshua Kirton, 1655), ch. 1, 4–6 and 9.

56 Marco Barducci, *Hugo Grotius and the Century of Revolution, 1613–1718: Transnational Reception in English Political Thought* (Oxford: Oxford University Press, 2017), 72.

57 Łukasz Opaliński, *Polonia Defensa contra Ioan. Barclaium* (Dantisci: Georg Förster, 1648); Łukasz Opaliński, 'Obrona Polski,' in *Wybór Pism*, ed. Stanisław Grzeszczuk (Wrocław et al., Zakład Narodowy im. Ossolińskich, 1959), 175; see also Maria O. Pryshlak, *Państwo w filozofii politycznej Łukasza Opalińskiego*, 97.

58 Knud Haakonssen, *Natural Law and Moral Philosophy. From Grotius to the Scottish Enlightenment* (Cambridge: Cambridge University Press, 1996), 5.

good. Only a strong foundation in morality could guarantee a peaceful outcome in this contest: 'Individuals with natural rights are the units of which all social organization is made. They are people who balance pure self-interest and social inclinations by entering in contractual relations with others about property and about modes of living together, especially about authority.'[59] This approach is well suited to the conditions of commercial Dutch society, but it also applies fittingly to Poland-Lithuania, where elective royal authority, rights such as *habeas corpus*, freedom of conscience and religion, the distribution of offices and the power over a subject rural population had to be constantly renegotiated. Echoing the political usefulness of religious toleration in Poland-Lithuania for sustaining civic liberty, Grotius linked property rights with the right to freely exercise one's religion: Just as 'every man is the governor and arbiter of affairs relative to his own property,'[60] the choice of religion was part of a set of wider civic liberties. The freedom of religious choice by citizens who were 'free and sui iuris' found justification in the duties that active citizens owed to a republic or commonwealth. Key to the loyal fulfilment of duty was a strong code of individual virtues. Based on a similar understanding of duty and drawing from the priorities set by his Jesuit education, Starowolski focused on a 'Reformation of habits'[61] and called for a renewal of noble virtues: it was the nobles' moral duty to fend against greed and disunity, including religious strife, to uphold the *res publica*.[62]

5 The Virtue of Duty and the Duty of Virtue

We find a similar catalogue of virtues and duties in Opaliński's work *Pauli Naeoceli de officiis libri tres* (1659). It stresses the importance of merging

59 Haakonssen, *Natural Law*, 28.

60 Hugo Grotius, *De Iure Praedae Commentarius*, trans. Gwladys L. Williams and Walter H. Zeydel (Oxford: Clarendon Press, 1950), 1:18.

61 Szymon Starowolski, 'Reformacja obyczajów Polskich [c.1650],' in *Wybór z pism*, ed. Ignacy Lewandowski. Biblioteka Narodowa, seria I: 272 (Wrocław et al.: Zakład Narodowy im. Ossolińskich, 1991), 286–316.

62 Haakonssen, *Natural Law*, 25. The tradition of Catholic political reform writing began before Starowolski. The classic seventeenth-century treatise focusing on the 'good citizen,' in contrast to 'hostes' who have no virtue and will be damned in the last judgement, is Kaspar Siemek's *Civis bonus* of 1632. After Machiavelli, Renaissance virtue was the duty of the citizen to preserve liberty, if need be through resistance in a *rokosz*. Teresa Baluk-Ulewiczowa, 'Z dziejów zwierciadła władzy,' in *O senatorze doskonałym. Prace upamiętające postać i twórczość Wawrzyńca Goślickiego*, ed. Aleksander Stępkowski (Warszawa: Kancelaria Senatu, 2009), 35–82.

reason, wisdom and religion: 'it is Christian to philosophize.'[63] Opaliński's intention here is to highlight the rational position of human beings and the virtues that citizens needed to fulfil their duties in office: *probitas, charitas, pietas*. In the struggle against the corruptions of original sin, weak human will and temptations, Opaliński argues that self-knowledge, the use of reason ('una enim est ratio recta'), and the classical virtues recommended by the Stoics prevent humans from falling victim to vice and licence, which are consequences of exaggerated self-love, heresy and arrogance (*superbia*).[64] Instead, citizens have to follow the golden middle (*modicum iusto*) and show *fortitudo*: courage to make free choices and be responsible.[65] One of the temptations which ensnares weak human beings is heresy. Opaliński classifies it as one of the confusions of the mind, which hinder the access of rational human beings to the will of God and the virtuous life of a citizen. Like Skarga, Opaliński derives a manichaeistic distinction between good and evil, virtue and vice, and reasonable godliness and ungodly folly from Suárez's definition of free will which gives human beings the ability to decide either to behave selfishly, or to act for the common good.[66] He then translates this behaviour to the bad or good exercise of civic office in the Commonwealth.

The date of Opaliński's publication matters. It followed the decision in the Sejm of 1658 to expel all Antitrinitarians who would not convert to Catholicism or leave the country voluntarily. By 1662 all remaining Antitrinitarians had to leave. Even nobles who had influential protectors, such as Jan Mierzeński from Wiłkomierz who served the Lithuanian Calvinist magnate Bogusław Radziwiłł (1620–1669), were not spared. The *Theatrum Europaeum* of 1662 reported how Mierzeński was unceremoniously removed from the chamber of deputies of the Polish-Lithuanian Sejm amidst sabres drawn and threats to throw him from a window. His recent conversion to Calvinism was not accepted as a valid reason to save him from expulsion from the Sejm.[67] The 'anarchy' of public dissent in the chamber of the Sejm had already become a stereotype

63 Łukasz Opaliński, *Pauli Naeoceli de officiis libri tres in quibus Sapientiae Christianae, id est, Moralis Philosophiae, Jurisprudentiae, immo et Theologiae pleraque et praecipua* [...] (Kraków: F. Cezary, 1659), 5.

64 Opaliński, *Pauli Naeoceli*, 53, 25. Opaliński absorbed Lipsian and Stoic ideas during his studies, 1626 to 1629, under Eric Puteanus, Lipsius's successor at the University of Leuwen (Louvain), see Kamila Schuster, *Biblioteka Łukasza Opalińskiego marszałka nadwornego koronnego (1612–1662)* (Wrocław et al.: Zakład Narodowy im. Ossolińskich, 1971), 19–20.

65 Opaliński, *Pauli Naeoceli*, 79–80.

66 Haakonssen, *Natural Law*, 23–24.

67 *Theatrum Europaeum*, ed. Johann Philip Abelin, vol. 9 (Frankfurt/M.: Merian, 1662): 619 (25 February 1662).

across Europe. In his *Polonia defensa contra Joannem Barclaium* of 1648, written against Barclay's negative depiction of Polish customs in *Icon Animorum* of 1614, Opaliński fought back against such depictions, praising the Poles who 'among all peoples of Europe embraced the plague of heresy but most persistently stuck with the Catholic faith, and most ardently and lovingly received from their ancestors a general godliness [...] [who] despite religious conflict, confusion of souls and all kinds of novelties, preserved the unanimity of their citizens and the public peace.'[68] Fortunately, so Opaliński, most were now returning to the Catholic church. He blamed all 'heresies' on foreign origin ('from foreigners did this poison arrive'), and the stereotype of the 'Polak-Katolik' [Pole-Catholic] would soon become a popular topos among Polish Catholic writers.

Opaliński's *De Officiis* presented a taxonomy of Christian and civic virtues and became a widely disseminated textbook published in many editions, well into the eighteenth century. In 1648, it boasted in response to Barclay that it had not been the fear of religious war that had produced toleration in Poland-Lithuania, but that the absence of religious war was in fact the result of Poland's tolerant spirit.[69] The absence of a systematic, institutionalized and targeted Catholic confessionalization at state level, at least until the first half of the seventeenth century, had indeed created a multi-religious Commonwealth that attracted religious dissenters from other parts of Europe. It might have been this non-institutional, non-territorial character of the multiplicity of churches and religions that endeared Poland-Lithuania to Hugo Grotius. As Jonathan Israel has observed, after his personal experience of persecution Grotius embraced the idea of the freedom of conscience and of expression, but rejected the institutionalization of dissent.[70]

In his polemic against Barclay, Opaliński's purpose had been to defend the Poles' love of liberty, the *forma mixta* and self-government, which included a non-institutionalised practice of toleration. For that reason Opaliński and other constitutionalist writers in Poland-Lithuania had little time or understanding for a state-focused natural law theory that, soon after Grotius's death, became the obligatory reading for German territorial rulers and the French

68 Opaliński, 'Obrona Polski,' 212–214.

69 'Tolerantia nempe hac consultum tantum est, ut inter cives pax & quies esset; non turbae, non seditiones, non mutuae caedes, non internecina bella, quae totam Europam hucusque exercent, & misere conficiunt.' Opaliński, *Polonia Defensa*, 115.

70 Jonathan Israel, 'The Intellectual Debate about Toleration in the Dutch Republic,' in *The Emergence of Tolerance in the Dutch Republic*, ed. Christiane Berkvens-Stevelinck, Jonathan Israel, and G.H.M. Posthumus Meyjes (Leiden: Brill, 1997), 12.

monarchy after Bodin. As Robert Frost has stressed in various contexts, in the understanding of its noble citizens the Commonwealth after 1569 consisted of two states – the kingdom of Poland and the Grand Duchy of Lithuania, but the union it had created was not a state and never wanted to become one. It was a republic.[71] For many natural law theorists in Europe's monarchies such as Samuel Pufendorf, royal or princely office included the power to determine the religion of its citizens, which was part of the process of state-building. Yet the Commonwealth had no ambition of state-building. If the choice of religion was part of the civic liberties of a nobleman and not a prescription by the state, there was no point in demanding the separation of state and church, or what Simone Zurbuchen called 'de-confessionalization.'[72] When Polish Reformers argued for unity, therefore, they did not evoke reason of state but the need for agreement.

Grotius's comment, that Poland did not legislate on religion, can be understood as a mark of approval for the Commonwealth's rejection of 'reason of state.'[73] His support for the consensus of 1570 indicates that he favoured the right to freely 'own' one's religion: 'Civilians call a faculty that Right which every man has to his own [...] this comprehends the power that we have ourselves, which is called liberty; to deprive another of what belongs to him, merely for one's advantage, is repugnant to the law of nature.'[74] For Grotius, mankind, due to its social and rational nature, was both source and agent of natural law.[75] This insight attracted him to the Polish approach which in 1573 sought toleration through a rights-based constitution to protect the free exercise of religion, albeit within the parameters of Trinitarian Christianity.

---

71 Robert Frost, *The Oxford History of Poland-Lithuania*, vol. I: *The Making of the Polish-Lithuanian Union, 1385–1569* (Oxford: Oxford University Press, ^{2}2018), 493–494; see also Frost, 'Medicinal Herbs,' 28–53, and James Collins, 'Wschód uczy Zachód – wpływ polskiej myśli konstytucyjnej na kulturę prawną w świecie zachodnim w latach 1572–1810,' in *Lex est Rex in Polonia et in Lithuania. Tradycje prawnoustrojowe Rzeczypospolitej – doświadczenie i dziedzictwo*, ed. Adam Jankiewicz (Warszawa: Wydawnictwo DIG, 2011), 127–155.

72 Simone Zurbuchen, *Naturrecht und natürliche Religon. Zur Geschichte des Toleranzbegriffs von Samuel Pufendorf bis Jean-Jacques Rousseau* (Würzburg: Königshausen und Neumann, 1991), 6–7.

73 Reason of state could dictate religion to preserve unity, but it could also allow toleration to prevent civil war. See Jon Parkin, 'Preface: Rethinking Toleration via Natural Law,' in *Natural Law and Toleration in the Early Enlightenment*, ed. Jon Parkin and Timothy Stanton (Oxford: Oxford University Press, 2013), xvi.

74 Hugo Grotius, *The Rights of War and Peace* [1625], from the edition by Jean Barbeyrac ed. Richard Tuck (Indianapolis: Liberty Fund, 2005), Book I, I, 5.

75 Haakonssen, *Natural Law*, 29. Also Jerzy Zajadło, 'Die Bedeutung der Hypothese "etiamsi daremus,"' *Archiv für Rechts- und Sozialphilosophie / Archives for Philosophy of Law and Social Philosophy*, 74 (1988/1): 83–92.

6 Antitrinitarianism and Natural Law

Polish-Lithuanian approaches to toleration also helped pave the way from Grotius's understanding of natural law to the natural law thinking of the later seventeenth century, particularly of John Locke (1632–1705), Samuel Pufendorf and his disciple, Christian Thomasius (1655–1728). One of the Reformed Radziwiłłs' most loyal agent, the Antitrinitarian Samuel Przypkowski (1592–1670), who studied in Leiden at a time when Remonstrants still enjoyed toleration,[76] became most closely connected with Grotian ideas. Deeply knowledgeable and influenced by humanist learning, which he acquired at the Academy of the (Antitrinitarian) Polish Brethren at Raków, Przypkowski divorced natural law more radically from revealed religion than Grotius himself. Przypkowski dispensed with the divine origin of all law because humans, in his view, had no way of knowing or proving the divine will or God's design. In his *Cogitationes Sacrae* of 1650, Przypkowski outlined that man was bound to the spiritual authority of the church only by his own free will, whereas secular authority demanded obedience and subordination. There are echoes here of Grotius's critique of Calvinist theocracy and his emphasis on the importance on *adiaphora*: only the dogmas absolutely necessary for salvation needed to be prescribed by a Christian prince or government.[77] At the same time, a well-governed body politic had to rely on the civic obedience of its citizens, independent from their religious beliefs. Przypkowski applied this model to the specific circumstances of the Antitrinitarian movement in Poland-Lithuania, split between a group of radical pacifists who refused taking up arms and offices, and a more compromising movement, led by himself. Przypkowski argued that the *Ecclesia Reformata Minor* (Polish Brethren church) had to prove its patriotic credentials and accept active citizenship when – as during the wars against Sweden and Muscovy – the survival of the fatherland was at stake. The fact that Christ did not lay down secular laws on trade or warfare did not mean, according to Przypkowski, that such secular laws should not be binding.[78]

---

76 Luisa Simonutti, 'Resistance, Obedience and Toleration: Przypkowski and Limborch,' in *Socinianism and Arminianism. Antitrinitarians, Calvinists and cultural exchange in seventeenth-century Europe*, ed. Martin Mulsow and Jan Rohls (Leiden: Brill, 2005), 194–195.

77 Marco Barducci, 'The Anglo-Dutch Context for the Writing and Reception of Hugo Grotius's De Imperio Summarum Potestatum Circa Sacra 1617–1659,' *Grotiana* 34 (2013/1): 138–161, here 153. Also, Simonutti, 'Resistance,' 201.

78 Samuel Przypkowski, 'Braterska deklaracja na niebraterskie napomnienie od autora pod imieniem szlachica polskiego ad dissidentes in religione uczynione [s.l., 1646],' in *700 lat*

Two years after the outbreak of the Cossack rebellion of 1648, Przypkowski asked his co-religionists to subordinate spiritual differences to political necessity. By following natural and common reason Przypkowski backed complete freedom of religion under the condition that the concept of heresy should be abolished, as it was not appropriate for the fatherland to persecute its loyal citizens.[79] Servile acceptance of religious dogma was counterproductive for the republic. This earned the Polish Antitrinitarians accusations by the Lutheran and Bohemian Brethren's theologians that 'they elevate reason above Scripture and [...] negate God's rule over the world, arguing that divine words are not truthful if reason does not recognize them.'[80] In this matter Przypkowski agreed with the sixteenth-century Dutch defender of toleration Dirck Cornheert, favoured by Grotius: 'Dubitatio studii et sapientiae initium et causa est.'[81] Political unity did not demand religious uniformity, while toleration was the 'mother of concord.'[82] Political pragmatism that created religious peace was led by reason, and so could Christian dogma be tamed by the power of rationalism.

This adoption of natural law divorced from its divine origin was a step too far for most of Przypkowski's contemporaries, Protestant or Catholic. Yet among the Catholic nobility, Przypkowski's own position came under scrutiny not only for theological reasons, but for his association with the Calvinist Radziwiłłs, the cousins Janusz and Bogusław, who had supported the Swedish king during the Second Northern War between 1655 and 1657. More Catholics had taken the same course of action, but the fact that many Protestants in the Radziwiłłs' service had made this choice intensified the hostility of the Catholic *szlachta* against dissidents. It increased noble paranoia about treason in their midst, scapegoated Protestants and undermined the defence of the Warsaw Confederation.

Grotius died ten years before the difficult years of the 'Swedish Deluge' of 1655–1660, often marked as the time when Poland-Lithuania lost its status as

myśli polskiej. Filozofia i myśl społeczna XVII wieku, ed. Zbigniew Ogonowski (Warszawa: PWN, 1979), 527–549, esp. 540–544.

79 [Samuel Przypkowski,] *Samuelis Przipcovii Equitis Poloni* [...] *Cogitationes sacrae ad initium Euangelii Matthaei et omnes Epistolas Apostolicas. Nec non tractatus varii argumenti, praecipue De jure Christiani magistratus* [...] (Eleutheropoli [Amsterdam]: n.p., 1692). See also Stanisław Kot, *Socinianism in Poland: The Social and Political Ideas of the Polish Antitrinitarians*, transl. Earl Morse Wilbur (Boston: Starr King Press, 1957), 183–200.

80 Zenon Gołaszewski, *Bracia Polscy* (Warszawa: Dom Wydawniczy Duet, 2004), 270.

81 Zbigniew Ogonowski, *Z zagadnień tolerancji w Polsce XVII wieku* (Warszawa: PWN, 1958), 189.

82 Przypkowski, 'Braterska deklaracja,' 540, 541–542.

an East-Central European great power. Its parliamentary institutions began to decline under foreign influence and the pressure of rival factions that accused each other of pursuing their self-interest in violation of the common good. Annabel Brett has pointed out Grotius's interest in civil philosophy and history, where the Polish example might indeed have influenced the Dutchman. Championing a balanced pact between the demands of the body politic and individual citizens' desire for liberty, Grotius developed a theory of sociability, foreshadowing Pufendorf, by declaring respect for the good of others as a consequence of self-love. The relationship that exists between individuals in a *res publica* (or *civitas*) and is based on mutual consent to pursue the common good also imposes obligations on each individual: *pacta sunt servanda*.[83] It is a moral demand that Paulus Vladimiri had already flung at the Teutonic Knights at the Council of Constance.

7 Conclusion

As a remedy for the practical political, military and economic problems of the Polish-Lithuanian Commonwealth, Lipsius's call for a monoreligious *res publica* offered a less complex and more decisive solution. Starowolski stated the obvious: that the negotiated agreement of 1573 was unenforceable as long as it depended on Catholic consent, which was short in supply. He offered 'the rest of Europe' as an example, where states usually accepted one religion to conduct their affairs and guide their citizens.[84] In the charged atmosphere of warfare during the 1650s, when Poland-Lithuania seemed encircled by non-Catholic enemies, the appeal of Opaliński's and Starowolski's Lipsian approaches and Skarga's sermons gained authority. The large number of conversions to Catholicism among the nobility was proof enough.[85] Blame was easily apportioned: the Orthodox Cossacks had rebelled and joined Muscovy, depriving the Commonwealth's eastern borderlands of its most effective defence force. The Antitrinitarian communities, many of whom had followed Swedish promises of protection, were exiled. Some of them went to

83 Annabel Brett, 'Natural Right and Civil Community: The civil philosophy of Hugo Grotius,' *The Historical Journal* 45 (2002/1): 31–51, here 41–44.

84 Szymon Starowolski, *Prawdziwe objaśnienie braterskiego napomnienia ad dissidentes in religione przed dwiema laty wydanego* (s.l. [Kraków, 1646]), 22–23.

85 Waldemar Kowalski, 'From the "Land of Diverse Sects" to National Religion: Converts to Catholicism and Reformed Franciscans in Early Modern Poland-Lithuania,' *Church History* 70 (2001/3): 482–526.

the Netherlands where posthumously Przypkowski's works were collected by Philip van Limborch, who integrated Przypkowski's ideas on toleration into his own publications in defence of the Arminian Remonstrant movement. While refusing to accept Przypkowski's Antitrinitarian theology, Limborch still applied the Pole's advocacy of civic unity to Dutch Arminianism, thinking it a political objective worth pursuing.

During their lifetimes, both Grotius and Przypkowski had to go into exile. Both called for a separation of matters of state and matters of faith: a Christian prince or authority should not define religious dogma or persecute dissidents. Poland-Lithuania came close to realizing this demand in legal terms in the Warsaw Confederation of 1573. Ever since, Protestants and moderate Catholics called for the implementation of the decisions of 1573 and a 'compositio inter status,' a civic pact that Grotius and Przypkowski had delineated for a harmonious, united commonweal. In practical reality this meant an agreement among the nobles of all denominations to find a legal *modus vivendi*: that local secular courts could not enforce ecclesiastical decision (implemented in Poland as early as 1565), no more than six clerics could sit on the Crown Tribunal (made into law in 1589), no appeals could go to Rome (from 1607), six lay deputies could sit on the Crown Tribunal to judge spiritual matters (from 1616), no noble lands could be sold to the clergy without the church giving up land in return (from 1588), and all ecclesiastical lands were subject to taxation (from 1633). The rebellion (*rokosz*) of Zebrzydowski in 1606–09, led by Protestants and Catholics alike against attempts by king Sigismund III Wasa and the episcopal hierarchy to expand their powers, failed to introduce completely separate jurisdictions for secular and ecclesiastical matters. But the 'compositio inter status' diminished interference by the Church in secular matters.

In the long term, such measures did not establish the kind of toleration that Wolan, Grotius, Przypkowski or many among the dissidents had hoped for. The 'compositio inter status,' however, helped to define more clearly the limits of the secular and ecclesiastical spheres in a framework of law, tempering religious conflict in a multi-confessional state. In 1633, Chancellor Jerzy Ossoliński travelled to Rome and convinced Pope Urban VIII to confirm and bless the 'compositio inter status.' In 1635, the Sejm passed it into law. Disputes about the paying of the tithe were also settled. After this achievement, debates about a further process of confederation slowed and died. Toleration became less attractive to an increasingly Catholic nobility which dominated Sejm decisions, denying dissidents the protection they once enjoyed. Natural law discourse is not easy to pinpoint in such practical discussions. Yet Poland-Lithuania did not produce a Hobbes, who, according to Timothy J. Hochstrasser, reduced the discussion about natural law to a debate about the nature of a contract.[86] The Sejm did not surrender its sovereignty to a Leviathan. Grotius's idea of sociability suited the civic humanism and the republican model of the Commonwealth more than a Lipsian prince who demanded obedience. In the Commonwealth's political philosophy, Neo-Stoic virtues however remained attractive. To that end, the Commonwealth's Sejm did legislate, not on religion, as Grotius rightly spotted, but on the manner that the relationship between state and church, religion and politics, commonweal and individual rights were negotiated. And that was a victory of a kind, at least for some time, for those who believed that the seat of natural law is human reason and that the common good in a civic society does not depend on relinquishing rights, but creating them, in order to maintain peace and sociability in the commonweal.

Bibliography

Primary Sources

Confoederatio Generalis Warsaviensis 1573, in *Volumina Legum II* [Saint Petersburg: s.l. 1859], ed. Jozafat Ohryzki, repr. Warszawa: Wydawnictwo Artystyczne i Filmowe, 1980.

Erstenberger, Andreas, *De autonomia, das ist von der Freystellung mehrerley Religion und Glauben*, Munich: Adam Berg, 1586.

Grotius, Hugo, *De Iure Praedae Commentarius*, trans. Gwladys L. Williams and Walter H. Zeydel, Oxford: Clarendon Press, 1950.

Grotius, Hugo, *Of the Authority of the Highest Powers about Sacred Things. Or, The right of the state in the Church. Wherein are contained many judicious discourses, pertinent to our times, and of speciall use for the order and peace of all Christian churches*, London: T.W. for Joshua Kirton, 1655.

[Grotius, Hugo,] *Hugonis Grotii Epistolae ad Israelem Jaski*, Dantisci: Rhetius, 1670.

Grotius, Hugo, *The Rights of War and Peace* [1635], from the edition by Jean Barbeyrac ed. Richard Tuck, Indianapolis: Liberty Fund, 2005.

Modrzewski, Andrzej Frycz, *Dzieła wszystkie*. Tom I: *O poprawie Rzeczypospolitej*, Warszawa: PIW, 1953.

Opaliński, Łukasz, 'Obrona Polski,' in *Wybór Pism*, ed. Stanisław Grzeszczuk, 125–232, Wrocław et al.: Zakład Narodowy im. Ossolińskich, 1959.

Opaliński, Łukasz, *Pauli Naeoceli de officiis libri tres in quibus Sapientiae Christianae, id est, Moralis Philosophiae, Jurisprudentiae, immo et Theologiae pleraque et praecipua* [...], Kraków: F. Cezary, 1659.

86 Timothy J. Hochstrasser, *Natural Law Theories in the Early Enlightenment* (Cambridge: Cambridge University Press, 2000), 102.

Opaliński, Łukasz, *Polonia Defensa contra Ioan. Barclaium*, Dantisci: Georg Förster, 1648.

Orzelski, Stanisław, *Bezkrólewia ksiąg ośmioro*, ed. Edward Kuntze, Kraków: Nakładem Polskiej Akademii Umiejętności, 1917.

Przyłuski, Jakub, *Leges Seu Statuta Ac Privilegia Regni Poloniae Omnia*, s.l., 1553.

Przypkowski, Samuel, 'Braterska deklaracja na niebraterskie napomnienie od autora pod imieniem szlachica polskiego ad dissidentes in religione uczynione [s.l., 1646],' in *700 lat myśli polskiej. Filozofia i myśl społeczna XVII wieku*, ed. Zbigniew Ogonowski, 527–549, Warszawa: PWN, 1979.

[Przypkowski, Samuel,] *Samuelis Przipcovii Equitis Poloni* [...] *Cogitationes sacrae ad initium Euangelii Matthaei et omnes Epistolas Apostolicas. Nec non tractatus varii argumenti, praecipue De jure Christiani magistratus* [...], Eleutheropoli [Amsterdam]: n.p., 1692.

Skarga, Piotr, *Upominanie do ewangelików y do wszystkich społem Niekatolików* [...], Kraków: Architypographia Lazarzowa, 1592.

Starowolski, Szymon, *Prawdziwe objaśnienie braterskiego napomnienia ad dissidentes in religione przed dwiema laty wydanego*, s.l. [Kraków, 1646].

Starowolski, Szymon, 'Reformacja obyczajów Polskich [c.1650],' in *Wybór z pism*, ed. Ignacy Lewandowski, 286–316, Wrocław et al.: Zakład Narodowy im. Ossolińskich, 1991.

Statut Wielkiego Xięstwa Litewskiego naprzód za Naiaśnieyszego Hospodara Króla Jegomości Zygmunta III w Krakowie w roku 1588. Drugi raz w Wilnie 1619 roku [...]. *Teraz zaś piąty raz ze szczęśliwie panuiącego Naiaśnieyszego Króla Jegomości Augusta Trzeciego przedrukowany*, Wilno: Drukarnia S.J., 1744.

Theatrum Europaeum, ed. Johann Philip Abelin, vol. 9, Frankfurt/M.: Merian, 1662.

Włodkowicz, Paweł, 'Traktat o władzy papieża i cesarza w stosunku do pogan,' in *700 lat myśli polskiej. Filozofia i myśl społeczna XVII wieku*, ed. Jan Domański, 184–203, Warszawa: PWN, 1978.

Wolan, Andrzej, *De Libertate Politica sive civile*, ed. Maciej Eder and Roman Mazurkiewicz, ed. acad. Wacław Uruszczak, Warszawa: Neriton, 2010.

[Wolan, Andrzej,] Andreas Volanus, *Oratio ad Senatum Regni Poloniae Magnique Ducatus Lituaniae quo boni Principis in Republica constituendi modus ostenditur*, s.l. [Kraków], 1573.

Secondary Sources

Baluk-Ulewiczowa, Teresa, 'Z dziejów zwierciadła władzy,' in *O senatorze doskonałym. Prace upamiętające postać i twórczość Wawrzyńca Goślickiego*, ed. Aleksander Stępkowski, 35–82, Warszawa: Kancelaria Senatu, 2009.

Bardach, Juliusz, 'Elity Wielkiego Księstwa Litewskiego a Polski przekład *De Republica Emendanda* Andrzeja Frycza Modrzewskiego,' in *Kultura staropolska – kul-*

tura europejska. Prace ofiarowane Januszowi Tazbirowi w siedemdziesiątą rocznicę urodzin, 307–314, Warszawa: Semper, 1997.
Barducci, Marco, 'The Anglo-Dutch Context for the Writing and Reception of Hugo Grotius's De Imperio Summarum Potestatum Circa Sacra 1617–1659,' *Grotiana* 34 (2013/1): 138–161.
Barducci, Marco, *Hugo Grotius and the Century of Revolution, 1613–1718: Transnational Reception in English Political Thought*, Oxford: Oxford University Press, 2017.
Bem, Kazimierz, *Calvinism in the Polish-Lithuanian Commonwealth, 1548–1648: The Churches and the Faithful*, Leiden and Boston: Brill, 2020.
Bieńkowski, Tadeusz, 'Nauczanie filozofii w Gdańsku w XVI–XVII wieku,' in *Nauczanie filozofii w Polsce w XV–XVIII wieku*, ed. Lech Szczucki, 157–165, Wrocław et al.: Zakład Narodowy im. Ossolińskich, 1978.
Blom, Hans W., 'Grotius and Socinianism,' in *Socinianism and Arminianism. Antitrinitarians, Calvinists, and cultural exchange in seventeenth-century Europe*, ed. Martin Mulsow and Jan Rohls, 121–147, Leiden: Brill, 2005.
Brett, Annabel, 'Natural Right and Civil Community: The civil philosophy of Hugo Grotius,' *The Historical Journal* 45 (2002/1): 31–51.
Brüning, Alfons, *Unio non est unitas: Polen-Litauens Weg im konfessionellen Zeitalter (1569–1648)*, Wiesbaden: Harrassowitz, 2008.
Charipova, Liudmila V., *Latin Books and the Eastern Orthodox Clerical Elite in Kiev, 1632–1780*, Manchester and New York: Manchester University Press, 2006.
Chemperek, Dariusz, ed., *Ewangelicyzm Reformowany w pierwszej Rzeczypospolitej: Dialog z Europą i wybory aksjologiczne w świetle literatury i piśmiennictwa XVI–XVII wieku*, Warszawa: Wydawnictwa Uniwersytetu Warszawskiego, 2015.
Collins, James, 'Wschód uczy Zachód – wpływ polskiej myśli konstytucyjnej na kulturę prawną w świecie zachodnim w latach 1572–1810,' in *Lex est Rex in Polonia et in Lithuania. Tradycje prawnoustrojowe Rzeczypospolitej – doświadczenie i dziedzictwo*, ed. Adam Jankiewicz, 127–155, Warszawa: Wydawnictwo DIG, 2011.
Daugirdas, Kęstutis, 'Rezeption der Theologie Calvins im Großfürstentum Litauen und Königreich Polen,' in *Calvin und Calvinismus. Europäische Perspektiven*, ed. Irene Dingel and Hermann Selderhuis, 155–220, Göttingen: Vandenhoeck & Ruprecht, 2011.
Dworzaczkowa, Jolanta, *Bracia Czescy w Wielkopolsce w XVI i XVII wieku*, Warszawa: Semper, 1997.
Frick, David, *Kith, Kin, and Neighbors: Communities and Confessions in Seventeenth-Century Wilno*, Ithaca and London: Cornell University Press, 2013.
Friedeburg, Robert v. and Michael J. Seidler, 'The Holy Roman Empire of the German Nation,' in *European Political Thought 1450–1700. Religion, Law and Philosophy*, ed. Howell A. Lloyd et al., 102–172, New Haven, Conn., Yale University Press, 2007.

Friedrich, Karin, 'Die Reformation,' in *Polen in der europäischen Geschichte. Ein Handbuch in vier Bänden*, general ed. Michael G. Müller, vol. ed. Hans-Jürgen Bömelburg, vol. II: Die Frühe Neuzeit, 123–143, Stuttgart: Hiersemann, 2011.

Frost, Robert, 'Medicinal Herbs and Poison Plants: Reading Machiavelli in the Polish-Lithuanian Commonwealth, 1560–1700,' in *Unie międzypaństwowe, parlamentaryzm, samorządność*, ed. Wacław Uruszczak et al., 28–53, Warszawa: Wydawnictwo Sejmowe, 2020.

Frost, Robert, *The Oxford History of Poland-Lithuania*, vol. I: *The Making of the Polish-Lithuanian Union, 1385–1569*, Oxford: Oxford University Press, 2018.

Gaay Fortman, Bas de, 'Between Principles and Practice: Grotius's commitment to religious peace in a contemporary context,' *Grotiana* 34 (2013): 25–40.

Garloff, Mona, 'Irenik als gelehrte Praxis. Religionspolitische Friedensprojekte im Zeitalter der europäischen Konfessionskonflikte,' *Daphnis* 45 (2017): 13–36.

Gelderen, Martin van, *The Political Thought of the Dutch Revolt 1555–1590*, Cambridge: Cambridge Univerity Press, 1992.

Gołaszewski, Zenon, *Bracia Polscy*, Warszawa: Dom Wydawniczy Duet, 2004.

Grunert, Frank, 'The Law of Nations in German historia literaria and Encyclopaedias in the Eighteenth Century,' in Simone Zurbuchen, ed., *The Law of Nations and Natural Law 1625–1800*, 89–105, Leiden: Brill, 2019.

Grzybowski, Stanisław, *Teoria reprezentacji w Polsce epoki Odrodzenia*, Warszawa: PWN, 1959.

Haakonssen, Knud, *Natural Law and Moral Philosophy. From Grotius to the Scottish Enlightenment*, Cambridge: Cambridge University Press, 1996.

Halecki, Oskar, *Zgoda Sandomierska 1570 r. Jej geneza i znaczenie w dziejach reformacyi Polskiej za Zygmunta Augusta*, Warszawa: Anczyca i spółki, 1915.

Hochstrasser, Timothy J., *Natural Law Theories in the Early Enlightenment*, Cambridge: Cambridge University Press, 2000.

Israel, Jonathan, 'The Intellectual Debate about Toleration in the Dutch Republic,' in *The Emergence of Tolerance in the Dutch Republic*, ed. Christiane Berkvens-Stevelinck, Jonathan Israel, and G.H.M. Posthumus Meyjes, 3–36, Leiden: Brill, 1997.

Jobert, Ambroise, *De Luther à Mohila: la Pologne pendant la crise de la chrétienté 1517–1648*, Paris: Collection historique de l'Institut d'Etudes Slaves, 1974.

Kaźmierczyk, Adam, Andrzej Link-Lenczowski and Mariusz Markiewicz, ed., *Rzeczpospolita wielu wyznań. Materiały z międzynarodowej konferencji. Kraków 18–20 listopada 2002*, Kraków: Księgarnia Akademicka, 2004.

Kempa, Tomasz, *Konflikty wyznaniowe w Wilnie od początku reformacji do końca XVII wieku*, Toruń: Wydawnictwo Naukowe Uniwersytetu Mikołaja Kopernika, 2016.

Kempa, Tomasz, *Wobec kontrreformacji: protestanci i prawosławni w obronie swobód wyznaniowych w Rzeczypospolitej w końcu XVI i w pierwszej połowie XVII wieku*, Toruń: Adam Marszałek, 2007.

Kleinmann, Yvonne et al., ed. *Kommunikation durch symbolische Akte. Religiöse Heterogenität und politische Herrschaft in Polen-Litauen*, Stuttgart: Steiner, 2010.

Knoll, Paul, 'Religious Toleration in Sixteenth-Century Poland. Political Realities and Social Constraints,' in *Diversity and Dissent. Negotiating Religious Difference in Central Europe, 1500–1800*, ed. Howard Louthan, Gary Cohen and Franz A.J. Szabo, 30–52, New York and Oxford: Berghahn, 2011.

Korołko, Mirosław, *Klejnot wolnego sumienia: Polemika wokół konfedercji warszawskiej w latach 1573–1658*, Warszawa: Instytut Wydawniczy PAX, 1974.

Kościelak, Sławomir, 'Dzieje wyznaniowe w Prusach Królewskich w XVI–XVIII w.,' in *Prusy Królewskie. Społeczeństwo, kultura, gospodarka, 1454–1772*, ed. Edmund Kizik, 204–263, Gdańsk: Muzeum Narodowe, 2012.

Kościelak, Sławomir, *Katolicy w protestanckim Gdańsku od drugiej połowy XVI do końca XVIII wieku*, Gdańsk: Wydawnictwo Uniwersytetu Gdańskiego, 2012.

Kosman, Marceli, 'Rola Radziwiłłów w ruchu Kalwińskim na Litwie,' *Miscellanea Historico-Archivistica* 3 (1989): 122–139.

Kot, Stanisław, 'Hugo Grotius a Polska,' in Stanisław Kot, *Polska złotego wieku a Europa. Studia i szkice*, ed. Henryk Barycz, 577–614, Warszawa: PIW, 1987.

Kot, Stanisław, *Socinianism in Poland: The Social and Political Ideas of the Polish Antitrinitarians*, transl. Earl Morse Wilbur, Boston: Starr King Press, 1957.

Kowalski, Waldemar, 'From the "Land of Diverse Sects" to National Religion: Converts to Catholicism and Reformed Franciscans in Early Modern Poland-Lithuania,' *Church History* 70 (2001/3): 482–526.

Kriegseisen, Wojciech, *Stosunki wyznaniowe w relacjach państwo-kościół między reformacją a oświeceniem: Rzesza Niemiecka, Niderlandy Północne, Rzeczpospolita polsko-litewska*, Warszawa: Semper, 2010.

Louthan, Howard, 'A Model for Christendom? Erasmus, Poland and the Reformation,' *Church History* 83 (March 2014): 18–37.

Makiłła, Dariusz, *Artykuły henrykowskie (1573–1576)*, Warszawa: Vizja Press, 2012.

Maliszewski, Kazimierz, 'Najnowsze zbiorowe dzieło z historii Gdańskiego Gimnazjum Akademickiego w dobie Rzeczypospolitej,' *Zapiski Historyczne* 78 (2013/3): 175–186.

Müller, Michael G., 'Der Consensus Sandomiriensis – Geschichte eines Scheiterns? Zur Diskussion über Protestantismus und protestantische Konfessionalisierung in Polen-Litauen,' in *Konfessionelle Pluralität als Herausforderung. Koexistenz und Konflikt in Spätmittelalter und Früher Neuzeit*, ed. Joachim Bahlcke et al., 397–407, Leipzig: Leipziger Universitätverlag, 2006.

Müller, Michael G., '"Nicht für die Religion selbst ist die Conföderation inter dissidentes eingerichtet…." Bekenntnispolitik und Respublica-Verständnis in Polen-Litauen,' in *Aspekte der politischen Kommunikation*, ed. Luise Schorn-Schütte, Beiheft *Historische Zeitschrift* 39 (2004): 311–328.

Müller, Michael G., *Zweite Reformation und städtische Autonomie im Königlichen Preußen. Danzig, Elbing und Thorn in der Epoche der Konfessionalisierung 1557–1660*, Berlin: Akademie Verlag, 1997.

Nowakowska, Natalia, *King Sigismund of Poland and Martin Luther: The Reformation before Confessionalization*, Oxford: Oxford University Press, 2018.

Obirek, Stanisław, S.J., *Jezuici w Rzeczypospolitej obojga narodów w latach 1564–1668. Działalność religijna, społeczno-kulturalna i polityczna*, Kraków: Wydział Filozoficzny Towarzystwa Jezusowego, 1996.

Obirek, Stanisław, S.J., *Wizja kościoła i państwa w kazaniach ks. Piotra Skargi S.J.*, Kraków: Wydawnictwo WAM, 1994.

Ogonowski, Zbigniew, *Z zagadnień tolerancji w Polsce XVII wieku*, Warszawa: PWN, 1958.

Olszewski, Henryk, *Historia doktryn politycznych i prawnych*, Warszawa: PWN, 1982.

Orzeł, Joanna, 'Rzeczpospolita Obojga Narodów w pismach Jeana Bodina,' in *Kontakty, tradycje i stosunki polsko-francuskie od XVI do początków XX wieku. Zbiór studiów*, ed. Joanna Orzeł and Mariusz Mróz, 44–56, Toruń: Wydawnictwo Adam Marszałek, 2012.

Parkin, Jon, 'Preface: Rethinking Toleration via Natural Law,' in *Natural Law and Toleration in the Early Enlightenment*, ed. Jon Parkin and Timothy Stanton. x–xxi, Oxford: Oxford University Press, 2013.

Pietrzyk-Reeves, Dorota, *Polish Republican Discourse in the Sixteenth Century*, Cambridge: Cambridge University Press, 2020.

Pryshlak, Maria O., *Państwo w filozofii politycznej Łukasza Opalińskiego*, transl. Grzegorz Chomicki, Kraków: Historia Iagiellonica, 2000.

Ptaszyński, Maciej, 'The Polish-Lithuanian Commonwealth,' in *A Companion to the Reformation in Central Europe*, ed. Howard Louthan and Graeme Murdock, 40–67, Leiden: Brill, 2015.

Ptaszyński, Maciej, *Reformacja w Polsce a dziedzictwo Erazma z Rotterdamu*, Warszawa: Wydawnictwo Uniwersytetu Warszawskiego, 2018.

Ptaszyński, Maciej, 'Religiöse Toleranz oder politischer Frieden? Verhandlungen über den Religionsfrieden in Polen-Litauen im 16. und 17. Jahrhundert,' in *Unversöhnte Verschiedenheit. Verfahren zur Bewältigung religiös-konfessioneller Differenz in der europäischen Neuzeit*, ed. Johannes Paulmann, Matthias Schnettger, and Thomas Weller, 161–178, Göttingen: Vandenhoeck & Ruprecht, 2016.

Pyszka, Stanisław, S.J., *Nauczanie filozofii moralnej w uniwersytetach i gimnazjach akademickich w Polsce i na Litwie od XV do XVII wieku w świetle podręczników wykładowych*, Kraków: Wydawnictwo WAM, 2011.

Scattola, Merio, *Das Naturrecht vor dem Naturrecht. Zur Geschichte des 'ius naturae' im 16. Jahrhundert*, Tübingen: Max Niemeyer, 1999.

Schuster, Kamila, *Biblioteka Łukasza Opalińskiego marszałka nadwornego koronnego (1612–1662)*, Wrocław: Zakład Narodowy im. Ossolińskich, 1971.

Simonutti, Luisa, 'Resistance, Obedience and Toleration: Przypkowski and Limborch,' in *Socinianism and Arminianism. Antitrinitarians, Calvinists and cultural exchange in seventeenth-century Europe*, ed. Martin Mulsow and Jan Rohls, 187–206, Leiden: Brill, 2005.

Skinner, Quentin, *The Foundations of Modern Political Thought*, vol. II, Cambridge: Cambridge University Press, 1978.

Spicer, Andrew, 'Luther, Adiaphora and the material culture of worship,' *Studies in Church History* 56 (2020): 246–272.

Stollberg-Rilinger, Barbara, 'Einleitung,' in *Konfessionelle Ambiguität. Uneindeutigkeit und Verstellung als religiöse Praxis in der Frühen Neuzeit*, ed. Andreas Pietsch and Barbara Stollberg-Rilinger, 9–26, Gütersloh: Gütersloher Verlagshaus, 2013.

Sucheni-Grabowska, Anna, *Spory królów ze szlachtą w złotym wieku: Wokół egzekucji praw*, Kraków: Krajowa Agencja Wydawnicza, 1988.

Tazbir, Janusz, *A State Without Stakes: Religious Toleration in Reformation Poland-Lithuania*, New York: Kościuszko Foundation, 1973.

Te Brake, Wayne T., *Religious War and Religious Peace in Early Modern Europe*, Cambridge: Cambridge University Press, 2017.

Tricoire, Damien, 'Beyond fundamentalism and tolerance narratives: Catholic representation of political-religious order and policy-making in the Holy Roman Empire and Poland-Lithuania,' in *Frühneuzeitliche Reiche in Europa*, ed. Tomasz Gromelski et al., 223–235, Wiesbaden: Harrassowitz, 2016.

Wagner-Rundell, Benedict, *Common Wealth, Common Good. The Politics of Virtue in Early Modern Poland-Lithuania*, Oxford: Oxford University Press, 2015.

Wajsblum, Marek, *Ex regestro arianismi. Szkice z dziejów upadku protestantyzmu w Małopolsce*, Kraków: Nakł. Towarzystwa Badań nad dziejów Reformacji w Polsce, 1937.

Wisner, Henryk, *Najjaśniejsza Rzeczpospolita. Szkice z dziejów Polski szlacheckiej XVI–XVII wieku*, Warszawa: PIW, 1978.

Wisner, Henryk, *Rozróżnieni w wierze. Szkice z dziejów Rzeczypospolitej schyłku XVI i połowy XVII wieku*, Warszawa: Książka i Wiedza, 1982.

Wünsch, Thomas, *Konziliarismus in Polen: Personen, Politik und Programme aus Polen zur Verfassungsfrage der Kirche in der Zeit der mittelalterlichen Reformkonzilien*, Paderborn: F. Schöningh, 1998.

Zajadło, Jerzy, 'Die Bedeutung der Hypothese "etiamsi daremus,"' *Archiv für Rechts- und Sozialphilosophie / Archives for Philosophy of Law and Social Philosophy*, 74 (1988/1): 83–92.

Zurbuchen, Simone, 'Introduction,' in Simone Zurbuchen, ed., *The Law of Nations and Natural Law 1625–1800*, 1–9, Leiden: Brill, 2019.

Zurbuchen, Simone, ed., *The Law of Nations and Natural Law 1625–1800*, Leiden: Brill, 2019.

Zurbuchen, Simone, *Naturrecht und natürliche Religon. Zur Geschichte des Toleranzbegriffs von Samuel Pufendorf bis Jean-Jacques Rousseau*, Würzburg: Königshausen und Neumann, 1991.

CHAPTER 3

Why Was the Political Discourse of the Polish-Lithuanian Nobility so Weakly Influenced by Natural Law?

Anna Grześkowiak-Krwawicz

1

The concept of natural law has been present in European political theory since the Ancient period and with the onset of the Modern age, it became a fundamental element of discussions relating to the state and law. Between the late sixteenth and the late eighteenth century, it was one of the central, if not the most important, subjects of theoretical debates. As Donald R. Kelley asserted, natural law was 'the main theme of early modern legal and political thought.'[1] Indeed, its significance was evident beyond theoretical discussions. As a classic author on the subject, Otto von Gierke, noted, '[t]he natural-law theory of the State was a guide to all the political efforts and struggles from which the modern state proceeds.'[2] The turn of the seventeenth century marked not only a watershed in European theories of natural law alongside the sudden rise to prominence of names such as Suárez, Althusius, Grotius and Pufendorf, but also the emergence of the concept as a key argument in political debates. French Monarchomachs had already turned to the idea in the sixteenth century, with the inhabitants of the Netherlands doing the same soon afterwards in the course of their disputes with the Spanish monarch. The English then adopted natural law in their struggle against the Stuarts. Indeed, in all of these cases, parties on both sides of the debates turned to arguments based in natural law.[3] It is also worth noting that those thinkers whose

1 Donald R. Kelley, 'Law,' in *The Cambridge History of Political Thought 1450–1700*, ed. James H. Burns with the assistance of Mark Goldie (Cambridge: Cambridge University Press, 1991), 89.

2 Otto Gierke, *Natural Law and the Theory of Society 1500–1800* (Boston: Beacon Press 1957), 35.

3 'The idea of natural rights could be used to defend either absolutist or liberal theories of government.' Brian Tierney, *The Idea of Natural Rights. Studies on Natural Rights, Natural Law and Church Law 1150–1625* (Grand Rapids, Michigan and Cambridge: William B. Eerdmans Publishing Co, 2001), 182.

 | DOI:10.1163/9789004545847_004

works we today consider as classics of natural law emerged in the course of the abovementioned and subsequent (Lockean) conflicts and struggles for power.

While they were perhaps less bloody, the political disputes and discussions in the Polish-Lithuanian Commonwealth were nevertheless extremely fierce and lively, and particularly so between the 1570s and 1620s. What is also important, they left behind a significant archive of political literature. Indeed, any issue that was of interest to the members of the nobility involved in political debate offered a reason for creating texts and notes. Most often, these took the form of manuscripts but this did not prevent them from being disseminated, read and commented upon (likewise in written form). Such statements, alongside more substantial declarations with greater theoretical ambitions, form the focus of my analysis of how modern theories of natural law were adapted by participants of public life in the Polish-Lithuanian Commonwealth. I examine whether they were indeed adapted at all and what shaped the paths along which nobles' political thought developed. It should be emphasized that the focus here is on the ideas represented by the nobility. Notwithstanding the interesting contributions stemming from the learned tendencies of some burghers of Gdańsk (Danzig) and Toruń (Thorn), it was the nobility that participated more or less directly in political struggles[4] and had the right to determine the affairs of the Commonwealth (or at least believed that they had the right to do so). The starting point of my analysis is 1569, the year when the union of the two nations was sealed in Lublin, or rather, to be more precise, 1573 – when the political form of the Polish-Lithuanian Commonwealth was officially established. My study ends in the 1770s, a time when such a far-reaching transformation of political language occurred that we might justifiably speak of a watershed.

2

A long-established argument in research has emphasized how modern conceptions of natural law in noble political discourse have been overlooked, with some scholars going as far as declaring that 'in pre-Enlightenment Poland,

4 This is why I omit, for example, the scholarly ideas of Aron Aleksander Olizarowski (*De politica hominum societate libri tres*, Gedani 1651) and Łukasz Opaliński's latin treatise (*De officiis libri tres*, Amsterdam 1668), as they clearly targeted foreign readers. Writing for a domestic audience, Opaliński quite evidently employed a different political idiom and language.

there was no real interest in new conceptions of natural law.'[5] The lack of interest is all the more striking in light of statements made by Polish Medieval and Renaissance theorists of the state. They considered the idea to be a product, on the one hand, of Stoic philosophy and, on the other, of classic Christian thinkers (first and foremost St. Thomas Aquinas) that offered crucial insight into visions of the state, society and the role of individuals in them. *Ius naturale* already played a significant role in Paweł Włodkowic's (1370–1435) fifteenth-century writings, as well as in the subsequent works of Andrzej Frycz Modrzewski (1503–1572), Wawrzyniec Goślicki (1530–1607) and Andrzej Wolan (1530–1610), to mention but the most significant names.[6] It could be argued that while they wrote serious treatises, what is being discussed here are merely the contemporary polemical pieces. However, natural law was also absent from more substantial essays which displayed a degree of theoretical ambition. The last thinkers from the period making reference to the idea were clerics who had drawn inspiration from Spanish Neo-Scholasticism and argued for increased powers for the monarchy in the late sixteenth century, namely bishop Józef Wereszczyński (1530–1598), Krzysztof Warszewicki (1543–1603) and the famous preacher Piotr Skarga (1536–1612). While Robert Frost suggests that in contrast to their humanist and Medieval predecessors, they were 'strongly influenced by the Jesuit natural law tradition,'[7] natural law was in fact used in their works as just another argument in favour of a more powerful monarchy and they did not develop the subject further. Natural law then disappeared from the discourse for almost two hundred years.

5 Anna Kochan, 'Prawo natury i prawo naturalne w dziełach autorów staropolskich,' in *Człowiek wobec natury. Humanizm wobec nauk przyrodniczych*, edited by Jacek Sokolski (Warsaw: Wydawnictwo Neriton, 2010), 41; see also Robert Frost, '"Liberty without Licence?". The Failure of Polish Democratic Thought in the Seventeenth Century,' in *Polish Democratic Thought from the Renaissance to the Great Emigration: Essays and Documents*, eds. Mieczysław B. Biskupski and James S. Paula (New York: Columbia Univ. Press, 1990), 47; Karin Friedrich, 'Polish-Lithuanian Political Thought, 1450–1700,' in *History of European Political Thought, 1450–1700*, eds. Howell A. Lloyd, Glenn Burgess, and S. Hodson (New Haven: Yale University Press, 2007), 221; Konstanty Grzybowski, 'Systematyka prawa w Polsce odrodzenia, jej rola i podłoże klasowe,' in *Odrodzenie w Polsce* (Warsaw: PIW, 1956), vol. 2, 199, although this applies rather to an earlier period.

6 Dorota Pietrzyk-Reeves, *Polish Republican Discourse in the Sixteenth Century*, transl. Teresa Bałuk-Ulewiczowa (Cambridge: Cambridge University Press, 2020), 78–85; Grzybowski, 'Systematyka prawa,' 194; Dariusz Makiłła, 'Prawo natury w szesnastowiecznej koncepcji prawa polskiego,' in: *'Nam hoc natura aequum est…' Księga jubileuszowa ku czci profesora Janusza Justyńskiego w siedemdziesięciolecie urodzin*, ed. Andrzej Madeja (Toruń: Towarzystwo Naukowe Organizacji i Kierownictwa 'Dom Organizatora,' 2012), 126sqq.

7 Frost, '"Liberty without Licence?,"' 42.

This does not mean that participants of political debate were ignorant either of norms that transcended the human realm (i.e. natural laws and the laws of God) or of their primacy in relation with positive norms. Nevertheless, this was something that was rarely addressed, though never completely absent, in their statements. The existence of natural laws, as they were termed in the Polish-Lithuanian Commonwealth, was mentioned occasionally in the works of more educated authors, sometimes as part of attempts to offer a systematic description of law. This was the case with an anonymous participant of the first free election of the monarch. He divided rights into those that are 'natural, those that form part of customs or are written down, and those that we call privilege.'[8] Natural rights were also raised as an argument in support of the nobles' freedoms, as happened in the controversies surrounding the 1665–66 trial of Marshal Jerzy Lubomirski, and in disputes based on faith.[9] However, any mention was usually brief, fairly arbitrary and tended to draw on pre-Modern traditions of natural law. As Robert Frost has noted, noble participants in political debates remained in their 'Aristotelian prison' until at least the end of the seventeenth century.[10]

This neglect is all the more striking in light of the fact that debates over the nature of the state were not only very lively but also conducted on a rather high level, at least during certain periods, such as the first free election (1573), the Zebrzydowski rebellion (*rokosz*) (1606–08) and the discussions over state reform under King John II Casimir (1648–1668). Meanwhile, those involved in these debates had not only failed to notice the watershed that had taken place in Western Europe in respect of understandings of natural law, but they also clearly had no need to refer to it in their disputes nor to develop ideas of the state based upon it. Why was this so? It would be too simplistic to

8 '[Prawa] przyrodzone, bądź te, które w obyczajach albo na piśmie są, bądź te, które zowiemy przywilej.' 'Naprawa Rzeczypospolitej do elekcyi nowego króla' (1573), in *Pisma polityczne z czasów pierwszego bezkrólewia*, ed. Jan Czubek (Kraków: Akademia Umiejętności, 1906), 201; in the same time period, another learned author wrote, citing Aristotle: 'Non hominem, inquit, imperare sinimus, sed rationem, hoc est legem naturae et iudicium de rebus agendis virorum sapientium.' 'Elekcyja krola Krześcijanska,' in *Pisma polityczne*, 324–325; see also Makiłła, 'Prawo natury,' 128.

9 Urszula Augustyniak has suggested the possibility of some form of reception of seventeenth-century conceptions of natural rights as a hypothesis worth testing in further research. Urszula Augustyniak, 'Polska i łacińska terminologia ustrojowa w publicystyce politycznej epoki Wazów,' in: *Łacina jako język elit*, ed. Jerzy Axer (Warsaw: Wydawnictwo DiG, 2004), 55.

10 Frost, "'Liberty without Licence?,'" 54; Kochan, 'Prawo natury,' 41, 48.

attribute this solely to the nobility's xenophobia and lack of openness towards foreign ideas, their supposed cultural backwardness and isolation from the mainstream of European thought. While these factors should not be ignored, they offer rather easy explanations and indeed oversimplify the entire issue. It would be worth adopting an alternative perspective that views the matter through the lens of nobles' political discourse. It is necessary to consider what the essential elements of that discourse were, what conceptual frameworks it employed and the extent to which natural law played a significant role in it. What is equally important is to examine the significance of the idea for Western European political disputes: how their participants employed the notion and whether similar references could have been of relevance to public debate in the Commonwealth. Were they necessary and was it indeed even possible to incorporate this concept into noble discourse?

3

A suitable opening statement would be that in Poland-Lithuania the law itself was not only a fixed presence in discourse between the sixteenth and eighteenth centuries, but was also of enormous significance to the image of the political world that developed during that period. It was an important element in debates and disputes over the nature of the state, society, relations between individuals and the order of the Commonwealth, as well as between the individuals involved in constructing this order. Besides creating and unifying the tissue of the body politic, the law also provided it with a vital force that permeated all aspects of its existence and deeds.[11] Symbolic of the significance attached to the law was the metaphor adopted from classical authors that equated it to the soul of the Commonwealth. As Stanisław Sarnicki (1532–1597) writes in the preface to his *Statut*, 'without the laws, the *Rzeczpospolita* is as though a body without soul, as Plato and Aristotle state in their *De Legibus* and *De Republica* volumes.'[12] Despite the importance of the role ascribed to the law, it would be difficult to find in Polish-Lithuanian statements an equi-

11 Pietrzyk-Reeves, *Polish Republican Discourse*, 80; Anna Grześkowiak-Krwawicz, *The Political Discourse of the Polish-Lithuanian Commonwealth. Concepts and Ideas*, transl. D. Sax (New York and London: Routledge, 2021), 42.

12 '[*B*]yć *abseque legibus* Rzeczpospolita jest jakoby ciało bez dusze, jako Plato i Aristoteles w księgach *de legibus* i *de Republica* wywodzą,' Stanisław Sarnicki, *Statuta i Metrika przywileiów koronnych: językiem polskim spisane* (Kraków, 1594), foreword, fol. *3v.

valent of what was termed *jurisprudence language* in Western Europe.[13] Even sixteenth-century authors, such as Modrzewski or Goślicki, who wrote a great deal about law in their works, did not make it the basis or framework for their ideas. While they included it as part of their broader constitutional-political treatises, they never based their ideas upon it. One important factor in this was the relatively limited knowledge of Roman law, which in some cases was completely rejected.[14] Polish authors drew their conceptions of law primarily from Roman philosophers, turning relatively rarely to Justinian's *Digests*. It could be argued that in the Commonwealth law was discussed using the language of politics, rather than politics being discussed in legal terms.[15] This is a significant difference meaning that *de facto* no strand of thought on the idea of the state emerged in Poland that could be considered analogous to the conceptions developed in the Netherlands, the Holy Roman Empire or England. In those countries, jurisprudential interpretations of the role of the law contributed to the formation of a discourse in which natural law became fundamental to visions of the state, power, and relations between the individuals that made up society.[16]

---

13 J.G.A. Pocock coined this term and applied it in numerous works, such as 'Virtues, Rights, and Manners. A Model for Historians of Political Thought,' *Political Theory* 9 (1981/3): 353–368, here 355sqq.; likewise Mark M. Goldsmith, 'Liberty, Virtue and the Rule of Law, 1689–1770,' in *Republicanism, Liberty and Commercial Society, 1649–1776*, ed. David Wootton (Stanford: Stanford University Press, 1994), 199–200.

14 On the Polish-Lithuanian nobility's aversion to Roman law see Adam Vetulani, 'Opory wobec prawa rzymskiego w dawnej Polsce,' *Analecta Cracoviensia* 1 (1969): 372–386; Claude Backvis, 'Jednostka i społeczeństwo w Polsce doby renesansu,' in Backvis, *Szkice o kulturze staropolskiej* (Warsaw: Państwowy Instytut Wydawniczy, 1975), 556–557; Stanisław Estreicher, *Kultura prawnicza w Polsce XVI wieku*, Kraków 1931, 44sqq.; Stanisław Grodziski, *Z dziejów staropolskiej kultury prawnej* (Kraków: Universitas, 2004), 166. It would seem that there has been relatively little research on this question with relation to Lithuania, where the influence of Roman law was significantly stronger. This is evident, for example, in the Statutes. See Juliusz Bardach, *Statuty litewskie a prawo rzymskie* (Warsaw: Ośrodek Badań nad Tradycją Antyczną w Polsce i w Europie Środkowo-Wschodniej, 1999); Andrzej Zakrzewski, *Wielkie Księstwo Litewskie (XVI–XVIII w.). Prawo – ustrój – społeczeństwo* (Warsaw: Campidoglio, 2013), ch. 12: 'Statuty litewskie,' ch. 13: 'Prawo w teorii i praktyce'; Sławomir Godek, *Elementy prawa rzymskiego w III Statucie litewskim (1588)* (Warsaw: Oficyna Naukowa, 2004).

15 See more: Grześkowiak-Krwawicz, *The Political Discourse*, Ch. 2: 'Prawo – the Law.'

16 John P. Reid, *Rule of Law. The Jurisprudence of Liberty in the Seventeenth and Eighteenth Centuries* (Dekalb: Northern Illinois University Press, 2004), passim; Kenneth Pennington, *The Prince and the Law, 1200–1600* (Berkeley: University of California Press, 1993), 119sqq.

This was not the only difference. Another was something that has been mentioned here already, namely that beyond the statements of sixteenth-century humanists, it was only positive law to which great significance was ascribed. Regardless of whether they were writing about the law in general as the embodiment of justice and a guide to how members of society should behave '*rationes honestatis, aequi et iniqui*,'[17] or rather as a guardian of civil liberties and source of protection from monarchs, the law in question was primarily positive or common law, although the latter form was less significant in Polish thought than, for example, in English conceptions.[18] Over time, with the crisis of political thought in the mid-seventeenth century and early-eighteenth century, references to the law increasingly focused on particular questions and aspects of its influence on the way the collective functioned, rather than on a totalizing conception of law. This state of affairs was not conducive to the adoption of a more general understanding of natural law.

4

This offers at least a partial explanation for the evident difficulties faced in adapting Western theories. However, when examining the adaptation or development of a particular idea, it is worth considering what purpose and whom it was to serve in ongoing political struggles. We should bear in mind certain fundamental questions relating to the early modern watershed in theories of natural law and contextualize them in terms of the conditions that shaped this watershed and the objectives that this idea was to serve. The aim here is not to outline natural law's significance for the development of philosophies of the state but rather to demonstrate which particular polemical objectives were expected to be fulfilled by natural law in light of the particular socio-political conditions in which the idea emerged. Certainly, one of the most important functions of natural law in its modern form, at least in the early phase of the idea's development, was to justify or rather legitimize the resistance practised by subjects towards rulers. This is something that scholars working on the history of French Monarchomachs[19] and on the struggle for the sovereignty of

17 'Naprawa Rzeczypospolitej,' 196.

18 However, it was important to court proceedings. See Grodziski, *Z dziejów staropolskiej kultury prawnej*, 162–163.

19 The appeal to natural law arguments 'enabled them to base their theory of popular sovereignty on the logical and not merely the chronological origins of commonwealth.' Quentin Skinner, *The Foundations of Modern Political Though* (Cambridge: Cambridge University Press, 1978), vol. 2, 322.

the Netherlands have noted. As Eco Haitsma Mulier argues, 'for long after the Revolt the principal concern of political theorists in the Netherlands was to emphasise the legitimacy of their rebellion against the Spanish crown.'[20] References to natural law made it possible to shift the focus of debate onto a higher theoretical plane, turning individual struggles with rulers into broader political issues that transcended national and religious boundaries. This leads into another, and perhaps the most important, role of the theory of natural law, one that soon provided the central axis and basis of seventeenth-century power struggles. Both supporters of the idea of the sovereignty of the people and those favouring the sovereignty of the monarch turned to it,[21] from Bacon's conviction that there was 'a natural right of kings to rule'[22] to Althusius's declaration of the natural law of the people's sovereignty.[23] After all, natural law not only provided the basis for a post-Bodinian conception of sovereignty, but also for the circumscription of monarchs' power – '*princeps autem legi naturae pareat*.'[24] In the case of absolutist ideas, it often constituted the sole limitation. Again, this was an important and often fundamental argument in the dispute. It was clear that what was at stake was not only natural law as something that was fundamental to life in a state community and regulated international relations, but also *natural rights* as something inviolable and inalienable, and due to each member of the community. It is worth recalling

20 Eco Haitsma Mulier, 'The language of seventeenth-century republicanism in the United Provinces: Dutch or European?,' in *The Languages of Political Theory in Early-Modern Europe*, ed. Anthony Pagden (Cambridge: Cambridge University Press, 1987), 180; Ernst H. Kossman, 'The Developement of Dutch Political Theory in the Seventeenth Century,' in *Britain and Netherlands. Papers delivered to the Oxford – Netherlands Historical Conference 1959*, ed. John S. Bromley and Ernst H. Kossmann (London: Chatto & Vindus, 1960) 90, 94; Gierke, *Natural Law*, 234.

21 Gierke, *Natural Law*, 42; Martin van Gelderen, 'Aristotelians, Monarchomachs and Republicans: Sovereignty and *respublica mixta* in Dutch and German Political Thought, 1580–1650,' in *Republicanism: A Shared European* Heritage, ed. Martin van Gelderen and Quentin Skinner (Cambridge: Cambridge University Press, 2002), vol. 1, 202.

22 Robert Zaller, *The Discourse of Legitimacy in Early Modern England* (Stanford, CA: Stanford University Press, 2007), 324; Cf. Richard Tuck, *The Sleeping Sovereign. The Invention of Modern Democracy* (Cambridge: Cambridge University Press, 2016), 51.

23 Howell A. Lloyd, 'Constitutionalism,' in *The Cambridge History of Political Thought*, 289.

24 Jean Bodin, *Six Livres de la République*, Lib. II, cap. 3; see also Janine Chanteur, 'La loi naturelle et la souveraineté chez Jean Bodin,' in: *Théologie et droit dans la science politique d'état moderne* (Rome: Ecole Française de Rome, 1991), 292; Skinner, *The Foundations*, 296; Howard Nenner, 'Liberty, Law, and Property: The Constitution in Retrospect from 1689,' in *Liberty secured? Britain before and after 1688*, ed. James R. Jones (Stanford: Stanford Univ. Press, 1992), 89; Pennington, *The Prince and the Law*, 278, 283.

that modern natural law emerged in the course of Protestant struggles for religious freedoms and thus formed one of the basic arguments in their defence.

5

This rather simplified outline of the contexts in which natural law was employed in political debates in the early modern period leads into a key question of this study, namely: to what extent was it possible to draw on these ideas in the debates taking place in the Polish-Lithuanian state? As was the case all over Europe, there was also no shortage of political disputes in the Commonwealth. They ranged from religious disputes (which were never as bloody as those in the West) to the incessant struggle for power in the state between monarchs and the nobility, which also led to serious conflicts with the rulers (Zebrzydowski's *rokosz* 1606–08 and Lubomirski's *rokosz* 1666). However, if we take into account also the significant debate that spread through the Commonwealth relating to its form of government following the first election of the monarch and, in particular, in the context of the governmental crisis of 1573–76, we could argue that there was a period of several decades of intensive discussion that also resounded in subsequent years, even if the quality of debate had declined noticeably by then. But did these debates include references to natural law?

A suitable starting point is that of the most extreme cases, namely the rebellions (*rokosze*), particularly Zebrzydowski's, which produced a wealth of interesting documents. While this was ultimately a challenge to the king that at some point escalated into a civil war, it would be difficult to apply the concept of resistance to power that developed in the writings of French and English opponents of the monarchy to the discussions taking place in Poland-Lithuania. It was certainly significant that those involved did not need to refer to resistance theory, which was derived from natural law, because they had recourse to positive law, namely the very specific article *de non praestanda oboedientia* that was inscribed in the Henrician Articles. The fundamental difference, however, was to be found elsewhere. In contrast to the Monarchomachs, the Dutch, or even the Stuarts' opponents, those involved in the Zebrzydowski rebellion did not consider their actions in terms of resistance to the monarch's rule but rather in terms realizing their rights and indeed executing their power. Interestingly, they sought to make the case, somewhat counter to reality, that their intention was not to undermine the existing order but rather to uphold it in light of the disruption to it resulting from the actions of King Sigismund III. They made reference to the older *rokosz* tradition whereby 'the nobility, having noted intolerable harm being done in the Commonwealth, whether as a result of the actions of the Lord, the senators or the nobility [...], left to douse the flames, came together and rallied.'[25] This was part of a common European trend of drawing on 'ancient' arguments and common law, with 'the law of the *rokosz*' declared 'older than the king, *magistratus* and all the statutes.'[26] What was most emphatically stressed, however, was that the highest authority in the state belonged to the nobility, or at least primarily to the nobility, with the rebellions being the expression of this. 'If this absolute power is held by all the estates, then it is consequently to be found in the hand of that estate which is most important to this kingdom and which has primacy in this kingdom.'[27]

Zebrzydowski's rebellion was just one of the stages in two ages of struggles for power between the noble 'people' (*lud*) and the monarch. However, the dispute took a different form to the conflicts that would emerge in Western Europe. One exception to this rule was during the period 1606–08, when participants of the *rokosz* tried to find alternative ways to express their demands and political ambitions. However, they did not wholly espouse natural law, as they remained within the limits imposed by traditional conceptual frameworks rather than introduce new concepts and ideas. On the one hand, it was too early to do so. New ideas were still emerging: the ink was not yet dry on Althusius's work, while Grotius's ideas concerning rights in war and peace would not appear for another twenty years or so. What was important in this case, however, was that the modern conception of natural law and the broader modern vision of the state and power were incompatible with the nobility's political language. This is why they failed to appear in the *szlachta*'s discourse for decades to come. This applies not only to natural law but also to the post-Bodinian idea of sovereignty. There was no place, either, for notions of the social contract, delegation of power, or the mechanistic vision of the state as

25 'Szlachta obaczywszy skazy jakie nieznośne w Rzeczypospolitej, bądź to z osoby pańskiej, bądź z koła senatorskiego, bądź też z stanu szlacheckiego pochodzące [...] do naprawy tych skaz, jako do gaszenia ognia rzucali się, do kupy się zwoływali i zjeżdżali.' 'Defensio ac definitio rokoszu' (1606), in *Pisma polityczne z czasów rokoszu Zebrzydowskiego 1606–1608*, 1–3 vols, ed. Jan Czubek (Kraków: Akademia Umiejętności, 1916–1918), vol. 2, 440.

26 'Starsze prawo rokoszowe, niż król, *magistratus* i statuta wszytkie.' 'Natura albo definitio rokoszu,' in *Pisma polityczne z czasów rokoszu*, vol. 2, 413.

27 'Jeśli ta *absoluta potestas* jest w ręku wszech stanów, tedy pogotowiu jest w ręku tego stanu, który jest *potissima huius regni portio* i który *primas parte habet in regno hoc.*' [Mikołaj Zebrzydowski], 'Apologia szlachcica polskiego,' in *Pisma polityczne z czasów rokoszu*, vol. 3, 234.

persona ficta. Instead, the nobility remained loyal to older conceptions that did not separate society and the state, seeing them as an organic whole – a *civitas* or commonwealth.[28] In debates over authority within the state – with whom power should reside, what its extent should be, and what executive force it had – the nobles involved in political discussions made reference to mixed government, liberty, and participation. They offered a total vision of the political world, or at least one that satisfied participants in the discussions. That vision did not encompass natural law, though, because it was necessary neither as the basis for rule (by whomever) nor as a limitation on power.

What are telling here are the discussions related to the scope and limitations of royal authority. The monarch was presented as one element in a mixed system of rule, who together with the two remaining parts – the senate and *szlachta* – formed the body of the Commonwealth. As an anonymous author from the mid-seventeenth century (and a royalist, no less) noted, '[t]he Lord and the Commonwealth, all three estates [in political meaning] form one single body and you cannot separate what is impossible to be divided.'[29] The king was indeed an essential element in this system, but his power was constrained in an effectively natural way by the complicated ties forming the structure of rule and without which he was unable to exert his power. The limitations imposed on the ruler were not only evident in the set of mutual restrictions in the *respublica mixta* but also, and perhaps most evidently, in the law. From at least the sixteenth century to the eighteenth century, what was stressed was not only the role of the law as the supreme set of rules for ruling the country, but also who possessed the most power according to it and who, therefore, was the sovereign who 'ruled both the king and the people.'[30] However, the question of the monarch's subordination to the law was considered

28 See more: Pietrzyk-Reeves, *Polish Republican Discourse*, passim; Grześkowiak-Krwawicz, *The Political Discourse*, ch. 1: '*Rzeczpospolita* – The Commonwealth.'

29 'Pan i Rzeczpospolita wszystkie *tres ordines* jedno ciało czynią *et quod dividi nequit – separari non potest*.' 'Respons panu Reklewskiemu,' (1663), in *Pisma polityczne z czasów panowania Jana Kazimierza Wazy 1648–1668. Publicystyka, eksorbitancje, projekty, memoriały*, ed. Stefania Ochmann-Staniszewska, vol. 2: 1661–1664 (Warsaw: Volumen, 1990), 200.

30 'Rządząc i królem i ludem.' [Mikołaj Kossobudzki], Jan Januszowski transl., *Zwierciadło królewskie z wielu miejsc ludzi wielkich zebrane i na polskie przełożone* (Kraków 1606), in *Sześć broszur politycznych z XVI i początku XVII stulecia*, ed. Bolesław Ulanowski (Kraków: Polska Akademia Umiejętności, 1921), 267; cf. Anna Sucheni-Grabowska, 'Obowiązki i prawa królów polskich w opiniach pisarzy epoki odrodzenia,' in *Między monarchą a demokracją. Studia z dziejów Polski XV–XVIII wieku*, ed. Anna Sucheni-Grabowska and Małgorzata Żaryn (Warsaw: Wydawnictwo Sejmowe, 1994), 79, 87 and Claude Backvis, 'Główne tematy polskiej myśli politycznej w XVI wieku,' in Backvis, *Szkice o kulturze staropolskiej*, 509.

exclusively in terms of existing law, thus in terms of either customary norms or positive norms that applied in the Commonwealth and could thus provide not only a theoretical but also a practical basis and restraints for the monarch's rule.[31] Indeed, more voluminous texts did consider the subordination of the monarch to divine and natural law, although such considerations were always accompanied by statements declaring the necessity of submitting him to positive laws.[32] It could be argued that all those involved in political discussions at the time would have accepted the view presented by Jakub Zawisza of Kroczów that natural laws are insufficient in so far as their transgression does not entail immediate legal sanctions.[33] Andrzej Frycz Modrzewski had already written that 'the Commonwealth was to be ruled not according to royal will but by written legislation.'[34] The key term here is *written*. What is particularly significant in the texts produced around the elections of monarchs is the oft-repeated phrase that the monarch was 'for the sake of the existing laws'[35] or was 'taken' by them.[36] The argument that the king was bound by 'old laws' was not peculiar to the discourse of the Polish nobility, as this was something that subjects throughout Europe made reference to. Yet, this tendency not only survived significantly longer in the Commonwealth than in other countries but was *de facto* the sole argument presented. Furthermore, it was much more common to speak of positive laws rather than of a mythical 'ancient constitution' or the no less mythical eternal 'laws of the land' or 'of the people.' Over time, the emphasis was increasingly shifted away from claims regarding the

31 Urszula Augustyniak, 'Granice wolności obywatela Rzeczypospolitej w XVI–XVII w. Jednostka wobec władzy, prawa i społeczeństwa,' in *Wolność i jej granice. Polskie dylematy*, ed. Jacek Kloczkowski (Kraków: Ośrodek Myśli Politycznej, 2007), 17.

32 For example, in *Zwierciadło* of Kossobudzki/Januszowski after chapter XVIII on the king's obedience to divine laws, the subsequent chapter (XIX) explained that '[n]ext to the law of God, the king should be submitted to the laws of the Crown and should guard them' (*[p]o prawie Bożym praw koronnych pilnować i im podlegać król ma*); cf. Backwis, 'Główne tematy,' 509.

33 Jakub Zawisza from Kroczów, *Wskrócenie prawnego procesu koronnego* (1613), ed. Alojzy Winiarz (Kraków: Akademia Umiejętności, 1899), 16.

34 'Rzeczpospolita nie wedle woli królewskiej, ale wedle praw pisanych ma być rządzona.' Andrzej Frycz Modrzewski, *O poprawie Rzeczypospolitej księgi czwore*, transl. Cyprian Bazylik (1577), ed. Mirosław Korolko (Piotrków Trybunalski: Naukowe Wydawnictwo Piotrkowskie, 2003), 325.

35 '[D]o gotowych praw przychodzi,' 'Naprawa praw, swobód i wolności, naszych,' [inc.] in *Pisma polityczne z czasów pierwszego bezkrólewia*, 187.

36 'Do których praw dobrze porządnych ma być nowy pan wzięt, aby nam wedle nich panował.' 'Summa tych rzeczy, które mają być opatrzone, postanowione przed obraniem nowego króla,' in *Pisma polityczne z czasów pierwszego bezkrólewia*, 172.

subordination of the king to the law and towards claims that this was the law that 'we [...] make and improve.'[37] The discussions focused no longer on the limitations imposed on the monarch but rather on the power and authority that belonged not to him but to the noble citizens.

It bears repeating that neither the idea of natural law as the source of power, nor the vision of natural rights 'of the people' as something that the king had no right to violate as doing so would be tantamount to tyranny, actually featured in Polish debates. Any traces of such claims were generally irrelevant and isolated.[38] This is hardly surprising since if they did find their way into discourse, then those involved in political discussions in Poland-Lithuania would necessarily need to transform their entire political language. Another matter was that this language had over time ossified and from around the seventeenth century had largely come to serve in the defence of the status quo rather than enable new programmes of reform to be applied to the increasingly deficient state structures. In some ways, this form of language not only made it more difficult to describe the problems that existed but also hindered the ability to take into account members of society beyond the nobility.

6

A notable feature of this language was that it lacked not only a conception of natural law as a basis of the structures of the state and power, but also of individual natural rights. The concept of natural rights was an idea that in Western Europe not only provided an argument in defence of religious liberties, or – more broadly – of the rights of the individual against the whims of the ruler, but also came to provide the foundation for the formulation of theories that

37 This was in the context of the struggle against the Jesuits: 'We make the law and improve upon it, not priests' ('My prawo stanowimy i naprawiamy, nie księża'). 'Jezuitom i inszem duchownym respons,' in *Pisma polityczne z czasów rokoszu*, vol. 3, 93.

38 There were nevertheless some references, cf. Michał Zwierzykowski, '"Sine iustitia in libertate żyć nie chcemy." Prawo i sprawiedliwość w dyskursie politycznym kampanii sejmowych lat 1696–1762,' in *Wartości polityczne Rzeczypospolitej Obojga Narodów. Struktury aksjologiczne i granice cywilizacyjne*, ed. Anna Grześkowiak-Krwawicz in collaboration with Jerzy Axer (Warsaw: Wydawnictwo Uniwersytetu Warszawskiego, 2017), 275. In the seventeenth century, the distant echo of natural law theory could be heard in speeches of Protestants defending their rights, e.g. 'Uniżona prośba do Króla Jego M[ił]ości i Rzeczypospolitej na sejm MDCXXVII pisana,' in *Państwo świeckie czy księże? Spór o rolę duchowieństwa katolickiego w Rzeczypospolitej w czasach Zygmunta III Wazy. Wybór tekstów*, ed. Urszula Augustyniak (Warsaw: Semper, 2013), 389.

considered the mutual relations among those who formed society. Indeed, humanists such as Modrzewski and Wolan did develop an idea of natural rights based on classical conceptions as the basis for their critique of the laws of the Commonwealth that harmed the plebeians and were thus incompatible with universal norms.[39] However, their successors, focusing on the rights of the noble citizens who formed the *szlachta*-centred Commonwealth, did not employ the concept in its modern sense. Compared to the Polish-Lithuanian nobility, participants of political disputes in the Netherlands or England found it much more convenient to refer to the laws of nature that they considered universally applicable to all 'the people.' Even if the Polish-Lithuanian noble citizens considered themselves to be 'the people' (*lud*) or 'the nation' (*naród*), it would have been difficult for them to refer to natural rights while ignoring completely other inhabitants of the Commonwealth. The republican language rooted in classical tradition was much more suited to their needs, as adopting such a narrative meant that certain concepts became superfluous.

An excellent example of this was natural liberty. Certainly, some Renaissance theorists of the state incorporated the idea into their thought,[40] while claims such as '*libertas est naturalis facultas*'[41] also appeared later. Nevertheless, this was an idea that remained firmly at the margins of Polish political thought and ultimately did not come to provide the foundation for noble discourse. In that discourse, in contrast to ideas that formed the basis of liberal thought, positive rights offered no guarantee of human liberty nor did they form a limit to it; instead, they were the basis of freedom itself. 'Our laws that

---

39 Cf. Steffen Huber, *Polifonia tradycji: filozofia polityczna i teoretyczna Andrzeja Frycza Modrzewskiego* (Warsaw: Wydawnictwo Naukowe Sub Lupa, 2014), 336; Jan Květina, *Mýtus Republiky. Identita a politický diskurz raně novověké polské šlechty* (Hradec Králové: Pavel Mervart, 2019), 514.

40 This was indeed familiar before this time. Cf. Jacek Wiesiołowski, 'Kultura szlachecka,' in *Kultura Polski średniowiecznej XIV–XV w.*, ed. Bronisław Geremek (Warsaw: Instytut Historii PAN, 1997), 174; Janusz Ekes, *Natura – wolność – władza. Studium z dziejów myśli politycznej Renesansu* (Warsaw: Instytut Wydawniczy PAX, 2001), 56.

41 *Respons przyjacielowi pewnemu od ziemianina jednego na straconą wolność narzekającemu. Z Liska 9 decembris 1697*, Scientific Library of the PAAS and the PAS in Cracow, ms. 1060, 279. 'Liberty, which wise nature took as a priceless jewel together with the original being in the world, *in dotem* of the Creator of all things to the people spread around the forests and fields' ('Wolność, którą rozumna natura, jako nieoszacowany klejnot z pierwszą zaraz na świecie bytnością, prawie *in dotem* Stwórcy wszechrzeczy wzięła pospołu z ludźmi po lasach i polach rozproszonymi') – rulers were said to be 'plundering' this liberty. [Walenty Pęski], *Domina Palatii regina libertas*, in Jan Dębiński, *Różne mowy publiczne, sejmikowe i sejmowe* ([Częstochowa], 1727), 4.

laid the foundations of Polish freedom'[42] was a typical phrase that made clear the reality of noble privileges while also making reference to a classical discourse that perceived the connections between rights and liberty. From this perspective, liberty was closely connected both to a particular form of rule and to membership of a particular collective, namely the nobility or the Commonwealth, without which freedom could not exist. Such a perspective had far-reaching social and political consequences. What is significant is that the question of liberty as a natural right simply had no place in this discourse. Typically, even in discussions on freedom of conscience, the noble participants involved preferred to make reference to noble liberties and Polish freedom than to liberty as a natural right. However, this is a question that still deserves closer investigation.

While liberty as a natural right seemed to be of little interest in the Commonwealth, freedom itself was a key element of the nobility's discourse. But another natural right, namely property, was almost completely absent. This is perhaps something of a simplification, but even if the absence of discussions on property was not total, its relative insignificance is nevertheless striking, particularly in light of Western European discussions, where it came to be one of the most common and perhaps even most important concepts.[43] This applied not only to theorists but also to all those involved in Western political debate for whom it was a key element of their political universe. The foundations of property, its role in the construction of the collective and in its activities, and its political significance were all subjects of analysis. Alongside the right to life, property was one of the most crucial natural rights that was supposed to guarantee the social contract and the state that it produced. It was also a basic and inviolable right of the individuals who created that society. Yet, those involved in debates in Poland-Lithuania did not tend to perceive these functions of property. On the one hand, this was a result of the particular socio-political realities. It was not property but membership of the noble class that enabled participation in power and guaranteed liberty. On the other hand, it was also a result of traditional political discourse, which attached greater significance to other values, while individual property (while desirable) was viewed in fairly ambivalent terms.[44] This began to change in the

42 'Prawa nasze, które polską ufundowały wolność.' Stanisław Konarski, *O skutecznym rad sposobie*, vol. 2 (Warsaw 1761), 185.

43 Cf. e.g. Ellen Meiksins Wood, *Liberty and Property. A Social History of Western Political Thought from Renaissance to Enlightenment* (London: Verso, 2012).

44 Cf. Grześkowiak-Krwawicz, *The Political Discourse*, ch. 9: 'In Conclusion, What Concepts Were Absent? Property.'

1770s when property came to be presented in Polish discourse not as wealth, luxury or even solely as noble possessions. Instead, it was spoken of in and of itself as something that was not marginal but rather crucial to the political world and thus a natural right – 'the natural rights to property.'[45] As Józef Wybicki (1747–1820) wrote, 'the right to property was based in nature. Its origins were to be found in nature and it derived its respect from it.'[46] The society and authority that were derived from the social contract were there merely to guarantee property.

7

This was symptomatic of a significant shift. Around this time, Polish political debate came to include a whole host of new concepts and ideas. These included, first and foremost, natural rights in the Enlightenment sense of individual human rights. This produced something of a feedback loop, as an entire group of authors emerged in the 1770s who sought to describe not only the noble Commonwealth but also all of society. They required suitable tools to do so and natural rights was one of them. At the same time, reference to this idea not only enabled but also indeed forced them into recognition of all those who formed the social collective. Natural rights could be, and indeed were, a tool that enabled the description of all the rights due to all members of the 'civil society' precisely in order to defend these rights. From Wybicki in the 1770s to Hugo Kołłątaj (1750–1812) around the turn of the 1790s, those responsible for introducing the concept into discourse emphasized that the rights of civil society had to be in accordance with natural rights.[47] The incorporation of natural rights into political discourse by the noble participants of public life was one of the most significant transformations that signalled a revival and modernization of the discourse. This took place comparatively late and on their own

45 'Przyrodzone prawa własności.' Konstantyn Bogusławski, *O doskonałym prawodawctwie* (Warsaw, 1786), 76.

46 'Prawo własności zasadzało się na naturze. Razem z nią miało swój początek i uszanowanie.' Józef Wybicki, *Listy patriotyczne* (1777–1778), ed. Kazimierz Opałek (Wrocław: Zakład im. Ossolińskich, 1955), 18.

47 It was Stroynowski, who went the furthest in this argument, arguing – following François Quesney and other Physiocrats – that people do not make laws but rather discover laws made by God as part of the natural order. Hieronim Stroynowski, *Nauka prawa przyrodzonego, politycznego, ekonomiki politycznej i prawa narodów* (Wilno, 1785), 108. Cf. Kazimierz Opałek, *Prawo natury u polskich fizjokratów* (Warsaw: Książka i Wiedza, 1953), 21 and 74.

terms, so to speak. Natural rights became an important element of discussions about society, its structures, and the rights of the individuals that formed it, though the concept did not influence political debates over the nature of the state. What prevailed in the latter were references, on the one hand, to traditional visions of the Commonwealth and, on the other (and more readily), to ideas drawn from Rousseau and Montesquieu, the thinkers less interested in natural rights theory.

As a consequence, I would argue that their long absence from Polish-Lithuanian debates was shaped less by ignorance of Western theories (although it would be worth investigating closely which works of political thought reached the Commonwealth and who, if anyone, read them) and more by their 'unsuitability' to the *szlachta*'s political discourse. Perhaps there was a degree of mistrust, as it is worth remembering that the greatest theorists of natural law, from Suárez to Pufendorf, supported strong monarchical rule, an unacceptable option in the Commonwealth. It could be argued that Polish discourses skipped the stage when natural law formed the basis of discussions about the state and power, instead turning to these ideas only when they became relevant to human rights and thus struck a chord with the growing need to describe not only the noble Commonwealth but also the entire social community.

Translated from Polish by *Paul Vickers*

Acknowledgement

The linguistic proofreading was supported by the Max Weber Centre for Advanced Cultural and Social Studies of the University of Erfurt.

Bibliography

Primary Sources

Bogusławski, Konstantyn, *O doskonałym prawodawctwie*, Warsaw, 1786.

Konarski, Stanisław, *O skutecznym rad sposobie*, Warsaw, 1760–1763.

[Kossobudzki, Mikołaj], Januszowski, Jan, transl., *Zwierciadło królewskie z wielu miejsc ludzi wielkich zebrane i na polskie przełożone* Kraków (1606), in *Sześć broszur politycznych z XVI i początku XVII stulecia*, ed. Bolesław Ulanowski, Kraków: Polska Akademia Umiejętności, 1921.

Modrzewski, Andrzej Frycz, *O poprawie Rzeczypospolitej księgi czwore*, transl. Cyprian Bazylik (1577), ed. M. Korolko, Piotrków Trybunalski: Naukowe Wydawnictwo Piotrkowskie, 2003.

Państwo świeckie czy księże? Spór o rolę duchowieństwa katolickiego w Rzeczypospolitej w czasach Zygmunta III Wazy. Wybór tekstów, ed. Urszula Augustyniak, Warsaw: Semper, 2013.

[Pęski, Walenty], *Domina Palatii regina libertas*, in Jan Dębiński, *Różne mowy publiczne, sejmikowe i sejmowe* [Częstochowa], 1727.

Pisma polityczne z czasów pierwszego bezkrólewia, ed. Jan Czubek, Kraków: Akademia Umiejętności, 1906.

Pisma polityczne z czasów rokoszu Zebrzydowskiego 1606–1608, 1–3 vols, ed. Jan Czubek, Kraków: Akademia Umiejętności, 1916–1918.

Pisma polityczne z czasów panowania Jana Kazimierza Wazy 1648–1668. Publicystyka, eksorbitancje, projekty, memoriały, ed. Stefania Ochmann-Staniszewska, vol. 2: 1661–1664, Warsaw: Volumen, 1990.

Respons przyjacielowi pewnemu od ziemianina jednego na straconą wolność narzekającemu. z Liska 9 decembris 1697, Scientific Library of the PAAS [PAU] and the PAS [PAN] in Kraków, ms. 1060.

Sarnicki, Stanisław, *Statuta i Metrika przywileiów koronnych: językiem polskim spisane*, Kraków, 1594.

Stroynowski, Hieronim, *Nauka prawa przyrodzonego, politycznego, ekonomiki politycznej i prawa narodów*, Wilno, 1785.

Wybicki, Józef, *Listy patriotyczne* (1777–1778), ed. Kazimierz Opałek, Wrocław: Zakład Narodowy im. Ossolińskich, 1955.

Zawisza from Kroczów, Jakub, *Wskrócenie prawnego procesu koronnego* (1613), ed. Alojzy Winiarz, Kraków: Akademia Umiejętności, 1899.

Secondary Sources

Augustyniak, Urszula, 'Granice wolności obywatela Rzeczypospolitej w XVI–XVII w. Jednostka wobec władzy, prawa i społeczeństwa,' in *Wolność i jej granice. Polskie dylematy*, ed. Jacek Kloczkowski, 13–36, Kraków: Ośrodek Myśli Politycznej, 2007.

Augustyniak, Urszula, 'Polska i łacińska terminologia ustrojowa w publicystyce politycznej epoki Wazów,' in *Łacina jako język elit*, ed. Jerzy Axer, 33–71, Warsaw: Wydawnictwo DiG, 2004.

Backvis, Claude, *Szkice o kulturze staropolskiej*, Warsaw: Państwowy Instytut Wydawniczy, 1975.

Bardach, Juliusz, *Statuty litewskie a prawo rzymskie*, Warsaw: Ośrodek Badań nad Tradycją Antyczną w Polsce i w Europie Środkowo-Wschodniej, 1999.

Chanteur, Janine. 'La loi naturelle et la souveraineté chez Jean Bodin,' in *Théologie et droit dans la science politique de l'état moderne*. Actes de la table ronde de Rome (12–14 novembre 1987), 283–294, Rome: Ecole Française de Rome, 1991.

Ekes, Janusz, *Natura – wolność – władza. Studium z dziejów myśli politycznej Renesansu*, Warsaw: Instytut Wydawniczy PAX, 2001.

Estreicher, Stanisław, *Kultura prawnicza w Polsce XVI wieku*, Kraków, 1931.

Friedrich, Karin, 'Polish-Lithuanian Political Thought, 1450–1700,' in *History of European Political Thought, 1450–1700*, eds. Howell A. Lloyd, Glenn Burgess, and S. Hodson, 212–231, New Haven: Yale University Press, 2007.

Frost, Robert, '"Liberty without Licence?". The Failure of Polish Democratic Thought in the Seventeenth Century,' in *Polish Democratic Thought from the Renaissance to the Great Emigration: Essays and Documents*, eds. Mieczysław B. Biskupski and James S. Paula, 29–54, New York: Columbia University Press, 1990.

Gierke, Otto, *Natural Law and the Theory of Society 1500–1800*, Boston: Beacon Press, 1957.

Godek, Sławomir, *Elementy prawa rzymskiego w III Statucie litewskim (1588)*, Warsaw: Oficyna Naukowa, 2004.

Goldsmith, Mark M., 'Liberty, Virtue and the Rule of Law, 1689–1770,' in *Republicanism, Liberty and Commercial Society, 1649–1776*, ed. David Wootton, 197–232, Stanford: Stanford University Press, 1994.

Grodziski, Stanisław, *Z dziejów staropolskiej kultury prawnej*, Kraków: Universitas, 2004.

Grześkowiak-Krwawicz, Anna, *The Political Discourse of the Polish-Lithuanian Commonwealth. Concepts and Ideas*, transl. D. Sax, New York and London: Routledge, 2021.

Grzybowski, Konstanty, 'Systematyka prawa w Polsce odrodzenia, jej rola i podłoże klasowe,' in *Odrodzenie w Polsce*, vol. 2, 175–212, Warsaw: PIW, 1956.

Haitsma Mulier, Eco, 'The language of seventeenth-century republicanism in the United Provinces: Dutch or European?,' in *The Languages of Political Theory in Early-Modern Europe*, ed. Anthony Pagden, 179–195, Cambridge: Cambridge University Press, 1987.

Huber, Steffen, *Polifonia tradycji: filozofia polityczna i teoretyczna Andrzeja Frycza Modrzewskiego*, Warsaw: Wydawnictwo Naukowe Sub Lupa, 2014.

Kelley, Donald R., 'Law,' in *The Cambridge History of Political Thought 1450–1700*, ed. James H. Burns with the assistance of Mark Goldie, 66–94, Cambridge: Cambridge University Press, 1991.

Kochan, Anna, 'Prawo natury i prawo naturalne w dziełach autorów staropolskich,' in *Człowiek wobec natury. Humanizm wobec nauk przyrodniczych*, ed. by Jacek Sokolski, 35–54, Warsaw: Wydawnictwo Neriton, 2010.

Kossman, Ernst H., 'The Developement of Dutch Political Theory in the Seventeenth Century,' in *Britain and Netherlands. Papers delivered to the Oxford – Netherlands Historical Conference 1959*, ed. John S. Bromley and Ernst H. Kossmann, 91–110, London: Chatto & Vindus, 1960.

Květina, Jan, *Mýtus Republiky. Identita a politický diskurz raně novověké polské šlechty*, Hradec Králové: Pavel Mervart, 2019.

Lloyd, Howell A., 'Constitutionalism,' in *The Cambridge History of Political Thought 1450–1700*, ed. James H. Burns with the assistance of Mark Goldie, 254–297, Cambridge: Cambridge University Press, 1991.

Makiłła, Dariusz, 'Prawo natury w szesnastowiecznej koncepcji prawa polskiego,' in: *'Nam hoc natura aequum est...' Księga jubileuszowa ku czci profesora Janusza Justyńskiego w siedemdziesięciolecie urodzin*, ed. Andrzej Madeja, 121–129, Toruń: Towarzystwo Naukowe Organizacji i Kierownictwa 'Dom Organizatora,' 2012.

Meiksins Wood, Ellen, *Liberty and Property. A Social History of Western Political Thought from Renaissance to Enlightenment*, London: Verso, 2012.

Nenner, Howard, 'Liberty, Law, and Property: The Constitution in Retrospect from 1689,' in *Liberty secured? Britain before and after 1688*, ed. James R. Jones, 88–121, Stanford, CA: Stanford University Press, 1992.

Opałek, Kazimierz, *Prawo natury u polskich fizjokratów*, Warsaw: Książka i Wiedza, 1953.

Pennington, Kenneth, *The Prince and the Law, 1200–1600*, Berkeley: University of California Press, 1993.

Pietrzyk-Reeves, Dorota, *Polish Republican Discourse in the Sixteenth Century*, transl. Teresa Bałuk-Ulewiczowa, Cambridge: Cambridge University Press, 2020.

Pocock, John G.A., 'Virtues, Rights, and Manners. A Model for Historians of Political Thought,' *Political Theory* 9 (1981/3): 353–368.

Reid, John P., *Rule of Law. The Jurisprudence of Liberty in the Seventeenth and Eighteenth Centuries*, Dekalb: Northern Illinois University Press, 2004.

Skinner, Quentin, *The Foundations of Modern Political Thought*, Cambridge: Cambridge University Press, 1978.

Sucheni-Grabowska, Anna, 'Obowiązki i prawa królów polskich w opiniach pisarzy epoki odrodzenia,' in *Między monarchą a demokracją. Studia z dziejów Polski XV–XVIII wieku*, ed. Anna Sucheni-Grabowska and Małgorzata Żaryn, 54–115, Warsaw: Wydawnictwo Sejmowe, 1994.

Tierney, Brian, *The Idea of Natural Rights. Studies on Natural Rights, Natural Law and Church Law 1150–1625*, Grand Rapids, MI and Cambridge: William B. Eerdmans Publishing Co, 2001.

Tuck, Richard, *The Sleeping Sovereign. The Invention of Modern Democracy*, Cambridge: Cambridge University Press, 2016.

Van Gelderen, Martin, 'Aristotelians, Monarchomachs and Republicans: Sovereignty and *respublica mixta* in Dutch and German Political Thought, 1580–1650,' in *Republicanism: A Shared European* Heritage, ed. Martin van Gelderen and Quentin Skinner, vol. 1, 147–166, Cambridge: Cambridge University Press, 2002.

Vetulani, Adam, 'Opory wobec prawa rzymskiego w dawnej Polsce,' *Analecta Cracoviensia* 1 (1969): 372–386.

Wiesiołowski, Jacek, 'Kultura szlachecka,' in *Kultura Polski średniowiecznej XIV–XV w.*, ed. Bronisław Geremek, 32–50, Warsaw: Instytut Historii PAN, 1997.

Zakrzewski, Andrzej, *Wielkie Księstwo Litewskie* (XVI–XVIII *w.*). *Prawo – ustrój – społeczeństwo*, Warsaw: Campidoglio, 2013.

Zaller, Robert, *The Discourse of Legitimacy in Early Modern England* Stanford, CA: Stanford University Press, 2007.

Zwierzykowski, Michał, '"Sine iustitia in libertate żyć nie chcemy." Prawo i sprawiedliwość w dyskursie politycznym kampanii sejmowych lat 1696–1762,' in *Wartości polityczne Rzeczypospolitej Obojga Narodów. Struktury aksjologiczne i granice cywilizacyjne*, ed. Anna Grześkowiak-Krwawicz in collaboration with Jerzy Axer, 264–288, Warsaw: Wydawnictwo Uniwersytetu Warszawskiego, 2017.

CHAPTER 4

Ernst König and the Teaching of Natural Law at the Academic Gymnasia of Royal Prussia

Gábor Góngó

1 Introduction

The subject matter of this study is the institutionalisation of natural law as an academic discipline at the gymnasia of Royal Prussia. The academic gymnasia in Gdańsk, Toruń and Elbląg (Danzig, Thorn and Elbing, respectively, in German) were outstanding institutions in the regional intellectual landscape of this region of the Polish–Lithuanian Commonwealth between the sixteenth and eighteenth centuries.[1] Similarly to a number of universities in Germany,[2] natural law was a foundational science (*Grundlagenwissenschaft*) in the teaching of moral philosophy, politics and jurisprudence at the academic gymnasia of Royal Prussia as well. The present study provides a chronological and thematic outline of the creative adaptation and (pedagogically motivated) devel-

---

1 Stanisław Salmonowicz, 'Die protestantischen Akademischen Gymnasien in Thorn, Elbing und Danzig und ihre Bedeutung für die regionale Identität im Königlichen Preußen (16.–18. Jahrhundert),' *Nordost-Archiv* 6 (1997/2): 528; Klaus Garber, 'Gymnasien als Agenturen literarischer und kultureller Innovation in der Frühen Neuzeit,' in *Das Akademische Gymnasium zu Hamburg (gegr. 1613) im Kontext frühneuzeitlicher Wissenschafts- und Bildungesgeschichte*, ed. Johann Anselm Steiger, Martin Mulsow, and Axel E. Walter (Berlin and Boston: De Gruyter, 2017), 24–29; Lech Mokrzecki, 'Protestant Grammar Schools of Royal Prussia in the Polish School System in the 16th and 17th Centuries,' in *Kulturgeschichte Preußens königlich polnischen Anteils in der Frühen Neuzeit*, ed. Sabine Beckmann and Klaus Garber (Tübingen: Niemeyer, 2005), 359–369; Marian Pawlak, 'Die Geschichte des Elbinger Gymnasiums in den Jahren 1535–1772. Trans. Joanna Braksiek,' in *Kulturgeschichte Preußens königlich polnischen Anteils in der Frühen Neuzeit*, ed. Sabine Beckmann and Klaus Garber (Tübingen: Niemeyer, 2005), 371–394. On the intellectual impact of the gymnasia and their professors in the context of Royal Prussia, see Karin Friedrich, *The Other Prussia: Royal Prussia, Poland and Liberty, 1569–1772* (Cambridge: Cambridge University Press, 2000), chaps. 3–5.

2 Dominik Recknagel, 'Naturrecht in der Lehre. Naturrechtliche Vorlesungen an der Friedrichs-Universität zu Halle bis zum Jahr 1850,' in *"Vernunft, du weißt allein, was meine Pflichten sind!" Naturrechtslehre in Halle. Katalog zur Ausstellung im Interdisziplinären Zentrum für die Erforschung der Europäischen Aufklärung, Halle (Saale), 10. Oktober 2013 bis 6. Januar 2014*, ed. Dominik Recknagel and Sabine Wöller (Halle [Saale]: Mitteldeutscher Verlag, 2013), 9.

 | DOI:10.1163/9789004545847_005

opment of modern natural law in the academic triad. However, a significant difference between German universities and these academic institutions consisted in the lack of a particular department of natural law; instead, elements of natural law were conveyed as basic knowledge for the academic triad within the well-established study programme.[3]

This study extends the scope of research into academic natural law in Europe to the Polish–Lithuanian Commonwealth.[4] The secondary literature on these gymnasia is based on printed and manuscript sources of their history.[5] To extend the sources of investigation, I also made use of various texts related to teaching: school year programmes, course descriptions, exercitations and disputations, as well as schoolbooks and research monographs written by professors at these academic gymnasia. The course descriptions constitute the most important sources, as they provide an account of the general educational objectives of the academic year and situate the courses on natural law within the entire study programme.

The fact that Ernst König (1635–1698), rector at Toruń (1667–81) and Elbląg (1688–98), was engaged with modern natural law in general and with the works of Samuel Pufendorf in particular seems decisive for the whole academic triad. At Toruń, König and, later, Johann Arndt, endeavoured to reshape the teaching of moral philosophy and politics, while making an effort, perhaps in emulation of Gdańsk, to incorporate jurisprudence-based natural law into the curriculum. After Arndt's departure around 1720, natural law remained in the school programme for two decades without any original contribution by its teachers. During his rectorship at Elbląg, König achieved a partial adoption of modern science and philosophy, including modern natural law, to the teaching programme. However, after his demise, the gymnasium returned to the humanist curriculum.

König played a paramount role in consolidating the functioning of the gymnasia at Toruń and Elbląg during the relatively stable period after the Swedish

3 On the university-like departments at Gdańsk, see Mokrzecki, 'Protestant,' 364–365.

4 See Frank Grunert, Knud Haakonssen, and Diethelm Klippel, 'Natural Law 1625–1850: An International Research Network,' in *Aufklärung. Interdisziplinäres Jahrbuch zur Erforschung des 18. Jahrhunderts und seiner Wirkungsgeschichte*, ed. Martin Mulsow, Gideon Stiening, and Friedrich Vollhardt. Vol. 30 (Hamburg: Meiner, 2018), 267–276.

5 Stanisław Tync, *Dzieje gimnazjum toruńskiego* [*A history of the gymnasium in Toruń*], vols 1–2 (Toruń: Nakład Towarzystwa Naukowego, 1928–1949); Stanisław Salmonowicz, *Toruńskie gimnazjum akademickie w latach 1681–1817* [The academic gymnasium in Toruń, 1681–1817] (Poznań: Państwowe Wydawnictwo Naukowe, 1973); Marian Pawlak, *Dzieje gimnazjum elbląskiego w latach 1535–1772* [A history of the gymnasium in Elbląg, 1535–1772] (Olsztyn: Pojezierze, 1972); Edmund Kotarski, ed., *Gdańskie Gimnazjum Akademickie* [The academic gymnasium in Gdańsk], 5 vols (Gdańsk: Wydawnictwo Uniwersytetu Gdańskiego, 2008).

wars. The rector's organisational and administrative achievement, thanks to which these declining institutions managed to regain their former educational standard to some extent, received due attention in the secondary literature. König's courses, research activity, and pedagogic or scholarly publications in ethics and politics are, however, only descriptively and incompletely covered. Furthermore, the reconstruction and interpretation of the main characteristics of König's scholarly practice, i.e. the fact that he based his courses and exercitations in ethics, politics and jurisprudence on Pufendorf's works on natural law, especially on his *De Officio hominis et civis*, has remained so far rather outside the scope of historians of these gymnasia.[6] My study discusses both periods of König's career in a unified narrative, embedding König's reception of Pufendorf in the context of the rector's scientific and pedagogic efforts. The study broadens the scope of investigation to the reception of natural law at Toruń, following in König's footsteps until the mid-eighteenth century, and at Gdańsk, under König's former colleague, Samuel Schelwig, until ca. 1700.

The study has three main parts, dealing with each gymnasium separately. In the first part, I offer an overview of König's activity at Toruń, as well as the revival of natural law studies in the gymnasium from the 1710s to the 1740s. The subsequent section presents König's Elbląg years: a story of declining standards in the teaching of natural law. The beginnings of the teaching of natural law at Gdańsk are then delineated in the third part.

2 Toruń

Considerable differences existed between the gymnasia in terms of their financial resources, teacher qualifications and the way students were recruited.

6 Tync, *Dzieje*, II 177–231; Marian Pawlak, 'Nauczyciele Gimnazjum Elblaskiego w latach 1535–1772 [Teachers at the gymnasium in Elbląg, 1535–1772]. Parts I–II,' *Rocznik Elbląski* 5 (1972): 139–158, here 150; 6 (1973): 127–177, here 151–152; Marian Pawlak, 'Młodzież elbląska w Toruńskim Gimnazjum Akademickim w XVI–XVIII wieku [Youth from Elbląg at the academic gymnasium in Toruń in the sixteenth to eighteenth centuries],' in *Księga pamiątkowa 400-lecia toruńskiego gimnazjum akademickiego*, ed. Zbigniew Zdrójkowski. Vol. 1 (Toruń: s.d., 1972), 209; [Zenon Hubert Nowak and Janusz Tandecki,] 'Einleitung,' in *Metryka uczniów Toruńskiego Gimnazjum Akademickiego 1600–1807*. Part I: 1600–1717, ed. Zenon Hubert Nowak and Janusz Tandecki (Toruń: Towarzystwo Naukowe w Toruniu, 1997), xxi; Stanisław Salmonowicz, 'Nauczanie filozofii w Toruńskim Gimnazjum Akademickim [The teaching of philosophy at the academic gymnasium in Toruń],' in *Nauczanie filozofii w Polsce w XV–XVIII wieku*, ed. Lech Szczucki (Wrocław: Zakład Narodowy im. Ossolińskich, 1987), 184–185; Stanisław Salmonowicz, 'Das protestantische Gymnasium Academicum in Thorn im 17. und 18. Jahrhundert,' in *Kulturgeschichte Preußens königlich polnischen Anteils in der Frühen Neuzeit*, ed. Sabine Beckmann and Klaus Garber (Tübingen: Niemeyer, 2005), 403.

The budget of the gymnasium in Gdańsk was more generous than that of some small universities. It was also better embedded in the German higher education system than Toruń or Elbląg: some of its professors shared their career between Gdańsk and a German university, such as that of Frankfurt an der Oder. The university-like structure of the teaching there and the established studies of jurisprudence created more favourable conditions for the reception of natural law than those at Toruń or Elbląg. The maritime commerce contributed to a receptiveness to natural law and the law of nations at Gdańsk.

The gymnasia of Toruń and Gdańsk represent two different models for the reception of natural law, with political science and jurisprudence, respectively, at the centre. At Toruń, new content appeared within the old pedagogic framework, as no fundamental change had occurred in the curriculum and in the teaching methods between 1661 and 1774.[7] For its students – future members of the political classes in East-Central Europe – natural law served as a common theoretical foundation for the subsequent appropriation of national political and juridical systems. Accordingly, König opted for Pufendorf's *On the Duty of Man and Citizen According to Natural Law* as a manual for ethics and politics. During his career, König built up a coherent corpus of texts, the aim of which was to adapt Pufendorf to the needs of the teaching of politics in a gymnasium. At Toruń, a translation and numerous exercitations supported the teaching of Pufendorf's tenets. At Elbląg, König had to simplify his teaching material further, and his educational objective consisted in the cultivation of his (lower middle-class) students, rather than instructing future members of the national political classes.

At Gdańsk, however, natural law theories served a different function, as the students had career prospects in international commerce. In jurisprudence, Roman law remained central during the seventeenth and eighteenth centuries. At the turn of the eighteenth century, however, a shift occurred in the commentary literature of the *Institutes* and the *Pandects* from the ancient natural law to the modern. As a result, the reception of modern natural law theories became instrumental to supplementing ancient juridical knowledge with new tenets. This rather smooth transition in studies of law also facilitated the integration of modern natural law into practical philosophy.

At Toruń and Elbląg, the shift seems to have triggered more conflicts in so far as Aristotelian political science had to be replaced by, or, despite some evident incompatibilities, reconciled with modern natural law. Perhaps inspired by the example of the Athenaeum, König and later Arndt intended to incorporate

7 Nowak and Tandecki, 'Einleitung,' xxii.

jurisprudence, interpreted from the perspective of modern natural law, into the curriculum. This was a difficult and, as it turned out, impossible task in the long run, as natural law challenged the whole curriculum, which, consisting of humanist material from classical languages to rhetoric to moral and political philosophy, transmitted the ancient ethics of virtue.

The son of a Lutheran pastor and great-grandson of the Swiss theologian Urban Regius, Ernst König was born in 1635 in the Pomeranian village of Uchtenhagen (now Krzywnica, near the town of Stargard Pomorski). He studied at the University of Leipzig under Jakob Thomasius, completing his studies in 1660.[8] Thereafter, König returned to Pomerania, where he served as a vice-rector at the Pädagogium in Szczecin (Stettin in German) until it was closed by the Swedish administration in 1667.[9] That year, he had transferred to Toruń, where he was the rector until 1681. An elementary introduction to logic has survived from his Szczecin years, with the title *Idea praeceptorum logices*, printed in 1664.

The most important account of König's dismissal from Toruń in 1681 is his *Ad bonarum artium patronos virosque doctos Provocatio a decreto abdicationis Thorunensi* (1683). Tellingly enough, König invoked in this book the '*bonâ fide*' acting Hugo Grotius defending his political and religious position in front of the Dutch States-General with a polemical writing, which König knew in its Latin version as *Apologeticus eorum qui Hollandiae … ex legibus praefuerunt* (1622).[10] The dismissed rector's book contains the fourteen points

8 As to the intellectual impulses that König might have received from Jakob Thomasius, further research is needed. According to Jakob's son, Christian Thomasius, his father must have acquainted his students with Grotius and the commentary literature on him. Frank Grunert, 'Naturrecht *nach* Grotius – Vor allem mit Blick auf Thomasius,' in *"Vernunft, du weißt allein, was meine Pflichten sind!" Naturrechtslehre in Halle. Katalog zur Ausstellung im Interdisziplinären Zentrum für die Erforschung der Europäischen Aufklärung, Halle (Saale), 10. Oktober 2013 bis 6. Januar 2014*, ed. Dominik Recknagel and Sabine Wöller (Halle [Saale]: Mitteldeutscher Verlag, 2013), 23. With reference to Christian Thomasius, Vorrede an die Herren Zuhörer gerichtet, in *Drey Bücher der Göttlichen Rechtsgelahrheit* (Halle/Saale: Renger, 1709), 2. Between König and Christian Thomasius there is, however, a gap of one generation. It is an open question whether Jakob Thomasius was of the same opinion of Grotius during his career, teaching Grotius's works as early as the 1640s in the vein described by Christian Thomasius. Christian Thomasius's account refers to the state of the art in the philology on Grotius in the early 1670s.

9 Zbigniew Ogonowski, ed., *Filozofia i myśl społeczna XVII wieku* [Philosophy and social thought in the seventeenth century]. Part 1 (Warszawa: PWN, 1979), 371.

10 Ernst König, *Ad bonarum artium patronos virosque doctos Provocatio a decreto abdicationis Thorunensi* (Szczecin: Daniel Starck, 1683), A2v; Hugo Grotius, *Apologeticus eorum qui Hollandiae … ex legibus praefuerunt* (Paris: Buon, 1622). Cf. [Hugo Grotius] Hugo de

of accusation both in their official form as well as in König's self-justificatory reformulation. Besides mentioning minor controversial issues in teaching and management, the accusations of the town magistrate concentrate over abuses of pupils, not rarely sons of local office holders. Above all, they reproached König's draconian punishments in retaliation for breaches of the school rules: expulsion, confinement, and ferule. Another anomaly was the rector's practice of demanding payment for private courses. König did not deny these charges. What he straightforwardly rebuked was the allegation that he had persecuted those pupils who attended the gymnasium just to learn Polish.[11]

An elite school for the Protestant nobility and the patricians, the gymnasium in Toruń prepared its students for public service.[12] Completing the curriculum at a gymnasium was seen as an educational minimum for a political post or that of town magistrate.[13] As a teacher, König's intention with natural law was to hand over 'suitable and, for the community, useful tools' to the youth.[14] Moreover, the gymnasium served the same function for foreign students from East-Central European countries. König addressed his target audience in his preparatory lecture *Diatribe synoptica de eumathia* in 1678 as 'futuri Politici.'[15] Since politics was the profession which students were prepared for in the gymnasium, politics became the integrative science to which the other disciplines were subordinated under König's rectorship. A successful examination in politics completed the curriculum. Hence, König's pedagogic objective consisted in the qualification of his international, East-Central European audience for careers in politics and administration on the local or regional level by conveying political knowledge equally useful in any political

Groot, *Briefwisseling van Hugo Grotius. Deel 17*, ed. by H.J.M. Nellen en Cornelia M. Ridderikhoff (Den Haag: Martinus Nijhoff, 2001), 208 and H.J.M. Nellen, *Hugo Grotius: A Lifelong Struggle for Peace in Church and State, 1583–1645*. Transl. from the Dutch by J.C. Grayson (Leiden: Brill, 2015), ch. 8 and 9, esp. 340–353. See also Nowak and Tandecki, 'Einleitung,' xxi.

11 König, *Ad bonarum artium patronos*, B3r–B4r and F2r–F3r.

12 Salmonowicz, 'Protestantische,' 400; Stanisław Salmonowicz, 'Das Thorner protestantische Gymnasium Academicum 1658–1793,' *Beiträge zur Geschichte Westpreußens* 14 (1996): 47. On the manner in which students were recruited for the gymnasium in Toruń, see 46–47, 52.

13 Salmonowicz, 'Protestantischen,' 522.

14 '[T]üchtige und dem gemeinen Wesen nützliche Werkzeuge.' From the lost autobiography by Ernst König quoted by Fritz Skrey, *Aus der Geschichte des Elbinger Gymnasiums 1535–1935* (Elbing: Wernich, 1935), 28.

15 Ernst König, *Diatribe synoptica de eumathia* (Manuscript, Książnica miejska im. Kopernika in Toruń Bibl. gimn. R 4° 16) § 172.

or urban community in the region. In Pufendorf's *De Officio hominis et civis*, he believed he had found the appropriate instrument for this goal.

Before his shift from Aristotle to Pufendorf, König taught Scholastic political science. He undertook the task of teaching law, politics and rhetoric, lecturing on Aristotle's *Politics* and Justinian's Roman Law. Among his public courses from 1670, there is an introduction to philosophy (*praecognita*), analytic and synthetic logic, and politics (*scientiae civilis praecepta*) based on Jakob Thomasius's *Philosophia practica* from 1661.[16] In 1668, König taught politics from Jakob Thomasius's practical philosophy[17] and Aristotle's *Politics*. In private lectures, he read Justinian's *Institutes*.[18] In 1670, he announced the same courses as in the previous year.[19]

As to his pre-Pufendorfian publications, König summarized Jakob Thomasius's practical philosophy in the form of an ethics manual for the gymnasium in 1671.[20] A dissertation under his leadership from this period also adhered to political Aristotelianism. Heinrich Fibing's *Diatribe Politica de Majestate* from 1671 discussed majesty based on ancient sources and the Bible using Grotius's *De jure belli ac pacis*, Jakob Thomasius's ethical tables and Marcus Zuerius Boxhornius's *Institutionum politicarum libri duo* as signposts. Not surprisingly, in

---

16 *Catalogus Lectionum Publicarum in Gymnasio Thorunensi Anno Aerae Christianae* M.DC.LXVIII (Toruń: Coepselius, 1668); Tync, *Dzieje*, II 193–194. Stanisław Salmonowicz, 'Nauczanie prawa i polityki w Toruńskim Gimnazjum Akademickim od XVI do XVIII w. [Instruction in jurisprudence and politics at the academic gymnasium in Toruń from the sixteenth to the eighteenth centuries],' *Czasopismo Prawno-Historyczne* 23 (1971/2): 53–86, 66–67.

17 '[F]inita expositione Tabellarum Politicarum V. Cl. Jacobi Thomasii.' *Catalogus Lectionum Publicarum in Gymnasio Thorunensi Anno Aerae Christianae* M.DC.LXVIII (Toruń: Coepselius, 1668). Cf. *Catalogus Lectionum et Exercitati*[o]*num Publicarum, in Gymnasii Thorunensis* [...] *Anno Aerae Christ.* M.DC.LXX. *per semestre aestivum* (Toruń: Coepselius, 1670), 2.

18 Tync, *Dzieje*, 183, 193–194.

19 'Rector, absolutae propè Cursoriae *Institutionum* D. *Justiniani* praelectioni pleniorem earundem interpretationem subjunget, Jurisprudentiaeque adeò propaediâ praemissâ, Textus obscura enodabit, LL. Rationes ex Practicae Philosophiae principiis ostendet, jus antiquatum ab usitato sequestrabit, factique species subinde adferet; sic ut Progymnasmata simul Oldendorpiana Instituto huic accomodet.' *Catalogus Lectionum 1670*, 3. Hence, König's intention to expose the practical philosophical foundations of the law dates back to 1670. He also taught Roman law: 'Rector proponit Elementa Jurisprudntiae Romanae, ex Institutionibus Justinianeis.' *Catalogus Lectionum et Exercitati*[o]*num Publicarum, in Gymnasii Thorunensis* [...] *Anno Aerae Christ.* M.DC.LXX. *per semestre aestivum* (Toruń: Coepselius, 1670), 4.

20 Ernst König, *Summarium Doctrinae Ethicae, à V. CL. M. Jacobo Thomasio Lips. Acad. Prof. P. Continuis Tabellis adornatum. In Gymnasio Thorunensi, Publicè praelegit & disputavit – –* (Toruń: Coepselius, 1671).

the light of his sources, Fibing explicitly distanced himself from the direction represented by the 'novaturients' (*novaturientium*).[21]

König's *Summarium doctrinae ethicae* from 1671 is an arrangement of the schemes and tables in ethics in Jakob Thomasius's *Philosophia practica* into grammatically complete sentences that left the original order of the chapters untouched. According to his statement in the Preface to his 1682 *Fasciculus*, König completed a similar adaptation of the political part of Thomasius's *Philosophia practica*, which does not seem to have survived. As the *Summarium* served the purpose of disputations, it presented the material to the students in half-sheet (eight-page) units. In addition to the discursive presentation, König inserted the table of the eleven virtues into his book as well.[22] Because of this decision, he might have felt personally addressed by a passage from Pufendorf's *De jure naturae et gentium* a few years later – an encounter which seems to have transformed his approach to politics. Notwithstanding this change, his excerpt from Thomasius continued to form an integral part of his teaching activity at Toruń, even more so at Elbląg.[23]

König's courses on natural law theory from 1675 display synchrony with tendencies in academic life in the Eastern part of Germany.[24] Yet, König seems to have accomplished this intellectual shift solely based on his readings of Pufendorf and without any external impulse. His position as rector entitled him to put this personal decision into institutional practice. König taught natural law (from Pufendorf's *De Officio hominis et civis*, which he published in 1679 as a course book[25]) as a foundational science for jurisprudence and moral philosophy.

21 'Nihil dicitur, quin dictum sit prius. Neque nos ex novaturientium censu sumus, qui ex singulari cerebelli foecundidate inaudita proferunt.' Henricus Fibing, *Diatribe Politica de Majestate quam suprema majestate favente, in Gymnasio Thorunensi, praeside M. Ernesto König, subjicit* – – (Toruń: Coepseius, 1671), A2r.

22 König, *Summarium*, 34–35.

23 'In Ethicis igitur post tabulas Viri Cl. Jacobi Thomasii, quas publicis praelectioni [...] notis nos illustravimus, et nunc Auctor ipse cum annotationibus auctiores edidit.' König, *Diatribe*, § 167.

24 The department of natural law at the University of Greifswald was established in 1674. Recknagel, 'Naturrecht,' 16, with reference to Notker Hammerstein, 'Die Naturrechtslehre an den deutschen, insbesondere den preußischen Universitäten,' in *Reformabsolutismus und ständische Gesellschaft. Zweihundert Jahre Preußisches Allgemeines Landrecht*, ed. Günter Birtsch and Dietmar Willoweit (Berlin: Duncker und Humblot, 1998), 8.

25 Ernst König, *D. Samuelis Pufendorfii Liber de Officio Hominis, Noscendis Ethicae Principiis genuinis ac solidis, in Gymnasio Thorun. per semestre aestivum* M. DC. LXXIX. *publicè praelectus, atque ad disputandum propositus à* – – (Toruń: Coepselius, 1679).

Between 1672 and 1675, a game-changing encounter must have taken place with Pufendorf's *Jus naturae et gentium* that touched the nerve of König's professional habitus. As he wrote in the Preface to the 1682 edition retrospectively:

> I would not deny that I hesitated long ago whether the ethical writers who came into my hands were sufficiently memorable to be dealt with intensely [...]. Now, I almost wonder that many, as Mr Pufendorf asks at the beginning of his work on the law of nature and nations, 'who have hitherto professedly treated moral Philosophy, have fancied the main Part of their Business and of their Science discharg'd, by explaining only the eleven Words that stand for so many Virtues.' (Book I, chap. 4, § 5 [recte: 6])[26]

The exercitation of another author and respondent in one, Gabriel Nakielski, from 1675, *Dissertatio Politica de Legibus Civitatis in genere*, displays the shift towards Pufendorf but not towards Pufendorf's *De Officio*. Nakielski brought works of jurisconsults into dialogue with not only Grotius's *De jure belli ac pacis* and Pufendorf's *De jure naturae et gentium*, but also with Hobbes's *De Cive*.[27] The exercitation written by Nakielski, as well as the passages on the link between practical philosophy and jurisprudence in the *Diatribe*,[28] confirm that Pufendorf's tenets on natural law as discussed in *De jure naturae et gentium* had already been integrated into König's philosophical courses by the mid-1670s. The *Diatribe* also shows the ways in which natural law could be legitimated within the curricula of the gymnasium by connecting the discipline of politics to jurisprudence – a science that was closer to civic life and more important in terms of the students' career opportunities than Aristotelian ethics.

26 'Neque enim negaverim, & olim me haesitasse, num auctores Ethicorum, quae in manus meas venerant, satis memores fuissent illius triti; [...], & nunc quoque propemodum mirari, quod plerique qui Philosophiam moralem se tradituros professi sunt, magnum, quod D. Pufendorfius, in principio operis de Jure naturae & gentium queritur, disciplinae suae partem, explicatis undecim virtutum vocabulis se repraesentasse crediderint. Lib. I. c. IV. n. 5 [recte: 6].' Cf. Samuel Pufendorf, *De jure naturae et gentium. Erster Teil: Text (Liber primus – Liber quartus)*, ed. Frank Böhling (Berlin: Akademie-Verlag, 1998), I 51. The English translation was taken from Samuel Pufendorf, *Of the Law of Nature and Nations. Eight Books*, trans. by Basil Kennett (London: J. Walthoe etc., 1729), 38–39.

27 Gabriel Nakielski, *Dissertatio Politica, de Legibus Civitatis in Genere. Quam in Gymnasio Thoruniensi, ... Praeside M. Ernesto König,* [...] *subjicit – –,* [...] *Autor & Respondens* (Toruń: Coepselius, 1675).

28 'Philosophiae activae filia esse Jurisprudentia.' § 174.

If we wish to reconstruct the shifts in König's pedagogic objectives as regards Pufendorf, the prefaces he wrote to both of his published books immediately after his dismissal from Toruń are of paramount importance: the second edition of *De officio hominis et civis* and his *Fasciculus exercitationum ethicarum et politicarum*, both printed in Gdańsk in 1682. König recollected the moment of a circumspect transition from old to new politics in the Preface to his 1682 edition of *De Officio* in these terms:

> I have neither acted nor sympathised with those for whom, while dealing with science and arts, the newest was the most beautiful too. Not that I would attribute absolute value to any ancient doctrine, a value that should be devalued while being exchanged. Still, I am worried about changes which might be dangerous even if they are changes for the better. That we should be less afraid of barbarism as long as Cicero remains in the schools, according to the judgement of Johann Sturm, the second greatest teacher in Germany after Philipp Melanchthon. Hence, the Scholastic sciences are, without any doubt, studied in the best way by those who praise Aristotle most of all the doctors of philosophy and recommend him to students of science. [...] In the meantime, however, it was not only allowed to schoolmasters, but also it became their duty to give milk, rather than solid food, to their weaker and, in philosophy, so to speak, two-pence pupils. The greatest of the philosophers did not write for them, and, as a matter of fact, lecturing on his works is not for them. For the sake of their understanding, as if to lead them by hand, it seems appropriate that the works of the moderns be highly valued by the professors as well as by their audience. When I faced the task of having to dictate the whole synopsis of ethical science to my students, I overcame my (if I am honest) mixed feelings concerning the plan, to present the ethical tables of the famous Jakob Thomasius, which were re-printed at this place, to the youth publicly, and to publicize them in more than twenty public disputations. Recently, the present book of a famous writer on the duties of men and citizens has undergone a number of disputations, a book in which, if I am not mistaken, the solid and original principles of ethics, as well as politics, are discussed.[29]

29 'Nunquam cum illis feci sensique, quibus, in disciplinis & artibus tradendis, recentissimum quodque pulcherrimum. Non quia antiqua quaelibet omnibus adeò numeris absoluta existimem, ut quae convertuntur, continuò in deterius mutentur; sed quod verear, ne mutatio ipsa, quamtumvis facta in melius, heîc quoque sit periculosa. Ut,

It was the methodological function Pufendorf's *De Officio* could and should perform in teaching that mattered for König. Both the exposition and (to some extent) the interpretation of Pufendorf's tenets were shaped by its function.

The 1679 edition of Pufendorf's *De Officio* is the most spectacular and, due to its new edition in 1682, the most widely known testimony to König's work with Pufendorf. This 1679 edition is the third earliest after the *editio princeps* in Lund and the second one in Erfurt in 1678.[30] König's subsequent readings of Pufendorf's *De officio hominis et civis* span twenty-three years: the edition, the Introduction, together with a summary for didactic purposes, and the treatise *Disquisitio ethica, super justitia particulari* from 1698. It seems evident that *De Officio* stood at the centre of his work as a teacher and a researcher after 1679, though with changing functions during the last two decades of König's career.

De Officio, sliced into units of nearly equal length for disputations, was printed for his special course on Pufendorf in 1679.[31] This was the original function of the text. The names of the disputants had been printed in the margins of the text; moreover, the typesetting was arranged such that every unit to be disputed continued from the beginning of a new sheet to the end. This was the only typesetting of König's edition of Pufendorf's *De Officio*: the 1682 Gdańsk edition contains the names of the disputants from 1679, not unlike the copy

quamdiu in scholis manet Cicero, minus est extimescenda barbaries, judicio magni illius post Philippum Melanchthonum Germaniae Praeceptoris, Joh. Sturmii; sic optimè procul dubio rei Scholasticae consulunt, qui Philosophiae inter Doctores Aristotelem ante omnes & magnificiunt, & commendant sapientiae studiosis. [...] At verò Scholarum interim licet Magistris, imo incumbit, lac potiùs quàm solidum cibum praebere alumnis infirmioribus, atque in Philosophiâ, ut sic dicerem, dupondiis. Quibus nec scripsit summus Philosophus, nec voluminum illius congruit praelectio. Ad horum intelligentiam, prout manu quasi ducunt recentiorum opere, simul magistris, simul auditoribus in pretio esse par est. Mihi, cum integrum esset in calamum dictare doctrinae Ethicae synopsin, praevaluit, istius instituti (fatebor verum) fastidio, Tabellas Ethicas & Politicas Viri Cl. Jacobi Thomasii hîc loci recusas publicè juventuti ut proponerem, ac disputationibus insuper viginti & amplius ventilarem. Quibus novissimè subjeci praesentem Celeberrimi Scriptoris libellum, de officio hominis & Civis, principia hinc Ethica, hinc Politica solida & genuina ni fallor, exhibentem[.]' Ernst König, 'Lectori S.' in *V. Cl. Samuelis Pufendorfii, De officio hominis et civis Libri duo. Commodo juventutis studiosae In Gymnasio Thorunensi, recudendos curavit, Ordinariis Lectionibus proposuit, itemque Solemni Studiosorum ac Eruditorum Virorum examini subjecit* – – (Gdańsk: Rhete, 1682), [unnumbered pages 1–3].

30 It is missing from the catalogue of the editions of Pufendorf's *De Officio*. Horst Denzer, *Moralphilosophie und Naturrecht bei Samuel Pufendorf: eine geistes- und wissenschaftsgeschichtliche Untersuchung zur Geburt des Naturrechts aus der praktischen Philosophie* (Goldbach: Keip, 1996), 362.

31 Ogonowski, *Filozofia*, 371; Tync, *Dzieje*, II 206–207.

used at Elbląg. König wrote about the genesis, function and functional typesetting of his edition in the Preface to his *Fasciculus* in these terms:

> Hence, besides other arguments discussed by respondents not without erudition [= exercitations by Fibing and Nakielski], I adapted some minor works of famous men [= Pufendorf's *De Officio*] for the purpose of useful exercises after I had presented them to the audience in public lectures [= lecture on Pufendorf's *De Officio*]. Moreover, I had them printed with the gymnasium type partly at my own expense, so the lack of copies should not be a hindrance to the advancement of my students [= *De Officio*, ed. 1679]. Because their modest distribution hardly surpassed one single sheet and I had been asked to develop some of them in more detail [= the eight exercitations 1677–1680], I found a task that was useful to me, in so far as after the excerpt of Aristotle's *Politics* I had accomplished, I discuss both parts of practical philosophy so that the studying youth should easily understand the true and solid foundations of Catholic Jurisprudence, together with that of a true and unaffected morality; or, at least, they should not approach with, as it is said, unwashed hands the lecture of works that Hugo Grotius, a man with an immortal memory, left to us on the law of nature and the nations. This is how these eight exercitations were born to me, with my wish that I would have the number of respondents who would lead my efforts, of whatever quality they are, to full success within the two years during which I had been dealing with politics, first and foremost.[32]

32 'Igitur inter alia, quae Respondentes ipsi non ineruditè pertractaverant, argumenta, Clarissimorum Virorum Opuscula quaedam utilissimo Exercitio accommodavi, postquam publicis ea praelectionibus Auditoribus exposueram, acne exemplarium inopia profectibus illorum antercederet, in Typographeo Gymnasii curaveram meis quoque sumptibus recudenda. Cum verò pro minutis istis partitionibus, quae dimidium pars quaternionem haud excederent, Themata aliquantò copiosius tractata nonnulla à me expeterent, operae me pretius facturum arbitrabar, si post epitomen Politicae Aristotelis, quam adornaveram, utramque Philosophiae Activae partem sic traderem, ut Jurisprudentiae Catholicae, ac verae adeò, non simulatae morum Philosophiae, principia genuina solidaquae studiosa juventus haud difficulter perciperet, aut saltem ad lectionem operis incomparabilis, quod de Jure Naturae ac Gentium reliquit immortalis memoriae Vir, Hugo Grotius, illotis, quod ajunt, manibus haud accederet. Inde mihi natae hae Exercitationes octo, non sine voto, ut ea mihi foret Respondentium copia, quae intra biennium ad summum qualescunque conatus meos ad exitum usque perduceret, cum praesertim Politicen haberem confectam. Ernst König, 'Lectori S.,' in *Fasciculus Exercitationum ethicarum et politicarum, Quas sub ejusdem praesidio, Solemni ventilationi subjecerunt Studiosi quidam Juvenes. Accesserunt nonnulla alia* (Gdańsk: Typis Rhetianis, 1682), [unnumbered pages 1–2].

As this account shows, the years between 1677 and 1680 saw König most consistently engaged with Pufendorf and his new political science. After he began dealing with Pufendorfian natural law theory, König wrote (or presided over) eight exercitations in total.[33] They were published in 1682 in Gdańsk in a thematically cohesive volume as a testimony to the scholarly teacher's work at Toruń under the title *Fasciculus exercitationum ethicarum*.[34] The eight new exercitations,[35] built on a more or less cohesive basis of sources, reflect the growing knowledge that König had accumulated during his intense orientation in the scholarly field of politics. As König's retrospective account emphasised, he himself was the author of these exercitations and not the students. This fact was put on the title page of these exercitations as well. In the case of an exercitation from 1677, the student, Jakob Merschier, as the title page confirms, 'had taken the role of the respondent on himself' (*partes sustin*[*uit*]. *respondentis*).

In these exercitations, König was drawing on Grotius's *De jure belli ac pacis*; Pufendorf's *Elementa jurisprudentiae universalis*, *De jure naturae et gentium* and *De officio hominis et civis*; and Hobbes's *De Cive*. For commentary literature, he made use of the standard works of the orthodox Lutheran interpretation of

33 Ernst König, *De Principiis Jurisprudentiae ethicis, Exercitatio Philosophica. Praeside – –, partes sustin. respondentis d. Decembr. A. M. DC. LXXVII.* [...] *Jacobus Merschier, Elbingensis* (Toruń: Coepselius, 1677); Ernst König, *De Natura & Constitutione Philosophiae Practicae. Resp. Simon Antonii, Topscha Hung. d. 27. Jan* (Toruń: Coepselius, 1678); Ernst König, *Exercitatio Ethica, De Eo, Qvod Justum Est. Praeside – –* [...] *subjicit* [...] *Johannes Gebhardus, Olsna-Siles. Respondens* (Toruń: Coepselius, 1678); Ernst König, *Exercitatio ethica, de bono hominis supremo, ejusque instrumentis. Praeside – –* [...] *subjicit* [...] *Michael Agnethler, Cibin. Trans. Respondens* (Toruń: Coepselius, 1678); Ernst König, *Exercitatio Politica, De Origine Civitatis, ac Rebus Huic Necessariis, Nominatim, Territorio & Publicis Reditibus. Praeside – –* [...] *subjicit* [...] *Boguslaus ab Unruh Eqves Polon. Respondens* (Toruń: Coepselius, 1679); Ernst König, *Exercitatio politica, De cive, et diversis hominum in civitate ordinibus, praeside – –* [...] *subjicit* [...] *Christianus Wernigke, Elbingens. respondens* (Toruń: Coepselius, 1680); Ernst König, *Exercitatio Politica, De Summis In Civitate Potestatibus, Harumq*[*ue*] *Praecipuis Administris / Praeside – –* [...] *Subjicit* [...] *Petrus Genschius, Ortr. Misnic. Respondens* (Toruń: Typ. Gymnasii, 1680); Ernst König, *De Collegiis & Urbibus. Ob defectum Respondentis non fuit ventilata*, this latter surviving as text no. VIII of Ernst König, *Fasciculus Exercitationum ethicarum et politicarum, Quas sub ejusdem praesidio, Solemni ventilationi subjecerunt Studiosi quidam Juvenes. Accesserunt nonnulla alia* (Gdańsk: Typis Rhetianis, 1682).

34 König, *Fasciculus*.

35 For disputations in gymnasia, see Manfred Komorowski, 'Das akademishe Schrifttum Altpreußens: Königsberg, Danzig, Elbing und Thorn,' in *Kulturgeschichte Preußens königlich polnischen Anteils in der Frühen Neuzeit*, ed. Sabine Beckmann and Klaus Garber (Tübingen: Niemeyer, 2005), 426.

natural law – David Mevius's *Prodromus jurisprudentiae gentium communis*, Johann Heinrich Boecler's commentary on *De jure belli ac pacis* and the works of Hermann Conring, Johann Heinrich Alsted, Veit Ludwig von Seckendorff, Caspar Ziegler, Johannes Felden and (the Remonstrant) Guilielmus Grotius.

König's publications bear the imprint of his teaching activity. At the academic gymnasia of Royal Prussia, the outcome of original research was published, as a rule, at the local printing press.[36] These publications were subservient to the teaching, or at least justified their existence with reference to their adaptability to pedagogic goals. This functionality determined their design. Typically, they had a simplified style, their subject matter was developed in the form of questions and responses for mnemonic reasons, and the texts were meant to be used for disputations. In contradistinction to universities, publications by gymnasium professors were destined for the institutional and regional public and rarely became part of the cultural transfer of the early modern republic of letters.[37] Re-issues of the works of some Gdańsk professors by renowned German publishers brought a shift in this trend. As a rule, with significant exceptions, exercitations were authored by the professor rather than the student. Disputations and defences of these theses took place (especially at Toruń and Elbląg) on a lower linguistic and scholarly level than at universities.

It seems useful to consider two points for a due evaluation of the life's work of a gymnasium professor such as König. First, his texts are not autonomous scientific works, even by early modern standards. Every text of his was expected to find its proper place in the process of teaching. Because of the expenses involved, this rule had to be respected in the case of printed materials even more strictly than in that of manuscripts. Secondly, König's administrative efforts as a gymnasium rector, on the one hand, and his scientific efforts as a professor of philosophy, on the other, seem to have failed to form a harmonious unity. The account in the secondary literature of König's rectorship in both places as the heyday of Baroque culture and science in Royal Prussia[38] is not entirely compatible with König's own experience of the constantly diminishing standard of teaching in general. Hence, the chronology of König's texts (treatises, compendia, editions and exercitations which had not only been defended with him presiding, but the overwhelming majority of which had also been written by him) are no less than his successive answers

36 Garber, 'Gymnasien,' 28–29.
37 Garber, 'Gymnasien,' 30–31.
38 Salmonowicz, 'Nauczanie prawa i polityki,' 67.

to continual challenges. By preferring Pufendorf to Aristotle, he chose a more reader-friendly author for a textbook and material for disputations. As we will see, even his printed texts (which cost him and were not used in their entirety for teaching) underwent functional changes over time.

3 Natural Law at Toruń after König

In 1681, König had to leave Toruń. The attitude of his successors seems to have contributed considerably to the discontinuities in the teaching of natural law. The new rectors, the orthodox Lutheran Paul Hoffmann and Georg Wende, fervently opposed any innovation in science and teaching. However, sporadic data show that two professors, Paul Pater[39] (1656–1724) and Johannes Sartorius (1656–1729), continued to deal with the natural sciences and natural law.[40] External causes also aggravated the crisis. The turn of the eighteenth century brought hard times for the town of Toruń and the gymnasium with it. The town was forced to endure the Swedish siege in 1703; between 1708 and 1710, it was afflicted by the plague.[41] As the gymnasium re-opened from 1710 onwards, skirmishes with the Catholics disrupted teaching. An escalating 'tumult' between students at the gymnasium and those at the Jesuit College in 1724 caused considerable damage, as a court in Warsaw punished the gymnasium, among other measures, by depriving it of some of its buildings.

During Peter Jänichen's rectorship, a newly engaged professor of philosophy, Johann Arndt,[42] authored a series of six exercitations on Pufendorf and

39 Paul Pater was at Toruń between 1689 and 1705, and then he was a professor of mathematics at Gdańsk; there, he was a participant in a dissertation presided over by Samuel Friedrich Willenberg and with Johann Wilhelm Hagdorn as respondent with the title *Disputatio Juris Gentium De Arbitris Et Mediatoribus Belligerantium*.

40 Cf. Johannes Sartorius, *De poena ob alienum delictum inflicta, Sub Praesidio – –,* [...] *publice disseret Johannes Czimmermann,* [...] (Thorunii: e Chalcographeo Gymnasii, [1699]); Salmonowicz, 'Protestantische,' 403.

41 Salmonowicz, 'Protestantische,' 401.

42 Arndt's biographical data are unknown. His inauguration: *Numine divino aspirante atque Magnifici et Amplissimi Senatus Thorunensis auctoritate ad solennem inaugurationis actum, in quo viro clarissimo atque doctissimo, Domino M. Ioanni Arndio, Gedanensi, professoris publici munus in Gymnasio Thorunensi D. XXIII. April. A. MDCCXVI more et ritu solito hora IX. conferetur, atque ad audiendas benevole orationes musarum patrones fautores literarumque aestimatores ea, qua decet reverentia, cultu et humanitate invitant, studiosam vero iuventutem peramanter convocant Gymnasii Rector et Professores* (Toruń: Johann Nicolai, 1716).

held courses based on them. Georg Peter Schultz and Johann Friedrich Bachstrom also had a share in the courses on natural law, but published no work related to this discipline.[43] Until the mid-1730s, Schultz was mainly responsible for courses on natural law. In 1716, Arndt took them over for a few years. Arndt must have arrived at Toruń from Gdańsk as an expert in natural law theory. Before his Toruń period, he published a book on Grotius in Rostock in 1712.[44]

Arndt also taught natural jurisprudence as useful knowledge for students of theology and philosophy, future citizens of a state in which they ought to live so that they must not harm or be harmed by anybody out of ignorance.[45] In addition, he offered courses on theoretical and practical philosophy. For the changing times at Toruń, it is telling that Arndt felt obliged to defend natural jurisprudence against the accusation of being useless ('*sine usu*')[46] and that his aim consisted in contributing to a more conscious passive citizenship, instead of preparing his pupils, like König did, for active political participation.

Written at Toruń, his *Collegium Pufendorfianum* is a six-piece series of disputations[47] and, as such, an emulation of König's *Fasciculus*. Of Disputation VI, the respondent's copy also survived with handwritten information about

---

43 Bachstrom was a respondent to a dissertation by Carl Friedrich Buddeus in Jena, which dealt with the duties of man on the basis of natural law: Carl Friedrich Buddeus, *Dissertatio I. De Officio Hominis Circa Eruditionem Acquirendam Quam* [...] *submittunt praeses – –* [...] *et respondens Io. Fridericus Bachstrom* (Jena: Müller, 1713).

44 Johann Arndt, *Specimen de Hugone Grotio a Commentatoribus Juris Belli & Pacis Aliisque Immerito vapulante* (Rostock: Nicolaus Schwieger, 1712); further publications of his with relevance to natural law: Johann Arndt, *Licitam esse medii loci occupationem ex necessitate factam, consensu facultatis philosophicae, praeses – –, Dantiscanus, & respondens Paulus Matthias Wunsch, Meva-Prussus* [...] *juxta Juris Nat. principia defendent* (Rostock: Schwiegerau, 1712); Johann Arndt, *Orationes binae, quarum altera inchoavit, finiit altera, Universale Philosophiae cursum, privatos inter cancellos institutum* (Gdańsk: s.d., 1715).

45 '& Theologiae & Philosophiae studiosi, cuiuscunque civitatis membra aliquando sint futuri, eam ex istis lectionibus utilitatem capiant, ne vel ipsi in vita communi, alios inscii laedant, neve ab aliis incauti laedantur.' Johann Arndt, *Collegii Pufendorfiani Exercitationem I. generalem de opere Pufendorfiano Juris Nat. et Gent. praeside – –* [...] *defendet Joannes Kownacki* (Toruń: Johann Nicolai, 1717), 3–4.

46 *Catalogus lectionum et operarum cum Deo in Gymnasio Thorunensi pertractandarum auctoritate nobiliss. et ampliss. scholarcharum ipso tempore Paschali publicatus anno 1716* (Toruń: Johann Nicolai, 1716), 7.

47 Arndt, *Collegii Pufendorfiani Exercitatio I.*; Johann Arndt, *Collegii Pufendorfiani exercitationem II. de geometrica juris naturalis demonstratione praeside – –* [...] *defendet Io. Gottlob Stoeckel* (Toruń: Johann Nicolai, 1717); Johann Arndt, *Collegii Pufendorfiani Exercitationem III. de actione morali una et de emendandis addendisque in toto Lib. I. Pufend. De J. N. & G. praeside – –* [...] *defendet Casparus Geelhaar* (Toruń: Johann Nicolai, 1717); Johann Arndt, *Collegii Pufendorfiani exercitationis IV. de existentia juris naturalis continu-*

the complete procedure for the defence. The introductory talk by the respondent shows that natural law in Arndt's courses was rather modestly conceived as a general tool of erudition: 'someone who wants to liberate himself from the rudeness of nature,' so the respondent, 'must refine his mind with natural law.'[48] The text was proposed by the presiding Arndt and not written by the student, whose Latin must have been insufficient for this task.[49]

Despite their interest in modern science, philosophy or natural law theory, professors at Toruń, with a few exceptions, did not publish original works in these fields, not even disputations.[50] Georg Peter Schultz (1680–1748) studied at Frankfurt an der Oder from 1696, and in Leipzig from 1698 to 1700, returning to Frankfurt an der Oder in 1700. Although he decided on medicine, he acquired a solid knowledge of natural law as well.[51] Schultz's inauguration speech (*De oblivione moris antiqui*, 1712) shows his sympathies with the science of the ancients. He used the works of his teacher and a colleague of his father's ('*Praeceptoris sui & Collegae olim B. Parentis*'), Heinrich von Cocceji – probably the series of dissertations on the law of nature and nations – as his teaching material.[52] Schultz also held the post of pro-rector of the gymnasium from 1711 to 1742.

---

ationem, praeside – – [...] *defendet Samuel Leonar: Zillich* (Toruń: Johann Nicolai, 1717); Johann Arndt, *Collegii Pufendorfiani Exercitationem v. de definitionibus juris naturalis praeside* – – [...] *defendet Mart. Dan. Serini* (Toruń: Johann Nicolai, 1718); Johann Arndt, *Collegii Pufendorfiani exercitationem vi. De proprietatibus juris naturalis, videlicet autore, promulgatione, forma, materia, subjecto, objecto et fine, praeside* – – [...] *defendet Christianus Martini* (Toruń: Johann Nicolai, 1718).

48 '[Q]uis ab hac Naturae ruditate liberari velit, animam suam per Jus N: excolat oportet.' Arndt, Johann, *Collegii Pufendorfiani exercitatio vi.* (Biblioteka Kórnicka, Sygn. 15720, handwritten note by the student.)

49 'Bene ergo facit Praes. Excell: quod hoc J: N: investigandam per hodiernam disputationem proposuerit.' Arndt, Johann, *Collegii Pufendorfiani exercitatio vi.* (Biblioteka Kórnicka, Sygn. 15720, handwritten note by the student.)

50 On the gymnasium in Toruń as the leading institution in Poland between 1713 and 1723 in terms of the propagation of the tenets of modern philosophy and science under Bachstrom, Schultz and Arndt, see Salmonowicz, *Dzieje*, 147.

51 'Außer dem Rechte der Natur und der deutschen Geschichte befliß er sich der Arzneykunst unter der Anführung der Doctorum und Professorum Vehrii und Johrenii. Hernach hörete er in Halle D. Hoffmannen und D. Stahlen, wie auch den Herrn Cellarius und Buddeus.' 'Georg Peter Schultz,' in *Preußische Lieferung alter und neuer Urkunden, Erörterungen und Abhandlungen, zur Erläuterung der Preußischen Geschichte für allerley Leser*, 1 (1753–55/3): 365–371, here 366.

52 *Catalogus lectionum et operarum cum Deo in Gymnasio Thorunensi pertractandarum auctoritate nobiliss. et ampliss. scholarcharum ipso tempore Paschali publicatus anno 1714* (Toruń: Johann Nicolai, 1714), [2].

Jänichen seems to have supported the re-introduction of natural law into the curriculum after the chaotic years, but Schultz did relatively little in this matter during the three decades of his employment at Toruń. In 1714, he read natural law as part of the practical philosophy (‘*praestantissima Philosophiae Practicae Pars*, Jus Naturae & Gentium’).[53] In 1716, when Arndt took over the teaching of natural law, Schultz switched to a course on the human body.[54] In 1718, Schultz taught his course on natural law as well as on Polish law, while Arndt taught jurisprudence in the highest year.[55] According to the *Catalogus Lectionum* for the year 1719, rector Jänichen chose Pufendorf's history of European politics as a model for his private lectures.[56] Arndt dealt with *Jus civilis* (with natural law as its foundation) with a view to the situation in Prussia in the highest year. He continued the *Collegium Pufendorfianum* with two new exercitations (of which the seventh is unknown or remained unwritten).[57]

1719 was Arndt's last academic year at Toruń. In 1720, the rector kept lecturing on Pufendorf's introduction to European history, while Schultz read the works of Johann Franz Budde in the highest year: his (Budde's) practical philosophy, together with his natural law.[58] In 1721, Schultz took back the courses on natural law.[59] Reinhold Friedrich Bornmann taught mathematics from manu-

---

53 *Catalogus lectionum et operarum cum Deo in Gymnasio Thorunensi pertractandarum auctoritate nobiliss. et ampliss. scholarcharum ipso tempore Paschali publicatus anno 1714* (Toruń: Johann Nicolai, 1714), 4.

54 ‘Porro loco *Juris Naturae & Gentium*, quod hactenus proposuit, *Noticiam & Cognitionem humani corporis Physicam & Medicam* ipsis inculcabit.’ *Catalogus lectionum et operarum cum Deo in Gymnasio Thorunensi pertractandarum auctoritate nobiliss. et ampliss. scholarcharum ipso tempore Paschali publicatus anno 1716* (Toruń: Johann Nicolai, 1716), 4.

55 *Catalogus lectionum et operarum bono cum Deo in Gymnasio Thorunensi pertractandarum auctoritate nobiliss. et ampliss. scholarcharum circa tempus Paschale publicatur anno 1718* (Toruń: Johann Nicolai, 1718), 4–5, 7.

56 *Catalogus Lectionum et operarum bono cum Deo in Gymnasio Thorunensi pertractandarum auctoritate nobiliss. et ampliss. scholarcharum anno 1719 autumnali tempore publicatus* (Toruń: Johann Nicolai, 1719), 3.

57 ‘Exercitationes Collegii Pufend. jam editas auxit duabus aliis, nempe Vita: de Proprietatibus Iuris Nat. & VIIma: de Origine Iuris Nat. in mente humana.’ *Catalogus Lectionum et operarum bono cum Deo in Gymnasio Thorunensi pertractandarum auctoritate nobiliss. et ampliss. scholarcharum anno 1719 autumnali tempore publicatus* (Toruń: Johann Nicolai, 1719), 3–5.

58 *Catalogus Lectionum et operarum bono cum Deo in Gymnasio Thorunensi pertractandarum auctoritate nobiliss. et ampliss. scholarcharum publicatus anno 1720* (Toruń: Johann Nicolai, 1720), 2–3.

59 ‘[S]eparatim vero Supremanos *Jus Naturae & Gent.* docuit [...]. His partim finitis, partim propediem, volente Deo, finiendis lectionibus, *Jus* quidem *Nat. & Gent.* continuabit. [...] Et haec quidem publice.’ *Catalogus Lectionum et operarum cum Deo in Gymnasio Thorunensi pertractandarum auctoritate nobiliss. et ampliss. scholarcharum ipso tempore autumnali publicatus anno 1721* (Toruń: Johann Nicolai, 1721), 2–3.

als written by Christian Wolff. In 1722, Schultz addressed himself to Pufendorf's *On The Duty of Man and Citizen* with a lecture, as well as disputations in the highest year. The teaching of arithmetic from Wolff's books was taken over by Samuel Theodor Schönwald.[60] Schultz continued to teach Budde's *Jus naturae et gentium*, publicly as well as privately, even in 1732.[61] In 1736, he dedicated half of a course to natural law.[62]

As his course descriptions show, Arndt intended to implement a clearly formulated pedagogic objective with his courses on natural law. After his departure, Georg Peter Schultz seems to have kept natural law in the curriculum out of duty, teaching Pufendorf and Budde. After Arndt, there is no sign of any link between jurisprudence and ethics or politics at Toruń, nor any trace of efforts to keep up with the growing literature on natural law. Roman law was no longer taught after Arndt's departure. The teaching of political science and practical philosophy was cut back, with Schultz's courses on natural law as all that was on offer. Classical languages and authors returned, together with the strengthened presence of theology and church history.

Further data can be retrieved from the library of the gymnasium to reconstruct the teaching of natural law at Toruń in the mid-eighteenth century. Exemplars of the works of Christian Wolff and Johann Gottlieb Heineccius can be found in the library there with reader annotations.[63] Another disputation by the pro-rector Gottfried Centner (1712–1774) has survived from 1745 under the title *Comparatio Motivorum quibus Homo Christianus ad servandam Legem Naturalem obligatur*.[64] Centner taught psychology and natural theology following a Wolffian philosopher, Ludwig Philipp Thümmig.

60 *Catalogus Lectionum et operarum cum Deo in Gymnasio Thorunensi pertractandarum auctoritate nobiliss. et ampliss. scholarcharum ipso tempore autumnali publicatus anno 1722* (Toruń: Johann Nicolai, 1722) 4, 6.

61 *Catalogus Lectionum et operarum propitio Deo in Gymnasio Thorunensi pertractandarum auctoritate nobiliss. et ampliss. scholarcharum publicatus anno 1732* (Toruń: Johann Nicolai, 1732), 4.

62 *Typus Lectionum et operarum publicarum et privatarum adiuvante Deo in Gymnasio Thorunensi pertractandarum auctoritate nobiliss. et ampliss. scholarcharum publicatus anno 1736* (Toruń: Johann Nicolai, 1736), 3.

63 On the dominance of Christian Wolff in the natural law instruction after 1750 in Toruń, see Salmonowicz, *Dzieje*, 397.

64 Cf. Joanna Kodzik, 'Aus der Mentalitätsgeschichte des Thorner Akademischen Gymnasiums von den Anfängen bis zu den Teilungen Polens,' in *Das Akademische Gymnasium zu Hamburg (gegr. 1613) im Kontext frühneuzeitlicher Wissenschafts- und Bildungesgeschichte*, ed. Johann Anselm Steiger, Martin Mulsow, and Axel E. Walter (Berlin and Boston: De Gruyter, 2017), 466.

4 Elbląg

König's scholarly achievement is generally seen as outstanding.[65] As a teacher, however, he failed. After his dismissal from Toruń, König seems to have oriented himself towards Gdańsk. At the Athenaeum, he published his *Fasciculus exercitationum ethicarum* and re-issued his edition of Pufendorf.[66]

Another shift that König completed was the juridical orientation of the teaching of politics. König, as Marian Pawlak wrote, 'confined the civil and the Roman law to Justinian's *Institutes* and in conformity with the prevailing conviction in Royal Prussia, which conceived civil law as part of Roman law.'[67] As a result of this shift, natural law was attached to jurisprudence at Elbląg, and not, as at Toruń, to ethics.[68]

The pedagogic difficulties of the Toruń years had prompted König to rearrange knowledge on politics at Elbląg on a more practical basis. At Toruń, König's programme consisted in training future members of the East-Central European political classes for jobs not reserved for aristocrats, while at Elbląg he had to prepare the sons of his fellow townsmen for the law and other professions.[69] At Elbląg, König could maintain neither the standard nor the thematic preferences, i.e. the preponderance of the moderns in teaching. His 'Ethicae & Politicae Breviarium' is a testimony to the co-existence of ancient and modern elements in his courses.

Pufendorf's *De Officio* was adapted to this new, lower standard of instruction by even more easily comprehensible texts surrounding it. Firstly, a new Introduction was written: *Introductio ad Libros duos V. Cl. Samuelis Pufendorfii, De Officio Hominis & Civis, in Usum Gymnasii Elbingensis*. This represents a

65 Pawlak, 'Nauczyciele,' I 150.

66 Ernst König, *V. Cl. Samuelis Pufendorfii, De officio hominis et civis Libri duo. Commodo juventutis studiosae In Gymnasio Thorunensi, recudendos curavit, Ordinariis Lectionibus proposuit, itemque Solemni Studiosorum ac Eruditorum Virorum examini subjecit – –* (Gdańsk: Rhete, 1682).

67 Pawlak, 'Młodzież,' 209.

68 Books on natural law were catalogued as 'Iuridici et politici' at Elbląg. Jerzy Sekulski, 'Księgozbiór biblioteki gimnazjum elbląskiego w XVIII wieku [The book collection at the library of the gymnasium in Elbląg in the eighteenth century],' *Komunikaty Mazursko-Warmińskie* 3 (1982), 187–199. The majority of Pufendorf's works fell under the 'history' heading. The works of Justinian were available in the library in nineteen copies, while Grotius's *De jure belli ac pacis* was only available in a single copy. Jerzy Sekulski, *Książka w Elblągu do roku 1772 [Books at Elbląg until 1772]* (Gdańsk: Wydawnictwo Morskie, 1990), 62.

69 Pawlak, 'Die Geschichte,' 389.

transition to Pufendorf from Aristotelian ethics, rather than a proper introduction to Pufendorf. The Introduction conceives philosophy as the science of divine and human things, divided accordingly into theoretical and practical philosophy; the goal of practical philosophy should be happiness, while the framework for pursuing happiness should be the state.[70] As König went on in the first part of his introduction on practical philosophy, he discussed the highest good first, then the principles of human actions, law, intellect, will and habitus, and, finally, the cardinal virtues which he had wanted to overcome with such determination in his Toruń years. In the transitory passages to Pufendorf's views, König's principal references were Paulus Slevogtius, Thomas Hobbes, Samuel Rachel, Jakob Thomasius and David Mevius. Knowingly ('*consultò*'), as he wrote, he omitted the first three chapters of *De Officio* and only used excerpts from the fourth chapter ('Duties towards God') and after.[71] There may have been good pedagogic reasons for the omission of the first three chapters with their detailed account of corrupt and fallible human nature. More importantly, König deleted the whole Pufendorfian concept of natural law as precepts of human co-existence, which were inconsistent with Justinian's definition of *ius naturae et gentium*. The concepts of sociality (*socialitas*) and weakness (*imbecillitas*) play no role in König's interpretation of Pufendorf, here or elsewhere. The *Introductio* is accomplished with a sketchy summary of *De Officio*, one sentence on each paragraph, not only to grasp (or sometimes to blur or dissimulate) their essence, but also to help students memorize its content.

At Elbląg, König used a collection of writings he called 'Ethicae & Politicae Breviarium' as a textbook. This small volume is mentioned under this name in his course description from 1689.[72] Some of his works survived between its hard covers: the Thomasius paraphrase, the edition of Pufendorf, an Introduction and an even more rudimentary summary of practical philosophy after Aristotle, the 'Praecognita,' together with Samuel Schelwig's *Idea Pneumaticae* which was taught by him at Elbląg as well.[73] The possessor of the copy to be found at Elbląg, Christian Kretschmer, commenced his studies at the

70 Ernst König, *Introductio ad Libros duos V. Cl. Samuelis Pufendorfii, De Officio Hominis & Civis, in Usum Gymnasii Elbingensis*, exhibita à – – (Toruń: Christianus Bekk, s.d.), § 3–5.

71 König, *Introductio*, G1r.

72 'Libri duo Sam. Pufendorfii, de Officio hominis & Civis, praemissâ perspicuâ Isagoge, ne quid desit *Ethicae & Politicae* Breviario.' *Elenchus praelectionum et operarum publicarum Gymnasii Elbingensis, Auctoritate Magnificorum et nobilissimorum D. D. scholarcharum, publicatus a M. Ernesto König, Gymnasii Rectore* (Elbląg: Achatius Corelli, 1689), 3.

73 'Idea Pneumaticae D. Sam. Schelguigii.' *Elenchus*, 2.

gymnasium on 27 September 1695.[74] Thus, while at Toruń, König had been entertaining higher pedagogic and scientific ambitions with Pufendorf's *De Officio* as his starting point, at Elbląg he had to reduce the book to even more concise summaries.

5 König's *Disquisitio ethica, super Justitia particulari* (1698)

A significant exception is his only treatise from 1698, *Disquisitio ethica, super Justitia particulari, viri perillustris, Samuelis L. B. de Pufendorf, libris duobus, De Off. Hominis et Civis, dilucidandis tributa* (An Ethical disquisition on particular justice, devoted to the elucidation of Pufendorf's two books on the Duty of Man and Citizen). My approach to this text aims to reconstruct the philosophical framework in which König situated his teaching within private law, challengingly novel in the context of the political community to which König addressed himself.

Disquisition signalled a shift in König's intellectual focus towards jurisprudence and, simultaneously, in his pedagogic goals. In the Preface, König (political philosopher that he was) felt the necessity to justify his competence in private law matters[75] and to re-adjust the historical narrative of his approach to Pufendorf. In harmony with his earlier accounts of his road to Pufendorf, he wrote he had chosen Pufendorf (with the permission of the supervising town magistrates of the gymnasia at Toruń and Elbląg) for didactic reasons and after long deliberation. As a new element, he restricted the scope of his investigations to the first book of *De Officio* to focus on the question of the extent to which Pufendorf's theses harmonized with Roman law.[76] In his Toruń years,

74 Hugo Abs, *Die Matrikel des Gymnasiums zu Elbing (1598–1786)* (Gdańsk: Danziger Verlags-Gesellschaft, 1936–1940), 189. The catalogue number of the Elbląg copy is SD. XVII. 26; the Toruń copy is marked with Sygn. 110440–110443.

75 'Eâdem ratione verissimè dixeris, quae Civilis Philosophiae sunt, eousque ab Ethicae & Politicae Professore exponenda & discutienda esse, donec nihil amplius CIVILE, quod quidem jurisprudentia naturalis, catholica & perpetua sibi vidicet, supersit examinandum' (a3r).

76 '[R]e multùm ac diu deliberatâ, Illustris Pufendorfii Epitomen ac summam J. N. quam ex majori opere octo librorum, de Jure Naturae ac Gentium, magno cum juventutis bono, excerptam publici juris fecit, primùm in Gymnasio Thorunensi, ante haec quatuor lustra, ac deinde in hoc Elbingensi, autoritate Magnifici Senatûs & Nobiliss. DD. Scholarcharum, publicè interpretarer, simulque prioris libri de O. H. themata omnia cum titulis Institutionum Juris D. Justiniani conferendo, argumentis haud obscuris indicarem, quid opis ad discendas posthac LL. Romanas in eruditissimo hoc libello foret' (a3v).

König taught natural law as presented in Pufendorf's *De Officio* as preparatory knowledge for a political career, while at Elbląg (or at least in the late phase of his Elbląg rectorship) he did so as a foundation of particular positive legal systems, with the claim that tenets of natural law overlap with particular national legal systems and even more with the *Corpus Juris Civilis* to a great extent.[77]

König achieved not only a shift from political philosophy towards jurisprudence, but also a shift from his adherence to modern philosophy, through the adoption of Pufendorf's perspective, back to Aristotelianism. The central concept of the book, particular justice (*justitia particularis*), was borrowed from the title of Book V, chapter 2 of the Latin version of *Nicomachean ethics*. König indeed referred to Aristotle a few times, though *Disquisition* draws on such authorities of modern natural jurisprudence as Hermann Conring and David Mevius, rather than Aristotle himself. Nonetheless, König did adopt some requisites of Scholastic philosophy in *Disquisition:* for example, discussing the subject matter in the order of its causes, effective, formal and final. Apparently, the restoration of the humanist curriculum and the end of the teaching of natural law in conformity with modern philosophy gained ground at Elbląg as early as König's final years.

Despite its close connection to jurisprudence, *Disquisition* was meant to be a book on ethics in so far as it established general precepts for the jurist's practical work. Drawing heavily on David Mevius's *Prodromus jurisprudentiae gentium communis, pro exhibendis ejusdem principiis et fundamentis* (1672), König justified the practical philosopher's competence in the field of (natural) jurisprudence in three steps: (1) by (partially) identifying the scope of ethics and natural jurisprudence;[78] (2) by interpreting particular jurisprudence as the adaptation of the tenets of universal (natural) jurisprudence to a national legal system;[79] and (3) by demarcating the competence of the political philosopher and the lawyer as dealing with universal and particular jurisprudence,

77 'Enimverò cum vix invenias jura Civitatum, quae merè positiva sint, non partem magnam naturalia; minimè omnium, quae sunt talia, Corpus Juris Civilis, quod *kat' exokhen* sic dicitur, continet' (a3v–a4r).

78 '[O]mne [...] naturale jus esse moralis philosophiae' (a2r). In the similar vein, confirming it with a reference to David Mevius's *Prodromus* (and via Mevius, to Hugo Grotius's *De jure belli ac pacis*, Prolegomena, § 7): 'ita philosophiam activam, Ethicam & Politicam, nihil aliud esse agnoscit, quàm jurisprudentiam universalem, seu, ut Hugo Grotius appellat, naturalem & perpetuam' (a2r).

79 'Neque dissimulat [*scil.* Mevius], ab universali illâ & communi gentium haud aliter differre particularem seu specialem jurisprudentiam, ac rivus differt ab ingenti flumine, ex hoc in locum fluens certum refluensque' (a2r). He invoked Pufendorf in this sense: 'So that, if we give the Law of Nature all that belongs to it, and take away from the Civilians what they have hitherto engross'd and promiscuously treated of; we shall bring the Civil

respectively.[80] The motto of *Disquisition* – '*Ubi desinit ethicus, ibi incipit jurisconsultus*' – urges the lawmaker to draw practical consequences from the ethical exposition, in the sense of Jacob Peter Hunter's distinction between an '*Ethicus*' and a '*Jurisconsultus*' in his interpretation of the dictum from 1631.[81]

Particular jurisprudence denotes – again in Aristotle's and Mevius's sense – the concrete legal system of private law of a particular societal community.[82] Among national legal communities, König mentioned Poland firstly, showing that the particular political community König had in mind was the Polish–Lithuanian Commonwealth.[83] He cited the words of the bishop of Cracow and Great Crown Chancellor Andrzej Lipski (1572–1631), who had reminded King Sigismund III that Roman civil law 'should be used here no less than elsewhere.'[84] In the Polish context, the proposal that Roman law be introduced was identical with the postulation of natural freedom and equality of the citizens before the law.[85] Understandably, König was not in a position to claim

---

Law to a much narrower Compass; not to say at present, that whenever the Civil Law is deficient, we must have recourse to the Law of Nature; and that therefore in all Commonwealths the natural Laws supply the Defects of the Civil.' Pufendorf, Samuel, *Of the Law of Nature and Nations. Eight Books*, trans. by Basil Kennett (London: J. Walthoe etc., 1729), 748 (VIII, 1, § 1), italics omitted.

80 '[N]ec alia supersit differentia inter Philosophum & JCtum, quàm quod ille in naturali & communi gentium jure subsistat: hic ex positivo ac speciali, quod ipsum jus commune est, sub diversis materiis & formis, ad certae civitatis & regni, v.c. Poloniae, Daniae, Svediae, statum, aulam, judicia, domos, &c. adplicatum, actiones in curiâ, foro, campo, formet' (a2r–a2v, with a literal quote from Mevius).

81 Jacobus Petrus Hunterus, *Epistolae Miscellanae* (Wien: Michael Rickhes, 1631), 14–15.

82 Aristotle, *Nicomachean Ethics* V.2 (1130b30–1131a1); 'Nec enim civilia jura aliud sunt, quam communis juris, sub diversis materiis & formis ad suas aulas, curias, fora, judicia, domos, applicatio.' David Mevius, *Prodromus jurisprudentiae gentium communis, pro exhibendis ejusdem principiis et fundamentis* (Stralsund: Otto Reumann, 1671), Praefatio, 4r.

83 a2v. For the conception of Polish political community in its religious and national heterogeneity, see [Karin Friedrich and Barbara M. Pendzich,] 'Preface,' in *Citizenship and Identity in a Multinational Commonwealth. Poland–Lithuania in Context, 1550–1772*, ed. by Karin Friedrich and Barbara M. Pendzich (Leiden and Boston: Brill, 2008), xix.

84 '[A]ttamen quia jus illud Civile Romanorum, ex praeceptis juris naturalis & gentium, (quorum apud nos etiam non minor quàm alibi usus esse debet) Iurisconsultus Ulpianus conflatum esse testetur.' Andrzej Lipski, *Practicarum observationum ex iure civili et saxonico* [...] *centuria prima* (Riga: Nicolaus Mollinus, 1602), **2r.

85 As put in the *Institutes* 1.2.2: 'by nature, from the outset, all human beings were born free and equal.' John Finnis, 'Natural Law Theories,' *The Stanford Encyclopedia of Philosophy* (Summer 2020 Edition), Edward N. Zalta (ed.), URL = https://plato.stanford.edu/archives/sum2020/entries/natural-law-theories/, ch. 2 (1.9.2021) On the legally guaranteed bodily integrity of the nobility, cf. Karin Friedrich, 'Poland–Lithuania,' in *European political thought 1450–1700: Religion, law and philosophy*, ed. by Howell A. Lloyd, Glenn Burgess, and Simon Hodson (New Haven and London: Yale University Press, 2008), 212, 221.

that the aim of his *Disquisition* was to exert influence (not even indirectly, through his students as jurists-to-be) on the Polish legal system. Instead, he pointed out the usefulness of knowledge on particular justice in civic life.[86]

Certainly, König's *Disquisition* did not elucidate on Pufendorf's *De Officio* as suggested in the title. It highlights elements of Pufendorf's work (and modern natural law tradition, in general) that could contribute to the modernization of the Polish legal system without challenging the political system as a whole and especially the origin, scope and limitations of political power. While König and his students at Toruń worked with *De Officio* in its entirety, and his Elbląg *Introductio* to Pufendorf already failed to focus on some parts of the book, König engaged in a further, radical thematic omission in *Disquisition*. His approach was confined to passages on private contracts embedded in a theory of obligations. More than three references are made to the following sections in *De Officio* alone: I.i ('On human action'); I.vi ('On the duty of every man to every man, and, first, of not harming others'); I.vii ('On recognizing men's natural equality'); I.xi ('On the duty of parties to agreements in general'); I.xii ('On duty in acquiring ownership of things'); and I.xv ('On contracts which presuppose value in things and on the duties they involve').[87]

The practical purposes of particular justice are further enumerated in Chapter I of *Disquisition* on the necessity and external causes of particular justice, where religion and particular justice are named, again with a quote borrowed from Mevius, as the cornerstones of human society.[88] König defined universal and particular justice, as well as their relation after Aristotle[89] and

---

86 'Et quoniam cura mihi praecipua est, quae fuit semper, ut vitae magis quàm scholae discant, qui me audiunt, cogitare non ita pridem coepi, quâ ratione ante alia Ethicae praecepta, quae justitiae particularis sunt, ad publicos accomodarem usus, & qualicunque de justitiâ particulari diatribe, quoad fieri per ingenii mei vites [vires?] posset, methodicâ atque inprimis perspicuâ, auditores meos ad juridprudentiae studium aliquatenus praepararem' (a4v).

87 Translation taken from Samuel Pufendorf, *On the Duty of Man and Citizen According to Natural Law*, ed. James Tully, trans. Michael Silverthorne (Cambridge etc.: Cambridge University Press, 1991).

88 'Pietas & justitia particularis societatum humanarum columina sunt' (A1r).

89 'Ut verò à nomine incipiamus, Latinis justitia particularis ex eo dicitur, quod Aristoteles illam vocat *dikaiosynēn kata meros*, ad differentiam latè acceptae justitiae, quae *universalis* appellatur, & constans ac perpetuum propositum est obtemperandi omni rationis rectae dictamini, seu legibus de omni agibili. Qua ratione haec non species certa virtutis moralis, sed tota virtus est, quae de virtutibus moralibus omnibus conjunctim praedicatur, ceu totum intergrale, de partibus integralibus, juxta versum Theognidis, [...] *Justitia in sese virtutes continet omnes*' (A3r).

the Melanchthon interpreter Viktorian Strigel.[90] Relying on Pufendorf, the effective causes of particular justice are defined by König in these terms:

> If we consider the causes of particular justice this way, we find its principal effective cause, in so far as it has a common feature with other virtues, as well as the *first* cause, GOD, and the state subordinated to Him, as the *second* one, namely the human being, who successively produces a habit in himself by free and recurrent actions; by actions which correspond to the conscience, or the dictates of the right reason, that is, to the law, and above all the *natural* law as forms, examples, norms and infallible measures necessary to actions, called duties by Pufendorf, and producing a habit, i.e. the active power through which the acts of the *perfect* virtue emerge, acts that were imperfect before the formation of the habit.[91]

The final causes of particular justice, on the other hand, consist in 'good fame among humans, the benevolence of others, a good social order, the tranquillity of everyone, and an increment of things, public and private.'[92]

Chapter II indicates the formal cause of particular justice in Ulpian's rule of *suum cuique tribuere*.[93] Three differences between universal and particular justice are provided here. There is no footnote to this passage, so König seems

90 'Sicut enim unus flosculus inserto se habet ad flores omnes, ex quibus sertus contextum est fragrantissimum: ita se particularis justitia ad universalem habet' (A3r).

91 'Causas justitiae particularis si inspiciamus, efficientem principalem cum caeteris virtutibus morum communem habet, tam *primam* DEUM, & huic subordinatam Civitatem, quàm *secundam*, nempe hominem, qui per actiones voluntarias crebras, conscientiae, seu dictamini rectae rationis, i.e. juri, seu legi praecipuè *naturali*, ceu formae exemplari, normae & mensurae infallibili, ad agendum necessariae, congruentes, (Pufendorfius officia appellat,) habitum successivè in se producit, i.e. talem potentiam activam, per quam eduntur actus virtutis *perfecti*, qui ante habitum productum erant imperfecti' (A3r–A3v).

92 '[B]ona fama inter homines, aliorum benevolentia, bonus societatis ordo, omnium tranquillitas, rerum incrementa publicè & privatim' (A4v).

93 'Causa formalis Particularis Justitiae in hoc consistit, quod cum promptitudine alteri tribuitur, quod ipsi jure debetur *perfecto*, ut à non tribuente actione in foro contra hunc intentatâ, aut, fori brachio deficiente, id per vim rectè exigatur, damnumque per injuriam datum autoritate privatâ reparetur. Ex quo intelligitur, non sufficere, si cuique seu homini, seu hominum societati, tribuantur sua bona, quae vel naturae, vel fortunae, vel suae industriae accepta refert: sed simul requiri, ut, quemadmodum in ceterarum actibus Virtutum, sic in suis cuique bonis tribuendis, circumstantiarum simul omnium, quas morales vocant, ratio habetur secundum illud pervulgatum: *bonum ex integrâ causâ est; malum ex quovis defectu*' (A4v).

to credit himself with this summary of generally accepted tenets of private law (which can, in any case, be inferred from Aristotle's writing):

> Particular justice differs from universal justice *in just three aspects*. *First*, [it differs] as concerns the persons who are its objects, as universal justice only demands what we owe not to others, but also to ourselves. Particular justice, however, only [demands what we owe] to others, namely, in an unqualified sense, not according to some particular aspect: the latter includes justice between parents and children, husband and wife. *Furthermore*, [it differs] as concerns its closest real objects, as universal justice directs all genera of actions, that is, virtues, towards the goal that, after our example, others should also strive towards all genera of virtues and a flourishing state should come into existence. Particular justice solely concerns those other-regarding actions by which external goods or evils, benefits and burdens are distributed or exchanged. *Besides*, [it differs] as concerns the subject to which justice belongs, as the subject of universal justice is none other than the good man, namely, he who [...] is instructed in the habit of all virtues. In contrast, that of particular justice is by no means a man who is always good, besides which its goal consists in the exertion of justice, private or public, by acts of distribution and exchange. [This is] an aspect which also directly concerns a man who is not good, provided he is not inexpert in jurisprudence.[94]

Chapter III treats the real objects of particular justice: liberty, dominion and authority over family and household members. The first standard right to private law,[95] bodily integrity, is here enumerated among 'internal' goods, in

94 'Differt autem justitia particularis ab universali potissimùm *tripliciter. Primùm* objecto personali, quatenus justitia universalis, id quod debetur, non alteri solùm tribuit, sed etiam sibi ipsi. Particularis autem alteri duntaxat, & quidem alteri simpliciter, non secundùm quid tali; in quo genere sunt parentes & liberi, maritus & uxor. *Deinde* objecto reali proximo, dum justitia universalis omne actionum seu virtutum genus ad alterum dirigit, eum in finem, ut suo exemplo alii quoque omnis generis virtutibus incumbant, sitque beata respublica. Particularis eas solummodo actiones ad alterum refert, quibus externa bona vel mala lucra & onera distribuuntur vel commutantur. *Praeterea* subjecto inhaesionis, quod jusitiae universali nonnisi vir bonus est, & quidem ille, qui omnium [...] virtutum habitibus instructus est. Particularis verò nequidem semper vir bonus est, propterea quod hujus finis est, per actus distributivos & commutativos justitiam privatim vel publicè exercere; id quod etiam subinde in virum non bonum cadit, dummodo jurisprudentiae non sit expers' (B2r).

95 Ernest J. Weinrib, 'Private law and public right,' *University of Toronto Law Journal* 61 (2011): 191–211, here 195.

contradistinction to external goods, possessed by *dominium* and *potestas*. In the notes to these passages, as well as in the further discussion of private law, König referred to parallel places in Pufendorf and Justinian's *Institutes*, showing where they agree:

> Under things which we own by strict law falls everything in which damage can be inflicted on others by injustice. Such things are, on the one hand, *internal* goods, such as life, bodily and mental health, freedom, chastity, safety of limbs, integrity of the sense organs, robustness, excellent form, natural dignity and equality originating from it in respect to those of whom a privilege is not demanded; on the other hand, *external* goods or fortunes, such as good reputation, fame, honour, nobility, family estate and richness, power, domestic and civil; and further obligations which others owe to us by *perfect* law, partly privately, partly publicly, the rulers as well as the subjects.[96]

Liberty and bodily integrity are not discussed in *Disquisition* in further detail. In Chapter IV, König touched upon privileges (Part XIV), private authority (*potestas privata*), such as the power of a husband, father or preceptor (Part XV), and public power, such as majesty (*maiestas*) and leadership over local communities (Part XVI). Here, in an excursion into Polish politics, König calls it an 'aberrant condition in the Commonwealth' (*statum reipublicae aberrantem*) that the Polish nobility is the judge of their own serfs.[97] Parts XVII–XX contain König's understanding of property, again following Pufendorf.

Chapter IV deals with the origins of obligation. These are threefold: (1) divine and human law, according to which humans are by their nature equals[98] (Part XXI); (2) contracts; and (3) torts, i.e. two types of legal transactions that maintain equality and give occasion to restore equality through corrective justice, respectively (Part XXII). The chapter also discusses the 'formal causes' (or pertinent acts) of particular justice, i.e. the basic features of a person's contractual performance (Part XXIII): '(1) not to harm others; (2) to

---

96 'Continentur verò sub eo, quod jure debetur stricto, omnia, in quibus alteri dari damnum per injuriam potest. Cujusmodi sunt bona tùm *interna*, ut vita, sanitas animae & corporis, libertas, pudicitia, incolumitas membrorum, sensuum integritas, robur, formae praestantia, dignatio à natura homini data, & quae hinc oritur aequalitas, respectu eorum, quibus peculiare jus non est quaesitum' (B3r).

97 C2v.

98 'Unus isque *primus* est lex Divina & Humana, quae homines sic inter se devincit, ut ne quis alterum injuriâ afficiat, sed eum aestimet tractetque tanquam naturaliter sibi aequalem' (D1r).

give satisfaction to damage caused by tort; (3) to offer a valid interpretation to words of obligation; (4) to observe contracts; (5) to further equality; and (6) to refrain from vigilantism.'[99]

König referred to distributive and commutative justice as parts of particular justice in Chapter V, after Georg Adam Struve's *Juris-Prudenz*. While not dealing with distributive justice any further, he divided commutative justice into *justitia directiva* and *justitia correctiva*: directive justice to maintain equality between partners in a transaction and corrective justice to restore it. A further component of particular justice is public or coactive justice, i.e. the public administration of justice to enforce equality.[100] These parts of particular justice are developed in each of the remaining three chapters with a final chapter on adjudication. In these chapters, König provided an overview of the basic features of private law, drawing again on parallel places in Pufendorf and Roman law. For König, as well as for other East-Central European natural law writers,[101] natural law becomes instrumental to the introduction into natural legal discourse of the notion of a person capable of contractual performance. As a result, the system of private law should become the sphere for legal equality, co-existing with actual inequalities as concerns social standing and political participation:

> It is beyond any doubt that even the highest ruler, i.e. the Pope or the Emperor, are no less obliged to observe contracts made with others than any private person; he is bound by the natural law or the law of nations. That is why he cannot act in breach of his own contract, being obliged by

99 '(1) Alteri se praestare innocentem; (2) De damno per culpam dato satisfacere; (3) Verba obligantia legitimè interpretari; (4) Pactis conventis stare; (5) Servare aequalitatem; (6) Vindictâ privatâ abstinere' (C4v).

100 'Est enim Justitia *distributiva* (utar definitionibus celeberrimi JCti G. Adami Struvii) quâ illa, quae civibus in societate civili communia sunt, ut honores, munera & onera, ipsis, secundùm cujusve qualitatem & conditionem, deferuntur, ita ut secundùm proportionem Geometricam aequalitas inter eos observetur. Contrà Justitia *commutativa* est, quae aequalitatem servat in iis, quae ad cives *singulos*, particulariter in societate civili spectant, nimirum quoad personas & res civium proprias, & in contractibus, inter cives celebratis, de rebus singulorum, nec non in poenis, ob delicta infligendis vel etiam damnis resarciendis. Harum utramque à parte actûs qui nunc magis perfectus, nunc minùs est, possis distinguere in *directivam*, quâ quis officium suum facit aequalitatem in principio observando; & *correctivam*, quâ qui alterum laesit, suum factum ipse emendat, atque illatam injuriam, restitutione factâ, suâ sponte delet' (D3r–D3v). Cf. Georg Adam Struve. *Juris-Prudenz oder Verfassung der Landüblichen Rechte* (Merseburg: Gottschick / Forberger, 1689), 5.

101 See József Simon's paper on Miklós Apáti in this volume.

> the contract he has entered with one of his subjects. For the ruler can be exempted from the laws and unbound by positive law [...], but he is not exempted from the dictates of the right reason as a rational being. And no authority whatsoever can exempt him from the dictates of natural law or the right reason, that is, the eternal law.[102]

Chapter VI discusses commutative justice in agreements and contracts, with common formal features, four in number (Part XXVIII), and kinds (Part XXIX). In Chapter VII (*De Justitia Commutativâ, in ordine ad delicta*), König enumerates the catalogue of torts as listed in Pufendorf's *De Officio*. In contrast, there is no reference to Pufendorf in Chapter VIII (*De Justitia publicâ, seu administrativa & coactivâ*), which deals with the enforcement of justice in a political society[103] and establishes criteria for a competent, nonpartisan, formally right and fair administration of justice. Chapter IX (*De Judicio, & in specie, de formà ejus; hoc est, de Processu judiciario*) covers the process of adjudication.

In sum, to make his message more compatible within existing pedagogic frameworks, König returned to Aristotelianism, placing the notion of particular justice into the centre of his argument – a concept mentioned only a single time in Pufendorf's *De Officio* out of obligation.[104] As König died the same year as the *Disquisition* was published, there is no evidence of how this treatise could have fit into the curriculum.

6 The Beginnings of the Teaching of Natural Law at Gdańsk

At Gdańsk, Samuel Schelwig, professor of philosophy and a former colleague of König's at Toruń, introduced natural law to the tuition. As a driving force behind the teaching of natural law at Toruń and Elbląg, König also made his mark, even if indirectly, at the third and the most renowned member of the academic triad in Royal Prussia to the reception of natural law. At the

---

102 'Indubitatum, quod etiam summus Princeps, id est, Papa vel Imperator, non minùs obligetur ad observantiam contractuum initorum cum aliis, quàm quilibet privatus, ex quo jure naturali sive gentium tenetur. Ideoque contra contractum suum venire non potest: obligaturque ex contractu suo cum subdito suo. Licet enim Princeps sit solutus LL. & lege positivâ non obligetur [...] tamen à dictamine rectae rationis non est solutus, quia est animal rationale. Neque ulla autoritas eum potest absolvere à lege naturae, vel à dictamine rectae rationis, seu legis aeternae' (E1v).

103 'Ut jus & aequum in civili societate cum effectu obtineatur, justitia opus est coactivâ, ideoque publicâ' (F4r).

104 I.ii.14.

Athenaeum in Gdańsk, natural law was not only firmly incorporated into the teaching of jurisprudence and philosophy between ca. 1680 and 1760, but also a number of professors greatly contributed to the research on natural law with their treatises, disputations and exercises.

Samuel Schelwig (1643–1715) matriculated at the University of Leipzig in 1661 and then in the same year at the University of Wittenberg. He obtained *venia legendi* in 1663 to become adjunct professor at Wittenberg in 1667. At König's bidding, Schelwig occupied the position of co-rector and professor of logic, metaphysics and poetics at Toruń.[105] In 1673, he went to Gdańsk as professor of philosophy and was appointed rector in 1685.

As professor, Schelwig introduced natural law at Gdańsk, and, as rector, he institutionalised its instruction there. As early as 1678, Schelwig held a course on natural law for the first year.[106] As two appointments (Johann Christoph Rosteuscher and Johann Gottfried von Diesseldorff) brought no lasting solution, Schelwig won over Samuel Friedrich Willenberg for Gdańsk. With Willenberg (whose activity is beyond the scope of the present paper), the teaching of natural law theory was guaranteed for half of a century. Schelwig's case exemplifies a different attitude towards natural law as an academic discipline than that of König. As rector, Schelwig subscribed to natural law (for example, in his welcome address to Diesseldorff[107]), while, as a fervently orthodox Lutheran theologian and scholar, he had other scholarly interests. Scientific and pedagogic attitudes towards natural law thus diverged from each other within a single career.

The early years of teaching natural jurisprudence was associated with Johann Schultz-Szulecki. Schultz-Szulecki started his studies in Königsberg

105 Salmonowicz, 'Das protestantische,' 403.

106 '[E]x philosophia Ethicam, classis primae Studiosis. ita proponet, ut quae Juris Naturae & Gentium praecepta, in Politica commodè exponi haud potuerunt, jam suis inserta sedibus, ordine enucleretur.' *Catalogus lectionum et operarum publicarum in Athenaeo Gedanensi* [...] *Anno MDCLXXIIX* (Gdańsk: Rhete, 1678), [B2].

107 Samuel Schelwig, *Proposito Numine, Jussu Magnifici Atque Amplissimi Senatus Gedanensis, Cum Viro Nobilissimo, Excellentissimo et Consultissimo Dn. Joh. Godofredo à Diesseldorf Gedanensi, J. U. D. Caesarei Palatini Comiti, Atque In Academia Lipsiensi Antea Concilii Perpetui Assessori, Nunc In Patria Jurium Et Historiarum Professio Publica Et Ordinaria, Atque Athenaei Inspectio, Solenni Ritu Committeretur, Ad Inaugurationis Actum A. C. M DC XCVII. D. XII. Decembris Celebrandum, Liberalium Artium Et Studiorum Patronos, Fautores, Cultores Et Aestimatores, Submisse, Reverenter, Officiose Et Peramanter Invitat; Studiosum Vero Coetum Paterne Convocat, Athenaei Rector, – –, S. Theol. D. Et Prof. Publ. Itemque Ecclesiae Ad SS. Trinit. Pastor* (Gdańsk: Stolle, 1697).

(present-day Kaliningrad in Russia). In 1682, he went to the University of Frankfurt an der Oder, where he earned his doctorate in 1688. His doctoral dissertation[108] and his early disputations[109] there reveal a lively interest in natural law theory. Under Schelwig's rectorship, Schultz-Szulecki opted for Gdańsk in 1688 to shift emphasis from Roman law to the law of nature and nations – disciplines that students at Gdańsk would put to better use in public service or business.[110]

His main work, *Harmonia Struvio-Grotio-Strobeliana*,[111] is a re-edition of Joachim Schnobelius's dissertations on the *Pandects*, supplemented with commentaries based on Grotius's *De jure belli ac pacis*. His treatise on Polish law, *Tractatus historico-politicus de Polonia nunquam tributaria*,[112] also contains a large number of references to Grotius, especially to his *De jure belli ac pacis*. This served as a textbook for exercitations in the gymnasium, with ten sections with a respondent for each section. A number of further exercitations were tied to this book.[113] In 1700, Schultz-Szulecki returned to Frankfurt an der Oder, where natural law was also an area of interest for him.

It took a decade before Pufendorf was incorporated into the curriculum. In 1689, Schultz-Szulecki taught *Jus Civilis* with a view to natural law. This course provided a logical deduction of private law based on Grotius's works and con-

108 Johannes Schultz, *Disputatio solennis Juridica, De Civilitate Proficua, quam* [...] *praeside* [...] *Samuele Strykio* [...] *Pro Summis In Utroque Jure Honoribus* [...] *submittit* – – (Frankfurt an der Oder: Coepselius, 1685).

109 Johann Samuel Stryk, *Disputatio iuris publici, De Philosophia Principum, quam* [...] *Praeside* [...] *Johanne Schultzen, J. U. D. Ejusdemque & Historiarum vocato Professore & Inspectore Athenaei Gedanensis,* [...] *exhibet* – – (Frankfurt an der Oder: Coepselius, 1688); Christian Georg Rötlin, *Disputatio Juridica in Quâ Decas Casuum Illustrium Moderni temporis Continetur, Quam* [...] *praeside* [...] *Johanne Schultzen* [...] *exhibebit* – – (Frankfurt an der Oder: Coepselius, 1688).

110 Tadeusz Maciejewski, 'Prawo i jego nauczanie w Gdańskim Gimnazjum Akademickim od XVI do XIX wieku (1558–1810) [Jurisprudence and its teaching at the academic gymnasium in Gdańsk from the sixteenth to the nineteenth centuries],' *Czasopismo Prawno-Historyczne* 67 (2015/2): 111–126, here 113.

111 Johannes Schultz, *Harmonia Struvio-Grotio-Strobeliana, Sive* [...] *Joachimi Schnobelii* [...] *Dissertationes XXV. ad Pandectas Perpetuis ad Syntagma Juris Civilis* [...] *Georg. Adam. Struvii, Remissionibus, quae commentarii vice esse poterant, atque indice locupletissimo auctae, Publicae luci iterataeque ventilationi in Alma Salanâ expositae à* [...] *Adriano Beier* [...] *& Nuper in Athenaeo Gedanensi repetitae atque Observationibus Grotianis Parallelis auctae â* – – (Gdańsk: Rhete, 1693).

112 Johannes Schultz, *Tractatus historico-politicus de Polonia nunquam tributaria* (Gdańsk: Rhete, 1694).

113 See Johannes Schultz, *Disputationis De Polonia Nunquam Tributaria, Sectio V. Quam* [...] *Praeside* [...] *Johanne Schultzio* [...] *submittit* [...] *Daniel Schrader* (Gdańsk: Rhete, 1693).

sequently presented natural law as a theoretical foundation of private law.[114] In 1691, he lectured on Justinian's *Institutes*, without any special consideration of natural law. Nor do Schultz-Szulecki's course descriptions contain any references to natural law in 1692, 1693 and 1694. Instead, Johann Christoph Rosteuscher taught Grotius in the 1693 academic year. Rosteuscher spoke about *De jure belli ac pacis* in a public lecture as well as in a series of thirty exercitations as part of the teaching of politics in the study programme for philosophy.[115] In 1694, Rosteuscher carried on his lecture on Grotius according to the wishes of the students and on the basis on Jan Klenck's compendium.[116] It seems that there was a division of labour between Schultz-Szulecki and Rosteuscher: Schultz-Szulecki provided instruction in jurisprudence, while Rosteuscher taught the foundations of jurisprudence in natural law, offering text-centred interpretations with regard to the commentary literature.[117]

114 'In Primô Auditoriô Institutiones Juris Civilis / consvetis horis explicare materiam praebuerunt, ex primis titulis, Juri N. & G. prolixè explicando. Continuabuntur eaedem, eô, quô par est, explicandi conatu, istiusque anni pensum constituent. Alterius verò partae studium, Juris Civilis & Canonici Historiae enucleandae destinatum, praemittendam mereri videbatur Juris N. & G. historiam, cum turpe sit rivulos sequi, spretis fontibus. Grotii hâc in materiâ ductus placuit, à quô Juris Civilis Historia per modum Genealogiae expressa legitur Proleg. §. 16. Dum ille Juris Civilis *matrem* appellat Jus. G., *aviam* Jus Naturae, *Proaviam* Naturam Humanam. Haec igitur Genealogia historicô sensu tractata hactenus fuit, docendo sc. per Exempla, de communi imprimis Juris N. à plerisque Gentibus receptione, à multis falsâ illius interpretatione, à paucissimis oblivione totali. Accesserunt Exempla de approbatione illius Divinâ, ter imprimis repetitâ, & de apparenti ejusdem immutatione. Ad ipsam igitur *Filiam*, Jus Civile sc. per DEI gratiam jam perventum. Cujus Historiae enucleandae futura impendetur cura.' *Catalogus lectionum et operarum publicarum in Athenaeo Gedanensi ... Anno* MDCXXCIX (Gdańsk: Rhete, 1689), [A2v–A3r].

115 'Ut interim ad istiusmodi solenniora exercitia praepararentur nondum satis in hâc palaestrâ versati nonnullorum animi, Commentationem Grotianam de Jure Belli ac Pacis, antidhâc à se publicè explicatam, in succintas theses redactam, triginta velitationibus in Auditorio Philosophico institutis excussit hactenus, cumque labor iste haud ita pridem ad finem perductus sit, in ejus locum thesium Politicarum Syllogen singulis septimanis ventilandam surrogare coepit.' *Catalogus lectionum et operarum publicarum in Athenaeo Gedanensi ... Anno* MDCXCIII (Gdańsk: Rhete, 1693), [A4v].

116 '[J]amque ab Auditoribus rogatus, ad explicanda operis Grotiani argumenta, quae per selectas quaestiones in compendium redigit Klenckius, animum adjecit.' *Catalogus lectionum et operarum publicarum in Athenaeo Gedanensi ... Anno* MDCXCIV (Gdańsk: Rhete, 1694), [A4r].

117 'Grotium ex ipsomet Grotio declaret, adjectis tamen subinde & in medium collatis, tum Interpretum ejusdem Auctorumque aliorum, quos aetas nostra in hoc studiorum genere veneratur, diversis saepè sententiis; tum, sicubi opus, perspicuis exemplis, quae ex recentiorum inprimis Historicorum monumentis selecta, Grotiana praecepta quàm maximè illustrant.' *Catalogus lectionum et operarum publicarum in Athenaeo Gedanensi ... Anno* MDCXCIV (Gdańsk: Rhete, 1694), [A4r].

In 1697, Rosteuscher, a priest and theologian, was already at his parish office, while the new teacher and librarian, Johannes Gottlieb Möller, announced in his study programme a return to Jakob Thomasius and his practical philosophy (hence a return to Aristotelian ethics and the virtue tables).[118] Privately, he held disputations on ethics, the outcome of which he wanted to synthesize in a book, 'Collegiô jam fermè finitô, Disputatorium Ethicum, ad *Libellum Memorialem ethicum Boeclerianum*, & Lectorium Politicum, publicabit.' He seems to have used a book on ethics by Johann Heinrich Boecler, published independently in 1654 and then re-printed for school purposes in Jena in 1681: a purely Aristotelian ethics.[119] In 1698, Diesseldorff took over the teaching of jurisprudence and history. He taught the historical works of Pufendorf privately.[120] Möller continued to hold his lectures on ethics with Boecler at hand;[121] at the same time, he held disputations on Pufendorf's *De officio*.[122] He also announced a private lecture 'ad Puffendorffianum *de officio Hominis & Civis* Libellum.'[123]

---

118 'Johannes Gottlieb Mollerus, Gedanensis, Auspice DEO, in Lectionibus Publicis, praemissâ ad studium Logices, Metaphysices, ac Philosophiae Practicae feliciter tractandum, manuductione, in Auditorio Primo, Metaphysicum & Ethicum; in Secundo, Logicum, *Ideâ Logices & Metaphysices Schelgvigianâ*, (quam hôc recudi fine curavit;) ac *Philosophiâ Practicâ Thomasianâ*, succintis inclusâ Tabulis, praeeunte, ingressus est curriculum, in quo, donec metam fuerit consecutus, more hactenùs receptô, perget, sedulam daturus operam, ut, quae cognitu sunt necessaria, cum suo in Superioribus usu, perspicuâ & sufficienti declarentur brevitate.' *Catalogus lectionum et operarum publicarum, in Athenaeo Gedanensi* [...] *Anno MDCXCVII* (Gdańsk: Stolle, 1697), [B3r].

119 Johann Heinrich Boecler, *Institutiones Politicae. Accesserunt Dissertationes Politicae Ad Selecta Veterum Historicorum Loca. Et Libellus Memorialis Ethicus* (Straßburg: Zetzener, 1674).

120 'Privatim quoque indefessum studium solertissimis Legalis ac Historiae scientiae cultoribus approbare non omittet: Quem in finem *Illustris Dn. Puffendorffii Introductionem in Historiam & Magnifici Dn. Hoppii Examen Institutionum* cupientibus exponent.' *Catalogus lectionum et operarum publicarum, in Athenaeo Gedanensi* [...] *Anno MDCXCVIII* (Gdańsk: Stolle, 1698), A3r–v.

121 '[I]n Auditorio autem Secundo, repetitioni Logicae, explanationem Ethices, ad ductum *Libelli memorialis Ethici Boecleriani*, adjunget.' *Catalogus lectionum et operarum publicarum, in Athenaeo Gedanensi* [...] *Anno MDCXCVIII* (Gdańsk: Stolle, 1698), C1r.

122 'Praeibunt iis [i.e., to disputations on metaphysics and ethics] propediem Nobilissimi aliquot Juvenes, aureum Illustris Puffendorffii *de Officio Hominis & Civis* Libellum, sub praelo apud nos jam sudantem, XXX. Disputationibus, in Auditorio Ordinario publicè expensuri; quorum vestigiis laudatissimis, ut & alii, praecipuè, qui tot à Partonis Munificentissimis mactari beneficiis, ad edenda industriae specimina prae reliquis obligantur, insistant, seriò exoptat.' *Catalogus lectionum et operarum publicarum, in Athenaeo Gedanensi* [...] *Anno MDCXCVIII* (Gdańsk: Stolle, 1698), C1v.

123 *Catalogus lectionum et operarum publicarum, in Athenaeo Gedanensi* [...] *Anno MDCXCVIII* (Gdańsk: Stolle, 1698), C1v–2r.

7 Conclusion

In the academic gymnasia of Royal Prussia, the teaching of natural law was mainly confined – ultimately because of König's decisions as a rector and professor – to Pufendorf's *De Officio* until the end of the seventeenth century (and until the mid-eighteenth century at Toruń). My paper has shown that Pufendorf's works served varying functions in terms of König's changing didactic objectives. These goals, despite König's administrative efforts to consolidate the institutional changes he had made had to be adapted to the declining quality of teaching, especially at Elbląg. Another factor that prompted König to adjust his exigencies to the changing circumstances was the difference in the manner in which students were recruited at Toruń and Elbląg, as well as their different career prospects. From an internationally renowned gymnasium attended by the offspring of patricians and noble families and attracting students from Silesia, Moravia, Hungary and Transylvania, König opted for an institution in which an overwhelming majority of the students were recruited from families of clerks, artisans and businessmen living in the town or its immediate vicinity.[124]

Under these circumstances, König's principal objective consisted in transforming the methodology of teaching political science via Pufendorf's works rather than in introducing modern science and philosophy into the curricula of the German gymnasia in Royal Prussia. In the main fields of his competence, ethics and politics, König did play a role in challenging Aristotelianism, at Toruń as well as at Elbląg. Similarily to the praxis of universities in the Protestant states of the Holy Roman Empire, it was political philosophy, and not Descartes's and Galileo's new tenets, that undermined the Scholastic tradition in the gymnasia of Royal Prussia. Just as with Christian Thomasius's thought, Aristotelian elements survived thanks to the influence of his father, Jakob Thomasius.[125] Hence, König, Jakob Thomasius's student, attempted to

124 Salmonowicz, 'Thorner,' 46–52; Novak and Tandecki, 'Einleitung,' xxii–xxiii; Salmonowicz, 'Die Protestantischen,' 522; Emil Waschinski, 'Das Thorner Stadt- und Landschulwesen vom Beginn der Reformation bis zum Ende der polnischen Herrschaft,' *Zeitschrift des Westpreußischen Geschichtsvereins* 56 (1916): 1–137.

125 Ian Hunter, 'Die Geschichte der Philosophie und die Persona des Philosophen. Trans. Sarah Erdmann and Sabrina Kessler,' in *Die Cambridge School der politischen Ideengeschichte*, ed. Martin Mulsow and Andreas Mahler (Berlin: Suhrkamp, 2010), 257; Salmonowicz, 'Nauczenie prawa i polityki,' 67; Stefania Ochmann, 'Rzeczpospolita jako "monarchia mixta" dylematy władzy i wolności [The Polish state as a "mixed monarchy" – dilemmas of power and liberty],' in *Kultura – polityka – dyplomacja. Studia ofiarowane Profesorowi Jaremie Maciszewskiemu w sześćdziesiątą rocznicę jego urodzin*, ed. Andrzej

find a compromise between ancient and new political science in his teaching practice.

Further, it has shown that the introduction of modern natural law as part of the new science and philosophy was not unique to the gymnasium in Toruń.[126] All three gymnasia took part in the adoption of early Enlightenment ideas and modern natural law; indeed, they did so in interaction with one another. We may identify König as a driving force behind these trends. On the other hand, jurisprudence and political science, rather than philosophy and natural sciences, also lent principal impulses to the challenge of the Aristotelian corpus of knowledge in Royal Prussia.[127] This shift from the ancient to the modern in science and philosophy was, however, not an irreversible process: in the first half of the eighteenth century, both gymnasia in Toruń and Elbląg returned to the humanist curriculum, dropping natural law or marginalizing it in their study programme.

Acknowledgements

The archives research in Poland and the writing of the first draft of this paper was made possible by a post-doctoral research grant at Erfurt University in 2018–19. The rewriting and the linguistic proofreading of this study was supported by the Hungarian Scientific Research Fund (NKFIH K-137963, 'History of Hungarian Philosophy in Early Modernity (1570–1710),' principal investigator: József Simon. The author thanks József Simon for his remarks and suggestions.

Bibliography

Primary Sources

Arndt, Johann, *Specimen de Hugone Grotio a Commentatoribus Juris Belli & Pacis Aliisque Immerito vapulante*, Rostock: Nicolaus Schwieger, 1712.

Bartnicki et al. (Warszawa: PWN, 1990), 268. Cf. Thomas Behme, 'Gegensätzliche Einflüsse in Pufendorfs Naturrecht,' in *Samuel Pufendorf und die europäische Frühaufklärung. Werk und Einfluß eines deutschen Bürgers der Gelehrtenrepublik nach 300 Jahren (1694–1994)*, ed. Fiammetta Palladini and Gerald Hartung (Berlin: Akademie Verlag, 1996), 74–82, with further literature.

126 See Salmonowicz, 'Das protestantische,' 405–406.

127 This thesis was formulated by Ian Hunter in terms of the European university system (*Rival Enlightenments: Civil and Metaphysical Philosophy in Early Modern Germany*, Cambridge: Cambridge University Press, 2001).

Arndt, Johann, *Licitam esse medii loci occupationem ex necessitate factam, consensu facultatis philosophicae, praeses – –, Dantiscanus, & respondens Paulus Matthias Wunsch, Meva-Prussus* [...] *juxta Juris Nat. principia defendent*, Rostock: Schwiegerau, 1712.

Arndt, Johann, *Orationes binae, quarum altera inchoavit, finiit altera, Universale Philosophiae cursum, privatos inter cancellos institutum*, Gdańsk: s.d., 1715.

Arndt, Johann, *Collegii Pufendorfiani Exercitationem I. generalem de opere Pufendorfiano Juris Nat. et Gent. praeside – –* [...] *defendet Joannes Kownacki*, Toruń: Johann Nicolai, 1717.

Arndt, Johann, *Collegii Pufendorfiani exercitationem II. de geometrica juris naturalis demonstratione praeside – –* [...] *defendet Io. Gottlob Stoeckel*, Toruń: Johann Nicolai, 1717.

Arndt, Johann, *Collegii Pufendorfiani Exercitationem III. de actione morali una et de emendandis addendisque in toto Lib. I. Pufend. De J. N. & G. praeside – –* [...] *defendet Casparus Geelhaar*, Toruń: Johann Nicolai, 1717.

Arndt, Johann, *Collegii Pufendorfiani exercitationis IV. de existentia juris naturalis continuationem, praeside – –* [...] *defendet Samuel Leonar: Zillich*, Toruń: Johann Nicolai, 1717.

Arndt, Johann, *Collegii Pufendorfiani Exercitationem V. de definitionibus juris naturalis praeside – –* [...] *defendet Mart. Dan. Serini*, Toruń: Johann Nicolai, 1718.

Arndt, Johann, *Collegii Pufendorfiani exercitationem VI. De proprietatibus juris naturalis, videlicet autore, promulgatione, forma, materia, subjecto, objecto et fine, praeside – –* [...] *defendet Christianus Martini*, Toruń: Johann Nicolai, 1718.

Boecler, Johann Heinrich, *Institutiones Politicae. Accesserunt Dissertationes Politicae Ad Selecta Veterum Historicorum Loca. Et Libellus Memorialis Ethicus*, Straßburg: Zetzener, 1674.

Budde, Karl Friedrich, *Dissertatio I. De Officio Hominis Circa Eruditionem Acquirendam Quam* [...] *submittunt praeses – –* [...] *et respondens Io. Fridericus Bachstrom*, Jena: Müller, 1713.

Catalogus lectionum et operarum publicarum in Athenaeo Gedanensi [...] *Anno MDCLXXIIX*, Gdańsk: Rhete, 1678.

Catalogus lectionum et operarum publicarum in Athenaeo Gedanensi [...] *Anno MDCXXCIX*, Gdańsk: Rhete, 1689.

Catalogus lectionum et operarum publicarum in Athenaeo Gedanensi [...] *Anno MDCXCIII*, Gdańsk: Rhete, 1693.

Catalogus lectionum et operarum publicarum in Athenaeo Gedanensi [...] *Anno MDCXCIV*, Gdańsk: Rhete, 1694.

Catalogus lectionum et operarum publicarum, in Athenaeo Gedanensi [...] *Anno MDCXCVII*, Gdańsk: Stolle, 1697.

Catalogus lectionum et operarum publicarum, in Athenaeo Gedanensi [...] *Anno* MDCXCVIII, Gdańsk: Stolle, 1698.

Catalogus Lectionum Publicarum in Gymnasio Thorunensi Anno Aerae Christianae M.DC.LXVIII, Toruń: Coepselius, 1668.

Catalogus Lectionum et Exercitati[o]*num Publicarum, in Gymnasii Thorunensis* [...] *Anno Aerae Christ.* M.DC.LXX. *per semestre aestivum*, Toruń: Coepselius, 1670.

Catalogus lectionum et operarum cum Deo in Gymnasio Thorunensi pertractandarum auctoritate nobiliss. et ampliss. scholarcharum ipso tempore Paschali publicatus anno 1714, Toruń: Johann Nicolai, 1714.

Catalogus lectionum et operarum cum Deo in Gymnasio Thorunensi pertractandarum auctoritate nobiliss. et ampliss. scholarcharum ipso tempore Paschali publicatus anno 1716, Toruń: Johann Nicolai, 1716.

Catalogus lectionum et operarum bono cum Deo in Gymnasio Thorunensi pertractandarum auctoritate nobiliss. et ampliss. scholarcharum circa tempus Paschale publicatur anno 1718, Toruń: Johann Nicolai, 1718.

Catalogus Lectionum et operarum bono cum Deo in Gymnasio Thorunensi pertractandarum auctoritate nobiliss. et ampliss. scholarcharum anno 1719 autumnali tempore publicatus, Toruń: Johann Nicolai, 1719.

Catalogus Lectionum et operarum bono cum Deo in Gymnasio Thorunensi pertractandarum auctoritate nobiliss. et ampliss. scholarcharum publicatus anno 1720, Toruń: Johann Nicolai, 1720.

Catalogus Lectionum et operarum cum Deo in Gymnasio Thorunensi pertractandarum auctoritate nobiliss. et ampliss. scholarcharum ipso tempore autumnali publicatus anno 1721, Toruń: Johann Nicolai, 1721.

Catalogus Lectionum et operarum cum Deo in Gymnasio Thorunensi pertractandarum auctoritate nobiliss. et ampliss. scholarcharum ipso tempore autumnali publicatus anno 1722, Toruń: Johann Nicolai, 1722.

Catalogus Lectionum et operarum propitio Deo in Gymnasio Thorunensi pertractandarum auctoritate nobiliss. et ampliss. scholarcharum publicatus anno 1732, Toruń: Johann Nicolai, 1732.

Elenchus praelectionum et operarum publicarum Gymnasii Elbingensis, Auctoritate Magnificorum et nobilissimorum D. D. scholarcharum, publicatus a M. Ernesto König, Gymnasii Rectore, Elbląng: Achatius Corelli, 1689.

Fibing, Henricus, *Diatribe Politica de Majestate; Quam suprema majestate favente, in Gymnasio Thorunensi, praeside M. Ernesto König,* [...] *subjicit – –* [...] *Autor & Respondens*, Toruń: Coepseius, 1671.

Grotius, Hugo, *Apologeticus eorum qui Hollandiae* [...] *ex legibus praefuerunt*, Paris: Buon, 1622.

[Grotius, Hugo] Hugo de Groot, *Briefwisseling van Hugo Grotius. Deel 17*, ed. by H.J.M. Nellen en Cornelia M. Riderikhoff, Den Haag: Martinus Nijhoff, 2001.

Hunterus, Jacobus Petrus, *Epistolae Miscellanae*, Wien: Michael Rickhes, 1631.

König, Ernst, *Ad bonarum artium patronos virosque doctos Provocatio a decreto abdicationis Thorunensi*, Szczecin: Daniel Starck, 1683.

König, Ernst, *D. Samuelis Pufendorfii Liber de Officio Hominis, Noscendis Ethicae Principiis genuinis ac solidis, in Gymnasio Thorun. Per semestre aestivum* M. DC. LXXIX. *publicè praelectus, atque ad disputandum propositus à – –*, Toruń: Coepselius, 1679.

König, Ernst, *De Collegiis & Urbibus. Ob defectum Respondentis non fuit ventilata* (= Fasciculus, no. VIII).

König, Ernst, *De Natura & Constitutione Philosophiae Practicae. Resp. Simon Antonii, Topscha Hung. d. 27. Jan.*, Toruń: Coepselius, 1678.

König, Ernst, *De Principiis Jurisprudentiae ethicis, Exercitatio Philosophica. Praeside – –, partes sustin. respondentis d. Decembr. A.* M. DC. LXXVII. [...] *Jacobus Merschier, Elbingensis*, Toruń: Coepselius, 1677.

König, Ernst, *Diatribe synoptica de eumathia*, Manuscript, Książnica miejska im. Kopernika in Toruń Bibl. gimn. R 4° 16.

König, Ernst, *Disquisitio ethica, super Justitia particulari, viri perillustris, Samuelis L. B. de Pufendorf, libris duobus, De Off. Hominis et Civis, dilucidandis tributa à – –*, Elbląg: Samuel Preus, 1698.

König, Ernst, *Exercitatio ethica, de bono hominis supremo, ejusque instrumentis. Praeside – – ... subjicit ... Michael Agnethler, Cibin. Trans. Respondens*, Toruń: Coepselius, 1678.

König, Ernst, *Exercitatio Ethica, De Eo, Qvod Justum Est. Praeside – –* [...] *subjicit* [...] *Johannes Gebhardus, Olsna-Siles. Respondens*, Toruń: Coepselius, 1678.

König, Ernst, *Exercitatio politica, De cive, et diversis hominum in civitate ordinibus, praeside – –* [...] *subjicit* [...] *Christianus Wernigke, Elbingens. respondens*, Toruń: Coepselius, 1680.

König, Ernst, *Exercitatio Politica, De Origine Civitatis, ac Rebus Huic Necessariis, Nominatim, Territorio & Publicis Reditibus. Praeside – –* [...] *subjicit* [...] *Boguslaus ab Unruh Eqves Polon. Respondens*, Toruń: Coepselius, 1679.

König, Ernst, *Exercitatio Politica, De Summis In Civitate Potestatibus, Harumq*[*ue*] *Praecipuis Administris / Praeside – –* [...] *Subjicit* [...] *Petrus Genschius, Ortr. Misnic. Respondens*, Toruń: Typ. Gymnasii, 1680.

König, Ernst, *Fasciculus Exercitationum ethicarum et politicarum, Quas sub ejusdem praesidio, Solemni ventilationi subjecerunt Studiosi quidam Juvenes. Accesserunt nonnulla alia*, Gdańsk: Typis Rhetianis, 1682.

König, Ernst, *Introductio ad Libros duos V. Cl. Samuelis Pufendorfii, De Officio Hominis & Civis, in Usum Gymnasii Elbingensis*, exhibita à – –, Toruń: Christianus Bekk, s.d.

König, Ernst, 'Lectori S.,' in *Fasciculus Exercitationum ethicarum et politicarum, Quas sub ejusdem praesidio, Solemni ventilationi subjecerunt Studiosi quidam Juvenes. Accesserunt nonnulla alia*, [1–2 unnumbered pages], Gdańsk: Typis Rhetianis, 1682.

König, Ernst, 'Lectori S.,' in *V. Cl. Samuelis Pufendorfii, De officio hominis et civis Libri duo. Commodo juventutis studiosae In Gymnasio Thorunensi, recudendos curavit, Ordinariis Lectionibus proposuit, itemque Solemni Studiosorum ac Eruditorum Virorum examini subjecit* – –, [1–6 unnumbered pages], Gdańsk: Rhete, 1682.

König, Ernst, *Summarium Doctrinae Ethicae, à V. CL. M. Jacobo Thomasio Lips. Acad. Prof. P. Continuis Tabellis adornatum. In Gymnasio Thorunensi, Publicè praelegit & disputavit* – –, Toruń: Coepselius, 1671.

König, Ernst, *V. Cl. Samuelis Pufendorfii, De officio hominis et civis Libri duo. Commodo juventutis studiosae In Gymnasio Thorunensi, recudendos curavit, Ordinariis Lectionibus proposuit, itemque Solemni Studiosorum ac Eruditorum Virorum examini subjecit* – –, Gdańsk: Rhete, 1682.

Lipski, Andrzej, *Practicarum observationum ex iure civili et saxonico* [...] *centuria prima*, Riga: Nicolaus Mollinus, 1602.

Mevius, David, *Prodromus jurisprudentiae gentium communis, pro exhibendis ejusdem principiis et fundamentis*, Stralsund: Otto Reumann, 1671.

Nakielski, Gabriel, *Dissertatio Politica, de Legibus Civitatis in Genere. Quam in Gymnasio Thoruniensi, ... Praeside M. Ernesto König,* [...] *subjicit* – –, [...] *Autor & Respondens*, Toruń: Coepselius, 1675.

Numine divino aspirante atque Magnifici et Amplissimi Senatus Thorunensis auctoritate ad solennem inaugurationis actum, in quo viro clarissimo atque doctissimo, Domino M. Ioanni Arndio, Gedanensi, professoris publici munus in Gymnasio Thorunensi D. XXIII. April. A. MDCCXVI more et ritu solito hora IX. conferetur, atque ad audiendas benevole orationes musarum patrones fautores literarumque aestimatores ea, qua decet reverentia, cultu et humanitate invitant, studiosam vero iuventutem peramanter convocant Gymnasii Rector et Professores, Toruń: Johann Nicolai, 1716.

Pufendorf, Samuel, *De jure naturae et gentium. Erster Teil: Text* (*Liber primus – Liber quartus*), ed. Frank Böhling, Berlin: Akademie-Verlag, 1998.

Pufendorf, Samuel, *Of the Law of Nature and Nations. Eight Books*, trans. by Basil Kennett, London: J. Walthoe etc., 1729.

Pufendorf, Samuel, *On the Duty of Man and Citizen According to Natural Law*, ed. James Tully, trans. Michael Silverthorne, Cambridge: Cambridge University Press, 1991.

Rötlin, Christian Georg, *Disputatio Juridica in Quâ Decas Casuum Illustrium Moderni temporis Continetur, Quam* [...] *praeside* [...] *Johanne Schultzen* [...] *exhibebit* – –, Frankfurt an der Oder: Coepselius, 1688.

Sartorius, Johannes, *De poena ob alienum delictum inflicta, Sub Praesidio* – –, [...] *publice disseret Johannes Czimmermann*, Thorunii: e Chalcographeo Gymnasii, [1699].

Schelwig, Samuel, *Proposito Numine, Jussu Magnifici Atque Amplissimi Senatus Gedanensis, Cum Viro Nobilissimo, Excellentissimo et Consultissimo Dn. Joh. Godofredo à Diesseldorf Gedanensi, J. U. D. Caesarei Palatini Comiti, Atque In Academia Lipsiensi Antea Concilii Perpetui Assessori, Nunc In Patria Jurium Et Historiarum Pro-*

fessio Publica Et Ordinaria, Atque Athenaei Inspectio, Solenni Ritu Committeretur, Ad Inaugurationis Actum A. C. M DC XCVII. D. XII. Decembris Celebrandum, Liberalium Artium Et Studiorum Patronos, Fautores, Cultores Et Aestimatores, Submisse, Reverenter, Officiose Et Peramanter Invitat; Studiosum Vero Coetum Paterne Convocat, Athenaei Rector, – –, S. Theol. D. Et Prof. Publ. Itemque Ecclesiae Ad SS. Trinit. Pastor, Gdańsk: Stoll, 1697.

Schultz, Johannes, *Disputatio solennis Juridica, De Civilitate Proficua, quam* [...] *praeside* [...] *Samuele Strykio* [...] *Pro Summis In Utroque Jure Honoribus* [...] *submittit – –*, Frankfurt an der Oder: Coepselius, 1685.

Schultz, Johannes, *Harmonia Struvio-Grotio-Strobeliana, Sive* [...] *Joachimi Schnobelii* [...] *Dissertationes XXV. ad Pandectas Perpetuis ad Syntagma Juris Civilis* [...] *Georg. Adam. Struvii, Remissionibus, quae commentarii vice esse poterant, atque indice locupletissimo auctae, Publicae luci iterataeque ventilationi in Alma Salanâ expositae à* [...] *Adriano Beier* [...] *& Nuper in Athenaeo Gedanensi repetitae atque Observationibus Grotianis Parallelis auctae â – –*, Gdańsk: Rhete, 1693.

Schultz, Johannes, *Disputationis De Polonia Nunquam Tributaria, Sectio V. Quam* [...] *Praeside* [...] *Johanne Schultzio* [...] *submittit* [...] *Daniel Schrader*, Gdańsk: Rhete, 1693.

Schultz, Johannes, *Tractatus historico-politicus de Polonia nunquam tributaria*, Gdańsk: Rhete, 1694.

Strigel, Victorinus, *In Epitomen Philosophiae Moralis Philippi Melanchthonis. Hypomnēmata – –: Excepta de ore ipsius in praelectionibus publicis: Quibus in Academia Lipsensi ante annos quindecim, ratione docendi ad captum iuventutis scholasticae accomodata, illustravit initia doctrinae Ethicae*, Neustadt an der Haardt: Matthaeus Harnisch, 1590.

Struve, Georg Adam, *Juris-Prudenz oder Verfassung der Landüblichen Rechte*, Merseburg: Gottschick / Forberger, 1689.

Stryk, Johann Samuel, *Disputatio iuris publici, De Philosophia Principum, quam* [...] *Praeside* [...] *Johanne Schultzen, J. U. D. Ejusdemque & Historiarum vocato Professore & Inspectore Athenaei Gedanensis,* [...] *exhibet – –*, Frankfurt an der Oder: Coepselius, 1688.

Typus Lectionum et operarum publicarum et privatarum adiuvante Deo in Gymnasio Thorunensi pertractandarum auctoritate nobiliss. et ampliss. scholarcharum publicatus anno 1736, Toruń: Johann Nicolai, 1736.

Secondary Sources

Abs, Hugo, *Die Matrikel des Gymnasiums zu Elbing (1598–1786)*, Gdańsk: Danziger Verlags-Gesellschaft, 1936–1940.

Behme, Thomas, 'Gegensätzliche Einflüsse in Pufendorfs Naturrecht,' in *Samuel Pufendorf und die europäische Frühaufklärung. Werk und Einfluß eines deutschen Bürgers der Gelehrtenrepublik nach 300 Jahren (1694–1994)*, ed. Fiammetta Palladini and Gerald Hartung, 74–82, Berlin: Akademie Verlag, 1996.

Denzer, Horst, *Moralphilosophie und Naturrecht bei Samuel Pufendorf: eine geistes- und wissenschaftsgeschichtliche Untersuchung zur Geburt des Naturrechts aus der praktischen Philosophie*, Goldbach: Keip, 1996.

Finnis, John, 'Natural Law Theories,' *The Stanford Encyclopedia of Philosophy* (Summer 2020 Edition), Edward N. Zalta (ed.), URL = ⟨https://plato.stanford.edu/archives/sum2020/entries/natural-law-theories/⟩ (1.9.2021).

[Friedrich, Karin and Barbara M. Pendzich,] 'Preface,' in *Citizenship and Identity in a Multinational Commonwealth. Poland–Lithuania in Context, 1550–1772*, ed. Karin Friedrich and Barbara M. Pendzich, xv–xix, Leiden and Boston: Brill, 2008.

Friedrich, Karin, *The Other Prussia. Royal Prussia, Poland and Liberty, 1569–1772*, Cambridge: Cambridge University Press, 2000.

Friedrich, Karin, 'Poland–Lithuania,' in *European political thought 1450–1700. Religion, law and philosophy*, ed. Howell A. Lloyd, Glenn Burgess, and Simon Hodson, 208–242, New Haven and London: Yale University Press, 2008.

Garber, Klaus, 'Gymnasien als Agenturen literarischer und kultureller Innovation in der Frühen Neuzeit,' in *Das Akademische Gymnasium zu Hamburg (gegr. 1613) im Kontext frühneuzeitlicher Wissenschafts- und Bildungesgeschichte*, ed. Johann Anselm Steiger, Martin Mulsow, and Axel E. Walter, 21–44, Berlin and Boston: De Gruyter, 2017.

'Georg Peter Schultz,' *Preußische Lieferung alter und neuer Urkunden, Erörterungen und Abhandlungen, zur Erläuterung der Preußischen Geschichte für allerley Leser*, 1 (1753–55/3): 365–371.

Grunert, Frank, 'Naturrecht *nach* Grotius – Vor allem mit Blick auf Thomasius,' in *"Vernunft, du weißt allein, was meine Pflichten sind!" Naturrechtslehre in Halle. Katalog zur Ausstellung im Interdisziplinären Zentrum für die Erforschung der Europäischen Aufklärung, Halle (Saale), 10. Oktober 2013 bis 6. Januar 2014*, ed. Dominik Recknagel and Sabine Wöller, 21–33, Halle [Saale]: Mitteldeutscher Verlag, 2013.

Grunert, Frank, Haakonssen, Knud, and Klippel, Diethelm, 'Natural Law 1625–1850. An International Research Network,' in *Aufklärung. Interdisziplinäres Jahrbuch zur Erforschung des 18. Jahrhunderts und seiner Wirkungsgeschichte*, ed. Martin Mulsow, Gideon Stiening, and Friedrich Vollhardt. Vol. 30, 267–276, Hamburg: Meiner, 2018.

Hammerstein, Notker, 'Die Naturrechtslehre an den deutschen, insbesondere den preußischen Universitäten,' in *Reformabsolutismus und ständische Gesellschaft. Zweihundert Jahre Preußisches Allgemeines Landrecht*, ed. Günter Birtsch and Dietmar Willoweit, 3–19, Berlin: Duncker und Humblot, 1998.

Hunter, Ian, *Rival Enlightenments: Civil and Metaphysical Philosophy in Early Modern Germany*, Cambridge: Cambridge University Press, 2001.

Hunter, Ian, 'Die Geschichte der Philosophie und die Persona des Philosophen. Transl. Sarah Erdmann and Sabrina Kessler,' in *Die Cambridge School der politischen Ideengeschichte*, ed. Martin Mulsow and Andreas Mahler, 241–283, Berlin: Suhrkamp, 2010.

Kodzik, Joanna, 'Aus der Mentalitätsgeschichte des Thorner Akademischen Gymnasiums von den Anfängen bis zu den Teilungen Polens,' in *Das Akademische Gymnasium zu Hamburg (gegr. 1613) im Kontext frühneuzeitlicher Wissenschafts- und Bildungesgeschichte*, ed. Johann Anselm Steiger, Martin Mulsow, and Axel E. Walter, 455–475, Berlin and Boston: De Gruyter, 2017.

Komorowski, Manfred, 'Das akademishe Schrifttum Altpreußens: Königsberg, Danzig, Elbing und Thorn,' in *Kulturgeschichte Preußens königlich polnischen Anteils in der Frühen Neuzeit*, ed. Sabine Beckmann and Klaus Garber, 411–431, Tübingen: Niemeyer, 2005.

Kotarski, Edmund, ed., *Gdańskie Gimnazjum Akademickie*, 5 vols, Gdańsk: Wydawnictwo Uniwersytetu Gdańskiego, 2008.

Maciejewski, Tadeusz, 'Prawo i jego nauczanie w Gdańskim Gimnazjum Akademickim od XVI do XIX wieku (1558–1810),' *Czasopismo Prawno-Historyczne* 67 (2015/2): 111–126.

Mokrzecki, Lech, 'Protestant Grammar Schools of Royal Prussia in the Polish School System in the 16th and 17th Centuries,' in *Kulturgeschichte Preußens königlich polnischen Anteils in der Frühen Neuzeit*, ed. Sabine Beckmann and Klaus Garber, 359–369, Tübingen: Niemeyer, 2005.

Nellen, H.J.M., *Hugo Grotius: A Lifelong Struggle for Peace in Church and State, 1583–1645*. Transl. from the Dutch by J.C. Grayson, Leiden: Brill, 2015.

[Nowak, Zenon Hubert and Janusz Tandecki], 'Einleitung,' in *Metryka uczniów Toruńskiego Gimnazjum Akademickiego 1600–1807*. Part I: 1600–1717, ed. Zenon Hubert Nowak and Janusz Tandecki, xvii–xxvii, Toruń: Towarzystwo Naukowe w Toruniu, 1997.

Ochmann, Stefania, 'Rzeczpospolita jako "monarchia mixta" dylematy władzy i wolności,' in *Kultura – polityka – dyplomacja. Studia ofiarowane Profesorowi Jaremie Maciszewskiemu w sześćdziesiątą rocznicę jego urodzin*, ed. Andrzej Bartnicki et al., 264–278, Warszawa: PWN, 1990.

Ogonowski, Zbigniew, ed., *Filozofia i myśl społeczna XVII wieku*. Part 1, Warszawa: PWN, 1979.

Pawlak, Marian, *Dzieje gimnazjum elbląskiego w latach 1535–1772*, Olsztyn: Pojezierze, 1972.

Pawlak, Marian, 'Elbląskie gimnazjum akademickie – jego dzieje i wychowankowie w historii miasta i regionu,' in *Tradycje akademickie Elbląga – dawniej i dziś*, ed. Józef Borzyszkowski, 17–32, Elbląg: Elbląska Uczelnia Humanistyczno-Ekonomiczna, 2006.

Pawlak, Marian, 'Die Geschichte des Elbinger Gymnasiums in den Jahren 1535–1772. Transl. Joanna Braksiek,' in *Kulturgeschichte Preußens königlich polnischen Anteils in der Frühen Neuzeit*, ed. Sabine Beckmann and Klaus Garber, 371–394, Tübingen: Niemeyer, 2005.

Pawlak, Marian, 'Młodzież elbląska w Toruńskim Gimnazjum Akademickim w XVI–XVIII wieku,' in *Księga pamiątkowa 400-lecia toruńskiego gimnazjum akademickiego*, ed. Zbigniew Zdrójkowski, vol. 1, 207–224, Toruń: s.d., 1972.

Pawlak, Marian, 'Nauczyciele Gimnazjum Elblaskiego w latach 1535–1772. Part I–II,' *Rocznik Elbląski* 5 (1972): 139–158; 6 (1973): 127–177.

Recknagel, Dominik, 'Naturrecht in der Lehre. Naturrechtliche Vorlesungen an der Friedrichs-Universität zu Halle bis zum Jahr 1850,' in *"Vernunft, du weißt allein, was meine Pflichten sind!" Naturrechtslehre in Halle. Katalog zur Ausstellung im Interdisziplinären Zentrum für die Erforschung der Europäischen Aufklärung, Halle (Saale), 10. Oktober 2013 bis 6. Januar 2014*, ed. Dominik Recknagel and Sabine Wöller, 9–19, Halle [Saale]: Mitteldeutscher Verlag, 2013.

Salmonowicz, Stanisław, 'Nauczanie filozofii w Toruńskim Gimnazjum Akademickim,' in *Nauczanie filozofii w Polsce w XV–XVIII wieku*, ed. Lech Szczucki, 137–197, Wrocław: Zakład Narodowy im. Ossolińskich, 1987.

Salmonowicz, Stanisław, 'Nauczanie prawa i polityki w Toruńskim Gimnazjum Akademickim od XVI do XVIII w.,' *Czasopismo Prawno-Historyczne* 23 (1971/2): 53–86.

Salmonowicz, Stanisław, 'Das protestantische Gymnasium Academicum in Thorn im 17. und 18. Jahrhundert,' in *Kulturgeschichte Preußens königlich polnischen Anteils in der Frühen Neuzeit*, ed. Sabine Beckmann and Klaus Garber, 395–409, Tübingen: Niemeyer, 2005.

Salmonowicz, Stanisław, 'Die protestantischen Akademischen Gymnasien in Thorn, Elbing und Danzig und ihre Bedeutung für die regionale Identität im Königlichen Preußen (16.–18. Jahrhundert),' *Nordost-Archiv* 6 (1997/2): 515–540.

Salmonowicz, Stanisław, 'Das Thorner protestantische Gymnasium Academicum 1658–1793,' *Beiträge zur Geschichte Westpreußens* 14 (1996): 41–54.

Salmonowicz, Stanisław, *Toruńskie gimnazjum akademickie w latach 1681–1817*, Poznań: Państwowe Wydawnictwo Naukowe, 1973.

Sekulski, Jerzy, 'Księgozbiór biblioteki gimnazjum elbląskiego w XVIII wieku,' *Komunikaty Mazursko-Warmińskie* 3 (1982): 187–199.

Sekulski, Jerzy, *Książka w Elblągu do roku 1772*, Gdańsk: Wydawnictwo Morskie, 1990.

Skrey, Fritz, *Aus der Geschichte des Elbinger Gymnasiums 1535–1935*, Elbing: Wernich, 1935.

Thomasius, Christian, 'Vorrede an die Herren Zuhörer gerichtet,' in Christian Thomasius, *Drey Bücher der Göttlichen Rechtsgelahrheit*, 1–57, Halle [Saale]: Renger, 1709.

Tync, Stanisław, *Dzieje gimnazjum toruńskiego*, vols 1–2, Toruń: Nakład Towarzystwa Naukowego, 1928–1949.

Waschinski, Emil, 'Das Thorner Stadt- und Landschulwesen vom Beginn der Reformation bis zum Ende der polnischen Herrschaft,' *Zeitschrift des Westpreußischen Geschichtsvereins* 56 (1916): 1–137.

Weinrib, Ernest J., 'Private law and public right,' *University of Toronto Law Journal* 61 (2011): 191–211.

PART 2

The Austrian Empire

CHAPTER 5

Natural Law in Austrian and Hungarian Science of Public Law in the Second Half of the Eighteenth Century: A Comparison

Martin P. Schennach

1 Introduction

'The Austrian states' – you will notice the plural – 'are remarkable in every regard. There is no other European state whose constitution consists of so many anomalies.'[1] These are the words Josef Marx von Liechtenstern uses to introduce his work on Austrian public law published in 1791. Liechtenstern's book reflects a growing interest of legal scholars in the constitutional law of the Habsburg monarchy in the second half of the eighteenth century which resulted in a considerable number of publications.[2] However, the preoccupation with Austrian public law was a challenge at that time: After all, there

1 Joseph Marx von Liechtenstern, *Staatsverfassung der Oesterreichischen Monarchie im Grundrisse* (Vienna: Kleinmayer, 1791), 5.

2 Cf. for instance Christian August Beck, *Specimen I. juris publici Austriaci, ex ipsis legibus, actisque publicis eruti, quod sub sacratissimis auspiciis sacrae caesareae Regiaeque majestatis in collegio regio Theresiano nobilium societatis Jesu* [...] (Vienna: Trattner, 1750); Christian August Beck, *Specimen II. juris publici Austriaci, ex ipsis legibus actisque publicis eruti quod in collegio regio Theresiano nobilium S. J. propugnavit Nicolaus S. R. I. Liber Baro a Wallhorn* (Vienna: Trattner, 1752); Franz Ferdinand von Schrötter, *Abhandlungen aus dem österreichischen Staatsrechte*, vol. 1: *Erste Abhandlung aus dem österreichischen Staatsrechte, von den Freyheitsbriefen des Durchläuchtigsten Erzhauses von Oesterreich, samt einer Einleitung in die österr. Geschichte und einem Anhange Beylagen*; vol. 2: *Zweyte Abhandlung aus dem Oesterreichischen Staatsrechte von den Titeln und Reichserzämtern des Durchläuchtigsten Erzhauses von Oesterreich. Mit einem Anhange von Urkunden versehen*; vol. 3: *Dritte Abhandlung aus dem Oesterreichischen Staatsrechte. Von den Erbhuldigungen und Kleynodien der Erzherzoge von Oesterreich. Mit einem Anhange Beylagen versehen*; vol. 4: *Vierte Abhandlung aus dem österreichischen Staatsrechten, von den vorzüglichen Rechten, welche den Durchläuchtigsten Erzherzogen mit und neben der Landeshoheit gebühren*; vol. 5: *Fünfte Abhandlung aus dem österreichischen Staatsrechte, von der Erbfolgs-Ordnung wie auch der Vormundschaft der Durchlauchtigsten Erzherzoge. Mit Urkunden* (Vienna: Kraus, 1762–1766); Franz Ferdinand von Schrötter, *Grundriß des österreichischen Staatsrechtes* (Vienna: Kurzböck, 1775); Klemens, *Grundriß der Staatsrechte der Habsburgisch-Oesterreich-Lotharingischen Erbmonarchie* (Vienna: Sonnleithner, 1782); Ignaz de Luca, *Vorlesungen über die Oestreichische Staatsverfassung*, vol. 1 [the only volume] (Vienna, 1792); Anton Wilhelm Gustermann, *Ver-*

 | DOI:10.1163/9789004545847_006

was no homogenous, let alone Austrian state: Around 1750, the Austrian monarchy was a 'composite' state, a 'monarchical union of estates-states,'[3] each individual country of the Habsburg reign having its own law, its own estates and 'constitution,' unified above all by the dynasty, the Austrian army and central authorities.[4] Only the reforms realised in the second half of the eighteenth century led to the emergence of an Austrian state; the unification of the Austrian composite state was not yet finished at the beginning of the nineteenth century. Even the adoption of the purely dynastic title 'Emperor of Austria' in 1804 left, as the proclamation bill pointed out, the 'constitutions and conditions in the independent states' unchanged.[5]

2 Austrian and Hungarian *Staatsrechtslehre*

Legal science supported and legitimised this process of integration. In fact, the Austrian science of public law, the Austrian *Staatsrechtslehre* flourished during this period and was, at least until the end of the eighteenth century, supported by the monarch and central authorities.[6] The Austrian *Staatsrechtslehre* developed in a specific scientific environment. The *Staatsrechtslehre* – the

such eines vollständigen österreichischen Staatsrechtes. Erster Theil [only volume] (Vienna: Wappler, 1793); Josef Kropatschek, *Oestreichs Staatsverfassung, vereinbart mit den zusammengezogenen bestehenden Gesetzen, zum Gebrauche der Staatsbeamten, Advokaten, Oekonomen, Obrigkeiten, Magistraten, Geistlichen, Bürger und Bauern, zum Unterrichte, für angehende Geschäfftsmänner*, 10 volumes and 2 supplementary volumes (Vienna: Mößle, 1794–1810).

3 '[M]onarchische Union von Ständestaaten:' cf. Otto Brunner, *Land und Herrschaft. Grundfragen der territorialen Verfassungsgeschichte Österreichs im Mittelalter*, 5th ed. (Vienna: Rohrer, 1965), 447.

4 Cf. Karin Schneider, 'Zwischen "Monarchischer Union von Ständestaaten" und Gesamtstaat. Die Habsburgermonarchie im 18. und 19. Jahrhundert,' in *Rechtshistorische Aspekte des österreichischen Föderalismus. Beiträge zur Tagung an der Universität Innsbruck am 28. und 29. November 2013*, ed. Martin P. Schennach (Vienna: Verlag Österreich, 2015), 34–49 (with many further literature suggestions).

5 Cf. Schneider, 'Zwischen "Monarchischer Union von Ständestaaten,"' 37–38; Wilhelm Brauneder, 'Kaiserwürde durch Verwaltungsakt: Der österreichische Kaisertitel von 1804,' in *Wahl und Krönung in Zeiten des Umbruchs*, ed. Ludolf Pelizaeus (Frankfurt: Lang, 2008), 207–220.

6 Cf. Martin P. Schennach, *Austria inventa? Zur Entstehung der österreichischen Staatsrechtslehre* (Frankfurt: Klostermann, 2020). An English summary can be found in Martin P. Schennach, '"There is no other European state whose constitution consists of so many anomalies." The Austrian Doctrine of Public Law in the Second Half of the 18th Century,' *Rechtsgeschichte – Legal History* 28 (2020): 95–118.

German term 'Staatsrecht' was only introduced at around 1750 – dealt with the constitutional basis of a state, but was not a homogenous academic discipline.[7] The *Allgemeine Staatslehre* (*ius publicum generale*), the natural-law branch of the *ius publicum*, presented the formation, the essence and the purpose of states, of state power and the relations between ruler and subjects in a general way, whereas the *Besonderes Staatsrecht* (*ius publicum speciale* or *particulare*) treated the positive public law of an individual state. With regard to the Holy Roman Empire, the *Besonderes Staatsrecht* dealt with the public law of the Holy Roman Empire itself, and this discipline, which had emerged at the beginning of the seventeenth century, was called *Reichspublizistik*. Under the umbrella of the *Reichspublizistik*, legal science started in the first decades of the eighteenth century to work on the public law of individual territories of the Holy Roman Empire.[8] The theoretical foundation of this *Territorialstaatsrecht* (*ius publicum specialissimum* or *particularissimum*) was created by Johann Jacob Moser,[9] and the Austrian *Staatsrechtslehre* was one of these *Territorialstaatsrechte*.

With regard to methods, sources of law, issues and contents, there was a strong similarity between *Reichspublizistik* and *Territorialstaatsrecht*; the latter was in fact a derivative of the *Reichspublizistik*. Whereas a large number of legal scholars were preoccupied with the public law of the Holy Roman Empire, they were reluctant to deal with the *ius publicum* of the territories, and only about two dozen of the territories were worked on by the end of the Holy Roman Empire in 1806. Contemporaries explained this phenomenon by referring to the resistance of the princely rulers who seemed to fear that as a consequence of the scientific presentation of the *Territorialstaatsrecht*, their actions could be examined and possibly found unconstitutional by the

7 Cf. the standard work of Michael Stolleis, *Geschichte des öffentlichen Rechts in Deutschland*, vol. 1: *Reichspublizistik und Policeywissenschaft 1600–1800* (Munich: C.H. Beck, 1988).

8 For a survey in English cf. Michael Stolleis, *Public Law in Germany. A Historical Introduction from the 16th to the 21st Century* (Oxford: Oxford University Press, 2017), 27–44.

9 Cf. Johann Jacob Moser, *Praecognita juris publici germanici generalissima. Oder Tractat Von der Lehre der heutigen Staats-Verfassung von Teutschland überhaupt Nemlich Von deren Natur, Nothwendigkeit, Nuzen* [!], *der Befügnus, solche zu lehren, und wie ferne? Deren gegenwärtigem Zustand, der besten Art, diese Staats-Verfassung zu erlernen, und denen im Druck vorhandenen theils besten, theils neuesten, sowohl vollständigern als kurtzen Einleitungen darzu entworffen* (Frankfurt/Leipzig: Stein, 1732); Johann Jacob Moser, *Allgemeine Einleitung in die Lehre des besonderen Staats-Rechts aller einzelen* [!] *Stände des Heil. Röm. Reichs, und in Sein von diesem Staats-Recht handlendes Werck* (Frankfurt/Leipzig, 1739); Dietmar Willoweit, 'Landesstaatsrecht als Herrschaftsverfassung des 18. Jahrhunderts,' *Rechtsgeschichte – Legal History* 19 (2011): 333–353, here 341; Stolleis, *Geschichte des öffentlichen Rechts*, 263.

public.[10] This was not true for the Austrian *Staatsrechtslehre*. As already mentioned, the discipline was promoted by the dynasty and central authorities, so that the Austrian public law was, among all *Territorialstaatsrechten*, the one that was by far the most intensely worked on by legal science, although the subject was especially difficult due to the character as a composite monarchy. Austrian legal scholars did not disappoint the high expectations. Three main subjects can be identified in almost all publications: the legitimation of absolutism and of the process of integration of the former 'monarchical union' as well as, closely linked to these topics, the dogmatic and discursive construction of an Austrian state.[11]

So far, I have mentioned only the Austrian and not the Hungarian *Staatsrechtslehre*. In fact, the relation between the Austrian and the Hungarian *Staatsrechtslehre* is quite complicated. Just like the Austrian hereditary lands – that is, the parts of the Habsburg monarchy belonging to the Holy Roman Empire – the Kingdom of Hungary as well as its *partes annexae*, the Principality of Transylvania and the Kingdom of Croatia, were ruled by the Habsburg dynasty and therefore part of the Austrian monarchy. From such a perspective, the Hungarian *Staatsrechtslehre* was only an element of the Austrian *Staatsrechtslehre*, and this perspective was adopted by most German speaking legal scholars. This attitude reveals the ambiguity of the concept of 'Austria' in the eighteenth century.[12] The concept of 'Austria' could not only refer to the individual countries Upper and Lower Austria, but could also be used as a collective term: be it for the totality of the Habsburg monarchy including Hungary, or be it for the Austrian hereditary lands only (and therefore excluding Hungary). Almost all German-speaking scholars chose the first option and included Hungary in their work; some of them, such as Christian August Beck or Anton Wilhelm Gustermann, even published separate monographs on Hungarian public law.[13]

---

10 Dietmar Willoweit, 'Das Staatsrecht Kreittmayrs,' in *Wiguläus Xaver Aloys Freiherr von Kreittmayr 1705–1790. Ein Leben für Recht, Staat und Politik. Festschrift zum 200. Todestag*, ed. Richard Bauer and Hans Schlosser (Munich: C.H. Beck, 1991), 101–117; Willoweit, 'Landesstaatsrecht.'

11 Cf. Schennach, *Austria inventa?*, 25–82.

12 Cf. Grete Walter-Klingenstein, 'Was bedeuten "Österreich" und "österreichisch" im 18. Jahrhundert? Eine begriffsgeschichtliche Studie,' in *Was heißt Österreich? Inhalt und Umfang des Österreichbegriffs vom 10. Jahrhundert bis heute*, ed. Richard G. Plaschka, Gerald Stourzh, and Jan Paul Niederkorn (Vienna: Verl. d. Österr. Akad. d. Wissenschaften, 1995), 149–220; Schennach, *Austria inventa?*, 268–276 and 313–324.

13 Beck's work *Specimen II. juris publici Austriaci* was reprinted with another title and additional notes in 1790, cf. Christian August Beck, *Jus publicum Hungariae. Cum notis autoris*

However, including Hungary did not necessarily mean that they dealt with Hungarian public law in an exhaustive way. Mostly, the authors focused on the public law of the Austrian hereditary lands and only mentioned the circumstances in Hungary in a comparative or in a complementary way. Hungarian writers adopted a completely different point of view and generally focussed exclusively on Hungarian public law without taking into account other territories ruled by the Habsburgs.[14] Languages of publication were nevertheless Latin and German; the first works written in Hungarian and dealing (among other subjects) with Hungarian public law were published only at the end of the eighteenth century and then not by legal scholars.[15] This is due to the fact that Latin was the official language in the kingdom of Hungary until 1848 and many of the Hungarian authors were German-speaking (originating for instance from the German minority in Transylvania or in Upper Hungary (that is, today's Slovakia). Furthermore, German publications could address a far broader public and were hence more interesting from a financial point of view.

As Hungary was definitely not part of the Holy Roman Empire, the Hungarian *Staatsrechtslehre* cannot be considered as a *Territorialstaatsrecht*. Nevertheless, the science of Hungarian public law was strongly linked to the *Reichspublizistik* and to the Austrian *Staatsrechtslehre*.[16] Despite the close and

---

et observationibus Josephi Benzur (Vienna: Kraus, 1790); Anton Wilhelm Gustermann, *Ungerisches Staatsrecht*, vol. 1 [it remained the only volume] (Vienna: Doll, 1818); Anton Wilhelm Gustermann, *Die Ausbildung der Verfassung des Königreiches Ungern; aus der Geschichte, und den Gesezen dieses Reiches dargestellet*, 2 volumes (Vienna: Doll, 1811).

14 Cf. Adam Frantisek Kollár, *Historiae iurisque publici regni Ungariae amoenitates*, 2 volumes (Vienna, 1783); Ignaz Stephan Horváth, *Institutionum juris publici particularis regni Hungariae. Pars I: De Territorio Regni Hungariae* (Bratislava: Weber, 1786); Franz Rudolf von Großing, *Ungarisches allgemeines Staats- und Regiments-Recht* (s.l., 1786); József Petrovics, *Introductio in ius publicum regni Hungariae* (Vienna: Kraus, 1790); Stephan Rosenmann [= József Ürményi and György Zsigmond Lakits], *Jus publicum Regni Hungariae ex combinatione veterum, recentiorumque legum, in compendium sistematicum redactum, et usibus maxime scholasticae juventutis adcommodatum* (Vienna: Baumeister, 1791) (one year later published in a German translation); Martin von Schwartner, *Statistik des Königreichs Ungern. Ein Versuch, Zweyter u. Dritter Theil* (Pest: Trattner, 1798); Michael Horváth, *Statistica Regni Hungariae, et partium eidem adnexarum*, 2nd ed. (Bratislava: Landerer, 1802). On the doctrine of Hungarian public law, see Schennach, *Austria inventa?*, 418–457.

15 Katalin Gönczi, *Die europäischen Fundamente der ungarischen Rechtskultur. Juristischer Wissenstransfer und nationale Rechtswissenschaft in Ungarn zur Zeit der Aufklärung und im Vormärz* (Frankfurt: Klostermann, 2008), 123–127; Schennach, *Austria inventa?*, 435–436.

16 Cf. Schennach, *Austria inventa?*, 418–423.

evident connection to the Austrian *Staatsrechtslehre*, this fact seems curious with regard to the *Reichspublizistik*. One further reason is probably the phenomenon of the *peregrinatio Hungarica*: There was only one university in the Kingdom of Hungary – the University of Trnava had been founded in 1635 and was transferred to Buda in 1777 and in 1784 to Pest;[17] five Royal Academies offered only two-year courses of law and were not allowed to award an academic title.[18] Thus, many Hungarians went to universities in the Holy Roman Empire: not only to universities in the Austrian hereditary lands such as Vienna or Prague, but also to universities in Protestant territories such as Göttingen or Halle whose faculties of law were very distinguished and hotspots of the *Reichspublizistik*. Some went even further afield, to the Dutch Republic.[19] When coming back to Hungary, these students of course applied the methods they had learnt on the study of Hungarian public law. Katalin Gönczi, who has done research on Hungarian students at the Viennese faculty of law, even speaks of a common Austro-Hungarian scientific community during the eighteenth century.[20]

To sum up, in legal sources, methods and issues, there are evident similarities, but also some remarkable differences between Austrian and Hungarian public law. What sources were used by legal scholars, and, in particular, what role did natural law play in this context?

---

17 Márta Fata and Anton Schindling, 'Peregrinatio Hungarica. Studenten aus Ungarn an deutschen und österreichischen Hochschulen vom 16. bis zum 20. Jahrhundert,' in *Peregrinatio Hungarica. Studenten aus Ungarn an deutschen und österreichischen Hochschulen vom 16. bis zum 20. Jahrhundert*, ed. Márta Fata, Gyula Kurucz, and Anton Schindling (Stuttgart: Steiner, 2006), 5 and 26; Gönczi, *Die europäischen Fundamente*, 21–24, 28 and 36; Matthias Asche, 'Studenten aus Ungarn und Siebenbürgen an katholischen Universitäten des Heiligen Römischen Reiches deutscher Nation im 18. Jahrhundert, in *Peregrinatio Hungarica. Studenten aus Ungarn an deutschen und österreichischen Hochschulen vom 16. bis zum 20. Jahrhundert*, ed. Márta Fata, Gyula Kurucz, and Anton Schindling (Stuttgart: Steiner, 2006), 137; Barna Mezey, 'Universitäten und Rechtsakademien (Anfänge und Entwicklungstendenzen der juristischen Ausbildung in Ungarn),' in *Die ungarische Universitätsbildung und Europa*, ed. Márta Font and László Szögi (Pécs: University, 2001), 192–193; Béla P. Szabó, 'Wissenschaftsgeschichtlicher Überblick,' in *Die Entwicklung der Verfassung und des Rechts in Ungarn*, ed. Gábor Máthé (Budapest: Dialóg Campus, 2017), 374.

18 Gönczi, *Die europäischen Fundamente*, 31–33; András Jakab, 'Wissenschaft vom Verfassungsrecht: Ungarn,' in *Handbuch Ius Publicum Europaeum, vol. 2: Offene Staatlichkeit – Wissenschaft vom Verfassungsrecht*, ed. Armin von Bogdandy, Villalón Cruz, and Peter M. Huber (Heidelberg: C.F. Müller, 2008), 778–779.

19 See the paper by Péter Balázs and Gábor Gángó in this volume.

20 Gönczi, *Die europäischen Fundamente*, 40–41.

3 *Leges fundamentales* and Customary Law ('Herkommen')

In accordance with *Reichspublizistik*, the positive sources of Austrian and Hungarian public law were written sources and customary law (the so-called *Herkommen*, which was to be extracted by a specific historical method widely applied by legal scholars).[21] The written sources were commonly called *leges fundamentales*, or in German *Grundgesetze*, that included a large number of different types of documents: not only laws in a narrower sense, enacted by a princely legislator, but also international treaties, contracts, privileges and dynastic regulations and the decisions of a Diet (*Landtagsabschiede*). *Leges fundamentales* laid down, at least partly, the legal basis of a territory (or, with regard to the *leges fundamentales imperii*, of the Holy Roman Empire) and often implied the limitation of princely power, for instance by fixing the rights and privileges of the Diet.[22] However, the Austrian scholars did not stress this particular function of the *leges fundamentales*; on the contrary, they highlighted an extensive monarchical power and marginalised or omitted all factors that could lead to a restriction of princely power. They focused, among others, on the *Privilegium maius* as a fundamental law of the entire Habsburg monarchy, which was used to define the legal status of the Habsburg ruler as absolute and not subject to any limitations.[23] Thus, Austrian legal scholars

21 Cf. e.g. Notker Hammerstein, *Jus und Historie. Ein Beitrag zur Geschichte des politischen Denkens an deutschen Universitäten im späten 17. und 18. Jahrhundert* (Göttingen: Vandenhoeck & Ruprecht, 1972), 225; Notker Hammerstein, 'Jus publicum Romano-Germanicum,' in *Diritto e potere nella storia Europea. Atti in onore di Bruno Paradisi; Quarto Congresso internazionale della Soc. Italiana di Storia del Diretto* (Florence: Olschki, 1982), 744; Michael Stolleis, 'Johann Jacob Moser (1701–1785), oder: der Erzpublizist des Alten Reichs,' in *Johann Jacob Moser. Politiker, Pietist, Publizist*, ed. Andreas Gestrich and Rainer Lächele (Karlsruhe: Braun-Verlag, 2002), 63.

22 Cf. Heinz Mohnhaupt, 'Von den "leges fundamentales" zur modernen Verfassung in Europa. Zum begriffs- und dogmengeschichtlichen Befund (16.-18. Jahrhundert),' *Ius Commune* 25 (1998): 121–159 (reprint 2000); Heinz Mohnhaupt and Dieter Grimm, *Verfassung. Zur Geschichte des Begriffs von der Antike bis zur Gegenwart. Zwei Studien*, 2nd ed. (Berlin: Duncker & Humblot, 2002), 62–66; Dieter Wyduckel, *Ius Publicum. Grundlagen und Entwicklung des öffentlichen Rechts und der deutschen Staatsrechtswissenschaft* (Berlin: Duncker & Humblot, 1984), 164–168; Heinz Mohnhaupt, 'The Object of Interpretation: Legislation and Competing Normative Sources of Law in Europe during the 16th to 18th Centuries,' in *Interpretation of Law in the Age of Enlightenment. From the Rule of the King to the Rule of Law*, ed. Yasumoto Morigiwa, Michael Stolleis, and Jean-Louis Halpérin (Dordrecht et al.: Springer, 2011), 78.

23 Martin P. Schennach, 'Die "österreichische Gesamtstaatsidee." Das Verhältnis zwischen "Gesamtstaat" und Ländern als Gegenstand rechtshistorischer Forschung,' in *Rechtshistorische Aspekte des österreichischen Föderalismus. Beiträge zur Tagung an der Universität*

had no interest in the power-limiting function of the *leges fundamentales* of individual countries. As the creation of a uniform authority across the entire Habsburg territories was a goal of vital interest not only for Habsburg reforms during the eighteenth century, but also for the Austrian *Staatsrechtslehre*, the 'rights and freedoms' of the estates of individual countries, such as Tyrol or Styria, were consequently ignored. Normally, they are not even mentioned by Austrian authors.[24] If they do so nevertheless, these *leges fundamentales* are not seen as contracts between rulers and estates or subjects, but as privileges granted by the ruler which could be revoked at any time.[25] Therefore the Austrian monarchy was always classified as a *monarchia illimitata* by Austrian *Staatsrechtslehre*. That is a fundamental difference to the views on Hungarian public law. Due to the political power structures in the kingdom and to the considerable rights preserved by Hungarian estates, it is impossible to consider Hungary as a *monarchia illimitata*,[26] and no author could ignore the Hungarian *leges fundamentales* restricting royal power,[27] for instance the *Bulla aurea* of King Andreas II.

With regard to unwritten sources of Hungarian and Austrian public law, the customary law or *Herkommen* was reconstructed by historical methods, which resulted in a growing interest in Austrian and Hungarian history; after all, the *Herkommen* could only be identified by historical facts, and historical knowledge, often gleaned from hundreds of age-old documents, was also vital for the interpretation of the fundamental laws.[28]

Innsbruck am 28. und 29. November 2013, ed. Martin P. Schennach (Vienna: Verlag Österreich, 2015), 20–23; Schennach, *Austria inventa?*, 292–298.

24 Cf. for instance Kropatschek, *Oestreichs Staatsverfassung*, vol. 1, 217–245, who explains the estates 'composition extensively, but does not mention their, iura et libertates'; see also Liechtenstern, *Staatsverfassung*, 254; Gustermann, *Versuch*, 132. See also Schennach, 'Die "österreichische Gesamtstaatsidee,"' 22–23; Schennach, *Austria inventa?*.

25 Cf. Schrötter, *Dritte Abhandlung*, 68–70.

26 There is only one exception: Großing, *Ungarisches allgemeines Staats- und Regiments-Recht*, 42, but the statement remains an outsider's opinion in the scientific community.

27 Cf. Schennach, 'Die "österreichische Gesamtstaatsidee,"' 21; Schennach, *Austria inventa?*, 441–452; Alexander Piff, *Mit Geschichte und Recht. Die Beschreibung von Österreich von 1775 bis 1808 im Zeichen einer eigenen Staatsrechtsposition* (Diploma Thesis, University of Innsbruck, 2014), 106–107; see for instance Ignaz de Luca, *Historisch-statistisches Lesebuch zur Kenntniß des Oestreichischen Staates. Zweyter Theil: Oestreichische Staatsverwaltungskunde* (Vienna: Rehm, 1798), 223; de Luca, *Vorlesungen*, 187.

28 Hammerstein, *Jus und Historie*; Ewald Grothe, 'Verfassungsgeschichte als Reichshistorie. Zur Vorgeschichte einer historischen und juristischen Teildisziplin im 18. Jahrhundert,' in *Gesellschaft – Region – Politik. Festschrift für Hermann de Buhr, Heinrich Küppers und Volkmar Wittmütz*, ed. Jörg Hentzschel-Fröhlings (Norderstedt: Books on Demand, 2006),

4 The Role of Natural Law as a Source of Austrian and Hungarian Public Law: General Remarks

As far as fundamental laws and customary law and their role as sources of law are concerned, Austrian and Hungarian *Staatsrechtslehre* are congruent with the *Reichspublizistik*. With regard to other sources, we can see fundamental differences between the Austrian *Staatsrechtslehre* on the one hand and, on the other, the Hungarian counterpart and the *Reichspublizistik*. When speaking of the sources of the *ius publicum imperii*, the latter distinguished between 'main sources' (including the fundamental laws and the *Herkommen*) and 'auxiliary sources.'[29] Analogy and natural law – in particular the *Allgemeines Staatsrecht* – were commonly considered as 'auxiliary sources,' though sometimes natural law or *Allgemeines Staatsrecht* were listed among the 'main sources' (which did not make a big difference, as the name did not reflect the legal status, but only the importance of each source of law).[30] The *Allgemeines Staatsrecht* (*ius publicum universale*) was rooted 'in the nature of states'[31] and

---

295–304; Wyduckel, *Ius Publicum*, 194–210; Manfred Friedrich, *Geschichte der deutschen Staatsrechtswissenschaft* (Berlin: Duncker & Humblot, 1997), 107–109 and 130; Brigitte Mazohl and Thomas Wallnig, '(Kaiser)haus – Staat – Vaterland? Zur "österreichischen" Historiographie vor der "Nationalgeschichte,"' in *Nationalgeschichte als Artefakt. Zum Paradigma "Nationalstaat" in den Historiographien Deutschlands, Italiens und Österreichs*, ed. Hans Peter Hye, Brigitte Mazohl, and Jan Paul Niederkorn (Vienna: Verl. d. Österr. Akad. d. Wissenschaften, 2009), 64.

29 For the distinction of 'main' and 'auxiliary sources' cf. for instance Johann Jacob Moser, *Kürzere Einleitung in das Teutsche Staats-Recht. Zum Gebrauch der Anfängere in diser Wissenschaft* (Frankfurt/Leipzig: Cotta, 1753), 5–15; this distinction was criticised already by contemporary scholars, see for instance Daniel Nettelbladt, 'Von dem rechten Gebrauche des allgemeinen Staatsrechtes in der teutschen Staatsrechtsgelahrtheit,' in *Erörterungen einiger einzelner Lehren des teutschen Staatsrechtes*, ed. Daniel Nettelbladt (Halle [Saale]: Rengersche Buchhandlung, 1773), 26–28.

30 Cf. Heinrich Gottlieb Francke, *Notitia subsidiorum juris publici maxime litteraria* (Leipzig, 1740), 23; Nettelbladt, 'Von dem rechten Gebrauche,' 26; Andreas Josef Schnaubert, *Anfangsgründe des Staatsrechts der gesammten Reichslande* (Jena: Akademische Buchhandlung, 1787), 11–16; Theodor Hartleben, *Dissertatio de origine, incrementis et fontibus iuris publici territoriorum Imperii Romano-Germanici communis, nec non de utilitate, illud in academiis Germanicis specialibus praelectionibus tradendi. Oratio inauguralis* (Salzburg: Mayer, 1796), 10; Johann Richard Roth, *Staatsrecht deutscher Reichslande. Akademische Vorlesungen. Nebst einem Abdrucke der neuesten kaiserlichen Wahlkapitulation und des westphälischen Friedens nach den Originalien des Reichsarchivs, Erster Theil* (Mainz: Winkopp, 1788), 8; Ernst Christian Westphal, *Das teutsche Staatsrecht* (Leipzig: Weygand, 1784), 72.

31 Klemens, *Grundriß*, 63 (transl. by Martin P. Schennach).

was considered of universal validity for all states of the world.[32] For example, Ludwig Höpfner defines *Allgemeines Staatsrecht* as:

> a part of natural law; a science dealing with rights and duties recognised by the use of reason and deriving from the nature of the civil constitution. That is why it is also called the philosophical or rational *Staatsrecht*. The rules presented by the *Allgemeines Staatsrecht* are common to all states and form the basis for the rules of each individual state.[33]

As already mentioned, the *Allgemeines Staatsrecht* dealt with the nature of states as such, their formation and purpose, with legislative, executive and judiciary power, with the rights and duties of rulers and subjects. Therefore, the development of the idea of fundamental and human rights took place within the *Allgemeines Staatsrecht*, and they were conceived as individual spheres of liberty protected from interference by the state and as relics of the former 'natural freedom' which all men had possessed before the conclusion of the social contract.[34]

---

32 Cf. Justus Henning Böhmer, *Introductio in ius publicum universale, ex genuinis iuris naturae principiis deductum, et in usum iuris publici particularis quarumcunque rerumpublicarum adornatum, adiecto indice duplici* (Halle [Saale]: Orphanotropheum, 1710), 90; Johann Salomo Brunnquell, *Eröffnete Gedancken / Von dem Allgemeinen Staats-Rechte, Und dessen Höchst-nützlichen Excolirung* (Jena: Fickelscherr, 1721), 10: 'weil es [das Allgemeine Staatsrecht] als ein Theil des natürlichen Rechts alle Staaten in der Welt ohne Unterscheid verbindet.'

33 Ludwig Julius Friedrich Höpfner, ed., *Deutsche Encyclopädie oder Allgemeines Real-Wörterbuch aller Künste und Wissenschaften* (Frankfurt: Varrentrapp und Wenner, 1778), 364 (transl. by Martin P. Schennach).

34 Cf. Diethelm Klippel, *Politische Freiheit und Freiheitsrechte im deutschen Naturrecht des 18. Jahrhunderts* (Paderborn et al.: Schöningh, 1976); Jörn Garber, 'Vom "ius connatum" zum "Menschenrecht." Deutsche Menschenrechtstheorien der Spätaufklärung,' in *Rechtsphilosophie der Aufklärung. Symposium Wolfenbüttel*, ed. Reinhard Brandt (Berlin and New York: De Gruyter, 1982), 107–147; Martin Fuhrmann and Diethelm Klippel, 'Der Staat und die Staatstheorie des aufgeklärten Absolutismus,' in *Aufgeklärter Absolutismus im europäischen Vergleich*, ed. Harm Klueting and Helmut Reinalter (Vienna, Cologne and Weimar: Böhlau, 2002), 239–240; Diethelm Klippel, 'Verfaßte Freiheit. Die Entdeckung der Freiheitsrechte als Verfassungsprinzip im 18. und 19. Jahrhundert,' in *Reich, Regionen und Europa in Mittelalter und Neuzeit. Festschrift für Peter Moraw*, ed. Paul-Joachim Heinig et al. (Berlin: Duncker & Humblot, 2000), 163–166; Diethelm Klippel, 'Die Allgemeine Staatslehre um 1800,' in *Festschrift für Jan Schröder zum 70. Geburtstag*, ed. Arndt Kiehnle, Bernd Mertens, and Gottfried Schiemann (Tübingen: Mohr Siebeck, 2013), 429–435; Stolleis, *Geschichte des öffentlichen Rechts*, 384–385.

Most authors demanded caution in the use of the *Allgemeines Staatsrecht* because of its vagueness.[35] Natural law was to be consulted in cases of incompleteness of positive law; this subsidiary use of natural law led to a certain hierarchy of the sources of public law in the Holy Roman Empire.

5 Austrian *Staatsrechtslehre*

Despite the big influence of the *Reichspublizistik* on Austrian *Staatsrechtslehre*, Austrian scholars did not adopt this classification of the sources of law for political reasons. Most of them, such as Christian August Beck, Ignaz de Luca or Josef Marx von Liechtenstern, tended to avoid general remarks on methods and on sources of law; if they did so, almost all restricted the number of legal sources, taking into account only *leges fundamentales* and 'customary law,' leaving aside both analogy and natural law.[36] One of the rare exceptions was Wilhelm Anton Gustermann who at least admitted analogy among the sources of law.[37] The reason for neglecting natural law was not a positivist approach to Austrian public law. The procedure of Austrian scholars was rooted in political considerations. All legal scholars were aware of the political implications of their work. To include natural law would have been a risk. It would have made possible interpretation in conflict with monarchical interests. It was far less problematic to confine oneself to the analysis of positive sources of law. In other words, the limitation of sources of law was aimed at limiting the range of possible interpretations.

Hence it is not surprising that Austrian authors did not list natural law among the sources of Austrian public law when outlining the theoretical basis of their work, even if German-speaking representatives of the *Allgemeines Staatsrecht* tended to legitimise absolute monarchical power and recognised only very narrow limitations on royal power. Until the 1780s, individual liberty was restricted by the goals of state. As long as the 'common welfare' and the 'happiness of the subjects' were defined as primary objectives of the state, there was hardly any place left for individual liberty. After all, it was the monarch who defined the 'common welfare' and who took care of the 'happiness' of

35 Cf. Nettelbladt, 'Von dem rechten Gebrauche,' 31–33; Roth, *Staatsrecht deutscher Reichslande*, 8–9.

36 Cf. Beck, *Specimen I.*; Liechtenstern, *Staatsverfassung*; de Luca, *Vorlesungen*; Schennach, *Austria inventa?*, 215–218.

37 Gustermann, *Versuch*, XXXIV.

his subjects.[38] This older concept of natural law was also accepted by Austrian scholars and it corresponds to the views of Carl Anton Martini's *Positiones de jure civitatis* which for decades served as the standard textbook in Austrian universities where natural law was taught since the 1750s.[39]

The fundamental changes taking place in the *Allgemeines Staatsrecht* in other German-speaking countries were ignored by Austrian authors. In the 1780s we note a shift: The primary objective of the state is limited to providing a framework of safety within which individuals are responsible for themselves and for the free development of their talents.[40] These changes, let alone the idea of human fundamental rights, are omitted by Austrian authors.

---

38 Cf. Klippel, *Politische Freiheit*; Jürgen Schlumbohm, *Freiheit. Die Anfänge der bürgerlichen Emanzipationsbewegung in Deutschland im Spiegel ihres Leitworts (ca. 1760–ca. 1800)* (Düsseldorf: Schwann, 1975); Klippel, 'Verfaßte Freiheit'; Fuhrmann and Klippel, 'Der Staat und die Staatstheorie'; Diethelm Klippel, 'Der liberale Interventionsstaat. Staatszweck und Staatstätigkeit in der deutschen politischen Theorie des 18. und der ersten Hälfte des 19. Jahrhunderts,' in *Recht und Rechtswissenschaft im mitteldeutschen Raum. Symposium für Rolf Lieberwirth anläßlich seines 75. Geburtstags*, ed. Heiner Lück (Köln, Wien, and Weimar: Böhlau, 1998), 82–92.

39 Cf. Carl Anton Martini, *Positiones de jure civitatis in usum auditorii Vindobonensis* (Vienna: Trattner, 1768); Carl Anton Martini, *Erklärung der Lehrsätze über das allgemeine Staats- und Völkerrecht, Erster Teil: Allgemeines Staatsrecht* (Vienna, 1791), and Carl Anton Martini, *Allgemeines Recht der Staaten. Zum Gebrauch der öffentlichen Verlesungen in den k. k. Staaten. Ganz neue von dem Verfaßer selbst veranstaltete Uebersetzung* (Vienna: Mößle, 1799); cf. Herbert Kalb, 'Grundrechte und Martini – eine Annäherung,' in *Naturrecht und Privatrechtskodifikation. Tagungsband des Martini-Colloquiums 1998*, ed. Heinz Barta, Rudolf Palme, and Wolfgang Ingenhaeff (Vienna: Manz, 1999), 235–260; that Martini's statements were very common is stated by Maria Rosa Di Simone, *Aspetti della cultura giuridica austriaca nel settecento* (Rome: Bulzoni, 1984), 87 and 95; László Péter, *Hungary's Long Nineteenth Century. Constitutional and Democratic Traditions in a European Perspective*, ed. Miklós Lojkó (Leiden: Brill, 2012), 71; similar is the opinion expressed by Friedrich, *Geschichte der deutschen Staatsrechtswissenschaft*, 100; Robert Schelp, *Das allgemeine Staatsrecht – Staatsrecht der Aufklärung. Eine Untersuchung zu Inhalt, Anspruch und Geltung des naturrechtlichen Staatsrechts im 17. und 18. Jahrhundert* (Berlin: Duncker & Humblot, 2001), 73–75.

40 Cf. Jan Rolin, *Der Ursprung des Staates. Die naturrechtlich-rechtsphilosophische Legitimation von Staat und Staatsgewalt im Deutschland des 18. und 19. Jahrhunderts* (Tübingen: Mohr Siebeck, 2005), 124–130; Fuhrmann and Klippel, 'Der Staat und die Staatstheorie,' 239–240; Klippel, 'Verfaßte Freiheit,' 163–166; Klippel, *Politische Freiheit*, 113–134; summarising Jörn Garber, 'Recht und Utilitarismus: Joseph von Sonnenfels und das späte Naturrecht,' in *Joseph von Sonnenfels*, ed. Helmut Reinalter (Vienna: Verl. d. Österr. Akad. d. Wissenschaften, 1988), 101–102; Ulrich Scheuner, 'Die Verwirklichung der Bürgerlichen Gleichheit. Zur rechtlichen Bedeutung der Grundrechte in Deutschland zwischen 1780 und 1850,' in *Grund- und Freiheitsrechte im Wandel von Gesellschaft und Geschichte. Beiträge zur Geschichte der Grund- und Freiheitsrechte vom Ausgang des Mittelalters bis zur Revolution von 1848*, ed. Günter Birtsch (Göttingen: Vandenhoeck & Ruprecht, 1981),

The Austrian *Staatsrechtslehre* is even stricter; a thorough search shows that natural law and *Allgemeines Staatsrecht* are mentioned in very few cases.[41] Among all authors, only Anton Wilhelm Gustermann refers – twice – to natural law as a hypothetical limit on monarchical power. When he comes to the question whether the Austrian ruler is entitled to sell a country, Gustermann denies his right to do so by invoking natural law: As subjects are not allowed to evade the monarch's governance, the ruler is not allowed to withdraw from his duties as a ruler, which consist in serving and protecting the *salus publica*.[42] When speaking of the protection of the property of the subjects and the lawfulness of expropriation, he notes the lack of a positive norm and that therefore, he must refer to natural law. In accordance with the concept of natural law, he declares that expropriation is only acceptable in cases of emergency when and, to the extent, required by common welfare.[43] These are the only examples where an Austrian author points out the subsidiary validity of natural law in the absence of a positive norm.

When 'innate,' 'civil liberties' of the individual are discussed, this is done by Austrian legal scholars dealing with private law and in particular during the codification of Austrian private law, which resulted in the enactment of the Austrian General Civil Code in 1811. But here, too, natural law has no emancipatory or even revolutionary content, but also stabilises the absolute rule and the existing system.[44] 'Civil liberty' was strictly limited to private law and had decidedly no political dimension. But even this entitlement to act freely under

383–384; on the role of Immanuel Kant and Wilhelm von Humboldt in this context cf. Volker Müller, *Staatstätigkeit in den Staatstheorien des 19. Jahrhunderts* (Opladen: Westdeutscher Verlag, 1991), 97–106; Wolfgang Kersting, *Wohlgeordnete Freiheit. Immanuel Kants Staatsphilosophie. Mit einer Einleitung zur Taschenbuchausgabe: Kant und die politische Philosophie der Gegenwart* (Frankfurt: Suhrkamp, 1993), 365–368.

41 Cf. Klemens, *Grundriß*, 65 (Klemens recognises that even an absolute monarch is bound by the duties imposed by natural law).

42 Cf. Gustermann, *Versuch*, 232.

43 Cf. Gustermann, *Versuch*, 234; see Franz von Zeiller in his lecture on *Allgemeines Staatsrecht* (Herbert Hofmeister, 'Bürger und Staatsgewalt bei Franz v. Zeiller. Erörterungen zu Zeillers Staatsrechtslehre anhand einer Vorlesungsmitschrift aus 1802,' in *Diritto e potere nella storia europea. Atti del quatro Congresso internazionale della Società Italiana di Storia del Diritto, in onore di Bruno Paradisi*, vol. 2 [Florence: Olschki, 1982], 1023).

44 Cf. Martin P. Schennach, 'Generalisierung und Differenzierung des Rechts und durch das Recht? Zu einem Vergleich von ALR, Code civil und ABGB,' in *Kontinuität im Wandel. 200 Jahre ABGB (1811–2011)*, ed. Heinz Barta et al. (Innsbruck: Innsbruck Univ. Press, 2012), 68–70; Martin P. Schennach, 'Privatautonomie oder paternalistischer Interventionsstaat? Das ABGB und sein kodifikatorisches Umfeld,' in *La codificazione del diritto fra il Danubio e l'Adriatico. Per i duecento anni dall'entrata in vigore dell'ABGB (1812–2012)*, ed. Pio Caroni and Riccardo Ferrante (Turin: Giappichelli, 2015), 57–70.

private law could, according to the understanding of contemporaries such as Joseph von Sonnenfels or Franz von Zeiller, be restricted by the regent if necessary for the common good.[45] Carl Anton Martini's conception of freedom, like Zeiller's, was also limited by the purpose of the state, which was bindingly determined by the monarch.[46]

Furthermore, the absence of references to the *Allgemeines Staatsrecht* is characteristic of the decisively pro-absolutistic tendency of Austrian *Staatsrechtslehre*.[47] However, it must be stressed that this orientation in favour of monarchical rights was not specific to Austrian *Staatsrechtslehre* but characterised the *Territorialstaatsrecht* in general. When we take a look at the publications of Carl Heinrich von Römer who worked on Saxon public law or of Carl Gerhard Wilhelm Lodtmann who sketched the public law of the Duchy of Osnabrück, they simply did not mention natural law, but limited the sources of law to fundamental laws and customary law.[48] In all *Territorialstaatsrecht* (and not only in the Austrian), natural law was far from developing an emancipatory, critical, let alone revolutionary potential.[49]

6 Natural Law and Hungarian *Staatsrechtslehre*

A few legal scholars who dealt with Austrian public law in the narrower sense (excluding Hungary) chose the same approach when writing on Hungarian law. When Christian August Beck published his second volume on Austrian

45 Cf. Martin P. Schennach, '"Allgemeines Bestes" und "bürgerliche Freiheit"? Staatsentstehung, Staatszweck und Staatstätigkeit bei Joseph von Sonnenfels,' in *Päpste, Privilegien, Provinzen. Studien zur Kirchen-, Rechts- und Landesgeschichte. Festschrift für Werner Maleczek zum 65. Geburtstag*, ed. Martin P. Schennach, Rainer Murauer, and Johannes Gießauf (Vienna and Munich: Böhlau and Oldenbourg, 2010, 367–375.

46 Cf. Kalb, 'Grundrechte und Martini.' A different view is taken by Dieter Grimm, 'Das Verhältnis von politischer und privater Freiheit bei Zeiller,' in: *Forschungsband Franz von Zeiller (1751–1828). Beiträge zur Gesetzgebungs- und Wissenschaftsgeschichte*, ed. Walter Selb and Herbert Hofmeister (Vienna, Graz and Cologne: Böhlau, 1980), 94–106.

47 Cf. Schennach, 'Die "österreichische Gesamtstaatsidee,"' 21.

48 Carl Heinrich von Römer, *Staatsrecht und Statistik des Churfürstenthums Sachsen und der dabey befindlichen Lande, Erster Theil* (Halle [Saale]: Curt, 1787); Carl Gerhard Wilhelm Lodtmann, *Delineatio iuris publici Osnabrugensis* (Osnabrück, 1767).

49 Therefore, the statement of Dietmar Willoweit, *Rechtsgrundlagen der Territorialgewalt. Landesobrigkeit, Herrschaftsrechte und Territorium in der Rechtswissenschaft der Neuzeit* (Cologne and Vienna: Böhlau, 1975), 365, who stresses the fact that *Allgemeines Staatsrecht* could be considered a way to critically analyse a territory's public law, seems to over-estimate the influence of natural law on this branch of legal science.

Staatsrecht – in which he presented the Hungarian constitution – he omitted to speak of natural law; in fact, he is the only one who managed to write of Hungarian public law without mentioning even the Hungarian *leges fundamentales*, e.g., the *Bulla aurea*.[50] That was a deliberate decision taken for political reasons, as the fundamental laws presented a real, and the *Allgemeines Staatsrecht* at least a potential, threat to monarchical power. Beck knew better: When he taught *ius publicum* to Maria Theresia's son, Archduke Joseph, from 1755 until 1759, he not only presented the *ius publicum Imperii* to the future Emperor, but also the Austrian *Staatsrecht* – as a matter of course neglecting natural law and its role in (Austrian) public law.[51]

It is not surprising that a fervent adversary of the Hungarian nobility and its rights like Franz Rudolph Großing not only avoided mention of natural law, but even classified Hungary as an absolute monarchy (*monarchia illimitata*).[52]

These examples of authors who entirely omit natural law when writing on Hungarian *ius publicum* are, however, exceptions.[53] In general, there is a noteworthy difference between writings on Austrian and those on Hungarian *Staatsrecht* as far as concerns the role of natural law as a source for public law.[54] The latter writings normally do include natural law among the legal sources. We see this in the *Staatsrecht des Königreichs Hungarn* that József Ürményi and György Zsigmond Lakits published under the pseudonym of Stephan Rosenmann.[55] Like their contemporaries, they defined the *Allgemeines Staatsrecht* as 'principles of the mutual rights and duties of rulers and subjects […] derived from natural law and deduced from the nature and

50 Beck, *Specimen II.*; republished as Beck, *Jus publicum Hungariae.*

51 Christian August von Beck, 'Kern des Natur- und Völkerrechts zum Unterricht eines großen Prinzen entworfen, ca. 1755,' in *Recht und Verfassung des Reiches in der Zeit Maria Theresias. Die Vorträge zum Unterricht des Erzherzogs Joseph im Natur- und Völkerrecht sowie im Deutschen Staats- und Lehnrecht*, ed. Hermann Conrad (Köln and Opladen: Westdeutscher Verlag, 1964), 145–394; cf. Anna Hedwig Benna, 'Der Kronprinzenunterricht Josefs II. in der inneren Verfassung der Erbländer und die Wiener Zentralstellen,' *Mitteilungen des Österreichischen Staatsarchivs* 20 (1967): 115–179, esp. 120–124, 132–135 and 139–150; Alfred von Arneth, *Johann Christoph Bartenstein und seine Zeit* (Vienna: C. Gerold's Sohn, 1871), 61–67; Friedrich Hartl, 'Die erbländischen Landstände im Zeitalter Maria Theresias. Bedeutung und Bewertung in den Kronprinzenvorträgen für Joseph (II.),' in *Gedächtnisschrift für Herbert Hofmeister*, ed. Werner Ogris and Walter H. Rechberger (Vienna: Manz, 1996), 200–201.

52 Cf. Großing, *Ungarisches allgemeines Staats- und Regiments-Recht*, 1786.

53 Schwartner, *Statistik des Königreichs Ungern*, also does not mention natural law and the *Allgemeines Staatsrecht.*

54 Cf. Schennach, *Austria inventa?*, 438–440.

55 Cf. Schennach, *Austria inventa?*, 218–219.

object of civil society.'[56] If these principles are applied to an individual state, they constitute a nation's *ius publicum specialissimum*.[57] The same is true for Ignaz Stephan Horváth[58] and for Anton Wilhelm Gustermann. As Gustermann was one of the scholars writing on Austrian as well as Hungarian public law, the differences between the Austrian and Hungarian legal tradition become particularly evident. When dealing with Austrian public law, Gustermann tends to omit natural law and *Allgemeines Staatsrecht*,[59] whereas it is taken into account when he writes on Hungarian *Staatsrecht*.[60] This observation leads to an important conclusion. At first sight and in particular in comparison with Austrian *Staatsrechtslehre*, the use of natural law seems to indicate an emancipatory, anti-absolutistic orientation of the Hungarian *Staatsrechtslehre*, especially if we take into account that all writers except Großing classify Hungary as a *monarchia limitata* where sovereignty is divided between the king and the Hungarian estates. However, this is misleading. While not all scholars dealing with Hungarian public law were 'king's men,'[61] neither did they support the estates. Most of the authors[62] taught either at universities or royal academies or held public offices and therefore cannot be assumed to be anti-monarchical. Ignaz Stephan Horváth, for instance, was a professor of natural law at the Royal Academy of Bratislava and a censor, and in addition he was awarded the title of royal chamberlain. He could hardly be expected to have an anti-monarchical orientation.[63]

Natural law and *Allgemeines Staatsrecht* fulfilled another function than in Austrian *Staatsrechtslehre*, and this was due to the structure and system of Hungarian works on public law. Hungarian authors regularly contrast particular sources of Hungarian public law (the fundamental laws and the *Herkommen*) with general ones and especially with natural law which serves as a framework. In most works on Hungarian *Staatsrecht*, the *Allgemeines Staatsrecht* has the function that the *Reichsstaatsrecht* has for Austrian public law.

---

56 Stephan Rosenmann [= József Ürményi and György Zsigmond Lakits], *Staatsrecht des Königreichs Hungarn. Nach der heutigen Verfassung dieses Reichs bearbeitet* (Vienna: Doll, 1792), 4 (transl. by Martin P. Schennach).

57 Rosenmann, *Staatsrecht*, 4–5.

58 Horváth, *Institutionum*, 7–8.

59 See above.

60 Gustermann, *Ungerisches Staatsrecht*, 4–5.

61 Péter, *Hungary's Long Nineteenth Century*, 71.

62 Cf. Gönczi, *Die europäischen Fundamente*.

63 Cf. the preface of Horváth, *Institutionum*, 1786; Constantin von Wurzbach, ed., *Biographisches Lexikon des Kaiserthums Oesterreich*, vol. 9 (Wien: Kaiserlich-Königliche Hof- und Staatsdruckerei, 1863), 332.

At the same time, we must not overestimate the emancipatory implications of natural law in the Hungarian context. Whenever the authors make references to literature on natural law and *Allgemeine Staatsrechtslehre*, they refer mostly to Martini's *Positiones de iure civitatis*, first published in 1768, or to the doctoral thesis of Matthias Anton Markovics on the sources of Hungarian law.[64] The shift in German speaking literature on natural law towards human rights and individual liberties did not affect Hungarian *Staatsrechtslehre*, so in this regard, there was no difference from the development in Austria.

The same is true when we consider the concrete use of natural law by legal scholars writing on Hungarian public law. References to natural law are almost as rare as in the works of their Austrian colleagues. Let us take a look at the work of Michael Bencsik, professor of natural law at the Academy of Trnava: In his treatise entitled *Novissima diaeta nobilissima principis, Statuumque, & Ordinum inclyti regni Hungariae* (1722) Bencsik explained that the king of Hungary was not bound by positive laws (not even by the *leges fundamentales*), as they were given by himself or by his predecessors and as there was no power which could force him. Nevertheless, Bencsik admitted that although the king was not bound by positive laws, this did not apply to natural or divine law which, according to Bencsik, had a binding character even for the king (which of course was a commonplace frequently repeated by most natural law theorists).[65] The resistance clause in the Golden Bull of 1222 could also be qualified as null and void with a (summary) reference to natural law.[66] Thus Gustermann sees the corresponding article as incompatible with the *Allgemeines Staatsrecht*: It was 'against the contract of submission to oppose the sovereign by force.'[67] Likewise, Beck had described the resistance clause as 'tanquam Juri Naturae & Gentium contraria.'[68]

Therefore we see that, despite the different role of natural law in the theoretical system of Austrian *Staatsrechtslehre* on the one hand and of Hungarian public law on the other, the practical impact of the *Allgemeines Staatsrecht* was not greater in Hungarian than in Austrian literature. That is not surprising:

64 Matthias Anton Markovics, *De Fontibus iuris hungarici, quam exantlatis ex omnigena iurisprudentia rigorisis examinibus, una cum adnexis ex universo iure positionibus* [...] (Trnava, 1776).

65 Nicolaus Bencsik (Respondent) and Michael Bencsik (Praeses), *Novissima diaeta nobilissima principis, Statuumquè, & Ordinum inclyti regni Hungariae, Partiumquè Eidem Annexarum. Sive propositiones academicae lege nobilitares. De Nobilitate Gentis Hungaricae, ejus Origine, Modis illam acquirendi* (Trnava: Gall, 1722), 94–95.

66 Cf. Schennach, *Austria inventa?*, 448.

67 Gustermann, *Ungerisches Staatsrecht*, 64.

68 Beck, *Specimen II.*, 29–35.

After all, the practice of censorship was the same in Austria and in Hungary, and a radical point of view would have had no chance to be published (at least not within the borders of the Austrian monarchy). Indeed, it can easily be seen that in the entire monarchy all works dealing with public law were thoroughly analysed by central authorities in order to be sure that no contents ran contrary to monarchical interests. This is also true for the Hungarian *Staatsrechtslehre*. In fact, the theory of the *filum successionis interruptum* developed by the Hungarian nobility opposing Joseph's centralising reforms was not even mentioned in works on Hungarian public law, although it was a theory deeply rooted in Hungarian *leges fundamentales*. Referring among others to the Hungarian *Bulla aurea* of Andreas II and the right to resist that was settled in this charter, Péter Ócsai Balogh led the Hungarian opposition to Joseph II. They claimed that since Joseph had never been crowned King of Hungary and never confirmed the kingdom's *iura et libertates*, the Hungarian nobility was entitled to elect a new king.[69] The theory of the *filum successionis interruptum* was not dealt with in works on Hungarian public law, but only as a matter of political debate.

7 The Work of Josef Hajnóczy

The writings of Josef Hajnóczy, who did make some references to natural law, do not primarily belong to the Hungarian *Staatsrechtslehre* but are above all political. In two treatises published anonymously in 1791 Hajnóczy not only dealt with Hungarian public law as it was at the beginning of the 1790s,[70] but he developed ideas strongly influenced by the French Revolution and natural

---

69 Cf. Horst Haselsteiner, *Joseph II. und die Komitate Ungarns. Herrscherrecht und ständischer Konstitutionalismus* (Vienna, Cologne and Graz: Böhlau, 1983), 73–86; Luisa Bussi, *Fra unione personale e stato sovranazionale. Contributo alla storia della formazione dell'impero d'Austria* (Milan: Guiffrè, 2003), 296–302; Tibor Iván Berend, *History Derailed. Central and Eastern Europe in the Long Nineteenth Century* (Berkeley: Univ. of California Press, 2003), 106–107; Helmuth Größing, 'Die ungarische Verfassung und der Konstitutionalismus des Jahres 1848. Aus den Berichten eines Hofrats der obersten Polizeistelle vom ungarischen Reichstag 1847/48,' *Mitteilungen des Instituts für Österreichische Geschichtsforschung* 81 (1973): 304–336, here 312; Heinrich Marczali, *Ungarische Verfassungsgeschichte* (Tübingen: Mohr, 1910), 120; Ákos Barcsay, *Herrschaftsantritt im Ungarn des 18. Jahrhunderts. Studien zum Verhältnis zwischen Krongewalt und Ständetum im Zeitalter des Absolutismus* (St. Katharinen: Scripta-Mercaturae-Verl., 2002), 46.

70 Cf. Josef Hajnóczy, *Dissertatio politico publica de regiae potestatis in Hungaria limitibus* (s.l., 1791); Josef Hajnóczy, *De comitiis regni Hungariae, deque organisatione eorundem dissertatio iuris publici Hungarici* (s.l. [Bratislava], 1791).

law.[71] Like other writers dealing with the Hungarian *leges fundamentales*, he mentions the abolition of the estates' *ius resistendi* by the Hungarian Diet in 1687, but he is the only one to pretend that the *ius resistendi* is nevertheless rooted in and justified by natural law: the right to resist a tyrant would be an indispensable result of the social contract. If not, the social contract would be a *contractus leoninus* only bearing advantages on the ruler's side.[72] In addition, despite the rules of dynastic succession fixed in the 'Pragmatic Sanction' of 1713, he declared that the Hungarian estates still had the right to elect a new king if such a measure was demanded by common welfare. This was once again justified by natural law. Otherwise, it would be a violation of the nation's *libertas naturalis*.[73] Of course, his terminology and his reference to the social contract are obviously rooted in natural law. Nevertheless, his argumentation is not based on important representatives of natural law (he does not cite a single relevant work), but exclusively on concrete Hungarian legal sources, in particular on resolutions of the Hungarian Diet.

8 The Perception of Hungarian *Staatsrechtslehre* by Central Authorities

Nevertheless, on the part of Viennese authorities and of the monarch, scepticism dominated the perception of Hungarian *Staatsrechtslehre*, especially in comparison to its Austrian counterpart. Whereas the science of Austrian public law could easily be exploited to legitimise absolutism and the forging of a central state, that was not true for Hungarian *Staatsrechtslehre*, whose representatives could not and did not omit the estates' rights or the kingdom's fundamental laws. They were not willing or able to classify the Kingdom as an 'unlimited monarchy.' These were the main reasons for the authorities' distrust of Hungarian public law. It was not so much the fact that natural law was assigned a different position in the system of sources of Hungarian *ius publicum* in comparison with Austrian legal scholars, although this might also have played a certain role. In the *Ratio Educationis* of 1777, which set the regulatory framework for academic teaching, the professor of public law was reminded to proceed with the utmost caution. As far as the estates and their

71 Cf. Schennach, *Austria inventa?*, 453–454; Gönczi, *Die europäischen Fundamente*, 140–142; Moritz Csáky, *Von der Aufklärung zum Liberalismus. Studien zum Frühliberalismus in Ungarn* (Vienna: Verl. d. Österr. Akad. d. Wissenschaften, 1981), 75–76.

72 Hajnóczy, *Dissertatio*, 118; Péter, *Hungary's Long Nineteenth Century*, 125.

73 Cf. Hajnóczy, *Dissertatio*, 115–116; Hajnóczy, *De comitiis regni Hungariae*, 118.

rights were concerned, the teacher should avoid dealing with any details and circumvent all potential controversies.[74]

During the reign of Joseph II, the teaching of Hungarian public law was suspended for political reasons.[75] A suggestion to teach Hungarian public law at the University of Pest was rejected by the Viennese State Council (*Staatsrat*) due to the revolutionary potential of the subject,[76] and even at the beginning of the nineteenth century, distrust persisted: In 1816, Franz von Zeiller stated that Hungarian public law should be skipped at universities and academies due to its potentially explosive contents.[77]

9 Summary

Austrian and Hungarian *Staatsrechtslehre* had very similar roots and origins in the *Reichspublizistik* and the theory of *Territorialstaatsrecht*. Nevertheless, natural law and *Allgemeines Staatsrecht* played different roles in Austrian and Hungarian public law. Whereas natural law and its use were thoroughly avoided by Austrian writers, who evidently were afraid of its emancipatory potential, Hungarian scholars had no fear of listing natural law among the sources of Hungarian *ius publicum*. This was due to the differing theoretical framework. In Austrian public law, legal questions not answered by positive law could be solved by referring to the subsidiary public law of the Holy Roman Empire. This solution was not possible as far as Hungary was concerned, as it was not part of the Holy Roman Empire. This theoretical gap was filled by referring to natural law or to the *Allgemeines Staatsrecht*. With regard to the practical use however, no significant discrepancies can be observed between Austrian and Hungarian *Staatsrechtslehre*. This did not change the sceptical attitude of Austrian central authorities towards the teaching of Hungarian public law. Whereas Austrian *Staatsrechtslehre* legitimised absolutism and the formation of a central state, this was not true for Hungarian scholars who did not keep quiet about the rights of Hungarian estates – not because of any anti-monarchical attitude, but because such an omission would evidently conflict with the actual political situation.

---

74 Cf. Anonymus, *Ratio educationis totiusque rei literariae per Regnum Hungariae et provincias eidem adnexas*, vol. 1 (Vienna: Trattner, 1777), § 186, 332–334.

75 Cf. Jakab, 'Wissenschaft vom Verfassungsrecht,' 779.

76 Cf. Schennach, 'Die "österreichische Gesamtstaatsidee,"' 23–24.

77 Österreichisches Staatsarchiv, Allgemeines Verwaltungsarchiv, Unterricht und Kultus, Studienhofkommission, Teil 2, Karton 239, Pos. 2, Zahl 471 ex 1816, 1816 March 10.

Acknowledgement

The linguistic proofreading was supported by the Max Weber Centre for Advanced Cultural and Social Studies of the University of Erfurt.

Bibliography

Primary Sources

[Anonymus], *Ratio educationis totiusque rei literariae per Regnum Hungariae et provincias eidem adnexas*, vol. 1, Vienna: Trattner, 1777.

Beck, Christian August, *Jus publicum Hungariae. Cum notis autoris et observationibus Josephi Benzur*, Vienna: Kraus, 1790.

Beck, Christian August, *Specimen I. juris publici Austriaci, ex ipsis legibus, actisque publicis eruti, quod sub sacratissimis auspiciis sacrae caesareae Regiaeque majestatis in collegio regio Theresiano nobilium societatis Jesu* [...], Vienna: Trattner, 1750.

Beck, Christian August, *Specimen II. juris publici Austriaci, ex ipsis legibus actisque publicis eruti quod in collegio regio Theresiano nobilium S. J. propugnavit Nicolaus S. R. I. Liber Baro a Wallhorn*, Vienna: Trattner, 1752.

Bencsik, Nicolaus (Respondent) and Bencsik, Michael (Praeses), *Novissima diaeta nobilissima principis, Statuumquè, & Ordinum inclyti regni Hungariae, Partiumquè Eidem Annexarum. Sive propositiones academicae lege nobilitares. De Nobilitate Gentis Hungaricae, ejus Origine, Modis illam acquirendi*, Trnava: Gall, 1722.

Böhmer, Justus Henning, *Introductio in ius publicum universale, ex genuinis iuris naturae principiis deductum, et in usum iuris publici particularis quarumcunque rerumpublicarum adornatum, adiecto indice duplici*, Halle [Saale]: Orphanotropheum, 1710.

Brunnquell, Johann Salomo, *Eröffnete Gedancken / Von dem Allgemeinen Staats-Rechte, Und dessen Höchst-nützlichen Excolirung*, Jena: Fickelscherr, 1721.

De Luca, Ignaz, *Historisch-statistisches Lesebuch zur Kenntniß des Oestreichischen Staates. Zweyter Theil: Oestreichische Staatsverwaltungskunde*, Vienna: Rehm, 1798.

De Luca, Ignaz, *Vorlesungen über die Oestreichische Staatsverfassung*, vol. 1 [only volume], Vienna, 1792.

Francke, Heinrich Gottlieb, *Notitia subsidiorum juris publici maxime litteraria*, Leipzig, 1740.

Großing, Franz Rudolf von, *Ungarisches allgemeines Staats- und Regiments-Recht*, s.l., 1786.

Gustermann, Anton Wilhelm, *Versuch eines vollständigen österreichischen Staatsrechtes. Erster Theil* [only volume], Vienna: Wappler, 1793.

Gustermann, Anton Wilhelm, *Die Ausbildung der Verfassung des Königreiches Ungern; aus der Geschichte, und den Gesezen dieses Reiches dargestellet*, 2 vols, Vienna: Doll, 1811.

Gustermann, Anton Wilhelm, *Ungerisches Staatsrecht*, vol. 1 [it remained the only volume], Vienna: Doll 1818.

Hajnóczy, Joseph, *De comitiis regni Hungariae, deque organisatione eorundem dissertatio iuris publici Hungarici*, s.l. [Bratislava], 1791.

Hajnóczy, Joseph, *Dissertatio politico publica de regiae potestatis in Hungaria limitibus*, s.l., 1791.

Hartleben, Theodor, *Dissertatio de origine, incrementis et fontibus iuris publici territoriorum Imperii Romano-Germanici communis, nec non de utilitate, illud in academiis Germanicis specialibus praelectionibus tradendi. Oratio inauguralis*, Salzburg: Mayer, 1796.

Höpfner, Ludwig Julius Friedrich, ed., *Deutsche Encyclopädie oder Allgemeines Real-Wörterbuch aller Künste und Wissenschaften*, Frankfurt: Varrentrapp und Wenner, 1778.

Horváth, Ignaz Stephan, *Institutionum juris publici particularis regni Hungariae. Pars I: De Territorio Regni Hungariae*, Bratislava: Weber 1786.

Horváth, Michael, *Statistica Regni Hungariae, et partium eidem adnexarum*, 2nd ed., Bratislava: Landerer, 1802.

Klemens, *Grundriß der Staatsrechte der Habsburgisch-Oesterreich-Lotharingischen Erbmonarchie*, Vienna: Sonnleithner, 1782.

Kollár, Adam Frantisek, *Historiae iurisque publici regni Ungariae amoenitates*, 2 vols, Vienna, 1783.

Kropatschek, Josef, *Oestreichs Staatsverfassung, vereinbart mit den zusammengezogenen bestehenden Gesetzen, zum Gebrauche der Staatsbeamten, Advokaten, Oekonomen, Obrigkeiten, Magistraten, Geistlichen, Bürger und Bauern, zum Unterrichte, für angehende Geschäfftsmänner*, 10 vols and 2 supplementary vols, Vienna: Mößle, 1794–1810.

Liechtenstern, Joseph Marx von, *Staatsverfassung der Oesterreichischen Monarchie im Grundrisse*, Vienna: Kleinmayer, 1791.

Lodtmann, Carl Gerhard Wilhelm, *Delineatio iuris publici Osnabrugensis*, Osnabrück, 1767.

Markovics, Matthias, *De Fontibus iuris hungarici, quam exantlatis ex omnigena iurisprudentia rigorisis examinibus, una cum adnexis ex universo iure positionibus*, Trnava, 1776.

Martini, Carl Anton, *Positiones de jure civitatis in usum auditorii Vindobonensis*, Vienna: Trattner, 1768.

Martini, Carl Anton, *Erklärung der Lehrsätze über das allgemeine Staats- und Völkerrecht, Erster Teil: Allgemeines Staatsrecht*, Vienna, 1791.

Martini, Carl Anton, *Allgemeines Recht der Staaten. Zum Gebrauch der öffentlichen Verlesungen in den k. k. Staaten. Ganz neue von dem Verfaßer selbst veranstaltete Uebersetzung*, Vienna: Mößle, 1799.

Moser, Johann Jacob, *Allgemeine Einleitung in die Lehre des besonderen Staats-Rechts aller einzelen* [!] *Stände des Heil. Röm. Reichs, und in Sein von diesem Staats-Recht handlendes Werck*, Frankfurt/Leipzig, 1739.

Moser, Johann Jacob, *Kürzere Einleitung in das Teutsche Staats-Recht. Zum Gebrauch der Anfänger in diser Wissenschaft*, Frankfurt/Leipzig: Cotta, 1753.

Moser, Johann Jacob, *Praecognita juris publici germanici generalissima. Oder Tractat Von der Lehre der heutigen Staats-Verfassung von Teutschland überhaupt Nemlich Von deren Natur, Nothwendigkeit, Nuzen [!], der Befügnus, solche zu lehren, und wie ferne? Deren gegenwärtigem Zustand, der besten Art, diese Staats-Verfassung zu erlernen, und denen im Druck vorhandenen theils besten, theils neuesten, sowohl vollständigern als kurtzen Einleitungen darzu entworffen*, Frankfurt/Leipzig: Stein, 1732.

Nettelbladt, Daniel, 'Von dem rechten Gebrauche des allgemeinen Staatsrechtes in der teutschen Staatsrechtsgelahrtheit,' in *Erörterungen einiger einzelner Lehren des teutschen Staatsrechtes*, ed. Daniel Nettelbladt, 21–36, Halle [Saale]: Rengersche Buchhandlung, 1773.

Petrovics, József, *Introductio in ius publicum regni Hungariae*, Vienna: Kraus, 1790.

Römer, Carl Heinrich von, *Staatsrecht und Statistik des Churfürstenthums Sachsen und der dabey befindlichen Lande, Erster Theil*, Halle [Saale]: Curt, 1787.

Rosenmann, Stephan [= József Ürményi and György Zsigmond Lakits], *Jus publicum Regni Hungariae ex combinatione veterum, recentiorumque legum, in compendium sistematicum redactum, et usibus maxime scholasticae juventutis adcommodatum*, Vienna: Baumeister, 1791.

Rosenmann, Stephan [= József Ürményi and György Zsigmond Lakits], *Staatsrecht des Königreichs Hungarn. Nach der heutigen Verfassung dieses Reichs bearbeitet*, Vienna: Doll, 1792.

Roth, Johann Richard, *Staatsrecht deutscher Reichslande. Akademische Vorlesungen. Nebst einem Abdrucke der neuesten kaiserlichen Wahlkapitulation und des westphälischen Friedens nach den Originalien des Reichsarchivs, Erster Theil*, Mainz: Winkopp, 1788.

Schnaubert, Andreas Josef, *Anfangsgründe des Staatsrechts der gesammten Reichslande*, Jena: Akademische Buchhandlung, 1787.

Schrötter, Franz Ferdinand von, *Abhandlungen aus dem österreichischen Staatsrechte*, vol. 1: *Erste Abhandlung aus dem österreichischen Staatsrechte, von den Freyheitsbriefen des Durchläuchtigsten Erzhauses von Oesterreich, samt einer Einleitung in die österr. Geschichte und einem Anhange Beylagen*; vol. 2: *Zweyte Abhandlung aus dem Oesterreichischen Staatsrechte von den Titeln und Reichserzämtern des Durchläuchtigsten Erzhauses von Oesterreich. Mit einem Anhange von Urkunden versehen*; vol. 3: *Dritte Abhandlung aus dem Oesterreichischen Staatsrechte. Von den Erbhuldigungen und Kleynodien der Erzherzoge von Oesterreich. Mit einem Anhange Beylagen versehen*; vol. 4: *Vierte Abhandlung aus dem österreichischen Staatsrechten, von den vorzüglichen Rechten, welche den Durchläuchtigsten Erzherzogen mit und neben der Landeshoheit gebühren*; vol. 5: *Fünfte Abhandlung aus dem österreichischen Staatsrechte, von der Erbfolgs-Ordnung wie auch der Vormundschaft der Durchlauchtigsten Erzherzoge. Mit Urkunden*, Vienna: Kraus, 1762–1766.

Schrötter, Franz Ferdinand von, *Grundriß des österreichischen Staatsrechtes*, Vienna: Kurzböck, 1775.

Schwartner, Martin von, *Statistik des Königreichs Ungern. Ein Versuch, Zweyter u. Dritter Theil*, Pest: Trattner, 1798.

Westphal, Ernst Christian, *Das teutsche Staatsrecht*, Leipzig: Weygand, 1784.

Secondary Sources

Arneth, Alfred von, *Johann Christoph Bartenstein und seine Zeit*, Vienna: C. Gerold's Sohn, 1871.

Asche, Matthias, 'Studenten aus Ungarn und Siebenbürgen an katholischen Universitäten des Heiligen Römischen Reiches deutscher Nation im 18. Jahrhundert,' in *Peregrinatio Hungarica. Studenten aus Ungarn an deutschen und österreichischen Hochschulen vom 16. bis zum 20. Jahrhundert*, ed. Márta Fata, Gyula Kurucz, and Anton Schindling, 135–154, Stuttgart: Steiner, 2006.

Barcsay, Ákos, *Herrschaftsantritt im Ungarn des 18. Jahrhunderts. Studien zum Verhältnis zwischen Krongewalt und Ständetum im Zeitalter des Absolutismus*, St. Katharinen: Scripta-Mercaturae-Verl., 2002.

Beck, Christian August von, 'Kern des Natur- und Völkerrechts zum Unterricht eines großen Prinzen entworfen, ca. 1755,' in *Recht und Verfassung des Reiches in der Zeit Maria Theresias. Die Vorträge zum Unterricht des Erzherzogs Joseph im Natur- und Völkerrecht sowie im Deutschen Staats- und Lehnrecht*, ed. Hermann Conrad, 145–394, Köln and Opladen: Westdeutscher Verlag, 1964.

Benna, Anna Hedwig, 'Der Kronprinzenunterricht Josefs II. in der inneren Verfassung der Erbländer und die Wiener Zentralstellen,' *Mitteilungen des Österreichischen Staatsarchivs* 20 (1967): 115–179.

Berend, Tibor Iván, *History Derailed. Central and Eastern Europe in the Long Nineteenth Century*, Berkeley: Univ. of California Press, 2003.

Brauneder, Wilhelm, 'Kaiserwürde durch Verwaltungsakt: Der österreichische Kaisertitel von 1804,' in *Wahl und Krönung in Zeiten des Umbruchs*, ed. Ludolf Pelizaeus (Frankfurt: Lang, 2008), 207–220.

Brunner, Otto, *Land und Herrschaft. Grundfragen der territorialen Verfassungsgeschichte Österreichs im Mittelalter*, 5th ed., Vienna: Rohrer, 1965.

Bussi, Luisa, *Fra unione personale e stato sovranazionale. Contributo alla storia della formazione dell'impero d'Austria*, Milan: Guiffrè, 2003.

Csáky, Moritz, *Von der Aufklärung zum Liberalismus. Studien zum Frühliberalismus in Ungarn*, Vienna: Verl. d. Österr. Akad. d. Wissenschaften, 1981.

Di Simone, Maria Rosa, *Aspetti della cultura giuridica austriaca nel settecento*, Rome: Bulzoni, 1984.

Fata, Márta and Anton Schindling, 'Peregrinatio Hungarica. Studenten aus Ungarn an deutschen und österreichischen Hochschulen vom 16. bis zum 20. Jahrhundert,' in *Peregrinatio Hungarica. Studenten aus Ungarn an deutschen und österreichischen Hochschulen vom 16. bis zum 20. Jahrhundert*, ed. Márta Fata, Gyula Kurucz, and Anton Schindling, 3–35, Stuttgart: Steiner, 2006.

Friedrich, Manfred, *Geschichte der deutschen Staatsrechtswissenschaft*, Berlin: Duncker & Humblot, 1997.

Fuhrmann, Martin and Diethelm Klippel, 'Der Staat und die Staatstheorie des aufgeklärten Absolutismus,' in *Aufgeklärter Absolutismus im europäischen Vergleich*, ed. Harm Klueting and Helmut Reinalter, 223–243, Vienna, Cologne, and Weimar: Böhlau, 2002.

Garber, Jörn, 'Vom "ius connatum" zum "Menschenrecht." Deutsche Menschenrechtstheorien der Spätaufklärung,' in *Rechtsphilosophie der Aufklärung. Symposium Wolfenbüttel*, ed. Reinhard Brandt, 107–147, Berlin and New York: De Gruyter, 1982.

Garber, Jörn, 'Recht und Utilitarismus: Joseph von Sonnenfels und das späte Naturrecht,' in *Joseph von Sonnenfels*, ed. Helmut Reinalter, 97–138, Vienna: Verl. d. Österr. Akad. d. Wissenschaften, 1988.

Gönczi, Katalin, *Die europäischen Fundamente der ungarischen Rechtskultur. Juristischer Wissenstransfer und nationale Rechtswissenschaft in Ungarn zur Zeit der Aufklärung und im Vormärz*, Frankfurt: Klostermann, 2008.

Grimm, Dieter, 'Das Verhältnis von politischer und privater Freiheit bei Zeiller,' in: *Forschungsband Franz von Zeiller (1751–1828). Beiträge zur Gesetzgebungs- und Wissenschaftsgeschichte*, ed. Walter Selb and Herbert Hofmeister, 94–106, Vienna, Graz and Cologne: Böhlau, 1980.

Größing, Helmuth, 'Die ungarische Verfassung und der Konstitutionalismus des Jahres 1848. Aus den Berichten eines Hofrats der obersten Polizeistelle vom ungarischen Reichstag 1847/48,' *Mitteilungen des Instituts für Österreichische Geschichtsforschung* 81 (1973): 304–336.

Grothe, Ewald, 'Verfassungsgeschichte als Reichshistorie. Zur Vorgeschichte einer historischen und juristischen Teildisziplin im 18. Jahrhundert,' in *Gesellschaft – Region – Politik. Festschrift für Hermann de Buhr, Heinrich Küppers und Volkmar Wittmütz*, ed. Jörg Hentzschel-Fröhlings, 295–304, Norderstedt: Books on Demand, 2006.

Hammerstein, Notker, *Jus und Historie. Ein Beitrag zur Geschichte des politischen Denkens an deutschen Universitäten im späten 17. und 18. Jahrhundert* (Göttingen: Vandenhoeck & Ruprecht, 1972).

Hammerstein, Notker, 'Jus publicum Romano-Germanicum,' in *Diritto e potere nella storia Europea. Atti in onore di Bruno Paradisi; Quarto Congresso internazionale della Soc. Italiana di Storia del Diretto*, 717–753, Florence: Olschki, 1982.

Hartl, Friedrich, 'Die erbländischen Landstände im Zeitalter Maria Theresias. Bedeutung und Bewertung in den Kronprinzenvorträgen für Joseph (II.),' in *Gedächtnisschrift für Herbert Hofmeister*, ed. Werner Ogris, and Walter H. Rechberger, 199–233, Vienna: Manz, 1996.

Haselsteiner, Horst, *Joseph II. und die Komitate Ungarns. Herrscherrecht und ständischer Konstitutionalismus*, Vienna, Cologne and Graz: Böhlau, 1983.

Hofmeister, Herbert, 'Bürger und Staatsgewalt bei Franz v. Zeiller. Erörterungen zu Zeillers Staatsrechtslehre anhand einer Vorlesungsmitschrift aus 1802,' in *Diritto e potere nella storia europea. Atti del quatro Congresso internazionale della Società Italiana di Storia del Diritto, in onore di Bruno Paradisi*, vol. 2, 1007–1029, Florence: Olschki, 1982.

Jakab, András, 'Wissenschaft vom Verfassungsrecht: Ungarn,' in *Handbuch Ius Publicum Europaeum, vol. 2: Offene Staatlichkeit – Wissenschaft vom Verfassungsrecht*, ed. Armin von Bogdandy, Villalón Cruz, and Peter M. Huber, 777–805, Heidelberg: C.F. Müller, 2008.

Kalb, Herbert, 'Grundrechte und Martini – eine Annäherung,' in *Naturrecht und Privatrechtskodifikation. Tagungsband des Martini-Colloquiums 1998*, ed. Heinz Barta, Rudolf Palme, and Wolfgang Ingenhaeff, 235–260, Vienna: Manz, 1999.

Kersting, Wolfgang, *Wohlgeordnete Freiheit. Immanuel Kants Staatsphilosophie. Mit einer Einleitung zur Taschenbuchausgabe: Kant und die politische Philosophie der Gegenwart*, Frankfurt: Suhrkamp, 1993.

Klippel, Diethelm, *Politische Freiheit und Freiheitsrechte im deutschen Naturrecht des 18. Jahrhunderts*, Paderborn et al.: Schöningh, 1976.

Klippel, Diethelm, 'Der liberale Interventionsstaat. Staatszweck und Staatstätigkeit in der deutschen politischen Theorie des 18. und der ersten Hälfte des 19. Jahrhunderts,' in *Recht und Rechtswissenschaft im mitteldeutschen Raum. Symposium für Rolf Lieberwirth anläßlich seines 75. Geburtstags*, ed. Heiner Lück, 77–103, Köln, Wien, and Weimar: Böhlau, 1998.

Klippel, Diethelm, 'Verfaßte Freiheit. Die Entdeckung der Freiheitsrechte als Verfassungsprinzip im 18. und 19. Jahrhundert,' in *Reich, Regionen und Europa in Mittelalter und Neuzeit. Festschrift für Peter Moraw*, ed. Heinig, Paul-Joachim et al., 149–169, Berlin: Duncker & Humblot, 2000.

Klippel, Diethelm, 'Die Allgemeine Staatslehre um 1800,' in *Festschrift für Jan Schröder zum 70. Geburtstag*, ed. Arndt Kiehnle, Bernd Mertens, and Gottfried Schiemann, 423–441, Tübingen: Mohr Siebeck, 2013.

Marczali, Heinrich, *Ungarische Verfassungsgeschichte*, Tübingen: Mohr, 1910.

Mazohl, Brigitte and Wallnig, Thomas, '(Kaiser)haus – Staat – Vaterland? Zur "österreichischen" Historiographie vor der "Nationalgeschichte,"' in *Nationalgeschichte als Artefakt. Zum Paradigma "Nationalstaat" in den Historiographien Deutschlands, Italiens und Österreichs*, ed. Hans Peter Hye, Brigitte Mazohl, and Jan Paul Niederkorn, 43–72, Vienna: Verl. d. Österr. Akad. d. Wissenschaften, 2009.

Mezey, Barna, 'Universitäten und Rechtsakademien (Anfänge und Entwicklungstendenzen der juristischen Ausbildung in Ungarn),' in *Die ungarische Universitätsbildung und Europa*, ed. Márta Font and László Szögi, 187–202, Pécs: University, 2001.

Mohnhaupt, Heinz, 'The Object of Interpretation: Legislation and Competing Normative Sources of Law in Europe during the 16th to 18th Centuries,' in *Interpretation of Law in the Age of Enlightenment. From the Rule of the King to the Rule of Law*, ed. Yasumoto Morigiwa, Michael Stolleis, and Jean-Louis Halpérin, 61–89, Dordrecht et al.: Springer 2011.

Mohnhaupt, Heinz, 'Von den "leges fundamentales" zur modernen Verfassung in Europa. Zum begriffs- und dogmengeschichtlichen Befund (16.-18. Jahrhundert),' *Ius Commune* 25 (1998): 121–159 (reprint 2000).

Mohnhaupt, Heinz and Dieter Grimm, *Verfassung. Zur Geschichte des Begriffs von der Antike bis zur Gegenwart. Zwei Studien*, 2nd ed., Berlin: Duncker & Humblot, 2002.

Müller, Volker, *Staatstätigkeit in den Staatstheorien des 19. Jahrhunderts*, Opladen: Westdeutscher Verlag, 1991.

Péter, László, *Hungary's Long Nineteenth Century. Constitutional and Democratic Traditions in a European Perspective*, ed. Miklós Lojkó, Leiden: Brill, 2012.

Piff, Alexander, *Mit Geschichte und Recht. Die Beschreibung von Österreich von 1775 bis 1808 im Zeichen einer eigenen Staatsrechtsposition*, Diploma Thesis, University of Innsbruck, 2014.

Rolin, Jan, *Der Ursprung des Staates. Die naturrechtlich-rechtsphilosophische Legitimation von Staat und Staatsgewalt im Deutschland des 18. und 19. Jahrhunderts*, Tübingen: Mohr Siebeck, 2005.

Schelp, Robert, *Das allgemeine Staatsrecht – Staatsrecht der Aufklärung. Eine Untersuchung zu Inhalt, Anspruch und Geltung des naturrechtlichen Staatsrechts im 17. und 18. Jahrhundert*, Berlin: Duncker & Humblot, 2001.

Schennach, Martin P., '"Allgemeines Bestes" und "bürgerliche Freiheit"? Staatsentstehung, Staatszweck und Staatstätigkeit bei Joseph von Sonnenfels,' in *Päpste, Privilegien, Provinzen. Studien zur Kirchen-, Rechts- und Landesgeschichte. Festschrift für Werner Maleczek zum 65. Geburtstag*, ed. Martin P. Schennach, Rainer Murauer, and Johannes Gießauf, 352–376, Vienna and Munich: Böhlau and Oldenbourg, 2010.

Schennach, Martin P., 'Generalisierung und Differenzierung des Rechts und durch das Recht? Zu einem Vergleich von ALR, Code civil und ABGB,' in *Kontinuität im Wandel. 200 Jahre ABGB (1811–2011)*, ed. Heinz Barta et al., 49–84, Innsbruck: Innsbruck Univ. Press, 2012.

Schennach, Martin P., 'Die "österreichische Gesamtstaatsidee." Das Verhältnis zwischen "Gesamtstaat" und Ländern als Gegenstand rechtshistorischer Forschung,' in *Rechtshistorische Aspekte des österreichischen Föderalismus. Beiträge zur Tagung an der Universität Innsbruck am 28. und 29. November 2013*, ed. Martin P. Schennach, 1–29, Vienna: Verlag Österreich, 2015.

Schennach, Martin P., 'Privatautonomie oder paternalistischer Interventionsstaat? Das ABGB und sein kodifikatorisches Umfeld,' in *La codificazione del diritto fra il Danubio e l'Adriatico. Per i duecento anni dall'entrata in vigore dell'ABGB (1812–2012)*, ed. Pio Caroni and Riccardo Ferrante, 35–78, Turin: Giappichelli, 2015.

Schennach, Martin P., *Austria inventa? Zur Entstehung der österreichischen Staatsrechtslehre*, Frankfurt: Klostermann, 2020.

Schennach, Martin P., '"There is no other European state whose constitution consists of so many anomalies." The Austrian Doctrine of Public Law in the Second Half of the 18th Century,' *Rechtsgeschichte – Legal History* 28 (2020): 95–118.

Scheuner, Ulrich, 'Die Verwirklichung der Bürgerlichen Gleichheit. Zur rechtlichen Bedeutung der Grundrechte in Deutschland zwischen 1780 und 1850,' in *Grund- und Freiheitsrechte im Wandel von Gesellschaft und Geschichte. Beiträge zur Geschichte der Grund- und Freiheitsrechte vom Ausgang des Mittelalters bis zur Revolution von 1848*, ed. Günter Birtsch, 376–401, Göttingen: Vandenhoeck & Ruprecht, 1981.

Schlumbohm, Jürgen, *Freiheit. Die Anfänge der bürgerlichen Emanzipationsbewegung in Deutschland im Spiegel ihres Leitworts (ca. 1760–ca. 1800)*, Düsseldorf: Schwann, 1975.

Schneider, Karin, 'Zwischen "Monarchischer Union von Ständestaaten" und Gesamtstaat. Die Habsburgermonarchie im 18. und 19. Jahrhundert,' in *Rechtshistorische Aspekte des österreichischen Föderalismus. Beiträge zur Tagung an der Universität Innsbruck am 28. und 29. November 2013*, ed. Martin P. Schennach, 34–49, Vienna: Verlag Österreich, 2015.

Stolleis, Michael, *Geschichte des öffentlichen Rechts in Deutschland, vol. 1: Reichspublizistik und Policeywissenschaft 1600–1800*, Munich: C.H. Beck, 1988.

Stolleis, Michael, 'Johann Jacob Moser (1701–1785), oder: der Erzpublizist des Alten Reichs,' in *Johann Jacob Moser. Politiker, Pietist, Publizist*, ed. Andreas Gestrich and Rainer Lächele, 57–70, Karlsruhe: Braun-Verlag, 2002.

Stolleis, Michael, *Public Law in Germany. A Historical Introduction from the 16th to the 21st Century*, Oxford: Oxford University Press, 2017.

Szabó, Béla P., 'Wissenschaftsgeschichtlicher Überblick,' in *Die Entwicklung der Verfassung und des Rechts in Ungarn*, ed. Gábor Máthé, 359–386, Budapest: Dialóg Campus, 2017.

Walter-Klingenstein, Grete, 'Was bedeuten "Österreich" und "österreichisch" im 18. Jahrhundert? Eine begriffsgeschichtliche Studie,' in *Was heißt Österreich? Inhalt und Umfang des Österreichbegriffs vom 10. Jahrhundert bis heute*, ed. Richard G. Plaschka,

Gerald Stourzh, and Jan Paul Niederkorn, 149–220, Vienna: Verl. d. Österr. Akad. d. Wissenschaften, 1995.

Willoweit, Dietmar, *Rechtsgrundlagen der Territorialgewalt. Landesobrigkeit, Herrschaftsrechte und Territorium in der Rechtswissenschaft der Neuzeit*, Cologne and Vienna: Böhlau, 1975.

Willoweit, Dietmar, 'Das Staatsrecht Kreittmayrs,' in *Wiguläus Xaver Aloys Freiherr von Kreittmayr 1705–1790. Ein Leben für Recht, Staat und Politik. Festschrift zum 200. Todestag*, ed. Richard Bauer and Hans Schlosser, 101–117, Munich: C.H. Beck, 1991.

Willoweit, Dietmar, 'Landesstaatsrecht als Herrschaftsverfassung des 18. Jahrhunderts,' *Rechtsgeschichte – Legal History* 19 (2011): 333–353.

Wurzbach, Constantin von, ed., *Biographisches Lexikon des Kaiserthums Oesterreich*, vol. 9, Wien: Kaiserlich-Königliche Hof- und Staatsdruckerei, 1863.

Wyduckel, Dieter, *Ius Publicum. Grundlagen und Entwicklung des öffentlichen Rechts und der deutschen Staatsrechtswissenschaft*, Berlin: Duncker & Humblot, 1984.

CHAPTER 6

The Chair of Natural Law in Prague (1748–1775)

Ivo Cerman

1 Introduction

In the Habsburg monarchy, the introduction of secular natural law was directed by the central government in Vienna and determined by the larger cultural context of Catholic Europe. It is the aim of this paper to reconstruct the cultural and administrative processes that resulted in the establishment and development of the chair of natural law in Prague. Legal scholars at Charles-Ferdinand University in Prague began to experiment with secular natural law in the early eighteenth century, then an experimental chair of natural law was founded in 1748, and the final breakthrough came with the university reforms in Vienna during 1752–54 which made natural law obligatory at all universities and established a network of chairs in the Habsburg hereditary lands. The scholars in Prague were then trying to find their own way – limited by the tight study regulations – until 1775, when new unitary instructions for Prague and Vienna made it obligatory to use the textbooks by Carl Anton Martini (1726–1800). This was the end of Prague's scholarly independence. In what follows we will explore the struggles of natural law thinkers during this period.

2 Prague and the Catholic Network

The history of natural law in Prague starts long before 1748, when it was officially introduced as a university discipline. The Charles-Ferdinand University, which was created by the unification of the old Carolinum with the Jesuit college, had existed as a part of a large network of Catholic universities, where the ideas of early modern Spanish theologians and lawyers were still kept alive and discussed.[1]

1 For the history of Charles University in Prague, see: Ivana Čornejová, ed., *Dějiny univerzity Karlovy II (1622–1802)* [*History of the Charles University II (1622–1802)*] (Prague: Carolinum, 1996). For the history of legal sciences in eighteenth-century Bohemia see Jiří Klabouch, *Osvícenské právní nauky v českých zemích* [*The Enlightenment Legal Sciences in the Bohemian Lands*] (Praha: Czechoslovak Academy of Sciences, 1958).

 | DOI:10.1163/9789004545847_007

This large network confronted and discussed the impulses coming from Grotius and Pufendorf in the late seventeenth century.[2] There was a school of Catholic experts on Roman law at the universities of Ingolstadt, Dillingen and Salzburg who admired the Belgian jurist Henricus Zoesius (1571–1627) and commented on issues of natural law theory quite early on. In terms of organization, the new Benedictine University of Salzburg played a groundbreaking role. It established a chair of jus publicum as early as 1652, a chair of jus gentium in 1718 and a chair of ius naturae in 1731.[3] Lastly, these Catholic pioneers include the University of Würzburg, which underwent sweeping reforms in the 1720s and 1730s when Johann Adam Ickstatt was asked to modernize the Faculty of Law. In 1731 Würzburg also established a chair of natural law.[4] The last of these reforming centres was the University in the territory of the Bishopric Bamberg. In 1735 it too went through a reform when the Bishop founded a new Faculty of Law.[5] The Salzburg scholars Josef Adam Glettle (Klettle) and Franciscus Schmier produced works discussing jus publicum, which showed the limits of what was acceptable in the Catholic world. Josef Adam Ayblinger then provided a manual of the public law of the Holy Roman Empire.[6] This discipline, closely coupled with systematic thought on natural law, found another template in the pro-Habsburg work of Philipp Reinhard Vitriarius who taught

2 Ivo Cerman, 'Nikolaus Ignaz Koenigsmann: Natural Law in Prague before 1752,' *Grotiana* 41 (2020): 177–197.

3 Peter Putzer, 'Aspekte der Wissenschaftspflege an der alten Salzburger Juristenfakultät,' in *Universität Salzburg 1622–1962–1972. Festschrift*, ed. Hans Wagner (Salzburg: Universität Salzburg, 1972), 121–163; Ivo Cerman, *Habsburgischer Adel und Aufklärung. Bildungsverhalten des Wiener Hofadels im 18. Jahrhunderts* (Stuttgart: Franz Steiner Verlag, 2010), 322.

4 Notker Hammerstein, *Aufklärung und katholisches Reich* (Berlin: Duncker und Humblot, 1977), 33–73; Anton Schindling, *Bildung und Wissenschaft in der Frühen Neuzeit 1650–1800* (München: Oldenbourg Verlag, 1999), 11–12; Katharina Beiergrösslein, Iris von Dorn and Diethelm Klippel, 'Das Naturrecht an den Universitäten Würzburg und Bamberg im 18. Jahrhundert,' *Zeitschrift für Neuere Rechtsgeschichte* 35 (2013/3–4): 172–192.

5 Berhhard Spörlein, *Die ältere Universität Bamberg (1648–1803). Studien zur Institutionen- und Sozialgeschichte* (Berlin: Scripvaz Verlag, 2004), 2 vols, vol. 2, 562–588; Heinrich Lang, 'Das Fürstbistum Bamberg zwischen katholischer Aufklärung und aufgeklärten Reformen,' in *Bamberg im Zeitalter der Aufklärung und der Koalitionskriege*, ed. Mark Häberlein (Bamberg: University of Bamberg Press, 2014), 11–71, esp. 62.

6 Josef Adam Glettle, *Jurisprudentia fundamentalis* (Salzburg: Jonnas Baptista Mayr, 1691); Josef Adam Ayblinger, *Institutiones imperiales* (Salzburg: Jonnas Baptista Mayr, 1718); Franciscus Schmier, *Jurisprudentia publica universalis, seu ex jure tum naturali tum divino positivo nec non jure gentium nova et scientifica methodo derivata et juris publici facta* (Salzburg: Joannes Joseph Mayr, 1722).

this subject at the University of Leiden in the Netherlands.[7] Even though this university found itself in a Protestant country, Vitriarius's commentaries on Grotius and on the public law became very popular with the Habsburg nobility. Later, when these noblemen began to outline the university reforms under Maria Theresa, they accepted these Dutch and South German works as the sources for courses in the new disciplines. The South German universities were also a source of personnel for the new chairs at Habsburg universities. The experiments made in South German institutions of higher education were extremely important for the university reform in the Catholic Habsburg monarchy.

Prague made its first experience in natural law on the margins of this intellectual world. In 1664 Matthias Alois Malanotte de Caldes made the first reference to Grotius in his tract on the law of war,[8] and Pufendorf was first referred to in 1723.[9] The most famous Prague lawyer of the era, Wenzel Xaver Neumann von Puchholz, provided an extensive discussion of South German theorists in his comment on Henricus Zoesius.[10] During this time, Catholic noblemen were already asking for lectures on natural law in Prague, and their pressure led to concessions in school policies. In 1725 it was permitted to teach natural law and public law in the private *collegia* provided by Prague professors.[11] They were encouraged to draw on *Struvii Syntagma* for public law, and on the *Tractatus Hugoni Grotii de Jure belli ac pacis* for natural law.[12]

7 Philipp Reinhard Vitriarius, *Institutiones iuris publici Romano-Germanici selectae* (Leiden: Van der Aa, 1686); Philipp Reinhard Vitriarius, *Institutiones iuris naturae et gentium* […] *ad methodum Hugonis Grotii conscriptae, editae et auctae a Johanne Jacobo Vitriario, accedit Johannis Francisci Buddei Historia juris naturalis* […] (Leiden: Jordan Luchtmann, 1704). See Cerman, *Habsburgischer Adel*, 272–277, 333–339.

8 Archiv Univerzity Karlovy, Prague, old prints, shelf number B 316 adl. 5, Matthias Alois Malanotte de Caldes, *Disputatio canonico-civilis de iure belli … pro consequenda in utroque iure licentia* (Prague, 1664).

9 Klabouch, *Osvícenské právní nauky*, 147. According to Klabouch, the first reference was in Wenzel Xaver Neumann, *Pacificatio nomothetica rempublicam per pacta publica domi forisque tranquillans* (Prague: Wolfgang Wickhart, 1723), 35.

10 Wenzel Xaver Neumann, *Annotationes ad viri clarissimi Henrici Zoesii Commentarium ad XXV libri Digestorum* (Nürnberg: Johann Friedrich Rudiger, 1732). Klabouch confused Henricus Zoesius of Louvain with Ulrich Zasius of Freiburg im Breisgau. See Klabouch, *Osvícenské právní nauky*, 154.

11 See Georg Norbert Schnabel, *Geschichte der juridischen Facultät an der vereinigten Carl-Ferdinandeischen Hochschule zu Prag* (Prague: Straschiripka, 1827), vol. 1, 65.

12 Schnabel, *Geschichte*, vol. 1, 65. *Hofdecret vom 4. Dezember 1725*. The original document was lost, together with the whole file of historical governmental regulations for the university, in 1945.

This regulation seems to be part of an attempt at a large-scale reform, because in the same year[13] we have similar permissions for the universities of Vienna and Louvain, the latter in the Austrian Netherlands, the largely francophone area of present-day Belgium that was part of the Habsburg Monarchy. A forerunner was the proposal by the superintendent Theodore Birelli in Prague to introduce *jus publicum* in a comprehensive reform for Prague in 1711.[14] His proposal was not implemented due to the plague epidemic.

Natural law became the object of intense discussion in Prague in the 1730s when Heinrich Peter Broichausen produced a tract on the question of toleration based on a systematic treatment of *leges permittentes*.[15] Since he was also drawing on historical examples and could not openly criticize Habsburg policies, he approved only of the toleration of non-Catholics in the Holy Roman Empire, but not in Bohemia. His conservative ideas provoked the response of Nikolaus Ignaz Koenigsmann who produced the first more extensive treatment of secular natural law in Prague. This forgotten legal scholar was born in East Prussia in 1688, but he had already come to Prague as a student before 1709. Since the University required an oath to the Immaculate Conception, we must assume that he had converted to Catholicism before his enrolment. He stayed at the Faculty of Law even after his graduation in 1721. From then on, he started his regular career as a tenured professor of law, which continued without interruption until his death in 1752. He was one of the first commentators on secular natural law in Prague. His most important work is

13 'Reformvorschläge von der Seite der Universität, 1725, 4. September, in Rudolf Kink, *Geschichte der kaiserlichen Universität zu Wien* (Wien: C. Gerold & Sohn, 1854), vol. II/1, 237–245, Document Nr. 85; Victor Brants, *Faculté de droit de l'université de Louvain à travers cinq siècles (1426–1906)* (Louvain: Peeters, 1906), 161–164; Charles Terlinden, 'Les avatars de la chaire de droit public dans l'Université de Louvain au XVIIIe siècle,' in *L'Université de Louvain à travers cinq siècles (1426–1926)*, ed. Léon van der Essen (Bruxelles: Lesigne, 1927), 203–243. Most recently, Martin P. Schennach argues that the changes started in Freiburg im Breisgau and also included the Jesuit Universities of Olomouc and Graz. However, these two Jesuit universities did not have fully developed faculties of law. See Martin P. Schennach, *Austria inventa? Zu den Anfängen der österreichischen Staatsrechtslehre* (Frankfurt am Main: Vittorio Klostermann, 2020), 361–366.

14 Karel Kučera, 'Raně osvícenský pokus o reformu pražské univerzity [An effort to reform the University of Prague during the Early Enlightenment],' *Acta Universitatis Pragensis – Historia Universitatis Carolinae Pragensis* 4 (1963/2): 61–86. The original manuscript of this reform proposal has been lost.

15 Heinrich Peter Broichausen, *Tolerantia exculpata per III. dissertationes juridicas naturam legis permittentis explicantes deducta* (Prague: Mathias Höger, 1732). See Cerman, 'Koenigsmann,' 184.

the *Prolegomena iuris* of 1737,[16] in which he responded to Broichausen. This tract is based on the discussion of three meanings of '*jus*.' Firstly, it means 'that which is just' (*justum*), secondly, the 'moral faculty to do something or to have something' and thirdly 'laws' (*leges*).[17] Each discussion of these three meanings leads, however, to deeper questions discussed by early modern natural lawyers. Koenigsmann draws heavily on Grotius, so that each of the three parts can be seen as a commentary on sections of the classic work *De jure belli ac pacis*. However, the tract is also an elaboration on older conceptions of Spanish theologians and German Catholic lawyers who are referred to throughout the whole work. In fact, the most influential source of Koenigsmann's views is Francisco Suárez, even though his name does not come up so often. In his approach to natural law, Koenigsmann simply integrates elements of Grotius's teachings into a longer Catholic tradition.

In keeping with the Catholic tradition of the freedom of the will, he rejects approaches which derive natural law from a highest principle and accepts Grotius's definition of '*dictatum rectae rationis*.' He also believes that natural law takes its name from rational human nature. It is law discovered by human reason. This optimistic view did not deny the divine origin of natural law, because rational human nature had been created by God. If God had created us as donkeys,[18] we would lack reason and our acts would lack any morality. Koenigsmann had one more reason for rejecting a deductive conception of natural law as derived from from a highest principle. He knew that we may find ourselves in a great variety of circumstances, and there is no general principle which would fit all of them. What we need is to examine the circumstances and consequences of each action, and then decide and create a circumstantial rule. In keeping with Suárezian tradition, he preferred circumstantial reasoning.[19] The foundation of natural law is not in *voluntas Dei*, nor in laws, but in *sana ratio* (sound reason) which God gave us.[20]

The other underlying issue of Koenigsmann's tract was the question whether permissions are a part of law. Natural law theorists tended to dismiss the conception that law not only prescribes and prohibits but also permits.

16 Nikolaus Ignaz Koenigsmann, *Prolegomena juris dissertatio unica* (Prague: Magnum Collegium Carolinum, 1737).

17 Königsmann, *Prolegomena*, 4. '[…] tres hodie praecipuas hujus vocis significationes statui, et primo, "illud quod justum est," deinde "facultatem moralem ad aliquid agendum vel habendum," et tertio "legem," seu jus constituens, hoc vocabulo denotari. Primam significationem […] de "jure" id est "justo," quam de "justitia" quae illud pro objecto habet.'

18 Koenigsmann, *Prolegomena*, 94.

19 Francisco Suárez, *De legibus ac Deo legislatore* (Coimbra: Didacum Gomez de Loureyro, 1612), vol. II, 16, 6.

20 Koenigsmann, *Prolegomena*, 186.

Permissions were perceived as either disguised commands, or as something which is not a part of law at all.[21] It was, however, a crucial question concerning the liberal culture which allowed some space of personal liberty to citizens even after the social contract. Koenigsmann solved this issue after the model of Suárez[22] by separating the *permissio* into a wide range of various degrees of permissions with different legal force.[23] What is perhaps even more important than the fact that he admitted a '*permissio iuris positiva*' is the fact that he admitted that positive laws may differ from natural law and the difference was not seen as a contradiction to be removed, but as a latitude to be preserved. Something that is neutral or bad in natural law may be permitted by positive law, and something that is permitted in natural law may be prohibited by positive laws. What was equally important was his assertion that if such a prohibition in positive law is removed, the act is again permitted without issuing a new positive enactment. In doing so, Koenigsmann acknowledged the original liberty as a premise that does not have to be proved.

The final remarkable feature of his tract was the historical part at the end,[24] in which he brought a biography of Grotius and appreciated his merits. Even though he still believed as a Catholic that natural law had been discussed even before Grotius, he admitted that Grotius was the first one to treat this subject '*in separatae doctrinae formam*.'[25]

In spite of this promising philosophical achievement, Koenigsmann did not become the first professor of natural law in Prague. His career was seriously disturbed when the French-Bavarian army occupied Prague during the War of the Austrian Succession and he joined the lawyers who supported the usurper. Even though he was cleared of all charges, he was not perceived as a reliable person. When the experimental chair of natural law was created in 1748, it was not given to Koenigsmann. In 1752, he died.

3 The Reforms of Maria Theresia

The state authorities began to show their support for the new discipline after the succession of Maria Theresia. Yet before the new discipline was introduced

21 For permissive law see Brian Tierney, *The Idea of Natural Rights. Studies on Natural Rights, Natural Law, and Church Law 1150–1625* (Grand Rapids, MI and Cambridge: William. B. Eerdemans Publishing Co., 2001); Brian Tierney, *Liberty and Law. The Idea of Permissive Natural Law, 1100–1800* (Washington, DC: Catholic University of America Press, 2014).

22 Suárez, *De legibus*, vol. I. 15. § 7–§ 8.

23 Koenigsmann, *Prolegomena*, 71–75.

24 Koenigsmann, *Prolegomena*, 123–176.

25 Koenigsmann, *Prolegomena*, 125.

in a systematic manner, it was tested in Prague. In 1746 Maria Theresia issued a new study plan which suggested a course in natural law, the *Institutes* and Bohemian law in the first year, plus courses in history, geography and auxiliary historical sciences.[26] In May 1748, an experimental chair of natural law was established at the Faculty of Law in Prague. It was given to Johann Franz Bourguignon von Baumberg (1722–1784) who was sent there from Vienna. The holder of this first experimental chair was assigned the task of teaching natural law in the state of nature and *jus publicum* of citizens after the social contract. He was also supposed to teach feudal law (*Lehensrecht*). The meaning of this move appears in a different light, if we consider that the other new chairs founded in the 1740s were all focused on history, i.e. empirical methods. In 1740 it was the chair of Bohemian justice (*Gerichtspraxis*)[27] and in 1746 it was the chair of *historia et eloquentia* which dealt with auxiliary historical disciplines.[28] In this context, the establishment of the chair of natural law cannot be interpreted as the beginning of an anti-historical rationalist system. It appears that the aim of the courses in natural law was from the outset to clarify terminology and create categories to systematise positive legal material and to understand historical facts.

However, when Maria Theresia started the reform in 1752 in Vienna, the system of disciplines changed and Bourguignon was called away from Prague. Natural law was divided between the chair of natural law and the chair of jus publicum. The old system which was based on the structure of Roman law was abandoned. The reforms in Vienna started with new regulations for the faculties of philosophy and theology in 1752, and after that continued with a competition for the chair of natural law in the Spring of 1753. It is not sure whether the Faculty of Law also received new regulations, but there is a handwritten project of Study Regulations from 1752 or 1753, which implies that it was the case.[29] The winner of the competition for the new chair was Benedict

26 Karel Beránek, 'Právnická fakulta [The Faculty of Law],' in *Dějiny univerzity Karlovy II (1622–1802)*, ed. Ivana Čornejová (Praha: Carolinum, 1996), 137–163, esp. 146.

27 In spite of the confusing terminology, the holder of the chair was teaching history of Bohemian law and not commenting on legal cases.

28 Klabouch, *Osvícenské právní nauky*, 138; Beránek, 'Právnická fakulta,' 146.

29 The undated manuscript version of the study regulations is preserved in the Archives of the *Studienhofkommission*. Even though it is preserved in the folder with documents from 1753, it is surrounded by documents dated to 1752. It is possible that the regulations for the faculty of law were also drafted in 1752. Allgemeines Verwaltungsarchiv Wien (hereafter AVA Wien), Studienhofkommission (hereafter StHK), carton 13, file 34 ex 753, 'Wie auf allergnädigsten Befehl der Ihrer Kayserl. Königl. Majestt. in Zukunfft das *studium juridicum* auf der hohen Schule zu Wienn einzurichten sey,' undated, fol. 199r–222r.

Schmidt (1726–1778) from Bamberg,[30] but it took one more year for the chair to become functional. Schmidt left Vienna before he even started his courses[31] and the chair was given to Carl Anton Martini after a new competition in 1754.[32]

It was only after this long process that the reforms were introduced in Prague. By then, the chair of natural law was vacant because Bourguignon was called to Vienna in 1753 to take up the position of director of the faculty of law.[33] The faculties in Prague received new instructions after the Viennese model in 1754–55, and in the next year the chair of natural law was given to Anton Finck (?–1758), while the chair of *jus publicum* was given to Johann Franz Lothar Schrodt (1727–1777) from Würzburg.[34] Finck was born in Westphalia but studied law in Prague. Regrettably, the minutes from the competitions for these new chairs are not extant. We may assume that they took place in 1755.

The contents of the courses and the opinions were determined by the study regulations, but the problem is that if we compare the extant regulations for Vienna and for Prague, we find that they are not the same sorts of documents and some of the Viennese documents are certainly missing.[35] The most important issues are the instructions for the courses in philosophy and the prohibition of peripatetic traditions. The instruction for the directors of the Faculties of Philosophy and Theology for Vienna of August 1752 contains a detailed section on the faculty of theology, but nothing on philosophy.[36] The instruction of 1754 for the same faculties in Prague contains a detailed section for the faculty of philosophy, which includes an important prohibition against drawing on 'peripatetic conjectures.'[37] We may assume that this was a

30 AVA Wien, StHK, carton 15, file 31 ex 1753, report about Benedict Schmidt's appointment, 16 October, 1753.

31 In the same year Schmidt took up a position at the University of Bamberg where he had studied. See Johann Friedrich Schulte, 'Schmidt, Benedikt' in *Allgemeine Deutsche Biographie* (Leipzig: Duncker-Humblot, 1890), vol. 31, 715–716.

32 AVA Wien, StHK, carton 15, file 31 ex 1754, Allerunterthänigstes Referat die Ersetzung der Cathedra juris naturae betreffend, 22. Aprilis 1754, fol. 12–15.

33 Klabouch, *Osvícenské právní nauky*, 138.

34 The list of all holders of the chairs is in Klabouch, *Osvícenské právní nauky*, 341–343; for a list of Finck's works see Klabouch, 198–200.

35 It may be hoped that the missing Viennese instructions are preserved in the archives of the Studienhofkommission in Vienna. I have discovered several hitherto unknown documents relating to the university reforms in Vienna, but a detailed assessment of the Viennese manuscipt documents is too a large topic here.

36 Kink, *Geschichte*, vol. II/2, 536–540.

37 *Gesetzeslexikon im Geistlichen-, Religions- und Toleranzfache* […] *für das Königreich Böhmen von 1601 bis 1801. Band 5* (*R–S*), ed. Peter Karl Jaksch (Prague: Gubernialregistratur, 1828), 602–605.

repetition of the same principle which had been applied in Vienna and which must be considered a landmark decision as it opened the Catholic universities in the Habsburg hereditary lands to new ideas and rejected scholastic Aristotelianism. This assumption is also supported by Rudolf Kink's summary of the missing instruction for the Faculty of Philosophy in Vienna of 1752, which asserts that it ordered that Aristotelian philosophy should be abandoned.[38] We may conclude that the prohibition was already spelt out in 1752 in the Instruction for the Faculty of Philosophy in Vienna.[39]

The introduction of natural law in Vienna was also based on such instructions for the professors of the new disciplines. The question is whether Prague also followed the model of Vienna. However, earlier research could not answer this question since the original instructions for the first professor of natural law were not known, and therefore we had nothing with which to compare the instruction for the professor in Prague. Now, this question can be already answered because our research in the archives of the *Studienhofkommission* in Vienna revealed handwritten study regulations for the Faculty of Law from 1752 or 1753[40] and even a handwritten instruction[41] for the first professor of natural law from 1753 and for the professor of the jus publicum.

As stated above, in the new system after 1752, natural law was divided between these two professors. The former was teaching first year students, the latter advanced fourth-year students.

The Instruction for the professor of natural law[42] shows that the professor was supposed to start his course with a history of famous legal scholars, and then proceed to explaining the fundamental principles (*Grund-Sätze*) and the

38 See Kink, *Geschichte*, vol. 1, 458–459. According to Kink, this instruction was in the *Statutenbuch der Universität Wien*, which he edited as part of his book. However, the instruction he edited contains only the theological part.

39 'Instruktion für den Direktoren Studii Juridici, 6. Februarii 1755' in Schnabel, *Geschichte*, vol. 2, 105–110.

40 AVA Wien, StHK, carton 13, file 34 ex 753, 'Wie auf allergnädigsten Befehl der Ihrer Kayserl. Königl. Majestt. in Zukunfft das *studium juridicum* auf der hohen Schule zu Wienn einzurichten sey,' undated, fol. 199r–222r.

41 The instructions were not printed in Kink's *Geschichte*. The instructions for the professor of natural law and public law have been used by Notker Hammerstein in his monograph on Catholic university reforms, but without a proper reference. Since then, it has been believed to be lost, until Martin P. Schennach in his recent monograph on Austrian *Staatsrecht* suggested that the documents are filed in carton 13 of the Archives of the *Studienhofkommission*. See Notker Hammerstein, *Aufklärung*, 185–187; Schennach, *Austria*, 370–371.

42 AVA Wien, StHK, carton 13, file 34 ex 753, Verhaltungsbericht für den Professoren *juris naturae et institutionum*, fol. 286r–310v.

way in which we use them to build up a system. His task was to help the students to sharpen their memory. The students would use these skills in their study of Roman law. Even though the instruction believed that the best systematic approach to Roman law was to be found in the works of Samuel von Cocceji, it encouraged the professor to draw also on the works of Grotius and Pufendorf (*De officio hominis et civis*). It recommended also Heineccius, Gundling and other German Protestant authors. However, the Instruction also believed that the works of Protestant authors were suspicious, and therefore strongly advised the professor to balance their errors with Catholic authors, such as St. Augustine, St. Thomas and others.[43] Supplements to the study regulations for the Faculty of Law explain that the professor was supposed to restrict his course to that part of natural law which considers people as private persons.[44] All these stipulations foreshadow the Instruction for Prague, where they are all repeated with more details.

The instruction for the professor of *ius publicum*[45] stipulates that the professor must focus on that part of natural law which considers people as citizens of states and investigates relations between nations. The instruction recommends also particular authors, even though not specific books. The courses of *jus publicum* should be based on 'Grotius, Pufendorf, Boecler, Heineccius, Hornius, Cocceji, Huber, and Böhmer.'[46] Aside from that, the lecturer was encouraged to use the works by the Benedictine Franciscus Schmier and an anonymous work titled *Essai sur le gouvernement civil*, which was believed to have been written by Fénelon.[47] In a more detailed commentary, the instruction highlighted Grotius's *De iure belli ac pacis*[48] and encouraged the professor to use it as a reliable basis for his courses and balance Grotius's

43 AVA Wien, StHK, carton 13, file 34 ex 753, fol. 193r.

44 AVA Wien, StHK, carton 13, file 34 ex 753, fol. 153r–165v (surveys of courses with short descriptions). The courses are described as 'institutiones iuris naturae privati' (fol. 153r), and 'Institutiones juris naturae in soweit solches die Richtschnur einzelner Menschen ist, und deren Handlungen entscheidet.' (fol. 153r). In the Study regulations for the Faculty of Law (fol. 206r), his task is described as 'Der erste [Professor] [...] das *jus naturae* so ferne es die Pflichten einzelner Menschen lehret und zu dem bürgerlichen Rechte (jus civile) unentbehrlich ist, abgehandelt hat.'

45 AVA Wien, StHK, carton 13, file 34 ex 753, 'Verhaltungsbericht für den Professoren iuris publici et feudalis,' fol. 257r–283v.

46 AVA Wien, StHK, carton 13, file 34 ex 753, fol. 258r–259r.

47 Today, it has been established that it was written by Andrew Michael Ramsay in 1719 and 1721 to support the Stuart claims to the thrones of England and Scotland. See Andrew Michael Ramsay, *Essais de politique. Edition critique*, ed. Georges Lamoine (Paris: Honoré Champion, 2009).

48 AVA Wien, StHK, carton 13, file 34 ex 753, fol. 260v–261r.

unspecified errors with other authorities according to his own discretion. All these hints were elaborated into more details in the instruction for Prague.

The Prague regulations only repeated principles and most of the authors which had been established in Vienna. According to the instruction for the professor of *jus naturae* in Prague,[49] his task was to teach first-year students the history of law, then *jus naturae* and finally *institutiones* of Roman law. He was ordered to restrict his lessons to the law of private persons in the state of nature, and not to progress to public law among citizens after the social contract. He was supposed to draw on the Protestant authors Grotius, Pufendorf, Thomasius, Heineccius and Glafey, but he was advised to balance their errors by consulting the teachings of Catholic theologians such as St. Augustine, Aquinas, Honoratus Tournellius, and the Jesuit Jacob Bonfrerius (Jacques Bonfrère). The list also included the renegade Calvinist theologian Samuel Huber. The elements of Roman law were supposed to be taught on the principles of natural law, as they were elucidated in Cocceji's commentaries.

The professor of *jus publicum* was teaching fourth-year students.[50] Again as in the Vienna instruction his task was to explain *jus publicum universale*, which was defined as 'the part of natural law which considers men as citizens and whole nations, their duties to each other, and which teaches the entitlements of the sovereign and the subjects.'[51] His exposition was supposed to start with a history of this discipline, after which he was to explain the subject matter on the basis of Böhmer's *Introductio in jus publicum*,[52] and of the compendium of the Benedictine Franciscus Schmier and, again, of the anonymous *Essai sur le gouvernement civil*. Also here famous Protestant authors such as Grotius, Pufendorf, Hornius, Boecler and Huber were recommended as additional authorities. However, the abstract discipline of *jus publicum universale* was to be combined with the *jus publicum* of the Holy Roman Empire, which was to be taught on the basis of Mascov's compendium.[53] In his discussion of the *jus publicum*, the professor was obligated to refute the 'misleading arguments of the Monarchomachs' and focus on the relation between the state and the Church and on the properties and entitlements of the supreme power in

49 *'Verhaltungs-Bericht für den Professoren iuris naturae et institutionum,'* in Schnabel, *Geschichte*, vol. II, 113–120.

50 *'Verhaltungs-Bericht für den Professoren iuris publici et feudalis'*, in Schnabel, *Geschichte*, vol. II, 130–136.

51 Schnabel, *Geschichte*, vol. II, 130.

52 Justus Henning Böhmer, *Introductio in jus publicum universale ex genuinis juris naturae principis deductum* (Halle: Waisenhausbuchdruckerei, 1710).

53 Johann Jakob Mascov, *Principia juris publici Imperii Romano-Germanici* (Leipzig: Jakob Schuster, 1729).

its relation to the subjects. The relations between states were to be taught on the basis of Grotius's *De jure belli ac pacis*, but the professor was encouraged to correct his errors. The remaining four months from April to September were to be devoted to *jus feudale*.

Since the regulations obligated the professors of the new disciplines to produce their own manuals, they might have stimulated prolific literary activity. In fact, only Finck, the professor of natural law, penned a manual on legal history,[54] and he was ready to go on with further disciplines. Schrodt did not publish anything in these early years. The only theoretical tract on natural law written in that time originated, surprisingly, from the professor of *Digests* and penal law Johann Wenzel Dworzak. His essay '*De aequitate naturali*' was published in 1754,[55] which suggests that he aimed to get the new chair of natural law. Considering the hierarchy of chairs, it would have made sense because he had held the low-ranking chair of *institutiones*. Dworzak's slim tract is quite interesting; it explores the relation between 'equity' (*aequitas*), which is informal justice, and 'justice' (*justitia*), which is based on positive laws. The achievements of the new professors are assessed in the inspection report by Johann Franz Bourguignon[56] who was sent to Prague in 1755 to check whether the study regulations were being respected. Bourguignon praised both of the new professors especially for their literary activities, even though he could not name a single work written by Schrodt. On the other hand, he levelled criticism at Dworzak, whom he accused of laziness while forgetting to mention his engaging printed thesis. Bourguignon noticed that the numbers of students were declining because the reform paradoxically prolonged the period of studies and also because the Jesuits were offering shorter and easier courses at the Faculty of Philosophy. In view of the abilities of Finck and Schrodt the inspector was optimistic about the future. Yet the promising times were brought to an abrupt end when Finck died at the beginning of 1758. It was during the Seven Years' War, and Prague was under constant threat from the Prussian army. The circumstances of his death are not clarified anywhere.

After his death, the two chairs were reunited again because Schrodt was asked to take over the course in natural law. The provincial government, called

54 Anton Finck, *Synopsis historiae legalis in tres partes divisa* (Prague: Magnum Collegium Carolinum, 1755).

55 Joannes Nepomucenus Wenceslaus Dworzak de Boor, *Dissertatio iuridica de aequitate naturali* (Prague: Magnum Collegium Carolinum, 1754).

56 AVA Wien, Studienhofkommission, kart. 41, Sign. 5, Alleruntertänigster Bericht den gegenwärtigen Zustand des Studii Iuridici auf der hohen Schule zu Prag betreffend. Wien 6. Aug. 1755, fol. 176–182.

Repräsentation und Kammer, started a competition for the new holder of the chair, which is very well documented.[57] The archival documents also include autobiographies of applicants which show that even a Catholic country was open to Protestant scholars. However, they had to convert to Catholicism. The first applicant was Johann August Gressl[58] who had come to Prague several years earlier and already participated in the first competition four years before (i.e. in 1755). After his failure, he was employed in the University library, and began to work as a tutor. He also provided legal opinions for the *Repräsentation und Kammer* but failed to provide any examples.[59] The second applicant was Carl David Lossius[60] from Saxony, who had attended the Universities of Leipzig and Wittenberg and graduated from Wittenberg in 1733. He was versed in *jus feudale*, *jus publicum* and *jus civile*, and he was also called to the bar in Saxony and admitted to the *Landesgericht* in Lower Lausitz. For some reason, he converted to Catholicism and moved to Prague, where he tried to secure a job as a lawyer. He also tried to get the job at the first interview for the chair of natural law, which he dates to 6 February, 1756, and after his failure accepted the job in the university archives. Lossius asked the sovereign to consider that he had abandoned all he had for the Catholic religion and stressed that the salary of the archivist was so low that it was not enough to provide a living.

A similar case of a wandering scholar might also have been Josef Anton Schuster (1720–1797), who submitted his application[61] while he was working at the Theresianum in Vienna as a private tutor (*Repetitor*). Since he claimed that he was employed at the Ritterakademie, we may assume that he was working at the short-lived aristocratic school, which was founded as a part of the Theresianum and which was by then on the point of abolition.[62] Schuster was

57 National Archives (hereafter NA) Praha, České gubernium (hereafter ČG) – publicum 1755–63, cart. 210, files 2–3. For the competition see Ivo Cerman, 'Konkurz na profesora přirozeného práva roku 1758 [The competition for the chair of natural law in Prague in 1758],' *Acta Universitatis Carolinae – Historia Universitatis Carolinae Pragensis* 40 (2020/2): 11–22.

58 NA Praha, ČG – publicum 1755–63, cart. 210, files 2–3, application of Johann August Grössl (or 'Gressl'), 17 January 1758, sine folio.

59 He is believed to have written two manuscripts on legal questions, which were not printed and are lost. See Klabouch, *Osvícenské právní nauky*, 134.

60 NA Praha, ČG – publicum 1755–63, carton 210, 1 February 1758, sine folio. For Lossius's employment in the archives see Miroslav Truc, 'K dějinám archivu pražské univerzity v polovině 18. století [On the History of the Archives of the University in Prague in the Middle of the Eighteenth Century],' *Acta Universitatis Carolinae – Historia Universitatis Carolinae Pragensis* (1960/1): 91–126, esp. 101.

61 NA Praha, ČG – publicum 1755–63, carton 210, application 24 January 1758.

62 It was closed in November 1758. See Johannes Schwarz, 'Die niederen und höheren Studien an der k. k. Theresianischen Akademie in Wien,' *Jahres-bericht des Gymnasiums der Theresianischen Akademie* 1902/1903, I, 1–28, esp. 11–16.

looking for a new job, and he stressed that the sovereign promised him that tutors from the Theresianum would be preferred in competitions for professorships at Habsburg universities. Schuster did not provide any details about his previous studies, but the Prague professors later argued that he had studied in Prague.

The last application came, surprisingly, from the Viennese professor of criminal law Johann Peter Baniza who filed it on behalf of his son Leonard Josef.[63] The Banizas belonged to the new acquisitions from Catholic Germany because the father of the family had taught at Bamberg. Baniza explained that his son had finished his legal studies in Vienna and had already collected some professional experience as tutor to the Counts of Trautson. The director of the Faculty of Law, Kressel von Qualtenberg, and the professors of the faculty then decided in favour of Schuster. In their decision, they pointed to the promise the sovereign had given, and to the good moral and professional qualities he displayed when he was attending the *collegia* in Prague.[64]

As a result of the competition, which was confirmed by the *Repräsentation und Kammer* in Prague and by the Directorium in Vienna, Schuster took up his post at the end of 1758.

4 Natural Law Theories

The competition for the chair of natural law in 1758 provided a long-needed stability. Schrodt was free to focus on *jus publicum* and *jus gentium*, and Schuster was given time for writing his manuals. The Directorium in Vienna also dealt with the illegal Jesuit competition at the Faculty of Philosophy. The teaching in question was mainly represented by Josef Jurain (1726–1773), a very prolific author who sought to cover singlehandedly all the sections of natural law, from relations between individuals to the relations between states. He provoked the authorities by his work *Lucubrationes ethicae in ius naturae*,[65] in which he made a polemic assault against Grotius and Pufendorf, whom he criticized for failing to understand that the true source of natural law was solely Divine will, and not *dictatum rectae rationis* or *socialitas*. The problem with

63 NA Praha, ČG – publicum 1755–63, carton 210, application of Leonard Josef Baniza, 11 January 1758, sine folio.

64 NA Praha, ČG – publicum 1755–63, carton 210, application of Leonard Josef Baniza, 11 January 1758, sine folio.

65 Josef Jurain, *Lucubrationes ethicae in jus naturae* (Prague: Jacob Schwaiger, 1760). This was an extended version of his work *Lucubrationes ethico-politicae in jus naturae* (Prague: Jacob Schwaiger, 1759).

his polemic texts was that he was not authorized as a theologian to interfere with secular natural law, plus the fact that his scathing criticism did not spare even Grotius, who had been accepted by official legal theorists as an authority on modern law. Jurain chose a different road from his secular colleagues at the faculty of law. In keeping with the reactionary views of Central European Catholic theologians which were developed in the 1740s, Jurain argued in favour of a very passive conception of man, which was a complete reversal of Catholic positions dating from the sixteenth and seventeenth centuries.[66] In 1760 the authorities in Vienna were appalled by his new manual on the law of nations, which was considered unclear and flawed.[67] In fact, it was based on literature that was generally accepted even in the Faculty of Law, and it did not polemicize against Protestant authors. It was quite timid compared to what Jurain had written earlier. However, the Viennese Directorium had to act, and it issued a strict order that Jurain must no longer call himself '*professor iuris naturae*' and suggested that he should not publish on the subject either.[68]

Now what kind of works did the two secular professors publish to take advantage of the situation? Schuster did not actually write the long-expected compendium on natural law. He only produced several tracts on particular problems of natural law, which were actually conceived as commentaries on particular passages in Grotius's *De iure belli ac pacis*. Only his treatise on the appropriation of things in the state of nature discusses a more general topic.[69] Schuster conceived it as a commentary on chapter 4 in Book II of Grotius's *De jure belli ac pacis*, which is connected to the question of seizure of goods in

66 The origin of this new trend was the work of the Bavarian Jesuit Ignaz Schwartz, who had precursors in the Italian theologians Giambattista Vico and Caste Ansaldi. See Ivo Cerman, 'Ethics and natural law: wolffianism in Prague 1750–1773,' *Studies on Voltaire and the Eighteenth Century* (2011/7): 131–146.

67 Josef Jurain, *Commentarius in jus gentium* (Prague: Jacob Schwaiger, 1760).

68 NA Praha, ČG – publicum, 1756–63, carton 203, M 1, *Reskript*, Wien 22. Novembris 1760, 'Endlich ist ein Buch zum Vorschein gekommen, unter der Unterschrift Commentarii in jus gentium authore Josephi Jurain S. J. Philosophiae Doctore, Ethicae et Juris Naturae Professore Pragae in 4to. Da nun dieseß Werck übel gerathen, und an vielen Ohrthen nicht einmal verständlich ist, als wirdt ihr diesem Professori P. Jurain recht gemessen untersagen sich künftighihn den Titul eines Professoris Juris naturae beyzulegen und dießes um so mehr, als Wier ohnehin in Prag einen besonderen Professoren Juris Naturae aufgestellt haben. Wie Wier dann überhaupt wollen, dass die Professores nicht extra sphaeram ihrer Facultät gehen, und nichts zum Druck befördern sollen, als welches der Universität eine Ehre bey dem Publico machen kann.'

69 Josef Anton Schuster, *Exercitatio academica de jure usucapionis in statu naturali* (Prague: Sophia Kirchneriana, 1759). He also wrote on testaments of priests, on the rights of testators, on entail (*fideicommissum*) and on the right to punish.

war.[70] It implies that the rules set for a just appropriation of things in the state of nature could also be applied to the conduct of parties at war.

Johann Franz Lothar Schrodt (1727–1777) was also supposed to write two elementary compendia, one for *jus publicum* and one for *jus gentium*, and he did so.[71] In his book on *jus publicum*, Schrodt draws on Grotius, Pufendorf and Wolff, but his immediate template was the work of Johann Justin Schierschmid (1707–1778) from the new university of Erlangen.[72] He applied deductive methods imitating Wolff, especially when he was deducing his principles from general notions.

Schrodt continued to develop the optimistic Catholic tradition which maintained that rules of natural law are discovered by human reason. God created man with a nature that also included reason, and that is why it is called natural law. This tradition also implied a certain relaxed conception of law which maintained that law includes not only prohibitions and prescriptions but also permissions.[73] This conception had been revived by Christian Wolff,[74] and Schrodt took it over from him. Natural law includes, according to him, rules that aim either at security or at the welfare of human society (*securitas ac salus rei publicae*). For this reason, natural law includes prohibitions pertaining to acts impeding these aims, and prescriptions pertaining to acts supporting these aims, and also an area of permissive rules, which pertain to neutral issues – adiaphora.[75]

This truly permissive conception of law could have led to statements concerning rights, but Schrodt did not opt for this way because it would violate the instructions. Instead, he skipped this topic completely and focused on the properties of supreme power (*imperans*).

---

70 Hugo Grotius, *De iure belli ac pacis libri tres*, ed. P.C. Molhuysen (Leiden: A.W. Sijthof, 1919) (hereafter IBP), II, 4–5.

71 Johann Franz Lothar Schrodt, *Systema iuris publici universalis* (Prague, 1765) (2nd edition Bamberg: Vinzent Dederich, 1780); Johann Franz Lothar Schrodt, *Systema iuris gentium* (Prague, 1768) (2nd edition Bamberg: Vinzent Dederich, 1780). We will refer to the editions of 1780, as the original Prague editions of 1765 are unavailable.

72 Johann Justin Schierschmid, *Elementa iuris naturalis et gentium* (Jena: Kroekeriana, 1742). (Schrodt makes frequent references to this work.)

73 For the fundamental principle of law see Schrodt, *Systema iuris gentium*, Prolegomena, I, § 12; § 20.

74 See Ivo Cerman, '"Universal Human Rights" and Social Compact in Christian Wolff,' *Das Achtzehnte Jahrhundert und Österreich. Jahrbuch der österreichischen Gesellschaft zur Erforschung des 18. Jahrhunderts 31* (2016): 123–146.

75 Schrodt, *Systema iuris gentium*, Prolegomena, I, § 20, 'Illa quae finis societatis civilis conveniunt, iure publico universali praecepta, quae huic fini repugnant, prohibita, quae relative ad hunc finem sunt adiaphora, seu indifferentia, in statu civili permissa sunt.'

He does not pause to discuss the creation of the *societas civilis*, even though he took over Pufendorf's conception of a double social pact.[76] His explanation is actually more straightforward than Pufendorf's, but slightly different.[77] The first social contract, which he calls *pactum associationis*, binds individuals to each other to establish a society. The second one, which he calls *pactum subjectionis*, subjects the society to the sovereign.[78] In his description of the civil society, Schrodt took over Hornius's conception, which was also used in the prescribed manual by the Benedictine Franciscus Schmier.[79] According to this model, society was built as a pyramid based on 'simple societies' (*societates simplices*), which contained families, family clans and communities. A plurality of such simple societies made up a 'complex society' (*societates compositae*), which shared the same laws and the same sovereign. Since they had their own law, and in this sense were complete, Schrodt also called them 'perfect societies' (*societates perfectae*) after Schmier's model. This intellectual tradition elaborated on the conceptions of Aristotle's *Politics*, which described society as a gradual combination of individuals, families and smaller communities. The trouble was that this model conceived only of unities of relatives as the basis of society, and failed to explain the transition from 'natural units' (e.g. family, clan) to artificial units or unmatched individuals. This model was actually in contradiction with the modern idea of a social contract, which was concluded by individuals, not by communities.[80] It is worth noting that Pufen-

76 Samuel Pufendorf, *De jure naturae et gentium* (hereafter DJN), VII, ch. 2, § 7–9; Samuel Pufendorf, *De jure naturae et gentium*, ed. Frank Böhlig (Berlin: Akademie Verlag, 1998), vol. II, 644–646.

77 Pufendorf's conception involved a compact, a decree about the form of the state, an election and a second compact.

78 It is worth mentioning that Pufendorf does not use this term in his discussion of the twofold social compact (DJN VII.2.7–9; DJN VII.3.1), but spoke of '*subjectionis pacto*' in his discussion of citizenship (DJN VIII.11.3). He also tackled the same subject in earlier works. Samuel Pufendorf, *De obligatione adversus patriam* (Heidelberg: Adrian Wyngerden, 1658), § 8, § 35; Samuel Pufendorf, *Elementorum jurisprudentiae universalis libri duo* (The Hague: Adrian Vlacq, 1660), Pars II, Axiom II, § 2; Pufendorf, DJN, VII.2.9; VII.3.1; DJN VIII.11.2.

79 See Ivo Cerman, 'Obraz společnosti raného novověku' [*The Idea of Society in the Early Modern Age*], in *Společnost českých zemí v raném novověku. Struktury, identity, konflikty* [*Society in the Bohemian lands of the early modern age. Structures, identities and conflicts*], ed. Václav Bůžek (Prague: Nakladatelství Lidové noviny, 2010), 54–74. For Johann Friedrich Horn see Heinrich De Wall, *Die Staatslehre Johann Friedrich Horns* (Aalen: Scientia, 1992).

80 The idea that it is individuals who conclude the social pact was proposed by Hobbes (*De cive*, ch. 5, § 10–12), but it was not accepted by natural law thinkers without reservations. Pufendorf, who described the two social pacts as conluded between *singuli cives*, added a comment, in which he asserted that wives and children were represented by

dorf criticized Hornius because he did not consider the consent of the people as a necessary condition of a legitimate ruler.[81]

In compliance with the instruction for his chair, Schrodt focused on exploring the properties of the supreme power. He insisted that the individual is totally subject to the sovereign (*imperans*), which has to provide the security and welfare (*securitas et salus*) that are the aims of civil society. The citizen may not criticize the supreme power, for he has not enough information to judge its decisions or offer resistance to it. The legal relation between the citizen and the sovereign power is defined by the fact that the system of law construed as a fabric of logical inferences from the highest principle compels the theorist to except the legislator from the system of enforceable legal bonds. The sovereign has enforceable rights against the citizen, but the citizen does not have such rights against the sovereign. If the citizens were allowed to enforce their rights by force or through the courts, it would result in the rejection of the civil state and a return to the state of nature. In the relationship with the supreme power, the citizen is the subject and has only duties. To be exact, the citizen has the duty to render obedience, faithfulness, goods and labour as required.

On the other hand, the supreme power has all rights against the subject, including the right of life and death (*jus vitae et necis*). It is interesting to see which logical construction Schrodt uses to deduce this alleged right. He made this task more difficult for himself by agreeing with Christian Wolff's opinion that the right to life cannot be alienated. For this reason, even the subject may not give the right to life to his sovereign. Schrodt argues, however, that since life comes from God, and the sovereign's duties to preserve the security and well-being of society also come from God, the sovereign has the right to use the subject's life to attain the common good. This right comes directly from

heads of households who were the only real citizens (Pufendorf, DJN, VII.2.20). His concession to the older tradition would have left many individuals outside the protection of law. Wolff sought to resolve the dilemma by adding that the social pact is concluded by houses and individuals ('*inter domos multas, seu ab ingente hominum multitudine*'). Christian Wolff, *Jus naturae methodo scientifica pertractatum*, 8 vols (Frankfurt an der Oder: Renger, 1740–1748), VIII, § 14). See Hanns Martin Bachmann, *Die naturechtliche Staatslehre Christian Wolffs* (Berlin: Duncker und Humblot, 1977), 128–129.

81 Pufendorf, DJN, VII.1.5. However, Pufendorf focused only on the case of a military occupation. Hornius in his work *Politicorum pars architectonica de civitate* (Utrecht: Wilhelm Klerck, 1664) sought to win the favour of the Danish king and glorify the absolute monarchy. Even though he discussed various kinds of social compacts he argued that it is always God who determines the future ruler, and not the people concluding the compact. He sought to prove that 'democracy,' as the state in which everybody is citizen and ruler, is logically impossible.

God and not from the subject's transfer of his own right to life. This truly is a very absolutist argument which may not be compared even to the deductions of Christian Wolff.

In spite of these deductions, the relation between the subject and the supreme power is not the focus of Schrodt's compendium. He only briefly suggests that the sovereign has the right to interfere with the subjects' property, i.e. collect taxes, and even with the subjects' conscience. After that follows the discussion of the relation between the Church and the state, which is the real focus of Schrodt's work. These chapters reveal the real reason for the interest of the enlightened monarchy in natural law. Schrodt even argues that the sovereign power's duty to safeguard the security and well-being of the subjects entitles it to use its *jus eminens* and interfere with the property and powers of the Church. Schrodt does not comment on religious policies, but his remarks about the sovereign's right to interfere with the subjects' conscience implies that he did not recognize religious toleration.

5 Centralizing the Studies in 1775

Schrodt's tract on *ius publicum* enjoyed a considerable reputation, but when the situation was ripe, the Viennese authorities prescribed textbooks written by Professor Carl Anton Martini from the University of Vienna. The original works by provincial authors were no longer needed. Even though Schuster and Schrodt were writing the manuals for their courses, the printed dissertations, which had been the most important genre before the reforms, were rapidly declining because the study regulations in 1754 abolished the obligation to have the final dissertations printed.[82] By the end of the 1760s Martini had covered all the levels of natural law from the state of nature through the civil state to relations between states. When the authorities began to prepare new study regulations after the abolition of the Jesuit order (1773), it was clear that the body of Martini's textbooks would provide a complete and universal overview over all the prescribed sections of natural law.

The study regulations for the Faculties of Law in Vienna and in Prague were written in 1775 by Franz Ferdinand Schrötter (1736–1780) under the title *Ratio studii juridici*.[83] The teaching obligations of the professor *juris naturae et*

82 Klabouch, *Osvícenské právní nauky*, 256.

83 Franz Ferdinand Schrötter, *Ratio studii iuridici* (Wien: Kurzböck, 1775). Cf. Kink, *Geschichte*, vol. II/1, 576–578, Document nr. 170, Verfassung der juridischen Facultät 8. Oktober 1774.

institutionum were still the same, but the textbooks were already definitively prescribed. Natural law was supposed to be taught on the basis of Martini's *De lege naturali positiones*,[84] and chapter VII of this book was to serve as the basis for the history of the discipline. At the end of the course in natural law, the professor was obligated to teach for two months an abbreviated history of civil law on the basis of Martini's *Ordo historiae juris civilis*;[85] the Roman *jus civile* had to be taught on the basis of Heineccius's *Elementa iuris civilis*.

As for the courses in *jus publicum*, Martini's books were supposed to be used only in the last year. It was prescribed to teach on the basis of Martini's *Positiones de jure civitatis*.[86] Since this discipline also pertained to positive law, the professor was encouraged not to restrict himself only to theoretical works, but also to use material from enacted laws. In his comments on law, he was also allowed to use other authors, such as Hugo Grotius, Samuel Pufendorf, Christian Wolff and Emer de Vattel.[87]

Ratio studii juridici introduced a uniform system of natural law in the whole of the Habsburg hereditary lands and terminated the independent attempts of Prague legal theorists. Yet scholarly life did not stay still, because the introduction of political and cameral sciences into the curriculum instigated a new reshuffling of sciences and started a push towards a more empirical exploration of society, which gradually replaced the monotonous *jus publicum universale*. At the same time, the progress of systemic codification of positive law created a completely new situation in legal sciences, which also contributed to the downgrading of natural law as a discipline.

6 Conclusion

The article sets out to reconstruct the institutionalization of natural law as a scientific discipline at the Charles-Ferdinand University in Prague and draw the intellectual profile of the doctrines taught in the successive stages.

84 Schrötter, *Ratio*, 11–12. The prescribed work is Carl Anton Martini, *De lege naturali positiones* (Vienna: Kaliwodia, 1762).

85 Schrötter, *Ratio*, 13. The prescribed work is Carl Anton Martini, *Ordo historiae juris civilis* (Wien: Johann Thomas Trattner, 1755).

86 Schrötter, *Ratio*, 19. The prescribed work is Carl Anton Martini, *Positiones de jure civitatis* (Wien: Johann Thomas Trattner, 1768).

87 Schötter, *Ratio*, 20.

The general character of the Bohemian version of natural law had been determined by the Catholic religion. A large network of Catholic Universities in southern Germany had already experimented with secular natural law in the seventeenth century and applied its methods to Roman law, public law and international law. Their experiments helped to make the teachings of leading Protestant works more acceptable in the Catholic environment. In the period before the establishment of the first chair of natural law in 1748, secular natural law had been discussed in several works by Prague scholars, mainly in connection with the issue of religious toleration. This debate resulted in Nikolaus Ignaz Koenigsmann's *Prolegomena juris* of 1737 where he outlined the history of secular natural law and discussed the meaning of *jus* on the basis of Grotius's *De jure belli ac pacis*.

The second period started with the establishment of the chair of natural law of 1748. The new discipline was, however, restructured in 1755, and separated into two chairs. The chair of *jus naturae* was to discuss only the relations between individuals, whereas the chair of *jus publicum universale* was to deal with citizens within a state and the properties of public power. This period ended with the introduction of a unitary plan of studies in 1775 which universally prescribed the textbooks by Carl Anton Martini of Vienna and made home-grown legal science redundant. The competition for the new professorship of natural law organized in 1758 showed that the Prague chair was actually attractive even to graduates from Protestant Germany.

In terms of intellectual history, Koenigsmann's work determined the limits of openness by its conceptions of free will and of human rationality capable of discovering law by their own reason. This led to the rejection of deductive methods deriving obligations and rights from a single highest principle. The works by specialised professors after 1755 were already determined by detailed instructions for their chairs which encouraged them to write their own textbooks. Whereas Josef Anton Schuster of the chair of natural law did not write any comprehensive tracts on the subject, Johann Franz Lothar Schrodt of the chair of *jus publicum* produced a large compendium on *jus publicum* as state law. In compliance with the official instructions, he focused on the properties of the supreme power and ignored the issue of rights of persons. An interesting feature of his method is the adaptation of Pufendorf's double social contract which he combined with the traditional idea that civil society emerged from smaller units, trying thus to explain the transition from natural units (families), to artificial ones (communities, states). In the last analysis, his teachings about supreme power supported absolute monarchy.

Bibliography

Primary Sources

Ayblinger, Josef Adam, *Institutiones imperiales*, Salzburg: Jonnas Baptista Mayr, 1718.

Böhmer, Justus Henning, *Introductio in jus publicum universale ex genuinis juris naturae principis deductum*, Halle: Waisenhausbuchdruckerei, 1710.

Broichausen, Heinrich Peter, *Tolerantia exculpata per III. dissertationes juridicas naturam legis permittentis explicantes deducta*, Prague: Mathias Höger, 1732.

Dworzak de Boor, Joannes Nepomucenus Wenceslaus, *Dissertatio iuridica de aequitate naturali*, Prague: Magnum Collegium Carolinum, 1754.

Finck, Anton, *Synopsis historiae legalis in tres partes divisa*, Prague: Magnum Collegium Carolinum, 1755.

Glettle, Josef Adam, *Jurisprudentia fundamentalis*, Salzburg: Jonna Baptista Mayr, 1691.

Grotius, Hugo, *De iure belli ac pacis libri tres*, ed. P.C. Molhuysen, Leiden: A.W. Sijthof, 1919.

Hornius, Johann Friedrich, *Politicorum pars architectonica de civitate*, Utrecht: Wilhelm Klerck, 1664.

Jurain, Josef, *Commentarius in jus gentium*, Prague: Jacob Schwaiger, 1760.

Jurain, Josef, *Lucubrationes ethicae in jus naturae*, Prague: Jacob Schwaiger, 1760.

Jurain, Josef, *Lucubrationes ethico-politicae in jus naturae*, Prague: Jacob Schwaiger, 1759.

Koenigsmann, Nikolaus Ignaz, *Prolegomena juris dissertatio unica*, Prague: Magnum Collegium Carolinum, 1737.

Malanotte de Caldes, Matthias Alois, *Disputatio canonico-civilis de iure belli* [...] *pro consequenda in utroque iure licentia*, Prague, 1664.

Martini, Carl Anton, *De lege naturali positiones*, Wien: Kaliwodia 1762.

Martini, Carl Anton, *Ordo historiae juris civilis*, Wien: Johann Thomas Trattner, 1755.

Martini, Carl Anton, *Positiones de jure civitatis*, Wien: Johann Thomas Trattner, 1768.

Mascov, Johann Jakob, *Principia juris publici Imperii Romano-Germanici*, Leipzig: Jakob Schuster, 1729.

Neumann, Wenzel Xaver, *Annotationes ad viri clarissimi Henrici Zoesii Commentarium ad XXV libri Digestorum*, Nürnberg: Johann Friedrich Rudiger, 1732.

Neumann, Wenzel Xaver, *Pacificatio nomothetica rempublicam per pacta publica domi forisque tranquillans*, Prague: Wolfgang Wickhart, 1723.

Pufendorf, Samuel, *De jure naturae et gentium*, ed. Frank Böhlig, 2 vols, Berlin: Akademie Verlag, 1998.

Pufendorf, Samuel, *De obligatione adversus patriam*, Heidelberg: Adrian Wyngerden, 1658.

Pufendorf, Samuel, *Elementorum jurisprudentiae universalis libri duo*, The Hague: Adrian Vlacq, 1660.

Schmier, Franciscus, *Jurisprudentia publica universalis, seu ex jure tum naturali tum divino positivo nec non jure gentium nova et scientifica methodo derivata et juris publici facta*, Salzburg: Joannes Joseph Mayr, 1722.

Schrodt, Johann Franz Lothar, *Systema iuris gentium*, Prague, 1768; 2nd edition Bamberg: Vinzent Dederich, 1780.

Schrodt, Johann Franz Lothar, *Systema iuris publici universalis*, Prague, 1765; 2nd edition Bamberg: Vinzent Dederich, 1780.

Schrötter, Franz Ferdinand, *Ratio studii iuridici*, Wien: Kurzböck, 1775.

Schuster, Josef Anton, *Exercitatio academica de jure usucapionis in statu naturali*, Prague: Sophia Kirchneriana, 1759.

Suárez, Francisco, *De legibus ac Deo legislatore*, 10 vols, Coimbra: Didacum Gomez de Loureyro, 1612.

Vitriarius, Philipp Reinhard, *Institutiones iuris naturae et gentium* [...] *ad methodum Hugonis Grotii conscriptae, editae et auctae a Johanne Jacobo Vitriario, accedit Johannis Francisci Buddei Historia juris naturalis* [...], Leiden: Jordan Luchtmann, 1704.

Vitriarius, Philipp Reinhard, *Institutiones iuris publici Romano-Germanici selectae*, Leiden: Van der Aa, 1686.

Wolff, Christian, *Jus naturae methodo scientifica pertractatum*, 8 vols, Frankfurt an der Oder: Renger, 1740–1748.

Secondary Sources

Bachmann, Hanns Martin, *Die naturrechtliche Staatslehre Christian Wolffs*, Berlin: Duncker und Humblot, 1977.

Beiergrösslein, Katharina, Iris von Dorn, and Diethelm Klippel, 'Das Naturrecht an den Universitäten Würzburg und Bamberg im 18. Jahrhundert,' *Zeitschrift für Neuere Rechtsgeschichte* 35 (2013/3–4): 172–192.

Beránek, Karel, 'Právnická fakulta,' in *Dějiny univerzity Karlovy II (1622–1802)*, ed. Ivana Čornejová, 137–163, Praha: Carolinum, 1996.

Brants, Victor, *Faculté de droit de l'université de Louvain à travers cinq siècles (1426–1906)*, Louvain: Peeters, 1906.

Cerman, Ivo, 'Ethics and natural law: wolffianism in Prague 1750–1773,' *Studies on Voltaire and the Eighteenth Century* (2011/7): 131–146.

Cerman, Ivo, *Habsburgischer Adel und Aufklärung. Bildungsverhalten des Wiener Hofadels im 18. Jahrhunderts*, Stuttgart: Franz Steiner Verlag, 2010.

Cerman, Ivo, 'Konkurz na profesora přirozeného práva roku 1758,' *Acta Universitatis Carolinae – Historia Universitatis Carolinae Pragensis* 40 (2020/2): 11–22.

Cerman, Ivo, 'Nikolaus Ignaz Koenigsmann: Natural Law in Prague before 1752,' *Grotiana* 41 (2020): 177–197.

Cerman, Ivo, 'Obraz společnosti raného novověku,' in *Společnost českých zemí v raném novověku. Struktury, identity, konflikty*, ed. Václav Bůžek, 54–74, Prague: Nakladatelství Lidové noviny, 2010.

Cerman, Ivo, '"Universal Human Rights" and Social Compact in Christian Wolff,' *Das Achtzehnte Jahrhundert und Österreich. Jahrbuch der österreichischen Gesellschaft zur Erforschung des 18. Jahrhunderts 31* (2016): 123–146.

Čornejová, Ivana, ed., *Dějiny univerzity Karlovy II (1622–1802)*, Prague: Carolinum, 1996.

Gesetzeslexikon im Geistlichen-, Religions- und Toleranzfache [...] für das Königreich Böhmen von 1601 bis 1801. Band 5 (R–S), ed. Peter Karl Jaksch, Prague: Gubernialregistratur, 1828.

Hammerstein, Notker, *Aufklärung und katholisches Reich*, Berlin: Duncker und Humblot, 1977.

Kink, Rudolf, *Geschichte der kaiserlichen Universität zu Wien*, vol. I; vol. II/1–2, Wien: C. Gerold & Son, 1854.

Klabouch, Jiří, *Osvícenské právní nauky v českých zemích*, Praha: Czechoslovak Academy of Sciences, 1958.

Kučera, Karel, 'Raně osvícenský pokus o reformu pražské univerzity,' *Acta Universitatis Pragensis – Historia Universitatis Carolinae Pragensis* 4 (1963/2): 61–86.

Lang, Heinrich, 'Das Fürstbistum Bamberg zwischen katholischer Aufklärung und aufgeklärten Reformen,' in *Bamberg im Zeitalter der Aufklärung und der Koalitionskriege*, ed. Mark Häberlein, 11–71, Bamberg: University of Bamberg Press, 2014.

Putzer, Peter, 'Aspekte der Wissenschaftspflege an der alten Salzburger Juristenfakultät,' in *Universität Salzburg 1622–1962–1972. Festschrift*, ed. Hans Wagner, 121–163, Salzburg: Universität Salzburg, 1972.

Ramsay, Andrew Michael, *Essais de politique. Edition critique*, ed. Georges Lamoine, Paris: Honoré Champion, 2009.

Schennach, Martin P., *Austria inventa? Zu den Anfängen der österreichischen Staatsrechtslehre*, Frankfurt am Main: Vittorio Klostermann, 2020.

Schierschmid, Johann Justin, *Elementa iuris naturalis et gentium*, Jena: Kroekeriana, 1742.

Schindling, Anton, *Bildung und Wissenschaft in der Frühen Neuzeit 1650–1800*, München: Oldenbourg Verlag, 1999.

Schnabel, Georg Norbert, *Geschichte der juridischen Facultät an der vereinigten Carl-Ferdinandeischen Hochschule zu Prag*, 2 vols, Prague: Straschiripka, 1827.

Schulte, Johann Friedrich, 'Schmidt, Benedikt,' in *Allgemeine Deutsche Biographie*, vol. 31, 715–716, Leipzig: Duncker-Humblot, 1890.

Schwarz, Johannes, 'Die niederen und höheren Studien an der k. k. Theresianischen Akademie in Wien,' *Jahres-bericht des Gymnasiums der Theresianischen Akademie* 1902/1903, I, 1–28.

Spörlein, Berhhard, *Die ältere Universität Bamberg (1648–1803). Studien zur Institutionen- und Sozialgeschichte*, 2 vols, Berlin: Scripvaz Verlag, 2004.

Terlinden, Charles, 'Les avatars de la chaire de droit public dans l'Université de Louvain au XVIIIe siècle,' in *L'Université de Louvain à travers cinq siècles (1426–1926)*, ed. Léon van der Essen, 203–243, Bruxelles: Lesigne, 1927.

Tierney, Brian, *The Idea of Natural Rights. Studies on Natural Rights, Natural Law, and Church Law 1150–1625*, Grand Rapids, MI and Cambridge: William. B. Eerdmans Publishing Co., 2001.

Tierney, Brian, *Liberty and Law. The Idea of Permissive Natural Law, 1100–1800*, Washington, DC: Catholic University of America Press, 2014.

Truc, Miroslav, 'K dějinám archivu pražské univerzity v polovině 18. století,' *Acta Universitatis Carolinae – Historia Universitatis Carolinae Pragensis* (1960/1): 91–126.

Wall, Heinrich De, *Die Staatslehre Johann Friedrich Horns*, Aalen: Scientia, 1992.

PART 3

Hungary and Transylvania

CHAPTER 7

The Dream of Freedom, Peace and Order

Natural and Divine Law in the Works of a Unitarian Bishop from Sixteenth-Century Transylvania

Borbála Lovas

1 Introduction

In his *De officio hominis and civis*, Pufendorf says:

> What is the character of natural law? What is its necessity? And in what precepts does it consist in the actual condition of mankind? These questions are most clearly answered by a close scrutiny of the nature and character of man. Just as one makes great progress towards an accurate knowledge of civil laws by first achieving a good understanding of the condition of a state and the customs and occupations of its citizens, so if one first takes a view of the common character and condition of mankind, the laws on which man's security rests will easily become clear.[1]

In the following pages, I will take a closer look at the works of a Unitarian writer in late-sixteenth-century Transylvania, Bishop György Enyedi (1555–1597), and I shall answer the question of whether Enyedi's views on politics and society – based on the texts of writers in classical Antiquity, authorities during the Reformation, and theorists of natural theology – point towards a conception of natural law which then unfolded in seventeenth-century Unitarian theology in Transylvania. Note that, if it can be found at all, proof of Enyedi's affinity for natural law can be found scattered in manuscript collections of his sermons and in his printed exegetical work. These sources show connections to seventeenth-century writers on natural law, as well as the classical sources, the waves of the Reformation and the ideas of natural theology. Thus, the question is rather whether it is possible to build up a conception of natural law from fragments held in collections of sermons and

1 Samuel Pufendorf, *On the Duty of Man and Citizen According to Natural Law*, ed. James Tully, transl. Michael Silverthorne (Cambridge: Cambridge University Press, 1991), 33 (I.3.1.).

 | DOI:10.1163/9789004545847_008

debates copied throughout a century and from old prints of biblical exegesis, for the result could well be the mere illusion of a synthesis.

2 The Third Unitarian Bishop and His Textual Heritage

György Enyedi was an accomplished and gifted preacher and theologian. He studied in Geneva and Padua, attending Giacomo Zabarella's lectures on Aristotelian philosophy. He was a teacher at Cluj,[2] then the rector of the Unitarian College. Before being elected bishop in 1592, he gave lectures on theology and philosophy there.[3]

Enyedi's theological arguments were appreciated and adopted by Dutch, Swiss, German and English theologians and biblical scholars, such as Lambert Bos, Jean Leclerc and Daniel Whitby, in the seventeenth century, as well as by Adolf Jülicher and Werner Wilhelm Jaeger in the nineteenth and twentieth centuries, especially passages where Enyedi made pioneering use of Antique texts to explicate biblical verses.[4] His virtuosity is evident in his sermon collection, which contains some two hundred texts and which was written between 1592 and 1597, an extensive source of study, even in its unfinished form.[5] Enyedi did not hold on to pure theological subjects and common preaching customs but instead created a sort of reference book, combining controversial theology, biblical exegesis and politics. This collection also served as a sermon handbook for the main feasts of the Church.[6] In it, he addressed numerous

2 The city has a rich history, and, although it has had various names (Cluj-Napoca, Kolozsvár, Klausenburg and Claudiopolis), I refer to it as Cluj in this article.

3 For his life and works, see Mihály Balázs and János Káldos, ed., *György Enyedi* (Baden-Baden: Editions Valentin Koerner, 1990), 11–18, 71–150.

4 For a more in-depth analysis of the most famous example, where Enyedi compared the text of Philippians 2:6 with a passage from Heliodorus's *Aethiopica*, cf. József Simon, *Explicationes explicationum: Filozófia, irodalom és egzegetika Enyedi György életművében* [Explicationes explicationum: Philosophy, literature and exegesis in the oeuvre of György Enyedi] (Budapest: Typotex, 2016), 193–229.

5 In this article, the notes on the sermons refer to the manuscripts. Modern printed editions of sermons 67–211 can be found in *Enyedi György prédikációi* [Sermons of György Enyedi], Vols. 1–3, ed. Borbála Lovas (Budapest: MTA–ELTE HECE, Magyar Unitárius Egyház, 2016–2018).

6 The sermons survived in seventeenth-century handwritten copies. Although the printing regulations in the principality of Transylvania stopped the Unitarians from publishing the sermons in the bishop's lifetime, the extensive manuscript culture of the Unitarians that helped to preserve their most important texts – sermons, songs and prayers, various versed stories, Psalm translations, religious debates, and philosophical and theological works – maintained Enyedi's sermons as well. On the censorship and the printing culture, see Carmen Florea, 'Shaping Transylvanian Antitrinitarian identity in an urban context,' in

issues with potential points of connection to natural law, including divinity, miracles, human behaviour, conscience, property, social order, state theory, ethics of war, morality and human law.

Enyedi's sermons are full of cross-references to his extensive exegetical work, *Explicationes locorum veteris et novi testamenti*, published in the year following his death.[7] While the first Latin edition reached mostly Central and Eastern European readers for geographical and political reasons, the second one, identified lately as an Amsterdam edition,[8] was commissioned from England and served its readership in the Low Countries, England, Ireland and later America.[9] The London publisher of the volume was John Dunmore, who had close business ties to Dutch printing houses and dealt in French, Latin and Greek books. In 1674, Daniel Elzevier sent him two thousand copies of Grotius's *De veritate religionis Christianae*.[10] As a rule, Enyedi's

Confessional Identity in East-Central Europe, ed. Maria Crăciun, Ovidiu Ghitta, and Graeme Murdock (Aldershot: Ashgate, 2002), 64–80.

7 György Enyedi, *Explicationes locorvm Veteris et Novi Testamenti, ex qvibvs Trinitatis dogma stabiliri solet* (Kolozsvár: [Heltai, 1598]). USTC 305892.

8 György Enyedi, *Explicationes locorvm Veteris et Novi Testamenti, ex qvibvs Trinitatis dogma stabiliri solet* (Amsterdam: [Johannes van Ravesteyn(?), ca. 1669]). Cf. Borbála Lovas, 'The Posthumous Reception of an Antitrinitarian Bishop at Home and Abroad: The Afterlife of György Enyedi's *Explicationes*,' in *Print Culture at the Crossroads: The Book and Central Europe*, ed. Elizabeth Dillenburg, Howard Louthan, and Drew B. Thomas (Leiden: Brill, 2021), 58–84.

9 The exegetical work of Enyedi was in the possession of John Locke and Sir Isaac Newton, Samuel Pepys and Robert Sharrock as well as by theologians and clerics like Richard Allestree, Sir Richard Ellys, Thomas Gataker, Peter Gunning, John Moore, William Owtram, Thomas Turner, William Wake and Thomas Sherlock. John Locke adopted elements of anti-Trinitarian or Socinian theology. For their relation to Locke's natural law theory, see David Wootton, 'John Locke: Socinian or natural law theorist?,' in *Religion, Secularization and Political Thought: from Thomas Hobbes to J.S. Mill*, ed. James E. Crimmins (London: Routledge, 1989), 39–67; John Marshall, 'Locke, Socinianism, "Socinianism," and Unitarianism,' in *English Philosophy in the Age of Locke*, ed. M.A. Stewart (Oxford: Oxford University Press, 2000), 111–182. For parallel elements in the views of John Locke and Enyedi on Christian faith, ecclesiastical moderation, and religious toleration, see Béla Mester, 'The Connection between the Unitarian thought and Early Modern political philosophy,' *Journal for the Study of Religions and Ideologies* 3 (2002 Winter): 142–157. On Socinianism as a source of inspiration for Newton, see Steven Snobelen, 'Isaac Newton, Socinianism and "the One Supreme God,"' in *Socinianism and Arminianism: Antitrinitarians, Calvinists, and Cultural Exchange in Seventeenth-Century Europe*, ed. Martin Mulsow and Jan Rohls (Leiden: Brill, 2005), 241–298. Newton's dog-eared copy is kept today at Trinity College, Cambridge (Newton's Library, No. H557). A dog-ear also marks the page of Cristopher Sand's *Nucleus historiae ecclesiasticae* owned by Newton, where Sand mentions Enyedi and Fausto Sozzini (Newton's Library, No. H1444).

10 Cf. Henry R. Plomer, *A Dictionary of the Booksellers and Printers who were at work in England, Scotland and Ireland from 1641 to 1667* (London: For the Bibliographical Society by Blades, East, and Blades, 1907), 108.

book was often sold together with the Socinian volumes of the *Bibliotheca Fratrum Polonorum* series, and his name is often mentioned along with that of Fausto Sozzini, Christoph Ostorodt, Valentine Smalcius and, last but not least, Johann Crell, whose *Ad librum Hugonis Grotii, quem de Satisfactione Christi adversus Faustum Socinum Senensem scripsit, responsio* (1623) provided arguments on the natural, social and political order based on Aristotelian natural law. The exchanges of opinions between the Socinians, especially those involving Grotius,[11] had a significant impact on the revision and improvement of their ideas.[12]

3 Original Sin and Human Nature

The Protestant conception of natural law in Enyedi's time drew heavily on the interpretation of the Fall and human depravity as its consequence. Although he rejected the views of Luther, Calvin, Melanchthon or Beza, ne nevertheless dismissed the intellectual trend in Renaissance Platonism of rejecting original sin and human corruptedness.[13] However, this attitude emerges in the hiatuses

11 Although there is no evidence of any direct connection between Enyedi and Grotius, their names were mentioned side by side in theological works or biblical commentaries. The Puritan theologian John Owen mentioned Grotius and Enyedi several times together in his enormous work, *An exposition of the Epistle to the Hebrews*, interpreting Enyedi's *Explicationes* to his English-speaking readers. He referred to Enyedi as one of the first to discuss the doctrine of the Trinity and 'whose writings, indeed, gave the first countenance to the Antitrinitarian cause.' John Owen, *Exposition of the Epistle to the Hebrews; with the Preliminary Exercitations*. Revised and abridged by the Rev. Edward Williams (London: James Black, 1815), Vol. 1, 280.

12 Sarah Mortimer, 'Human Liberty and Human Nature in the Works of Faustus Socinus and His Readers,' *Journal of the History of Ideas* 70 (2009): 191–211; Sarah Mortimer, *Reason and religion in the English revolution: The challenge of Socinianism* (Cambridge, Cambridge University Press, 2010), 28–33.

13 A more detailed analysis of the Reformed Protestant idea of natural law and its seventeenth-century development connected to Luther and Melanchthon is provided by Kari Saastamoinen, *The morality of the fallen man: Samuel Pufendorf on natural law* (Helsinki: SHS, 1995), 38–52. For an overview of the doctrine of original sin in the Protestant context, as regards Luther and Melanchthon in particular, see Peter Harrison, *The Fall of Man and the Foundation of Science* (Cambridge: Cambridge University Press, 2007), 52–66. Enyedi already composed notes on the annotations of Theodore Beza on the New Testament during his studies in Geneva. (His work – still in a manuscript copy – entitled *Annotationes in Novum Testamentum*, finished on 22 June 1584, in Geneva, is held today in the Cluj Branch of the Romanian Academy Library: Biblioteca Academiei Române, Filiala Cluj, Ms. C. 628.). Later in his sermons and printed works, he refers to Beza often. More

within his text where he does not follow the way of thinking in reference to the Fall and its consequences.[14] Nor did he agree with the theses put forward by Sozzini on the rejection of the doctrines of original sin, salvation and faith as a source of obedience that precedes commands followed through free will.[15] As József Simon reminds us in his detailed philosophical analysis of Enyedi's *Explicationes*, Sozzini's *Praelectiones theologicae* was an important work in the criticism and refutation of the traditional doctrine of original sin as the most basic component of human nature. Further, although Enyedi rather restrains himself from discussing any other topic than the Trinity in most of the relevant chapters of his exegetical work, he discusses in detail the teachings on man and his ability of cognition in the chapter on John 1. In the passages on John 1, a critical read of Calvin's commentary can be found on the postlapsarian fate of the intellect, which leads Enyedi to an alternative understanding of Sozzini's anthropological theses. Enyedi criticises Calvin's statement, 'the light of understanding is not wholly extinguished, for, amidst the thick darkness of the human mind, some remaining sparks of brightness still shine.'[16] The Unitarian bishop asks if the light of men (John 1:4) is the same light which shines in the darkness, does not comprehend it (John 1:5) and dims after the Fall, Calvin's explanation that the light was not extinguished entirely in John's case leads to a contradiction.[17] In addition, as Enyedi says, if Calvin is right, John's Gospel is incoherent, which is not the case with the verses.[18] Simon also covers Enyedi's sermon written against his former student, János Szilvási, especially

detailed analysis of Renaissance Platonism and criticism of Calvin's and Beza's theses can be found in József Simon, *Explicationes explicationum*, especially 121–125.

14 For further details, see József Simon, 'A természetjog eszméje Enyedi György prédikációiban [The Idea of Natural Law in György Enyedi's Sermons],' in *Dávid Ferenc és a kortárs prédikációirodalom. A reformáció első generációi*, ed. Borbála Lovas and Dávid Molnár (Budapest: A kora újkori unitárius prédikációirodalom története Erdélyben és Magyarországon Kutatócsoport – Kolozsvári Protestáns Teológiai Intézet, 2022), 87–100.

15 Mortimer, *Reason and religion in the English revolution*, 120–123.

16 John Calvin, *Commentary of the Gospel According to John*, Vol. 1, transl. William Pringle (Edinburgh: The Calvin Translation Society, 1847), 33.

17 György Enyedi, *Explicationes* [1598], 144–147.

18 On Enyedi's explication based on the Prologue of the Gospel of John, see József Simon, *Explicationes explicationum*, 121–128. Simon also emphasises in his analysis how Enyedi turns to Aristotelian interpretations instead of conciliating the 'progressive-critical potential of Platonism with the anti-Platonist orientation of anti-Trinitariansim.' This is even more interesting in terms of the attitude of the early Reformers towards Aristotle. It is enough to recall Luther's critical notes on the 'fabulator' with the 'un-Christian, profane, meaningless babblings.' Peter Harrison, *The Fall of Man and the Foundation of Science*, 55–58.

the part of the debate where Enyedi states, 'the intellect which refers from a metaphysical perspective to its own objects is equal to the "intellect planted in man by God," thus discrediting the dogma of the Trinity.'[19] For the Unitarians in general and for Enyedi in particular, morality had no supernatural origin. Their anthropological optimism shared the view that man will be able to perform good acts without supernatural help; this intellectual capacity should provide the basis for the pre- and postlapsarian continuity.[20]

Amongst the Unitarians, this thesis was notorious. As late as 1701, Ferenc Petrityevity Horváth in his *Apologia Fratrum Unitariorum*, the only vernacular interpretation of the Socinian–Remonstrant ideas, wrote in these terms: 'When God created man, he endowed him with intellect and wisdom. And after the creation, the first man had the talent with which he could reason, and so we have it today; and he did not lose this ability with his sin.'[21]

4 The Anti-trinitarian Development in Transylvania

In the second half of the sixteenth century, the Transylvanian city of Cluj, which hosted different Protestant denominations, was the centre of the new

19 József Simon, *Explicationes explicationum*, 126. On the details of the debate, see the later chapter. The paragraphs on the text and interpretations of the meaning of light and darkness in John 1:5 are also echoed in Sermon 124 (today only available in a fragmented copy). Sermon 124, Codex of Sárospatak (Great Library of the Reformed Protestant College in Sárospatak, Kt 7.), 2/275–277. This textual parallelism is even more interesting if we consider the year in which the sermon was supposedly written and delivered in Hungarian. The sermon is part of the fourth triacas, dated to the first half of 1595, while Enyedi's sermon on his former student, János Szilvási, in the text of which Simon completes his arguments, is dated to the end of 1593.

20 In the seventeenth century, this Unitarian doctrine was discussed widely, since Dutch Remonstrant theologians, the likes of Conrad Vorstius and Hugo Grotius, were accused of Socinianism. Jan Rohls, 'Calvinism, Arminianism and Socinianism in the Netherlands until the Synod of Dort,' in *Socinianism and Arminianism. Antitrinitarians, Calvinists and Cultural Exchange in Seventeenth-Century Europe*, ed. Martin Mulsow and Jan Rohls (Leiden: Brill, 2005), 22–44.

21 '[M]ikor Isten az embert teremté, értelemmel és okossággal ruházá-fel [...]. [V]alamint az első embernek teremtetése után meg-vólt ő néki az ő tehetsége, melly által okoskodhatott, szintén ugy meg-vagyon mostan-is; és ezt, az ő vétke által el nem vesztette [...].' Ferenc Petrityevity Horváth, *Apologia Fratrum Unitariorum* (Kolozsvár: Az Unitária Ecclesia Typusival, 1701), 5–6. Cf. Tamás Túri, 'Unitárius prédikációalkotás a 17. század végén: Egy nyilvánosságra szánt iskolai prédikációskötet [Unitarian Preaching at the End of the Seventeenth Century: A Book of Sermons by Theology Students for the Public],' in *Kultúrjav: Írásbeliség és szóbeliség irodalma újrahasznosítva*, ed. Zsófia Ágnes Bartók et al. (Budapest: Reciti, 2015), 201, 204–205.

Unitarian Church. This paper shall focus on the last decade of the century, when the majority of the population was Unitarian. Enyedi's sermons reflect an image of this community in many aspects. They reveal the views of the Unitarian Church on and its relationship to the city and show the extent of their author's cooperation with the magistracy, the council of the hundred, or the *centumviri*, during his episcopacy.[22] In contrast to the harsh polemical tone in early Unitarian, Calvinist and Lutheran sermons, each sermon reveals Enyedi's diplomacy in addressing political, social and everyday issues within the principality. These texts will form the basis for my disquisition. Although Enyedi's sermons were written under the reign – unwelcoming for the Unitarians – of the Catholic Prince Sigismund Báthory, they survived in a dozen or so codices dated between 1614 and 1696.[23] These sermons were presumably delivered by Enyedi in the main church of Cluj, on the main square, surrounded by a market and the houses of the wealthiest citizens, in the very heart of the city. Enyedi's sermons display this geography and its complex connotations, cultural and historical. Cluj was the beneficiary of the uniquely enlightened 1568 edicts, which codified the co-existence of various denominations in Transylvania. During Enyedi's episcopacy, in 1595, they were re-issued by Prince Sigismund Báthory. Four denominations, Catholic, Lutheran, Calvinist and Unitarian (referred to as Arian), were granted equal rights.[24] Consequently, Transylvania and Poland were the two countries in

---

22 The council of the hundred was the principal legislative forum in Cluj, while the first judge and the inner council were responsible for justice. The centumvirate rarely supervised the judge or the inner council. This occurred mostly in judicial cases when office holders were involved in order to help the inner council and to 'preserve self-governance and the independent judicial control of the town.' László Pakó, 'Hatalmi konfliktus vagy testületi összefogás? A kolozsvári százférfiak tanácsa és a városi igazságszolgáltatás a 16. század második felében [Conflict of power or corporative bond? The assembly of the centumviri and the justice system in Cluj in the second half of the sixteenth century],' *Erdélyi Múzeum* 72 (2010/3–4): 87, in the English summary. Cf. also László Pakó, 'The inquisitors in the judicial practice of Cluj at the end of the sixteenth century,' *Transylvanian Review* 21, Supp. No. 2: *Institutional Structures and Elites in Sălaj Region and in Transylvania in the 14th–18th Centuries*, ed. András W. Kovács (2012): 181–197.

23 For further research on the sermons and their textual tradition, see Borbála Lovas, 'Enyedi György prédikációskötetének eredeti szerkezete [The original structure of György Enyedi's sermon collection],' in *Enyedi 460. Tanulmánykötet Enyedi György születésének 460. évfordulójára rendezett kamarakonferencia előadásaiból*, ed. Borbála Lovas and Krisztina K. Kaposi (Budapest: MTA–ELTE HECE, 2016), 71–141; Borbála Lovas, 'Enyedi György szerkesztett prédikációskötete új megvilágításban. A prédikációgyűjtemény triacasainak újrarendezése [The sermon book of György Enyedi in a new light: The rearrangement of the sermon collection's triacades],' *Irodalomtörténeti Közlemények* 120 (2016): 47–54.

24 The acts of Sigismund Báthory were mainly intended to strengthen the Catholic Church.

Europe in the second half of the sixteenth century which overtly tolerated the anti-Trinitarians.

Socinianism in Poland and Transylvanian Unitarianism are close but not identical in terms of their theological theses. While in the Polish case, the denomination represented a moderate theological point of view, the Italian Giorgio Biandrata, a close collaborator with Sozzini during the Polish Reformation, inspired the anti-Trinitarian community differently in Transylvania, and the progression of the theological doctrines was more radical. As a result, Biandrata had arguments with Ferenc Dávid, the first elected bishop of the Transylvanian Unitarians, and even invited Sozzini as a mediator. However, their attempts to eliminate radical ideas, such as non-adorantism – denial the validity of religious worship or prayer for aid addressed to Jesus Christ –, from the theological discussions, and to persuade the bishop to recant, led to dissensions and to the imprisonment of Dávid in the 1570s.[25] As his successor, Demeter Hunyadi, attempted to consolidate the Church with Biandrata's help, Transylvania became a haven for radical thinkers. A number of international figures of radical Protestantism were active in the principality. Among them were Jacobus Palaeologus, a former Dominican friar, leading theoretician of non-adorantism and supporter of Dávid against Sozzini, the German Matthias Vehe-Glirius, known for his famous work, *Mattanjah*, and Adam Neuser from Heidelberg, who later converted to Islam. Further, mention should also be made of the Transylvanian Saxon (German) theologian, Johann Sommer, who is best known as the biographer of Despot Vodă,[26] and, finally, a former Jesuit, Christian Francken.[27] In consequence, non-adorantism and Sabbatarianism

---

25 George H. Williams, 'The christological issues between Francis Dávid and Faustus Socinus during the Disputation on the invocation of Christ, 1578–1579,' in *Antitrinitarianism in the Second Half of the 16th Century*, ed. Róbert Dán and Antal Pirnát (Budapest – Leiden: Akadémiai – Brill, 1982), 287–321; Mihály Balázs, 'Antitrinitarianism,' in *A Companion to the Reformation in Central Europe*, ed. Howard Louthan and Graeme Murdock (Leiden: Brill, 2015), 188–189.

26 Domenico Caccamo, *Eretici italiani in Moravia, Polonia, Transilvania (1558–1611). Studi e documenti* (Florence – Chicago: Sansoni – Newberry Library, 1970); Róbert Dán, *Matthias Vehe-Glirius: Life and Work of a radical antitrinitarian with his collected writings* (Budapest – Leiden: Akadémiai – Brill, 1982); *The Heidelberg Antitrinitarians: Johann Sylvan, Adam Neuser, Matthias Vehe, Jacob Suler, Johann Hasler*, ed. Christopher J. Burchill (Baden-Baden: Koernerm, 1989); Mihály Balázs, *Early Transylvanian Antitrinitarianism 1561–1571. From Servet to Palaeologus* (Baden-Baden: Editions Valentin Koerner, 1996).

27 For Francken and his ideas of natural law and a theology consistent with it, see József Simon, *Die Religionsphilosophie Christian Franckens (1552–1610?). Atheismus und radikale Reformation im Frühneuzeitlischen Ostmitteleuropa* (Wiesbaden: Harrassowitz Verlag, 2008); Alexander Schmidt, 'Irenic patriotism in sixteenth and seventeenth-century German political discourse,' *The Historical Journal* 53 (2010): 243–269; Mario

gathered ground and gained strength in this period, especially at the turn of the sixteenth and seventeenth centuries.[28] The radicalization of the theological ideas was accompanied by the production of radical works circulated in rare prints and in manuscript copies, which caused recurring conflicts within the Unitarian community. The third bishop, György Enyedi, who copied and used the works of Palaeologus and others, knowing their theses in great depth, endeavoured to unify the Unitarian doctrines in his written works, especially in *Explicationes*. As a result, he was labelled by contemporaries, such as Sozzini (who sent him a copy of his *De Jesu Christi invocatione*), as an unscrupulous non-adorantist, a non-Christian, a Judaizer and sometimes even an idiot. In subsequent centuries, his doctrines and explications of the Bible were nonetheless considered as a subject of disputation by Lutheran, Calvinist and Catholic theologians.[29]

While the 'alternative path towards state-building'[30] in the Transylvanian principality may have been a weak attempt for a ruler to build a confessional state, it had the effect of making the Unitarian sect a well-received church in a multicultural and multiconfessional territory[31] which was also known

Biagioni, *The Radical Reformation and the Making of Modern Europe. A Lasting Heritage* (Leiden: Brill, 2016); József Simon, 'Philosophical Atheism and incommensurability of religions in Christian Francken's thought,' *Magyar Filozófiai Szemle* 61 (2017): 57–67.

28 For the Transylvanian Sabbatarian tradition and its key figures, see Antal Pirnát, 'Gerendi János és Eőssi András [János Gerendi and András Eőssi],' *Irodalomtörténeti Közlemények* 74 (1970): 680–684; Róbert Dán, *Az erdélyi szombatosok és Péchi Simon* [The Transylvanian Sabbatarians and Simon Péchi] (Budapest: Akadémiai, 1987); István Keul, *Early Modern Religious Communities in East-Central Europe: Ethnic Diversity, Denominational Plurality, and Corporative Politics in the Principality of Transylvania (1526–1691)* (Leiden: Brill, 2009), 129–133.

29 A more detailed description of the polemical discussions can be found in Borbála Lovas, 'Magyar török, kicsiny pogány, zsidózó és vaddisznó: Enyedi György és az unitarizmus kritikája a 17. században [Hungarian Turk, little Pagan, Judaizer and the boar: György Enyedi and criticism of Unitarianism in the seventeenth century],' in *Viszály és együttélés: Vallások és felekezetek a török hódoltság korában*, ed. Gábor Ittzés (Budapest: Universitas, 2017), 223–250. About the period: *Antitrinitarianism in the Second Half of the 16th Century*, ed. Róbert Dán and Antal Pirnát (Budapest – Leiden: Akadémiai – Brill, 1982); *György Enyedi and Central European Unitarianism in the 16–17th Centuries*, ed. Mihály Balázs and Gizella Keserű (Budapest: Balassi, 2000).

30 Maria Crăciun, Ovidiu Ghitta, and Graeme Murdock, 'Religious reform, printed books and confessional identity,' in *Confessional Identity in East-Central Europe*, ed. Maria Crăciun, Ovidiu Ghitta, and Graeme Murdock (Aldershot: Ashgate, 2002), 3.

31 For further scrutiny, see Graeme Murdock, 'Multiconfessionalism in Transylvania,' in *A Companion to Multiconfessionalism in the Early Modern World*, ed. Thomas Max Safley (Leiden: Brill, 2011), 393–416; István Pásztori-Kupán, 'The spirit of religious tolerance,' in

for being made up of three nations – the Hungarians, Saxons, and Szeklers (a distinct Hungarian subgroup). In the city of Cluj (as well as in the Unitarian congregation), two of these nations were proportionally represented: the centumviri had fifty elected Saxon citizens and fifty elected Hungarian citizens (with the position of judge, like that of bishop, alternating – mostly – between a Saxon and a Hungarian). The free royal city was a bastion of the Unitarian Church; this relationship between the ruling prince and the Church is displayed in many of Enyedi's sermons. These details, as well as the whole history of the Unitarian Church in Transylvania, show that the Unitarians did not construct their doctrines on an apolitical basis. Their texts, debates, theological works and sermons served as priceless tools to fight political and theological battles. The Church, with more influence in the sixteenth century and less in the seventeenth, subsisted in close symbiosis with the political powers, which transformed into a politically powerless interaction between Church and state after the end of the Ottoman occupation and the territory being taken over by the Habsburg emperor. These changes also caused a shift in the ecclesiastical canon. In the new historical and political milieu, Enyedi's sermons were no longer relevant.

In the sixteenth century, Reformed natural law theorists were few in number. Even the most important Protestant writers, such as Martin Luther, gave but a fragmented account of their ideas on the topic. Philipp Melanchthon is thought to have been the first Protestant natural law theorist.[32] While the works of these Reformers are also well-known in East-Central Europe, an otherwise receptive field did not welcome their legal ideas. At the end of the sixteenth century, the Romanisation of Hungarian customary law was aborted, only having peripheral significance with relation to the *Tripartitum* by István Werbőczy.[33] While in the seventeenth century, natural law became an academic discipline in Western Europe, in Hungary and Transylvania this change took place only a century later.

Calvinism on the peripheries: Religion and Civil Society in Europe, ed. Ábrahám Kovács (Budapest: L'Harmattan, 2009), 167–176; and, especially, Mihály Balázs, 'Tolerant Country – Misunderstood Laws: Interpreting Sixteenth-Century Transylvanian Legislation Concerning Religion,' *Hungarian Historical Review* 2 (2013/1): 85–108.

32 A recently published monograph provides a detailed account of the political philosophy and natural law theory of Philipp Melanchthon: Mads Langballe Jensen, *A Humanist in Reformation politics: Philipp Melanchthon on Politics and Natural Law* (Leiden: Brill, 2020).

33 Martyn C. Rady, *Customary law in Hungary: Courts, texts and the Tripartitum* (Oxford: Oxford University Press, 2015).

5 György Enyedi and His Sermons

Enyedi was a priest, not a social philosopher. Arguments in his sermons borrowed from political authors were instrumental in biblical exegesis. However, even his sermons, in their incompleteness, together with the few surviving items from his library and manuscript notes, allow us to reconstruct a basic outline of Enyedi's social thought. The political views of the Unitarian bishop seem to complement and even modify, to some extent, the overall picture of the relation of Church and state in Socinian thought. As Sarah Mortimer put it, Socinians attempted to reject the 'mainstream language of natural law' in an effort to insulate Christianity from natural law and, consequently, to separate the Church from the state.[34] The latter case was just partly an issue connected to Transylvania, since the ruling princes were of other denominations. However, the close connection between the Church and the political elite, as well as the cooperation between the Church and the council in their most important centre, Cluj, led to a more complicated situation.

Hence, Enyedi's detailed vision of his society, revealing strong affinities with natural law thinking, was a unique phenomenon in the late-sixteenth-century intellectual landscape of Hungary and Transylvania.[35] Enyedi adhered to the Christian natural law tradition, which regarded God as the main governor of the world. As all laws come from God, the Bible is for him the highest legal authority: the source of law, the full statement of divine law, a summary of natural law and the only guide for positive law. Accordingly, he did not seek an autonomously valid foundation for natural law in human reason, independent of God. He described society as a well-designed structure, using the popular image of the human community as the co-responsibly functioning ensemble of the members of a human body. The various bonds between people define the status of everyone within the community as its useful member.[36] He touched upon the practical questions of communication, ecclesiastical debates, political discussions, and polemics, as well as theoretical issues of the common good and other underlying moral principles. As to these principles, Enyedi believed in universal understanding, even if his tone

34 Mortimer, *Reason and religion in the English revolution*, 2.

35 Merio Scattola, *Das Naturrecht vor dem Naturrecht: Zur Geschichte des 'ius naturae' im 16. Jahrhundert* (Tübingen: Max Niemeyer Verlag, 1999).

36 Here Enyedi does not echo the Calvinist idea of community, where '[a]ctive participation in society is a necessary duty because it helps in part to restore the original prelapsarian social order.' Peter Harrison, *The Fall of Man and the Foundation of Science*, 62.

turned vigorously polemical now and then. In the next sections, I will exemplify Enyedi's views on social and human experience in correlation with the dynamism of the Transylvanian community.

6 The Rulers and Their Subjects

In Sermon 184, entitled 'De subditorum officio' (The subjects' duty), based on 1 Peter 2:13 ('Keep all the laws of men because of the Lord'), Enyedi's focus was on the community, as well as the obedience of the people, especially the nobility.[37] Thus, the bishop examines the usage of law in the community here from a different perspective from the one discussed in the sermons on judges. Enyedi outlines the structure of his society and lists the deeds that provide for the subsistence of the community. The first is the punishment of the wicked and reward of the good, the responsible task of rulers, princes and magistrates. He also notes that the Christians' reasoning about the heathen Greeks and Romans is usually superficial and imprudent, as 'in many cases they act in conformity with nature; hence, they are closer to the law of God than us.' Or, as a variant of the text states in a somewhat more flamboyant way, 'they imitate and follow nature in many of its matters; hence, they are a thousand times closer to the truth, the law of the Great Lord.'[38] This can be interpreted as Enyedi's idea on a common foundation of moral life in natural law, leading to and perfected by divine reason, irrespective of one's religion and faith.

The second reason for why human communities subsist is, according to Enyedi's argument based on the Holy Scriptures (1 Peter 2:15), 'because this is the will of God.' And this should be kept in mind, since people, even the wisest, are not without fault. Enyedi uses the well-known maxim here: 'Sic volo, sic iubeo, sit pro ratione voluntas.'[39] He goes on to say, 'It is a great sin for

37 The biblical verse is frequently used (and often together with Romans 13:1–5) by sixteenth-century authors in connection with their views on natural law, the nature of civil government and the household codes propagated by the Reformers.

38 Sermon 184, 5th Codex of Kolozsvár (Biblioteca Academiei Române, Filiala Cluj, Ms. U. 1228), fol. 82v: 'Szoktunk az pogánok felől csak imígy-amúgy emlékezni és ítílni, de bizony sok dolgokban azok az természetnek tulajdonságát követvén közelb járnak nállunknál az Isten törvényéhez.' / Codex of Székelykeresztúr (Teleki-Bolyai Library, Târgu Mureș, No. 0439), 458: 'Csak imígy, amúgy szoktunk ám az pogánok felől szóllani, emlékezni és ítéletit tenni, de él az Úr, hogy nagy sok dolgában azok csak az természetnek tulajdonságát imitálván, követén ezerszer közelebb járnak nállunknál az igazsághoz, azaz Nagy Úrnak törvényéhez, csak arányozásból.'

39 Juvenalis, *Satyrae*, VI. 223.

a man to do this. But it is necessary that the cause of his actions should not be his will, but other wisdom and goodness.'[40] Here he turns the focus from good rulers to tyrants, who do not rule for the common good and trust their own will instead of God's. Right after this passage, however, he mentions the story of Abraham and Isaac as a biblical example to follow: once the orders of the ruler are issued, the subjects are not allowed to question them.

Thus, Enyedi stresses here, as well as in other sermons, that Christians are not allowed to rebel against their rulers, even if their political or religious liberties are under threat. This prohibition of resistance (a widespread idea in the period) is based upon the commands in the New Testament and as such is superior to the natural right of self-defense. Interestingly, Enyedi combines these two behaviours in sermons delivered at the beginning of 1597, arguing that both are right and valid. By that time, the prince of Transylvania, Sigismund Báthory, had already left his throne once in July 1594 to return a few months later, celebrating it with a slaughter of the Transylvanian nobility, his own cousin among them. Although Enyedi would not live to see it, Sigismund would leave and return to take up the throne three more times between 1598 and 1602.

The third precept of a lasting community is to stop the offence of faithless people, based on 1 Peter 2:15 ('Because it is God's pleasure that foolish and narrow-minded men may be put to shame by your good behaviour'). In his commentary, Enyedi gives political advice to his believers on their stance against those who insinuated to the prince and the political elite that the Unitarian Church posed a threat to the community, as their leaders instigate their believers to rebel against their rulers. As he highlights, any theory of resistance is an argument of factionalist powers which must be trumped by lawful obedience. As the bishop puts these thoughts into a sermon, he reminds his audience of the importance of the true faith and moral responsibility.

The interpretation of 1 Peter 2 shows Enyedi's connection to the Erasmian humanist tradition as the decreasing relevance of the Fall re-legitimized ancient political–rhetorical thought. Enyedi ascribes the structure and natural institutions of his society, from the individual, to a reinterpreted paternal authority, and the love of God to political authority. The first grade, as he calls it, is that we are all humans. That is why our first duty is to not hate anybody and to honour everyone. He also quotes a saying: 'Good words will not

40 Sermon 184, 5th Codex of Kolozsvár (Biblioteca Academiei Române, Filiala Cluj, Ms. U. 1228), fol. 83r: 'Ezt embernek cselekedni nagy vétek, hanem szükség, hogy az ő cselekedetinek oka ne csak az ő akaratja, hanem egyéb okosság és jóság legyen.'

have a broken wing.'[41] The second grade is kinship, concerning which Enyedi expands the meaning of the word 'family' from blood relatives to members of the church, with the bishop as its head. The third grade is belief in God. The fourth is respect for and obedience to the king, or, in the case of Transylvania, the prince.

In the last paragraph, Enyedi discusses servitude, stating that subjects should submit themselves to their superior, good or evil and be obedient to the authorities, as far as their obedience is not counter to God's law. It does not matter if the lord is unjust or ungrateful: if he does not pay in time or in the due amount, or if he forces his people to overwork. If the duties are against the law, it is not the subject's sin, but that of the superior, and God is the only one who will punish him for these acts. Still, subjects should disobey in the cases of homicide of innocent and harmless persons, destruction of cities and forced recantation of faith. Moreover, this is not only a divine commandment, but one inscribed on our hearts and mind. As Enyedi states:

> And where he says to be obedient not only to the good, but also to the wicked, here first remember that it is the servant's duty to receive the word of his lord in things that are not contrary to the truth and the law of God. But if his lord commands him to kill the innocent, to set his city on fire, to deny his God and so on, it is not appropriate to accept his word in these matters.[42]

Enyedi also teaches the suffering to comport themselves with dignity and to endure their hardship with grace. He exemplifies with the death of Socrates that as Socrates, condemned to death though innocent, obeyed the laws of Athens, so too should the subjects obey their superiors, irrespective of their position in the community. This argument shows how human law falls under natural law and natural law under the divine order. For another example of the idea that human nature requires that some should be ruled by others in societies, we can quote Sermon 180:

---

41 Sermon 184, 5th Codex of Kolozsvár (Biblioteca Academiei Române, Filiala Cluj, Ms. U. 1228), fol. 85v: 'Jó beszédnek nem szegik meg a szárnya.'

42 Sermon 184, 5th Codex of Kolozsvár (Biblioteca Academiei Române, Filiala Cluj, Ms. U. 1228), fol. 86v: 'Ahol penig azt mondja, hogy ne csak az jóknak, hanem az gonoszoknak is engedelmességgel legyenek, itt elsőben azt vedd eszedben, hogy tartozik az szolga uránák szavát fogadni oly dolgokban, az kik az közönséges igazsággal és az Isten törvényével nem ellenkeznek. De ha azt parancsolná, hogy az ártatlant megölje, városát felgyújtsa, Istenét megtagadja etc., ezekben nem illik szavát fogadni.'

> Although freedom is dear to everybody, and by nature anybody would rather rule and command than to serve and to depend on somebody else, it is no small glory to know oneself and be humble before the powerful and to show obedience.[43]

Let us explore this point more closely. As to different magistrates, Enyedi talks about them, as a rule, with a critical overtone, especially about the prince and his duties. While other writers of the Reformation, finding biblical comparisons for contemporary rulers, mentioned Moses, David, Solomon and Gideon,[44] Enyedi, finding fault with young prince Sigismund Báthory, compares him to Zedekiah, Jehoiakim, king of Judah, and even to Rehoboam, 'the fool of the nation.' The prince, the city, the judges and all the citizens are involved in a sermon on Ecclesiastes: 'Since Rehoboam was king,' Enyedi says, commenting on the passages of the Wisdom of Sirach, 'he [*scil.* the prophet] calls his foolishness the mindlessness of the whole country, the whole community. For the morality of the prince and his behaviour is not exclusively his own character, but it affects people under him and becomes ordinary.'[45] Enyedi's free translation of Scripture includes not only the prince, but also the head of the city, the judge and the magistrates, making his audience think of their own city of Cluj. He reminded the citizens that in electing officials, they should 'put one on the shelf,' selecting them from among themselves for their habits, trustworthiness and morality. Pointedly, Enyedi zooms in from the whole principality to the city and to the individual citizen. It is also clear from his critical tone that he believes in the idea of obedience toward the prince, provided his acts are just, and takes care of his people so that he expects them to serve him. Notwithstanding, Enyedi emphasises multiple times that no law can justify the murder of a ruler, not even of a tyrant.[46]

---

43 Sermon 180, 5th Codex of Kolozsvár (Biblioteca Academiei Române, Filiala Cluj, Ms. U. 1228), fol. 56v: 'Noha az szabadság mindeneknél kedves, és természet szerént akárki is inkább akar uralkodni, parancsolni, hogynem mint szolgálni és mástól függeni, de azért nem kisebb dicsíret magát megismernie, az nállánál hatalmasb előtt magát megalázni és engedelmességet mutatni.'

44 Cf. Graeme Murdock, 'The Importance of Being Josiah: An Image of Calvinist Identity,' *Sixteenth Century Journal*, 29 (1998): 1043–1059.

45 Sermon 35, 4th Codex of Kolozsvár (Biblioteca Academiei Române, Filiala Cluj, Ms. U. 737/IV), fol. 12r: 'Mert mivelhogy az Roboám király vala, az ő bolondságát az egész országnak és közönségnek esztelenségének híja. Azért, mert az fejedelem erkölcse és magaviselése nem valami kiváltképpen egy személynek tulajdonsága, hanem kihat és kiterjed minden alatta való népre és közönségessé leszen.'

46 The idea of laying down one's life instead of resisting the magistrate forcibly is certainly not Enyedi's original idea but a fine early realization of the political points we can find in works such as Hugo Grotius's *Via ad pacem ecclesiasticam* (first publication: Paris, 1641).

7 The Principality, the Turks, the Habsburgs and Taxation

Through his exegesis, Enyedi also invited his congregation to observe their current situation in Transylvania from a broader historical perspective. A tributary state to the Ottoman Empire, Transylvania also attempted to maintain good relations with the Catholic Habsburgs. Enyedi raises this point with a typical Reformation motif of the *chosen people*. With this concept, also applied to a diverse array of nations, including the English and the Czechs, Enyedi draws an analogy between the Hungarians and the Jews. Enyedi re-vitalises this overused motif with a new interpretation, according to which Nebuchadnezzar, compared to the sultan, becomes a positive figure:

> So, Nebuchadnezzar was a pagan; the Turk is also a pagan. Yet, as he managed to occupy the entirety of the Land of the Jews twice, leaving them a king from their own nation out of benevolence, surely in such a way Hungary and Transylvania were in the hands of the Turk. Still, they left us a king, a reigning prince, from our nation. But every time we attempted to break away from them, we always hit the dust. Nebuchadnezzar waited for Zedekiah to return in peace. It seems that if the Transylvanian Lords were in peace with the Turks, we could keep ourselves in our religion and heritage [i.e. property]. Nebuchadnezzar expected only loyalty and tribute from Zedekiah. What else does the Turkish emperor want from us?[47]

47 Sermon 53, Codex of Székelykeresztúr (Teleki-Bolyai Library, Târgu-Mureş, Romania, No. 0439), 233: 'No, pogán vala Nabukodonozor, pogán az török is, de valamint amaz teljességgel occupálhatja, elfoglalhatja vala Zsidóországot kétszer, de nem cselekedé. Hanem mégis jó akaratjából királt hagya az zsidó nemzetségből. Bizony szintén azonképpen Magyarország és Erdély talám kétszernél többször is kezében volt az töröknek, de mégis pogán lévén királt, fejedelmet hagyott az mi nemzetségünkből országunkban. De valamennyiszer elszakadánk tőlle, mindannyiszor vertök a portot[!]. Békességben tartá Nabukodonozor Sedékiást. Úgy tetszik, hogy az mi országunkbeli urak ha jók volnának az török miatt, mind vallásunkban, s mind örökségünkben szabadon megnyughatnánk. Sedékiástól csak hűséget, adót kéván vala Nabukodonozor. Mit kéván egyebet valaha mitőllünk török császár?' Modern Hungarian ed. of the variants in: *Enyedi György válogatott művei* [Selected works of György Enyedi], ed. Mihály Balázs and János Káldos (Bukarest and Kolozsvár: Kriterion, 1997), 134. The sermon is also quoted by Béla Mester, 'Politikai közösség és vallásszabadság: Párhuzamok John Locke-nak és Enyedi György erdélyi unitárius teológusnak a vallási türelemről alkotott nézeteiben [Political community and freedom of religion: Parallelism in the views of John Locke and György Enyedi, Transylvanian Unitarian theologian, on religious tolerance],' *Keresztény Magvető* 107 (2001): 25–36.

Enyedi emphasises the importance of contracts between countries and states, pointing out that the only way to keep the peace is to respect agreements and pay taxes. He made use of this analogy to offer a moderating position in the conflict between the ruling prince of Transylvania and the sultan. To stress this analogy, Enyedi also mentions the age of Zedekiah, the king of Judah, who was young (as Enyedi says, twenty-one years old); in 1593, when the sermon was delivered, Sigismund Báthory was the same age.

One year later, events took a dramatic turn. At the time of Enyedi, the political elite of Transylvania was divided into two main fronts. The mostly Unitarian political elite and nobility were engaged in pro-Turkish politics. This group faced the pro-Habsburg Catholic prince and his circle, who forced a pact with Emperor Rudolph II and wanted to join the anti-Turkish league of Europe. Sermon 82 shows that the metaphor of a two-sided power struggle transmuted into a more complex, three-sided image with the sultan as the ruler of Babylon and the emperor as the pharaoh of Egypt:

> So to understand […], the country and empire of Zedekiah were given by Nebuchadnezzar, whom he did ally with. When the power of the Babylonian king grew, the surrounding kings were becoming worried and began to confer on how to stop Nebuchadnezzar. Therefore, they sent a legate to Zedekiah, king of Judah, lured him away from Nebuchadnezzar and made him break their alliance.[48]

This was an important topic for the Unitarian church, since it was located almost exclusively in Transylvania. The conflict led to one of the biggest political disasters in Transylvania. In the spring of 1594, the prince attempted to convince the political elite to agree with his Habsburg-friendly policies. As his scheme failed, he resigned at the end of July. A few weeks later, the political winds shifted, and Sigismund returned. On 28 August 1594, he called upon his cousin Boldizsár Báthory, the Chancellor, and the members of the political elite who attended the Diet of Cluj, to accompany him at mass. He captured more than a dozen of these lords: some were executed, some sent to jail and

48 Sermon 82, 2nd Codex of Kolozsvár (Biblioteca Academiei Române, Filiala Cluj, Ms. U. 737/II), fol. 76r–v: 'Mert hogy megértsed, […] ez Sedékiás királynak az országát és birodalmát Nabukodonozor adta vala, kivel frigye vala. De mikor az babilóniai királynak hatalma igen megnevekedett volna, az környül való fejedelmek igen megfélemlének és tanácskozni kezdének egymással, miképpen állhatnának Nabukodonozor ellen, és mint ronthatnák meg. Küldenek azért Sedékiáshoz, Júda királlyához is követeket, hogy őtet is elvonnák Nabukodonozor mellől és az frigyet megszegetnék vélle.'

some converted to Catholicism shortly after. The Unitarian political elite were beheaded, figuratively and literally. In August and September, the Diet and the city council accepted all the orders of the prince. The sharp-tongued Enyedi refrained from an overt attack this time. The following paragraph illustrates the moderate and desperate voice of the bishop:

> It is not easy to fight against an overpowering enemy but even harder to tussle against your prince. Because the prince not only has power, but also majesty and honour. Not to mention his servants who carry out his orders.[49]

8 The Well-Being of the Citizens

In sermons from this period, Enyedi talks frequently about good behaviour and suitable preaching in difficult times, the nature of understanding and the importance of the well-being of the citizens under political pressure. As to the broader target, the audience of these strictures, his sermons, featuring rhetorical flourishes, philosophical debates, philological details and theological expositions, addressed a large cross-section of Cluj society. Peasants, craftsmen, members of the middle class, and the petty and high nobility were there, as we shall see, to understand the functions of the community and the administration of the city, and to advocate for Unitarian doctrines.

In Sermon 104, Enyedi talks about the value of human life, and the natural desire and importance of self-preservation. Drawing on Proverbs 24:3 ('Through wisdom is a house built, and by understanding is it established'), he says that there are three important precepts as concern humans' life. Human beings must build themselves up. That is, they must take care of their own needs and preserve themselves to protect their own property and wealth from others, and, if anybody attempts to attack their safety, they should confront and resist the attacker.[50] While acknowledging the importance of private

---

49 Sermon 110, Codex of Sárospatak (Great Library of the Reformed Protestant College in Sárospatak, Kt 7.), 2/113: 'Nehéz dolog náladnál hatalmasbbal víni, de nehezebb fejedelem ellen tusakodni. Mert az fejedelemnek nemcsak ereje, hanem méltósága is és böcsületi vagyon. Ez mellett sok szolgái vadnak, kik akaratját teszik.'

50 Sermon 104, Codex of Sárospatak (Great Library of the Reformed Protestant College in Sárospatak, Kt 7.), 2/41. A different echo of this argument appears in Sermon 182, based on 2 Kings 7:3 ('And there were four leprous men at the entry to the gate, and they said one to another: Why sit we here until we die?'). In the third part of the sermon, Enyedi lists

property,[51] he values human life over it and reminds his people that their most valuable possession is their own life. He repeatedly warns his audience that if they have a chance to commute their property for lives, they should never hesitate to do so: '[…] But life and man are more valuable than property and goods, like the sheep is more precious than the wool.'[52]

The idea of self-preservation is a recurring topic in Socinian and anti-Trinitarian works. Property and sovereignty were areas of conflict. While Sozzini's pacifism was often discussed, anti-Trinitarian writers, such as Johann Crell, shifted away from this concept, advocating ideas similar to Enyedi's.[53] As concerns wars, Enyedi refers not only to the violent acts of soldiers, but also to ransom during wars. From a financial point of view and with the renewed commitment of his earlier sermons, he stresses that if anybody, even the prince, can buy peace with money in wartime, it is a better solution than bloodshed. But he also emphasises in several sermons that all wars and violent attacks occur by God's will to remind His people to be penitent and to punish the disobedient. This argument, emphasising personal responsibility, reiterates the well-known ancient and Protestant tradition of the continuity of collective responsibility through time.

---

the grades and course of human life: the first is alimentation and preservation of life. The second is the acquirement of pleasure. The third is the apportionment of the acquired things among the members of the community. Sermon 182, 5th Codex of Kolozsvár (Biblioteca Academiei Române, Filiala Cluj, Ms. U. 1228), fol. 72r.

51 The connection between natural law and property rights is a perennial topic of discussion connected to sixteenth- and seventeenth-century works on the topic, such as those of Melanchthon, Grotius and Locke. The protection of the natural right to life supplements this subject. For example, Pufendorf establishes the link between natural law and the importance of the protection of one's life in his *De officio* (1.3.2.). See Kari Saastamoinen, 'Pufendorf and the stoic model of natural law,' in *Grotius and the Stoa*, ed. Hans W. Blom and Laurens C. Winkel (Assen: Royal van Gorcum, 2004), 266. Socinians challenged the idea that subjects of a ruler have the right to defend their property by force. The debate, based on Sozzini's words, between John Webberley, who translated Socinian texts into English, and Francis Cheynell, who mentioned this translation in his *The Rise, Growth and Danger of Socinianism*, is discussed by Mortimer, *Reason and religion in the English revolution*, 108–113.

52 Sermon 180, 5th Codex of Kolozsvár (Biblioteca Academiei Române, Filiala Cluj, Ms. U. 1228), fol. 58v: 'Másodszor, hogy az nem bolond cselekedet legyen, az okosság is megmutatja, mert jobb az kisebben az nagyobbat megváltani. De az élet és az ember drágább és böcsülletesb az marhánál, miképpen az gyapjúnál az juh. Azért mikor ember marháján életét megváltja, eszesen cselekeszik.'

53 Francesco Quatrini, 'Reassessing the Polish Brethren on magistracy, pacifism, and warfare in the seventeenth century,' *The Historical Journal* 63 (2020): 1–21.

9 The Laws, the Judges and the Magistracy

As to the election of officials, there are some sermons associated directly with the legislative and judicial figures of the city. The first sermons of the third triacas (Sermon 67 and 68) are connected to electing judges.[54] Regular elections began every year on 25 December, before the election of the members of the council. These texts are followed by two Christmas sermons (Sermons 69 and 70), a New Year's sermon (Sermon 71) and, finally, one about the power of the tongue (Sermon 72). The reference made in this sermon to the possibility of manipulation through speech cannot be accidental: one should rather connect it to the beginning of the new council's work.[55]

In the dual sermon about the election of judges, Enyedi explains what society is and why society needs judges, as well as what virtues and qualities are required in such people. As the bishop states, the existence of human society is an empirical fact, and he describes the function of judges together with their regulations as the iron nails in the roof or the lime in the wall. Without judges, the city could not work, and people could not live in an ordered community, as he puts it.[56] He also reminds his audience that although law means right thinking and people form a communion with God through the law, the law is silent and powerless and cannot be enforced by the people: 'Have you ever seen the law walking in the market square? I believe you would not find it in city hall either.'[57] The ones who make the law visible are the elected judges, the members of the centumviri and the magistrates.

At the beginning of his sermon, Enyedi talks at great length about the nature of society and its laws. After he quotes the well-known verses of Romans 13:1–2,[58] Enyedi offers a more in-depth analysis of the question of why people have to elect judges, choosing the structure of the society as a natural

54 The sermons are based on Deuteronomy 16:18 ('Judges and officers shalt thou make thee in all thy gates') and Sirach 10:1 ('A wise magistrate educates his people, and the rule of an intelligent person is well ordered').

55 These sermons are in the 2nd Codex of Kolozsvár (Biblioteca Academiei Române, Filiala Cluj, Ms. U. 737/II).

56 A more accurate and detailed analysis of the sermon can be found in Simon, 'A természetjog eszméje,' 89–92.

57 Sermon 67, 2nd Codex of Kolozsvár (Biblioteca Academiei Române, Filiala Cluj, Ms. U. 737/II), fol. 4r: 'Láttad-e valaha, hogy az törvény az piacon sétált volna? Azt hiszem, hogy az tanácsháznál is nehezen találnád.'

58 On Paul's letter and its importance in the Reformation: David M. Whitford, 'Robbing Paul to pay Peter: The reception of Paul in sixteenth century political theology,' in *A Companion to Paul in the Reformation*, ed. R. Ward Holder (Leiden: Brill, 2009), 573–606.

construction rather than the original sin for his starting point. He begins the discussion with the following statement:

> It is evident that no multitude, no congregation can be kept together for long without some rope that binds them. As in a stone foundation, the stones cannot remain on top of each other unless you bind them with iron or lime. [...] And if dead and unlively things cannot remain side by side for long without a rope, living and moving creatures surely cannot either [...]. But it is not appropriate for you to know this only from the external and empirical things, but also from those you do not see. For God has given us wisdom to ascend, not to be carried away by our senses at all times.

The invisible rope that keeps people in a society is no less than the law, ordinances, and decrees. This *ratio summa* is rooted in nature. Enyedi explains why the existence of the law therefore presumes government, which, in this way, has natural causes, and he mentions Demosthenes, who held that the law is nothing but the soul and, as the body perishes without the soul, the town falls apart without the law because 'its soul has flown away.'[59] József Simon points

59 Sermon 67, 2nd Codex of Kolozsvár (Biblioteca Academiei Române, Filiala Cluj, Ms. U. 737/II), fol. 3v–4r: 'Nyilván vagyon az, hogy semmi sokaság, gyülekezet együtt sokáig nem maradhat valami kötél nélkül, az ki őket öszvekapcsolja, mint a kőlábban, nem maradhatnak meg a kövek egymáson, ha vagy vassal, vagy mésszel öszve nem raggatod őket. [...] Ha penig az megholt és elevenség nélkül való dolgok meg nem maradnak egymás mellett sokáig kötél nélkül, bizony az eleven és mozgó állatok inkább nem [...]. De nem illik ezt csak az külső és megtapasztalható dolgok felől tudjad, hanem azok felől is, az kiket nem látsz. Mert arra adott Isten okosságot, hogy feljebb is emelkedjék az ember: nem mindenkor viseltessél csak az érzékenségtől. Mivelhgy azért látod, hogy az tapasztalható dolgoknak gyülekezetiben szükség valami kötél, minthogy látod azt, hogy az emberek között vagyon társaság és gyülekezet és egymás mellett való megmaradás, tehát bizony szükséges, hogy valami kötél legyen, az ki őket egymás mellett tartja, és nem engedi, hogy elszéledjenek, egymástól elkalandozzanak. De micsoda az kötél? Bizony nem kőfal, kivel bekeríttik az várost. Mert egy az, hogy sok helyen nincsen kerítése az városnak, de vagyon gyülekezet. Más az, hogy igen erőtlen kötél volna ez, mert az ember az kőfalnak vagy az kapuján kimehet, vagy az tetején kihághat. Micsoda tartja tehát együtt őket, hogy illyen eleven állatok lévén, mint egy ketrecben, együtt lakjanak? Nem egyéb, hanem az törvény, rendtartások és végzések. [...] Igen igazan mondta tehát egy pogány bölcs, Demosthenes, *Az törvény*, úgymond, *lélek*. Mert miképpen az test az lélektől megfosztván elromol, azonképpen ha törvény nincs az városban, elromol. Tudd-e, az míg az lélek az testben vagyon, minden ízek, csontok jól vadnak, de mihelt az lélek, ki öszvekapcsolja vala őket, kimúlik belőlle, ottan elszakadoznak egymástól, s végre el is senyved. Szintén így vagyon az városnak dolga, azt mondja az bölcs, mert az míg az tör-

out that Enyedi's notes on the bond of civil society reproduces Cicero's definition of law: 'lex sit civilis societatis vinculum.'[60] 'Since the law is powerless and weak,' continues Enyedi, alluding again to Cicero, 'on paper or in one's mind, it is insufficient to govern the people.[61] The cause of it is that people are made of flesh, and that is why the unseen law must be made visible by electing members of the society, who protect and serve the law.'[62]

In another sermon, Enyedi calls this bond that keeps his society together an 'agreement,' and notes that humans cannot live without society.[63] In other words, Enyedi argues that society and political power are based on natural reason. This justifies the election of magistrates from among the ranks of the community by its very members.[64] However, as he later explains in agreement with Melanchthon, Calvin and others, all magistrates and civil power

vény fennáll, addig jól vagyon dolga, de mihelt elvész, az város nem maradhat meg, mert elrepült az lelke.'

60 Cicero, *De Republica*, 1, 49. Cf. Simon, 'A természetjog eszméje,' 90–91.

61 The link between these sections and the Ciceronian idea of the function of the law is strengthened with a direct quotation: 'Lex est mutus magistratus, et magistratus est lex loquens' (Cicero, *De Legibus*, 3.1.).

62 Sermon 67, 2nd Codex of Kolozsvár (Biblioteca Academiei Române, Filiala Cluj, Ms. U. 737/II), fol. 4r: 'Tehát hol vagyon a törvény? Papírosra írták meg az decretomát, de az könnyű senkit nem bánt, senkit meg nem szólít. Az bölcs embernek elméjében vagyon, de azt senki nem látja, és az gondolat senkit meg nem sért, tehát hogy volna, hogy az törvény volna kötele az társaságnak és az foglalná őket egyben? Úgy vagyon, hogy ha az törvént csak őmagában tekénted meg, alkalmatlan és elégtelen arra, hogy az embereket igazgassa. mert az emberek testből állnak, azért az láthatatlan törvény őket nem gubernálhatja, hanem láthatóvá kell tenni. [...] Az emberek hallás után tanolnak. Azért az néma törvént szólóvá kell tenni. Miképpen lehet az meg? Úgy, hogy ha ollyanokat választunk közüllünk, az kik az törvénynek őrzői és kiszolgáltatói lennének.'

63 Sermon 79, Codex of Marosvásárhely (Teleki-Bolyai Library, Târgu Mureș, 0636), fol. 181r–v: 'Mert mi emberek azért születtünk, hogy egymással jóltegyünk, kegyességet cselekedjünk, és azért gyűltünk egy társaságban, hogy egymásnak mint tagok segétséggel legyünk, mert külömben egymás társaságában nem lehetünk. Az társaságnak és együtt való lakásnak penig kötele az egyesség, ha azért az egyesség nem volna, az társaság sem volna, ha az társaság nem volna, az ember sem volna, mert társaság nélkül nem élhet az ember.'

64 For Enyedi's argument on human beings as essentially social creatures, it is worth mentioning Melanchthon's interpretation of Aristotle's *Politics*, 'man is created for society,' and his subsequent claim that society cannot exist without authorities. Mads Langballe Jensen, 'By convention or by nature: Melanchthon's criticism of late medieval Ockhamist political thought in the *Commentarii in Aliquot politicos libros Aristoteles*,' *History of Political Thought*, 35 (Spring 2014): 14–16; and Jensen, *A Humanist in Reformation politics*, 77–80. These ideas can be found in the subsequent century, such as in Pufendorf: 'Man's nature, then, is so constituted that humans cannot be secure without social life and the human mind is seen to be capable of ideas which serve this end.' Pufendorf, *On the duty of man and citizen*, 36.

are ordained by God, meaning that even tyrannical governments should be obeyed.[65] This position, as we have seen above, did not restrain him from criticising the prince, judges or other authorities.

In late-sixteenth-century Transylvania, the question of true religion formed the subject matter of a complex controversy, and the bishop could not separate this problematic topic from that of civil society. In Sermon 67, Enyedi speaks out against the religious current of Anabaptism, which attempted to remove the judges, council and magistrates from society. In this, as well as in other sermons, he compares the ideas that the Unitarian community, the Catholics and other Protestant denominations entertained individually as to the best order of the city and concludes that the ideal political and social order can only be established based on ideas of the first of the three.[66] Enyedi likens the judges to a castle on a mountain or a candle on a table and warns his audience that it is not enough for magistrates to think about their duties; they must also prepare themselves for their responsibilities. He revisits the issue of the responsibility of elector citizens, emphasising that an election is a serious decision, the result of which predetermines the subsequent period. He introduces an exposition of the question of the right sentence with a quote from

65 In Sermon 44, although its chosen textus is Exodus 4:10, Enyedi inserts Romans 13:1 into his explanation and refers to it on two occasions. On the first occasion, he mentions it, together with John 19:11, as proof of the idea that God is the source of every good thing and that He is the one who dignifies and positions everyone; hence, any duty or position is granted by divine will. In the second case, he uses it, along with 1 Peter 2:17, to justify being subject to one's superiors (in this case, the kings and princes) and the obligation of obedience to rulers, good or evil. See also Sermon 51, 4th Codex of Kolozsvár (Biblioteca Academiei Române, Filiala Cluj, Ms. U. 737/IV), fol. 60r–61v.

66 It is important to mention an as yet little studied direction of the research on the political ideas of the Unitarians and their concept of natural, divine and positive law. In Enyedi's time, notable members of the Unitarian community criticised the system and function of the magistrate in Cluj, the centre of the Unitarian Church. Even in the late sixteenth century, critical voices were strong. Following closely the ideas of Jacobus Palaeologus on the ideal role of the magistrate, Enyedi rewrites and interprets the theses of the radical thinker in his sermons. Mihály Balázs has highlighted this connection at several conferences, mentioning the *Catechesis Christiana* and the *Disputatio Scholastica* as main sources for Enyedi's vision on the ideal function of the governing entity. For more details on Palaeologus, see Mihály Balázs, 'Fikció és valóság Palaeologus Disputatio Scholastica című művében [Fiction and reality in Palaeologus's Disputatio Scholastica],' in *'Tenger az igaz hitrül való egyenetlenségek vitatásának eláradott özöne…': Tanulmányok XVI–XIX. századi hitvitákról*, ed. János Heltai and Réka Tasi (Miskolc: Miskolci Egyetem BTK Régi Magyar Irodalomtörténeti Tanszék, 2005), 1–11. Modern ed. of the text: Jacobus Palaeologus, *Catechesis Christiana Dierum Duodecim*, ed. Ruzena Dostálová (Warsaw: PAN, 1971); Jacobus Palaeologus, *Disputatio Scholastica*, ed. Juliusz Domański and Lech Szczucki (Utrecht: Bibliotheca Unitariorum, 1994).

Aristotle, saying that 'neither evening nor morning star shines as bright as justice,'[67] and with the harmonising words of God from Ezekiel 45:9, 'execute judgement and justice,' According to Enyedi, two things are needed for a judge to pronounce the right sentence: they must understand what justice is, and they must administer justice. In another explanation, he goes further. Talking about the character of a good and a bad judge, he notes that if you see that a judge is corrupt, vicious and godless, you should still go to them with your righteous case. They will then be *just* with you, since God seated them there and he wants it to happen. Hence, the bishop not only touches on the virtues of judges, but also offers a practical guide on governance, based on the natural capacity of human judgement and divine law.[68] According to Enyedi's argument, if the magistracy and the judges must use their power in any way to protect or re-establish order within the community, they enjoy God's approval.[69]

Enyedi mentions the important personalities of the city a number of times in his sermons. In a sermon about lawyers and unnecessary legal cases, the bishop comments on issues such as the importance of peace, the function of the law, corruption and the link between the unnecessarily large number of rules and the high number of transgressions and misdeeds.[70] He quotes 1 Timothy 1:9–10:

> With the knowledge that the law is made not for the upright man, but for those who have no respect for law and order, for evil men and sinners,

67 Sermon 67, Ibid., fol. 5r: 'Nem ok nélkül mondja egy bölcs, hogy sem az estvéli, sem az hajnali csillag nem fénlik úgy, mint az igazság.' Cf. Aristotle, *Nicomachean Ethics*, v. (1129b29–31): 'And therefore justice is often thought to be the greatest of virtues, and "neither evening nor morning star" is so wonderful' (transl. David Ross).

68 As Cluj was a free royal town, the local government was the most important body for justice and legislation. It only had to obey the prince of Transylvania. One of the reasons why Enyedi discusses this matter at length is that there had been recurrent conflicts between the first judge and the twelve jurors in the last two decades. To solve this problem, the centumvirate was commissioned to prepare a regulatory order and call upon the jurors to obey the judge. As the conflicts continued, the centumviri had to renew the regulatory orders, in 1592 for the last time. Pakó, 'Hatalmi konfliktus vagy testületi összefogás?,' 74–75.

69 A similar argument can be found in Jonasz Szlichtyng's *Quaestiones duae*. For further information, see Stanisław Kot, *Socinianism in Poland: The Social and Political Ideas of the Polish Antitrinitarians*, transl. Earl Morse Wilbur (Boston: Starr King Press, 1957), 143–145; and Mortimer, *Reason and religion in the English revolution*, 31–32.

70 Sermon 39, 4th Codex of Kolozsvár (Biblioteca Academiei Române, Filiala Cluj, Ms. U. 737/IV), fol. 10v–15r. The sermon is based on 1 Corinthians 6:7–9: 'More than this, it is not to your credit to have causes at law with one another at all' etc.

> for the unholy and those who have no religion, for those who put their fathers or mothers to death, for takers of life, for those who go after loose women, for those with unnatural desires, for those who take men prisoner, who make false statements and false oaths, and those who do any other things against the right teaching.

This part alludes to the Thomist tradition of the Law being written on the heart, even if somebody does not obey the written law. It harmonises with Enyedi's main attitude to put religion and trust in God at the centre, while addressing political and ecclesiastical frictions. He also envisions the early times of humankind, when communities did not need any written law, since everyone did their own duty of their own free will.

10 The Well-Being of the Community and True Religion

Besides giving powerful sermons, Enyedi also had access to the council of the hundred, the city judges, of Cluj. He had an effect on their decision-making, through his preaching on morality and the natural order or that tied to true faith and worship, and his ideas were later translated into regulations by the council. During these weeks, he also preached about the role of the army and its soldiers, referring to the army of Sigismund posted around the city. Presumably, these sermons were also addressed to the city council.[71] He also

71 The second triacas can be dated roughly to early spring of 1593, and, as we have seen, they contain several sermons on political topics. While Enyedi is still more critical and straightforward in this triacas and is mostly talking about the value of peace in the city and in the principality, in the next triacas he talks more and more about war and warfare. While Cluj and Transylvania are slipping slowly into the Long Turkish War, we can sense the growing tension in the city. Blasphemy (like sodomy, adultery, lying etc.) emerges in one of the sermons. Blaspheming the Holy Ghost (*convitium in spiritum sanctum*) was a special type of blasphemy, which was banned and caused punishment all around Hungary and Transylvania during the Reformation. The custom was based on Matthew 12:32: 'And whosoever speaketh a word against the Son of man, it shall have forgiven him: but whosoever speaketh against the Holy Ghost, it shall not be forgiven him, neither in this world nor in the world to come.' In the sermon, Enyedi discusses the long fight of the church against blaspheming the Holy Ghost. The beginning of the arguments is about the unusual natural phenomena, floods, eathquakes, droughts, storms and comets, as well as a description of the recent hail which destroyed the lands – the trees, grapevines and other crops – around the city. In this regard, Enyedi complains about the people who, even after the disasters, do not care about God and his servants and that in the city there are so few people listening to the sermons that it seems the sermons are delivered to

had sermons addressed to the Catholic prince, who left the city with his army in early October 1593. During these weeks, his former student, János Szilvási, appeared in Cluj and attacked the bishop in a sermon. The bishop answered, sparking a long debate.[72] One of the key problems specified in the debate is unity and its various meanings (referring to Ephesians 4:1) and questions of

---

the sparrows and the city walls. In the sermon, delivered in July of 1594, Enyedi refers to the rules declared in 1584 by the centumviri (council of the hundred) that selling and buying is forbidden on market days during the sermons and that the city gates should be closed, and he mentions that the city gates are open all day and people can ride to their vineyards and fields whenever they like. He also notes the regulation against blaspheming the Holy Ghost. In 1592, the punishment for cursing was regulated and led to a one forint fine or three days in the stocks. As the bishop said, 'Despite this, a few days ago, a man in the market square took out his sword and began to shout and blaspheme the Holy Ghost' (Sermon 45). As Enyedi says, the man was throwing up his soul with a full mouth so intensely that people stepped out onto the balconies and opened the windows to look at it, even members of the council, but there was no man who acted or penalized the man. The outcome of these natural disasters was so serious that a few weeks later the city council requested the bishop to order public prayer and penitence to propitiate God. The council also had new regulations, keeping the city gates closed during the sermons, and tightened the rule on blaspheming the Holy Ghost. From this it is clear, that the bishop's prestige and his critical observations played an important role in the decrees of the council, at numerous times by restricting the freedom of individuals for the common good.

72 I mention only one paragraph from his cover letter attached to the Latin version of the sermon, Enyedi's first reply, which says a great deal about the bishop's attitude: 'there is a need for an entirely different encouragement and discipline now, for the well-being of the country, when you should rather preach about fasting, prayer, penitence and conversion and when you should remind the soldiers, leaders and princes of their duties and talk about how to fight and how to obtain useful aids. And when you should cite such paragraphs from the Bible, you unashamedly stir up, before the elite, inconvenient, malignant and bloody enmity amongst the Churches, and come up with the idiot flummery of your mind' ('miközben az ország jóléte érdekében egész másfajta biztatásra és fegyelmezésre volna szükség, amikor böjtöt, könyörgést, bűnbánatot, megtérést kellene prédikálnod, amikor a katonákat, vezéreket, fejedelmeket hivatásukra kellene figyelmezetned, hogy miképpen hadakozzanak, hogy szerezzenek maguknak hasznos segítőtársakat, amikor tehát a Szentírásból ilyen s ehhez hasonló dolgokat kellene előhoznod, neked van képed éppen akkor az ország előkelősége előtt, a felekezetek között időszerűtlen, gyűlölködő, véres visszavonást szítani, és agyad ostoba sületlenségeivel előhozakodni'). A modern Hungarian translation of the Latin text can be found in János Kénosi-Tőzsér and István Uzoni-Fosztó, *Az erdélyi unitárius egyház története* [A History of the Transylvanian Unitarian Church], Vol. 1, trans. Albert Márkos, preface Mihály Balázs, ed. Gizella Hoffmann, Sándor Kovács, and Lehel Molnár B. (Kolozsvár: Erdélyi Unitárius Egyház, 2005), 346. Enyedi's 60th sermon is known today in Hungarian and Latin versions. The modern ed. of the former: *Enyedi György válogatott művei*, 154–180.

true religion. Enyedi says that there is nothing more dangerous than the disruption of the community, and it is an unfortunate time for religious debates.[73] Enyedi talked about religious freedom and believed that violent conversion is against any law. His statement about the harmonisation of the Christian faiths is relevant here. Enyedi is not as concessive as Jacobus Palaeologus, the well-known radical thinker, connected in various ways to the Unitarians, who includes the Muslims (the Turci Christiani) and members of all other monotheistic religions, and argued in his works that all of them could have the same basis for their beliefs. Enyedi excludes non-Christians and Catholics (for obvious reasons, but, most importantly, for their heresy) and only discusses the harmonisation of the Protestant churches. Although, at the time of the Reformation, it was common to think that God's written word should certainly be the origin and the basis for morality, the great problem of contemporary thinkers was to harmonise natural moral law with divine law. In his *Defensio*, tied to this debate with Szilvási, Enyedi brings up the same idea with the interpretation of the *Decalogue*. Explaining the Ten Commandments, especially the fifth, he states that the virtues listed are in harmony with the natural sense, and this shows how pagans were, in many cases, more right-thinking than Christians, even if they did not have the same conception of virtue as do the followers of Christ. As regards this problem, the example of the Greeks (as in most cases, referred to as the 'good' pagans) offered Enyedi an opportunity to manage this task, and to show a morality and legislation to follow was like a synthesis of natural and biblical laws.[74]

---

73 In Hungarian, he says: 'Mert miképpen a külső társaságban, városban, országban nincs veszedelmesb dolog a hasadásnál, pártütésnél, azonképpen az Istennek egyházában és gyülekezetében nincs ennél gonoszabb és ártalmasabb dolog.' *Enyedi György válogatott művei*, 159.

74 György Enyedi, 'Defensio concionis Georgii [Eniedini] adversus Apolog[iam Johannis Zilvasii]…,' in *Enyedi-Codex* (Biblioteca Academiei Române, Filiala Cluj, Ms. U. 474), fol. 73r–75r. It is worth mentioning that although Enyedi does not offer a full analysis of the Decalogue in his sermons on natural law, as Melanchthon does (see e.g. Jensen, *A Humanist in Reformation politics*, 103–106), he regularly reminds his readers of it (e.g. in Sermons 52, 55, 59, 72 and 81). He sometimes also connects these to the non-Christians, building up an explanation compatible with the ideas of the Enlightenment, when he says the pagans, without revelation, on the basis of reasoning, could come to a supreme God. He states that although the pagans did not have God's commandments and could only use their 'external sapience,' they still concluded that first everybody should ask for God's help in all tasks: 'Mely erőtelen és elégtelen legyen az ember az ő dolgainak véghezvitelire isteni segítség nélkül, nemcsak az Istennek könyve, az régi szenteknek példája bizonítja, hanem az pogánoknak is cselekedetek megmutatják. Mert noha ők csak az külső okosságtól, nem az Istennek megíratott és kiadott törvényétől viseltettek, de mégis

11 Enyedi's Dream and His Legacy

Enyedi considered the city of Cluj, the centre of the Unitarian Church, as an experiment for a perfect community, based on divine law, natural law and common law. During his episcopacy, Enyedi influenced not only ecclesiastical growth, but also the work of the legislative body. The debates outlined in the 1560s–70s and developed at the end of the century concerned the political culture of Transylvania in the following century. More importantly, Enyedi saw the city as a testing ground for his socio-political vision in his discussions of the social order, the duty of the rulers and legal representatives, and the rights and obligations of the individuals within society. He was a dedicated churchman who closely followed the political shifts within the community and never stopped criticising unfortunate ways of effecting change. He also experienced, if not the collapse, the beginning of the downfall of the regnant political order and his own community within it. His widespread ideas on the order of the Unitarian community served as an example for the coming generations. But the Church was unable to retain its power and influence under the Calvinist princes, and the concept of peace and perfect order became part of a utopian dream. A few decades after Enyedi's death, the Transylvanian Unitarians held a rather fragile position within the principality. The ecclesiastical and political struggle of the Church can be understood through a passage of Valentin Radecius's *Apologia*, dated to October 1618. Radecius begins his text with the following lines:

> Every person accused in a common way is allowed to defend himself by both the laws of God and those of nature, such as the laws of the pagans and other denominations, because none of these laws make it possible to have this person punished for the reason behind the accusation.[75]

---

egyebeknek is azt hatták, és őmagok is azt mívelték, hogy minden dolgoknak kezdetiben az Istent hítták segítségül, és tőlle kértek azoknak elvégzésére való erőt.' Sermon 106, Codex of Sárospatak (Great Library of the Reformed Protestant College in Sárospatak, Kt 7.), 2/61.

75 'Minden közönségesen vádaltatott embernek minden törvények, hogy magát mentse, megengedik, mind az Isten és természet törvénye, mind az pogányok és egyéb társaságoknak törvények, mert egyik sem engedi meg ezek közül, hogy valaki a vádaltatott okért megbüntettessék.' The transcription of the Latin manuscripts and the text's nineteenth-century Hungarian translation were published in Dávid Molnár, 'Valentius Radecius: Apologia (1618),' *Irodalomtörténeti Közlemények* 117 (2013): 39–60. The texts are found on pages 47–55 (Lat.) and 55–60 (Hung.).

The work was an opposition to the accusations against the Unitarians, delivered at the Diet in Transylvania, which stated that the religion of the Unitarians adheres to Turkish (Muslim) practices rather than to Christian ones, and its followers, the Unitarians, prevent the recognition and worship of Christ. This *Apologia* followed a debate held in 1618. The work of Benedek Szentkirályi, *Vindicatio Locorum Veteris Testamenti*, published a year later, refers in many points to this debate, while it confutes the *Explicationes* by György Enyedi. This polemical work was followed by numerous Calvinist pamphlets in Hungary, putting Enyedi's exegetical work into focus (with versions of his sermons in it) for long decades. The polemical works against Enyedi appeared in Europe earlier, then continued to be published even a half century after the bishop's death, and a new wave of interest rose with the second edition in Western Europe from 1669. While his main theological work had its own life in the centuries that followed, his notions on humanity, cognition, consensus and religious freedom – also appearing in the sermons – can show us a practical understanding of civil, natural and divine law and society in the late sixteenth century.

Acknowledgement

The research was supported by the Hungarian Scientific Research Fund (NKFIH FK-135165, 'The History of Early Modern Unitarian Sermon Literature in Transylvania and Hungary'), principal investigator: Borbála Lovas. The linguistic proofreading of this study was supported by the Hungarian Scientific Research Fund (NKFIH K-137963, 'History of Hungarian Philosophy in Early Modernity (1570–1710),' principal investigator: József Simon.

Bibliography

Primary Sources

Calvin, John, *Commentary of the Gospel According to John*, Vol. 1, transl. William Pringle, Edinburgh: The Calvin Translation Society, 1847.

Enyedi, György, *Explicationes locorvm Veteris et Novi Testamenti, ex qvibvs Trinitatis dogma stabiliri solet*, Kolozsvár: [Heltai, 1598].

Enyedi, György, *Explicationes locorvm Veteris et Novi Testamenti, ex qvibvs Trinitatis dogma stabiliri solet*, Amsterdam: [Johannes van Ravesteyn(?), ca. 1669].

Enyedi György prédikációi, Vols. 1–3, ed. Borbála Lovas, Budapest: MTA–ELTE HECE, Magyar Unitárius Egyház, 2016–2018.

Palaeologus, Jacobus, *Catechesis Christiana Dierum Duodecim*, ed. Ruzena Dostálová, Warsaw: PAN, 1971.

Palaeologus, Jacobus, *Disputatio Scholastica*, ed. Juliusz Domański and Lech Szczucki, Utrecht: Bibliotheca Unitariorum, 1994.

Petrityevity Horváth, Ferenc, *Apologia Fratrum Unitariorum*, Kolozsvár: Az Unitária Ecclesia Typusival, 1701.

Pufendorf, Samuel, *On the Duty of Man and Citizen According to Natural Law*, ed. James Tully, transl. Michael Silverthorne, Cambridge: Cambridge University Press, 1991.

Secondary Sources

Balázs, Mihály, 'Antitrinitarianism,' in *A Companion to the Reformation in Central Europe*, ed. Howard Louthan and Graeme Murdock, 188–189, Leiden – Boston: Brill, 2015.

Balázs, Mihály, *Early Transylvanian Antitrinitarianism 1561–1571. From Servet to Palaeologus*, Baden-Baden: Editions Valentin Koerner, 1996.

Balázs, Mihály, 'Fikció és valóság Palaeologus Disputatio Scholastica című művében,' in *'Tenger az igaz hitrül való egyenetlenségek vitatásának eláradott özöne…': Tanulmányok XVI–XIX. századi hitvitákról*, ed. János Heltai and Réka Tasi, 1–11, Miskolc: Miskolci Egyetem BTK Régi Magyar Irodalomtörténeti Tanszék, 2005.

Balázs, Mihály, 'Tolerant Country – Misunderstood Laws: Interpreting Sixteenth-Century Transylvanian Legislation Concerning Religion,' *Hungarian Historical Review* 2 (2013/1): 85–108.

Balázs, Mihály and Gizella Keserű, ed., *György Enyedi and Central European Unitarianism in the 16–17th Centuries*, Budapest: Balassi, 2000.

Balázs, Mihály and János Káldos, ed., *Enyedi György válogatott művei*, Bukarest and Kolozsvár: Kriterion, 1997.

Balázs, Mihály and János Káldos, ed., *György Enyedi*, Baden-Baden: Editions Valentin Koerner, 1990.

Biagioni, Mario, *The Radical Reformation and the Making of Modern Europe. A Lasting Heritage*, Leiden, Boston: Brill, 2016.

Burchill, Christopher J., ed., *The Heidelberg Antitrinitarians: Johann Sylvan, Adam Neuser, Matthias Vehe, Jacob Suler, Johann Hasler*, Baden-Baden: Koernerm, 1989.

Caccamo, Domenico, *Eretici italiani in Moravia, Polonia, Transilvania (1558–1611). Studi e documenti*, Florence – Chicago: Sansoni – Newberry Library, 1970.

Crăciun, Maria, Ovidiu Ghitta, and Graeme Murdock, 'Religious reform, printed books and confessional identity,' in *Confessional Identity in East-Central Europe*, ed. Maria Crăciun, Ovidiu Ghitta, and Graeme Murdock, 1–30, Aldershot: Ashgate, 2002.

Dán, Róbert and Antal Pirnát, ed., *Antitrinitarianism in the Second Half of the 16th Century*, Budapest – Leiden: Akadémiai – Brill, 1982.

Dán, Róbert, *Az erdélyi szombatosok és Péchi Simon*, Budapest: Akadémiai, 1987.

Dán, Róbert, *Matthias Vehe-Glirius: Life and Work of a radical antitrinitarian with his collected writings*, Budapest – Leiden: Akadémiai – Brill, 1982.

Florea, Carmen, 'Shaping Transylvanian Antitrinitarian identity in an urban context,' in *Confessional Identity in East-Central Europe*, ed. Maria Crăciun, Ovidiu Ghitta, and Graeme Murdock, 64–80, Aldershot: Ashgate, 2002.

Harrison, Peter, *The Fall of Man and the Foundation of Science*, Cambridge: Cambridge University Press, 2007.

Jensen, Mads Langballe, 'By convention or by nature: Melanchthon's criticism of late medieval Ockhamist political thought in the *Commentarii in Aliquot politicos libros Aristoteles*,' *History of Political Thought*, 35 (Spring 2014): 14–16.

Jensen, Mads Langballe, *A Humanist in Reformation politics: Philipp Melanchthon on Politics and Natural Law*, Leiden: Brill, 2020.

Kénosi-Tőzsér, János and István Uzoni-Fosztó, *Az erdélyi unitárius egyház története*, Vol. 1, trans. Albert Márkos, preface Mihály Balázs, ed. Gizella Hoffmann, Sándor Kovács, and Lehel Molnár B., Kolozsvár: Erdélyi Unitárius Egyház, 2005.

Keul, István, *Early Modern Religious Communities in East-Central Europe: Ethnic Diversity, Denominational Plurality, and Corporative Politics in the Principality of Transylvania (1526–1691)*, Leiden: Brill, 2009.

Kot, Stanisław, *Socinianism in Poland: The Social and Political Ideas of the Polish Antitrinitarians*, transl. Earl Morse Wilbur, Boston: Starr King Press, 1957.

Lovas, Borbála, 'Enyedi György prédikációskötetének eredeti szerkezete,' in *Enyedi 460. Tanulmánykötet Enyedi György születésének 460. évfordulójára rendezett kamarakonferencia előadásaiból*, ed. Borbála Lovas and Krisztina K. Kaposi, 71–141, Budapest: MTA–ELTE HECE, 2016.

Lovas, Borbála, 'Enyedi György szerkesztett prédikációskötete új megvilágításban: A prédikációgyűjtemény triacasainak újrarendezése,' *Irodalomtörténeti Közlemények* 120 (2016): 47–54.

Lovas, Borbála, 'Magyar török, kicsiny pogány, zsidózó és vaddisznó: Enyedi György és az unitarizmus kritikája a 17. században,' in *Viszály és együttélés: Vallások és felekezetek a török hódoltság korában*, ed. Gábor Ittzés, 223–250, Budapest: Universitas, 2017.

Lovas, Borbála, 'The Posthumous Reception of an Antitrinitarian Bishop at Home and Abroad: The Afterlife of György Enyedi's *Explicationes*,' in *Print Culture at the Crossroads: The Book and Central Europe*, ed. Elizabeth Dillenburg, Howard Louthan, and Drew B. Thomas, 58–84, Leiden: Brill, 2021.

Marshall, John, 'Locke, Socinianism, "Socinianism," and Unitarianism,' in *English Philosophy in the Age of Locke*, ed. M.A. Stewart, 111–182, Oxford: Oxford University Press, 2000.

Mester, Béla, 'The Connection between the Unitarian thought and Early Modern political philosophy,' *Journal for the Study of Religions and Ideologies* 3 (2002 Winter): 142–157.

Mester, Béla, 'Politikai közösség és vallásszabadság: Párhuzamok John Locke-nak és Enyedi György erdélyi unitárius teológusnak a vallási türelemről alkotott nézeteiben,' *Keresztény Magvető* 107 (2001): 25–36.

Mortimer, Sarah, 'Human Liberty and Human Nature in the Works of Faustus Socinus and His Readers,' *Journal of the History of Ideas* 70 (2009): 191–211.

Mortimer, Sarah, *Reason and religion in the English revolution: The challenge of Socinianism*, Cambridge, Cambridge University Press, 2010.

Murdock, Graeme, 'The Importance of Being Josiah: An Image of Calvinist Identity,' *Sixteenth Century Journal*, 29 (1998): 1043–1059.

Murdock, Graeme, 'Multiconfessionalism in Transylvania,' in *A Companion to Multiconfessionalism in the Early Modern World*, ed. Thomas Max Safley, 393–416, Leiden: Brill, 2011.

Owen, John, *Exposition of the Epistle to the Hebrews; with the Preliminary Exercitations*. Revised and abridged by the Rev. Edward Williams, London: James Black, 1815.

Pakó, László, 'Hatalmi konfliktus vagy testületi összefogás? A kolozsvári százférfiak tanácsa és a városi igazságszolgáltatás a 16. század második felében,' *Erdélyi Múzeum* 72 (2010/3–4): 73–87.

Pakó, László, 'The inquisitors in the judicial practice of Cluj at the end of the sixteenth century,' *Transylvanian Review* 21, Supp. No. 2: *Institutional Structures and Elites in Sălaj Region and in Transylvania in the 14th–18th Centuries*, ed. András W. Kovács (2012): 181–197.

Pásztori-Kupán, István, 'The spirit of religious tolerance,' in *Calvinism on the peripheries: Religion and Civil Society in Europe*, ed. Ábrahám Kovács, 167–176, Budapest: L'Harmattan, 2009.

Pirnát, Antal, 'Gerendi János és Eőssi András,' *Irodalomtörténeti Közlemények* 74 (1970): 680–684.

Plomer, Henry R., *A Dictionary of the Booksellers and Printers who were at work in England, Scotland and Ireland from 1641 to 1667*, London: For the Bibliographical Society by Blades, East, and Blades, 1907.

Quatrini, Francesco, 'Reassessing the Polish Brethren on magistracy, pacifism, and warfare in the seventeenth century,' *The Historical Journal* 63 (2020): 1–21.

Rady, Martyn C., *Customary law in Hungary: Courts, texts and the Tripartitum*, Oxford: Oxford University Press, 2015.

Rohls, Jan, 'Calvinism, Arminianism and Socinianism in the Netherlands until the Synod of Dort,' in *Socinianism and Arminianism. Antitrinitarians, Calvinists and Cultural Exchange in Seventeenth-Century Europe*, ed. Martin Mulsow and Jan Rohls, 22–44, Leiden Brill, 2005.

Saastamoinen, Kari, *The morality of the fallen man: Samuel Pufendorf on natural law*, Helsinki: SHS, 1995.

Saastamoinen, Kari, 'Pufendorf and the stoic model of natural law,' in *Grotius and the Stoa*, ed. Hans W. Blom and Laurens C. Winkel, 257–269, Assen: Royal van Gorcum, 2004.

Scattola, Merio, *Das Naturrecht vor dem Naturrecht: Zur Geschichte des 'ius naturae' im 16. Jahrhundert*, Tübingen: Max Niemeyer Verlag, 1999.

Schmidt, Alexander, 'Irenic patriotism in sixteenth and seventeenth-century German political discourse,' *The Historical Journal* 53 (2010): 243–269.

Simon, József, *Explicationes explicationum: Filozófia, irodalom és egzegetika Enyedi György életművében*, Budapest: Typotex, 2016.

Simon, József, 'Philosophical Atheism and incommensurability of religions in Christian Francken's thought,' *Magyar Filozófiai Szemle* 61 (2017): 57–67.

Simon, József, *Die Religionsphilosophie Christian Franckens (1552–1610?). Atheismus und radikale Reformation im Frühneuzeitlischen Ostmitteleuropa*, Wiesbaden: Harrassowitz Verlag, 2008.

Simon, József, 'A természetjog eszméje Enyedi György prédikációiban,' in *Dávid Ferenc és a kortárs prédikációirodalom. A reformáció első generációi*, ed. Borbála Lovas and Dávid Molnár, 87–100, Budapest: A kora újkori unitárius prédikációirodalom története Erdélyben és Magyarországon Kutatócsoport – Kolozsvári Protestáns Teológiai Intézet, 2022.

Snobelen, Steven, 'Isaac Newton, Socinianism and "the One Supreme God,"' in *Socinianism and Arminianism: Antitrinitarians, Calvinists, and Cultural Exchange in Seventeenth-Century Europe*, ed. Martin Mulsow and Jan Rohls, 241–298, Leiden: Brill, 2005.

Túri, Tamás, 'Unitárius prédikációalkotás a 17. század végén: Egy nyilvánosságra szánt iskolai prédikációskötet,' in *Kultúrjav: Írásbeliség és szóbeliség irodalma újrahasznosítva*, ed. Zsófia Ágnes Bartók et al., 197–214, Budapest: Reciti, 2015.

Whitford, David M., 'Robbing Paul to pay Peter: The reception of Paul in sixteenth century political theology,' in *A Companion to Paul in the Reformation*, ed. R. Ward Holder, 573–606, Leiden, Boston: Brill, 2009.

Williams, George H., 'The christological issues between Francis Dávid and Faustus Socinus during the Disputation on the invocation of Christ, 1578–1579,' in *Antitrinitarianism in the Second Half of the 16th Century*, ed. Róbert Dán and Antal Pirnát, 287–321, Budapest – Leiden: Akadémiai – Brill, 1982.

Wootton, David, 'John Locke: Socinian or natural law theorist?,' in *Religion, Secularization and Political Thought: from Thomas Hobbes to J.S. Mill*, ed. James E. Crimmins, 39–67, London: Routledge, 1989.

CHAPTER 8

Protestant Schooling and Natural Law in Transylvania and Hungary

Péter Balázs and Gábor Gángó

1 Introduction

Recent studies have shown that political culture in early modern Hungary and Transylvania was more complex in terms of language and tradition than we used to think.[1] Especially the reception of the indisputably important classical republicanism and ancient constitutionalism has been researched. However, it is important to complement this work with systematic exploration and reinterpretation of the impact of natural law ideas on political culture in the Kingdom of Hungary and in Transylvania. The rather underexplored reception of Protestant (Grotian and Pufendorfian) or even Catholic natural law traditions played a significant role in Hungarian and Transylvanian philosophical discourse and thereby, indirectly, in the political culture and communication in these countries.

---

1 Zoltán Gábor Szűcs, 'Természet, jog, teológia: egy fejezet a politikai diskurzus történetéből a 18. századi Magyarországon [Nature, law and theology: A chapter in the history of political discourse in eighteenth-century Hungary],' *Aetas* 26 (2011/2): 99–115; Márton Zászkaliczky, 'A Bocskai-felkelés politikai nyelvei: Vázlat [Political languages of the Bocskai uprising: An outline],' in *Politikai nyelvek a 17. század első felének Magyarországán*, ed. Gábor Kármán and Márton Zászkaliczky (Budapest: reciti, 2019), 11–84; Sándor Bene, 'Szinkretisták és szamaritánusok. Címszavak a kora újkori magyar politikai szótárból [Syncretists and Samaritans: Entries from the Early Modern political vocabulary in Hungary],' in *Politikai nyelvek a 17. század első felének Magyarországán*, ed. Gábor Kármán and Márton Zászkaliczky (Budapest: reciti, 2019), 327–379; Márton Zászkaliczky, 'The Language of Liberty in Early Modern Hungarian Political Debate,' in *Freedom and the Constitution Europe. Vol. 1., Religious Freedom and Civil Liberty*, ed. Quentin Skinner and Martin van Gelderen (Cambridge: Cambridge University Press, 2012), 274–295; Sándor Bene, 'Eszmetörténet és irodalomtörténet: a magyar politikai hagyomány kutatása [Intellectual history and literary history: Research on the Hungarian political tradition],' *BUKSZ* 19 (2007/1): 50–64; Balázs Trencsényi, 'The Intellectual History of Patriotism and the Legacy of Composite States in East-Central Europe,' in *Whose Love of Which Country: Composite States, National Histories and Discourses in Early Modern East Central Europe*, ed. Balázs Trencsényi and Márton Zászkaliczky (Leiden: Brill, 2010), 735–757.

 | DOI:10.1163/9789004545847_009

Intellectual life in Hungary or in Transylvania does not compare with the complexity of the German or the French scene, and we have to be aware of the important differences that exist between the political contexts as well. On the German lands, after the reinforcement of the system of independent sovereign states by the Peace of Westphalia, the new jurisprudence proved to be a useful political instrument for the statist deconfessionalization and politically imposed pacification of society.

We need to address the question: to what extent is this pattern adaptable to the Kingdom of Hungary, governed by the Habsburgs, and to Transylvania, a multiconfessional principality long governed by Calvinist princes with a status as Turkish vassals and later, after the expulsion of the Turks, administered directly from the Court in Vienna? In Transylvania, minority confessions (for example, the Unitarians) were frequent victims of state-building processes directed from the centre of power. The institutionalization of natural law in the various denominational schools took place in this minority situation. However, it must be stressed that the Unitarian and Reformed colleges did not train jurists, but primarily Protestant ministers and catechists. While obviously interested in the suspension of religious persecution and the extension of tolerance advocated by modern natural law, they would hardly have welcomed its doctrine aimed at the separation of morality and theology.

One might wonder the extent to which exponents of natural law in Hungary – most of them teachers in the highest classes of the denominational secondary schools and colleges – were receptive to the potential ideological implications of these ideas. Were they, for example, conscious at all of the differences between the anthropological foundations of the metaphysical and of the civic Enlightenment, or between the Leibnizian and the Pufendorfian conception of natural law? We should investigate the extent to which Ian Hunter's representation of Pufendorf and Thomasius as destroyers of metaphysical rationalism and bearers of an intensive wave of deconfessionalizing politics or Timothy J. Hochstrasser's interpretation on the role of 'the histories or morality' can be applied to the Hungarian or Transylvanian context.[2]

---

2 Ian Hunter, *Rival Enlightenments: Civil and Metaphysical Philosophy in Early Modern Germany* (Cambridge: Cambridge University Press, 2001); Ian Hunter, 'Introduction to Christian Thomasius, Cautelen zur Kirchenrechts-Gelahrheit (2015),' ms., 1–51. https://espace.library.uq.edu.au/view/UQ:374464 (accessed 3 September, 2021); Timothy J. Hochstrasser, *Natural Law Theories in the Early Enlightenment* (Cambridge: Cambridge University Press, 2000); Timothy J. Hochstrasser, 'The Institutionalization of Philosophy in Continental Europe,' in *The Cambridge History of 18th-Century Philosophy*, ed. Knud Haakonssen (Cambridge: Cambridge University Press, 2005), 69–95.

For the Unitarian community in Transylvania, which faced serious difficulties in the seventeenth century under the Calvinist princes as well as later in the eighteenth century under the Catholic Habsburgs, the extension of the secular magistrates' power could only be a desirable goal if it went hand in hand with the gradual deconfessionalization of politics. Such a process would imply the disentangling of the nefarious linkage between religious and political authority, the abandoning of the state's pursuit of confessional objectives and, finally, the stripping of all civil power from the clergy.

2 The Reformation in Hungary: The Process and Its Consequences

In the second decade of the sixteenth century, Hungary adopted the ideas of the religious Reformation and the attendant institutional transformations in synchrony with other European countries.[3] The draconian though rarely implemented countermeasures – for example, the '*Lutherani comburantur*' decree of the 1524 Diet – show the early appeal of the new creed.[4] Erasmus's and Luther's theses took strong root at the royal court of Wladislas II (1490–1516) and that of the young Louis II (1516–1526) before the collapse of the Hungarian state at the Battle of Mohács in 1526. In the wake of this turning point, the territory of Hungary was divided into three parts for a period of 150 years. Consequently, the progress of Protestantism took different paths in Royal Hungary, Ottoman-occupied Hungary and Transylvania. To an unusual degree in the history of the Reformation, a large number of Protestant denominations spread and gained recognition in the trisected country. Due to the chronic political instability of the war-torn country, the ruling elite – the Catholic Habsburgs in North-Western Hungary as well as the Calvinist princes of Transylvania – had to pursue a moderate and circumspect denominational policy in order to avoid estrangement among potential political supporters. This circumstance explains the relatively low degree of confessional violence in the sixteenth century.

3 For the period in general, see István György Tóth, 'Old and New Faith in Hungary, Turkish Hungary and Transylvania,' in *A Companion to the Reformation World*, ed. R. Po-Chia Hsia (London: Blackwell, 2004), 205–220; László Kontler, *A History of Hungary* (Budapest: Atlantisz, 2009); Márta Fata, 'The Kingdom of Hungary and Transylvania,' in *A Companion to the Reformation in Central Europe*, ed. Howard Louthan and Graeme Murdock (Leiden: Brill, 2015), 92–119; and István Bitskey, 'Spiritual Life in the Early Modern Age,' in *A Cultural History of Hungary: From the Beginnings to the 18th Century*, ed. László Kósa (Budapest: Corvina/Osiris, 1999), 229–284.

4 Kontler, *History*, 160.

Thus, the population of the country was highly diverse in terms of confession. The German-speaking inhabitants of the mining and market towns of Upper Hungary (Kremnica, Banská Štiavnica and Banská Bystrica), the regions of Zips Land and Transylvania were, for obvious linguistic reasons, particularly responsive to Luther's theses. Therefore, the ecclesiastical organisation of Lutheranism did not take long to consolidate in these parts of the country. Hungarian students visiting the University of Wittenberg efficiently promoted the spread of the new tenets in various social milieus.[5]

The 'German creed,' however, proved to be unfit to satisfy the spiritual and ecclesiastical expectations of the majority of Hungarians. Then, by the mid-sixteenth century, the second wave of the Reformation arrived in the dismembered Kingdom. The Helvetian confession became particularly popular with the Hungarian-speaking nobility, as well as with the inhabitants of market towns, merchants and guild artisans. By the end of the sixteenth century, the majority of the Hungarian-speaking population of the country was to congregate in the Calvinist church. This occurred in spite of the intellectually remarkable efforts of some personalities within the irenic movement[6] at uniting the two major Protestant denominations and creating an efficient anti-Catholic theologico-political platform, but the separation of Calvinists and Lutherans had become irreversible as early as the first third of the sixteenth century.

According to the estimations of historians, at least eighty per cent of the inhabitants of Hungary had become Protestants by around 1580–1590. Among them, Calvinists were more numerous than all other denominations (Lutherans, Unitarians and Anabaptists) combined.[7] The rapid and spectacular success of Protestantism in Hungary seems to proceed from the fact that its preachers were able to offer a convincing theological response to the central problem that absorbed the Hungarians: the Ottoman occupation. According to the Protestant view, the Hungarians were supposed to be God's latest chosen people, who, if they showed firmness in their beliefs and kept the true Evangelical faith, would be liberated from the Turkish yoke through God's providence, as was the people of Israel from the Babylonian captivity.[8]

5 See Borbála Kelényi, 'Krakkótól Wittenbergig. Magyarországi hallgatók a krakkói, bécsi és wittenbergi egyetemeken [From Cracow to Wittenberg: Hungarian students at the universities of Cracow, Vienna and Wittenberg],' *Gerundium. Egyetemtörténeti közlemények* 8 (2017): 23–50.

6 See *Magyar Harmónia* (1628) by the Calvinist bishop, János Samarjai.

7 Kontler, *History*, 162.

8 Kontler, *History*, 162.

The early seventeenth century saw an important turning point in the confessional history of the country with a major transformation of the power relations among the various denominations. While Calvinism remained the religion of the majority of the Hungarian-speaking population in Transylvania as well as in the Ottoman-occupied part of the trisected country, the dominance of Catholicism was gradually restored in Royal Hungary. This shift was due mainly to a return to the old faith by the leading families, who came to see and condemn the spirit of rebellion as inherent in all forms of Protestantism as a consequence of a mutually acceptable political compromise with the Habsburgs at the beginning of the century.

The gradual re-Catholization of the majority of the population in the first half of the seventeenth century took place relatively peacefully. The driving force of this process was Péter Pázmány (1570–1637), Archbishop of Esztergom. His oeuvre is marked by ecclesiastical reforms, by influential educational and polemical works and by an important contribution to the foundation of the University of Trnava in 1635 (modelled mainly on that of Graz).[9] The violent Counter-Reformation crusade launched by the Habsburgs in the 1670s, together with the gradual re-population of the country by mainly Catholic settlers after the expulsion of the Ottomans represented only the final steps in this process. As a result, Roman Catholics again outnumbered Protestants by the beginning of the eighteenth century. Emperor Leopold I, after the expulsion of the Turks with the help of an international coalition, never meant to make things easy for his Protestant subjects in Hungary. Although the Peace of Szatmár that established the peace after Francis II Rákóczi's war of independence in 1711 promised to maintain freedom of worship for the Protestants, subsequent decrees and laws reversed this compromise. They not only secured Catholic ascendency in the reunited country and gave the Roman Catholic Church the possibility of proselytizing in every conceivable way, but, most importantly, also excluded Protestants from holding office. This Counter-Reformation period lasted until the promulgation of Joseph II's Patent of Toleration in 1781.[10] Reformed schooling was among the major victims of the hostility of the Court of Vienna towards the Protestants.

9 Paul Shore and Peter Tusor, 'Péter Pázmány, archbishop of Esztergom, primate of Hungary,' *Journal of Jesuit Studies* 7 (July 2020): 526–544.

10 Kontler, *History*, 207.

3 Transylvania: Politics and Confessions

The Principality of Transylvania emerged as a state in the turbulent times following the Battle of Mohács in 1526 when the forces of the Kingdom of Hungary were defeated by those of the Ottoman Empire. Prince John of Szapolyai, proclaimed King of Hungary, left to his widow, Isabella of Jagellon, and to his son, John Sigismund, the eastern parts of Hungary and Transylvania on his death in 1540. John Sigismund managed to preserve this territory for his family during his acrimonious rivalry with Ferdinand of Habsburg. Transylvania became a semi-independent state governed by the Prince and a Diet,[11] while paying tribute to the Ottoman Empire. Austrian and Turkish influence vied for supremacy until Transylvania was incorporated into the Habsburg Empire in 1691. The golden age of Transylvania – if there was one – had ended around 1657, when the ambitious Prince George II Rákóczi, coveting the Polish crown, was defeated by Polish–Lithuanian forces and their allies. The installation of his successor, Michael I Apafi, brought with it the reduction of the principality to the status of little more than a vassal state of the Ottoman Empire. Once the Ottoman Turks were ousted from Hungary at the end of the seventeenth century, the principality lost the quasi-independence it had enjoyed under the Turks. However, it was not reunited with the Hungarian Crown. Instead, it was administered directly by the Court in Vienna, obviously because of its important role in seventeenth-century independence struggles.[12]

Although the princes between 1540 and 1680 – with the notable exception of John Sigismund (who flirted with anti-Trinitarianism) and Stephan Báthory (the Catholic King of Poland as well) – belonged to the Reformed faith, they never intended or managed to impose one dominant religion on the population. After the establishment of the principality in 1541, the efforts of its Diet to assure political stability led to the confirmation of legal equality for the four established confessions (*religiones receptae*)[13] and thereby the preservation of the multidenominational situation.[14] Due to this tolerant legislative spirit, a great number of confessions coexisted in Transylvania, making it an excep-

11 It consisted of three estates: the Hungarian, Saxon (German) and Szekler. The Eastern Orthodox Romanian population received no political recognition.

12 Kontler, *History*, 207.

13 The Catholic, Reformed, Lutheran, and Unitarian confessions.

14 See István Keul, *Early Modern Religious Communities in East-Central Europe: Ethnic Diversity, Denominational Plurality and Corporative Politics in the Principality of Transylvania (1526–1691)* (Leiden: Brill, 2009).

tional territory in Reformation Europe.[15] As in Royal Hungary, the German-speaking (Saxon) burghers adopted Luther's creed. They remained faithful to it over the centuries, clearly distancing themselves from any further radical theological innovation at all. From 1550, the Calvinist Reformation spread rapidly among the Hungarian-speaking population to become the strongest of the rival confessions. Anti-Trinitarian (Unitarian) radicalism, imported into the principality by Italian heretics, took root largely through the support of John Sigismund. In 1638, in the Des agreement (or *complanatio Deesiana*), Prince George I Rákóczi imposed on the moderate wing of the Unitarian church the divine adoration of Jesus Christ as well as the violent elimination of any deniers of the legitimacy of such adoration, the non-Adorantists, and of the Sabbatarians, who had compromised them in the eyes of the other confessions.

Robert J. Evans has underlined that Transylvania provided the best illustration that absolutism did not necessarily entail homogeneity.[16] During the eighteenth century, the Reformed Protestants and particularly the Unitarians never ceased complaining about the intense attempts by the government in Vienna to promote the cause of Catholicism in the principality, but the central government never achieved a Catholic majority in Transylvania. Transylvania was a special case because of its particular political traditions, its multiconfessionalism, recognised officially in the Diploma Leopoldinum (1691), and the close links that its Protestant (Lutheran, Calvinist, and Unitarian) elite always maintained with Western academic circles.

4 Protestant Schooling in Early Modern Hungary

As Calvin stated a number of times, a true faith should be an intelligent faith. Thus, Calvinism and education were necessarily intimately linked: the diffusion of the new creed gave a powerful impulse to schooling. The lack of a

---

15 See Mihály Balázs, 'Tolerant country – misunderstood laws: Interpreting sixteenth-century Transylvanian legislation concerning religion,' *Hungarian Historical Review* 2 (2013/1): 85–108.

16 R.J.W. Evans, 'Die Grenzen der Konfessionalisierung, Die Folgen der Gegenreformation für die Habsburgerländer,' in *Konfessionalisierung in Ostmitteleuropa. Wirkungen des religiösen Wandels in 16. und 17. Jahrhundert in Staat, Gesellschaft und Kultur*, ed. Joachim Bahlcke and Arno Strohmeyer (Stuttgart: Franz Steiner Verlag, 1999), 395–412. For an evaluation of recent historiography, see Bálint Keserű, 'Shaping Protestant networks in Habsburg Transylvania (1686–1699),' in *A Divided Hungary in Europe: Exchange, Networks and Representations, 1541–1699*. Vol. 1., ed. Gábor Almási (Newcastle: Cambridge Scholars Publishing, 2014), 183–200.

Protestant university increased the significance of the practice of *study tours*, since highly qualified religious and lay intellectuals in the Reformed Protestant (and Unitarian) communities mainly studied abroad. In the seventeenth century, as a guarantee for maintaining the religious and cultural standards of Protestant schools and, ultimately, the Churches themselves, students went abroad continuously. This *peregrinatio academica* provided fresh intellectual reinforcements almost without interruption, even in difficult times of oppression and crisis.[17] Visitors to foreign – mainly German and Dutch – universities brought home natural law-related books and ideas. The pearl of Reformed Protestant education was, at least for a short period of time, the college of Alba Iulia that Prince Gabriel Bethlen wanted to develop into a real university with the invitation of illustrious foreign scholars, such as Martin Opitz, Johann Heinrich Bisterfeld and Johann Heinrich Alsted.[18] The devastation of the castle and the city of Alba Iulia by the Turks in 1658 led to the relocation of the college to the town of Aiud, also in Transylvania.

Schools in Hungarian territories were deeply integrated into the international Calvinist network of institutions, and those who founded and maintained the Reformed Protestant colleges also opted to follow the available Western models. For example, the philosopher and theologian Albert Szenczi Molnár published, under the title *Institutio iuventutis in paedagogiis illustribus Inferioris Palatinatus* (The education of youth in the illustrious schools of the Lower Palatinate, 1621), the educational methodology accepted at the academy of Heidelberg and adopted by higher education institutions in the Palatinate. Szenczi Molnár intended this scheme to serve as a model for all reformed schools in Hungary and Transylvania,[19] but eventually, each college pursued its own programme of studies.

These colleges – in Debrecen, Pápa, Oradea, Cluj and Sárospatak – provided education at a very high standard. As for the general content of the curriculum, grammar, poetics and rhetoric prepared students for access to the higher disciplines of philosophy and theology. The language of tuition was Latin. In these schools, the curricula were only broadly outlined, and (with the remark-

17 See the studies in *A Divided Hungary in Europe: Exchange, Networks and Representations, 1541–1699. Vol. 1. Study Tours and Intellectual-Religious Relationships*, ed. Gábor Almási (Newcastle: Cambridge Scholars Publishing, 2014).

18 Howard Hotson, *Johann Heinrich Alsted, 1588–1638: Between Renaissance and Reformation* (Oxford: Oxford University Press, 2000), 21.

19 József Barcza, ed., *A Debreceni Református Kollégium története* [A History of the Reformed College in Debrecen] (Budapest: A Magyarországi Református Egyház Zsinati Irodájának Sajtóosztálya, 1988), 32.

able exception of Debrecen) the framework was filled largely according to the individual professors' interests and preferences and the pedagogical material available. Due to this considerable professorial latitude, Protestant (Reformed and Unitarian) religious and scientific culture was much more diverse and rich than that of the Catholics. The majority of graduate students, installed later as pastors in villages, never lost contact with their college. A statute of the college of Debrecen from 1657 highlights in more detail the organisational structure of the studies. Once the lower division of studies (lasting six or seven years) had been completed, students were entitled to join the college proper, as it was called.[20] The completion of the *cursus philosophicus* or *cursus academicus* within two or three years was a must for every future theologian. In the regulations of Sárospatak, the students enrolled in basic education were referred to as *pueri*, those in secondary education as adolescents, and older students were called *studiosi* – either *togati* (theology students with a uniform) or *non togati* (not participating in the theology programme).[21]

As one of the last offshoots of the Reformation, the Transylvanian Unitarian Church differed in many respects from similar organisations, and even more radically from some of the short-lived sects of the time. Brilliant Unitarian freethinkers, for example György Enyedi (1555–1597), author of the *Explicationes locorum veteris et novis Testamenti* (1598), gained a reputation in Western Europe.[22] However, the average parishioner and the majority of the Church's leadership, who were bound to their homeland, had to work hard for the approval of the secular powers and a minimal level of political support for their organisation. Like other Protestant churches, the Unitarian Church always laid great stress upon teaching and education. During a brief period of direct princely support (1568–1571), they entertained the hope of running their own college and even began preparations for the foundation of a university. Their oldest educational institution, the Unitarian College in Cluj, together with its Main Library, was founded in 1557.

After the Peace of Szatmár in 1711, Protestant schooling came under serious pressure. After 1750, the situation grew even worse: in 1752, a decree issued by the Governing Council forced the college of Pápa to be handed over to the

20 Barcza, *Debreceni*, 536.

21 Dénes Dienes and János Ugrai, *History of the Reformed Church College in Sárospatak* (Sárospatak: Hernád Kiadó, 2013), 27.

22 See Borbála Lovas's paper in this volume. For recent literature in Hungarian, see József Simon, *Explicationes explicationum: Filozófia, irodalom és egzegetika Enyedi György életművében* [Explicationes explicationum: Philosophy, literature and exegesis in the oeuvre of György Enyedi] (Budapest: Typotex, 2015).

Catholics and in 1754, the college of Satu Mare was abolished (as well as those of Tata and Baia Mare).[23]

5 Sárospatak

In the Kingdom of Hungary, the most significant Reformed Protestant colleges were in Debrecen, Sárospatak, and Oradea. The college in Oradea was incorporated into Debrecen College in the mid-seventeenth century.[24] In addition, another dozen or so similar institutions existed in Hungary. Such as the college in Pápa, they were not complete colleges, as they had no instruction in philosophy: after grammar, poetics, rhetoric and logic, they taught theology directly. Thus, these institutions are not relevant for the reception of natural law, which was taught in the philosophy classes.[25]

The first flourishing period of the college in Sárospatak was during the reign of George I Rákóczi, Prince of Transylvania, and his consort, Zsuzsanna Lorántffy (1600–1662). They established the system of organisation and operation and covered the salaries of the professors as well as a subsistence for poor students.[26] The great European teacher Johann Amos Comenius came to Sárospatak at Zsuzsanna Lorántffy's invitation. The title 'illustris' for the college appears for the first time in Comenius's scheme of instruction, the *Illustris Patakinae scholae idea* (1650).[27] His student at Sárospatak, the Cartesian János Pósaházi, was the first to acquaint students with modern scientific and philosophical trends.[28]

There was no uniform curriculum for the Protestant colleges. In institutions such as Sárospatak, Latin, Greek, philosophy and theology were taught.[29]

---

23 Barcza, *Debreceni*, 115.

24 Géza Nagy, *A református egyház története 1608–1715*, Vols I–II. [A History of the Reformed Protestant Church 1608–1715 I–II]. (Máriabesnyő and Gödöllő: Attraktor, 2008), II 189. Barcza, *Debreceni*, 51.

25 József Hudi, 'A Pápai Református Kollégium szervezete és működése a XVI–XIX. században [The Reformed College in Pápa: Its Organisation and Functioning in the sixteenth to nineteenth centuries],' in *A Pápai Református Kollégium diákjai 1585–1861* [Students of the Reformed College in Pápa, 1585–1861] (Pápa: Pápai Református Gyűjtemények, 2006), 35.

26 József Ködöböcz, *Tan'ıtóképzés Sárospatakon: A kollégiumi és középfokú képzés négy évszázada* [A Teacher Training College in Sárospatak: Four Centuries of College and High School Training] (Budapest: Tankönyvkiadó, 1986), 34.

27 Nagy, *Református*, I 345.

28 Nagy, *Református*, II 219–221.

29 Ködöböcz, *Tanítóképzés*, 58.

This was complemented by the natural sciences. According to an instruction from the time of the college's patroness, Zsuzsanna Lorántffy, only knowledge necessary for piety and public life (*ad usum necessarium in ecclesia et politia*) was required for instruction and both theology and philosophy.[30] Reformed Protestant instruction regarded theology as its main discipline, and the lay sciences were instrumental to theology (*instrumentales disciplinae*).

Instruction in natural law at Sárospatak seems to have begun at the turn of the eighteenth century. From the late seventeenth century, the teaching of theology was complemented by profane subjects as service to society became the objective of instruction.[31] The Western European corpus of academic natural law provided an excellent means to this end and was easily adaptable to the pedagogic goals at Sárospatak. According to a memorandum by János Csécsy Jnr, director of the college, politics, morality, church history and Hungarian grammar were taught at the end of the seventeenth century. In 1709, however, this curriculum was complemented by natural law, the law of nations and experimental physics.[32]

The last third of the seventeenth century and the first decades of the eighteenth century brought persecution, exile and internal crisis to the college. After the demise of Zsuzsanna Lorántffy, the Catholic Zsófia Báthory not only denied the college support, but also took its building in 1671.[33] During the religious and Turkish wars, the college found itself in exile in various towns in Transylvania and Upper Hungary, but it returned to its hometown as Francis II Rákóczi, leader of an anti-Habsburg uprising, recaptured Sárospatak in 1703.[34]

The curriculum with a focus on piety was first challenged when János Csécsy (1689–1769), rector and professor of philosophy, returned from the universities of Western Europe with modern views. Csécsy's ambitious plans to teach Cartesian philosophy and natural theology rather than the old curriculum triggered vehement opposition.[35] Sources on instruction in natural law survive from 1734 during the professorship of Csécsy's successor, Dávid Sárkány.

30 Ködöböcz, *Tanítóképzés*, 59; Nagy, *Református*, I 325.

31 Ködöböcz, *Tanítóképzés*, 61.

32 Ködöböcz, *Tanítóképzés*, 60.

33 Nagy, *Református*, II 197; Ködöböcz, *Tanítóképzés*, 28, 35.

34 Nagy, *Református*, II 198.; Ködöböcz, *Tanítóképzés*, 29.

35 Kálmán Benda, 'A Kollégium története 1703-tól 1849-ig [History of the College, 1703–1849],' in *A Sárospataki Református Kollégium. Tanulmányok alapításának 450. évfordulójára* (Budapest: A Református Zsinati Iroda Sajtóosztálya, 1981), 90; Nagy, *Református*, II 185–187; Ködöböcz, *Tanítóképzés*, 43.

Texts accompanying the instruction of natural law in Western Europe as in the Lutheran gymnasia of Royal Prussia were typically prints. Curricula and course descriptions duplicated at the printing press of the academic institution, primary texts (distributed in the form of half- or one-sheet-long 'handouts') as well as printed exercises (*exercitationes*), disputations and dissertations provide the primary sources of historical research. In contrast, the college of Sárospatak had no printing press during the period under scrutiny, from the mid-seventeenth century to the early nineteenth century.[36] Consequently, neither printed curricula nor printed disputations have survived. The only form of dissemination for locally produced knowledge was the manuscript lecture notes, copied by the students by way of dictation. In addition, lists of exam questions divulging the teaching practice of some professors survived. A third manuscript genre was the manuscript book that gave an account of the professors' research. They only served an educational function indirectly. Their primary aim consisted in the documentation of new outcomes for the internal audience of the college.

Books on natural law were acquired from abroad, typically from the Netherlands and Germany, by the library or the professors.[37] The intensification of the acquisition in the last decades of the eighteenth century shows their importance in teaching. The library's collection was, however, insufficient for independent research: manuscript treatises were penned by professors who came home from years-long research stays at Western universities. On the other hand, the increase in the number of natural law books in the library coincided with the general increase of the library collection between 1766 and 1785 from 2500 to 3500 titles.[38] Around that time, the number of students in each class also doubled from approximately fifty to a hundred.[39]

36 Béla Takács, 'A sárospataki nyomda [The printing press at Sárospatak],' in *A Sárospataki Református Kollégium. Tanulmányok alapításának 450. évfordulójára* (Budapest: A Református Zsinati Iroda Sajtóosztálya, 1981), 306; Ködöböcz, *Tanítóképzés*, 61; János Román, *A Sárospataki Kollégium* [The College of Sárospatak] (Budapest: Képzőművészeti Alap Kiadóvállalata, 1956), 28.

37 Ködöböcz, *Tanítóképzés*, 61.

38 Mihály Szentimrei, 'A kollégium tudományos gyűjteményei [The Scientific Collections of the College],' in *A Sárospataki Református Kollégium. Tanulmányok alapításának 450. évfordulójára* (Budapest: A Református Zsinati Iroda Sajtóosztálya, 1981), 279.

39 Richard Hörcsik, *A Sárospataki Református Kollégium diákjai 1617–1777* [Students of the Reformed College in Sárospatak, 1617–1777] (Sárospatak: A Sárospataki Református Kollégium Tudományos Gyűjteményei, 1998), 36–38; Román, *Sárospataki*, 18. For the number of students in the second part of the eighteenth century, see Benda, *Kollégium*, 96.

For all courses, there was only a single, narrow lecture hall at Sárospatak. In the absence of printed manuals, dictating and excerpting made the teaching slow and laborious. Each month, a disputation in theology and philosophy took place.[40] There also existed a student circle (*collatio*) for friendly discussions.[41]

The staff was equally modest. Between 1713 and 1742, two professors were employed for the upper years at Sárospatak, three from 1742 to 1771, four from 1771 to 1796, six from 1796 to 1810 and seven to ten from 1810 to 1857.[42] A coryphe of Hungarian literary culture of the early nineteenth century, Ferenc Kazinczy (1759–1831), recalled his four professors in his *Memory of my career*, those of natural law and philosophy among them:

> The professor of philosophy was suffering from a fatal illness when I became his student, and he was ailing for a couple of months. He who taught history and natural law did not deliver a single lecture for half a year because of the almost complete darkening in his eyes. The teacher of theology went through his science in five years, whereas newer and newer students came to him every six months. No one wanted to attend the lectures of the fourth one, who taught physics and mathematics, because of his unimaginable rudeness.[43]

As Kazinczy's memoirs indicate, the surviving lecture texts and notes are helpful to reconstruct the curriculum, but they are by no means sufficient proof of its effective dissemination.

Natural law was incorporated into the teaching of practical philosophy and moral theology at Sárospatak. The newly established department of jurisprudence under the professorship of Sándor Kövy (1763–1829, professor 1793–1829)

---

40 Mátyás Bajkó, *Kollégiumi iskolakultúránk a Felvilágosodás idején és a reformkorban* [College School Culture in Hungary during the Enlightenment and the Reform Era] (Budapest: Akadémiai, 1976), 66.

41 Bajkó, *Kollégiumi*, 67.

42 Ködöböcz, *Tanítóképzés*, 41–42.

43 'A Philosophia professzora halálos betegségben fekvék midőn keze alá jutottam, és néhány hónapokig sínlett, a históriákat s természeti törvényt tanító félesztendeig sem tartott leczkét, szemeinek csaknem teljes elsötétedések miatt, az ki theológiát tanított, öt esztendő alatt mene végig tudományán, pedig keze alá minden hatodik hónapban új hallgatók jövének által; a negyediket, ki Phisicát és Mathesist tanított senki sem akará hallgatni, képzelhetetlen nyerseségei miatt.' Cited in Mátyás Bajkó, *A magyarországi és az erdélyi protestáns kollégiumok 1777 és 1848 között* [Protestant Colleges in Hungary and Transylvania between 1777 and 1848] (S.l.: Kinizsi Mg. Szakszöv. Nyomdája, 1991), 13.

and János Gortvay (professor 1829–1853) was not influenced by natural law.[44] Jurisprudence relieved the instruction of philosophy in so far as there was no longer any need to teach juridical knowledge as part of philosophy. Ultimately, it contributed to a phasing out of natural law instruction, since the backbone of juridical instruction was Hungarian law, which remained uninfluenced by the natural law tradition.

Professors of philosophy at Sárospatak were as follows: Mihály Buzinkay (1656–1683), János Pósaházi (1657–1686), János Csécsy Jnr (1686–1708, 1713–1734), Dávid Sárkány (1734–1758), Pál Szathmári Paksi (1759–1766), István Szentgyörgyi (1767–1791), Mihály Tóth-Pápai (1791–1805), József Rozgonyi (1797–1823), István Nyíri (1824–1838), József Milotay (1839–1846) and Gábor Szeremley (1841–1851). From 1743, natural law and history obtained a newly established professorship. This chair was occupied by István Bányai (1743–1767), János Szentesi (1767–1781) and János Szombathy (1783–1823).

Dávid Sárkány (1700–1762) studied at Sárospatak and Tărgu Mureş. He matriculated in 1729 at Utrecht University and in 1730 at Franeker University. His manuscript book entitled *Philosophia moralis* dates from the year 1745.[45] This monumental construction reveals its author's wide and deep knowledge of philosophical schools in general and modern natural law in particular from Hugo Grotius to Jean Barbeyrac. In his book, Sárkány divided the history of humankind into the Paradise, fallen and restored stages (*status institutus, status destitutus, status restitutus*).[46] Within a detailed critique of Hobbes, Sárkány argued that the integral status of humans, rather than their corrupted condition, should serve as a basis for natural law. Sárkány's book is an outstanding example of Protestant Scholastics in Hungary, which opens intriguing comparative vistas with Scottish Protestant moral theology, especially with James Dundas's *Idea philosophiae moralis* (1679).[47]

---

44 Cf. Gábor Bolvári-Takács, 'Ballagi Géza és a pataki jogakadémia [Géza Ballagi and the academy of law in Sárospatak],' in *Zempléni Múzsa* 7 (2007 ősz): 92–94, here 93.

45 Dávid Sárkány, *Philosophia moralis, opera – – in Kolleg. Ref. S. Patak. Prof. Publ. concinnata*, 1745 (Kt. 195). Cf. József Börzsönyi, *A Tiszáninneni Református Egyházkerület Nagykönyvtárának (Sárospatak) kéziratkatalógusa: 1850 előtti kéziratok* [The Catalogue of Manuscripts in the Great Library of the Cistibiscan Reformed Protestant Diocese: Manuscripts before 1850] (Budapest: Országos Széchényi Könyvtár, 1986), item 190.

46 'Index Generalis / Conspectus brevis operis / In hoc opere Cl. Auctor tradit Ethicam secundum triplicem respectum, triplicis status hominis nempe 1. Ad statum institutum, 2. ad statum Destitutum, 3. Ad statum Restitutum' (Sárkány, *Philosophia moralis*, [361]).

47 See Alexander Broadie, 'The Reformed Scholasticism of James Dundas,' in *The history of Scottish theology Vol. 1. Celtic origins to reformed orthodoxy*, ed. David Fergusson and Mark W. Elliott (Oxford: Oxford University Press, 2019), 259; Giovanni Gellera, 'Christian

Another anonymous and undated manuscript with the title *Institutionum juris naturae et gentium libri duo* can be tied to Sárkány's activities as well. Within the framework of a course on natural law, the manuscript displays a structure and argument similar to those of his *Theologia moralis*. It takes the history of the discipline into consideration until Jean Barbeyrac's 1724 contribution, i.e. the edition of Hugo Grotius's *De jure belli ac pacis* in French translation with annotations. It also provided a reason why it was desirable to introduce natural law into the curriculum at Sárospatak. This is because the illustrious college had to adhere to contemporary European trends, where 'these days, the name of Grotius resounds at every university' (*Et hodie, in omnibus Academiis Grotius resonat*).[48]

István Bányai (1711–1767) studied at Bratislava, Franeker and Harderwijk. Two lectures of his survived under the title *Jus naturae et gentium secundum Auctorem Clar[issimum] Vitriarium* (1765) and *Quaestiones Juris Naturalis*. At Leiden, Bányai probably attended courses by Johann Jacob Vitriarius (1679–1745). Johann Jacob was the son of Philipp Reinhard Vitriarius (1647–1720), author of the schoolbook *Institutiones Juris Naturae et Gentium, … ad methodum Hugonis Grotii conscriptae* (Halle 1701). His lecture manuscript *Jus naturae et gentium* is a compilation of selected theses from Vitriarius's *Institutiones*,[49] apart from the introduction, which is an original work on the question of the existence of natural law.

Also, István Bányai's personal library testifies to his orientation in natural law. He purchased Hugo Grotius's *De jure belli ac pacis* at Leiden in 1742, excerpting some basic theses from volume I, probably for lecture purposes. In addition, he annotated chapters one and twelve from volume II. He made notes for himself theses concerning the argumentation, the main claims and their counterarguments.[50] Bányai probably used the volume in his teaching: both chapters are of paramount importance: chapter one on the causes of wars and chapter twelve on contracts. These two areas formed the bulk of instruction in public and private law, respectively.

---

tolerance and tolerance of the Christians: Natural law and conscience in James Dundas's *Idea Philosophiae Moralis* (1679),' *Global Intellectual History* 5 (2020/2), 171–190.

48 *Institutionum juris naturae et gentium libri duo* (Kt. 580), 7.

49 Dienes and Ugrai, *History*, 69.

50 Hugo Grotius, *De Jure Belli ac Pacis libri tres* (Utrecht: Guilielmus vande Water, 1696, sign. DD 167); Hugo Grotius, *De Jure Belli ac Pacis libri tres*. Tomus secundus (Utrecht: Guilielmus vande Water, Guilielmus Broedelet, 1700, sign. DD 168, with reading track on pages 21–41, 406–444). For Bányai's library record, see *Catalogus Librorum, e Bibliotheca Clariss. D. Professoris Stephani Bányai in Bibliothecam publicam Ill. Collegii S. Patekiensis translatorum* (Kt. 1110).

Pál Szathmári Paksi (1733–1766) worked at Sárospatak as a teacher of philosophy between 1759 and 1766. He studied medicine at the Franeker University; this discipline was his unique field of publication. He taught natural law after Johann Gottlieb Heineccius and Christian Wolff. A set of student notes from the years of his professorship, *Study in moral philosophy by Sámuel Mándy, student in Sárospatak*, from 1763,[51] often makes mention of natural law authors and arguments.

János Szentesi (1735–1781) studied at Sárospatak and Franeker and returned to Sárospatak as a professor in early 1767. He published two treatises on biblical theology at Franeker in 1761 and 1762. The text of his lecture survived under the title *Syncope Juridica Seu Compendium Juris Naturae & Gentium* (1776).[52] Two series of questions for examination have survived from the years 1777 and 1781 under the titles *Magis momentosa universi Juris Naturae seu Gentium capita* (on the basis of which Ferenc Kazinczy and his brother had taken their exams) and *Asserta e Jure Naturae, seu Gentium, recollecta*.[53] Szentesi's horizon did not reach beyond Grotius, Hobbes and Pufendorf. He referred to them in the chapter on parental rights in his *Syncope*.[54] His questions from 1777 mainly concerned royal prerogatives, parental rights and contracts, with a question or two on the rights of war. Similarly, his questions from 1781 remain within the field of private law. Szentesi held enlightened views on the education of children. For example, he would only allow the exercise of paternal power in the interest of the child's well-being and 'perfection.'[55] Servitude, according to him, is against the law of nature. For the driving force of establishing society,

---

51 *Mándy Sámuel pataki diák erkölcs-filozófiai studiuma 1763-ból* [A study in moral philosophy by Sámuel Mándy, student at Sárospatak, from 1763] (Kt. a.162).

52 János Szentesi, *Syncope Juridica Seu Compendium Juris Naturae & Gentium*, 1776 (Kt. 397).

53 János Szentesi, *Magis momentosa universi Juris Naturae seu Gentium capita*, LVI. *assertis inclusa, quae ... sub praesidio ... – –, In Illustri Collegio Helv. Conf. addict. S. Patakiensi, Juris Naturae, Historiarum, & eloquentiae Professoris P. O. ... defendent ... Daniel Bártzay ..., Franciscus Kazinczy ..., Georgius Horváth de Pálotz, Dionysius Kazinczy ..., Albertus Szemere* (Cassovia: Landerer, 1777) (Kt. 3217, Fol. 74.); János Szentesi, *Asserta e Jure Naturae, seu Gentium, recollecta. Quae In Speciem Annuae Diligentiae ... Sub Praesidio – –, Juris Nat., Hist. & Eloqu. Profess. ... In Auditorio Maiori Disputationi Submissa sunt*, 1781, in *Liber Thesibus* (Kt. 1134, fol. 12r–13r).

54 Szentesi, *Syncope*, 58–59.

55 'XI. Post mutua conjugium officia & Iura, ex hac coniugali societate, nova sequitur obligatio: generandi nimirum, & rite educandi liberos. / XII. Quae obligatio Jus dat Parentibus in Liberos, quod Paternae potestatis nomine Bene venire potest. / XIII. Effectus hujus potestatis non sunt majores in Liberos, quam eorundem salutis, conservationis, & perfectionis ratio exigit' (Szentesi, *Asserta*, 12v).

he did not consider family ties or need for sociability in Grotius's and Pufendorf's sense, but rather, in Hobbes's vein, deprivation, fear and the search for security.[56]

János Szombathy (1749–1823) studied at Rimska Sobota, Sárospatak, Zürich, Franeker and Paris. He obtained his doctorate at Utrecht with a Cartesian-Coccejan dissertation, an anti-Socinian polemical writing at the same time: *Dissertatio de praescientia futurorum contingentium* (Utrecht: Abr. Paddenburg, 1778). The series of his questions for examination survived from the years between 1783 and 1792.[57]

In contradistinction to the Cartesian-Coccejans (Bányai, Szentesi and Szombathy), who advocated the interlocking of philosophy and theology, 'positive rationalists' defended the independence of theology. The first of them, István Szentgyörgyi, did not study abroad. He studied at Sárospatak with Dávid Sárkány, and thereafter went to Rimska Sobota to return to his home institution to be Pál Szathmári Paksi's successor as the chair in philosophy. Szentgyörgyi based his instruction on Wolff. His manual *Theologia naturalis*,

56 'XIX. Societatem civilem, quam Civitatem, seu Rempublicam vocamus primam, potius ex integris familiis, quam singulis hominum individuis, quae perpetuitatem non promittunt, coaluisse censendum. / XX. Nec eandem sanguinis, cognationisque vinculo, aut aliquo socialitatis studio, sed indigentiae & metus stimulis, hisque oppositorum commodorum, et securitatis spe convocatam fuisse' (Szentesi, *Asserta*, 12v).

57 János Szombathy, *Theses e Jurisprudentia Naturali depromtae, ac in Specimen Diligentiae semestris, sub Praesidio – – ... publicè disputandae*, 1783, in *Liber Thesibus* (Kt. 1134, fol. 13v–14r); János Szombathy, *Theses e Juris Prudentia Naturali juxta primas lineas Sam. Christ. Holmanni pertractata, recollectae, ac in Specimen diligentiae annuae sub Praesidio – – ... publice disputandae*, 1784, in *Liber Thesibus* (Kt. 1134, fol. 14v–15r); János Szombathy, *Positiones e Jure Publico Universali depromptae in specimen industriae et Profectus Studiosorum Jurisprudentiae ... Sub Praesidio – – ... publice ventilandae*, 1785, in *Liber Thesibus* (Kt. 1134, fol. 15v–16v); János Szombathy, *Positiones e Jure Naturae & Gentium item Publico Universali Seu Civitatis Depromtae ac in Specimen Diligentiae & Profectûs Studiosorum Juris-Prudentiae Praeside – – ... Publice disputendae*, 1786, in *Liber Thesibus* (Kt. 1134, fol. 17v–18v); János Szombathy, *Theses e Jure Naturae & Gentium Item Publico Universali depromtae ac in Specimen diligentiae & profectus Studiosorum Jurisprudentiae Praeside – – ... publice disputandae*, 1787, in *Liber Thesibus* (Kt. 1134, fol. 19r–19v); János Szombathy, *Positiones e Jure Naturae & Gentium Item Publico Universali depromtae quas Juris prudentiae Cultores diligentiae suae Specimen exhibituri sub Praesidio – – ... publice ventilabunt*, 1788, in *Liber Thesibus* (Kt. 1134, fol. 20r–20v); [János Szombathy,] *Theses Juridicae, Occasione Examinis Publici Ao. 1789. die 8a Julii disputandae*, in *Liber Thesibus* (Kt. 1134, fol. 21r); [János Szombathy,] *Theses Juridicae, pro Examine Publico Anni 1790*, in *Liber Thesibus* (Kt. 1134, fol. 21v); [János Szombathy,] *Theses Juridicae, pro Examine Publico Anni 1791*, in *Liber Thesibus* (Kt. 1134, fol. 22r); [János Szombathy,] *Theses Juridicae Pro examine Publico Anni 1792*, in *Liber Thesibus* (Kt. 1134, fol. 22v).

printed in Bratislava in 1784, was also used by his successors at Sárospatak. Manuscript works of his complement the picture of a thirty-year-long academic career. As his list of theses from 1770 under the title *Scholia ad Heineccii Philosophiam Moralem* shows, he taught moral philosophy at the early stage of his career after Johann Gottlieb Heineccius.[58] From the subsequent year, a lecture of his entitled *De Philosophiae moralis natura et constitutione* survived in the unreliable transcription of a subteen student.[59] It seems that the text reveals similarities to the lecture notes we have at our disposal from Pál Szathmári Paksi. His examination questions between 1781 and 1792 bear scant relevance to natural law.[60] The topics in another anonymous manuscript, *Dissertatio ex Jure Naturae et Gentium de Poenis*, however, can be linked to these examination questions in various ways.[61] In any case, a further anonymous manuscript under the title *Jurisprudentia naturalis* confirms that Szentgyörgyi was treated as a natural law writer at Sárospatak. He was mentioned in the same breath with other writers of ancient and modern natural law, held by the author as the sole authorities in issues of moral philosophy:

> Question: Is morality objective or intrinsic or rather subjective or extrinsic? Response: It is considered as intrinsic by the Stoics, Cicero, the ancient Scholastics; and among the moderns by Grotius, Pierre Bayle, Leibniz, Wolff, Canz, the illustrious Martini, the renowned István Szentgyörgyi etc. It is held as extrinsic by the Academics, Pyrrhonists, Pufendorf, Heinrich and Samuel Cocceji, Johann Franz Budde, Achenwall and our author, the renowned János Szentesi.[62]

József Rozgonyi (1756–1823) was the most significant professor of philosophy at Sárospatak. It was his *alma mater*, and then he went on to attend the universities of Vienna, Utrecht, Oxford and Göttingen. Rozgonyi accomplished a shift

---

58 István Szentgyörgyi, *Scholia ad Heineccii Philosophiam Moralem*. A Jove principium est Die 13ª 7bris Anno 1770. Sub Praesidio Celeberrimi ac Clarissimi Viri Stephani Sz. Györgyi (Kt. 428).

59 István Szentgyörgyi, *De Philosophiae moralis natura et constitutione*, 1771 (Kt. 1885).

60 Kt. 1134, fol. 34r–41v.

61 Kt. 551.

62 'Qs. An moralitas autem sit Objectiva sive Intrinseca vel Subjectiva sive Extrinseca? Rs. Intrinsecam docuerunt Stoici, Cicero, Scholastici antiqui, et recentioribus autem H Grotius, Pet Baelius, Leibnitzius, Wolfius, Canzius & Ills Martini Cl. Steph. SzGyörgyi &c. Extrinsecam Academici; Pirhonici, Puffendorf, Henr. & Sam. L. B. de Coccei, Joh. Franc. Buddeus, Achenwall & Auctor Noster Cl. Joh. Szentesi' (*Jurisprudentia naturalis* (Kt. 558), § 11, unpaginated).

in the teaching of natural law in so far as he taught it as an academic discipline that had its history, foundations, and critically verifiable principles and tenets rather than an applied social theory, in a word, as philosophical knowledge rather than practical knowledge of social life. Rozgonyi had a broad and up-to-date knowledge of natural law writers from Grotius, Pufendorf and Christian Thomasius to Heinrich and Samuel Cocceji, Holmann, Feder, Johann August Heinrich Ulrich, Achenwall and Burlamaqui to Kant, Jakob, Fichte and Hufeland.[63]

In Rozgonyi's time (not least due to his efforts), a printing press was once again put to his service at Sárospatak. His philosophical works in the genre and under the title of *aphorismi*, founding or accompanying his lectures, saw the light of day in print. With the help of these printed works, Rozgonyi's manuscript lecture notes can be identified on the basis of similarities in content. Hence, besides the already identified *Breves quaestiones a philosophia* from 1817, the manuscripts *Prolegomena Philosophiae* (1808), *Introductio ad Philosophiam* (1808/9) and *Brevis conspectus philosophiae* (1819) can also be considered as the work of Rozgonyi.[64] The lecture *Prolegomena philosophiae* discusses natural law with the same structure as his book *Aphorismi Juris naturae* does.[65] In both texts, Rozgonyi's starting point was Kant's moral philosophy. He stated the fundamental difference between their approaches. In contradistinction to Kant, Rozgonyi intended to link natural law to the sphere of morality rather than, as in Kant, to legality.[66] In harmony with the teach-

63 'Pro primo Juris Naturae principio posuit [*scil.* Hugo Grotius] *appetitum socialitatis tranquillae.* Tamen inquit: homo natus est ad socialitatem quare illam cole, atque custodi. Hinc ipse Grotius et omnes qui illum sequebantur dicti sunt *Socialistae* ut Sam: Puffendorfius, Christianus Thomasius; sed qui divinae voluntatis principium assumsit pro fundamento Juris Naturae. Praeter hos, auctores Juris Naturae celebrantur Henricus et Sam: Coccei plurimum meriti de codice Borussico; Holmann, Feder professor uterque Göttingensis, Ulric professor Jenensis, Achenwallius, Bürlamacki, Kant, Jacob, Fichte, Hufeland' (József Rozgonyi, *Prolegomena Philosophiae*, 1808 (Kt. 3401), § 4, unpaginated).

64 József Rozgonyi, *Breves quaestiones a philosophia*, 1817 (Kt. 2821); József Rozgonyi, *Introductio ad Philosophiam*, 1808/9 (Kt. a. 360); József Rozgonyi, *Brevis conspectus philosophiae*, 1819 (Kt. 677).

65 József Rozgonyi, *Aphorismi Juris Naturae, perpetua Juris Romani, Hungarici, Juris Naturae Kantiani ratione habita* (Sárospatak: András Nádaskay, 1822).

66 'Vox Moralis ambiguum habet sensum v. sumitur *lato* sensu et tam Philosophia moralis continet Jus Naturae et Ethicam; si *stricto* sensu sumitur tum solum Ethicam. et hoc posteriori sensu sumant Kantiani, penitus avellentes Jus Naturae a morali Philosophia. – Aliquas actiones illi dicunt esse *Legales*; quae pertinent v. ad Jus Naturae; v. ad Jus positivum: aliquas esse *morales*, quas producit reverentia honestatis, has retulerunt ad Ethicam. Kantianis ergo qui justus est i.e. legi conformiter agit, necdum est honestus. Nos lato sensu sumimus Moralitatem' (Rozgonyi, *Prolegomena*, § 1, unpaginated).

ing traditions at Sárospatak, Rozgonyi taught moral philosophy as a discipline open to common sense and not requiring the revolution of moral reasoning. He did not argue for an overlapping of the spheres of natural law and ethics. He saw Grotius as a renewer of the science of politics since, as he put it, the Dutchman achieved the separation of these spheres. Instead, he (Grotius) argued that sciences, ethics and natural law, though separated from one another, yield morally relevant knowledge.[67]

Among the professors of natural law at Sárospatak, Rozgonyi developed the argument in the most detailed form that the demands of Protestants for religious freedom can be effectively supported with natural law arguments. In his lectures, he treated Hungarian religious legislation (as written promises of the ruler for the Protestants) as well as the confessional elements of the *jus gentium* on the basis of natural law.[68] Freedom of religion for Protestants, according to Rozgonyi, hinges on the respect for contracts; Carneades's concept of justice, in contrast, would annihilate Protestantism in Hungary. The principal identitarian events of the Protestants in Hungary, the wars of liberation led by Stephan Bocskai, Gabriel Bethlen and Francis II Rákóczi, were evaluated by Rozgonyi, using the terminology of the Grotian *jus gentium* as mixed wars rather than rebellions, as the official historiography of the Habsburg Empire classified them.[69]

Rozgonyi discussed the subject matter of the origin of property in detail. His own opinion included in his extensive commentary is like that of Rousseau.[70] Rozgonyi's commentary on the origin of property is instructive for his conception of natural law as a whole. After Rozgonyi delineated the principal concepts on the basis of Roman law, he touched upon related philosophical

67 Rozgonyi, *Prolegomena*, § 2, unpaginated.

68 'Liberum nostrae religionis exercitium insistit pacificationibus Niccelburgensi, Viennensi, et Lincensi, cum Bethlenio, Botskaio, Rákózio, de aula triumpharunt initis. Hi itaque quaedam articulos praescripserunt, quos aula de Jure gentium debet servari quamvis Jesuitae non deberi servari ex eo quod metu injusto et vi extorti sint, dixerint. – At hinc conclusio esset nullos articulos pacis esse servandos, quod non consistit cum prudentia politica, et Jure Gentium' (Rozgonyi, *Prolegomena*, § 36, unpaginated).

69 '*Mixtum* [*scil.* bellum] quod ab usu parte a privata, ab altera a summa Majestate geritur, – v. quod geritur ab Imperante et Subditis e. gr. Bellum Botskaianum, Bethlenianum et Rákótzianum cum Imperatoribus Austriacis gestum' (Rozgonyi, *Prolegomena*, Caput VII, § Bellum varia ratione dividitur, unpaginated).

70 'Nos dicimus nunquam fuisse communionem primaevam; necunquam futuram; quia non est possiblis. Inter paucos et desides fors posset subsistere ut fuit inter Apostolos. Sed jam inter plures subsistere non potest, si sc: illi sint laboriosi; unus enim in laborando alium minus diligentem superat; consequenter abundantius etiam vult participari' (Rozgonyi, *Prolegomena*, § 36, unpaginated).

problems, such as the justification of the origin of property. He regarded the natural law tradition as the proper philosophical approach to the subject matter. In other words, natural law for Rozgonyi is nothing but a philosophy of rights as the foundational science of positive law.

In his lectures, Rozgonyi sees the scholarship of natural law from Hugo Grotius to Immanuel Kant as one single tradition. In this sense, his lectures link his critique on Kant's transcendental philosophy from 1792 (*Dubia initiis idealismi Kantiani*) with his book on natural law thirty years later (*Aphorismi Juris Naturae, perpetua Juris Romani, Hungarici, Juris Naturae Kantiani ratione habita*, 1822). Rozgonyi's polemical stance against Kant's practical philosophy can be reconstructed on the basis of his lectures.

István Nyíri (1776–1838) studied at Sárospatak, Lučenec, Košice and Vienna. At Sárospatak, he was István Szentgyörgyi's student. A polymath professor, Nyíri taught drawing, education science, arithmetic, statistics and philosophy between 1797 and 1838. Moreover, he played a role in the construction of a new college building.[71] He took over the instruction of philosophy (and natural law as a part of it) after Rozgonyi's demise. According to an 1825–26 report on the faculty members, 'Docet nunc [*scil.* Nyíri] Philosophiam Theoreticam, et practicam, Jus Naturae publicum item Universale, et Gentium.'[72] A lecture text of his survived from the year 1835 under the title *Philosophia practica*. Within his practical philosophy, Nyíri taught classical virtue ethics with biblical references. His natural law, on the other hand, functioned as a social theory.[73] It seems that Nyíri did not aspire to harmonize his ethical and natural law teaching. He was a partisan of a Kantian, perfectionist anthropology, believing in personal enlightenment and advocating social contract theories. At the same time, he rejected the political consequences of these theories, as becomes clear from the historical evaluation of the French Revolution in his encyclopaedic work on the history of science.[74]

The political conservatism was just one aspect of a general setback in pedagogic goals and methods at Sárospatak. The Protestant Scholasticism of Keckermann, Alsted, Bisterfeld and Voetius was replaced, as in other Reformed

---

71 Román, *Sárospataki*, 32.

72 Sárospatai Református Kollégium Nagykönyvára, Levéltár, Theológiai Akadémiai Igazgatói Irattár [Great Library of the Reformed Protestant College in Sárospatak, Archives, Records of the Director of the Theological Academy] (K. K. III. 6).

73 István Nyíri, *Philosophia practica* (Kt. 85).

74 István Nyíri, *A' tudományok öszvességének III-dik kötetje a' tulajdon história tudományai* [The entirety of the sciences. Vol. III: The science of history strictly speaking] (Sárospatak: András Nádaskay, 1831), 266.

Protestant colleges in Hungary and Transylvania, by a modern curriculum with disciplines within the natural and historical sciences.[75] In this lay context, natural law was also incorporated into the curriculum.[76] In the early nineteenth century, however, this process made a U-turn. After the death of the engaged and enlightened curator at Sárospatak, József Vay, in 1821, the old humanist curriculum emerged triumphant from the rivalry with modern pedagogy and shaped the new study programme in 1828. In this programme, the mathematical and natural sciences were pushed into the background in favour of the reinforcement of Latinity.[77] Thus, István Nyíri's courses on natural law in 1828 are part and parcel of this conservative turn in instruction.[78]

6 Debrecen

The Reformed Protestant college in Debrecen was founded in 1550. The number of chairs rose to five in 1798 with the establishment of an independent chair in philosophy.[79] By the turn of the nineteenth century, it had ca. 2,500 students, four hundred in the academic classes, 1350 in the gymnasium and 700 in the elementary school.[80]

The principal figures of the teaching of natural law at Debrecen were Miklós Sinai, József Lengyel and Dániel Ercsey. Their activity covers practically the whole period during which the teaching of natural law can be retrieved in the curriculum between 1760 and ca. 1840.[81] An overview of the activity of the professors and the manuals they used shows that the teaching material was prescribed by the Transtibiscan Reformed Protestant Diocese's consistory,

75 Nagy, *Református*, I 364 and II 184.

76 Mátyás Bajkó, 'A Sárospataki Kollégium a reformkorban [The College of Sárospatak in the Reform Era],' *Acta Paedagogica Debrecina* 9 (1963/1): 7.

77 Bajkó, *A sárospataki*, 21.

78 Bajkó, *A sárospataki*, 22.

79 Ferenc Balogh, *A Debreceni Református Kollégium története adattári rendszerben* [A History of the Reformed Protestant College in Debrecen in a data storage system] (Debrecen: Hoffmann és Kronovitz, 1904), 11 and 16.

80 Balogh, *Debreceni*, 17.

81 According to data in the secondary literature, the teaching of natural law (and, with it, that of jurisprudence) started in Debrecen in 1742, with courses by István Szilágyi Tönkő. (Botond G. Szabó, *A Debreceni Református Kollégium a "pedagógia századában." Neveléstörténeti tanulmány XVIII. századi forrásgyűjteménnyel* [The Reformed Protestant College in Debrecen in the 'century of pedagogy': A study on educational history with a collection of sources from the eighteenth century] (Debrecen: Kinizsi Nyomda, 1996), 86.) There is no surviving source from this early period.

which left no place for individual preferences. According to the situation in 1778, two professors lectured in the major hall, i.e. their lectures were compulsory, and they taught universal history, physics, natural law, ethics and theology in a concise form and at a forced pace.[82]

At Debrecen, the professors' and students' notes are much more concise than those at Sárospatak. The teaching material was to be poured into the mould of a semester's time, while at Sárospatak it was shaped by the professor's preferences. At Debrecen, no printed (or even manuscript) works on natural law were created. Only lecture notes survived, sometimes penned by the professors but, as a rule, in the simplified and incorrect transcription of the students that are not suitable for an in-detail analysis. With an exception or two, no documentation of exams seems to have survived either.

The works of Johann Gottlieb Heineccius and later of Gottfried Achenwall stood at the centre of teaching. According to the *Ordo studiorum* from 1781, natural law should be taught after Heineccius.[83] In agreement with the study plan from 1792, natural law was the task of the professor of philosophy, who had to teach after Achenwall, in the fourth semester of the academic programme, and in the minor hall, which means it was no longer compulsory, only optional.[84] It was a degradation for the discipline of natural law to set it back to the third philosophy class. In 1795, a decree issued by the Diocese ordered the teaching of every discipline in the Hungarian vernacular.[85] In 1798, it can be read among József Lengyel's tasks: 'Philosophia Moralis, Jus Naturae

82 G. Szabó, *Debreceni*, 77.

83 'Studiosis Secundae Classis Christiani Volfii Logica tradatur. Pro Praelectionibus Metaphysicis Ethicis Juris Naturae Politicis, et Physicis modo provisorio ordinatur Winclerus. Hejneccii Logica Ethica, Jus Naturae, et Fundamenta Stili cultioris in Auditoriis deponantur, et Loco Fundamentorum Stili assumatur Quintilianus, Proprio autem arbitrio nullum Authorem assumant Dni Professores.' Tiszántúli Református Egyházkerület Levéltára. Főiskolai tanács iratai [Archives of the Transtibiscan Reformed Protestant Diocese: Papers of the College Council.] In the following: TtREL I. 1. p. 4. doboz. Cited in G. Szabó, *Debreceni*, 363. cf. 77 and 442–448.

84 'A' 4-dikben reggel a' N. Auditoriumban Physica, dél után Jus Naturae, talám Achenwall szerént, a' kis Auditoriumban [In the fourth semester of the academic year, in the Great Auditorium, physics in the morning; in the afternoon natural law, perhaps after Achenwall, in the Minor Auditorium]' (G. Szabó, *Debreceni*, 412.); 'Jus Naturae ex Achenvallo' (G. Szabó, *Debreceni*, 491.); cf. Mátyás Bajkó, 'A debreceni felsőoktatás a felvilágosodás korában [Higher education in Debrecen in the Enlightenment era],' *Közlemények a Kossuth Lajos Tudományegyetem Pedagógiai Intézetéből* 1 (1954): 49. A copy of Achenwall's work in the College library (which cannot be the copy used for teaching as it had a private user from 1810): Gottfried Achenwall, *Prolegomena Iuris Naturalis in usum auditorium* (Göttingen: Bossiegel, 1781) (sign. N 198).

85 Balogh, *Debreceni*, 17.

& Gentium, & breve Politices compendium.'[86] An instruction plan compiled in 1807 designated the place of natural law as twinned with moral philosophy.[87] This system was confirmed and re-confirmed in 1817 and 1818, with the consolidation of the teaching of natural law in the third philosophy class.[88] In 1810, Dániel Ercsey taught 'Jus Naturale, Psychologiam Empiricam Historiam Philosophiae et Metaphysicam, diebus Mercurii et Saturni.'[89] The list of the courses held by Ercsey from October 1819 contains 'Jus Naturale, Publicum, et Gentium universale.'[90] In 1842, natural law remained in the curriculum, for the third philosophy class, taught by József Vécsey.[91]

Like the library at Sárospatak, the one at Debrecen also procured the natural law literature from Grotius up to the turn of the nineteenth century within a relatively short period (the second half of the eighteenth century) as the teaching of natural law was undergoing a consolidation. It holds a number of copies of works by Grotius, Pufendorf, Heineccius and Christian Wolff. Often, they were donated to the college by students, perhaps as a sign of orientation and motivation, or they were bought by the library from them.[92] A number of copies with a reading track were used by more than one student – these

86 TtREL I. 1. p. 4. doboz. Cited in G. Szabó, *Debreceni*, 459. Cf. Bajkó, *Debreceni*, 50–51.

87 'Philosophiae denique Professor, omnem uno conspectu Philosophiae, tam Theoreticae quam Practicae, campum aperiet, praecipuam Anthropologiae, Philosophiae Morum et Juris Naturae rationem habiturus.' *Ratio Institutionis* (Debrecen: Gregorius Csáthy, 1807), 12.

88 'Anno Tertio: Philosophia, et quidem Pars ejus Theoretica (cum pleniori Logica) priori: Practica, cum Jure Naturae, Jure item Publico Universali et Gentium, posteriori Semestri explicabitur.' Az egyházkerület által kiküldött bizottság jelentése az álmosdi tanácskozáson született határozatokról a felső tudományok tanításával kapcsolatban, 1817. aug. 10–11. [Report of the commission sent by the Diocese on the decrees of the Álmosd negotiations concerning the teaching of the higher sciences, 10–11 August 1817]; and Ordo Studiorum, in Consistorio Ven. Superintendentiae Helv. Conf. Trans. Tibiscanae, diebus 19, 20, 21 Julii, a 1818 habito, denuo revisus, et confirmatus (both TtREL I. 1. p. 4. doboz).

89 TtREL I. 1. p. 4. doboz.

90 TtREL I. 1. p. 5. doboz.

91 A Debreczeni Reform. Collegiumban taníttatni szokott Felsőbb Tudományok elrendelésének terve, 1842. április 18–21. [Class schedule of the higher sciences taught at the Reformed Protestant College in Debrecen, 18–21 April 1842]; Collegiumi tanítás rende, órák és teremek szerént, az 1842/3 iskolai év első felére [Class schedule of the College by course and room, for the first semester of the 1842–43 academic year] (both TtREL I. 1. p. 5. doboz).

92 Such as Samuel Pufendorf, *De officio hominis et civis*, 1696 (M 238); J.G. Heineccius, *Praelectiones academicae in Hugonis Grotii De jure belli et pacis libros tres*, 1744 (M 232); and Christian Wolff, *Jus gentium methodo scientifica pertractatum*, 1749 (M 131).

copies were probably used during their studies.[93] There are also copies with annotations showing their functions in teaching.[94] At Debrecen, natural law and its writers were treated as figures of the history of philosophy, among the innovators of practical philosophy (*Novatores philosophiae practicae*), with Hugo Grotius at their head with their principal tenets.[95] The teaching took place in the form of reading out the lecture notes and allowing the students to make notes of their own. There was no manual, let alone access to the original texts. As the notes of István Szoboszlai Papp show, the students could not even see the names of principal natural law writers in written form.[96]

The first professor to teach natural law, Miklós Sinai (1730–1808), studied at Debrecen and later at Vienna, Oxford, Groningen and Franeker. He was professor of history, Greek language, and Latin rhetoric between 1760 and 1790. Fragmentary lecture notes from Heineccius's *Elementa iuris naturae et gentium* survived in Sinai's handwriting.[97] It comments on the first thirty-seven paragraphs of Heineccius's work, with copious references to the Bible and classical authorities. It seems that Sinai's plan was to re-interpret the compulsory manual from the perspective of a historian and classical philologist.

93 For example, J.G. Heineccius, *Elementa juris naturae et gentium*, 1758 (Y 359); J.G. Heineccius, *Elementa philosophiae rationalis et moralis*, 1742 (N 741); J.G. Heineccius, *Elementa philosophiae rationalis et moralis*, 1761 (Y 280); and Christian Wolff, *Grundsätze des Natur- und Völkerrechts*, 1769 (M 262). Furthermore, a number of copies with one identifiable student user survived. For their identification, see István Szabadi, ed., *Intézménytörténeti források a Debreceni Református Kollégium Levéltárában I. A kollégiumi levéltár repertóriuma – Diáknévsor 1588–1792 – Iskolán kívül lakók névsora* [Sources for institutional history in the Archives of the Reformed Protestant College in Debrecen. I. Directory of the College Archives – List of students' names 1588–1792 – List of students' names living outside the school] (Debrecen: Tiszántúli Református Egyházkerület, 2013) and István Szabadi, ed., *Intézménytörténeti források a Debreceni Református Kollégium Levéltárában II. Diáknévsor 1792–1850 – Classificatio Generalis (osztályzati sorjegyzékek) 1820–1850* [Sources for institutional history in the Archives of the Reformed Protestant College in Debrecen. II. List of students' names 1792–1850 – General list of classifications 1820–1850] (Debrecen: Tiszántúli Református Egyházkerület, 2013).

94 For example, Christian Thomasius: *Institutionum jurisprudentiae divinae libri tres*, 1730 (M 94).

95 As, for example, in lecture notes by Pál Sárvári from the year 1783, based on Johann Gottlieb Heineccius's account of the history of philosophy: *Heineccius: Brevis tractatus historiae philosophiae* (Ms. R 84, fol. 351–363). Sárvári matriculated in 1782 and became a substitute professor of history in 1792 (Szabadi, *Intézménytörténeti*, I 645).

96 To the passage 'Juridicum systemák. Lásd a Természeti Jusban [Juridical systems: see natural law],' Szoboszlai Papp added in the margins: 'Grotius, Puffendorf [!], Hobbez [!], Tomasius [!], Glundling [!]' (108r).

97 Ms. R 509/29.4.

On the basis of similarities with this excerpt, as well as the date of the manuscript, 1773, we can suppose that an annotated excerpt from Heineccius's *Praelectiones academicae in Hugonis Grotii De Iure belli et pacis libros III* was also authored by Sinai.[98] These excerpts only offer an account of the first passages of voluminous works. Sinai added his own commentaries to the texts, the aim of which seems to be to harmonize what he was lecturing with existing Hungarian law – a rhetorical adaptation rather than normative-critical remarks in order to challenge Hungarian law from the point of view of natural law. Another interesting addition to the original account is the equation of natural law with the precepts of conscience – a position advocated by Jean Barbeyrac.[99] From this standpoint, Sinai agreed with those who posited the principle of natural law in human sociability:

> It does not seem absurd to me to place the principle of natural law into self-love and fear of others, i.e. into this inborn drive of self-preservation. Society also grows out of this self-love. For example, this rule of natural law or dictate of reason, what you do not want for yourself, do not do to others, is observed in the state of nature, for I suspect that if I harm others, they will give it back to me sometime. Therefore, out of self-love and fear of others, I feel I am within the boundaries set up by myself as a judge, i.e. my conscience, and refrain from harming someone. It seems that natural law, i.e. the law posited by nature itself, originates from here. This law is capable of obliging man to rightful action and deterring them from actions of another kind.[100]

98 '[Observationes] Diversis Auctoribus, maxime vero ex H. Grotii Libris de Jure Belli et Pacis, et Praelectionibus Heineccii in eosdem Libros Grotii collectae; adjectis interdum propriis etiam Sentimentis et considerationibus. Anno 1773. die 21a Decembris conscribi inchoatae,' in *Observationes iuris* (Ms. R 96, fol. 2–18).

99 'Mihi videtur Jus Naturae sic etiam definiri posse. Quod sit omnibus Hominibus recta ratione praeditis connatum Justitiae Studium. Quod quidem Jus Naturae aut ipsa Conscientia esse debet; aut in eodem Jure Conscientia Judex esse potest, seu pro Judice praesumi potest' (2v). For Barbeyrac's theory of natural law, see Timothy J. Hochstrasser, 'Conscience and Reason: The Natural Law Theory of Jean Barbeyrac,' *The Historical Journal* 36 (1993): 289–308.

100 'Non absurdum mihi videtur, Principium Juris Naturae ponere amorem sui ipsius et metum ab alio: sive connatum cuique semet conservandi studium. Ex illo enim suimet amore, societas etiam enata est. Ex. gr. Hanc regulam Legis Naturalis, seu dictamen rationis: Quod sibi fieri non vis, alteri non feceris, observo in statu naturae propterea, quia suspicor, quod si alterum laesero, ille laesus aliquando mihi vicem reddere possit. Ergo ex amore mei ipsius et metu ab alio, me in terminis a Judice meo, sive conscientia positis, contineo, et alium laedere supersedeo. Unde Lex aliqua naturalis, sive Lex ab

As the study plan for the year 1791 shows, after Sinai's dismissal there was no philosophy in the curriculum (and accordingly, no natural law either) for a short period.[101]

József Lengyel (1770–1821), who studied at Debrecen and Göttingen, was professor of philosophy and mathematics between March 1798 and March 1802.[102] His tasks included the teaching of logic, metaphysics and history of philosophy in the first semester of the first year and moral philosophy, the law of nature and nations, and the rudiments of politics in the second semester.[103] He started lecturing natural law from Achenwall but in 1801 opted for Ludwig Julius Friedrich Höpfner's *Naturrecht des einzelnen Menschen, der Gesellschaften und der Völker*.[104] In a letter to the Diocesan consistory from 24 March 1801, Lengyel attempted to justify his choice in these terms:

> Fourthly, the natural law. In this, I have followed Achenwall so far, but the following difficulties have presented themselves: (1) No copies of the author can be bought anymore, not in any bookshop; (2) the work is very broad and subtle, and it surpasses, according to my experience, the capacities of my first-year students. – I thought it better to translate Höpfner's work entitled *Naturrecht der einzelnen Menschen, der Gesellschaften und Völker* into Hungarian and to place it in the hands of my students this way. Indeed, it is the manual at every academy in Germany, though I have to confess that it is brief and consequently very dry.[105]

---

ipsa natura posita originem suam et essentiam sumere videtur, quae hominem ad certas actiones obligare, et a nonnullis depellere potest' (4v–5r).

101 G. Szabó, *Debreceni*, 333–335 (in Latin), 360–362 (in Hungarian).

102 József Lengyel accepted the invitation for the professorship of philosophy and mathematics in his letter from 7 March 1798 (TtREL I. 1. p. 3. doboz).

103 'Philosophiae Professor Tiszteletes Lengyel Jósef Uram az elsö esztendös Deakoknak [...] fogja tanitani az elsö Semesterben mind a két orán a Logicat Metaphysicat, és Historia Philosophicat. A' második Semesterben hasonlóképpen mint a' két óránn a' Philosophia moralist, Jus naturae et gentiumot és rövid Politicat [Venerable József Lengyel, professor of philosophy, will teach logic, metaphysics and history of philosophy in both classes to first-year students in the first semester. In the second semester, similarly in both classes, moral philosophy, the law of nature and nations, and, briefly, politics].' Proiectum a Tanitás Rendiröl, 1798. április 22. [Class schedule, 22 April 1798] (TtREL I. 1. p. 4. doboz), cited in G. Szabó, *Debreceni*, 434.

104 As in the instruction plan for the year 1801: 'Ordo Studiorum in Collegio Ref. Debreczinensi Determinationibus Venerabilis Superintendentiae Trans Tibiscanae de dato 25. Martij, item de dato 21. Aprilis Anni 1801. Conformatus: Lengyel József: "Jus Naturae ad ductum Höpfneri"' (TtREL I. 1. p. 4. doboz).

105 '4° A Jus Naturae. Ebben eddig követtem Achenwallt. de illyen nehézségek adtál elő magokat: 1ör Hogy az Auctornak examplárjait többé kapni nem lehet, semmi féle bibli-

As this source shows, Achenwall's work was supposed to be used as a student manual. Lengyel decided to overcome methodological difficulties with manuals, by providing one in the vernacular. His decision met with a vehement rebuke from the Diocese. As the ad hoc commission wrote in its report on 10 December 1801, they 'found in it [*scil.* in Höpfner's work] many forbidden, dangerous and imprudent things, as well as faults of various kinds.' Therefore, they judged that 'a worse book than this could hardly have been found, and it is completely impossible to use for teaching.'[106] The following March, Lengyel left the college.[107]

Among Lengyel's lecture notes, a number of manuscripts on natural law have survived. As prescribed by the consistory, he drew on various works by Gottfried Achenwall at the beginning. He held a lecture in Hungarian from 1799 to 1800,[108] starting from free actions, then speaking on imputation, and then on natural rights in general, on the state of nature, its liberty and equality. Then came property and contracts, punishments and right of war. Then he returned to unequal societies (husband and wife, household etc.). This was followed by a short exposition of politics: administration and government, and its three forms, with a Solomonic decision concerning their rank: 'Whatever it be, the best is that which is the best governed.'[109]

He had also written *Short aphorisms from moral philosophy*.[110] This practical guide to life informs an ethics of virtues and duties, towards God, ourselves and our neighbours. It places civic duties before duties towards another man, since their omission causes damage to the whole community.[111] Another work

---

opoliumban. 20r Maga a munka igen széles és szövevényes, úgy hogy az én első esztendős Deák hallgatóim capacitássát tapasztalásom szerént felűl múlja. – Jobbnak látom azért, hogy Höpfnernek illyen titulusú munkáját: Natur-Recht, der einzelnen Menschen der Gesellschaften und Völker; magyarra fordítsam, és úgy adjam halgatóim kezekbe. Csak ugyan minden német országi akadémiákban ez a manualis, ambár meg kell felőle vallanom hogy rövid, és annál fogva igen száraz' (TtREL I. 1. p. 4. doboz).

106 'Benne sok tilalmas és veszedelmes dolgokat, maga gondolatlanságokat, és mindenféle hibákat találtunk; [...] úgy ítélünk, hogy ennél roszszabb könyvet keresve sem lehetett volna találni, és ezt a tanításra felvenni tellyességgel lehetetlen' (TtREL I. 1. p. 4. doboz).

107 Lengyel resigned for health reasons in his letter from 28 March 1802 (TtREL I. 1. p. 3. doboz).

108 József Lengyel: *Filozófiai előadások* [*Lectures in philosophy*] (Ms. R 241, 4th lecture). A Latin version of it: *Elementa juris naturae* (Ms. R 241, 7th lecture).

109 'Akármelyik legyen, a melyiket leg jobban igazgatnak, az a legjobb' (76r).

110 *Rövid aphorismusok az erköltsi filozófiából* (Ms. R 241, 6th lecture, fol. 1–30.)

111 'A Polgár kötelességek sokkal erősebbek és szorosabbak mint az egygyes emberek eránt való kötelességeink. Mert azoknak elmúlatásából nem tsak egyes hanem egész közönség vall kárt [Civic duties bind us much more strongly and strictly than our duties towards individuals, since the omission of the former causes harm not only to individuals, but to the whole community]' (30r).

on natural law of his is *Elementa Juris Naturae brevibus Aphorismis Comprehensa*.[112] In Achenwall's sense, the argument is centred on human liberty, postulating the precept of 'neminem laedere,' the first principle of natural law.[113] Like Achenwall, Lengyel divided the exposition of natural law into four parts: absolute, hypothetical and civil law, and the law of nations.[114] Interestingly, Lengyel used the liberty thesis from Achenwall for a justification of *ius resistendi* as a privilege of the Hungarian nobility:

> If someone harmed someone else this way or thought about harming them, it would be permitted to oppose them by force or coerce them in order to defend the rights of our liberty. For this kind of force is only used against those who harm us and violent self-defense is not illegal. For they who oppose force to unjust force do nothing but [...] make impossible what is morally impossible, i.e. forbidden. It is right to coerce those who harm us.[115]

Between Lengyel and Ercsey, a manuscript in Hungarian survived from ca. 1801 that provides an overview of private law on the basis of natural law.[116]

---

112 Ms. R 241, 6th lecture, fol. 31–59. Another similar text: *Elementa juris naturae* (Ms. R 242, fol. 1–33).

113 '§ 9. Summum Juris Naturae Principium. Principium Juris Naturalis est Propositio, vel Sententia, cui quodcunque humanum factum subsumatur, ejus legalitas, aut illegalitas illico patescet. Principium hoc sequens Regula complectentur Neminem laede, atque huius sententiae Veritas ex Natura humana deducenda erit. § 20. Deductio Principii 1. Homines qui vivimus sumus Entia Moralia, nostrae Moralitatis fundamentum est libertas' (33r–v).

114 '§ 29 Partitio Juris Naturalis. Quatuor partibus hoc Jus N. absolvetur. Pars prima vocatur Jus N. Absolutum in quo Jura, quae horum qua homini debentur nullo aliquo facto praecedente enumerabantur. [...] In secunda parte enarrabuntur Jura Hypothetica i.e. Jura et obligationes Naturales, quae factum aliquod praecedens supponunt [...]. Tertia pars complectetur Jura Civitatis i.e. mutua regentis et Subditorum in se invicem Jura. [...] Quarta pars continebit Jura Gentium i.e. jura et obligationes quibus gens erga gentem tenetur' (35r.). The same division can be found in the form of an exam question among fifty-three other questions and responses. *Extractus Iuris naturalis secundum questiones* (Ms. R 762/39, fol. 2r). It was jotted down by András Molnár in 1811 (12r).

115 'Si quis itaque aliquem laeserit, aut certo laedere cogitarit *vim* ei opponere, aut ipsum cogere licet, ad salvanda libertatis nostrae jura. Atque vis talis laedenti illata justa est, ne que violenta sui defensio illegalis. Qui enim vim injustam vi reprimit, nihil aliud agit, quam [...] reddet impossibile, quod moraliter impossibile est id est prohibitum. Laedentem itaque cogere fas est' (34r).

116 'A természet Jussa [The law of nature],' in *Természetjog és államjog* [Natural law and public law] (Ms. R 1563, fol. 81–135). The preceding manuscript is dated from 1801: 'Az Erköltsi

Dániel Ercsey (1781–1836), an alumnus of the college in Debrecen with a doctorate from Göttingen, accepted the invitation of the college in August 1805.[117] He was a professor of philosophy between 1805 and 1836.[118] Ercsey's lectures on philosophy survived in the student notes of the future Reformed Protestant superintendent István Szoboszlai Papp from the academic year 1805–06.[119] Ercsey saw natural law as part of practical philosophy, besides moral philosophy. The latter science teaches how to attain our highest goal through the fulfilment of our duties, while natural law contains the precepts of acting according to the law of prudence.[120]

In Ercsey, politics was treated within an Aristotelian–communitarian framework, as in his lecture notes entitled *Politica* from 1809.[121] Natural law as part of moral philosophy, in contrast, was supposed to deal with the goals of the state from the point of view of the individual. He taught the correlativity of rights and duties, and the difference between moral philosophy and natural law as sciences of the morality vs. legality of human actions, respectively. Then he went on to the absolute rights of man without society and the hypothetical rights within society, then again on *jus publicum universale* and *jus gentium*.

Tudományra vagy az erköltsi philosophiára való bé vezetés [Introduction to the science of morals, i.e. moral philosophy]' (Ms. R 1563, fol. 1r–80r).

117 In his letter from 23 August 1805. (TtREL I. 1. p. 3. doboz). He was among a handful of professors at Debrecen who had a doctoral degree from a Western university. (István Rácz, *Az ország iskolája. A Debreceni Református Kollégium gazdasági erőforrásai* [The school of the country: The economic sources of the Reformed Protestand College in Debrecen] (Debrecen: Debreceni Református Kollégium, 1995), 72.)

118 Balogh, *Debreceni*, 44.

119 *Szoboszlai Papp István diákjegyzetei. 5. Ercsey: A philosophia compendiuma* [István Szoboszlai Papp's student notes. 5. Ercsey: A compendium of philosophy] (Ms. R 258/5, fol. 1–83.)

120 'A Practica Philosophia részei ezek 1° Moralis Philosophia az a tudomány melly az embernek legfőbb tzélját amellyen kötelességeinek bétöltése által érhet el adja elő 2° Jus Naturae természeti juss melly arról tanit mit szabad vagy nem szabad tselekedni az okosság törvénye szerént [The parts of practical philosophy are these: 1. Moral philosophy, a science which teaches the highest goal of the human being that they can achieve by fulfilment of their duties; 2. Jus nature, natural law, which teaches what should or should not be done according to the law of prudence]' (2r).

121 'A Politica az ojan tudomány, melly a Polgári Társaság igazgatását tanitja az a tudomány melly azokat a rendeléseket adja elő mellyek által minden társaságok [elérik] Fő Végeket, melly által a közönséges Boldogság el érődhetik [Politics is a science which teaches the government of civil society; [it] is a science which delivers the precepts through which each society achieves its highest goal through which public happiness can be achieved]' (*Szoboszlai Papp István diákjegyzetei. 3. Politica [István Szoboszlai Papp's student notes. 3. Politics]*. Ms. 258/3., 1r).

In his lecture notes entitled *History of philosophy*,[122] he did not treat natural law, but referred back to his philosophical compendium, classifying the systems of natural jurisprudence not as part of moral philosophy, but as 'juridical systems.'[123]

The lecture notes with the best transcription quality are in Hungarian from 1809.[124] In it, Ercsey sees the role of natural law in setting limitations on the individual's liberty in society and the precept '*neminem laede*' as its first principle.[125] He advocated the right of the individual to defend their rights in the face of violations even with force.[126] Consequently, Ercsey denied the right to equity, i.e. claiming a right to the respect of which others are not correspondingly obliged,[127] as right and obligation are for him different aspects of the same action.

122 'Philosophia historiája,' in *Szoboszlai Papp István diákjegyzetei. 5. Ercsey: A philosophia compendiuma* [István Szoboszlai Papp's student notes. 5. Ercsey: A compendium of philosophy] (Ms. R 258/5, fol. 84–128.)

123 'Juridicum systemák. Lásd a Természeti Jusban [Juridical systems: see natural law]' (108r).

124 *Természeti jus* [*Natural law*] (Ms. R 2779).

125 'A Természeti Jus problémája ez. Mit szabad tselekedni? Hogy nem mindent szabad, mindjárt szemünkbe tűnik, ha meg gondoljuk, hogy más szinte ugy ember, mit mi. Ha hát nékünk szabad minden, másnak is szabad; melyből látszik, hogy bizonyos határának kell lenni annak, mi szabad (vagy mit szabad tselekedni) a határ pedig ez, hogy senkit meg ne sértsünk (neminem laede) tsak azt szabad hát tselekedni, a mivel mást meg nem sértünk [The problem of natural law is this. What am I allowed to do? That not everything is allowed becomes evident, if we consider that others are humans like us. Now, if we are allowed to do everything, others are as well; from this appears that licit things (or what it is allowed to do) must have a certain boundary. The boundary is this: we must not harm anyone (neminem laede). Consequently, we are only allowed to do that through which we do not harm anyone]' (2r).

126 'Ha nékem tsak addig szabad, a meddig mást meg nem sértek, bizonyosan másnak is tsak addig szabad, a meddig éngem meg nem sért, a minn ha túl megy, minden Jusson túl teszi magát; és az által éngem arra szabadít, hogy a Jussomat ellene erővel fel tartsam; szabad hát Jussomat erővel is fel tartani [If I am allowed to do things as long as I do not harm others, others are also allowed to do things as long as they do not harm me. If they go beyond this, they transgress every kind of law, and this entitles me to assert my right against them by force. Hence, it is allowed to assert my right even by force]' (2r–v).

127 'Abbol, hogy Jussomat erővel is fel tarthatom következik: Iször Hogy tsak az a Jus, a minek tekintetbe való tartására másokat is kénszerithetek, és igy hát nints ugy nevezett egyenesség Jussa (Jus aequalitatis) melly ollyan volna, mellyel mások nem tartoznának, és ez annyit tenne, hogy valami Jus, még sem Jus [From the fact that I can maintain my right even by force, it follows first that a right is solely that which I can also force others to respect. Hence, there is no such thing as the right to equality [*scil.* equity] (Jus aequalitatis [*scil.* aequitatis]). It would be a right that does not involve an obligation by others, which would mean that something is a right and a non-right [at the same time]]' (2v).

Another set of lecture notes by Ercsey, *Introductio in Jus Naturae*, was written down in September 1827.[128] It also follows the structure of Achenwall's exposition and names the four figures as main representatives of natural jurisprudence: Grotius, Hobbes, Pufendorf and, finally, Gundling, 'qui perfecit Jus naturale.'[129] The same theorists are treated in Ercsey's *Conspectus historiae philosophiae* from subsequent years, as belonging to juridical systems of practical philosophy of the moderns.[130]

The same tradition can be noticed in another manuscript, *Introduction to the history of philosophy*, which must also belong to Ercsey.[131] This only contains biographies of Hobbes and Pufendorf, together with a critical remark on Grotius who did not demarcate natural law either from revealed law or the customs of nations turning into rights.[132] Gundling was seen to have taken the final step towards the 'perfection' of natural law by separating it from moral philosophy, positing in the former only those rights and duties 'the fulfilment of which the other can also be constrained by force (jura cogentia).' Thus natural law became an independent discipline.[133] He distinguished two sources

128 'Introductio in Jus Naturae' as part of the manuscript *Praelectiones excerptae philosophicae* (Ms. R 309, fol. 2–51). The manuscipt was in the possession of several people in the late 1820s and early 1830s, showing that Ercsey lectured it for a long period. For the year of matriculation of the users Antal Kovács, Menyhért Szabó, Károly Tóth and Lajos Kiss, see Szabadi, *Intézménytörténeti*, II 1044, 1050, and 1060.

129 5r.

130 'Philosophia recentium,' 'Systemata practica,' 'Juridica' (*Conspectus historiae philosophiae*, Ms. R 311, fol. 1v). The user of the manuscript, Lajos Kiss, matriculated in 1829–30. (Szabadi, *Intézménytörténeti*, II 1060). A similar manuscript of Ercsey's lecture from 1811 survived in Sárospatak: Dániel Ercsey, *Extractus Philosophia secundum quaestiones elaborata tradente -- descripsit Josephus Bonyhai anno 1811. die 3. Julii* (Kt. 3317a).

131 'Bévezetés a Philosophia históriájára [Introduction to the history of philosophy],' in *Extractus Philosophiae illius Walserianae Diis iratis conceptae atque natae* (Ms. R 608/15, fol. 86–122).

132 'Grotius a természeti Just, sem a Revelatioban levő Justól, sem a Nemzetek Jussá vált szokásaitól meg nem különbözteti [Grotius does not distinguish natural law either from revealed law or from the customs of nations becoming law]' (114v).

133 'Egy nagy lépés volt még hátra a Természeti Jus tökéletességére, hogy az a Moralis Philosophiától külön választodna. Ezt a lépést tette Gundling a Természeti Jusban tsak az ollyan jussokat s kötelességeket vévén fel, mellyeknek tellyesítésére masokat erővel is lehet kenszeriteni (Jura Cogentia). Ez által szabódott ki a határa a Természeti Jusnak; ez által lett az egy különös és magában állo Tudománnya [One big step was still to be taken for the perfection of natural law: to separate it from moral philosophy. This step was achieved by Gundling, who only assumed the rights and duties into natural law, through the fulfilment of which others can be coerced even by force (Jura Cogentia). Thereby, a boundary was set to natural law; thereby, it became a particular and independent sci-

of the individual's rights: natural law and positive law, citing the French Code and the Hungarian *Corpus Juris*, signalling that he finds natural law relevant for the Hungarian legal community.[134]

Ercsey defined natural law in contradistinction to positive law, claiming that (1) natural law is valid universally for every human being and not only in particular countries; (2) it is valid for cases not covered by positive law; and (3) it allows things forbidden by positive law (e.g. polygamy). For humans (1) living outside a society regards 'jus naturae primarium'; (2) living in a society regards 'jus societatis universale, vel naturale'; (3) living in a state regards 'jus publicum naturale, vel universale'; and (4) the rights of nations towards each other regard 'Jus Gentium naturale, vel universale.'[135] Further, he distinguishes absolute and hypothetical natural rights.

In another set of lecture notes with the title *Conspectus historiae philosophiae*, he gave the most detailed portraits of the protagonists of the natural law tradition: Grotius, Hobbes, Pufendorf and Gundling, according to which Grotius's major merits and shortcomings consist in the following:

> In his much-praised work in which he wished to discuss the rights of nations in war and peace, Grotius first inquired about the rights of physical persons so as to apply them to nations as moral persons later. Therefore, he considers man as a social being that, driven by this affect, associated with others and, in order to let society be established, grants rights to others over them. Now, the rights derived from this social affect are the natural rights of man. The rights of nations towards each other come to these; rights which were observed by every cultivated nation from the beginning. Natural rights correspond to divine rights (i.e. rights taken from the relation with God) in every aspect. And they should also correspond to each other. From this can be seen that (1) Grotius did not present the whole system of natural law, only one part of it, the universal law of nations. What is added to this is added to elucidate it; (2) he was not expected to deduce the rights of man from one single principle,

---

ence]' (115v). The same evaluation of these authors can be found in a student note on a lecture by Ercsey from 1811: *Molnár András hagyatéka. 1. A philosophia historiája* [András Molnár's papers: 1. History of philosophy] (Ms. R 762/1., 28r–29v).

134 '[P]. o. Frantzia Codex, a Corpus Juris [the French Code, the Corpus Juris [Hungarici]]' (2v).

135 3rv. Cf. Gottlieb Hufeland, *Lehrsätze des Naturrechts und der damit verbundenen Wissenschaften zu Vorlesungen*. Zweyte gänzlich umgearbeitete Ausgabe (Jena: Christian Heinrich Cunos Erben, 1795), 18–20.

> for they are retrieved partly from the customs of nations, partly from the reason. Grotius even confounded natural law with divine law and the customary law of nations.[136]

According to Ercsey, Hobbes only developed universal public law, i.e. the relation of ruler and subjects,[137] while Pufendorf discussed Grotius's tenets systematically:

> In order to distinguish natural law from divine law and customary law, Pufendorf [...] limited and systematically developed natural law. [...] Like Grotius, Pufendorf also posited the human predisposition towards sociability; hence, his followers are called Socialists.[138]

And Gundling is seen as the finalizer of the natural law tradition:

> One thing remained for the perfection of natural law, i.e. its separation from ethics. This was achieved, at Christian Thomasius's (died in 1728) initiative, by Gundling who included universal perfect duties in natural law. As a result, natural law became circumscribed by certain limits, the

---

136 'Grotius in opere laudato jura gentium in Bello et Pace expositurus, in jura primum personarum physicarum, naturalia inquirit, eaque postea Gentibus, qua personali moralibus applicat. hinc hominem pro animali Sociali habet, qui hoc affectu impulsu, in societatem se cum aliis confert, et ut Societas consistere possit, jus alteri in se dat. Jam quae jura ex hoc affectu sociali derivatur sunt Jura hominis naturalia. His immituntur jus Gentium erga se invicem, quae quidem inde ab initio omnes cultae gentes observarentur. Jura naturalia in omnibus conveniunt, cum Juribus divisis (s. ex relatione divina depromtis) Et debent quoque inter se convenire. Ex his vedere est – 1° Grotium haut totius Juris naturalis systema: verum autem universi Juris Gentium tradidisse: caeteraque quae adferuntur, ad luciora haec reddenda mediate tantam esse adlata. – 2° Non esse expectandum eundem ex uno eodemque principio, jura hominis deduxisse; cum illae nunc ex relatione mos consvetudine gentium, mox iterum ratione cernatur; atque adeo Grotium jus naturale cum Jure divino, et consvetudine Gentium confundisse' (Dániel Ercsey, *Conspectus historiae philosophiae*, Ms. R 310, fol. 57v–58r). The user of the manuscript, Lajos Kiss, matriculated in the academic year 1829–30 (Szabadi, *Intézménytörténeti*, II 1060).

137 4v.

138 'Pufendorfius erat qui jus Naturale a Jure Divino, ut et consvetudinario distincturus primus [...] circumscripsit limitibus, systematiceque elaboravit. Hic ergo est, qui, primus Jus Naturale in ordinem praecipium systematicum redigit. Uti Grotius: ita et Puffendorfius, pro fonte Juris Naturalis indolem humanam socialem assumit; unde sectatores ejus Socialistas sunt dictae' (Ercsey, *Conspectus*, fol. 59v) The latter characteristics were probably taken from Hufeland, *Lehrsätze*, 28.

> transgression of which was forbidden, but he created a whole and particular discipline.[139]

As compendia of natural law, Ercsey recommended the following titles to his students: Christian Wolff, *Institutiones Juris naturae et gentium*, Halle 1750; Gottfried Achenwall, *Elementa juris naturae*, Göttingen 1755; Gottlieb Hufeland, *Lehrsätze des Naturrechts und der damit verbundenen Wissenschaften zu Vorlesungen*, Jena 1795; Ludwig Heinrich von Jakob, *Philosophische Rechtslehre oder Naturrecht*, Halle 1795, Immanuel Kant, *Metaphysische Anfangsgründe der Rechtslehre*, Königsberg 1797, and perhaps Ludwig Julius Friedrich Höpfner's *Jus naturae singulorum hominum societatum et gentium*, Lingen 1793 – if this book stands for an otherwise unidentifiable, further item.[140] That would be the very same book in Latin translation, for which József Lengyel was dismissed a few years before for proposing it be used for students. Tellingly enough, Ercsey dictated the titles of German books in Hungarian, indicative of the fact that the pupils would have been unable to write them down in the original language. As another set of lecture notes from 1842 shows, the situation did not improve in the first half of the nineteenth century.[141]

Ercsey's principal pedagogical tenet was independent of the manuals he suggested as further reading. He started his exposition of natural law from the question fundamental to the Hungarian nobleman or Reformed Protestant burgher: What do I have a right to? Instead of duties, he laid emphasis on the rights of the individual. As to the practical benefits of natural law, Ercsey held that natural law proved helpful to ascertain the truth in social

139 'Unum adhuc deerat ad perfectionem Juris naturalis, ut scilicet ab Ethica sejungeretur. Hoc effecit Gundlingius, auctore Christiano Thomasio (mort. 1728) qui officia universi perfecta in Jure Naturali complectetur. Hoc facto Jus Naturalis certis limitibus est circumscriptum; hoc facto ei in alieno vagari vetitum erat; sed totum ac praecipium studium constituit' (Ercsey, *Conspectus*, fol. 59v).

140 'A természeti Jusra compendiumul lehet commendálni [As a compendium for natural law, it can be recommended]. Volfii Institutiones Juris Naturae, et Gentium Halae 1750 in 8°; Achenvallii elementa Juris naturae Göttingae 1755 in 8°; Heffners Jus naturae 1790 in 8°; Hufeland Természeti Jusra való propositiok [Propositions concerning natural law]. Jéna 1795 in 8°; Jacobs Philosophia. Jus Tudománnya [Science of philosophical law]. Halae 1795 in 8°; Kánt Természeti Jus Tudományának metaphysicum Elementumai [Metaphysical elements in the science of natural law] Königsberg 1797 in 8°' (6v).

141 Vécsey József: Filozófia. 6. A Lehozott Philosophia Második Része. A Gyakorlati Philosophia (Philosophia Practica). Leirtam T. Vecsey Jósef Úr után, Pólya Pál Debrecenben 1842 April 21. [József Vécsey: Philosophy. 6. Second part of applied philosophy: practical philosophy (Philosophia practica). I, Pál Pólya, wrote it after esteemed Mr József Vécsey, Debrecen, 21 April 1842] (R 1552/6.).

and political matters, as it started from true principles. This principle-based reasoning seemed to him to be instrumental in avoiding discontentment with the state and, consequently, in preventing revolutions.[142] Thus, Ercsey criticised those 'fantast philosophers, in whose mouths liberty and equality sound incessantly,'[143] who strive to retain all innate rights of individuals in the state of nature even after the social contract. As regards the relation of the governed to the governors, Ercsey developed a communitarian political vision that claimed that individuals formed a societal association in order to promote the highest common good of the very society.[144] Similarly, the duty of the sovereign consists in using all means to overcome the hindrances in the way of attaining the goal of the state.[145] These theses are developed without any reference to the precepts of natural law.

Consequently, no social or political emancipation claims were derived from Ercsey's account of natural law. Instead, this functioned as a theory to justify the rights of the nobility, not only in individual terms, but as a collective person as well. Before the rise of modern, liberal nationalism, the law of nations (in Ercsey's formulation) provided arguments in Hungary for safeguarding the constitution, self-determination and Protestant religious freedom against the Habsburg court:

> Each nation is free, so no nation whatsoever has a right to subdue another nation, to constrain it to accept a religion at all, to impose a

---

142 'Hasznos is tudni ex principiis mi igasság? mi nem? kell tudni a Polgárnak mi a Status tzélja? mit kiván az? ennek nem tudása többnyire a male contentusságnak, és revolutionak kútfeje [Indeed, it is useful to know from principles, what is truth and what is not. The citizen must know what the goal of the state is. What does this require? The ignorance of this is the source of malcontent behaviour and revolution]' (6v).

143 '[N]émely Phantasta Philosophusok, kiknek szájokban szüntelen a szabadság és egyenesség [egyenlőség] peng' (8r).

144 'A Társaság tzélja, mely minden társaságnak is közös tzélja, neveztetik Társaság Fő Javának (bonum publicum) és ennek elérésében áll a társaság fő java (salus publica). Az édgyesség által hát arra kötelezték magokat a társaság tagjai, hogy a társaságnak fő Javát, közül [közös?] akaratul munkálkodják [The goal of society, which is a common goal of each society, is called the highest good of the society (bonum publicum); the highest good [!] (salus publica) of the society consists in its achievement. Hence, the members of the society obliged themselves through the contract to work with their united will towards the highest good of the society]' (21r).

145 'A Felsőségnek az a kötelessége, hogy a Status tzélját végre hajtsa, van tehát Jussa élni azokkal az eszközökkel, mellyek által arra a tzélra nézve minden akadájok el háritodnak [The duty of the sovereign consists in the implementation of the goal of the state. Consequently, he has the right to use the means through which all hindrances will be brushed aside as concerns that goal]' (29v).

> constitution on it. [...] A nation has a real right to its territory and to use it as a private person uses their property.[146]

After the 'awakening' of the non-Magyar nations in Hungary, these theses reverberated in the complaints of non-Magyar nations against Hungarian supremacy in territories inhabited by Slovaks and Romanians. Perhaps Ercsey realised this counterproductive character of his development of the law of nations in 1809, which went missing from his lecture notes in subsequent years.

Natural law only lost its significance in the curriculum after Ercsey's demise, though it did not disappear completely. Ercsey's successor, József Vécsey, taught empirical constitutional studies and basic knowledge about representational systems in his courses on politics, embedded in a European or even global perspective, including the colonial systems. Instead of modern (even less Classical) natural lawyers, his exposition was grounded exclusively on German sources, such as the works of Pölitz, Bülau, Craig, Dahlmann, Rotteck and Weitzel. This thematic shift was accompanied by a methodological one. Vécsey lectured on the basis of a more flexible and continually expanded set of card files rather than from a complete set of manuscript notes that would have been in use for years.[147] As prescribed in the curriculum, Vécsey did lecture natural law separately, partly as a 'General introduction to agathology,' enumerating the tradition of natural jurisprudence from Socrates via Gundling, Thomasius, and Grotius to Krug and Pölitz,[148] partly as *Vernunftrecht*.[149]

It seems that the major practical difficulty in the teaching of natural law at Debrecen consisted in the transition from Latin as both source language and classroom language to German as source language and Hungarian as classroom language. Until the late eighteenth century, the Latin syntheses,

---

146 'Minden nemzet szabad, nints hát arra jussa égy nemzetnek is, hogy más nemzetet hatalma alá vessen, hogy azt valamely vallás bevételére kenszerittsen, hogy annak constitutiot diktáljon. [...] Reale Jussa a Nemzetnek ez, hogy Jussa van minden Nemzetnek a maga Territoriumához, és azzal ugy élhet, mint a privatus a maga birtokával' (40v–41r).

147 'Az országlástan (Politica) [Governmental studies (Politics)],' in *Vécsei József filozófiai előadásainak fogalmazványa* [Drafts of József Vécsey's lectures on philosophy] [1843] (Ms. R 1536).

148 'Általános bévezetés az agathológiába [A general introduction to agathology] [1841]'; 'Természeti Törvény Tudomány [The science of natural law],' in Vécsey József: *Filozófia* [*Philosophy*] (Ms. R 1552/5, 1r, on the natural law tradition: 4r).

149 Vécsey József: Filozófia. 6. A Lehozott Philosophia Második Része. A Gyakorlati Philosophia (Philosophia Practica). [József Vécsey: Philosophy. 6. Second part of applied philosophy: Practical philosophy (Philosophia practica)] (R 1552/6.).

manuals and compendia of modern natural law indeed played a role in teaching even if they were too voluminous to use during a very tight, one-semester window for the discipline of natural law as a whole. The fact that students bought natural law books for the college library or donated them shows that there was an interest and an expectation on the part of the students towards the institution with respect to the teaching of natural law. The double shift at the turn of the nineteenth century – making Hungarian the medium of instruction on the one hand and choosing German-language books as teaching resources on the other – proved to be detrimental to the standard of teaching at Debrecen. Teaching in Hungarian eliminated the canonical texts from the class praxis and caused terminological difficulties, as practically each teacher had to develop his own legal vocabulary in the vernacular. German compendia were inaccessible for the student, and therefore the teaching of natural law was reduced to a mere doxographical account the relevance of which to ongoing social processes was quite impossible to show. This problem was indicated earlier by József Lengyel, but his observations and proposals were set aside for theological reasons.

7 Transylvania

This part of our study provides an introduction to the reception of natural law by the Unitarians and the Reformed Protestants in Transylvania, with the main focus on the schools of the city of Cluj, populated by Saxon (German) and Hungarian inhabitants. Timothy J. Hochstrasser's seminal study on the institutionalization of philosophy in continental Europe helped us to formulate our research questions.[150] As one of the last offshoots of the Reformation, the Transylvanian Unitarian Church differed in many respects from similar organisations and even more radically from some of the short-lived sects of the time. While historians of ideas seem mainly interested in brilliant Unitarian freethinkers, for example, György Enyedi, the average parishioner and the majority of the Church's leadership, bound to their homeland, were driven more towards gaining the approval of the secular powers and a minimal level of legal support for their organisation. The Unitarian Church, like other Protestant churches, has always laid great stress upon teaching and education. Thus, during a brief period of direct princely support (1568–71), leaning on the numerical majority that they enjoyed at the time in the city, they managed to appropriate for themselves the building in Cluj that had housed a

150 Hochstrasser, *Institutionalization.*

pre-confessional Protestant school since the 1530s. They were even beginning preparations for the opening of a university. The College has often had to change its location under duress in the course of its history.[151] Its Main Library also suffered considerable losses: for instance, the precious sixteenth-century manuscript collection was completely destroyed.[152]

The Reformed Protestants had a school of their own in the city of Cluj (where they gradually managed to outnumber the Unitarians) since 1610, due to princely support. The heyday of this Calvinist college began in 1656 as the theologian and philosopher János Apáczai Csere (1625–1659) had fallen out of favour with Prince George II Rákóczi for his presbyterian views and was shifted from Alba Iulia to Cluj.[153]

Although no detailed or systematic description of the curricula prevailing at the two colleges in Cluj survived from the period preceding the promulgation of the Ratio Educationis in 1777, some elements may still provide us with clues.[154] In the eighteenth century, Reformed Protestant colleges seemed to be much more impregnated with natural law doctrines than Unitarian schools. There are more traces of natural law works in the former institutions than in the latter ones. Several documents on the history of the Reformed Protestant college confirm the presence of natural law in the second year of the philosophical cursus (seen as part of practical philosophy) in the curriculum of the Reformed schools.[155] Also, a list of the useful *compendia* survived, compendia which the leaders of the Reformed Church had recommended to teachers of natural law. It contained Samuel Pufendorf's *De Officio hominis et civis*, Johann Gottlieb Heineccius's *Elementa juris naturae et gentium*, Christian Wolff's *Institutiones juris naturae et gentium* and, finally, Carl Anton Martini's *De lege*

151 The Unitarian Church of Transylvania attracted suspicion and aversion from the Calvinist princes in the seventeenth century and from the Catholic Habsburgs in the eighteenth century. Their oppression by Calvinist rulers was thus to be followed by an all-out persecution of all forms of Protestantism by the Court in Vienna. See, for example, Earl Morse Wilbur, *History of Unitarianism in Transylvania, England, and America* (Cambridge, Mass.: Harvard University Press, 1977).

152 Kelemen Gál, *A kolozsvári unitárius kollégium története*, vols I–III [A History of the Unitarian College in Cluj I–III] (Kolozsvár: Minerva, 1935), I 323.

153 István Török, *A kolozsvári ev. ref. collegium története*, vols I–III [A History of the Reformed Evangelical College in Cluj I–III] (Kolozsvár: Stief Jenő és társa, 1905), I 37–41.

154 Even if the Protestant Churches were unwilling to accept Ratio Educationis (a decree and not a law formally adopted by the Diet) which was promulgated in 1777, they were eager to illustrate the conformity of the education provided in the colleges to the spirit of the decree.

155 See, for example, Török, *A kolozsvári*, I 181.

naturali positiones.[156] Another example illustrates the importance of natural law in Calvinist education. In 1769, the High Consistorium of the Church took pains to improve the quality of teaching and called upon the most illustrious professors to put forward suggestions. One of the most respected teachers at the Cluj college, Sámuel Pataki (1731–1804), picked out four sciences in his reply, which, given their importance, simply must not be assigned to senior students (*preses*) or unqualified teachers; instead, they should be taught in lectures by specialized professors. These four subjects were *theologia dogmatica, physica, jus naturae* and *historia universalis*.[157]

Another remarkable element is the presence of Samuel Pufendorf's works in the Cluj Academic Library. A number of them contain users' marks and some of them marginal notes in Hungarian or in Latin. Since its foundation in 1949, the Cluj Academic Library has been home to the nationalized corpus of the Reformed College, the Unitarian College, the Catholic Lyceum (founded in the eighteenth century), and finally the Greek Catholic (Uniate) school of Blaj.[158] Pufendorf's various works were present in all four collections. A careful review of the data provided by these file cards shows that Pufendorf was among the most popular authors in Reformed and Unitarian scholarly circles: the former and the latter each had three copies of *De jure naturae et gentium*. The more easily decipherable résumé of this major work, *De Officio hominis et civis* – which served an educational function – can be found in both collections in about a dozen exemplars (even in French translation). The file cards show that the Unitarians held other works authored by Pufendorf as well: the library had one exemplar each of *De Statu Imperii Germanici, Elementa jurisprudentiae universalis* and *Disquisitio de republica irregulari*. As for the Reformed Protestants, they can take pride in their possession of *Jus feciale* and *Eris Scandica*.

The intensity of the attention that the Reformed Protestants and the Unitarians in Cluj devoted to Pufendorf and the natural law tradition is borne out by an unfinished manuscript translation of his monumental introduction to

156 Török, *A kolozsvári*, I 246. The (unknown) author of the list was convinced that the science of natural law (*scientia juris naturalis*) was artfully elaborated by the divine Hugo Grotius. The four philosophers mentioned above did nothing but explain and develop the intuitions of the founding father into compendia that could be used by the young generations.

157 Török, *A kolozsvári*, I 148.

158 The books from various places are intermingled, but, as a rule, the file cards bear a letter, which makes it possible to identify the provenance of the items: R stands for the Reformed Protestant College, U for the Unitarian College, C for the Catholics and CF for Blaj.

the history of the principal states of Europe (*Einleitung zu der Historie der vornehmsten Reiche und Staaten*, 1684) into Hungarian.[159] The fragment ends with the eighth part of the first chapter, which deals with Macedon under the rule of Philip. It is the final part of a compiled manuscript containing three other works, all of them from a Unitarian context. Hence, we are entitled to assume that its (unknown) author belonged to that confession.[160] Furthermore, a law teacher from the Reformed College of Cluj, Mihály Csomós (1722–1796),[161] completed a pirated edition of the 1753 edition of Pufendorf's *De Officio* (the famous one with Jean Barbeyrac's commentaries and Gottfreid Wilhelm Leibniz's criticism) in 1773. This edition, dedicated to Count Sámuel Wass, who apparently sponsored it, shows the educational purpose of this work. In his preface, Csomós presented *De Officio* as a most useful work with which every law student must be familiar.

Besides the works of Pufendorf, those of Hugo Grotius, Christian Thomasius and Johann Gottlieb Heineccius also abound in the catalogue with the provenance mark of the Unitarian College – this fact shows the importance of these authors in the curriculum. A detailed enumeration of the compulsory classes for all students of the *cursus academicus* from the year 1787 shows that lectures on natural law were held in both semesters of the second year of the four-year-long college programme.[162]

After the reform of the *ordo studiorum* in 1792, no lectures specifically dedicated to natural law can be found in the curriculum. The ideas of Grotius, Pufendorf and Heineccius were, however, not neglected: they seem to emerge in lectures on *philosophia moralis*. Elements of philosophical natural law in lectures can at least partly be reconstructed on the basis of student-made manuscript notes. This is a feature shared by university education in Western Europe, which retained its dominantly oral character in the eighteenth century. We have shown a few examples of such notes from the Calvinist milieu.

Study tours at Dutch and German universities were essential for the development of library collections. For example, a former student at the faculty of philosophy and theology at Leiden and later on at Franeker, Unitarian

159 Academic Library of Cluj, MsR 1144–47.

160 As a modest contribution to the list of the early modern translations of the *Einleitung:* [Seidler, Michael,] 'Appendix 2. A List of Early Modern Editions and Translations,' in Samuel Pufendorf, *An Introduction to the History of the Principal Kingdoms and States of Europe*, trans. Jodocus Crull (1695), ed. Michael J. Seidler (Indianapolis, IN: Liberty Fund, 2013), 615–628.

161 Csomós studied at Leiden and Frankfurt an der Oder. He seems to be the author of two important treatises on Hungarian and Transylvanian public law.

162 Gál, *Kolozsvári*, II 68.

Bishop Zsigmond Pálfi Várfalvi (1672–1737), donated more than ninety books to the Unitarian college library. During his professorship from the turn of the seventeenth and eighteenth centuries, Pálfi Várfalvi must have made use of the editions of Pufendorf and Heineccius that he had brought home from abroad.[163]

The dimensions of academic migration are remarkable in terms of the size and wealth of the Unitarian Church. In the seventeenth century alone, the Church sent sixty-nine young people on study tours. As far as we know, fifty-seven of them were selected from among the senior students of the Unitarian College in Cluj. When departing, often two or three at a time, they had to sign a promissory note stating that they would stay true to their religion and return home. Those who accepted this condition returned not rarely after four-, five- and even six-year-long study trips to start work as teachers. The general book of records at the Cluj Unitarian College, *Fasciculus rerum scholasticarum* (1626–1801), contains every outbound and homeward trip together with the welcome speech as well as the subsequent history of the teachers.[164] Surviving sources often reveal the subject matter studied, and in some cases in detail. Disputations and dissertations also survived in the rich college library as well as handwritten accounts of foreign study trips and domestic educational programmes. In this aspect, further research is needed on the courses in natural law which these Unitarian students attended at Western universities.

The most remarkable exponent of natural law in Transylvania is Bishop Mihály Szentábrahámi Lombard (1683–1758), a central figure of eighteenth-century Unitarianism. Szentábrahámi Lombard studied at Leiden and Halle in the 1710s. He became professor at the Unitarian College of Cluj and went on to serve as bishop of the Unitarian Church between 1737 and 1758. On his return in 1716 from Holland and Halle (where he probably assisted Christian Thomasius with his lectures), Szentábrahámi Lombard immediately received permission from his superiors to reform the curriculum by introducing law studies. By law, as we will see, he meant mainly natural law. The agenda of the school leadership behind this decision is unknown.

Szentábrahámi Lombard's most important work, written for students at the Unitarian college, is a Latin manuscript on the history of the Church entitled *Precautiones ad historiam ecclesiam tenendae*. The author considered this work

163 See József Hajós, *Barangolás a kolozsvári könyvtárakban* [Wandering in the libraries of Cluj] (Kolozsvár: Kriterion, 1999), 170 and 174.

164 Edit Dományházi and Miklós Laczkovits, ed., *Fasciculus rerum scholasticarum Collegii Claudiopolitani Unitariorium: 1626–1690* (Szeged: Universitas: 1997).

as an important appendix to the synthesis *Summa Universae Theologiae Christianae*, published as late as 1785, when censorship was more permissive in the Josephine decade. In the *Precautiones*, Szentábrahámi Lombard largely drew upon Jean Leclerc's (Johannes Clericus) *Ars critica* and *Historia ecclesiastica*, as well as Pufendorf's works. His sources include another scholar that can be linked to Halle: Friedrich Gladow and his *De erroribus historicum vulgaribus*. Nonetheless, his main source is Christian Thomasius's *Cautelae circa iurisprudentia ecclesiasticae*, a text that grew out of his author's lectures as professor and dean of the law faculty at the University of Halle.[165] The choice of this work by a Unitarian scholar can seem a little delicate, as Thomasius, who here, as in other works, draws on Lutheran theological voluntarism and warns his readers against Socinianism for its depreciation of the supernatural dimensions of Faith. Szentábrahámi's interest in church history in general and in Thomasius's work in particular originates without doubt in the situation of his community. The oppression by the clergy of a dominant church (the Reformed Protestant church), which never ceases to slander and vilify the weaker confession, was an everyday experience for Unitarians. Thomasius's conception of the church as an institution that exists in profane historical time rather than as a sacred institution existing perennially or at least from its apostolic foundation was consistent with Unitarian convictions and also served their political pursuits well.

Szentábrahámi's *Precautiones* seem to be a historical reflection on the possible solution – or at least the easing – of the problem of confessional conflict and of heresy: a common subject of controversy in Germany and the rest of Europe. The main reason for this interest must have been the contemporary problem of religious dissent. Szentábrahámi's argumentation is clear: he wanted to offer a historical and relativized interpretation of the fundamentally problematic concept of heresy as an excuse for the clergy of a dominant faith as well as for the secular magistrates to persecute those whom they consider as their opponents. On this point, his line of thinking very closely approaches Gottfried Arnold's *Unparteyische Kirchen und Ketzer-Historie*. Szentábrahámi offered a very appealing description of early, uncorrupted Christianity, characterised by the absence of complex and compulsory theological doctrines

165 See Mihály Balázs, 'Szentábrahámi Lombard Mihály és Halle [Mihály Szentábrahámi Lombard and Halle],' *Keresztény Magvető* 126 (2020/3): 239–254. This work 'belongs to a form of early modern German Protestant humanist jurisprudence that was seeking to transform the historical disposition and juridical status of church law. It was envisaged that church law would change from law made by the church in the exercise of its religious authority – pre-eminently the canon law tradition – to law made about the church by the princely state in the exercise of a secular jurisdiction.' Hunter, *Introduction*, 1.

as well as the lack of persecution of theological heterodoxy. It takes a great deal of effort indeed on the part of faithful Christians to return to this happy state of things, but Szentábrahámi does not fail to reiterate Thomasius's warning: before attempting to restore perfection lost, we have to see if the present state of things and the instruments at our disposal make it conceivable. The main objective of Szentábrahámi's work, discussed at the very beginning and repeated throughout the text, was a reconsideration of church history, written hitherto from particular confessional or sectarian perspectives, in the spirit of complete impartiality. This approach has an evident political (or civil) implication: a vindication of religious pluralism, in which the Unitarians were deeply interested.

8 Conclusion

Our survey, based on extended archival and library research, aimed to show the rich variety of the reception of natural law in Protestant schools in Hungary and Transylvania in order to invite further, detailed inquiry. Some outstanding individual achievements, in particular those of Dávid Sárkány and Mihály Szentmihályi Lombard, require further investigation. Still, we hope that some generalizations do not seem out of place even at this early stage of the research.

Teaching natural law at Protestant educational institutions extended from the mid-eighteenth to the mid-nineteenth century in Hungary, while it was confined to the last decades of the eighteenth century in Transylvania. It was based on impulses received during study stays at Western universities, on which even the acquisition of books depended. The tradition from Grotius to Wolff was present at every Protestant school with an academic course on philosophy. At Sárospatak and Debrecen, instruction in natural law continued into the early nineteenth century as *Vernunftrecht* and political science based on German authors.

Natural law was conceived as an applied social science within the philosophical curriculum. Within this broad framework, each institution had its own profile, teaching tradition and pedagogical method. At Debrecen, emphasis was laid on the separation of natural law as another part of practical philosophy from moral philosophy, while at Sárospatak, it interfered with moral philosophy and even moral theology. In lecture notes on natural theology in Debrecen, there is no trace of using natural law writers.[166] In

166 *Theologia naturalis* (Ms. R 281); *Theologia naturalis* (Ms. R 306).

Transylvania and at Sárospatak, the instruction was rather systematic, while at Debrecen it was of a doxographical character.

Within the time frame of about a century, natural law fulfilled changing functions in terms of its social contexts. From the 1760s to the 1780s, Grotius arrived at Sárospatak with an asynchrony of one-and-a-half centuries. The asynchrony was one century in Pufendorf's case and half a century in Wolff's and Heineccius's case. In the last decades of the ancient regime in France, in the context of a society of estates, natural law favoured individual liberty and social equality in so far as it provided arguments for social emancipation based on written law and contracts concerning private law as well as the legal conditions of Protestant denominations. After the French Revolution of 1789, the same efforts to achieve individual and confessional emancipation within the existing political framework lent natural law a conservative character. At Debrecen, as at Sárospatak, the conservative function of natural law came to the foreground after the French Revolution.

Another characteristic phenomenon of academic natural law in Hungary and Transylvania, due to its chronological overlapping with the overall vernacular turn in European science, is the difficulties tied to the medium of instruction. Latin became obsolete and difficult to understand. Hungarian terminology, on the other hand, was in the making, and the professors had to present the material with their own terminological neologisms, the majority of which gained no acceptance.

Acknowledgement

The archives work in Debrecen and Sárospatak was financed by the mobility programme of the Research Centre for the Humanities, Budapest. The writing phase as well as the linguistic proofreading of this study was supported by the Hungarian Scientific Research Fund (NKFIH K-137963, 'History of Hungarian Philosophy in Early Modernity (1570–1710)'), principal investigator: József Simon. The authors thank József Simon for his critical reading of an earlier draft of the paper as well as Thomas Williams for his critical remarks and suggestions going far beyond the proofreader's task.

Note on the Text

The sub-chapters on Sárospatak and Debrecen are based on the following forthcoming publications: Gábor Gángó, 'A természetjog oktatása a

Sárospataki Református Kollégiumban [Teaching of natural law in the Reformed Protestant College in Sárospatak],' in Béla Mester and András Mészáros, ed., *A magyar filozófia történetírása. Módszertan és kutatói gyakorlat* [*Historiography of Hungarian philosophy: Methodology and research praxis*], Bratislava and Budapest: SZMAT – BTK Filozófiai Intézet, 2022; Gábor Gángó, 'A természetjog oktatása a Debreceni Református Kollégiumban [Teaching of natural law in the Reformed Protestant College in Debrecen],' in Gyula Klima and József Nagy, ed., *Magyar keresztény gondokodók az Árpád-kortól napjainkig* [*Christian thinkers in Hungary from the Era of the Árpáds to present days*], Budapest: Magyarságkutató Intézet, 2023.

Bibliography

Primary Sources

Manuscript Sources

The Great Library of the Reformed Protestant College in Sárospatak

Bányai, István, *Jus naturae et gentium secundum Auctorem Clar[issimum] Vitriarium per Clarissimum Dominum U[nive]rsalis H[isto]riae Juris prudentiae Professorem -- In Illustri Schola S. Patakiensi in publico Auditorio professum. In minus Systema contractum Scholae ejusdem S. Patakiensis pt. Contra Scriba H: D. Joh. Tsepel. ad calamum dictavit suis discipulis Auditoribus*. Anno 1765 (Kt.237).

Bányai, István, *Quaestiones Juris Naturalis* (Kt. 404).

Dissertatio ex Jure Naturae et Gentium de Poenis (Kt. 551).

Ercsey, Dániel, *Extractus Philosophia secundum quaestiones elaborata tradente -- descripsit Josephus Bonyhai anno 1811. die 3. Julii* (Kt. 3317a).

Institutionum juris naturae et gentium libri duo (Kt. 580).

Jurisprudentia naturalis (Kt. 558).

Mándy Sámuel pataki diák erkölcs-filozófiai studiuma 1763-ból (Kt. a.162).

Nyíri, István, *Philosophia practica* (Kt. 85).

Rozgonyi, József, *Breves quaestiones a philosophia*, 1817 (Kt. 2821).

Rozgonyi, József, *Brevis conspectus philosophiae*, 1819 (Kt. 677).

Rozgonyi, József, *Introductio ad Philosophiam*, 1808/9 (Kt. a. 360).

Rozgonyi, József, *Prolegomena Philosophiae*, 1808 (Kt. 3401).

Sárkány, Dávid, *Philosophia moralis, opera -- in Kolleg. Ref. S. Patak. Prof. Publ. concinnata*, 1745 (Kt. 195).

Szentesi, János, *Syncope Juridica Seu Compendium Juris Naturae & Gentium*, 1776 (Kt. 397).

Szentesi, János, *Asserta e Jure Naturae, su Gentium, recollecta. Quae In Speciem Annuae Diligentiae ... Sub Praesidio – –, Juris Nat., Hist. & Eloqu. Profess. ... In Auditorio Maiori Disputationi Submissa sunt*, 1781, in *Liber Thesibus* (Kt. 1134, fol. 12r–13v).

Szentesi, János, *Magis momentosa universi Juris Naturae seu Gentium capita*, LVI. *assertis inclusa, quae ... sub praesidio ... – –, In Illustri Collegio Helv. Conf. addict. S. Patakiensi, Juris Naturae, Historiarum, & eloquentiae Professoris P. O. ... defendent ... Daniel Bártzay ..., Franciscus Kazinczy ..., Georgius Horváth de Pálotz, Dionysius Kazinczy ..., Albertus Szemere* (Cassovia: Landerer, 1777) (Kt. 3217, fol. 74).

Szentgyörgyi, István, *De Philosophiae moralis natura et constitutione*, 1771 (Kt. 1885).

Szentgyörgyi, István, *Scholia ad Heineccii Philosophiam Moralem*. A Jove principium est Die 13ª 7bris Anno 1770. Sub Praesidio Celeberrimi ac Clarissimi Viri Stephani Sz. Györgyi (Kt. 428).

Szombathi, János, 'Theses e Jurisprudentiae Naturali depromtae, ac in Specimen Diligentiae semestris, sub Praesidio – – ... publicè disputandae,' 1783, in *Liber Thesibus* (Kt. 1134, fol. 13v–14r).

Szombathi, János, *Theses e Juris Prudentia Naturali juxta primas lineas Sam. Christ. Holmanni pertractata, recollectae, ac in Specimen diligentiae annuae sub Praesidio – – ... publice disputandae*, 1784 in *Liber Thesibus* (Kt. 1134, fol. 14v–15r).

Szombathi, János, *Positiones e Jure Publico Universali depromptae in specimen industriae et Profectus Studiosorum Jurisprudentiae ... Sub Praesidio – – ... publice ventilandae*, 1785, in *Liber Thesibus* (Kt. 1134, fol. 15v–16v).

Szombathi, János, *Positiones e Jure Naturae & Gentium item Publico Universali Seu Civitatis Depromtae ac in Specimen Diligentiae & Profectûs Studiosorum Juris-Prudentiae Praeside – – ... Publice disputendae*, 1786, in *Liber Thesibus* (Kt. 1134, fol. 17v–18v).

Szombathi, János, *Theses e Jure Naturae & Gentium Item Publico Universali depromtae ac in Specimen diligentiae & profectus Studiosorum Jurisprudentiae Praeside – – ... publice disputandae*, 1787, in *Liber Thesibus* (Kt. 1134, fol. 19r–19v).

Szombathi, János, *Positiones e Jure Naturae & Gentium Item Publico Universali depromtae quas Juris prudentiae Cultores diligentiae suae Specimen exhibituri sub Praesidio – – publice ventilabunt*, 1788, in *Liber Thesibus* (Kt. 1134, fol. 20r–20v).

[Szombathi, János,] *Theses Juridicae, Occasione Examinis Publici Ao. 1789. die 8a July disputandae*, in *Liber Thesibus* (Kt. 1134, fol. 21r).

[Szombathi, János,] *Theses Juridicae, pro Examine Publico Anni 1790*, in *Liber Thesibus* (Kt. 1134, fol. 21v).

[Szombathi, János,] *Theses Juridicae, pro Examine Publico Anni 1791*, in *Liber Thesibus* (Kt. 1134, fol. 22r).

[Szombathi, János,] *Theses Juridicae Pro examine Publico Anni 1792*, in *Liber Thesibus* (Kt. 1134, fol. 22v).

The Great Library of the Reformed Protestant College in Debrecen

'A természet Jussa,' in *Természetjog és államjog* (R 1563, fol. 81–135).

Ercsey, Dániel, 'Bévezetés a Philosophia históriájára,' in: *Extractus Philosophiae illius Walserianae Diis iratis conceptae atque natae* (R 608/15, fol. 86–122).

Ercsey, Dániel, *Conspectus historiae philosophiae* (R 311).

Ercsey, Dániel, *Introductio in Jus Naturae* (R 309).

Ercsey, Dániel, *Molnár András hagyatéka. 1. A philosophia historiája* (R 762/1, fol. 28r–29v).

Ercsey, Dániel, *Szoboszlai Papp István diákjegyzetei. 3. Politica* (R 258/3).

Ercsey, Dániel, *Szoboszlai Papp István diákjegyzetei. 5. Ercsey: A philosophia compendiuma* (R 258/5, fol. 1–83).

Ercsey, Dániel, 'Philosophia historiája,' in: *Szoboszlai Papp István diákjegyzetei. 5. Ercsey: A philosophia compendiuma* (R 258/5, fol. 84–128).

Ercsey, Dániel, *Természeti jus* (R 2779).

Lengyel, József, *Elementa juris naturae* (R 241, 7th lecture).

Lengyel, József, *Elementa Juris Naturae brevibus Aphorismis Comprehensa* (R 241, 6th lecture, fol. 31–59).

Lengyel, József, *Filozófiai előadások* (R 241, 4th lecture).

Lengyel, József, *Rövid aphorismusok az erköltsi filozófiából* (R 241, 6th lecture, fol. 1–30).

Sinai, Miklós, *Elementa iuris naturae et gentium* (Ms. R 509/29.4).

[Sinai, Miklós,] '[Observationes] Diversis Auctoribus, maxime vero ex H. Grotii Libris de Jure Belli et Pacis, et Praelectionibus Heineccii in eosdem Libros Grotii collectae; adjectis interdum propriis etiam Sentimentis et considerationibus. Anno 1773. die 21a Decembris conscribi inchoatae,' in *Observationes iuris* (R 96, fol. 2–18).

Vécsey, József, 'Az országlástan (Politica),' in *Vécsei József filozófiai előadásainak fogalmazványa [1843]* (R 1536).

Vécsey, József, 'A Lehozott Philosophia Második Része. A Gyakorlati Philosophia (Philosophia Practica)' [1842], in József Vécsey, *Filozófia* (R 1552/6).

Printed Sources

Achenwall, Gottfried, *Prolegomena Iuris Naturalis in usum auditorium*, Göttingen: Bossiegel, 1781.

Heineccius, Johann Gottlieb, *Elementa philosophiae rationalis et moralis. Praemissa est historia philosophica*. Editio x. emendatior, Frankfurt/Oder: Christian Kleibe, 1752.

Heineccius, Johann Gottlieb, *Praelectiones academicae in Hugonis Grotii De Iure belli et pacis libros III.*, Berlin: Iohann Andreas Rüdiger, 1744.

Höpfner, Ludwig Julius Friedrich, *Naturrecht des einzelnen Menschen, der Gesellschaften und der Völker*. 6. ed., Gießen: Johann Christian Krieger, 1795.

Hufeland, Gottlieb, *Lehrsätze des Naturrechts und der damit verbundenen Wissenschaften zu Vorlesungen.* Zweyte gänzlich umgearbeitete Ausgabe, Jena: Christian Heinrich Cunos Erben, 1795.
Jakob, Ludwig Heinrich von, *Philosophische Rechtslehre oder Naturrecht*, Halle: Renger, 1795.
Nyíri, István, *A' tudományok öszvességének III-dik kötetje a' tulajdon história tudományai*, Sárospatak: András Nádaskay, 1831.
Ratio Institutionis, Debrecen: Gregorius Csáthy, 1807.
Rozgonyi, József, *Aphorismi Juris Naturae, perpetua Juris Romani, Hungarici, Juris Naturae Kantiani ratione habita*, Sárospatak: András Nádaskay, 1822.
Rozgonyi, József, *Dubia initiis idealismi Kantiani*, Pest: Trattner, 1792.

Secondary Sources

Almási, Gábor, ed., *A Divided Hungary in Europe: Exchange, Networks and Representations, 1541–1699. Vol. 1. Study Tours and Intellectual-Religious Relationships*, Newcastle: Cambridge Scholars Publishing, 2014.
Bajkó, Mátyás, 'A debreceni felsőoktatás a felvilágosodás korában,' *Közlemények a Kossuth Lajos Tudományegyetem Pedagógiai Intézetéből* 1 (1954): 29–54.
Bajkó, Mátyás, 'A Sárospataki Kollégium a reformkorban,' *Acta Paedagogica Debrecina* 9 (1963/1): 5–31.
Bajkó, Mátyás, *Kollégiumi iskolakultúránk a Felvilágosodás idején és a reformkorban*, Budapest: Akadémiai, 1976.
Bajkó, Mátyás, *A magyarországi és az erdélyi protestáns kollégiumok 1777 és 1848 között*, s.l.: Kinizsi Mg. Szakszöv. Nyomdája, 1991.
Balázs, Mihály, 'Szentábrahámi Lombard Mihály és Halle,' *Keresztény Magvető* 126 (2020/3): 239–254.
Balázs, Mihály, 'Tolerant country – misunderstood laws: Interpreting sixteenth-century Transylvanian legislation concerning religion,' *Hungarian Historical Review* 2 (2013/1): 85–108.
Balogh, Ferenc, *A Debreceni Református Kollégium története adattári rendszerben, azaz a Kollégium adattára a Református Konvent és Egyetemes Tanügyi Bizottság által előírt pontozatok keretében*, Debrecen: Hoffmann és Kronovitz, 1904.
Barcza, József, ed., *A Debreceni Református Kollégium története*, Budapest: A Magyarországi Református Egyház Zsinati Irodájának Sajtóosztálya, 1988.
Benda, Kálmán, 'A Kollégium története 1703-tól 1849-ig,' in *A Sárospataki Református Kollégium. Tanulmányok alapításának 450. évfordulójára*, 87–115, Budapest: A Református Zsinati Iroda Sajtóosztálya, 1981.
Bene, Sándor, 'Eszmetörténet és irodalomtörténet: a magyar politikai hagyomány kutatása,' BUKSZ 19 (2007/1): 50–64.

Bene, Sándor, 'Szinkretisták és szamaritánusok. Címszavak a kora újkori magyar politikai szótárból,' in *Politikai nyelvek a 17. század első felének Magyarországán*, ed. Gábor Kármán and Márton Zászkaliczky, 327–379, Budapest: reciti, 2019.

Bitskey, István, 'Spiritual Life in the Early Modern Age,' in *A Cultural History of Hungary. From the beginnings to the 18th Century*, ed. László Kósa, 229–284, Budapest: Corvina/Osiris, 1999.

Bolvári-Takács, Gábor, 'Ballagi Géza és a pataki jogakadémia,' in *Zempléni Múzsa* 7 (2007 ősz): 92–94.

Börzsönyi, József, *A Tiszáninneni Református Egyházkerület Nagykönyvtárának (Sárospatak) kéziratkatalógusa: 1850 előtti kéziratok*, Budapest: Országos Széchényi Könyvtár, 1986.

Broadie, Alexander, 'The Reformed Scholasticism of James Dundas,' in *The history of Scottish theology. Vol. 1. Celtic origins to reformed orthodoxy*, ed. David Fergusson and Mark W. Elliott, 253–264, Oxford: Oxford University Press, 2019.

Dienes, Dénes and János Ugrai, *History of the Reformed Church College in Sárospatak* (Sárospatak: Hernád Kiadó, 2013).

Dományházi, Edit and Miklós Laczkovits, ed., *Fasciculus rerum scholasticarum Collegii Claudiopolitani Unitariorium: 1626–1690*, Szeged: Universitas: 1997.

Evans, R.J.W., 'Die Grenzen der Konfessionalisierung, Die Folgen der Gegenreformation für die Habsburgerländer,' in *Konfessionalisierung in Ostmitteleuropa. Wirkungen des religiösen Wandels in 16. und 17. Jahrhundert in Staat, Gesellschaft und Kultur*, ed. Joachim Bahlcke and Arno Strohmeyer, 395–412, Stuttgart: Franz Steiner Verlag, 1999.

Fata, Márta, 'The Kingdom of Hungary and Transylvania,' in *A Companion to the Reformation in Central Europe*, ed. Howard Louthan and Graeme Murdock, 92–119, Leiden: Brill, 2015.

G. Szabó, Botond, *A Debreceni Református Kollégium a "pedagógia századában." Neveléstörténeti tanulmány XVIII. századi forrásgyűjteménnyel*, Debrecen: Kinizsi Nyomda, 1996.

Gál, Kelemen, *A kolozsvári unitárius kollégium története*, vols I–III, Kolozsvár: Minerva, 1935.

Gellera, Giovanni, 'Christian tolerance and tolerance of the Christians: Natural law and coscience in James Dundas's *Idea Philosophiae Moralis* (1679),' *Global Intellectual History* 5 (2020/2): 171–190.

Hajós, József, *Barangolás a kolozsvári könyvtárakban* (Kolozsvár: Kriterion, 1999).

Hochstrasser, Timothy J., 'Conscience and Reason: The Natural Law Theory of Jean Barbeyrac,' *The Historical Journal* 36 (1993): 289–308.

Hochstrasser, Timothy J., 'The Institutionalization of Philosophy in Continental Europe' in *The Cambridge History of 18th Century Philosophy*, ed. Knud Haakonssen, 69–95, Cambridge: Cambridge University Press, 2005.

Hochstrasser, Timothy J., *Natural Law Theories in the Early Enlightenment*, Cambridge: Cambridge University Press, 2000.

Hont, István, 'The Language of Sociability and Commerce: Samuel Pufendorf and the Theoretical Foundations of the "Four-stages" Theory,' in *Jealousy of Trade. International Competition and the Nation-State in Historical Perspective*, 159–184, Cambridge, MA and London: The Belknap Press of Harvard University Press, 2005.

Hotson, Howard, *Johann Heinrich Alsted, 1588–1638: Between Renaissance and Reformation*, Oxford: University Press, 2000.

Hörcsik, Richard, *A Sárospataki Református Kollégium diákjai 1617–1777*, Sárospatak: A Sárospataki Református Kollégium Tudományos Gyűjteményei, 1998.

Hudi, József, 'A Pápai Református Kollégium szervezete és működése a XVI–XIX. században,' in *A Pápai Református Kollégium diákjai 1585–1861*, 7–111, Pápa: Pápai Református Gyűjtemények, 2006.

Hunter, Ian, 'Introduction to Christian Thomasius, Cautelen zur Kirchenrechts-Gelahrheit (2015),' ms., 1–51. https://espace.library.uq.edu.au/view/UQ:374464 (3.9. 2021).

Hunter, Ian, *Rival Enlightenments: Civil and Metaphysical Philosophy in Early Modern Germany*, Cambridge: Cambridge University Press, 2001.

Kelényi, Borbála, 'Krakkótól Wittenbergig. Magyarországi hallgatók a krakkói, bécsi és wittenbergi egyetemeken,' *Gerundium. Egyetemtörténeti közlemények* 8 (2017): 23–50.

Keserű, Bálint, 'Shaping protestant networks in Habsburg Transylvania (1686–1699),' in *A Divided Hungary in Europe: Exchange, Networks and Representations, 1541–1699*. Vol. 1., ed. Gábor Almási, 183–200, Newcastle: Cambridge Scholars Publishing, 2014.

Keul, István, *Early Modern Religious Communities in East-Central Europe. Ethnic Diversity, Denominational Plurality and Corporative Politics in the Principality of Transylvania, 1526–1691*), Leiden: Brill, 2009.

Ködöböcz, József, *Tanítóképzés Sárospatakon: A kollégiumi és középfokú képzés négy évszázada*, Budapest: Tankönyvkiadó, 1986.

Kontler, László, *A History of Hungary*, Budapest: Atlantisz, 2009.

Nagy, Géza, *A református egyház története 1608–1715*, vols I–II, Máriabesnyő and Gödöllő: Attraktor, 2008.

Rácz, István, *Az ország iskolája. A Debreceni Református Kollégium gazdasági erőforrásai* (Debrecen: Debreceni Református Kollégium, 1995).

Román, János, *A Sárospataki Kollégium*, Budapest: Képzőművészeti Alap Kiadóvállalata, 1956.

[Seidler, Michael,] 'Appendix 2. A List of Early Modern Editions and Translations,' in Samuel Pufendorf, *An Introduction to the History of the Principal Kingdoms and States of Europe*, trans. Jodocus Crull (1695), ed. Michael J. Seidler, 615–628, Indianapolis, IN: Liberty Fund, 2013.

Shore, Paul and Peter Tusor, 'Péter Pázmány, archbishop of Esztergom, primat of Hungary,' *Journal of Jesuit Studies* 7 (July 2020): 526–544.

Szabadi, István, ed., *Intézménytörténeti források a Debreceni Református Kollégium Levéltárában I. A kollégiumi levéltár repertóriuma – Diáknévsor 1588–1792 – Iskolán kívül lakók névsora*, Debrecen: Tiszántúli Református Egyházkerület, 2013.

Szabadi, István, 'Intézménytörténeti források a Debreceni Református Kollégium Levéltárában,' in *Intézménytörténeti források a Debreceni Református Kollégium Levéltárában I. A kollégiumi levéltár repertóriuma – Diáknévsor 1588–1792 – Iskolán kívül lakók névsora*, ed. István Szabadi, I 11–31, Debrecen: Tiszántúli Református Egyházkerület, 2013).

Szabadi, István, ed., *Intézménytörténeti források a Debreceni Református Kollégium Levéltárában II. Diáknévsor 1792–1850 – Classificatio Generalis (osztályzati sorjegyzékek) 1820–1850*, Debrecen: Tiszántúli Református Egyházkerület, 2013.

Szentimrei, Mihály, 'A kollégium tudományos gyűjteményei,' in *A Sárospataki Református Kollégium. Tanulmányok alapításának 450. évfordulójára*, 275–299, Budapest: A Református Zsinati Iroda Sajtóosztálya, 1981.

Szűcs, Zoltán Gábor, 'T*ermészet, jog, teológia: egy fejezet a politikai diskurzus történetéből a 18. századi Magyarországon,' Aetas* 26 (2011): 99–115.

Takács, Béla, 'A sárospataki nyomda,' in *A Sárospataki Református Kollégium. Tanulmányok alapításának 450. évfordulójára*, 300–319, Budapest: A Református Zsinati Iroda Sajtóosztálya, 1981.

Török, István, *A kolozsvári ev. ref. collegium története*, vols I–III, Kolozsvár: Stief Jenő és társa, 1905.

Tóth, István György, 'Old and New Faith in Hungary, Turkish Hungary and Transylvania,' in *A Companion to the Reformation World*, ed. R. Po-Chia Hsia, 205–220, London: Blackwell, 2004.

Trencsényi, Balázs, 'The Intellectual History of Patriotism and the Legacy of Composite States in East-Central Europe,' in *Whose Love of Which Country: Composite States, National Histories and Discourses in Early Modern East Central Europe*, ed. Balázs Trencsényi and Márton Zászkaliczky, 735–757, Leiden: Brill, 2010.

Wilbur, Earl Morse, *History of Unitarianism in Transylvania, England, and America*, Cambridge, Mass: Harvard University Press, 1952.

Zászkaliczky, Márton, 'A Bocskai-felkelés politikai nyelvei: Vázlat,' in *Politikai nyelvek a 17. század első felének Magyarországán*, ed. Gábor Kármán and Márton Zászkaliczky, 11–84, Budapest: reciti, 2019.

Zászkaliczky, Márton, 'The Language of Liberty in Early Modern Hungarian Political Debate,' in *Freedom and the Constitution Europe. Vol. 1., Religious Freedom and Civil Liberty*, ed. Quentin Skinner and Martin van Gelderen, 274–295, Cambridge: Cambridge University Press, 2012.

CHAPTER 9

Moral Indifference and Hypothetical Moral Necessity in Miklós Apáti's *Vita triumphans civilis* (1688)

József Simon

1 Introduction

The present study investigates Miklós Apáti's main intellectual achievement, *Vita triumphans civilis*, which was published in Amsterdam in 1688.[1] Hungarian researchers have long studied *Vita triumphans civilis* and deemed it as an important work of Hungarian Cartesianism.[2] Interpretations have rightly emphasised the parallels between the structure of Apáti's work and that of Antoine Le Grand's *Institutio philosophiae*.[3] Analyses of Apáti's Cartesianism concentrated on Descartes's late psychology and doctrine of the passions as developed in *Passions de l'âme* by the French philosopher.[4] Beyond the Cartesian philosophy of passions, Poiret's influence has also been stressed in the research.[5] However, the aim of the approach in this paper differs essentially from previous studies inasmuch as it accentuates the problem of human freedom in relation to obligation against the background of natural law theory. As will be shown, this is the decisive question with which Apáti struggles in *Vita triumphans civilis*. In order to develop his dilemmas concerning freedom and obligation, it is important to shed light on several influences on this

1 Miklós Apáti, *Vita triumphans civilis sive universa vitae humanae peripheria, ad mentem illustris herois et philosophi, D. Renati Des Cartes, ex unico centro deducta* (Amsterdam: Abraham a Someren, 1688).

2 József Turóczi-Trostler, 'Magyar cartesianusok [Hungarian Cartesians],' *Minerva-könyvtár* 12 (1933/1): 20–68, esp. 32–44 (reprint: József Turóczi-Trostler, *Magyar irodalom – világirodalom* (Budapest: Akadémiai, 1961), vol. I., 173–216); Zádor Tordai, 'A magyar kartezianizmus történetének vázlata [An outline of the history of Hungarian Cartesianism],' *Magyar Filozófiai Szemle*, 6 (1961/1): 54–79.

3 Turóczi-Trostler, 'Magyar cartesianusok,' 43–44.

4 The most important contribution is Gyula Laczházi, 'A karteziánus szenvedélyelmélet magyar recepciójáról [On the Hungarian reception of the Cartesian theory of passions],' *Kellék* 32 (2007): 119–125.

5 Turóczi-Trostler, 'Magyar cartesianusok,' 40–42. Laczházi, 'A karteziánus,' 122.

 | DOI:10.1163/9789004545847_010

work. As a first step, the paper outlines the presence of Poiret's *indifference* theory of human freedom in Apáti. As a second step, I will reconstruct Le Grand's Cartesian theory of freedom as an *affirmation of compelling mental content* as well as Apáti's attitude towards this doctrine, which stands in clear contrast to Poiret's conception. As a third step, the study investigates the problem of free will in Apáti's paraphrases of Le Grand's compilations of Pufendorf's *De officio hominis et civis*. The paper aims to show that Apáti was much more conscious of the problems of free will and Pufendorfian natural obligation than Le Grand, who incorporated Pufendorf's texts into his *Institutio* without reflecting on the (in)compatibility of moral necessity with Cartesian theory of freedom. The findings indicate that even Apáti did not succeed in reconciling the two motifs. However, the key historiographical question[6] on the relation of Cartesian philosophy to the early modern theory of natural law appears in its most transparent form in *Vita triumphans civilis*.

Miklós Apáti was born in Debrecen, Hungary, in 1662 to an upper middle class family; his father was a member of the city council.[7] After completing his elementary and secondary education, he attended several universities in the Low Countries. A stay abroad for the purposes of higher education in the Low Countries was a usual chapter in the biographies of Hungarian students of the Calvinist confession in Early Modernity.[8] His enrolment at the University of Leiden dates from 20 August 1685.[9] He defended two theological disputations[10] before leaving Leiden commencing his medical studies in Utrecht around the end of 1687 and remaining there until December 1688. Apáti left the Low Countries on 15 September 1689 with Miklós Misztótfalusi's mandate

6 See, for example, Ian Hunter, *Rival Enlightenments: Civil and Metaphysical Philosophy in Early Modern Germany* (Cambridge: Cambridge University Press, 2001).

7 For biographical details, cf. István Weszprémi, *Succincta medicorum Hungariae et Transilvaniae biographia, Centuria tertia*, decas I. et II. Tom. IV. (Vienna: Trattnern, 1787), 15–27; József Angyal, *Barock in Ungarn* (Budapest, Leipzig and Milano: Danubia, 1947), 88–89; Imre Bán, 'Adatok Apáti Miklós életrajzához [Details on Miklós Apáti's biography],' *Filológiai Közlöny* 4 (1958/3–4): 433–439; Róbert Oláh, 'Egy református lelkész könyves műveltsége: Apáti Madár Miklós olvasmányai I–II. [The erudition of a Calvinist preacher: The lectures of Miklós Apáti Madár],' *Magyar Könyvszemle* 129 (2013/2): 145–164 and 129 (2013/3): 322–335.

8 See Péter Balázs's and Gábor Gángó's chapter in this volume.

9 William N. Du Rieu, *Album studiosorum Academiae Lugduno Batavae MDLXXV–MDCCCLXXV* (Hagae Comitum: Nijhoff, 1875), 676.

10 Miklós Apáti, *Disputatio theologico-critica tripertita naturae tōn ūrīm we-tūmīm Urim et Thummim ad mentem Scripturae Sacrae* [...] *pars I–III* [praes. Christoph Wittich (1625–1687)] (Lugduni Batavorum: Elzevier, 1686); Miklós Apáti: *Disputatio theologica de virga Mosis* [praes. Jacob Gaillard (1620–1688)] (Lugduni Batavorum: Elzevier, 1687).

to deliver thousands of printed Bibles to Transylvania. The adventurous journey lasted almost a year. Apáti and his fellows were arrested and imprisoned in Poland several times before the intervention of Michael II Apafi, Prince of Transylvania secured their release and free movement.[11] From 1690 onwards, Apáti worked as a preacher in towns and villages in the south-eastern part of Upper Hungary (in present-day Slovakia). In contrast to Miklós Bethlen, he never managed to become an appreciated figure of the intellectual scene of early modern Hungary after his return. He died in Debrecen in 1724.

Let us turn to Apáti's Utrecht period in 1688. Some sources show that he visited Amsterdam several times during that year. Besides the fact that the *Epistola nuncupatoria* in his *Vita triumphans civilis*[12] is signed in Amsterdam on 10 February 1688, there are other traces of Apáti's presence in Amsterdam in 1688 that attest to his personal contact with the mystical Cartesian Pierre Poiret (1646–1719). It must have happened during Poiret's so-called 'Amsterdam period'[13] that the French philosopher contributed an entry to Apáti's *album amicorum* and donated three books[14] to his Hungarian friend. Apáti might have composed his *Utilitas pathematum animorum*, a work never published and only known today by its title in this intellectual milieu as well. In a letter written later in Hungary in 1713, Apáti recalls Poiret's appreciative judgement of his psychological work: 'No Cartesian has ever exceeded it' (*Nunquam Cartesianorum ullus hoc praestitit*).[15] Even if Apáti's 'unique friend' (*amicus noster singularis*[16]) might ultimately have overestimated the value of Apáti's lost work, Poiret's evaluation reveals the context of the framework within which Apáti's thoughts on natural law theory are situated: the philosophy of Descartes and Cartesianism in the late seventeenth century.

The interpretation developed in this paper faces a complexity of philological-philosophical problems. I have thus included the following section to explain the facts of philology on which the further analysis will rely.

---

11 Bán, 'Adatok,' 437.

12 Apáti, *Vita, n.p.*

13 Gustav A. Krieg, *Der mystische Kreis. Wesen und Werden der Theologie Pierre Poirets* (Göttingen: Vandenhoeck & Ruprecht, 1979), 20–37.

14 These were volumes of Antoinette Bourignon's works as edited by Poiret in Amsterdam after her death. The volumes contain Apáti's inscription testifying to their being donations from Poiret. Cf. Róbert Oláh, 'Egy református lelkész,' II 334, and Róbert Oláh, 'Pierre Poiret ajándéka, Adalék Apáti Madár Miklós peregrinációjához [Donation from Pierre Poiret: A contribution to Miklós Apáti Madár's study stay],' *Könyv és Könyvtár* 28 (2006): 183–192.

15 Apáti's letter to Mihály Vári, quoted in Weszprémi, *Succincta*, 26–27.

16 Apáti, *Vita*, 28.

2 Philological Approach

At first glance, Apáti's *Vita triumphans civilis* is a compilation of other works. It consists of twenty-nine sections, most of them either following their sources word for word or providing close paraphrases of them, sometimes changing the structure of the original argumentations. Sections 1 and 3–5 are taken from Pierre Poiret's extensive notes to the 'Libertas' chapter in the third edition of his *Cogitationum rationalium de Deo, anima et malo*,[17] which was published in Amsterdam in 1685 (pages 454–472). Sections 6–29 in Apáti's *Vita triumphans* rely mostly on the last book of Antoine Le Grand's summary of Cartesian philosophy, *Institutio philosophiae secundum principia D. Renati Descartes*, which was first published in London in 1672. As in Poiret's case, one can identify the edition used by Apáti: it is the 1683 Nuremberg[18] edition which claims to be a reproduction of the second edition in London 1675. The versions of Poiret's *Cogitationum rationalium* and Le Grand's *Institutio* used by Apáti in both cases underwent considerable additions and changes compared to their first editions.

There are some other philological details that need to be clarified: it is not only Apáti who can be accused of compilation in our story, but the author of his main source, Antoine Le Grand, as well. In his scholarly paper published in 2000, Thomas Mautner highlighted the fact that Le Grand introduced extensive chapters to the last book of his Cartesian handbook while dealing with problems of social philosophy.[19] Mautner proved that chapters 22–37 in Part 10 (*De Vita hominis recte instituenda*) of the second London edition (1675) of Le Grand's *Institutio* are equivalent to several chapters of Samuel Pufendorf's *De officio hominis et civis juxta legem naturalem*[20] (Lund: Junghans, 1673). As many of Apáti's headings match the titles of Le Grand's chapters that summarise

17 Pierre Poiret, *Cogitationum rationalium de Deo, anima et malo libri quatuor* (Amsterdam: Blaeu, 1685). The first edition (1677) had not yet contained Poiret's remarks paraphrased by Apáti. For the differences between the first and second editions of Poiret's *Cogitationum*, cf. Krieg, *Der mystische Kreis*, 87–102.

18 Antoine Le Grand, *Institutio philosophiae secundum principia D. Renati Descartes: Nova Methodo Adornata, & Explicata* (Nürnberg: Zieger, 1683).

19 Thomas Mautner, 'From Virtue to Morality: Antoine Le Grand (1629–1699) and the New Moral Philosophy,' *Jahrbuch für Recht und Ethik / Annual Review of Law and Ethics*, 8 (2000): 209–232.

20 I refer to Pufendorf's works according to the critical edition: Samuel Pufendorf, *De officio hominis et civis juxta legem naturalem*, ed. Gerald Hartung (Berlin: Akademie Verlag, 1997); Samuel Pufendorf, *De jure naturae et gentium*, ed. Frank Böhling (Berlin: Akademie Verlag, 1998).

Pufendorf's theory, I cannot help accounting for the Franciscan friar's attempt to incorporate natural law theory into a Cartesian framework of ethics, or, as Mautner puts it, for this 'discreet acceptance of a new paradigm.'[21] After the explanation of Le Grand's version of Pufendorf's passages, I will focus on the much-disputed problem of the relationship between Pufendorf's natural law theory and Cartesianism in Apáti's work again, in the form of the serious difficulties proposed by the special Cartesianism represented by Poiret's philosophy in his Amsterdam period.

However, before beginning with the interpretation, let me summarise the philological facts of Apáti's *Vita triumphans civilis* in three templates.

Poiret's texts in Apáti's *Vita triumphans civilis*

Apáti, *Vita triumphans civilis* (Amsterdam 1688)	**Poiret, *Cogitationes*, Lib. 3, 19 (Amsterdam 1685)**
1. De Doxa Fati breviter eversa	p. 463
3. De voluntate Dei Creandum Hominem Liberum	pp. 461–463
4. De Libero Hominis Arbitrio, quae etiam consistit in Indifferentia	
4. 1–19	pp. 455–457
4. 22–25	p. 460
4. 28–32	pp. 464–465

Le Grand's texts in Apáti's *Vita triumphans civilis* (without equivalences to Pufendorf)

Apáti, *Vita triumphans civilis* (Amsterdam 1688)	**Le Grand, *Institutio*, pars 10 (Nuremberg 1683)**
5. 6–9	6.
6. De Contiunationone Valoris Liberi Arbitrii, cum Remediis quibusdam, contra impetum Passionum excogitatis	18. De Regimine passionum, earumque Generalioribus remediis

21 Mautner, 'From Virtue,' 224.

7. De Continuationone ejusdem Valoris, Mente Libertate Bene Disposita ex Passionibus Animi exasciante Virtutes	
8. De Prudentia	9. De Prudentia
9. De Fortitudine	11. De Fortitudine
10. De Temperantia	10. De Temperantia
11. De Justitia	12. De Justitia
12. De Summo Hominis Bono, quod naturale dicitur, & Beatitudine s. Mentis gaudio & Satisfactione ex possessione Summi Boni resultante	3. Quid Summum Bonum 6. Quid demum sit in hac Vita, summum hominis Bonum, ejusque finis ultimus.

Le Grand's texts in Apáti's *Vita triumphans civilis* (with equivalences to Pufendorf)

Apáti, *Vita triumphans civilis* (Amsterdam 1688)	**Le Grand, *Institutio* (Nuremberg 1683)**	**Pufendorf, *De officio* (Lund 1673)**
13. De Munere Hominis in Genere, & de ejus actionum Regula	22. De humanarum Actionum Regula	1.1 De actione humana 1.2 De norma actionum humanarum, seu de lege in genere
14. De Obligatione, vel si mavis, Obsequio in Genere	–	
15. De Officio Hominis erga Pium Opificem	23. De hominis erga Deum Munere	1.4 De officio hominis erga Deum, seu de religione naturali
16. De Officiis erga Nosmet-ipsos	24. De hominis Officiis erga seipsum	1.5 De officio hominis erga seipsum
17. De officiis erga Proximum	25. De Legibus erga alios homines servandis	1.6 De officio quorumlibet erga quoslibet [...]
18. De Dominandi Jure variaque ejus Forma	35. De Dominandi Jure, variaque ejus forma	2.8 De formis rerumpublicarum 2.9 De affectionibus imperii civilis 2.10 De modis adquirendi imperium, inprimis monarchium

19. De Imperantium in Civitate Summarum Officiis	36. De Supremorum Dominorum officiis	2.11 De officio summorum imperantium
20. De Civium in Civitate Muneribus erga Majestates Humanas	37. De Civium Muneribus	2.18 De officiis civium
21. De Civium erga totam Civitatem Muneribus, quae & in Conjugio contemplantur	32. De Conjugatorum muneribus	2.2 De officiis conjugalibus
22. De Parentum & Liberorum Muneribus ut Civitati bene sit	33. De genitorum & Liberorum muneribus	2.3 De officiis parentum et liberorum
23. De Dominorum Servorum atque Famulorum Muneribus, ut Civitati inde consulatur	34. De Dominorum ac Servorum muneribus	2.4 De officiis dominorum et servorum
24. De Civium erga Concives Muneribus		
25. De civium in Civitate Loquentium & Jurantium legibus	30. De Loquentium & Jurantium Legibus	1.10 De officio sermocinantium
26. De Legibus, quas Civis in Conventionibus & Pactis tenetur observare	27. De legibus, in Conventionibus, seu pactionibus observandis	1.9 De officio pasciscentium seu pactionibus, in genere
27. De Contractibus, seu Pactis in Specie	28. De Contractibus seu pactis in specie	1.15 De contractibus, qui pretia rerum praesupponunt, et fluentibus inde officiis
28. De Modis, quibus contracta Civium Obligatio ex Pactis, solvitur	29. Quibus modis contracta ex pactis Obligatio tollatur	1.16 Quibus modis solvantur obligationes, quae ex pactis oriuntur
29. De Specialibus Hominum in Civitate Muneribus	37. De Civium Muneribus	2.18 De officiis civium

3 Human Freedom as Moral Indifference (Poiret)

Apáti opens his work with a massive critique of Spinoza's determinism.[22] He raises Poiret's question about the ontological status of *fate*: if the world is determined absolutely by inevitable necessity, what kind of existence is appropriate to fate? It cannot be *res cogitans* because it should exist either by its very nature or by the virtue of another thing as *res cogitans*. In the former case, fate would be God, and, in the latter case, fate would not be fate because it would be dependent on the thing by the virtue of which fate exists. If fate is *res extensa*, there are two options again. If it exists by its own virtue, fate ceases to be a merely extended thing because no *res extensa* is able to exist by its own virtue without being animated, i.e. connected to some *res cogitans*. If fate exists by the virtue of another thing as *res extensa*, then, again, fate cannot be fate because of its dependence.

There is no need to recapitulate the rest of the argumentation against Spinozism: the refutation runs into the idea of freedom existing in the world. Human freedom is created freedom: above all, freedom exists as the property of God. In Section 2, Apáti addresses the Cartesian problem of the relationship between God's freedom and the eternal truths, citing Descartes's famous claims from the *Sixth Set of Replies*: God is indifferent 'with respect to everything which has happened or will ever happen.'[23] Nothing can be thought of in the divine intellect as true or good 'prior to the decision of the divine will to make it so.'[24] Omitting Descartes's examples, Apáti quotes the French philosopher's conclusion: 'Thus the supreme indifference to be found in God is the supreme indication of his omnipotence.'[25] However, in Section three, Apáti does not follow Descartes's explicit distinction between created human freedom and divine freedom, only attributing total indifference to the latter.[26]

---

22 Apáti, *Vita*, 1–3; cf. Poiret, *Cogitationum rationalium*, 463.

23 René Descartes, 'Meditationes de prima philosophia,' in *Oeuvres de Descartes*, vol. VII. ed. Charles Adam and Paul Tannery (Paris: Cerf, 1904) (further: AT), 431–432, René Descartes, *The Philosophical Writings*, transl. John Cottingham, Robert Stoothoff and Dugald Murdoch (Cambridge: Cambridge University Press, 1984) (CSM), vol. II 291.

24 AT VII 432; CSM II 291.

25 Apáti, *Vita*, 5: 'Est ista summa Indifferentia in Deo, summum est ejus omnipotentiae argumentum'; cf. AT VII 432; CSM II 292.

26 For the problem of indifference in Descartes, see Vere Chappell, 'Descartes' Compatibilism,' in *Reason, Will, and Sensation: Studies in Descartes' Metaphysics*, ed. John Cottingham (Oxford: Clarendon Press, 1994), 177–190 and Joseph Keim Campbell, 'Descartes on Spontaneity, Indifference, and Alternatives,' in *New Essays on the Rationalists*, ed. Rocco J. Germaro and Charles Huenemann (New York and Oxford: Oxford University Press, 1999), 179–199.

Instead, the Hungarian author turns to Poiret's notes to the 'Libertas' chapter in the third book of his *Cogitationum rationalium*. An interpretation of human beings' created freedom requires an investigation of God's will particularly from the perspective of creating human freedom. As human freedom is different from God (and from God's freedom, which is identical with God), it falls under God's indifference. God could have created the world without freedom.[27] God was free to create human freedom and did so, but the creation of human freedom implies that God's creature bears an eminent similarity to him. Following Poiret's discussion, the central problem of the nature of human freedom is joined to the question of whether God was free to create something to His similitude as free. Does God's relation to His own freedom allow for reduplicating it in a created thing? On the one hand, God is necessarily free in the sense of His all-embracing indifference; on the other hand, all created essences and values depend indifferently on His unconstrained will. According to Poiret, God's omnipotence is unlimited to such a degree that His indifferent will can even create a being similar to Himself, that is, a creature with free will being exactly indifferent in the way God's free will is. God is able to will that his total indifference be *represented* in a creature distinct from Him.[28] The distinctive mark of indifference in created freedom does not turn the act of its creation into a necessary process: although humans resemble God due to their indifferent freedom, God created them and their freedom '*ex hypothesi, si velit; non ex necessitate*.'[29] Following Poiret's argumentative strategy on this point as well, Apáti conceals the problem of free will and intellectual certainty in Descartes – implying serious difficulties for freedom as indifference – and addresses Spinozistic determinism again: the theory of human freedom is not a mere consequence of prejudice and uncritical ignorance of 'fatal causes' that necessarily determine the world.

Human will is essentially indifferent to its objects. Following Poiret, Apáti describes individual freedom as 'always determining and never determined'[30] and as something to which nothing external is added. Freedom determines the faculties of will, desire and love as well as the attention of the intellect; nevertheless, nothing can determine freedom without freedom's own activity. These features are part of human will essentially, and they are inseparable

27 Apáti, *Vita*, 6–7; cf. Poiret, *Cogitationum rationalium*, 461.

28 Apáti, *Vita*, 6–7.

29 Apáti, *Vita*, 7; cf. Poiret, *Cogitationum rationalium*, 461.

30 Apáti, *Vita*, 11: 'Vera & Individua Libertas, sive Principium mere determinans, in hoc Puncto indivisibili consistit, quod semper determinet, & nunquam determinetur'; cf. Poiret, *Cogitationum rationalium*, 456.

from it. Further, human freedom cannot undergo changes. It remains the same in the various scenes of its presence: in the heavens, in our world, in hell, in good persons (*in probis*), in vicious persons and in persons who convert themselves from evil to good or from good to evil.[31] Apáti establishes a systematic order for Poiret's rather dispersed notes on this theme. Even if the angels' freedom is related to bright and good (*luminosa & bona*) objects, it is determined to accept and contemplate these objects without any constraint.[32] In our world, where good things are mixed with evil things and vice versa, freedom is determined neither through good nor evil objects alone.[33] The presence of evil cannot destroy the freedom to choose good; similarly, human will is not determined to choose good, even if bright and good objects are presented to it, as in the case of angels. In the latter case, Apáti introduces a slight interpolation to the text: 'according to the dreams and the nonsenses of the Arminians.'[34] For Apáti, the indifference theory of human freedom, as he learned it from Poiret, is obviously an appropriate polemical tool against the Arminian concept of human freedom. On the other hand, the confused objects of evil do not turn out to be irresistible for the damned; the wretched always have freedom as regards their election.[35] The fourth scene of the immunity of indifferent freedom is the case of 'good persons': here culminates the challenge against the *indifference* theory of freedom raised by intellectual or theological *irresistibility*. At first glance, God's proposal for 'good persons' is compelling: God offers them preparations through His inner touch in their minds; His offer contains contents from which the mind cannot turn away: the cognition of truth, the love of divine good or true faith in God.[36] Nevertheless, there still remains a moment of human freedom. At a last instance, the human mind affirms cognition of truth and inner divine touch because 'it absolutely pleases the mind not to will to admit' the *contrary* of God's offer.[37] Of course, 'good persons' will never refuse God's offer. The human mind (of 'good persons') freely subscribes to God's eminently irresistible offer, even if the human mind would never opt to reject it.

---

31 Apáti, *Vita*, 12; cf. Poiret, *Cogitationum rationalium*, 457.

32 Apáti, *Vita*, 12; cf. Poiret, *Cogitationum rationalium*, 456.

33 Apáti, *Vita*, 12–13; cf. Poiret, *Cogitationum rationalium*, 457.

34 Apáti, *Vita*, 13: 'tunc etiam objecta bona aut luminosa non efficiet Libertas, ut somniant & nugantur *Arminiani*.'

35 Apáti, *Vita*, 13; cf. Poiret, *Cogitationum rationalium*, 457.

36 Apáti, *Vita*, 13–14; cf. Poiret, *Cogitationum rationalium*, 457.

37 Apáti, *Vita*, 13: 'nihil etiam est magis impossibile, quam ut Mens eo flectatur, quo ipsi absolute placet non velle verti.'

However, the immunity of freedom does not result in its complete separation from perceptions, whether intellectual or sensual. Apáti illustrates the relationship of freedom to these external factors by citing Poiret's similitude.[38] Freedom relates to perceptions as a prince to his counsellors: while being independent of them in his voluntarily decisions, the prince respects their counsel and does not refute a thing without their dissent.

Chapters 11–21 in Section 4 outline a taxonomy of the properties of human freedom under various considerations: human freedom can be considered as positive, spontaneous, negative, directive, privative, admissive, rejective etc., but, in a most eminent way, it is *indifferent*.[39] Under the last aspect, the typology of indifference also follows Poiret's discussion.[40] Having warned his readers of the more sophisticated content of the subsequent passages with Virgil (*Eclogue* IV, 1), *Muses of Sicily, let me sing a little more grandly*, Apáti refers to Descartes's letter to Voetius,[41] in which he claims the freedom to philosophise. The ideal of *libertas philospandi* means, however, that he will continue compiling Poiret's remarks.

Indifference of the will is understood in *theological moral* terms[42] as related to adiaphora, that is, actions that can be performed or omitted without sin being committed. From a *logical* point of view,[43] indifference represents hesitation, incertitude and dubitation related to judgement about dubious objects. In the *physical* sense,[44] indifference is the suitability of some subject to receive various forms as well as the mind's aptitude to contemplate different objects indifferently. These aspects do not pertain to the essence of liberty: Apáti omits the theological moral sense as appropriate to a theological discussion instead of to his philosophical point of view – a remark missing in Poiret's passage. While Poiret deduces logical indifference from ignorance or from intellectual obscurity, Apáti omits this problem from his analysis. The physical aspect considers the subject as passive matter as such; it does not pertain to the discussion of indifference as a feature of an essentially active free will – for either Apáti and Poiret.

Indifference of freedom is essentially *metaphysical* indifference.[45] In this respect, 'indifference is not a necessarily established principle for the determ-

38 Apáti, *Vita*, 16; cf. Poiret, *Cogitationum rationalium*, 457.
39 Apáti, *Vita*, 16–18; cf. Poiret, *Cogitationum rationalium*, 455–456.
40 Apáti, *Vita*, 19–28; cf. Poiret, *Cogitationum rationalium*, 460–465.
41 AT VIII-2, 3.
42 Apáti, *Vita*, 19–20; cf. Poiret, *Cogitationum rationalium*, 460.
43 Apáti, *Vita*, 20; cf. Poiret, *Cogitationum rationalium*, 460.
44 Apáti, *Vita*, 20; cf. Poiret, *Cogitationum rationalium*, 460.
45 Apáti, *Vita*, 20–22; cf. Poiret, *Cogitationum rationalium*, 460.

ination of one's actions according to a certain and determined consideration or a particular mode.'[46] There are infinite modes, according to which human freedom can perform or suspend its actions without limitations.[47] After introducing criticism of Spinoza again, Poiret continues with a discussion of God's free will related to the creation of created indifferent freedom.[48] These arguments have already been incorporated into Section 3 of the *Vita triumphans civilis* by Apáti, as I have presented above. Apáti picks up the line of Poiret's thinking in describing the four elements of metaphysical indifference: endurance, illimitation, independence and indifference.[49] The arguments rely on the idea of the similitude of created metaphysical indifference to God's freedom. Apáti summarises his paraphrases from Poiret concerning human indifference: indifference determines itself for one or another object only because it wills that option so that its nature consists merely in its will; in turn, this essential will follows the internal principle of indifference without any necessity or external motif. This is the indifference that resides in metaphysical indifference.

Here, Apáti completes his compilation based on Poiret's *Cogitationum rationalium*. The last chapter of Section 4 explains 'the value of free will' from different points of view. The indifference theory of freedom enables us to understand ourselves as certain images of and similitude to God. However, there are new elements provided by the previous discussions on free will that anticipate the following sections.[50] The theory of free will has its value as

---

46 Apáti: *Vita*, 20: 'Indifferentia est principium non necessario alligatum ad determinandum actus suos certo determinatoque consilio aut modo particulari'; cf. Poiret, *Cogitationum rationalium*, 460.

47 Here, Apáti readily quotes Descartes's degrading statement on the indifference conception of human freedom from the Fourth Meditation, 'indifference [...] is the lowest grade of freedom; it is evidence not of any perfection of freedom, but rather of a defect of knowledge' (Apáti: *Vita*, 20; cf. AT VII, 58; CSM 70). Apáti obviates this challenge by referring Descartes's claim to the *logical* realm of indifference. Indifference as the '*lowest grade of freedom*' is logical indifference explaining human freedom as ignorance or a defect of knowledge. *Metaphysical* indifference, in contrast, has no such limits: human freedom is boundless even if the mind grasps at clear and distinct notions without any doubt. For the same thought, see Poiret: *Cogitationum rationalium*, 563.

48 Poiret, *Cogitationum rationalium*, 460–461.

49 Apáti, *Vita*, 22–28; cf. Poiret, *Cogitationum rationalium*, 464–466.

50 Let us quote Apáti's passage, where he extends the competency of indifferent freedom of will to the supreme good of ethics first and then to the obligations of political theory. Apáti, *Vita*, 30: 'Utilis & Jucunda est Libertatis Arbitrii scientia, immo necessaria; tantus enim est Valor L[iberi] A[rbitrii] ut ejus ratione rectoque usu Nos-ipsos Imaginem quandam & Similitudinem Dei redolere intelligere: Passionibus generose succensere: Virtutes

regards our distant attitude toward passions, acquiring virtues and living in accordance with them. Free will makes us familiar with the supreme good possible for humans as regards our natural condition, and it allows us to realise the satisfaction and delight of the mind's possessing knowledge of this supreme good. These claims may awaken a certain surprise in the reader because there is at least a little bit more accent on the *intellectual* grasping at the supreme good than could be expected against the background of the *indifference* theory of free will. However, the continuing series of themes that fall within the competency of free will provides an even wider perspective. Free will makes us realise the duties of humans in general and the duties of citizens in particular: it lets us recognise which action is to be taken as good (*honestum*) and which action is to be avoided as bad (*turpe*) *according to the prescription of nature.* These claims may seem suspicious for us as well: Poiret's special version of Cartesian philosophy thoroughly lacks the social dimension adumbrated in Apáti's claims. In his closing remarks in Section 4, Apáti introduces the two main topics in the rest of his work: the passions and social life. At the same time, he explicitly establishes a strong link between these new themes and the indifference theory of human freedom. Let us see whether they can stand together.

4 Paraphrases and Omissions from Le Grand

Antoine Le Grand's *Institutio philosophiae secundum principia D. Renati Descartes* has a strictly organised structure. After the introductory parts about logic and natural theology, it proceeds towards a description of inorganic and organic being and towards an explanation of the human body and mind accounting for passions, virtues and, finally, social life. Apáti's paraphrases target Le Grand's exposition of the latter themes. Le Grand provides the reader with an account of the passions following Descartes's *Les Passions de l'âme*[51] and develops the Cartesian ethical programme of the rule of the mind over

acquirere & exercere: Summum nobis Bonum, *naturale quod dicitur*, comparare, & ex eo Beatitudinem seu Mentis gaudium & satisfactionem ex possessione Summi Boni resultantem legitime creare: Munera Hominis in genere, mox boni Civis in specie, & quid uterque tanquam *Honestum* apprehendere, & quid tanquam *Turpe* omittere secundum naturae praescripta debeant, insinuare' (italics in the original).

51 AT IX, 291–497. On Le Grand's Cartesian psychology, see Gary Hatfield, 'The Cartesian Psychology of Antoine Le Grand,' in *Cartesian Empiricisms*, ed. M. Dobre and T. Nyden (Dordrecht: Springer, 2013), 251–274.

the passions being the supreme good for humans and assuring the exertion of cardinal virtues. As concerns the ethical perspective of the passions, Le Grand remained true to his sympathy towards Stoic ethics proper in his *L'homme sans passions*[52] (1662) before his Cartesian turn. Reading the headings of the closing chapters 22–37 in the Part 10 of the *Institutio*, one may have the impression that Le Grand simply ties his passages, which he took from Pufendorf's *De Officio*, to the theory of passions and virtues.[53]

With rich additions of historical examples, Apáti's Sections 5–7 follow Le Grand's treatment of the passions (*Institutio* Part 9)[54] but sometimes refer directly to Henri Desmaret's (1633–1725) Latin version[55] of Descartes's *Les Passions de l'âme*: one reads an exact quotation of the classification of mental cogitations (PA 1, 17), of the general definition of the passions (PA 1, 27) and of the explication of its elements (PA 1, 28). Apáti agrees with Descartes that the primary cause of the passions is the agitation of spirits on the little gland (PA 2, 51). Sections 8–11, which explain the cardinal virtues, are equivalent to Le Grand's *Institutio* 10, chapters 9–12[56] and there are essential similarities between Apáti's (Section 12) and Le Grand's (*Institutio* 10, 3–6) account of the supreme good naturally possible for humans.[57] However, there are two important chapters (*Institutio* 10, 19–20)[58] that function as a bridge between the Stoic-Cartesian theory of ethics asserting the mind's control over the passions and the theory of civic obligations that close the whole book. Apáti passes over these passages of Le Grand's in silence, and he had urgent theoretical reasons for this.

Le Grand dedicates *Institutio* 10, chapters 19–20 to the problem of human freedom. His point of departure is that passions and virtues can only contribute to the happiness of human life incompletely. Happiness of human life, i.e. the supreme human good consisting in a satisfied state of mind, can only be realised if there is a free will to rule over the passions and exercise virtues. Everyday experience teaches us the existence of free will: performing speech acts or remaining silent, walking or being at rest, lending a hand to

52 Antoine Le Grand, *Le sage des Stoïques, ou l'homme sans passions* (LaHaye: Broune & L'Escluse, 1662).

53 Compare the templates above.

54 Apáti, *Vita* 31–57; cf. Le Grand, *Institutio*, 682–735.

55 *Passiones Animae per Renatum Des Cartes. Gallice ab ipso conscripta, nunc autem in exterorum gratiam Latina civitate donatae Ab H.D.M* [Henri Desmaret], in Renati Des-Cartes *Opera Philosophica* (Amsterdam: Elzevirius, 1651).

56 Apáti, *Vita*, 57–95; cf. Le Grand, *Institutio*, 763–780.

57 Apáti, *Vita*, 96–115; cf. Le Grand, *Institutio*, 743–753.

58 Le Grand, *Institutio*, 799–805.

the wretched or just passing them by – these all depend on our free decision. Similarly, establishing laws, rewarding good acts and punishing bad ones presuppose elementary freedom as a human feature. Therefore, as Le Grand concludes, God allowed human beings to have the power of free will and to be influenced by His will instead of necessity in their actions.

> However, even if each person experiences this ability of choice and perceives that his will is not dependent on any created agent in his determinations, it should not yet be supposed that it [*scil.* his will] is wholly independent. For *if we attend merely to us*, as Descartes claims,[59] free will *cannot* be thought of as *not* being independent. But if we turn our mind to the infinite power of God, we are *not* able *not* to believe that all things depend on him. Therefore, even our free will is not released from his authority. It would imply a contradiction to claim that God created humans with nature such that the actions of their will did not depend on God's will. This would be the same as someone claiming that his power is finite and infinite simultaneously: finite, because there would be something not dependent on him, yet infinite because he could have created this thing to be independent.[60]

This is, of course, a short outline of Descartes's attempt at a theodicial justification[61] of human free will and its compatibility with unlimited divine freedom.[62] Le Grand walks around opposite sides of the problem. Even if my

59 This is a verbatim quotation from Descartes's letter to Princess Elizabeth, AT IV 330–334. For the Latin version cf. René Descartes, *Epistolae* (Amsterdam: Bleau, 1682), vol. I 24–26, esp. 25.

60 Le Grand, *Institutio*, 801 (10, 19): 'Sed quamvis quisque eam *eligendi* potentiam experiatur, sentiatque Voluntatem suam a nullo Agente creato, in suis determinationibus pendere; non est tamen existimandum, omnimode esse Independens, quia scilicet liberum Arbitrium, ut ait *Cartesius*, si ad nos tantum attendamus, non possit non concipi *Independens*; si vero ad Infinitam Dei *Potentiam*, Animum advertimus, non possumus non credere, omnia ab illo pendere, & proinde liberum nostrum Arbitrium, ejus imperio solutum non esse. Implicat enim contradictionem, Deum creasse Homines ejusmodi naturae, ut Voluntatum eorum Actiones ab *ejus* Voluntate non pendeat. Quia idem est, ac si quis diceret, Potentiam ejus finitam esse, simul & infinitam: *finitam*, cum aliquid sit, quod ab illo non pendet; *Infinitam* vero, quum potuerit rem hanc independentem creare' (italics in the original, but not in Descartes).

61 For a detailed analysis, see Clyde P. Ragland, *The Will to Reason. Theodicy and Freedom in Descartes* (Oxford: Oxford University Press, 2016).

62 The argument of the present paper moves along the borderline between Poiret's unconditional indifference and Descartes's intellectually motivated freedom. In this constellation, Poiret's metaphysical indifference is situated outside of Descartes's conception

cognition of divine existence bears the greatest certainty, it cannot refute the certitude as concerns my free will. On the other hand, the cognition of our free will should not raise any doubt about the existence of God. The independence we experience in human freedom is not incompatible with the dependence of that other kind according to which all things are subjected to God. Le Grand perceives that this problem should be observed in more detail and devotes chapter 20 to the relationship between human freedom and divine omnipotence.

The difficulty of the inconsistency between human freedom and divine omnipotence can be avoided if one claims that, although God is the total and universal cause of all things, He still does not relate in the same way to everything. As regards the production of things which are not subject to any created will, God regarded only His own will and decreed them absolutely in a certain way. On the other hand, as concerns those things to which human will has a certain right, God had not regarded His will as exclusive. Instead, He had included the consent of our will into His decree as well.

Le Grand illustrates the conflict between divine and human freedom by quoting Descartes's famous letter to Princess Elizabeth, in which he presents the king and the duellers.[63] As to his *absolute* will, God wills everything to happen as it appears; however, as to His *relative* will, He wills that humans obey His laws in contingent states of affairs. Le Grand enumerates three motifs that, according to authors on moral matters, can impede our use of free will – these are more important for our purposes than Descartes's illustration of the problem in his letter to Princess Elizabeth. The performance of acts in respect of freedom of will is hindered either by fear, ignorance or coercion. In the case of fear, there are two aspects of free will that can be affected psychologically: the spontaneity and freedom of our acts. While one can imagine a situation for the first kind of hindrance (there are acts performed only and exactly due to fear of the contrary of the favourable outcome of a situation), fear cannot impede freedom of will in the second sense

> because the nature of free will does not consist in *indifference*, as *we stated above*. We do nothing voluntarily and freely, but what we are

---

of indifference as the 'lowest grade of freedom.' We are therefore not delving into the subtle details of the problem of Cartesian freedom. However, for this problem, cf. Marcelo de Araujo, *Scepticism, Freedom and Autonomy* (Berlin and New York: De Gruyter, 2003), passim; and Dániel Schmal, *A kezdet nélküli kezdet. Descartes és a kartézianizmus problémája* [*Beginning without Beginning: Descartes and the Problem of Cartesianism*] (Budapest: Gondolat, 2012), 243–272.

63 AT IV 351–357.

> determined to do by urgent causes. This happens when we are pressed by *fear*. Even if the object displeases us and we would rather choose the contrary if it were possible [...], we accomplish it and prefer the lesser evil instead of the greater.[64]

Le Grand's obvious rejection of the indifference theory of human freedom must have been a decisive reason for Apáti's omission of his chapters on liberty. For Le Grand, there must exist some urgent causes that determine the very act of free will: either freedom of will is determined by these urgent causes or it ceases to be free will. Choosing the lesser evil can provide the persons in the situation with the appropriate urgent cause to avoid the menacing greater evil, even if they are motivated by fear. The psychological state of fear is stronger than the immunity that the allegedly indifferent will might have to it.

Le Grand refers to his previous passage, i.e. the second part of his work.[65] Here, while developing his natural theology, he attributes indifference to divine will and denies that any object could have existed in and for the divine mind prior to its creation proceeding from God's absolute and indifferent free will. It is only the essence of humans, with regard to which indifference implies an imperfection, which is the lowest level of freedom. As the free author of the world, God is devoid of any coercion. God's will has been indifferent from eternity in relation to whatever has been created and whatever has occurred in the world.

5 Apáti, Le Grand and Pufendorf

Apáti's attempt to engage certain elements of Poiret's and Le Grand's moral philosophy into a united argumentation faced incredible challenges. Obviously, he wanted to emphasise the indifference of human freedom against all intellectual motifs that determine will, and he likewise insisted on the theoretical programme of an intellectual ruling over the passions on the basis of irresistible cognition appropriate to the mind. For the purpose of maintaining

64 Le Grand, *Institutio*, 803: 'quia liberi Arbitrii natura, non in Indifferentia consistit, ut *dictum est antea*, quum nihil aeque voluntarie, atque adeo libere faciamus, quam ea, ad quae urgenti Causa determinamur. Quod accidit, quando *metu* premimur; quoniam etsi tunc objectum displiceat, mallemusque, si fieri posset, contrarium eligere [...], illud amplectimur, & minus Malum majori anteponimus' (italics in the original).

65 Le Grand, *Institutio*, Part 2, ch. 12, 154–155.

both of these positions – freedom as *indifference* and freedom as *affirmation of compelling mental cognition* – Apáti did not hesitate to invent his own concept to describe a state of mind that bears the feature of freedom. *Mens humana libero arbitrio bene disposita*:[66] for Apáti, there must exist a state of mind disposed appropriately by the freedom of will. On the one hand, the mind in this well-disposed state should behave indifferently toward its objects. On the other hand, it should have evident cognitions that assure the voluntary affirmation of intellectual cognition as well as the critique of passions. These two concepts imply a certain theoretical tension in sections of *Vita triumphans civilis* that deal with human freedom, passions and virtues – concealed cautiously by the author. However, the concern about the divergent conceptions of freedom must become apparent once we arrive at the Pufendorfian idea of obligation,[67] which is treated in detail by Le Grand as well as by Apáti.

First of all, it is important to shed light on Le Grand's revision of Pufendorf's doctrine. The first parallel headings read 'De humanarum Actionum regula' by Le Grand (*Institutio* 10, 22)[68] and 'De actione humana' and 'De norma actionum humanarum seu de lege in genere' by Pufendorf (*De officio* I, 1–2).[69] Following Pufendorf, Le Grand classifies the rules of human actions as pertaining either to the intellectual act of conscience or to the voluntary feature of obligation. As regards obligation, Le Grand introduces the definition of Roman law: obligation is a legal bond, according to which we are necessarily compelled to perform some act. There is a certain coercive power residing in our mind by the virtue of obligation that does not allow one to act against one's conscience. It restricts our free will in a certain way and compels us with necessity, even if we cognise ourselves as free and even if we are able to desire that which is contrary to the intended thing/act. Le Grand presents much of the essential elements from Pufendorf's first chapters. Only humans are able to stand under obligation. This feature of humans requires a Superior whose will imposes an obligation on His subjects. Beyond authority, the Superior must provide good reasons (*justae causae*) in explaining the voluntarist imposition of obligation. The rule of human actions is law or decree, through which the

66 Cf. Apáti, *Vita*, 48, 51–53.

67 For general presentations, cf. Craig L. Carr and Michael J. Seidler, 'Pufendorf, Sociality and the Modern State,' in *Grotius, Pufendorf and Modern Natural Law*, ed. Knud Haakonssen (Dartmouth: Ashgate, 1999), 133–157, and Knud Haakonssen, *Natural law and moral philosophy. From Grotius to the Scottish Enlightenment* (Cambridge: Cambridge University Press, 1996), 37–43.

68 Le Grand, *Institutio*, 807–811.

69 Pufendorf, *De officio*, 13–21.

Superior, aided by His public authority, obliges the subjects to perform acts in accordance with His law.

Two things must be noted in connection with Le Grand's paraphrase of Pufendorf's short discussion of obligation at the very beginning of *De officio*. First, the description of the initial state of liberty lacking the motif of obligation is missing in Le Grand's work. Pufendorf describes his abstract individuals in the theoretical stance prior to obligation as disposing of a kind of freedom, which is indifferent toward its objects.[70] Due to absolutely different theoretical aims and backgrounds, the freedom of Pufendorfian natural persons in their abstract individuality is entirely *indifferent* just like the freedom of Poiret's Cartesian individuals with their mystical leanings. However, one may explain why Le Grand abandoned the idea of the initial freedom in abstract natural persons without the motif of obligation. The Franciscan Cartesian must have realised that the original Pufendorfian indifference is hardly compatible with his own concept of freedom as the affirmation of *compelling* mental content. Undisturbed by this obvious contradiction, Le Grand holds that Pufendorfian natural obligation makes up the essence of natural laws that are engraved in each human heart and common to all nations. There is not the least reference to or reflection on the previously articulated theory of human freedom as an affirmation of irresistible mental content in Le Grand's whole summary of Pufendorf's moral necessity. This unreflective recitation of the theory of the German philosopher breaks the unity of Le Grand's *Institutio* into fragments. If there is any kind of order of values, offering themselves to be grasped at irresistibly for the intellect, then the obligation imposed on human will cannot totally determine it. According to Pufendorf, the possibility of any – say, Stoic or even Cartesian – moral philosophy independent of natural law theory destroys the holistic totality of obligation. Moral necessity must originate in the formal idea of obligation without any reference to any positive ethical content. The one and only ethical content that provides true moral necessity is the purely formal idea of being obligated. According to Pufendorf's theory, this was the very motif that Grotius failed to notice: if we take away God, nothing is left at all for natural morality. Moral necessity is not a property inherent in an objective order of values, but is rather produced by the will of God as the Superior imposing on us our state of being under obligation. In sum, as Le Grand reiterates the Pufendorfian doctrine of moral obligation more or less faithfully, he cannot remain faithful to himself and to his previously developed theory of human freedom.

---

70 Cf. Samuel Pufendorf, *De jure naturae et gentium. Dritter Teil: Materialien und Kommentar*, von Frank Böhling (Berlin and Boston: De Gruyter, 2014), 72–73.

Apáti begins his Section 14 (*De Obligatione, vel si mavis, Obsequio in Genere*)[71] with a clear diagnosis: the necessity contained in the idea of *obligation* contradicts the *indifference* theory of freedom. Indifferent freedom cannot be compelled by necessity; it cannot take on determination of any kind. Determined will ceases to be appropriately disposed free will. For Apáti, the impossibility of constraining free will is a common doctrine among authors writing on ethical matters. As regards jurisprudence, however, Apáti announces a new observation on obligation.

Like Le Grand, Apáti introduces the definition of obligation according to Roman law,[72] qualified by Pufendorf as the vulgar conception (*De officio*, I.ii.3).[73] Obligation is a legal bond. Further, civic obligation is the bond of civil rights, and natural obligation is the bond of equity. Following Vinnius's commentaries on the Justinian codex,[74] Apáti regards the Justinian definition as pertaining only to *civic* obligation and clearly distances his own approach from the juridical meaning in Roman law. He observes obligation in the widest sense to embrace natural, civic and *mere* civic obligation, the latter resulting from the penultimate under contingent circumstances. Compared to Le Grand, Apáti rejects the Roman law conception of obligation much more consciously in favour of modern approaches.

In order to maintain the indifference of freedom concerning acts prescribed by rules, Apáti draws a terminological distinction between *obligation* and *obsequiousness*.[75] In contrast to obligation, obsequiousness excludes necessity. Apáti warns his reader that even if the term 'obligation' occurs in the following passages, he will use it in this sense

> inasmuch as a human being is freely ready to grasp at a certain duty, that is, inasmuch as he or she determines himself or herself to will or not to will this or another thing, to will to will, to will not to will, to will to act or to will to omit, while freedom remains within his or her own power.[76]

71 Apáti, *Vita*, 120–130.

72 Apáti, *Vita*, 121; cf. Le Grand, *Insitutio*, 808.

73 Pufendorf, *De officio*, 18.

74 Arnold Vinnius, *In quatuor libros Institutionum imperialium commentarius academicus et forensis* (Amsterdam: Elzevir, 1569), 572–579, esp. 574–575.

75 As regards this distinction, Apáti refers to Ulrik Huber, *De Jure Civitatis libri tres* (Franeker: Gyselaar, 1684), 318.

76 Apáti, *Vita*, 123: 'Eatenus sumitur, quatenus ipse Homo se libere accingit alicui muneri capessendo: hoc est, se determinat ad hoc aut illud velle aut nolle, vult velle, vult nolle, vult facere, vult negligere, Libertate manente in sua potestate.'

Equipped with this distinction (and emphasising the presence of freedom even in obligation and thus somewhat confusing his readers), Apáti replaces the term *obligatio* with the term *obsequium* in several passages, expressing the idea of natural obligation, while leaving the rest of the sentences unchanged. In this sense, natural laws inscribed in the heart of each human being are the most legitimate ones; 'therefore, they must be obeyed (*obsequi*) following even our natural drive.'[77] In the hypothetical case that civil law commands citizens to observe something that is alien to divine law or contrary to the right reason, civil law 'destroys its capacity to call citizens to obey' (*ad Obsequium alliciendi*).[78] This is the reason why divine and natural law must be obeyed (*Obsequium*) above all.[79] The most striking example is the paraphrase of Pufendorf's claim that moral obligation requires a Superior who imposes obligation on moral persons. This idea is expressed by Apáti as follows: 'someone, in order to become *obsequious* in this way, must have a Superior and must recognise that he is subjected to the laws established by the Superior.'[80]

Even if this terminological trick seems odd at first glance, Apáti was aware of the difficulties inherent in his method. In order to save human freedom as indifference within the framework of the language appropriate to theories of natural law, he had to face the problem of the metaphysical status of natural law. To elaborate this problem, Apáti inserts extensive passages from Johannes Behrent's disputation *De prima inter homines lege, ex jure mundi*[81] proposed at the University of Leiden in 1686 under the presidency of Johannes Voet.

Natural law is eternal law. As such, it cannot be changed by humans or God. For the idea of immutability of eternal law from God's perspective, Behrent quotes Johann Georg von Kulpis's[82] (1652–1698) interpretation of Grotius from

77 Apáti, *Vita*, 124: 'Leges Naturales inscriptae omnium hominum cordibus cum sint opus Pii Opificiis, sunt justissimae & legitimae, unde illis Obsequi vel ex naturae ductu debemus.'

78 Apáti, *Vita*, 124: 'immo hoc si fiat, vim suam perdit Cives ad Obsequium alliciendi.'

79 Apáti, *Vita*, 124.

80 Apáti, *Vita*, 124: 'Ac idcirco oportet, ut quis hoc modo *Obsequiosus* fieri queat Superiorem habeat, & conditis ab eo Legibus, debere se obtemperare agnoscat.' Cf. Le Grand, *Institutio*, 809: 'Ac idcirco oportet, ut quis *obligari* possit, Superiorem habeat, & conditis ab eo legibus, debere se obtemperare agnoscat'; further: Pufendorf, *De officio*, 19 (I.ii.4): 'Sequitur ergo, ut ille *obligationis* sit capax, qui & superiorem habeat, & normam praescriptam potest cognoscere' (my italics – JS).

81 Johannes Behrent, *Disputatio inauguralis De prima inter homines lege, ex jure mundi* (Leiden: Elzevier, 1686).

82 For Kulpis's career as a jurist and diplomat in the service of the Duke of Württemberg, cf. Bernd Roeck, 'Kulpis, Johann Georg von,' in *Neue Deutsche Bio-*

his popular *Collegium Grotianum*.[83] Apáti incorporates Behrent's argumentation without indicating Kulpis's work as its original source. God cannot change eternal law because *God*, proceeding from His absolutely indeterminate consideration, after imposing moral necessity on certain actions of the rational nature created by Him, *obliged Himself* to this necessity as well. This is the core argument of the first *Exercitatio* in Kulpis's *Collegium Grotianum* which aims to reconcile Pufendorfian voluntarism and Grotian moral realism. In Behrent's version, the argument serves as a tool to refute both voluntarist and intellectualist approaches to God's relation to natural law. There are two lines of interpretation of God's self-subjection to eternal law that threatens God's omnipotence. First, this self-submission should not be interpreted as if there were a Superior who could impose an obligation on God to subject Himself to eternal law. Second, divine will revealing itself in self-subjection to eternal law should not be conceived of as honest or right because of its conformity to the eternal law to which it is subjected. Behrent supports his refutation of both voluntarist and intellectualist arguments against Kulpis's theory of God's self-determination to eternal law with a quotation from Anselm's *Cur Deus Homo*.[84] Again, Apáti follows Behrent's wording exactly and without reference to its original source. God is free from any subjection to any law. The values of justice and equitability are dependent on His will alone, while the negative values of injustice and inequitability do not pertain to His will. The latter claim is not a limitation of divine omnipotence resulting from some higher instance of law prescribing the negative validity of these values independently

---

graphie 13 (1982), 280–282 [Online-Version]; URL: https://www.deutsche-biographie.de/pnd100212204.html#ndbcontent, accessed on 15 February 2021. Unlike Behrent, Kulpis's name had a certain renown among jurisconsults of the late seventeenth century as a specialist in public and constitutional law. From the former point of view, Kulpis belonged to the Giessen school of public law. Cf. Michael Stolleis, 'Reformation und öffentliches Recht in Deutschland,' *Der Staat* 24 (1985/1): 51–74, esp. 57, and Johann Stephan Pütter, *Litteratur des Deutschen Staatsrechts*, vol. 1 (Göttingen: Wittwe Vandenhoek, 1777), 254–256. However, his fame was established by his critical commentary on Pufendorf's *De statu imperii Germanici*, Pufendorf's chief contribution to German constitutional law, published under the pseudonym Monzambano in 1667. Johann Georg von Kulpis, *In Sev. de Monzambano, de statu Imperii Germanici librum commentationes academicae* (Stuttgart: Zubrot, 1688, several editions later). Cf. Detlef Döring, 'Untersuchungen zur Entstehungsgeschichte der Reichsverfassungsschrift Samuel Pufendorfs (Severinus de Monzambo),' *Der Staat*, 33 (1994/2): 185–206, esp. 186; Fiammetta Palladini, *Discussioni seicentesche su Samuel Pufendorf. Scritti latini 1663–1700* (Milano: Il mulino, 1978), 154sqq.

83 Johann Georg von Kulpis, *Collegium Grotianum, Super Iure Belli Ac Pacis In Academia Giessensi XV. Exercitationibus Institutum* (Frankfurt am Main: Faber, 1682), 9.

84 S. Anselmus Cantuariensis, *Libri duo Cur Deus homo*, ed. Hugo Laemmer (Berlin: Schlawitz, 1857), 23–24 (1, 12).

of divine will. Injustice is simply beyond the competency of divine freedom. Apáti follows Behrent's conclusion: in the sentence 'God subjected himself to eternal law,' the word 'law' does not function in the proper sense. If law in this case were understood with its proper signification, it should be either natural or positive law. However, as regards God, neither the higher instance of moral objectivism nor the voluntarist obligation of a Superior applies.

If eternal law were natural law, that would oblige God. According to the theory of moral objectivism, it would dispose of the principle of law, which also determines God's will. Following Behrent's discussion closely, Apáti imports the standard terminology of the critique of intellectualist conceptions of natural law: natural law merely *indicates* how values are naturally disposed instead of commanding them.[85] Hence, the correct theory of God's self-obligation to eternal law is the following: God decreed absolutely freely that a certain act should not be performed. After His decision, God is not able to act against His own decree, i.e. he is not able to implement a new decree that prescribes acts contrary to the former. The reason for God's inability does not lie in the prohibition He has put into force by His decree. It results from the following contradiction: if God performed an act against His absolute decree, then He would have contrary decrees concerning one and the same thing at the very same time and from eternity. In other words, in this case, God would absolutely be willing two contradictory things at the same time. Therefore, the impotence of divine will in performing an act against His decree does not result from the prohibition, but from the nature of the thing (*natura rei*). Otherwise, we should suppose imperfection and privation in God, which cannot be considered 'without the utmost wickedness.'

This allusion to Grotius's famous formulation *etiamsi daremus* is a strange reversion of the classical argument. First of all, it runs against Grotius's intention: God's existence is necessary for the explanation of the metaphysical status of natural law. However, in Apáti's argument taken from Behrent, God's existence does not play the role of the voluntarist warrant for obligation as stated in classical conceptions.[86] Instead, God's entirely perfect existence functions as an *intellectual* explanation for His self-submission to the natural law decreed by His absolutely indifferent will.

---

85 Francisco Suárez, *De legibus ac Deo legislatore* (Coimbra: Didacum Gomez de Loureyro, 1612), 120 (II.6.iii): 'In hac re prima sententia est, legem naturalem [...] esse legem *indicantem*, quid agendum, vel cauendum sit, quid natura sua intrinsece bonum, ac necessarium, vel intrinsece malum sit' (my italics – JS). Cf. Haakonssen, *Natural Law*, 16–24.

86 Cf. Suárez, *De legibus*, 121 (II.6.iv).

Apáti continues by quoting Behrent and enters the sphere of human freedom. Eternal law cannot be changed by humans either. God gave human beings a nature such that it was impossible for them not to be conjoined with moral *necessity* as regards the performance or the omission of certain acts that are naturally good or bad. It is in this sense that the law is eternal for humans. According to Apáti, following Behrent,[87] the necessity in question must be fine-tuned by the distinction between absolute and hypothetical necessity. Whether an act conforms to natural or eternal law is demonstrated by its accordance with or its divergence from the rational and social nature of humans. However, the social nature of humans had not been inserted into humans by inevitable and immutable necessity, but according to the arbitrariness of divine will. Therefore, as regards the very time of its constitution, it was not eternal, as if it could not have been otherwise. Nevertheless, it became eternal and immutable after its constitution. This is why in *De jure naturae et gentium* I.ii.6 – thus the explicit reference by both Behrent and Apáti – Pufendorf claims that the fact that human beings are endowed with a rational and social nature was not imposed by absolute necessity, but only by hypothetical necessity.[88] However, this hypothetical necessity does not imply that natural law could be altered by humans.

6 Conclusion

If we consider Apáti's patchwork compiled from divergent sources, we cannot but suspect it of being fragmentary at least to the degree that Le Grand's *Institutio* is. If Le Grand can be accused of not paying attention to the incompatibility of his own concept of free will with Pufendorf's theory, then Apáti can be similarly criticised because of the insufficient elaboration of indifference theory of will within the framework of natural law theory. Both Le Grand and Apáti experience the challenge posed by Pufendorf's theory against their conceptions of freedom. Le Grand had to remain silent about Pufendorf's point of departure, the indifference of human will as abstracted from natural obligation; Le Grand paid this price for incorporating the social philosophy of the German scholar into his Cartesian handbook. In contrast, Apáti

87 Behrent, of course, is thinking of Pufendorf's *De jure naturae et gentium*, I.ii.6.

88 Pufendorf, *De jure* (as in note 20), 32 (I.ii.6): 'Ut adeo ista his ⟨attributa sit &⟩ competat non ex necessitate absoluta, sed hypothetica, posita ea conditione, quam homini prae reliquis animantibus DEUS libere assignavit.'

developed an explicit indifferent theory of free will while formulating paraphrases of Poiret's *Cogitationum rationalium* in the introductory sections of *Vita triumphans civilis*. He had to face the Pufendorfian challenge from quite the opposite point of view than Le Grand did. For Pufendorf, the preliminary and miserable state of isolated individuals with their indifferent will was something to be surpassed or left behind via the moral necessity of obligation. Being fascinated by Poiret's theory, Apáti did not subscribe to Pufendorf's ascribing moral indifference only to the miserable state of individuals.

It is beyond doubt that Apáti endeavoured to maintain the indifference theory of free will within the paradigm of natural law on which he likewise insisted. His strategy of composing the text bears clear witness to his efforts. Apáti disregards Le Grand's paraphrase of Pufendorfian obligation in the equivalent Section 14 of his *Vita triumphans civilis* and substitutes it for Behrent's much more sophisticated discussion of the topic. Apáti's decision to change his source testifies to his worries about Le Grand's revision of *De officio* I.i–ii. Indeed, Apáti showed sensitivity to Behrent's metaphysical account of obligation concentrated in the Pufendorfian idea of hypothetical moral necessity. He emphasised the hypothetical character of moral obligation to avoid moral objectivism, which threatens the indifference theory of human freedom. In this sense, Apáti solved the problem that emerged in the last part of Le Grand's *Institutio*. Despite all his awareness of related problems, Apáti did not succeed in developing a collection of compiled texts without contradiction. There was too much at stake: Poiret's indifferent will could not be incorporated into the world of natural law theory introduced by Grotius and Pufendorf.

Acknowledgement

The research was supported by the Hungarian Scientific Research Fund ('OTKA 137963 History of Hungarian Philosophy in Early Modernity (1570–1710)'). I am indebted to Gábor Gángó for his comments and to Thomas Williams for the proofreading.

Bibliography

Primary Sources

Apáti, Miklós, *Disputatio theologico-critica tripertita naturae tōn ūrīm we-tūmīm Urim et Thummim ad mentem Scripturae Sacrae* [...] *pars I–III* [praes. Christoph Wittich (1625–87)], Lugduni Batavorum: Elzevier, 1686.

Apáti, Miklós, *Disputatio theologica de virga Mosis* [praes. Jacob Gaillard (1620–1688)], Lugduni Batavorum: Elzevier, 1687.

Apáti, Miklós, *Vita triumphans civilis sive universa vitae humanae peripheria, ad mentem illustris herois et philosophi, D. Renati Des Cartes, ex unico centro deducta*, Amsterdam: Abraham a Someren, 1688.

Behrent, Johannes, *Disputatio inauguralis De prima inter homines lege, ex jure mundi*, Leiden: Elzevier, 1686.

Descartes, René, *Correspondance. Juillet 1643 – Avril 1647*, Oeuvres de Descartes, vol. IV. ed. Charles Adam and Paul Tannery, Paris: Cerf, 1901.

Descartes, René, *Epistolae. Partim ab Auctore Latino sermone conscriptae, partim ex Gallico translatae*, vols I–II, Amsterdam: Blaeu, 1682.

Descartes, René, *Meditationes de prima philosophia*. Oeuvres de Descartes, vol. VII, ed. Charles Adam and Paul Tannery, Paris: Cerf, 1904.

Descartes, René, *Passiones Animae per Renatum Des Cartes. Gallice ab ipso conscripta, nunc autem in exterorum gratiam Latina civitate donatae Ab H.D.M* [Henri Desmaret], in Renati Des-Cartes *Opera Philosophica*, Amsterdam: Elzevirius, 1651.

Descartes, René, *The Philosophical Writings*, transl. John Cottingham, Robert Stoothoff, and Dugald Murdoch, vols I–III, Cambridge: Cambridge University Press, 1984.

Huber, Ulrik, *De Jure Civitatis libri tres*, Franeker: Gyselaar, 1684.

Kulpis, Johann Georg von, *Collegium Grotianum, Super Iure Belli Ac Pacis In Academia Giessensi XV. Exercitationibus Institutum*, Frankfurt am Main: Faber, 1682.

Kulpis, Johann Georg von, *In Sev. de Monzambano, de statu Imperii Germanici librum commentationes academicae*, Stuttgart: Zubrot, 1688.

Le Grand, Antoine, *Institutio philosophiae secundum principia D. Renati Descartes: Nova Methodo Adornata, & Explicata*, Nürnberg: Zieger, 1683.

Le Grand, Antoine, *Le sage des Stoïques, ou l'homme sans passions*, LaHaye: Broune & L'Escluse, 1662.

Poiret, Pierre, *Cogitationum rationalium de Deo, anima et malo libri quatuor*, Amsterdam: Blaeu, 1685.

Pufendorf, Samuel, *De jure naturae et gentium*, ed. Frank Böhling, Berlin: Akademie Verlag, 1998.

Pufendorf, Samuel, *De jure naturae et gentium. Dritter Teil: Materialien und Kommentar*, von Frank Böhling, Berlin and Boston: De Gruyter, 2014.

Pufendorf, Samuel, *De officio hominis et civis juxta legem naturalem*, ed. Gerald Hartung, Berlin: Akademie Verlag, 1997.

S. Anselmus Cantuariensis, *Libri duo Cur Deus homo*, ed. Hugo Laemmer, Berlin: Schlawitz, 1857.

Suárez, Francisco, *De legibus ac Deo legislatore*, Coimbra: Didacus Gomez de Loureyro, 1612.

Vinnius, Arnold, *In quatuor libros Institutionum imperialium commentarius academicus et forensis*, Amsterdam: Elzevir, 1569.

Secondary Sources

Angyal, József, *Barock in Ungarn*, Budapest, Leipzig and Milano: Danubia, 1947.

Araujo, Marcelo de, *Scepticism, Freedom and Autonomy*, Berlin and New York: De Gruyter, 2003.

Bán, Imre, 'Adatok Apáti Miklós életrajzához,' *Filológiai Közlöny* 4 (1958/3–4): 433–439.

Campbell, Joseph Keim, 'Descartes on Spontaneity, Indifference, and Alternatives,' in *New Essays on the Rationalists*, ed. Rocco J. Germaro and Charles Huenemann, 179–199, New York and Oxford: Oxford University Press, 1999.

Carr, Craig L. and Michael J. Seidler, 'Pufendorf, Sociality and the Modern State,' in *Grotius, Pufendorf and Modern Natural Law*, ed. Knud Haakonssen, 133–157, Dartmouth: Ashgate, 1999.

Chappell, Vere, 'Descartes' Compatibilism,' in *Reason, Will, and Sensation: Studies in Descartes' Metaphysics*, ed. John Cottingham, 177–190, Oxford: Clarendon Press, 1994.

Döring, Detlef, 'Untersuchungen zur Entstehungsgeschichte der Reichsverfassungsschrift Samuel Pufendorfs (Severinus de Monzambo),' *Der Staat*, 33 (1994/2): 185–206.

Du Rieu, William N., *Album studiosorum Academiae Lugduno Batavae* MDLXXV–MDCCCLXXV, Hagae Comitum: Nijhoff, 1875.

Haakonssen, Knud, *Natural law and moral philosophy. From Grotius to the Scottish Enlightenment*, Cambridge: Cambridge University Press, 1996.

Hatfield, Gary, 'The Cartesian Psychology of Antoine Le Grand,' in *Cartesian Empiricisms*, ed. M. Dobre and T. Nyden, 251–274, Dordrecht: Springer: 2013.

Hunter, Ian, *Rival Enlightenments: Civil and Metaphysical Philosophy in Early Modern Germany*, Cambridge: Cambridge University Press, 2001.

Krieg, Gustav A., *Der mystische Kreis. Wesen und Werden der Theologie Pierre Poirets*, Göttingen: Vandenhoeck & Ruprecht, 1979.

Laczházi, Gyula, 'A karteziánus szenvedélyelmélet magyar recepciójáról,' *Kellék* 32 (2007): 119–125.

Mautner, Thomas, 'From Virtue to Morality: Antoine Le Grand (1629–1699) and the New Moral Philosophy,' *Jahrbuch für Recht und Ethik / Annual Review of Law and Ethics*, 8 (2000): 209–232.

Oláh Róbert, 'Egy református lelkész könyves műveltsége: Apáti Madár Miklós olvasmányai I–II,' *Magyar Könyvszemle* 129 (2013/2): 145–164 and 129 (2013/3): 322–335.

Oláh, Róbert, 'Pierre Poiret ajándéka, Adalék Apáti Madár Miklós peregrinációjához,' *Könyv és Könyvtár* 28 (2006): 183–192.

Palladini, Fiammetta, *Discussioni seicentesche su Samuel Pufendorf. Scritti latini 1663–1700*, Milano: Il mulino, 1978.

Pütter, Johann Stephan, *Litteratur des Deutschen Staatsrechts*, vol. 1, Göttingen: Wittwe Vandenhoek, 1777.

Ragland, Clyde P., *The Will to Reason. Theodicy and Freedom in Descartes*, Oxford: Oxford University Press, 2016.

Roeck, Bernd, 'Kulpis, Johann Georg von,' in *Neue Deutsche Biographie* 13 (1982), 280–282 [Online-Version]; URL: https://www.deutsche-biographie.de/pnd100212204.html#ndbcontent, accessed on 15 February 2021.

Schmal, Dániel, *A kezdet nélküli kezdet. Descartes és a kartézianizmus problémája*, Budapest: Gondolat, 2012.

Stolleis, Michael, 'Reformation und öffentliches Recht in Deutschland,' *Der Staat* 24 (1985/1): 51–74.

Tordai, Zádor, 'A magyar kartezianizmus történetének vázlata,' *Magyar Filozófiai Szemle* 6 (1961/1): 54–79.

Turóczi-Trostler, József, 'Magyar cartesianusok,' *Minerva-könyvtár* 12 (1933/1): 20–68 (reprint: Turóczi-Trostler, József, *Magyar irodalom – világirodalom*, vol. I., 173–216, Budapest: Akadémiai, 1961.

Weszprémi, István, *Succincta medicorum Hungariae et Transilvaniae biographia, Centuria tertia*, decas I. et II. Tom. IV., Vienna: Trattnern, 1787.

CHAPTER 10

Political Psychology and Natural Law in Miklós Bethlen's Preface to His *Autobiography* (1708)

József Simon

1 Introduction

The topic of the present paper is situated between two strong perspectives found in studies on the history of political ideas in Hungary. On the one hand, reflections on political concepts in seventeenth-century Hungary are dominated by contextual methodology. According to the mainstream of research, political individuals are defined by their representations in the social space, whether in terms of secular Machiavellianism/Tacitism[1] or in the manner of self-representation found in Protestant martyrology.[2] For the latter interpretation, political concepts affecting individuals' actions of the period, such as patriotism,[3] power and obedience, are available through the reconstruction of strategies that articulate the individual's social representation. Consequently, the chief sources for the history of political ideas are texts that reflect on political agency within the hard facts of political history – allusions to natural

1 Sándor Bene, *Theatrum politicum: Nyilvánosság, közvélemény és irodalom a korai újkorban* [Theatrum Politicum: Public sphere, public opinion and Literature in Early Modern times] (Debrecen: Kossuth Egyetemi Kiadó, 1999); Tibor Klaniczay, 'Niccolo Zrínyi, Venezia e la letteratura della ragione di Stato,' in *Mélanges de littérature comparée et de philologie offerts à Mieczyslaw Brahmer* (Warszawa: PWN-Éditions scientifiques de Pologne, 1967), 265–273; Tibor Klaniczay, 'Korszerű politikai gondolkodás és nemzetközi látókör Zrínyi műveiben [Modern political thinking and an international perspective in Miklós Zrinyi's works],' in *Irodalom és ideológia a 16–17. században* [Literature and ideology in the sixteenth and seventeenth centuries], ed. Béla Varjas (Budapest: Akadémiai, 1987), 337–400; Gábor Förköli, 'Miklós Zrínyi: un traité tacitiste hongrois et la réception tardive de l'étatisme,' in *Tacite et le tacitisme en Europe à l'époque moderne*, ed. Alexandra Merle and Alicia Oïffer-Bomsel (Paris: Honoré Champion, 2017), 501–516.

2 Zsombor Tóth, 'Calvinian Anthropology and the Early Modern Hungarian Devotion: The Case of István Nagy Szőnyi, the First Hungarian Martyrologist,' in *Anthropological Reformations – Anthropology in the Era of Reformation*, ed. Hannah Wälzholz (Göttingen: Vandenhoeck & Ruprecht, 2015), 415–428.

3 Balázs Trencsényi and Márton Zászkalicky, ed., *Whose Love of Which Country? Composite States, National Histories and Patriotic Discourses in Early Modern East Central Europe* (Leiden: Brill, 2010).

 | DOI:10.1163/9789004545847_011

law are instrumentalized under factual political aims.[4] On the other hand, there is an established branch of studies on the legal thinking of Hungarian authors within the framework of practical and theoretical jurisprudence in the eighteenth- and nineteenth-century Habsburg Empire.[5] In the latter perspective, the Enlightenment tradition of natural law proves to be an organic part of the history of political ideas – but the relevant sources only emerged in the mid-eighteenth century. The paradigm shift between the two perspectives draws our attention to the turn of the seventeenth and eighteenth centuries, raising the question: Had there really been no signs of the reception of the Grotian–Hobbesian–Pufendorfian paradigm before it became an essential part of law studies at universities in the mid-eighteenth century?[6]

My paper is an attempt to offer a case study of the Hungarian reception of modern natural law tradition in the early eighteenth century through a reconstruction of the theoretical claims developed in Miklós Bethlen's[7] Preface to his extended *Autobiography*[8] in 1708. I contend that Bethlen was deeply influ-

4 As happens most recently in Márton Zászkaliczky, 'A Bocskai-felkelés politikai nyelvei: Vázlat [Political languages of the Bocskai uprising: An outline],' in *Politikai nyelvek a 17. század első felének Magyarországán* [Political languages in Hungary in the first half of the seventeenth century], ed. Márton Zászkaliczky and Gábor Kármán (Budapest: reciti, 2019), 11–84.

5 See Martin P. Schennach's contribution to this volume. There are only a few examples of Hungarian research in this area: Anna Petrasovszki, 'The Significance of Natural Law as a Part of Legal Education in the Codification Process of 19th Century in Hungary,' in *Codification Achievements and Failures in the 19th–20th Century: 7th Conference on Legal History in Szeged*, ed. Mária Homoki-Nagy and Norbert Varga (Szeged: University of Szeged, Faculty of Law and Political Sciences, 2018), 125–130; Zoltán Gábor Szűcs, 'Természet, jog, teológia: egy fejezet a politikai diskurzus történetéből a 18. századi Magyarországon [Nature, law and theology: A chapter in the history of political discourse in eighteenth-Century Hungary],' *Aetas* 26 (2011/2): 99–115.

6 The Hungarian contributions to this volume are clearly devoted to making up for this shortage of reflections on the history of ideas in Hungarian Early Modernity.

7 There is an extended corpus of research on Bethlen's literary and diplomatic activities in the Hungarian language. Zsombor Tóth's bibliography is a helpful introduction to these studies: Zsombor Tóth, ed., *Bethlen Miklós – Válogatott bibliográfia* [Miklós Bethlen – A selected bibliography] (Budapest: reciti, 2016). For a general presentation of Bethlen's intellectual profile in English, I recommend George Gömöri, 'Miklós Bethlen,' in *Encyclopedia of Life Writing: Autobiographical and Biographical Forms*, ed. Margaretta Jolly (London and Chicago: Fitzroy Dearborn Publishers, 2001), 102–103; and Albert Tezla, 'Bethlen Miklós,' in Albert Tezla, *Hungarian Authors. A Bibliographical Handbook* (Cambridge, MA: Belknapp Press of Harvard University Press, 1970), 97–99.

8 All references to the Hungarian version follow the standard edition edited by Éva V. Windisch: Miklós Bethlen, 'Élete leírása magától,' in Éva V. Windisch, ed., *Kemény János és Bethlen Miklós művei* (Budapest: Szépirodalmi, 1980), 399–981. Although the text was not edited until 1858, it was read and copied in a wide circle of intellectuals. More than twenty

enced by the idea of natural law, as well as by the problems perceived by contemporaries related to this theoretical construction. I suggest that Bethlen did not unreservedly accept the theory of natural law as an ultimate explanation of the human social community. However, his themes (public communication, reputation, honour, shame and ambition as political passions) are clearly situated within the theoretical language established by classic authors of the Enlightenment natural law tradition.

Bethlen's text is part of a very special literary genre. Unlike sources analysed by other papers in this volume, it is neither a school text used to educate future lawyers or public officials nor a scientific work composed with the aim of a scholarly exchange of ideas on natural jurisprudence. Bethlen introduces his thoughts in his Preface as a kind of philosophico-theological treatise to provide readers of the extended narration of his life with the theoretical device of a body politic in which his political activity took place. Before going into detail on his concept of human society, let us familiarize ourselves with some information on his biography to enable us to sketch the intellectual milieu surrounding him.

Miklós Bethlen was born in 1642 to one of the most ancient families in the Transylvanian high nobility. Members of his family played an important role in early modern Transylvania throughout the sixteenth and seventeenth centuries, struggling in the political arena between the Ottoman and Habsburg Empires. Bethlen grew up in the immediate circle of Transylvanian princes in an exclusive group of youths of the same high social background. In the 1650s, he listened to lectures held in Cluj by János Apáczai Csere, a scholar known as the first Cartesian thinker in Hungary.[9]

Between 1661 and 1663, Bethlen attended the University of Heidelberg in Germany and the Universities of Utrecht and Leiden in the Low Countries. He

copies have been handed down to us from the eighteenth and nineteenth centuries. I will not discuss philological problems of manuscripts and editions: I will quote Bethlen's text according to my own studies to reconstruct an *ultima manus* version of his Preface which in some cases proves to be different from the formulations of the standard edition (cf. József Simon, 'Filológiai és filozófiatörténeti megjegyzések Bethlen Miklós *Önéletírás*ának Elöljáró beszédéhez [Philosophical and philological considerations of the Preface to Miklós Bethlen's *Autobiography*],' in *Irodalomtörténeti közlemények* 120 (2016/3): 299–314). For the English version, I follow Bernard Adams's translation (*The Autobiography of Miklós Bethlen*, transl. Bernard Adams (London: Paul Kegan, 2004)), but I have made essential emendations on some passages relevant to our topic. For a general exposition of Bethlen's *Autobiography* in the history of older Hungarian literature, see Gábor Tolnai, 'Miklós Bethlen un classique des anciens mémoires hongrois,' in *Acta Litteraria Academiae Scientiarum Hungaricae* 12 (1970/3–4): 251–272.

9 Tibor Hanák, *Geschichte der Philosophie in Ungarn* (München: Trofenik, 1990), 29–31.

had studied with Apáczai Csere, a Ramist-Cartesian, in 1659, and, not long after the death of his teacher, he heard lectures held by the young Samuel Pufendorf in Heidelberg over the summer of 1661.[10] Bethlen mentions his German professor in the usual laconic manner of the *Autobiography*. Nevertheless, he does not fail to note that the young Pufendorf lectured on Grotius's masterwork *De jure belli ac pacis*.[11] One cannot overestimate the striking difference in intellectual milieu between Transylvania and Heidelberg; while attending Pufendorf's lectures, Bethlen must have immediately experienced his professor's most intensive dilemmas on *a priori* mathematical argumentation as opposed to an historical argumentation for the theory of natural law or on the removal of moral theology from the realm of natural rights.[12]

The other setting for his higher education was the Low Countries. He attended both public and private lectures held by leading intellectuals, who belonged either to the philosophical movement of Cartesianism[13] (Johannes de Raey and Henry de Roy) or to the theological camp of Cocceianism[14] (Frans Burman, Abraham Heidanus and Johannes Cocceius himself). Bethlen acquired his basic cultural identity as a Reformed Cartesian in Utrecht and Leiden, due to the decisive role played by intellectuals in the Low Countries in the emergence of Cartesian philosophy within the mainstream of contemporary philosophical reflections.

After his studies, Bethlen became one of the most prominent politicians of his time, that is, of the last decades of Ottoman rule in Hungary and

10 See Benrath's publication of the advertisements of lectures at the University of Heidelberg in 1661: Adolf Benrath, 'The Heidelberger Vorlesungsverzeichnisse aus den Jahren 1655, 1658 bis 1662 und 1685,' in *Heidelberger Jahrbücher* 5 (Berlin, Göttingen and Heidelberg: Springer, 1961), 95; and Frank Böhling, 'Einleitung,' in Samuel Pufendorf, *De jure naturae et gentium. Dritter Teil: Materialien und Kommentar* (Berlin and Boston: De Gruyter, 2014), 12.

11 Bethlen, *Autobiography*, 185; Bethlen, *Élete*, 573: 'I went to the lectures by Samuel Pufendorf, then a young man but later a great and famous, learned *juris doctor*, who lectured on Hugo Grotius's *de jure belli et pacis*.' On Bethlen's visit to Heidelberg, cf. Peter Meusburger and Ferenc Próbáld, 'Scientific and Cultural Relations between Heidelberg University and Hungary over Five Centuries,' in *Geographies of the University*, ed. Peter Meusburger, Michael Heffernan, and Laura Suarsana (Cham: Springer, 2018), 43–134, esp. 67–69.

12 Horst Dreitzel, 'Samuel Pufendorf,' in *Grundriss der Geschichte der Philosophie. Die Philosophie des 17. Jahrhunderts*, ed. Helmut Holzhey and Wilhelm Schmidt-Biggemann, vol. 4/2 (Basel: Schwabe & Co AG, 2001), 779.

13 Tad Schmaltz, *Early Modern Cartesianisms: Dutch and French Constructions* (Oxford: Oxford University Press, 2016).

14 Willem J. van Asselt, *The Federal Theology of Johannes Cocceius (1603–1669)* (Leiden: Brill, 2001).

Transylvania and the first decade of their integration into the Habsburg Empire. It is no exaggeration to say that the whole history of Hungary and Transylvania between 1660 and 1704 can be described through the footnotes to his autobiography.[15] His main political achievement was *Diploma Leopoldinum* (1691), which declared the legal status of the Principality of Transylvania within the Habsburg Empire after its liberation from Ottoman rule.[16] In the course of his negotiations with Emperor Leopold I, Bethlen succeeded in securing guarantees for a much more liberal legal status than had previously been expected.[17] The regulations in *Diploma* proved to be enduring. Indeed, they remained in force until the revolutionary events of 1848.

It is more than puzzling that the only text that provides us with the possibility of reconstructing his philosophical ideas was written in the very late period of his life; Bethlen remained silent on philosophical matters until 1708, when, after he had been arrested in 1704 on a charge of high treason,[18] he was moved from Sibiu to Vienna. He was imprisoned along the way for a number of weeks in May of 1708 in Osijek. According to his own account, he composed the Preface to his *Autobiography* here, as he produced the rest of the manuscript containing the extended narration of his own life later while imprisoned in Vienna during the years 1708 to 1710.

The basic context for Bethlen's approach to natural law is provided by his interpretation of phenomena in social psychology, such as honour, shame and ambition. In a somewhat Hobbesian way, Bethlen makes these psychological phenomena closely dependent on speech acts in the public sphere of the community. To gain a better insight into the interrelated topics of social psychology and the public use of speech in Bethlen's thought, we must analyse his account of reputation (esteem expressed through signs of speech) as the most fundamental linguistic entity of intersubjective relations. Further, to describe communicative speech performances, we must turn to certain topics in the

---

15 Cf. Ágnes R. Várkonyi, 'The last decades of the independent principality (1660–1711),' in *History of Transylvania*, ed. László Makkai and Zoltán Szász, vol. II: From 1606 to 1830 (New York: Columbia Press, 2002), 325–397.

16 Várkonyi, 'The last decades,' 372–378.

17 In recognition of his diplomatic efforts, Bethlen was elected a member of the Gubernium as chancellor of Transylvania. His office remained vacant after his arrest, which fact led to an interesting chapter in Leibniz's biography, as he had made great efforts to secure his own appointment to Bethlen's former office as chancellor of Transylvania during his stay in Vienna from 1712 to 1714. For more details, see Gábor Gángó, 'G.W. Leibniz's Candidature for the Chancellorship of Transylvania,' in *Studia Leibnitiana* 47 (2015/1): 44–66.

18 For details, see Zsombor Tóth, 'A Man for All Seasons: Exile, Suffering and Martyrdom in the Autobiography of Miklós Bethlen,' *Hungarian Studies*, 26 (2012/2): 273–284, esp. 275.

philosophy of mind which underpin Bethlen's conceptions of public speech acts and social psychology. In line with this scheme, I have divided my paper into five sections. After accounting briefly for Bethlen's views on the philosophy of mind (Sec. 1), I will provide an outline of his definition of reputation and civic-moral qualities (Sec. 2) and of his description of honour, shame and ambition as eminent moral qualities (Sec. 3) embedded in a theory of natural passions (Sec. 4); afterwards, I close my paper with short conclusion (Sec. 5).

2 Philosophy of Mind

> Does not even the simplest of men experience this within himself; if his mind is fixed on something, he knows nothing about whatever he may hear or see apart from that which he then perceives. Indeed, he often does not know whether or not he has said that to which his tongue is accustomed; he may say a prayer or whatever, but his mind is far away. Sometimes he will even speak to another and answer, but he will not know of it when questioned later, and it will merely seem like a familiar dream that comes to mind. This everyone may experience best of all in church, during the divine service, when repeating a prayer after the preacher or listening to a sermon; if one's soul is far away, one will know nothing of what one's tongue is saying or one's ears are hearing, but one will be perfectly well aware of that which one's mind has perceived.[19]

According to Bethlen's conviction, social behaviour among individual agents in a society lacks conscious reflection in general or is realised at a very low level of consciousness at best. Speech performances as paradigmatic examples of social behaviour are no exceptions to this thesis. The problem stated here in Bethlen's passage is one central to Cartesian philosophy. According to the new Cartesian physiology, there are cases of human behaviour that can be

---

19 Bethlen, *Autobiography*, 52; Bethlen, *Élete*, 434: 'Nem tapasztalja-é a legegyügyűbb ember is meg ezt magában; ha az elméje valamire figyelmez, azonkívül, amire az figyelmez akkor, akármit halljon, lásson, semmit benne nem tud. Sőt sokszor amire a nyelve szokott, imádságot vagy mit a nyelve is elmond, de az elméje másutt járván, azt sem tudja, mondotta-é vagy nem. Néha másnak is szól, felel, de nem tudja, ha osztán rá kérdik, még csak úgy is, mint sokszori álma eszébe nem jut. Ezt legjobban megtapasztalhatja kiki magán, kiváltképpen a templomban, az isteni szolgálatban, mikor az imádságot a pap után mondja, vagy a prédikációt hallgatja; ha a lelke másutt jár, sem a nyelve szólásiban, sem a füle hallásiban semmit sem tud, de tudja azt jól, amire akkor az elméje figyelmezett.'

accounted for without the supposition of a soul determining them. The sharp distinction between the mind, described as *res cogitans*, and the mechanical world, described as *res extensa*, assures the entirely mechanical interpretation of sensual *enticements* of the human body and the basic biological and physical *responses* the human body gives to them as reflections. For an explanation of this responsive ability of the extended human body, there is no need to suppose any kind of sensitive or vegetative function of the soul involved between the mechanical stimulus and the mechanical response.

However, Bethlen narrows the perspective of the problem: he treats this enticement-response relationship within the context of using language. We all learned the Cartesian lesson on the speaking automaton from Part 5 of *Discours de la méthode* (Leiden 1637).[20] For Descartes, the ability to speak is a strong argument for the existence of an immaterial mind because we can account for the complicated structure of extended bodies of signs in a much more economical way by allowing for an immaterial mind producing it than by deriving it from an accidental realisation of the mechanical laws of nature. Bethlen – among several thinkers of his time – does not accept Descartes's view. Bethlen's example is an automatically praying man whose mind is intended for an entirely different object than the content expressed and whose mind directs the bodily organs to perform a speech act without consciousness.[21] Bethlen introduces two solutions for this problem. According to his *vitalistic* solution,[22] there is a *sensual* soul which moves the speaking organs without being conscious of the content of the prayer, that is, without the oper-

20 See the *locus classicus* in René Descartes, 'Discours de la méthode,' in *Oeuvres de Descartes*, ed. Charles Adam and Paul Tannery, vol. VI (Paris: Cerf, 1902), 56–57.

21 The automatically praying man served as a paradigmatic example in mechanistic descriptions of human behaviour; Claude Clerselier's Preface to the French edition of Descartes's *De l'homme* may have been the most influential passage to use this striking image; cf. Claude Clerselier, 'Preface,' in René Descartes, *L'Homme de René Descartes et vn traitté de la formation du foetus dv mesme avthevr. Auec des Remarques de Louys de La Forge* (Paris: Charles Angot, 1664), ooii–ooiii. For a detailed interpretation, cf. József Simon, 'Bethlen Miklós és az imádkozó automata [Miklós Bethlen and the praying automaton],' *Magyar Filozófiai Szemle* 61 (2017/4): 147–167.

22 Bethlen, *Autobiography*, 53 (Bethlen, *Élete*, 435): 'for the soul has two sorts of task in man, one which is purely that of the soul, spiritual, intellectual, and the other which is animal, physical, which consists of making one's senses and members, such as the mouth, tongue, ears etc., fit to perform human tasks; this the soul which attends to other thoughts does without abandoning them, and the limbs too can function without the *conscientia* or knowledge of the soul, for if it were with the awareness and the knowledge of the soul, one would not forget it so quickly.'

ation of the *spiritual* mind. According to his *mechanistic* solution,[23] the effect on the ears, the enticement of the 'strings of the body' up to the brain, and the reverse causal line from the brain through the 'bodily strings' down to the speaking organs is an entirely mechanical movement that lacks any intervention of any kind of soul or mind. Bethlen does not deny that humans have an immaterial mind, nor does he specify its mode of existence or argue for it based on the human ability to speak. For our present purpose, only the result of these investigations is of any importance: human speaking and communication, as well as other types of social behaviour, are characterised by only a very low level of consciousness. Human use of linguistic signs is a kind of mechanical or vitalistic process.

3 Reputation and Moral Qualities

Having in mind Bethlen's theory of speech acts as almost unconscious social behaviour, now let us turn to his definition of *reputation* as a basic structural constituent of the public sphere of community. The Hungarian equivalent of 'reputation' is *hírnév*, a compound word containing the elements *hír* (roughly 'message' in English) and *név* ('name' in English). Bethlen splits the two elements of the compound word and defines them separately. He introduces the definition of 'name' as follows:[24]

> A name is
> I. a *sign* invented and contrived
> I.1 for the distinguishing of one person or thing from another and
> I.2 for the better cognition of it and
> I.3 for having it acknowledged by another person, such as God, angel, man, sky, earth, sea, horse, ox; the distinct name and surname of countries, towns and people;
> II. the description, the name of a town, a village or any *mark* that separates them from each other, respectively;

23 Bethlen, *Autobiography*, 53 (Bethlen, *Élete*, 434–435): 'Rather it may be believed that its accomplishment is like the string of a cimbalom or virginals being struck at the end; the shock runs along it and it vibrates; or in the organ, when the wind enters a pipe and it sounds. So the sound of the word from the preacher's mouth enters your ear and by certain nerves affects your tongue and you make an utterance, especially if those physical members which, in dumb animals that have no comprehending souls, perform such functions as hearing, sight, speech etc.'

24 Subdivisions and emphases are my own – JS.

III. these all are but *signs* that help you and me to make our minds able to think of those [things] and to communicate our thoughts concerning them to each other as far as it is necessary.[25]

The definition reflects a conception of language which approaches the properties of language from a communicative perspective and which makes epistemology dependent on using it. Names are means for the epistemological function of successfully distinguishing between and thinking about things, instead of expressing mental content accessible only privately to separate individuals. Bethlen's definition of 'name' shows Hobbesian leanings in its emphasis on communication vis-à-vis linguistic meaning and reference.[26]

Bethlen applies this conception of 'name' to his views on *reputation*.

IV. This name is only a word, as is reputation, neither the reputation nor the name which we give to a certain person, or which we think, speak or write concerning him/her,

(IV.1) causes or produces any quality, reality or change; without it, he/she remains constantly in the condition given to him/her by God without any decrease, as long as, that is to say, the reputation and name of the given person uttered by another remain within the bounds of sincere, real simplicity of reputation and name.

(IV.2) But when the tongue goes beyond it, as James the Apostle finely describes in chapter 3, then the person spoken of begins to

25 Bethlen, *Autobiography*, 24–25 (emendations and emphases added – JS); Bethlen, *Élete*, 410: 'A név az emberektől a dolgok vagy emberek egymástól való megkülönböztetésére és annak jobban való megismerésére és mással is megismertetésére találtatott, szereztetett jegy, p. o. Isten, angyal, ember, ég, föld, tenger, ló, ökör; országoknak, városoknak, embereknek külön-külön a neve, vezetékneve; városról, faluról vagy akármi egyéb jelről másoktól megkülönböztető leírása, nevezése; mind csak olyan jegy, amely téged s engem segít arra, hogy azokról az én elmém s a tiéd jobban gondolkozhassunk és arról való gondolatunkat a szükséghez képest egymással közölhessük.'

26 Philip Pettit treats the transformative potential of the Hobbesian theory of language as an essential feature of Hobbes's social philosophy; see Philip Pettit, *Made with Words: Hobbes on Language, Mind, and Politics* (Princeton and Oxford: Princeton University Press, 2008); the important role language plays in Hobbes's contract theory has been reissued since Hungerland and Vick's article: Isabel C. Hungerland and George R. Vick, 'Hobbes's Theory of Signification,' *Journal of the History of Philosophy* 11 (1973/4): 459–482. In my rendering of the Hungarian terms 'jel'/ 'jegy' in English, I endeavoured to follow Hobbes's famous and controversial distinction between mark and sign; cf. Thomas Hobbes, *De Corpore. Elementorum Philosophiœ Sectio Prima* (London: Crook, 1655) I, 2, 1–2, 8–10; cf. Thomas Hobbes, *Leviathan Or The Matter, Forme, & Power Of A Common-Wealth Ecclesiasticall And Civill* (London: Crook, 1651), chaps. 4, 12–17, esp. 12–13.

> suffer and to be affected as good or evil are spoken of him, and in this way his advancement either aided or impeded in the condition given to him/her by God. And thence there come into the world these words and moral or civic qualities [*morális vagy civilis qualitasi*] of men: good or bad reputation, reproach, slander, scold, accusation or praise, honour, dignity, and good or bad remembrance in their lives as well as after their deaths. These, when later they become reality and actions affecting men, cause progress or hindrance and ruining of the person's life, property, freedom, peace and health either by the speaker or by those to whom he speaks; now that is good or bad reputation which one must desire or evade.[27]

The distinction between IV.1 and IV.2 seems to introduce a kind of differentiation between natural and social status. Reputation in the first sense has no causal capacity to influence the physical state of the person contained in the message of reputation. 'Reputation' and 'name' are merely words – as such, they cannot stand in a causal relationship with the physical world. The meaning implied by 'reputation' cannot cause any change in the state of the individual existing in the physical world: it does not 'cause or produce any quality, reality or change' in the person. This causal inefficacy presupposes that the meaning of 'reputation' must remain within the bounds of its sincere, real simplicity: Bethlen deduces this inefficacy from a kind of moral straightforwardness of the speaker. Even if Bethlen attributes some sort of reality to

27 Bethlen, *Autobiography*, 25; cf. Bethlen, *Élete*, 410–411: 'Ez a név is csak szó, mint a hír, és abban, akiről már én s te beszélünk, sem az a név, sem az a hír, amelyet mü néki adunk, vagy róla gondolunk, szólunk, vagy írunk, semmi qualitast, valóságot, vagy változást nem okoz, nem szerez; és ő anélkül az ő Istentől adott állapotjában minden fogyatkozás nélkül megmarad s megáll, valamíg tudniillik a hír és név, melyet őfelőle más elkövet, csak a hírnek és a névnek őszinte, való együgyűségének határában marad. De mikor osztán azon túl mégyen a nyelv, amint Jakab apostol szépen leírja *capite 3*. bezzeg már akkor kezd szenvedni, megillettetni az, akiről a szó vagyon, amint a szólók őróla jól avagy rosszul szólanak, és ő azáltal az ő Istentől adatott állapotjában vagy segíttetik, vagy akadályoztatik. És így innét jöttek már a világba bé ezek a szók és az embereknek morális vagy civilis qualitasi: jó vagy rossz hírnév, gyalázat, rágalmazás, szidás, vádlás vagy dícséret, becsület, méltóság, és éltekben is, holtok után is jó vagy rossz emlékezet. Melyek mikor osztán olyan valósággá és az embert megillető cselekedetté válnak, hogy az embernek azáltal élete, jószága, szabadsága, békessége s egészsége, vagy akármijében, akár maga a szóló által, akár akiknek szól, azok által, vagy előmenetele vagy akadálya, romlása légyen: már az a jó vagy rossz hírnév, amelyet embernek kívánni vagy távoztatni kell.'

this straightforward simplicity, the ontological status of the meaning of 'reputation' is strictly separated from the physical world: it cannot impose a causal effect on physical reality – and, conversely, it cannot be affected by physical entities.

In a second step, Bethlen exceeds this ideal framework of private communication with a rather obscure formulation: 'the tongue goes beyond it.' In this sense, the meaning spills over its original borders constituted within private communication and affects the person contained in the message of reputation. This effect proves to be twofold: the person in question can be aided or impeded by the content of reputation. Bethlen supplies an accurate description of the ontological status of these bizarre entities which can influence the physical state of the rumoured individual: they are 'moral or civic qualities' carried by communicative speech acts in a society. Although these qualities, i.e. 'a good or bad reputation, reproach, slander, scold, accusation, or praise, honour, dignity etc.,' are not physical items; they can still be manifested in the physical world as real actions. As a result of the causal impact of reputation, some changes will be induced in the physical state of the person: his/her *well-being*, *property* and *health* undergo some changes – and Bethlen seems to speak about the person's *freedom* or *peace* in this physical sense as well. This causal mechanism depends on the participants of the communicative situation in various ways: the positive or negative effect can be induced by the speaker as well as by the recipient of the message. Further, the causal context of these moral or civic qualities makes the person, a subject of rumour or reputation, articulate his own strategy in society: 'now that is good or bad reputation which one must desire or evade.'

The key term 'moral or civic qualities' in this passage is clearly of Pufendorfian origin. As noted above, Bethlen attended the young Pufendorf's lectures on Grotius's *De jure belli ac pacis* in Heidelberg during the 1661 academic year. At this time, Pufendorf had just published his first important work *Elementa jurisprudentiae universalis*,[28] in which the theory of moral qualities had already been elaborated.[29] But Bethlen's theory does not seem to match Pufendorf's conception of sociality. The German scholar considers moral status

---

28 Samuel Pufendorf, *Elementorum Jurisprudentiae Universalis Libri II* (Den Haag: Adrian Vlacq, 1660). I refer to *Elementa* according to the new edition in the series of Pufendorf's *Gesammelte Werke*: Samuel Pufendorf, *Elementa jurisprudentiae universalis*, ed. Thomas Behme (Berlin: Akademie Verlag, 1999).

29 Cf. Pufendorf: *Elementa*, 37 (Def. VIII, 1): '[...] vocabulum juris [...] sumatur pro *qualitate illa morali*, qua recte vel personis imperamus, vel res tenemus, aut qua eaedem nobis debentur'; or ibid., 44 (Def. XII, title): 'Obligatio est *qualitas moralis* operativa, qua quis praestare aut admittere vel pati tenetur aliquid' (my emphases – JS).

parallel to a physical world in which moral substances are imposed on physical bodies and carry the civic-moral qualities of power (*potestas*), right (*jus*) and obligation (*obligatio*).[30] Despite all the references Pufendorf makes in the direction of social psychology,[31] moral qualities essentially function as subjects of deductive inferences of social philosophy.[32] Bethlen presupposes public speech acts for the genesis of moral qualities; Pufendorf rather emphasises the mental act of their imposition by social agents. Pufendorf never developed any articulated theory of mind[33] but clearly presupposes a much higher level of consciousness of social behaviour[34] than Bethlen.

As regards the use of language, Pufendorf follows the Grotian topic of natural obligations of speech. Straightforwardness in communication is a basic natural obligation among humans. Although exceptional cases – such as danger to one's own life – may revoke this rule, the natural obligation of straightforward communication of mental contents and intentions attributes *moral* truth value to our utterances – despite *logical* truth consisting in the correspondence between words and things on a fundamental level. The idea of moral truth value enables Pufendorf to introduce a kind of criterion of truth into the social context of communication:

> From these Principals and fundamental Rules, it is easy to understand both the Nature of *Truth*, which Men are obliged to speak and profess; and the Nature of *Lye*, which is so abhorr'd by all the good and honest,

30 Samuel Pufendorf, *De jure naturae et gentium libri octo* (Lund: Junghans, 1672), 15–18 (I, 1, 18–21).

31 As in Pufendorf, *De jure*, 18 (JNG, I, 1, 21): 'Dantur enim qualitates morales patibiles, quae certo modo judicium hominum afficere intelliguntur; sicut inter qualitates physicas eo nomine vocantur, quibus facultas sensitiva afficitur; ut est honor, ignominia, auctoritas, gravitas, claritas, obscuritas, & similia.' For a seminal interpretation emphasising the role of moral passions in Pufendorf's theory, see Haara's recent publication: Heikki Haara, *Pufendorf's Theory of Sociability: Passions, Habits and Social Order* (Cham: Springer, 2018).

32 Pufendorf, *De jure*, 30 (JNG I, 2, 8): 'Adhibentur igitur potissimum demonstrationes in moralibus circa qualitates morales hactenus, ut eas actionibus & personis certo competere [...] constet; puta, an haec actio sit justa vel injusta, an in hanc personam, in genere consideratam, cadat hoc jus, aut haec obligatio.'

33 However, consciousness plays an important role in guiding egoistic and social passions; cf. Haara, *Pufendorf's theory*, 74–80.

34 This consciousness is a feature of voluntaristic imposition of moral entities and does not imply, of course, any rational access to a set of natural values as by Grotius. For this difference between Grotius and Pufendorf, see Knud Haakonssen, *Natural law and moral philosophy. From Grotius to the Scottish Enlightenment* (Cambridge: Cambridge University Press, 1996), 41.

> and the imputation of which every Man looks on as the foulest Disgrace.[35]

On the other side of this obligation of honest speech appears the right of the recipient to understand the speaker. Pufendorf aims at expounding these natural obligations and rights related to human communication. The role of speech performances played in the imposition of moral qualities is not central to Pufendorf's theory of language; or, at least, it is a matter of interpretation to explain the degree to which moral epistemology is dependent on the public use of speech.[36]

Bethlen seems to occupy an indifferent position on the Pufendorfian-Grotian natural conditions of social communication, even if he couples the genesis of civic-moral qualities with a conventional use of language in intersubjective human relations. Instead of treating the problem of the truth value of reputation,[37] Bethlen establishes a narrow relationship between public speech acts and moral epistemology. Use of language is void of truth value: performative speech acts simply produce physically effective civic-moral qualities. The distinction between the ineffective simplicity of reputation in private communication, on the one hand (IV.1), and the reputation's transcending this original situation, on the other (IV.2), does not imply the truth of reputation in the former case and in the falsity of reputation in the latter. Bethlen's distinction rests on the difference of causal deficiency in the former and effectiveness in the latter. A true or false reputation *may* as well induce physical changes as *not*. This, of course, is in harmony with Bethlen's conception of the low-level consciousness of speech acts: Pufendorf's natural obligation of straightforwardness presupposes a high level of consciousness of human utterances. Timothy J. Hochstrasser pointed out very convincingly how the late Pufendorf emphasised that only an adult with complete speech competence is able to perform communicative speech acts that are bearers of the imposition of the

---

35 Pufendorf: *Of the Law of Nature and Nations*, transl. Basil Kennett. The Fourth Edition (London: [Aris], 1729), 316. Cf. Pufendorf, *De jure*, 394 (JNG, 4, 1, 8): 'Ex hisce igitur fundamentis liquido judicari potest, quid sit veritas, ad quam dicendam homines obligantur; quid item mendacium, tantopere omnibus honestis detestatum.'

36 I follow Hochstrasser's interpretation here: Timothy J. Hochstrasser, *Natural Law Theories in the Early Enlightenment* (Cambridge: Cambridge University Press, 2000), 82–95.

37 Nor did Jean Barbeyrac, Pufendorf's French editor, accept the Pufendorfian truth value of utterances – for him, these natural rules of using signs would imply the extreme consequence that each violation of them should be qualified as committing a crime. Cf. Avi Lifschitz, 'The Arbitrariness of the Linguistic Sign: Variations on an Enlightenment Theme,' *Journal of the History of Ideas*, 73 (2012/4): 537–557, esp. 541–543.

entities of moral sphere. This is the reason why Pufendorf rejected a strong innate theory of natural law: recognising natural law presupposes a conscious use of language. According to an innate theory of natural law, children should be aware of the complete knowledge of natural law – which contradicts the plain fact of experience that children learn language gradually.

Against this background, Bethlen's use of the Pufendorfian term 'moral or civic qualities' cannot imply acceptance of the German scholar's political theory. The differences in the field of the philosophy of mind and concerning the problem of the true value of public human speech witness Bethlen's essential departure from his master's doctrine in Heidelberg. However, the differences cannot be accounted for as simple misunderstandings, but rather as a kind of reinterpretation of the ontology proper to the Pufendorfian political and moral sphere. To gain a better insight into Bethlen's reading of 'moral or civic qualities,' I suggest a simple intertextual experiment. Let us substitute the Pufendorfian expression 'civic and moral qualities' for the Hobbesian phrase 'means of power' in Bethlen's text quoted above.

> And thence there come into the world these words and *means of power* by men: good or bad reputation, reproach, slander, scold, accusation or praise, honour, dignity, and good or bad remembrance in their lives as well as after their deaths.[38]

All that Bethlen explores under the Pufendorfian label of *civic and moral qualities* relates in fact the *means of Hobbesian power* as described from either a psychological or an intersubjective perspective in chapter 6 or 10 of *Leviathan* (1651) or in the introductory passages of *De Cive* (1642), respectively. Although Hobbes's name is mentioned only once in the Preface to *Elementa*, the new edition of Pufendorf's early publication identified no fewer than 27 passages where Pufendorf alludes either critically or affirmatively to Hobbes.[39] Consid-

38 See the passage under my subsection IV.2. For a textual basis of this terminological change, cf. Hobbes: *Leviathan*, 41 (chap. 10): '*Naturall Power*, is the eminence of the Faculties of Body, or Mind: [...] *Instrumentall* are those *Powers*, which acquired by these, or by fortune, are *means* and Instruments to acquire more: as Riches, Reputation, Friends, and the Secret working of God [...]. For the nature of Power, is in this point, like to Fame, increasing as it proceeds; or like the motion of heavy bodies, which the further they go, make still the more hast.'

39 Cf. Thomas Behme, 'Einleitung,' in Samuel Pufendorf, *Elementa jurisprudentiae universalis*, ed. Thomas Behme (Berlin: Akademie Verlag, 1999), xvii. For a detailed analysis of the Hobbesian roots of Pufendorf's social theory, cf. Fiammetta Palladini, 'Pufendorf disciple of Hobbes: The nature of man and the state of nature: The doctrine of *socialitas*,' *History of European Ideas*, 34 (2008/1): 26–60.

ering the Heidelberg lectures, attended by Bethlen in 1661, Pufendorf might have treated Hobbes's philosophy in a more explicit way than he did in *Elementa*. Consequently, the German scholar's lectures in Heidelberg could ultimately have supported Bethlen in implementing the Pufendorfian phrase 'moral or civic qualities' with Hobbesian content. As regards *Leviathan*, in the chapters that introduce the psychological states of humans in the natural state, Hobbes did not yet proceed to his positive theory of a normative conception of absolute power – the preliminary discussions of phenomena in social psychology, particularly in the context of social communication, have the function of ideological critique. As later passages bear witness, Bethlen does not go on to accept the ultimately Hobbesian view on politics – however, the close relationship between social passions and interactions of language is a common feature in Bethlen's and Hobbes's thinking. Bethlen's claim that *civic and moral qualities* promote or impede one's advancement in the human community implies a Hobbesian strategy of the individual's survival among intersubjective relations prior to contractual relations. Individual advancement is expressed in the same way: 'Also, what quality soever maketh a man beloved, or feared of many; or the reputation of such quality, is Power';[40] consequently, Bethlen's reputation is best characterised by the famous Hobbesian formulation: 'Reputation of power is power.'[41]

4 Honour, Shame and Ambition

Section Two of Bethlen's Preface considered the maintenance of self-interest as dependent on civic-moral qualities. The individual – so to say – must survive in social interactions, and his survival demands a strategy of avoiding impediments or using opportunities provided by society. Bethlen's main theme is not social peace or maintenance of a commonwealth; his theoretical interest is focused on the individual in society and not on the society of individuals constituted through the establishment of political authority.

Bethlen picks up the quality of honour from the series of civic-moral qualities that result in the definition of reputation: 'And thence comes that lovely Helen or idol which the world worships under the name of honour.'[42] In the first instance, Bethlen makes a distinction between secular and spiritual

40 Hobbes: *Leviathan*, 41 (ch. 10).

41 Hobbes: *Leviathan*, 41 (ch. 10).

42 Bethlen, *Autobiography*, 27; Bethlen, *Élete*, 411: 'És ebből jő már ki a világnak az a szép Helénája vagy bálványa, amelyet becsület neve alatt imád a világ.'

honour. Spiritual honour is explained theologically within the framework of trinitology: the Father honours in his Son the Son's honourable values; these values are emanated to the created world. Individuals possessing these values of divine origin are honoured by others who discover them in the former. Honoured individuals honour in turn those others because they observe the fact that their honoured values are not their own but are of divine origin. That is why spiritual honour is reciprocal: men cannot vindicate honoured values for themselves. The honoured persons do not deserve honour self-sufficiently, and, consequently, the honour directed upon them merits honour in return.

This spiritual honour demands that humans meet overly strict requirements. After some passages, Bethlen leaves these strict theological demands behind and makes *secular* honour his main subject. Honour is expressed with outward signs that may as well be non-linguistic signs, such as letting someone enter a place ahead of one and bending one's knees. However, fear, silent hearkening, obedience and recognition of political power over the individual (expressed by the Hungarian term *uralás*[43]) are all among the sensual manifestations of honour. Linguistic expressions of honour are paradigmatically honouring speech, praise, flattery and ascribing social labels.

Bethlen introduces shame and ambition as some kinds of meta-passions of honour:

> From these [i.e. from one's honour from the perspective of others – JS] there arise and are born naturally in a man two things: *amibitio* or *generositas*, *gloriae cupido*, which is the desire for favourable judgement upon him, and shame, disgrace, *pudor*, which is fear and horror of unfavourable judgement.[44]

Ambition and shame are passions related or superadded to socially constructed honour. They are affective extensions of civic-moral qualities: civic-moral qualities produce the passions of shame and ambition in the same mechanical way as if they were produced by performative speech acts. Shame and

43 Bethlen, *Autobiography*, 27; Bethlen, *Élete*, 411. – Bernard Adams's translation of the term *uralás* using the English word *domination* is misleading, insofar as the Hungarian phrase refers to the recognition of domination from the perspective of a person subjected to someone else's power.

44 Bethlen, *Autobiography*, 28; Bethlen, *Élete*, 413: 'Ezekből származik vagy ugyan természet szerént születik az emberben kettő: az ambitio vagy generositas, gloriae cupido, mely annak az ő felőle való jó ítíletnek kívánása; és a szégyen, szemérem, pudor, mely attól a bal ítílettől való félelem, irtózás.'

ambition function as a kind of emotional management of social honour and recognition. They aim to articulate an individual strategy which enables the social agent to avoid negative evaluations and to promote positive ones in others.

However, neither shame nor ambition as one's psychological disposition depends on whether the evaluative judgements of others are correct or false. Should my fellows in a society make a *false* judgement of my intended act, I will intend *not* to perform the act in question; that is, I will feel ashamed to do so *as if* the expected evaluations of my fellows in a society were *right*. According to Bethlen, the certainty of the ultimately correct judgement about myself made by my conscience is not so strong that it would be able to eliminate my naturally-felt shame caused by the expected unfavourable judgement of others, even if the latter is false. It is the same with ambition: Even if the morsel of conscience informs me correctly concerning the evil of my planned act in the future, I will ambitiously intend to perform it because of the expected favourable judgement of others in society. This is not Bethlen's last word on the problem of naturally-felt shame and ambition, but before investigating them outside of the social context in the next section, let us remain within the bounds of human social status.

Honour and associated passions penetrate the whole society. Bethlen lists four levels on which honour determines the life of the human community.[45] Social institutions, such as family and church, are based on honour, as well as the recognition of different types of practical knowledge in industrial society. Interestingly, the social institution of the church is deduced from the secular honour felt by the members of the church towards their superiors: the high claims of theological honour play no role in its legitimation.

The most important level is the relationship between political authority and political subjects. Empowerment of representatives of political authority, or any kind of political office, is based alone on their honour, felt and expressed by the political subjects. The subjects feel real honour toward them; this feeling entails the people's hope and faith that the representatives not only have the qualities required for governance, but also the corresponding *will* to act according to these honoured qualities. Bethlen's emphasis is on the holistic nature of honouring as political recognition: there is no possibility for the legitimation of political power other than deriving it from the politico-psychological phenomenon of honour. Therefore, the mechanical and causal series of *unreflected speech performances – reputation – civic-moral qualities –*

45 Bethlen, *Autobiography*, 31–32; Bethlen, *Élete*, 414–416.

honour and other social passions results in the *legitimation of political authority*.

However, the Hobbesian line of thinking on the human condition in its pre-contractarian perspective ends here. After quoting the famous claim of Cicero, 'Salus populi suprema lex' (Cicero, *De legibus* 3, 3, 8), Bethlen continues his Hungarian text in Latin:

> Cuicumque et quomodocumque tandem populus in se dominandi supremam potestatem et suam erga illos obedientiam detulit, id cum suae salutis et summae majestatis penes se reservatione fecit.
>
> Finally, to whomsoever and in whatever way the people have transferred the *supreme power* that he may rule over it and be obeyed by it, this the people have done with the reservation to itself of its own salvation and of the *supreme majesty*.[46]

Through the roundabout way of passions, Bethlen makes political authority completely dependent on the sovereignty of people. The idea of limiting the political power of the ruler by deducing *suprema potestas* from *majestas populi* reveals Bethlen's sympathy for the Monarchomachs' theory[47] – one may suspect the influence of Johannes Althusius[48] (1557–1638) in these lines.[49] Even if Bethlen follows the Hobbesian method of reducing political behaviour to psycho-physiological states of humans, he nevertheless rejects the normative consequence of the unlimited power of political authority Hobbes drew from this method. Bethlen's theory of political authority is not a normative one: he does not speak about certain conditions, the fulfilment of which grants a right or imposes a duty of resistance. Bethlen's method is descriptive: if political subjects do not feel honour toward representatives of a political magistrate, they may resist and withdraw political legitimation.

---

46 Bethlen, *Autobiography*, 31; Bethlen, *Élete*, 414 (emphases added – JS).

47 Horst Dreitzel, 'Die Monarchomachen,' in *Grundriss der Geschichte der Philosophie. Die Philosophie des 17 Jahrhunderts*, ed. Helmut Holzhey and Wilhelm Schmidt-Biggemann, vol. 4/1 (Basel: Schwabe & Co AG, 2001), 613–625.

48 Horst Dreitzel, 'Johannes Althusius,' in *Grundriss der Geschichte der Philosophie. Die Philosophie des 17 Jahrhunderts*, ed. Helmut Holzhey and Wilhelm Schmidt-Biggemann, vol. 4/1 (Basel: Schwabe & Co AG, 2001), 625–638.

49 For the classic exposition of Althusius's theory of *majestas*, see Otto Friedrich von Gierke, *Johannes Althusius und die Entwicklung der naturrechtlichen Staatstheorien* (Breslau: Koebner, 1880), 18–36.

So far, the line of thought remained within the boundaries of a positive political community that outlined a political psychology that underlies social life. If people's sovereignty based on a political psychology of honour is apt to construct limitations against the political power of authority, then Bethlen has something to say about honour, shame and ambition as psychological states *outside* of a political community; that is, he must present a theory of these basic passions as *natural* endowments of mankind. This is exactly what happens in Part Eight of the Preface.

5 Natural Passions

Part Eight begins by establishing an optimistic anthropology. Historical evidence of consensus of all nations demonstrates that even original sin could not annihilate the basic moral distinction between good and bad, human conscience and belief in any kind of god. One of Bethlen's most fascinating statements is that intellectual understanding functioning in the basic moral distinction relies on the affective capacity of men. The purpose of the present paper does not require a deeper analysis of this claim.

In accordance with the contemporary comparative studies of religions, in the fashion of Gerardus Joannes Vossius[50] and Herbert of Cherbury,[51] Bethlen states that all nations 'adore stone, tree, snake and frog, rather than living without a god.'[52] However, Bethlen changes the perspective immediately from the worship of phenomena in the physical world to the general features of political psychology.[53]

---

50 Gerardus Joannes Vossius, *De theologia gentili et physiologia christiana sive de origine ac progressu idololatriae* [...] *Libri IX* (Amsterdam: Blaeu, 1668).

51 Herbert of Cherbury, *De religione gentilium, errorumque apud eos causis* (Amstelodami: Blaeu, 1663). For Vossius's and Cherbury's comparative investigations of religion, see Martin Mulsow, 'Antiquarianism and Idolatry: The *Historia* of Religions in the Seventeenth Century,' in *Historia: Empiricism and Erudition in Early Modern Europe*, ed. G. Pomata and N.G. Siraisi (Cambridge, MA and London: The MIT Press, 2005), 181–210.

52 Bethlen, *Autobiography*, 45; Bethlen, *Élete*, 427: 'Készebb követ, fát, kígyót, békát imádni, mintsem magát Isten nélkül hagyni.'

53 This change of perspective is in accordance with Martin Mulsow's thesis on the idea of an early modern political theology based on comparative studies of religion; cf. Martin Mulsow, *Moderne aus dem Untergrund* (Hamburg: Meiner, 2002), 173–181.

> There is no nation on earth in which there is no worship, oath-taking, blessing, cursing [*átok*], reproach [*szitok*], some slight modesty, glory, outrage, reward and punishment.[54]

The above thesis that social passions originate mechanically is settled within the framework of the psychological aspects of natural religion. Consequently, Bethlen directs his line of thinking to the borderline between positive social status and the natural condition of humans. One may suppose that the phenomena of social psychology exist only under the circumstances of a positive state of a commonwealth:

> Now let us suppose that glory, outrage, reward and punishment are entirely human inventions for the maintenance of society.[55]

Bethlen expresses the volatile and unstable feature of these social emotions in describing *reproach* as 'the blazing up of the angry heart, as it were, the burning of a sooty chimney.'[56] Here, we have the idea discussed above: inclination to glory is ambition towards expecting reward and honour because of acting in accordance with the interest of the common good or, as Bethlen puts it, 'maintenance of society.' *Outrage*, on the other hand, is punishment for violation of the interest of the common good. Should these emotions have their origin deep in human nature, the content of the common good directing them in a social context proves to be contingent in its very nature, or, as Bethlen writes, they 'are entirely *human inventions* for the maintenance of society.' However, mere fear of punishment, in cases when the common good is violated, cannot account perfectly for feeling shame, nor can the hope of reward, in the case of acting in accordance with the common good, account perfectly for keeping promises in oath-taking.

> Would there be worship, oath-taking, blessing and cursing if man did not believe in God, who has the power and the will, if you pray, to listen

54 Bethlen, *Autobiography*, 45, Bethlen, *Élete*, 427: 'Nincs nemzetség a világon, akiben imádság, esküvés, áldás, átok, szitok, és valami kis szemérem, dícsíret, gyalázat, büntetés, jutalom ne légyen.'

55 Bethlen, *Autobiography*, 45; Bethlen, *Élete*, 427: 'Már tegyük fel bár, hogy a dícsíret, gyalázat, jutalom, büntetés egészen csak emberi találmány a közönséges békesség megtartására.'

56 Bethlen, *Autobiography*, 45; Bethlen, *Élete*, 427: 'a szitok mintegy a megharagutt, felgyúladott kormos kéménynek, a szívnek kigyúlása.'

> and come to your aid; to punish him that swears falsely; to implement blessing and cursing? For surely everyone knows that that is all merely words, the motion of the tongue and the air, and if there is none to give it power, it is all futility and the wind bears it away. Would he that swears have any regard for that or he to whom he swears, he that blesses or curses or those to whom these are directed? Would they make use of them? Would they fear them? If they had no faith in them. Would the powerful man who fears no punishment blush and feel ashamed where no one can see him if his conscience did not prick him?[57]

While leaving the positive social context behind, Bethlen arrives at the domain of the natural state of humans. Bethlen appeals to God as an occasional guarantor of the causal efficacy of speech performances, such as oath-taking, blessing or cursing. However, this does not mean that the occurrence of these social phenomena and speech behaviours beyond the positive legal state relies on *supernatural* moments of belief. An inclination towards pursuing honour or avoiding shameful actions represents *natural* endowments of mankind. Addressing the Hobbesian figure of the *powerful individual* in the natural state, Bethlen declares that he feels shame even if knowledge of society, negative evaluation and potential punishment for violating the common good are suspended. Therefore, shame proves to be not only an emotional management of esteem and honour in a community, but also an emotion which mirrors the non-conventional, natural order of values.

At first glance, Bethlen's theory of natural passions seems to reiterate the traditional view of the correspondence between objective moral values and naturally-felt passions. Pufendorf argues explicitly against a theory of this kind in *De jure naturae et gentium* I, ii, 7, observing the general conviction that naturally-felt shame and its physical sign of blushing are proof of moral realism.[58] According to Pufendorf, the psychological phenomena of shame and

---

57 Bethlen, *Autobiography*, 45; Bethlen, *Élete*, 427–428: 'De az imádság, esküvés, áldás, átok volna-é, ha az ember az Istent nem hinné, akinek vagyon arra ereje s akaratja, hogy ha imádkozol, meghallgassa és segítsen; ha hamisan esküszik valaki, megbüntesse; az áldást és az átkot teljesítse? Mert hiszen azt minden tudja, hogy az mind csak szó, nyelvnek és aërnek mozgása, és ha nincs, aki erőt adjon néki, mind csak hijábanvalóság, elviszi a szél. Ezt az esküvő, és akinek esküsznek, az áldó vagy átkozó, és az, akire az igazgattatik, becsülné-é? élne-é véle? félne-é tőle? ha úgy nem hinné. Megpirulna-é, szégyenlene-é az ember ott is, ahol senki sem látja, a hatalmas, aki a büntetéstől nem fél, ha a lélekismereti nem ijesztené.'

58 Pufendorf, *De jure*, 28–30 (JNG, I, ii, 7). For a detailed analysis, cf. Kari Saastamoinen, *The Morality of the Fallen Man* (Helsinki: SHS, 1995), 150–152. Saastamoinen described very convincingly the extent to which Pufendorf had relied on Descartes's treatment of shame

ambition are related to the pursuit of esteem in society, and, as such, they express conventional values. While denying the moral realism implicated by natural passions, Pufendorf concedes that it is not without reason that God implanted these passions in mankind. According to Pufendorf, the divine origin of human shame does not contradict his anti-realistic claim that they are expressions of values in a positive social state. Natural passions and their physical signs are beneficial for human society, but they only function within the boundaries of the moral space imposed by human agents. Every plausible interpretation of natural passions has to presuppose a human imposition of moral qualities, as well as the ontology of social phenomena built on it.

While relating shame and ambition to honour, Bethlen explicitly perceives the social context of shame. However, he seems to accept moral realism, while attributing an evaluative function to shame outside of society. However, the anti-intellectualistic vein of his argumentation prevents him from adopting a world view like that of the Thomists, who emphasised the *intellectual* capacity of humans to realise acts that further basic inclinations towards self-preservation, the propagation of the species and the rearing of offspring. Instead of Aristotelian inclinations towards social integration, Bethlen drew upon basic egotistical-psychological traits of societies at the doorstep of industrialisation – albeit in terms of natural religion.

In this sense, shame is strongly tied to conscience. Even if Bethlen introduced conscience as a natural faculty of humans with a theistic origin, without the condition of revealed religion, one might ask whether feeling shame beyond and independently of the conventional positive state of a community has its origin in the anthropological standard of original sin.

Bethlen, a devout Calvinist, is aware of this challenge of Augustinian theological anthropology and addresses the relationship between shame and original sin directly:

> From this it is immediately apparent that the words of Moses are no *fabula* and that clothing is Adam's invention, not only against warm or cool, but also against shame. [...] In vain and falsely have certain atheists and profaners postulated that Moses and others like him wished to obtain

and pride in *Les Passions de l'âme* (§ 205–207). Since Bethlen discredited any theory of an independent mind for the explanation of both social and pre-social behaviour, his views must essentially differ from Pufendorfian hermeneutics of Cartesian passions. Bethlen's maintenance of naturally-felt shame proves to be a rather a deistic trust in a holistic system of the mechanical universe instead of turning back to the all-penetrating harmony of a Thomistic universe.

> honour for themselves, domination over others and the obedience of the simple, and therefore invented God, the soul, heaven, hell etc.[59]

One should not be misguided by Bethlen's apology of the Mosaic narrative against allegedly atheistic or profane interpretations. His vision of the relationship between shame and original sin is entirely rational and part of Enlightenment thinking. It is not the Mosaic law, which provides us with a theological interpretation of natural shame; it is the rational theory of naturally-felt shame which justifies the *truth* of the inspired Mosaic narrative of Adam's fall. In other words, we do not feel shame beyond social conventions because we are heirs to the theologically established original sin, but we as Christians inherit original sin because we, like members of other confessions, are naturally ashamed to perform various acts. Bethlen explores a thin area for shame as a natural emotion between the robust interpretative perspectives of social psychology and theological anthropology. He does not deny that one may feel shame because he or she experiences dishonour from his or her fellow citizens, and he does not rule out the possibility that one has a bad conscience while feeling shame. It is rather the natural emotion of shame which allows for shame as an individual strategy for avoiding dishonour in society and for upholding the *truth* of the Mosaic narrative of Adam's feeling of shame after the Fall.

Therefore, the mechanistic interpretation of passions relies on a religious anthropology outside of society. Bethlen develops his idea of natural religion against a double background of desire for honour in ancient religions and in the present human condition.

First, the main feature of this basic instinct contains the desire to be honoured even after one's death in the ancient pagan world. Bethlen agrees with Pierre Bayle's famous essay *Pensées diverses sur la comète*[60] that this expectation is a false one: after one's death, the surviving soul will not be affected through the honour of people living in this physical world. However, Bayle and Bethlen draw different conclusions from this view. While Bayle holds that an

59 Bethlen, *Autobiography*, 45–46; Bethlen, *Élete*, 428: 'És immár ebből látszik ki, hogy a Mózes írása nem fabula, a köntös nemcsak hideg, meleg, hanem a szégyen ellen való találmánya is Ádámnak. [...] Hijába s hamisan vetették némely bolond atheusok s profánusok azt is elé, hogy Mózes és más hasonlók magoknak becsületet, másokon való uralkodást, és az együgyű embereknek hozzájuk való engedelmességeket akarták szerzeni, és úgy költötték az Istent, a lelket, mennyországot, poklot etc.'

60 Pierre Bayle, *Pensées diverses sur la comète: écrites à un docteur de Sorbonne, à l'occasion de la comète qui parut au mois de décembre 1680* (Amsterdam: Reinier Leers, 1683), 529–531 (§ 173).

atheist would pursue honour just like a pagan or a Christian believer, without the hope of being affected by worldly honour after death, Bethlen maintains that the very fact of pursuing honour has natural theistic presuppositions. For him, the present-time passion to secure honour after death through building monuments etc. has in fact existed in humans in the past. This anthropological standard of mankind has a religious character, as it presupposes a belief in the survival of one's soul after death, even if the conception of the immortal soul's being affected by earthly affairs is a false one.[61]

What the present human condition concerns, the passion of shame for those in power, independent of prospects of social punishment, does not destroy the human instinct of pursuing honour. In this sense, natural shame is driven by a kind of eschatological recognition, whereby the scene of honour is changed from human society to the relationship between God and man. Bethlen never seems to forsake human selfishness: even the individual feeling shame outside of a community is driven by his desire to be honoured by God.[62]

6 Conclusion

Bethlen's intellectual life was situated at the crossroads of two types of Enlightenment. First, he became involved in the cultural and political life of the De Witt brothers' Low Countries during his university studies in the early 1660s,[63] he gained rich experience of everyday life in London at the same time,[64] and he promoted close relations with English and Dutch diplomats later during his political career.[65] On the other hand, he was faced with the 'actual'

61 Bethlen, *Autobiography*, 17–21, 51; Bethlen, *Élete*, 403–407, 433.

62 Bethlen, *Autobiography*, 45–46; Bethlen, *Élete*, 427–428.

63 Bethlen, *Autobiography*, 187–191; Bethlen, *Élete*, 573–580.

64 Bethlen, *Autobiography*, 196–198; Bethlen, *Élete*, 585–587.

65 In this study, I cannot outline the complex theme of Bethlen's diplomatic activities. However, Bethlen's early orientation in Transylvanian anti-Habsburg foreign policy towards an alliance with France and Poland in the 1660s was replaced by a pro-Habsburg policy with a balance of power supported by the Brandenburg-Dutch-English line of diplomacy at the Vienna court. Within the latter political context, Bethlen had personal ties to English and Dutch politicians, such as to England's ambassador William Paget (1637–1713) and to the Dutch ambassadors Conrad Heemskerck (1646–1702) and Jacob Jan Hamel-Bruyninx in Vienna. The former two were personally informed about Bethlen's Diploma Leopoldinum project before he submitted it to Emperor Leopold's foreign affairs faction; Bethlen, *Autobiography*, 409–410; Bethlen, *Élete*, 820–821. On Hamel-Bruyninx, referred

Enlightenment of the Vienna Court, in introducing the new political, economic and legal system in Transylvania after its liberation from Ottoman rule during the last decade of the seventeenth century.[66] Drawing on this opposition, one may somewhat metaphorically say that Bethlen's Preface mirrored the ideas of the *ideal* Enlightenment in the prison of the '*actual*' Enlightenment. But the natural law theory of Bethlen's envisaged ideal Enlightenment was in crisis itself. Bethlen's approach to developing a vision of society based on the self-interested pursuit of honour reflects the transformative process of social philosophy from continental natural law theory into the common-sense explanation of human society in eighteenth-century British thinking.[67]

In composing the Preface to his *Autobiography* in 1708, Bethlen shared many of his contemporaries' mistrust of the contractual framework of the community based on an abstract natural law. However, his political publications during the preceding decades demonstrate that, at some point, he had been convinced of the natural moral necessity obliging him to obey the political authority of the Vienna Court.[68] Nonetheless, his hopes for an economically prosperous Transylvania with political stability within the body politic of the Habsburg Empire dissipated in 1704 at the latest. His trust in natural law theory explaining political legitimacy and moral obligation in public affairs faded away with the abandonment of the recognition of Habsburg claims of political superiority. From a theoretical point of view, Bethlen no longer accepted the step from unsocial individuals towards constituting community and did not allow for the social contract, either in its totally artificial Hobbesian version or in its voluntarist Pufendorfian version. According to Knud Haakonssen's detailed analysis, the crisis of natural law proved to be a prolific one as regards

to as 'my old friend, the Dutch ambassador' by Bethlen, see Bethlen's correspondence between 1704 and 1712, József Jankovics, ed., *Bethlen Miklós levelei* [*The correspondence of Miklós Bethlen*] (Budapest: Akadémiai, 1987), vol. 2 (1699–1716), passim.

66 For an outline of this process in Habsburg policy in Transylvania from a Protestant point of view, see Bálint Keserű, 'Shaping Protestant Networks in Habsburg Transylvania: The Beginnings (1686–1699),' in *A Divided Hungary in Europe: Exchanges, Networks and Representations, 1541–1699*, vol. 2 – *Diplomacy, Information Flow and Cultural Exchange*, ed. Szymon Brzeziński and Áron Zarnóczki (Newcastle upon Tyne: Cambridge Scholars Publishing 2014), 183–202.

67 Haakonssen, *Natural law*, 58–62.

68 The best example of Bethlen's recognition of the Vienna Court's political authority against the background of natural law theory is his public letter to Franz Ulrich Kinsky, the counselor of the Vienna Geheimrat. For a modern edition of the Latin text, see József Jankovics and László Szörényi, 'Bethlen Miklós ismeretlen "nyílt levele" Franz Ulrich Kinskyhez (1691)' ['Miklós Bethlen's unknown "open letter" to Ulrich Kinsky'], *Irodalomtörténeti Közlemények* 117 (2013/6): 692–721.

the development of the Scottish Enlightenment. The representative thinkers of that movement sought a moral basis for the community in the immediate qualities of individuals deserving to be objects of other-respecting passions of other fellows in a society. Bethlen's Preface to his *Autobiography*, being itself an Eastern European momentary snapshot of these phenomena in Western Europe, occupies an intervening position between the poles of this development. He *already* rejects the contractual ramifications of society based on the explanatory power of natural law theory, but, at the same time, he does not *yet* substitute them for the other-respecting sentiments of social agents. For Bethlen, a contract among individuals consciously abandoning rights and attributing this to a sovereign is impossible. Enabling a political authority with power is an unconscious act of the social passion of honour. On the other hand, honour never forsakes its perspective of realising self-interest. There is no sign of either a *disinterested affection* in the fashion of Hutcheson[69] or of a Humean *moral sentiment*[70] or of the Smithian passion of *sympathy*.[71] For Bethlen, human desire for honour will never respect the interest of others. In order to avoid Mandeville's anarchistic conception of '*private vices, publick benefits*,'[72] Bethlen makes an effort to sanctify the private vice of pursuing self-interest through the passionate seeking of honour within a conception of natural religion. However, where the shame of those in power might seem to be a self-limiting moment in respect of the interests of others in a society on the surface, the real reason for his behaviour proves to be his selfishness on a higher level. The shame of the powerful equals his ambition to be recognised by God.

Acknowledgements

The research was supported by the Hungarian Scientific Research Fund ('NKFIH 137963 History of Hungarian Philosophy in Early Modernity (1570–1710)'). I am indebted to Gábor Gángó for his comments and to Thomas Williams for the proofreading.

69 Francis Hutcheson, *Inquiry into the original of our ideas of beauty and virtue* (London: Darby, 1725), 143.

70 David Hume, *An Enquiry Concerning the Principles of Morals* (London: Millar, 1751), 197–213 (Appendix I. Concerning moral sentiment).

71 Adam Smith, *The Theory of Moral Sentiments* (London-Edinburgh: Millar-Kincaid and Bell, 1761), 1–10 (Part I, Sec. 1, ch. 1 Of Sympathy).

72 Mandeville, Bernard, *The fable of the bees: or, private vices, publick benefits* (London: Roberts, 1714).

Bibliography

Primary Sources

Bayle, Pierre, *Pensées diverses sur la comète: écrites à un docteur de Sorbonne, à l'occasion de la comète qui parut au mois de décembre 1680*, Amsterdam: Reinier Leers, 1683.

Bethlen, Miklós, 'Élete leírása magától,' in Éva V. Windisch, ed., *Kemény János és Bethlen Miklós művei*, 399–981, Budapest: Szépirodalmi, 1980.

Bethlen, Miklós, *The Autobiography of Miklós Bethlen*, transl. Bernard Adams, London: Paul Kegan, 2004.

Clerselier, Claude, 'Preface,' in René Descartes, *L'Homme de René Descartes et vn traitté de la formation du foetus dv mesme avthevr. Auec des Remarques de Louys de La Forge*, e–ooiii, Paris: Charles Angot, 1664.

Descartes, René, 'Discours de la méthode,' in *Oeuvres de Descartes*, ed. Charles Adam and Paul Tannery, vol. VI, 1–78, Paris: Cerf, 1902.

Herbert of Cherbury, *De religione gentilium, errorumque apud eos causis*, Amstelodami: Blaeu, 1663.

Hobbes, Thomas, *De Corpore. Elementorum Philosophiæ Sectio Prima*, London: Crook, 1655.

Hobbes, Thomas, *Leviathan Or The Matter, Forme, & Power Of A Common-Wealth Ecclesiasticall And Civill*, London: Crook, 1651.

Hume, David, *An Enquiry Concerning the Principals of Morals*, London: Millar, 1751.

Hutcheson, Francis, *Inquiry into the original of our ideas of beauty and virtue*, London: Darby, 1725.

Mandeville, Bernard, *The fable of the bees: or, private vices, publick benefits*, London: Roberts, 1714.

Pufendorf, Samuel, *De jure naturae et gentium libri octo*, Lund: Junghans, 1672.

Pufendorf, Samuel, *Elementa jurisprudentiae universalis*, ed. Thomas Behme, Berlin: Akademie Verlag, 1999.

Pufendorf, Samuel, *Elementorum Jurisprudentiae Universalis Libri II*, Den Haag: Adrian Vlacq, 1660.

Pufendorf, Samuel, *Of the Law of Nature and Nations*. Transl. Basil Kennett. The Fourth Edition, London: [Aris], 1729.

Vossius, Gerardus Johannes, *De theologia gentili et physiologia christiana sive de origine ac progressu idololatriae* [...] *Libri IX*, Amsterdam: Blaeu, 1668.

Secondary Sources

Asselt, Willem J. van, *The Federal Theology of Johannes Cocceius (1603–1669)*, Leiden: Brill, 2001.

Behme, Thomas, 'Einleitung,' in Samuel Pufendorf, *Elementa jurisprudentiae universalis*, ed. Thomas Behme, ix–xxiv, Berlin: Akademie Verlag, 1999.

Bene, Sándor, *Theatrum politicum: Nyilvánosság, közvélemény és irodalom a korai újkorban*, Debrecen: Kossuth Egyetemi Kiadó, 1999.

Benrath, Adolf, 'The Heidelberger Vorlesungsverzeichnisse aus den Jahren 1655, 1658 bis 1662 und 1685,' in *Heidelberger Jahrbücher* 5, 85–103, Berlin, Göttingen and Heidelberg: Springer, 1961.

Böhling, Frank, 'Einleitung,' in Samuel Pufendorf, *De jure naturae et gentium. Dritter Teil: Materialien und Kommentar*, 3–57, Berlin and Boston: De Gruyter, 2014.

Dreitzel, Horst, 'Die Monarchomachen,' in *Grundriss der Geschichte der Philosophie. Die Philosophie des 17 Jahrhunderts*, ed. Helmut Holzhey and Wilhelm Schmidt-Biggemann, vol. 4/1, 613–625, Basel: Schwabe & Co AG, 2001.

Dreitzel, Horst, 'Johannes Althusius,' in *Grundriss der Geschichte der Philosophie. Die Philosophie des 17 Jahrhunderts*, ed. Helmut Holzhey and Wilhelm Schmidt-Biggemann, vol. 4/1, 625–638, Basel: Schwabe & Co AG, 2001.

Dreitzel, Horst, 'Samuel Pufendorf,' in *Grundriss der Geschichte der Philosophie. Die Philosophie des 17 Jahrhunderts*, ed. Helmut Holzhey and Wilhelm Schmidt-Biggemann, vol. 4/2, 751–812, Basel: Schwabe & Co AG, 2001.

Förköli, Gábor, 'Miklós Zrínyi: un traité tacitiste hongrois et la réception tardive de l'étatisme,' in *Tacite et le tacitisme en Europe à l'époque moderne*, ed. Alexandra Merle and Alicia Oïffer-Bomsel, 501–516, Paris: Honoré Champion, 2017.

Gángó, Gábor, 'G.W. Leibniz's Candidature for the Chancellorship of Transylvania,' *Studia Leibnitiana* 47 (2015/1): 44–66.

Gierke, Otto Friedrich von, *Johannes Althusius und die Entwicklung der naturrechtlichen Staatstheorien*, Breslau: Koebner, 1880.

Gömöri, George, 'Miklós Bethlen,' in *Encyclopedia of Life Writing: Autobiographical and Biographical Forms*, ed. Margaretta Jolly, 102–103, London and Chicago: Fitzroy Dearborn Publishers, 2001.

Haakonssen, Knud, *Natural law and moral philosophy. From Grotius to the Scottish Enlightenment*, Cambridge: Cambridge University Press, 1996.

Haara, Heikki, *Pufendorf's Theory of Sociability: Passions, Habits and Social Order*, Cham: Springer, 2018.

Hanák, Tibor, *Geschichte der Philosophie in Ungarn*, München: Trofenik, 1990.

Hochstrasser, Timothy J., *Natural Law Theories in the Early Enlightenment*, Cambridge: Cambridge University Press, 2000.

Hungerland, Isabel C. and George R. Vick, 'Hobbes Theory of Signification,' *Journal of the History of Philosophy* 11 (1973/4): 459–482.

Jankovics, József, ed., *Bethlen Miklós levelei*, vol. 1–2, Budapest: Akadémiai, 1987.

Keserű, Bálint, 'Shaping Protestant Networks in Habsburg Transylvania: The Beginnings (1686–1699),' in *A Divided Hungary in Europe: Exchanges, Networks and*

Representations, 1541–1699, vol. 2 – *Diplomacy, Information Flow and Cultural Exchange*, ed. Szymon Brzeziński and Áron Zarnóczki, 183–202, Newcastle upon Tyne: Cambridge Scholars Publishing 2014.

Klaniczay, Tibor, 'Korszerű politikai gondolkodás és nemzetközi látókör Zrínyi műveiben,' in *Irodalom és ideológia a 16–17. században*, ed. Béla Varjas, 337–400, Budapest: Akadémiai, 1987.

Klaniczay, Tibor, 'Niccolo Zrínyi, Venezia e la letteratura della ragione di Stato,' in *Mélanges de littérature comparée et de philologie offerts à Mieczysław Brahmer*, 265–273, Warszawa: PWN-Éditions scientifiques de Pologne, 1967.

Lifschitz, Avi, 'The Arbitrariness of the Linguistic Sign: Variations on an Enlightenment Theme,' *Journal of the History of Ideas*, 73 (2012/4): 537–557.

Meusburger, Peter and Ferenc Próbáld, 'Scientific and Cultural Relations between Heidelberg University and Hungary over Five centuries,' in *Geographies of the University*, ed. Peter Meusburger, Michael Heffernan, and Laura Suarsana, 43–134, Cham: Springer, 2018.

Mulsow, Martin, 'Antiquarianism an Idololatry: The *Historia* of Religions in Seventeenth Century,' in *Historia: Empiricism and Erudition in Early Modern Europe*, ed. G. Pomata and N.G. Siraisi, 181–210, Cambridge, MA and London: The MIT Press.

Mulsow, Martin, *Moderne aus dem Untergrund*, Hamburg: Meiner, 2002.

Palladini, Fiammetta, 'Pufendorf disciple of Hobbes: The nature of man and the state of nature: The doctrine of *socialitas*,' *History of European Ideas*, 34 (2008/1): 26–60.

Petrasovszki, Anna, 'The Significance of Natural law as a Part of Legal Education in the Codification Process of 19th Century in Hungary,' in *Codification Achievements and Failures in the 19th–20th Century: 7th Conference on Legal History in Szeged*, ed. Mária Homoki-Nagy and Norbert Varga, 125–130, Szeged: University of Szeged, Faculty of Law and Political Sciences, 2018.

Pettit, Philip, *Made with Words. Hobbes on Language, Mind, and Politics*, Princeton and Oxford: Princeton University Press, 2008.

Saastamoinen, Kari, *The Morality of the Fallen Man*, Helsinki: SHS, 1995.

Schmaltz, Tad, *Early Modern Cartesianisms: Dutch and French Constructions*, Oxford: Oxford University Press, 2016.

Simon, József, 'Bethlen Miklós és az imádkozó automata,' *Magyar Filozófiai Szemle* 61 (2017/4): 147–167.

Simon, József, 'Filológiai és filozófiatörténeti megjegyzések Bethlen Miklós Önéletírásának Elöljáró beszédéhez,' *Irodalomtörténeti közlemények* 120 (2016/3): 299–314.

Smith, Adam, *The Theory of Moral Sentiments*, London and Edinburgh: Millar-Kincaid and Bell, 1761.

Szűcs, Zoltán Gábor, 'Természet, jog, teológia: egy fejezet a politikai diskurzus történetéből a 18. századi Magyarországon,' *Aetas* 26 (2011/2): 99–115.

Tezla, Albert, 'Bethlen Miklós,' in Albert Tezla, *Hungarian Authors. A Bibliographical Handbook*, 97–99, Cambridge MA: Belknapp Press of Harvard University Press, 1970.

Tolnai, Gábor, 'Miklós Bethlen un classique des anciens mémoires hongrois,' *Acta Litteraria Academiae Scientiarum Hungaricae* 12 (1970/3–4): 251–272.

Tóth, Zsombor, ed., *Bethlen Miklós – Válogatott bibliográfia*, Budapest: reciti, 2016.

Tóth, Zsombor, 'A Man for All Seasons: Exile, Suffering and Martyrdom in the Autobiography of Miklós Bethlen,' *Hungarian Studies*, 26 (2012/2): 273–284.

Trencsényi, Balázs and Márton Zászkalicky, ed., *Whose Love of Which Country? Composite States, National Histories and Patriotic Discourses in Early Modern East Central Europe*, Leiden: Brill, 2010.

Várkonyi, Ágnes R., 'The last decades of the independent principality (1660–1711),' in László Makkai and Zoltán Szász, eds.: *History of Transylvania*, vol. II. From 1606 to 1830, 325–397, New York: Columbia Press, 2002.

Zászkaliczky, Márton, 'A Bocskai-felkelés politikai nyelvei: Vázlat,' in: Márton Zászkaliczky and Gábor Kármán, eds., *Politikai nyelvek a 17. század első felének Magyarországán*, 11–84, Budapest: reciti, 2019.

PART 4

Russia

CHAPTER 11

Strube de Piermont: The Passionate Natural Law in Russia

Ivo Cerman

1 Introduction

In his short history of natural law, Carl Anton Martini remarked in the final sections that 'even Russia received a system of natural law from Struben.'[1] It appears then that 'Struben' – whose exact name was not specified there – was perceived as the founding father of natural law in Russia and yet he remains a figure literally unknown even to many specialists. Even Martini got his name wrong. It may come as a surprise that the name refers to a certain Strube de Piermont who is known from the history of French materialism as the author of a scandalous work on passions, which preceded Claude Adrien Helvétius by more than a decade.[2]

In what follows we try to reconstruct the profile of Strube's natural law theory and trace its relation to its intellectual sources and to the politics of legislation in Russia. We will start with the biographical context of his work in Russian diplomatic service and scientific institutions. The analysis of his work will be divided into a section on the outline of his natural law theory, a section on international law and finally a section about his reflections on Russian laws and Montesquieu.

1 Carl Anton Martini, *Lehrbegriff des Natur-, Staats und Völkerrechts*, vol. 1 (Wien: Sonnleithnerische Buchhandlung, 1784), 126, § 299 ('Auch Rußland hat von Struben ein System des Naturrechts erhalten.'); Carl Anton Martini, *De lege naturali positiones* (Wien: Joseph Kurzböck, 1762), 84, § 299 ('Vidit et Russia Stubsii J. N. systema').

2 See Lester G. Crocker, *Nature and Culture. Ethical Thought of the French Enlightenment* (Baltimore: Johns Hopkins University Press, 1963), 24–25, 206–215. He has even been mistaken for a French author: see Albert Soboul, Guy Lemarchand, and Michèle Fogel, *Le siècle des Lumières. L'essor (1715–1750)* (Paris: Presses universitaires de France, 1977), 573–574.

 | DOI:10.1163/9789004545847_012

2 Early Career and Arrival in Russia

Fréderic Henri Strube de Piermont who wrote mostly in French, was actually born Germany in 1704.[3] It is not certain whether he was a native of Hanover, Hällesprüng, Piermont, or Rugmont. On his entrance into Russian service, he claimed to have been born a Hanoverian subject. He also linked himself to the town of Piermont, which is the present-day Bad Pyrmont in Lower Saxony, where his alleged Francophone ancestors had settled.

The data about his early life are scanty, and his biography has not altered much since Pekarskiy's classic *History of the Imperial Academy of Sciences in Petersburg* of 1870.[4] Strube attended the University of Helmstedt where he graduated in 1727 with a dissertation on the substitutes of slaves in Roman and medieval law.[5] Strube himself claimed a more distinguished intellectual ancestry because he alleged that he was a disciple of Christian Thomasius.[6] In the preface to his most important work *Ebauche des lois naturelles*, he also claimed to have studied at the University of Halle.[7] In 1729 he demonstrated his connection with Halle when he published an obituary of Nikolaus Hieronymus Gundling.[8] Some scholars have called this intellectual linkage into doubt,[9]

3 For biographies of Strube see Peter Pekarskiy, *История императорской Академии наук в Петербурге* [History of Imperial Academy of Sciences in Petersburg] (Saint Petersburg: Imperatorskaya akademia nauk, 1870), vol. 1, 671–689; Grigoriy Samuilovich Feldstein, *Главные течения в истории науки уголовного права в России* [The Main Currents in the History of the Science of Penal Law in Russia] (Yaroslav: Typographia gubernskogo pravlenya, 1909), 151–166; Vladimir Emanuilovich Grabar, *Материалы к истории литературы международного права в России 1647–1917* [Sources for the History of Literature on International Law in Russia 1647–1917] (Moscow: Zercalo, 2003; 1st edition Moscow: Akademia nauk SSSR, 1958), 309–334; William E. Butler, 'F.G. Strube de Piermont and the Origins of Russian Legal History,' in *Russia in the Age of Enlightenment. Essays for Isabel de Madariaga*, ed. Roger Bartlett and Janet M. Hartley (London: Palgrave Macmillan, 1990), 125–141; Michael Silnizki, *Geschichte des gelehrten Rechts in Rußland. Jurisprudencija an den Universitäten des Russischen Reiches 1700–1835* (Frankfurt am Main: Vittorio Klostermann, 1997), 68–80; Konstantin Dimitriyevich Bugrov and Mikhail Aleksandrovich Kiselev, *Естественное право и добродетель* [Natural Law and Virtue] (Ekaterinburg: Ural University Press, 2016), 146–171.

4 Pekarskiy, *История*, vol. 1, 671–689.

5 Frédéric Henri Strube de Piermont, *Observata diplomatico-historica de servis servorum* (Helmstedt: Paul Dietrich Schnorr, 1727).

6 Frédéric Henri Strube de Piermont, *Ebauche des lois naturelles et du droit primitif* (Amsterdam: J. Ryckhoff, 1744), iii.

7 Strube, *Ebauche*, iii.

8 Frédéric Henri Strube de Piermont, *Elégie sur la mort de l'illustrissime Nicolas Jerome Gundling* (Halle: Hendel, 1729).

9 Georges Dulac, 'Strube de Piermont,' at http://dictionnaire-journalistes.gazettes18e.fr/journaliste/758-frederic-strube-de-piermont (accessed on 1/11/2020). Dulac claims that Strube's name is not to be found in the register of the University of Halle.

but the fact is that Strube's approach to natural law does bear the stamp of Thomasius's passionate law. Strube maintained also in the same preface that he published the first preliminary version of his work on passions already in 1732.[10] Just a few copies of the first edition have survived. During these years of early professional experience, he also produced several short essays on international relations, which we will discuss later.[11] Between 1730 and 1738 he was already working for the Russian diplomatic service as secretary to the embassies in Vienna, London and Warsaw.[12] In Poland, he entered the service of Johann Ernst Biron, Duke of Courland, who was a favourite of the Empress Anna Ivanovna.

By then, he had learnt about the vacant professorship of law at the Academy of Sciences in Saint Petersburg, and decided to apply for this job. In spite of its name, the Imperial Academy of Sciences was not restricted only to research; it also included institutions of higher education. It also had a chair of jurisprudence, which had been given to the German scholar Johann Simon Beckenstein. However, Beckenstein was disappointed by the circumstances in Saint Petersburg and left the job in 1735. It was his position that Strube de Piermont wanted. It should be said that there was also a chair of ethics at the Academy, where another German scholar, Christian Friedrich Gross, lectured on natural law on the basis of Pufendorf's *De officio hominis et civis*. Finally, natural law was taught also at the Sokhoputniy Kadetten School, founded in 1731, where it was again a German scholar who was giving the courses, based on Johann Gottlieb Heineccius, Nikolaus Hieronymus Gundling and Adam Friedrich Glafey.[13]

In addition to that, some of the aristocrats in the Russian diplomatic service had also become familiar with secular natural law. Prince Antiochus Cantemir, who was serving as a diplomat in Western Europe for a couple of years, discussed natural law in his *Second Satire*, where he reproached the aristocrats for ignoring Grotius, Pufendorf and Roman law.[14] The high official and amateur

---

10 Frédéric Henri Strube de Piermont, *Recherche de l'origine et des fondemens du droit de la nature* (Amsterdam, 1732). Strube makes reference to it in the preface to the reedition of 1740 (xii).

11 [Frédéric Henri Strube de Piermont], 'Réflections d'un patriote allemand et impartial sur la demande de la garantie de la pragmatique sanction impériale,' in *Les intérêts présens et les prétensions des puissances de l'Europe*, ed. Jean Rousset de Missy (The Hague, Adrien Moutjens, 1734), vol. 1, 210–246; [Frédéric Henri Strube de Piermont], 'Examen des réflections d'un patriote allemand,' in: *Les intérêts*, vol. 1, 247–292. Frédéric Henri Strube de Piermont, 'Dissertation sur le droit de bienséance (1734),' in: Strube, *Ebauche*, [Supplement], 1–58.

12 Pekarskiy, *История*, vol. 1, 671.

13 Bugrov and Kiselev, *Естественное право*, 131–133.

14 Bugrov and Kiselev, *Естественное право*, 173.

historian Vasiliy Nikitich Tatishchev also stressed the significance of 'natural laws' (*законы естественного правила*) in his manuscript essay on education.[15] In his pedagogical philosophy, natural law was supposed to help achieve physical well-being because we feel good when we are sure that we have not hurt anybody. It is for this reason that we need the knowledge of 'natural laws,' according to Tatishchev. Natural law concepts also played a certain role in his famous *History of Russia from the Earliest Times*,[16] which he had already begun even before Strube came to Russia.

Finally, we should not forget that the works of Pufendorf had been translated into Russian in the time of Tsar Peter the Great to address a wider readership. It should be stressed, however, that the Tsar was not actually the driving force behind these translations. Most of his direct orders only concerned translations of existing laws and service codes of foreign countries, for he was interested in practical manuals. It was the governor of 'Ukraine,' Dimitriy Golitsyn, who first commissioned translations of theoretical works. It was upon his orders that the scholars of the Orthodox Mohyla academy in Kyiv produced Russian versions of Pufendorf's *De Officio* and fragments of Grotius's *De jure belli ac pacis* and John Locke's *Second Treatise*.[17] However, these translations were not printed. Peter the Great took an interest in these works in the last years of his reign and ordered the Most Holy Synod to translate Pufendorf's *De officio* and his book on the history of European states.[18] The translation of *De Officio* was printed in 1726, after the Tsar's death, and for a long time it remained the only printed Russian work on the subject.[19] As it later turned out, a certain Simon Kokhanovskiy, a teacher of poetics at the Kyiv Academy and a member of Golitsyn's team, translated Pufendorf's main work

---

15 Vasily Nikitich Tatishchev, *Разговор о пользе наук и училищ* [Dialogue on the Benefits of Sciences and Schools] (at http://pedagogic.ru/books/item/f00, accessed on 2/11/2020).

16 Vasily Nikitich Tatishchev, *История Российская с самых древнейших времен* [*History of Russia from the Earliest Times*] (Moscow: Imperatorskiy moskovskiy universitet, 1768), vol. 1.

17 Bugrov and Kiselev, *Естественное право*, 86–89.

18 Peter Pekarskiy, *Наука и литература в России при Ретри Великом* [Science and Literature in the Time of Peter the Great] (Saint Petersburg: Obshchestvennaya polza, 1862), vol. 1, 213–214; Sergei Ivanovich Nikolaev, 'Об атрибуции переводных памятников Петровской эпохи [On the Attribution of Translations from the Petrine Era],' *Русская литература* 30 (1988/1): 162–172; Sergei Ivanovich Nikolaev, *Литературная культура Петровской Епохы* [Literary Culture of the Petrine Era] (Saint Petersburg: Dmitriy Bulanin, 1996), 16; Bugrov and Kiselev, *Естественное право*, 92–93.

19 Samuel Pufendorf, *О должности человека и гражданина по закону естественному* [On the Duties of Man and Citizen according to the Law of Nature] (1726), ed. Viktor Makarovich Kruglov (Saint Petersburg: Nestor Istoria, 2011).

De jure naturae et gentium.[20] Regrettably, this accomplished translation was not printed either. Apart from that, Tsar Peter the Great indirectly supported the diffusion of natural law when he commissioned a German scholar, Heinrich von Huyssen of the University of Strasbourg, as preceptor to the Tsarevich Alexei Petrovich.[21] In his manuscript plan of studies, Huyssen recommended the works of Grotius, Pufendorf and Jean Domat for the lessons in law.

From this we see that Strube was entering a territory where secular natural law was already known, at least within the circles of Russian diplomats and German scholars at the two academies in Saint Petersburg. Some of the aristocrats mentioned were continuing their own reflections on natural law, while others purchased books by classical authors for their libraries. Later events showed that natural law was a handy and flexible tool that could be utilized in situations such as violent changes on the throne and declarations of war, but also for efforts to bind a despotic ruler by written rules. Furthermore, Russia was making ongoing efforts to systematize existing law, and secular natural law turned out to be useful in this enterprise.

3 At the Imperial Academy of Sciences (1738–1757)

In September 1738, Strube signed a contract with the Academy of Sciences, but only for five years.[22] He was hired as a 'professor of law and politics' (*профессор прав и политики*). In this capacity, Strube reedited his major work entitled *Recherche nouvelle de l'origine et des fondemens du droit de la nature* in 1740.[23] This francophone work, which was published under the auspices of the Imperial Academy of Sciences, was perceived as a scandal.[24] Surprisingly, the negative reviews did not make any impact on Strube's standing in Russia. He also produced several contributions to the journal *Supplements to the News*

20 Nikolaev, 'Об атрибуции,' 166; Bugrov and Kiselev, *Естественное право*, 138–139.

21 Bugrov and Kiselev, *Естественное право*, 122–123.

22 Pekarskiy, *История*, 671.

23 Frédéric Henri Strube de Piermont, *Recherche nouvelle de l'origine et des fondemens du droit de nature* (Saint Petersburg: Imprimerie de l'académie des sciences, 1740).

24 See the reviews in *Bibliothèque française* 30 (Amsterdam, 1740), Article II, 22–45; 31 (Amsterdam, 1740), Article I, 185–200; *Bibliothèque germanique* 99 (Amsterdam, 1740), Article VI, 113–133; 'Lettre aux éditeurs à l'occasion du nouveau Traité du Mr. de Piermont sur le droit naturel,' in *Journal helvétique* (Juin 1741, Neuchâtel), 536–547; *Bibliothèque raisonnée des ouvrages des savans de l'Europe*, 28, janvier-mars 1742 (Paris, 1742), Article IV, 75–91; *Nöthiger Beitrag zu den Neuen Zeitungen von den gelehrten Sachen*. Siebenter Theil (Leipzig, 1742), 375–384, 513–522.

(*Примечаня к ведомостям*) in 1739, just as other members of the academy did.[25] Most of these obligatory articles discussed theatre, and Strube utilized this opportunity to explore his favourite issue of passions. He discussed the power of the theatre in taming human passions, then the pantomime of the ancients and the distinction between wisdom and wit.[26] It appears that Strube pursued this topic even after he left the academy because as late as in 1742 he submitted to the academy an essay entitled *Schema actionum et passionum animae*.[27] However, he abandoned his academic position quite early because he joined the diplomatic mission of Count Piotr Grigoryevich Chernyshev to Copenhagen in 1741. The reason for his departure might also have been the efforts of the president of the academy to make him write an official history of the Turkish wars of Anna Ivanovna.[28] Moreover, his courses turned out to be a failure, for he could not speak Russian. He had few students, and even they petitioned the academy to be excused from attending his lectures.[29]

As secretary to Count Chernyshev, Strube went from Copenhagen to Berlin in 1742, where he was given another opportunity to rejoin the academy in Saint Petersburg. At the same time, the young Count Kirill Grigoryevich Razumovskiy was passing through Berlin on his grand tour, and Strube was commissioned to be his tutor in law. Since his new student was the prospective president of the Academy of Sciences, Strube could prepare the ground for a comfortable return. Even before his arrival in Russia, Strube, who never resigned his academic membership, was reaffirmed in his position at the Academy as a foreign corresponding member in September 1742. His former pupil Razumovskiy took up his position as president on 21 May 1746, and Strube followed him to Russia. On 1 July 1746 he signed a new contract as a 'professor of jurisprudence, i.e. natural rights and politics' (*профессор*

25 Butler, 'F.G. Strube,' 136. On the journal see Pavel Naumovich Berkov, *История русской журналистики XVIII. веку* [History of Russian journalism in the eighteenth century] (Moscow: Izdatelstvo akademiy nauk SSSR, 1958), 68.

26 *Материалы для истории академии наук* (1725–1743) [Documents on the History of the Academy of Sciences], vol. VI (Saint Petersburg: Imperatorskaya akademia nauk, 1890), 493. According to Butler, there are unedited manuscripts of his essays in the archives of the Academy of Sciences: Exercitatio philosophica de natura et usu actionum atque passionum animae; Exercitatio philosophica de feria et nexu actionum et passionum animae; Schema philosophicum actionum et passionum animae. See Butler, 'F.G. Strube,' 141.

27 Report on the activities of 1742 in: *Материалы для истории академии наук*, vol. IV, 557.

28 Pekarskiy, *История*, 673.

29 The petition is printed in: *Материалы для истории академии наук*, vol. IV, 207; Feldstein, *Главные течения*, 152.

юриспруденции то есть прав натуральных и политики).[30] In addition, he was also charged with the duties of secretary for French, German and Latin.

Before his return to Russia Strube had published the final version of his central work, *Ebauche des loix naturelles*, in 1744, and there already styled himself as a member of the Imperial Academy of Sciences of Saint Petersburg.[31] This edition did not provoke any hostile reactions, which may be explained by the public focus on the ongoing War of the Austrian Succession. It included also his juvenile essay on international relations of 1734[32] and one of his essays on the passions of the soul from 1739.[33]

Since the Imperial Academy of Sciences underwent a deep structural reform, which was regulated in the new *Réglement* of 1747, Strube saw his duties specified by the new rules. It was his obligation to teach the 'laws of nations and of nature' (*натуралная и народная права*). Strube described the content of his course in a printed *Programme*, in which he regretted the focus on military education among the Russian aristocracy and underscored the importance of law and laws for the public service.[34] It is interesting to note that this *Programme* was bilingual, in Russian and in Latin. However, the structural reform of the Academy also forced him to decide about the position of natural law in the system of sciences. One conception, advanced by Gerhard Friedrich Müller, saw natural law as a part of philosophy, whereas the other conception, advanced by Johann Daniel Schumacher, considered the same discipline as a part of jurisprudence. The discussion also attended to the practical question of whether Strube should also teach the laws of Russia, or just abstract natural law. Strube responded to this question with an unpublished memorandum[35] in which he argued that natural law is perceived in a

30 Pekarskiy, *История*, 676.

31 Strube, *Ebauche* [1744].

32 Strube, 'Dissertation.'

33 Frédéric Henri Strube de Piermont, 'Exercitatio philosophica de actionibus et passionibus animae,' in Frédéric Henri Strube de Piermont, *Recherche nouvelle de l'origine et des fondemens du droit de nature* (Saint Petersburg: Imprimerie de l'académie des sciences, 1740) [Supplements], 59–121.

34 [Frédéric Henri Strube de Piermont], *Программа, в которой равную пользу военной и судебной науки показывает; и купно желающих упражняться в основательнейшем учении на свои лекции призывает Фридрих Генрих Штрубе* [Programme which shows the equal benefit of the military and the legal science. Those who wish to exercise themselves together are invited by Frédéric Heinrich Strube] (Saint Petersburg: Imperatorskaya akademia nauk, 1748).

35 Bugrov and Kiselev, *Естественное право*, 155.

different light by a philosopher and by a lawyer, but he sided with the view that he should teach this discipline as a part of jurisprudence. He offered, however, to add research in Russian law because he believed that holders of chairs at faculties of law usually discuss the law valid in the country where they live. He believed that his enterprise might be useful because existing laws should comply with natural law.

Maybe it was this dilemma that prompted Strube to ask the Chancellery of the Academy for an assignment to draft a compendium of Russian laws. The Academy gave him this assignment, but he did not manage to bring the project to completion before the deadline. When his four-year contract of 1746 expired, Strube applied for 'the status of a Russian subject' on 27 May 1750.[36] After his application was accepted, he enrolled in Russian service permanently. Since it turned out that his work on the compendium of Russian laws did not make any progress, Strube was relieved of his duties as secretary in 1749 to focus on his most important task. Besides, the scope of his project was narrowed because it turned out that the original plan of a comprehensive compilation of Russian laws would be too difficult. Now he just had to prepare a short compendium of Russian laws for the education of Russian youth. However, this job also took a long time, as Strube was still not able to read Russian sources unaided and needed assistance with his research as well as with the translation of his own text into Russian. In 1753 the Chancellery of the Academy ordered him to submit what he had and then took two years to read it. The final verdict was devastating. The manuscript was evaluated as insufficient and not suitable for the purpose of education. The manuscript of *Compendium juris rutheni* (*Short compendium of Russian laws*) actually contained interesting theoretical introductions, but the body of the work consisted merely of excerpts from various Russian laws from the Middle Ages to the present.[37]

Strube managed to hold his position at the Academy even after 1755, but he lost it definitively when he refused to act as translator of the francophone journal *Gazette de Saint Petersbourg*, which the academy was obligated to publish.[38] He actually wanted to influence the content as well; the position of a mere translator did not satisfy him. The chancellery dismissed him from its service in 1757.

36 Bugrov and Kiselev, *Естественное право*, 158.

37 The excerpts have been published as a supplement to Bugrov and Kiselev, *Естественное право*, 322–339.

38 Pekarskiy, *История*, 685–686; Butler, 'F.G. Strube,' 130; Bugrov and Kiselev, *Естественное право*, 166.

4 The Legislative Commission of 1754–1760 and after

By then, Strube was already testing natural law in practice because he had become a member of the small commission for the new compilation of Russian laws that was established by the Senate in 1754.[39] The commission, headed by Count Peter Ivanovich Shuvalov, had explicit theoretical aims similar to parallel efforts in Bavaria, Prussia, and the Habsburg monarchy. The purpose of the reform was to 'render laws clear' and systematize them.[40] Since the body had only eight members, it may be assumed that Strube was supposed to be the main theoretical mind of the project, which drew on new principles of divine and natural law.[41] His efforts were not without results.

He presented a theoretical outline of his work in an address entitled *Discourse on the origin and changes of Russian laws* to the Imperial Academy of Sciences in 1756.[42] This address was the beginning of a new period in his research. It was his contribution to the debate about the origin of the Russians, and also the beginning of his criticism of Montesquieu. The *Compendium of Russian laws*, on which he had been working, was perhaps meant to provide solid ground for reforms, but Strube's failure in this field also jeopardized his position on the Commission. In 1760, the membership of the commission was altered. The erudite senator Roman Illarionovich Vorontsov entered the Commission and soon took over its intellectual leadership. Wishing to make it operational, Vorontsov dismissed three members, including Strube. The change of personnel was perhaps part of a coup by Vorontsov's party against the supporters of the Shuvalovs.[43]

However, this was not the end of Strube's influence within the Commission, nor the end of his engagement with Montesquieu. The Commission continued without him, but when Empress Catherine II summoned a new Legislative Commission in 1767, the members recalled Strube's com-

39 Oleg Anatolevich Omelchenko, *Кодификация права в России в период абсолютной монархии (вторая половина XVIII. века)* [Codification of Law in Russia in the Period of the Enlightened Monarchy (Second Half of the eighteenth Century)] (Moscow: Redaktsyonno-izdatelskiy sovet VYUZI, 1989), 7–29; Bugrov and Kiselev, *Естественное право*, 176.

40 Omelchenko, *Кодификация*, 16.

41 Omelchenko, *Кодификация*, 27–28.

42 Frédéric Henri Strube de Piermont, *Discours sur l'origine et les changements des lois russiennes* (Saint Petersburg: Imprimérie de l'académie impériale, 1756).

43 See Omelchenko, *Кодификация*, 18.

pilation of Russian laws and took it as their starting point.[44] He was also asked to write a francophone summary of his manual under the title *Introduction aux loix modernes de l'empire de Russie*,[45] which is, however, not extant.

Strube himself pursued his polemic against Montesquieu in further writings. Even before his dismissal from the Commission, he published the famous *Lettres russiennes*, in which he sought to provide an alternative explanation of the spirit of Russian laws, defend serfdom and engage with Montesquieu's views on principles.[46]

His destiny after 1760 is unclear. Ever since Pekarskiy's fundamental biography of 1870[47] it was believed that he entered the Collegium of Foreign Affairs, i.e. ministry of foreign affairs, and continued his work as a translator and propagandist. However, Mikhail Kiselev in his recent monograph on natural law in Russia pointed out the fact that Strube's collaboration with the Collegium did not start until 1771.[48] When he entered the service of the ministry, he reedited his old work on passionate natural law once again, now under the title *Catéchisme de la nature*.[49] After he retired, he published a tract on the origin of the Russians, which was his final contribution to the old debate discussed among German scholars in Saint Petersburg in the middle of the century.[50] The date of his death is not certain, but it is believed that he passed away around 1790.

44 Aleksander Sergeyevich Lappo-Danilevskiy, *Собрание и свод законов Российской империи, составленные в царствование императрицы Екатерины II*. [Collection and Compilation of Laws of the Russian Empire, compiled during the Reign of Empress Catherine II] (Moscow: Librokom, 2011, 1st edition 1897), 48.

45 Pekarskiy, *История*, vol. 1, 687.

46 [Frédéric Henri Strube de Piermont], *Lettres russiennes* ([Saint Petersburg], 1760).

47 Pekarskiy, *История*, vol. 1, 686.

48 Bugrov and Kiselev, *Естественное право*, 169; In a letter from 1779 reprinted by Pekarskiy, Strube complains that he had been working for the Collegium for four years, which would set 1774 as the beginning of his employment. See Pekarskiy, *История*, 686.

49 Frédéric Henri Strube de Piermont, *Catéchisme de la nature, ou l'on a taché de mettre dans un plus grand jour les fondemens de la jurisprudence naturelle, de la morale strictement due et de la politique privée* (Saint Petersburg, 1774?). The work is known to exist on the basis of Pekarskiy's biography, but no copy of it has yet been located.

50 Frédéric Henri Strube de Piermont, *Dissertation sur les anciens Russes par F. H. S. D. P.* (Saint Petersburg, 1785). Translated into Russian by Lev Pavlovskiy as *Рассуждение о древнихъ Россиынахъ учиненное Ф. Г. С. Д. П.* [Reflection on the Ancient Russians, written by F. H. S. d. P.] (Moscow: Universitatskaya typographia, 1791).

5 Strube's Passionate Natural Law

We will now reconstruct his theory of passionate natural law as it appeared in its mature form in the *Ebauche des loix naturelles* [*Laws of nature delineated*] of 1744.[51] In this conception, passions are literally part of law; they are the driving force which somehow impels humans to compose their human laws. Strube himself suggested that he was merely removing contradictions inherent in the system of Pufendorf, who allegedly based his natural law on self-love, and developing the system of Christian Thomasius and Adam Friedrich Glafey, who were sceptical about the power of human reason.[52] Strube did not reject Scripture but questioned the common understanding of biblical moral commands. He believed that our understanding of what is moral changes over time because morality is defined by the 'Great Law of preserving Mankind' and each historical period requires us to adopt different means to attain this moral end. He gave the example of public nudity and incest, which are now considered as immoral, but in ancient times when human beings were few, people would walk around naked, and when the survival of mankind required it, even the Bible approved of incestuous relationships.[53]

His advocacy of the passion-based natural law basically followed two aims. Firstly, he sought to weaken the belief in the power of reason, which was in his view a totally passive element, unable to incite us to any acts.[54] He proved this with references to the sceptical French Jesuit Pierre-Daniel Huet[55] and the anti-Cartesian naturalist poet Madame de Deshoulières,[56] but also with reference to Locke's *Essay*.[57] Secondly, he sought to refute conceptions which argued that our moral judgement must be based on a rule. Thinkers like Pufendorf[58] believed that we needed a rule to judge what is good or evil, because without a rule there is not even such an elementary distinction.

51 Strube, *Ebauche* [*1744*].

52 Strube, *Ebauche*, xiii–xv and 7–10. It should be noted that Strube made references only to Christian Thomasius, *Institutiones jurisprudentiae divinae* (1688), and not to *Fundamenta juris naturae et gentium* (1705).

53 Strube, *Ebauche*, xvi.

54 Strube, *Ebauche*, v.

55 Pierre-Daniel Huet, *Traité philosophique de la foiblesse de l'Esprit humain* (Amsterdam: Pierre du Sauzet, 1723).

56 See John J. Conley, 'Deshouières, Antoinette Ligier de la Garde,' in *Internet Encyclopedia of Philosophy*, at iep.utm.edu/deshouli/ (accessed on 9/11/2020).

57 Strube, *Ebauche*, 34–35.

58 Strube, *Ebauche*, xi–xiv. See Samuel Pufendorf, *De jure naturae et gentium libri octo. Editio secunda* (Frankfurt am Main: Johann Philip Andreae, 1684), book 1, ch. 2, § 6.

Unlike many religious and conservative thinkers who also repudiated this rule-based approach,[59] Strube sought to 'extract the general notions of just and unjust from the foundations of human nature.'[60] He believed in the psychological discoveries of Claude Perrault, who described the connections between ideas which he called 'associations,' but also in the philosophy of John Locke.[61] These thinkers explained the physical transmission of a sensation to become an idea. It is actually remarkable that Strube also drew on a wide range of writers of fiction and journals which far exceeded the narrow circle of natural law experts. His sources even included the religious sceptics Pierre Gassendi, Pierre Charron, Pierre Bayle, the *Spectator* (in French), and Pope's poems (in French). He also made frequent reference to the religious thinkers Nicolas Malebranche and William Wollaston, from whom he borrowed the title of his book.[62] He even referred to the philosophy of Confucius as rendered by the Flemish Jesuit Philippe Couplet.[63] To sum up, his passion-based natural law drew on French antagonists of Descartes, on German natural law theories and on French religious sceptics. What united them was their doubts about the power of human reason.

In accordance with a pessimistic view of man, Strube refuses to take the prelapsarian innocent man as the subject of natural law and the 'golden age' as the original state of man (*état de perfection*).[64] He admits only corrupted man, as Luther and Melanchthon did, but silently rejects Melanchthon's explanation

59 For discussions of tensions related to rule-based ethical judgements see Knud Haakonssen, *Natural Law and Moral Philosophy. From Grotius to the Scottish Enlightenment* (Cambridge: Cambridge University Press, 1996); Jerome Schneewind, *The Invention of Moral Autonomy. A History of Modern Moral Philosophy* (Cambridge: Cambridge University Press, 1998).

60 Strube, *Ebauche*, xii. 'Mais ce sont les premiers Principes, les notions générales du juste et de l'unjuste, que je tâche de tirer du fond de la Nature humaine.'

61 Strube, *Ebauche*, xix. See Claude Perrault, 'Des sens extérieurs,' in: *Oeuvres diverses de physique et de méchanique de M. C. P. Perrault* (Leiden: Pierre van der Aa, 1721), 517–683; John Locke, *An Essay Concerning Human Understanding*, ed. Pauline Phemister (Oxford: Oxford University Press, 2008).

62 In the index of names in Strube's book, Wollaston's '*The Religion of Nature Delineated*' is translated as '*Ebauche de religion naturelle.*'

63 Philippe Couplet, *Confucius Sinarum philosophus, sive scientia sinensis latine exposita* (Paris: Daniel Horthemel, 1687). Strube (on page 40) refers to a French translation titled '*L'Extrait de Confucius*,' which appears only in Jean Barbeyrac's preface to his translation of Samuel Pufendorf's *Le droit de la nature et des gens* (Amsterdam and Paris: Briasson, 1734), vol. 1, xl.

64 Strube, *Ebauche*, xv, and 25–27.

of natural law as remaining *notitiae* of divine wisdom inside us.[65] However, Strube needs to show human agents as capable of making and understanding law, even though he did not believe that the reason of the postlapsarian humanity was strong enough to fulfill this task. He believed that people are able to understand their 'Destination,' but their reason does not suffice to uncover the proper means to attain it.[66] He solves this quandary by claiming that only some sages, such as Socrates, preserved the original integrity, and implies that mankind may learn principles of natural law from them. Since this concession would still not be enough to explain how unreasonable human beings would be able to understand law, Strube turns to passions, which are the only surviving original urges in humans. In defiance of Descartes, Strube treats passions literally as innate principles which drive us to save ourselves, while our reason merely regulates our behaviour to others.[67] In order to prevent a conflict between reason and passions, Strube argues that man needs harmony to live. His proof of the value of harmony is the German phrase '*mit sich selbst einig sein*,' which has a positive meaning.[68] He also added a metaphysical belief in the existence of a 'trick of nature' that we will discuss below, in connection with the power of reason and passions.

Strube basically understood natural law as divine commands transmitted through Nature, not as human inventions, and when he set to define the essential parts of law, he was still speaking about notions that surpassed the human world, and not about parts of man-made laws. While other thinkers after Pufendorf were already speaking about punishment as a necessary part of an accomplished law,[69] Strube defined the three essential parts of an accomplished law as follows:

---

65 Merio Scattola, *Das Naturrecht vor dem Naturrecht. Zur Geschichte des 'ius naturae' im 16. Jahrhundert* (Tübingen: Max Niemeyer Verlag, 1999), 39–40, 42–47, 84, 89; Mads Langballe Jensen, *A Humanist in Reformation Politics. Philipp Melanchthon on Political Philosphy and Natural Law* (Leiden: Brill, 2020), 99.

66 Strube, *Ebauche*, 35.

67 Strube, *Ebauche*, 50.

68 Strube, *Ebauche*, xvii and 51.

69 Pufendorf, *De jure naturae et gentium*, book I, ch. 6, § 14. In this passage Pufendorf stipulates that a law is complete when it includes not only the proposition describing 'quid faciendum quidve ommittendum,' but also the punishment that is incurred by the offender who violates the law ('eaque pars solet vocari sanction'). Before Pufendorf, Hobbes had proposed that the punishment should be a part of law, but he made this proposition only in a passing remark about the proprieties which differentiate 'civil laws' from 'laws of nature.' (See Thomas Hobbes, *Leviathan*, ed. Richard Tuck (Cambridge: Cambridge University Press, 2005), 185 [= book II, ch. 26, § 4].)

(1) *intérêt commun et des principes sûrs et invariables* (i.e. they guarantee harmony),
(2) *un Être et autorité à la donner* (i.e. there must be a lawgiver),
(3) *des êtres réunis et reduits à la recevoir* (i.e. there must be someone to receive the law).[70]

The detailed elaboration of these essential parts of law in the following chapters repeats the simple idea that humans had been created by God and they received natural laws in the form of passions which were preserved even after the Fall. Yet Strube comes dangerously close to the idea that humans had been created good by God and corrupted themselves in civilization. He corroborates this principle with historical examples of the ancient Scythians and the recent fate of the Amerindians.[71] Strube regrets the barbaric acts committed against the inhabitants of the Americas, and with reference to the *Histoire morale des iles Antilles* argues that Europeans introduced '*crimes et déreglemens*' there.[72] In spite of this Rousseauist turn, Strube refuses to consider man in the state of innocence as his starting point, just as he refused to consider the reestablishment of an '*état de perfection*' as the goal of his natural law theory. Even though Christian Wolff, who was writing at the same time as Strube, returned to the idea of a '*homo integer*' as the bearer of natural law,[73] Strube did not seek to establish 'any kind of a society of perfect and uncorrupted humans.'[74] The moral agent he considers must simply be a person healthy enough to be able to exercise the basic bodily functions that make natural laws possible.

In terms of the formal properties of a law, Strube did say that law must have a proposition stating what we want and must be backed up by force.[75] Yet he did not go on to state that there must be a defined sanction, a punishment. The aim of the laws is, in his view, to assist us in achieving our self-preservation (*conservation*). The oddity of his way of thinking is revealed in what he understood as the 'publication' of laws.[76] While other thinkers meant 'publication' as

70 Strube, *Ebauche*, 5–11.
71 Strube, *Ebauche*, 23.
72 Strube, *Ebauche*, 23; [Charles de Rochefort], *Histoire naturelle et morale des iles Antilles de l'Amerique* (Rotterdam: Arnould Leers, 1658).
73 Christian Wolff, *Jus naturae methodo scientifica pertractatum* (Frankfurt am Main and Leipzig: Renger, 1740), vol. 1, § 75–§ 77. See Ivo Cerman, '"Universal Human Rights" and Social Compact in Christian Wolff,' *Jahrbuch der österreichischen Gesellschaft zur Erforschung des 18. Jahrhunderts* 31 (2016): 123–146.
74 Strube, *Ebauche*, 27. '[*U*]*ne espèce de société composée d'hommes parfaits ou non corrompus.*'
75 Strube, *Ebauche*, 11.
76 Strube, *Ebauche*, 34.

rendering the text of the law public by writing, or another form of announcement, Strube believed natural law was 'published,' i.e., made manifest, by the passions that drive our behaviour.[77] He did not fail to note that these were not only good ones.

In his view, human passions can be reduced to two classes: first, *passions principales*, which are *amour* (love) and *haïne* (hate). After these follow, secondly, *passions concomitantes* which intensify the principal passions.[78] The *amour propre*[79] is the strongest of all passions, and it also gives us the strongest pleasure and satisfaction. This is why Strube concluded that all kinds of hate are actually disguised *amour propre*.

Now this would mean that Strube was advocating immoral behaviour, but he was trying to explain how submission to seemingly evil passions makes us do good. He believed it is a trick of Nature which makes us act for our *amour propre* to achieve pleasure (or satisfaction for our own interest), but thereby arranges that we do good unknowingly. There is even a 'chain of interests' (*liaison d'intérêt*) arranged by Nature which manipulates us to achieve Harmony.[80] In seeking our own pleasure for our *amour propre*, we do good for a common benefit.[81]

This passion-based approach would conflate the science of law and the medical science of human anatomy, so Strube had to differentiate between the two areas. He emphasized that 'natural law' (*droit naturel*) is a complex of laws, and not just individual laws (*lois naturelles*). In so doing, he secured a specific area of study for legal sciences, for whereas the anatomical origin of passions could be seen as the task for a medical scientist, the reconstruction of their reciprocal systemic relations was the task for a legal scientist. His definition of this specific complex is reminiscent of the geometrical method

---

77 Yet Strube argues (on page 9) that he borrowed this idea from Glafey's *Droit de Raison, Liv. II, Chap. II, § 23*, which appears to be Adam Friedrich Glafey, *Vernunft- und Völckerrecht* (Frankfurt am Main and Leipzig: Christoph Riegel, 1723), 216.

78 Strube, *Ebauche*, 39–40.

79 It should be noted that French of the seventeenth and eighteenth centuries distinguished between a positive *amour de soi*, and a selfish negative *amour propre*. Even though both could be translated as 'self-love' they had different meanings. See Jacques Voisine, 'Amour de soi/amour propre,' in *Dictionnaire de Jean-Jacques Rousseau*, ed. Raymond Trousson and Frédéric S. Eigeldinger (Paris: Honoré Champion, 2006), 32–33; Patrick Riley, *The General Will before Rousseau. The Transformation of the Divine into the Civic* (Princeton, NJ: Princeton University Press, 1986).

80 Strube, *Ebauche*, 51 and 56.

81 Strube, *Ebauche*, 56–60.

of deriving natural law from a highest principle[82] because he proceeds to define it by one general definition. 'Precepts or rules which Nature, or rather God himself, prescribed to us by means of passions, about what we ought to do, or forbear, regarding everything that corresponds to these rules.' The second meaning of natural law was '[e]verything that corresponds to these rules.'[83]

Our acting upon these rules is not secured by reason, according to Strube, but by passions. As we have mentioned, reason is a completely passive factor, incapable of giving us laws, but capable of interpreting those we already have.[84] Passions move us through pangs of conscience (*remords vifs*) and the motions of the conscience function as punishments and rewards (*punitions et recompenses*).[85] Conscience (*La Conscience*) is understood as the ability to choose by comparing our actions with the innate rules.[86] Strube does not hesitate to infer some practical rules of moral conduct which imply that good conscience and inner calm are the criteria of moral conduct.[87] Even though it would seem that Strube was an advocate of Stoicism, his passionate conception made him actually reject this school of thought because the Stoics appreciated apathy, i.e. the status of being free of passions.[88]

The person as the subject of law has 'duties' (*devoirs*) and 'powers' (*pouvoirs*), which are set within the framework of relations to oneself and to others. This framework does not include the relation to God. Strube's understanding of duties and rights is based on the recognition that we live naturally in a state of life (*l'état de vie*), liberty (*l'état de liberté*) and perfection (*l'état de perfection*)[89] and we are naturally obligated to preserve these three statuses. In his description of 'duties to ourselves' (*devoirs envers nous même*) Strube derives them from a core of inalienable goods which we are obligated to hold. These are 'life, liberty and honesty' (*la vie, la liberté, la honnêteté*),[90] which is a

82 See Wolfgang Röd, *Geometrischer Geist und Naturrecht. Methodengeschichtliche Untersuchungen zur Staatsphilosophie im 17. und 18. Jahrhundert* (München: Verlag der Bayerischen Akademie der Wissenschaften, 1970).

83 Strube, *Ebauche*, 62. 'Préceptes ou règles que la Nature, ou plutot Dieu même, nous a préscrites par le moyen des passions, sur ce qu'il nous convient de faire, ou de ne pas faire, pour tout ce qui est conforme à ces règles. Tout ce qui est conforme à ces règles.'

84 Strube, *Ebauche*, 67.

85 Strube, *Ebauche*, 70.

86 Strube, *Ebauche*, 69.

87 Strube, *Ebauche*, 70.

88 Strube, *Ebauche*, 11; 39.

89 Strube, *Ebauche*, 71–75.

90 Strube, *Ebauche*, 75–84.

conception strongly reminiscent of Grotius's account of inalienable goods in *De jure belli ac pacis*.[91] The duty to respect these inalienable goods in others is the basis of his description of 'duties to others' (*devoirs envers les autres*). It compels us to comply with the principle 'not to deprive others of what belongs to them, nor harass them'(*ne pas les priver de ce qui leur appartient, ni les troubler en ce qu'ils font*).[92] If inalienable goods are at stake, then we may speak of 'perfect right' (*droit parfait*). Life, honour and comfortable life (*vie, l'honneur, les commodités de la vie*) are the basis of our imperfect 'duties of humanity' (*offices de l' humanité*).[93]

His application of this category of duties on human society starts with the relationship between man, wife and their children and only then proceeds to relations to our neighbours. The idea of applying the rules of natural law on relations between married partners turns to a discussion of incestuous relationship. Strube believes that even here the aim is to secure the conservation of mankind by producing offspring for the common benefit, but he asks also whether Nature wills us to match people inside the family, which is a practical and effective way of making couples.[94] However, he reveals that Nature arranged that siblings would not fall in love with each other because they would know each other's faults from early childhood. This trick of Nature secures that incestuous relationships would not even start. Strube does not, however, explain why incestuous relationships should be immoral. What is also puzzling is the fact that the application of natural law to neighbours is not general; in fact, Strube always speaks only about specific pairs of categories (e.g. the relationship between the rich and the poor, or between the superior and the inferior).

While this account was all about duties, and not about empowerments, Strube applied 'powers of man' (*pouvoirs de l'homme*) only to explain our power over things (*les choses*). He did not utilize them as a general category to be applied to relations in a society of equal citizens. The 'empowerments' (*pouvoirs*) of which he was speaking pertained only to property relations among family members (e.g. community of goods between man and wife, inheritance *ab intestato*), but not to property relations in general. His narrative about the power over oneself (*pouvoir de l'homme sur lui-même*) and one's neighbours (*pouvoirs de l'homme sur ses semblables*) resulted in a defence of

91 Hugo Grotius, *De jure belli ac pacis* (1625), ed. P.C. Molhuysen (Leiden: A.W. Sejthof, 1919), 328 (II.17.§ 2).

92 Strube, *Ebauche*, 86.

93 Strube, *Ebauche*, 89–90.

94 Strube, *Ebauche*, 97–100.

serfdom (*servitude*) because he suggested that people subjected to someone's power should be treated as goods.[95] This was unusual with German natural law thinkers who used the metaphor of the social contract, because they argued that people in the state of nature were equal and only the transition into the civil state turned some of them into serfs, war captives, etc. However, Strube did not recognize any transition of this kind in his naturalistic conception, which is why he considered the subjection of serfs as a natural condition.

This conception of law which understood legal rules as natural phenomena, and actually discussed only subjective duties and powers, failed to provide rules for determining the limits between individual empowerments. In this regard, Strube offered the very traditional explanation that our duties had to be measured by their relation to the aim, and that the aim was the 'general conservation of mankind.'[96] However, he did not provide any rule for relations between the subjects and the sovereign because his work did not include any sections on public law. He only suggested a scale of aims which should be used in case of a conflict between duties. Duties to others which support the common benefit take priority over duties supporting merely individual benefits, and the last place is taken by duties concerning our comfort and luxury (*nos aises et bienséances*).[97]

Another remaining question was whether Strube accepted 'permissions' as a part of law – in other words, whether he recognized any legal rights. He admitted the existence of '*droit préceptif*' and '*droit permissif*,' even though he had some scruples against using these terms in French.[98] However, he denied the legal character of such a *droit permissif* because natural law may not permit anything that is not in compliance with the Laws of Nature. Permissions in natural law make no sense because natural law must be clear-cut, without any latitude.[99] In his view, permissions have their place in international law and in man-made civil laws.

95 Strube, *Ebauche*, 131–154 and 185.

96 Strube, *Ebauche*, 122. 'La proportion du rapport de nos devoirs avec la conservation commune des hommes.'

97 Strube, *Ebauche*, 124–125.

98 Strube, *Ebauche*, 127–128.

99 Strube, *Ebauche*, 128. '[C]omme les Lois de Nature décident généralement de ce que nous sommes en état de faire ou d'empêcher qu'il ne se fasse, et qu'il n'y a proprement rien indifférent, on sent aisement que l'epithète de permissif ne convient pas au droit naturel dans un sens rigoureux; vû que celui-ci ne peut rien permettre qui ne s'accorde exactement avec les Lois d'où il résulte.'

6 On International Law

Natural law tracts usually proceeded from individuals living in the state of nature to relations between citizens in a state and finally to relations between states. Strube limited his inquiry to the first two stages merged into one, but he did write some shorter tracts on questions of international law when he was involved in diplomatic service. In fact, he used his juvenile tract *Treatise on the aims of war and the right of occupation* (*Dissertation sur la raison de guerre et le droit de bienséance*) of 1734 in his mature works on natural law of 1740 and 1744[100] where it was appended as a supplement. For this reason, we may consider this essay as his interpretation of international law and discuss it here.

The essay was about the entitlement of great powers to seize the territory of neutral states. Strube approaches this question by deductive methods, which start with the obligation of self-preservation. To achieve this, we must sometimes act out of necessity, and only necessity gives rise to real rights.[101] In compliance with his strict conception of natural law, he remarked that care for one's own self-preservation should not be taken as a legal permission.[102] Necessity was in his view the 'fundamental rule of [international] law' (*règle fondamentale de droit*) from which he also derives the 'aim of war' (*raison de guerre*). In a phrase anticipating Montesquieu, Strube argues that necessity is 'the spirit of military laws' (*esprit des lois militaires*).[103]

This is also used in deriving the rules of '*bienséances*,' which is his term for a peaceful occupation. Can necessity justify the occupation of a neutral territory? Strube argues that 'peaceful occupations' are allowed, but only in cases of necessity, because then they are justified by care for self-preservation.[104] However, he sets two conditions that the occupying power must meet. The first one is that other great powers guaranteeing the neutral status must be informed about the intended move and asked for their consent.[105] Secondly, the occupying power is obligated to restitute the territory and repair damage after the war.[106] Indemnities are a matter of honesty and not of law, but they should be paid.[107]

---

100 Strube, *Recherche nouvelle*, 237–308; Strube, *Ebauche*, [Supplement], 1–58.
101 Strube, *Ebauche* [Supplement], 8.
102 Strube, *Ebauche*, [Supplement], 11.
103 Strube, *Ebauche*, [Supplement], 33.
104 Strube, *Ebauche*, [Supplement], 10.
105 Strube, *Ebauche*, [Supplement], 44.
106 Strube, *Ebauche*, [Supplement], 45.
107 Strube, *Ebauche*, [Supplement], 46–48.

He substantiated this rule by the example of Louis XIV's occupation of German territories during the Dutch War of 1672–78.[108] This was, in his view, an unjustified move because Louis XIV failed to inform other powers about his plan and did not repair the damage he did during the occupation. Louis XIV blackmailed the German princes by threats and abused the Peace Treaty of Münster of 1648 because he argued that it prohibited the Emperor and the princes from entering any alliances and getting involved in war. He provided promises of respect and restitution only after he effectually occupied the territories. In reality, the French king failed to live up to his obligations.

7 On Russian Laws

Strube was progressing from abstract essays on general principles to investigations of real Russian laws, just as conjectural histories evolved in investigations of real legal history. The beginning of this period of his career was his preoccupation with the debate about the origin of the Russians in the 1750s, to which he later added a polemic against Montesquieu and against his negative image of Russian laws and Russian serfdom.[109]

Strube expressed his conclusions about the origin of the Russians in his *Discourse on the origin and changes of Russian laws* (*Discours sur l'origine et les changemens des lois russiennes*) delivered at the Academy of Sciences on 6 September 1756.[110] He joined his German colleagues who believed that the Russians were originally the governing elite that came from Scandinavia. This theory is based on the twelfth-century chronicle *Tales of Bygone Years* (*Повесть временных лет*), but it is no longer accepted as true.[111] Strube's investigation proceeds from the assumption that Russia was founded by two different nations – the Russians, who came from Scandinavia, and the indigenous Slavs, whom he calls '*esclavons*.' The Russian laws originated from a

108 Strube, *Ebauche*, [Supplement], 51–58.

109 For this reason he has been included in some histories of abolitionism; see Carminella Biondi, *Ces esclaves sont des hommes. La lotta abolizionista e la letteratura negrofilia nella Francia del Settecento* (Pisa: Goliardica, 1979), 145. For more context see Peter Kolchin, 'In defense of servitude. American proslavery arguments and Russian proserfdom arguments 1760–1860,' *American Historical Review* 85 (1980): 809–827; Peter Kolchin, *Unfree Labor. American Slavery and Russian Serfdom* (Cambridge, MA: Harvard University Press, 1987), 157–194.

110 Strube, *Discours*.

111 Vladimir Seraphimovich Buzin, *Етнография восточных Славян* [Etnography of Eastern Slavs] (Petersburg: Nestor-Istoria, 2012), 7.

merger of the laws of both nations, which he proves by investigating parallels between medieval Russian laws and the laws of ancient Germanic tribes from Germany, plus Sweden and Denmark. The greatest difficulty for him is the question whether even the ancient Slavs had any laws so that they could also contribute to this amalgam. He proves the existence of ancient Slavic laws by analogy with other Slavic nations, which presumably must have had some laws.[112] The difficulty is that Strube does not provide any particular example of such a Slavic law and therefore does not conduct any comparison.

What was perhaps more important for the Legislative Commission of 1754 were his opinions on the subsequent evolution of laws. Strube believed that the main driving force behind continuous changes was the effort to stop the corrupt behaviour of judges. At one point, the Russian rulers even allowed a return to dueling because that was still a better and more impartial way of rendering justice than a court trial.[113] The ancient Russian laws were deficient in a particular way, for they allegedly did not have any regulations concerning public crime. Strube explained this lacuna by the fact that punishments for crimes such as high treason and rebellion were common knowledge and there was no need to write them down.[114] Regrettably, the efforts to stop corruption were futile and laws continued to become complicated, and therefore the *Sobornoe Uloženie* (*Council Code*) of 1649 was issued to render laws clear. Since this last attempt also failed, the new Commission, of which Strube was a member, was asked to reform the laws. Strube's explanation of the necessary changes demonstrates that he hoped that the systematic nature of natural law would be helpful. The laws had to be cleansed of contradictions and rendered clear, and they also had to be based on general rules. Otherwise, the amendments would fail. Strube concluded:

> it was only with the help of the sciences and a theory of law, which people did not have at that time, that anyone could manage to discover and fix the rules which give laws the highest degree of perfection which they can have.[115]

Strube believed that the aim of the Commission was more than a compilation of laws, he believed they convened to draft a new Code. A logical structure

112 Strube, *Discours*, 4.
113 Strube, *Discours*, 25.
114 Strube, *Discours*, 29.
115 Strube, *Discours*, 37. 'Mais ce n'est qu'à l'aide des sciences et de la théorie du droit dont on manquoit alors, que l'on peut parvenir à decouvrir et à fixer ces vues et ces règles, qui donnent aux loix le plus haut degré de perfection dont elles sont susceptibles.'

of general rules would make it possible for judges to derive conclusions for particular cases and render the Code general, so that it would cover all the possible cases. His reasoning shows that Russia was following the fashion of creating such systematic codes, which were being created in Central European monarchies.

Strube disclosed his interpretation of contemporary Russian laws in the unpublished *Short Compendium of Russian Laws* of 1755, which survives only in the Russian translation. So far, only an excerpt of the first theoretical sections has been published.[116] It repeated the same methodological aims that had been stated in Strube's previous works: rendering the laws clear and providing tools for their interpretations.[117] The Table of Content of the whole work, which has also been published by Mikhail Kiselev, demonstrates that theoretical reflections were to be discussed only in the first part, whereas the second part was to provide rules for actual Russian institutions. If the same structure were to be applied to the proposed collection of Russian laws, it would result in a kind of Constitution. The theoretical part of the *Compendium* provides very short definitions of rights and laws and then rights pertaining to persons and property. The exposition does not include any narrative of social contract or conjectural history of society, but it does contain an interesting classification of inhabitants into free and unfree persons.[118] It shows again that Strube was deviating from general precepts of modern natural law which stressed equality, whereas Strube applied the distinction between persons and slaves, which was common in Roman law. The section on property is divided into articles on individual estates, which is reminiscent of the instructions given to the Legislative Commission of 1754.[119] The same structure based on institutions of administration, army and justice is applied in the second part of Strube's *Compendium*.

The *Discours sur l'origine* also opened Strube's last research topic, which was his effort to refute Montesquieu's image of Russia. At the beginning of his address, he explains that he hoped to find inspiration in the works of great minds, but when he looked at Montesquieu's *De l'esprit des lois*, he recognized that the great thinker had false information about Russia. Montesquieu

116 Excerpts from the Russian version were published as a supplement in Frédéric Henri Strube de Piermont, 'Краткое руководство к Российским правам [1755]. Избранные фрагменты [A Short Compendium of Russian Laws, 1755. Selected Fragments],' in Bugrov and Kiselev, *Естественное право*, 321–341.

117 Strube, 'Краткое руководство,' 328–329.

118 Strube, 'Краткое руководство,' 334–335.

119 Omelchenko, *Кодификация*, 20–26.

claims there that commerce in Russia does not flourish because Russians are not allowed to export goods freely. [120] Strube argued that this was a false allegation[121] and decided that he would devote a whole book to explaining Montesquieu's errors.

This polemic was the subject matter of his *Lettres russiennes* of 1760.[122] They were conceived on the model of Montesquieu's *Lettres persanes* as a correspondence between two visitors to Russia who were supposed to have opposing views on Russian serfdom and despotism. Even though the basis of their discussion is the criticism of *De l'esprit des lois*, they actually digress from this topic into more general discussions on these two subjects. Considering the fact that both correspondents actually share the same opinions, the book is not in fact a dialogue but a coherent essay.

In his discussion of serfdom,[123] Strube uses the French word 'servitude,' which may mean slavery or serfdom but also the forced labour of convicts. He argues that servitude is good for some people who are too stupid to survive on their own and who are serfs by nature, in a similar way to what Aristotle maintained.[124] To the question of what servitude meant and how far the power of the master extended, Strube provided answers that went far beyond acceptable ideas at the time. Unlike other contemporary natural law thinkers, Strube defined servitude as the power of the master over the life and goods of the slave. He justified the power over the slave's life by the contention that correctional means are used only when the serf fails to discharge his duties, which means they are not used excessively. Servitude was, in his view, compatible with the laws of nature because it did not deprive the person of anything that Nature had given to them. Strube also believed that Montesquieu's opinions on the origin of servitude from war were old-fashioned and that he misled himself in his conclusion that servitude had never been useful. Strube maintained that forced labour as a punishment for people dangerous to society was a useful form of servitude.

Another question pertains to Montesquieu's assertion about the despotic nature of the Russian government. Strube argues that there is just as much liberty in Russia as in Western countries, and all the countries referred to by Montesquieu as despotic actually respect the private property of their

120 Montesquieu, *De l'esprit des lois*, book XXII, ch. 14.

121 Strube, *Discours*, 2.

122 Strube, *Lettres*.

123 Strube, *Lettres*, Lettre quatrième, 33–38, Lettre septième, 70–88.

124 Strube, *Lettres*, 80–81.

citizens. Strube implied that Western thinkers were misinformed about the Russian regime because they proposed limitations of despotism, not knowing that such institutions actually had existed for a long time. One anonymous author had suggested the establishment of the Senate, even though such an institution had existed in Russia from the time of Peter the Great onwards.[125] Strube agreed that the sovereign limited by fundamental laws was happier than a despot but maintained that Russia was actually a limited monarchy.[126] His exploration of civil liberty in well-known absolute monarchies such as Denmark, France or Spain led him to the conclusion that Russia was no worse than any of these countries. In the very important *Lettre douzième* Strube addressed the question of the fundamental principles and embraced the Montesquieuan argument that the right principle is necessary to keep the state alive. However, unlike Montesquieu, he believed that such a principle – or a set of instruments – was always the same, and not different with each type of government.[127]

This question was developed in his discussion about the power of laws. Strube was apparently not enthusiastic about Montesquieu's decision to restrict 'fear' (*crainte*) only to despotic states because fear of punishments is an elementary instrument of law.[128] Montesquieu's belief that religious codes like the Koran in the Ottoman Empire could play a similar role to laws was erroneous. Strube argued that such religious Codes were still not as good juridical instruments as real Codes of civil law. Experience showed, Strube believed, that human nature needed punishments which were better incentives to good acts than positive counsels of religion. Religious codes such as the Koran do not produce such detailed and well-thought-out regulations as the Codes of law. In a provocative comparison of monarchy, despotism and republic Strube concluded that 'fear is the principle common to all governments.'[129] However, he also acknowledged that fear is a purely negative force which prevents people from doing evil but does not incite them to do good. For this reason, Montesquieu should not discourage rulers from employing a broader range of instruments inciting citizens to do good. Apart from honour and vir-

125 Strube, *Lettres*, 249–250.

126 See Bugrov and Kiselev, *Естесевенное право*, 207–229; Mikhail Aleksandrovich Kiselev, 'Montesquieu's Treatise De l'esprit des lois and fundamental Laws in Russia in the Early 1760s,' *Quaestio rossica* 5 (2017/4): 1131–1148. DOI 10.15826/qr.2017.4.271.

127 Strube, *Lettres*, 161–162.

128 Strube, *Lettres*, 165–166.

129 Strube, *Lettres*, 163. 'Crainte de peine est le principe commun à tous les gouvernements.'

tue, these should include also religion, prejudice and education.[130] Elaborating on Montesquieu's famous distinction between virtue, honour and fear as the moving principles of democracy, despotism and monarchy, Strube argued that virtue was necessary only in a democracy where all the citizens were lawgivers and for that reason needed to restrain themselves by virtue. Monarchies and despotic governments can actually subsist even without virtue, which means that civic virtue is not the fundamental value. What can be generalized, according to Strube, is honour, which appears to be necessary in all types of government. However, Montesquieu argued that Russians did not even have a word for '*honneur*,' and Strube felt compelled to explain that Russians actually did have the word '*tchest*' (*честь*), which had the same meaning.[131]

The defence of codes was already related to the final topic of the *Lettres russiennes*, which was the glorification of the Legislative Commission of 1754, established by Empress Elizabeth Petrovna and led by Count Peter Ivanovich Shuvalov. Strube was furious over Montesquieu's assertion that people in Russia easily would sell themselves into servitude because people in despotic monarchies would not esteem their own freedom.[132] The difference between liberty and servitude is not great in such states. Montesquieu drew his image of Russian laws from John Perry's account of Russia, which described the situation during the reign of Peter the Great.[133] Strube argued that not all people in Russia were serfs and that free persons possessed their property and fiefs. Actually, he believed that civil liberty in Russia existed. He also had to refute Perry's account as obsolete because Perry was not aware of the changes occurring after he left Russia. Strube provided the example of the way subjects were supposed to present their requests to the Tsar. While Perry argued that Peter the Great ordered that submitters of requests should be punished by capital penalty, the Tsar actually issued ordonnances in 1714, 1718 and 1722, the aim of which was to alleviate him and block unnecessary requests which prevented him from dealing with governmental duties. Strube was apparently writing in the good faith that the Commission of 1754 would produce a new Code for Russia, not yet knowing that he would be dismissed from this legislative body.

---

130 Strube, *Lettres*, 165–166. 'Je veux dire n'avoir recours non seulement à l'honneur et à la vertu, mais encore à la religion et à tous les préjugés favorables à la conservation des Etats et de se regler à ce sujet sur les circonstances.'

131 Strube, *Lettres*, 151.

132 Montesquieu, *De l'esprit*, book XV, ch. 6.

133 John Perry, *The State of Russia under the present Tsar* (London: Benjamin Tooke, 1716); French translation: *État présent de la Grande Russie ou Moscovite* (Paris: André Cailleau, 1718). Montesquieu makes references to Perry in *De l'esprit*, book III, ch. 8 (discussion on despotism), and book XV, ch. 6 (discussion on servitude).

8 Strube's Achievements and Impact

In 1990 William E. Butler argued in the conclusion to his seminal article on Strube that, 'an assessment of his influence in eighteenth-century Russia and Europe would be premature.'[134] Even though the Russian authors Mikhail Kiselev and Konstantin Bugrov in their comprehensive study of Russian natural law managed to put Strube in the context of Russian intellectual history, we could still argue that an assessment of Strube's achievement on a European scale would as yet be premature. The present article shows that a reconstruction of his natural law theory and reflections on the German and French contexts of his work open up for new questions which have not yet been answered.

The summary of his life provided above shows him as a cosmopolitan author who belonged to several cultural milieus and was employed in different professions. But this biography leaves many open questions. Not only are there as yet no details of his life after 1757 and until his also unknown date of death, but it is not clear what his connection to France actually was. As of now, it seems that he never stayed in the country, either as a student or as a diplomat. Yet he was writing mainly in French, and some historians have even considered him as part of the French Enlightenment. We have shown here the scandal provoked by his 1740 edition of *Recherche nouvelle*, but this topic needs more investigation. It is also not clear whether the scandal really went unnoticed in Russia, or whether it could have been responsible for his 'flight' from the Academy in 1741. It is finally not clear whether his dismissal from the Academy in 1757 and from the Legislative Commission in 1760 could have been caused by his discussions of Montesquieu and Russian despotism. Even though he sought to defend the Russian regime, he proceeded from the assumption that despotism was a bad thing.

On the other hand, it may be asked whether his naturalistic conception of natural law was connected with his effort to defend serfdom (*servitude*) and win the support of Russian rulers. Strube was one of the naturalistic thinkers who did not believe in the social contract and perceived social life as a continuation of natural relations. In his conception, the decisive transition was that from the prelapsarian innocent man to the fallen man of our times, not the subjection of humans to the sovereign. The question he asked was: what were the deepest natural sources of principles of justice in humans? – and his answer was that these were the passions which even fallen humanity retained,

134 Butler, 'F.G. Strube,' 136.

and which connected it to the prelapsarian stage. Reason, in his conception, had only a regulatory power, viz. to regulate the impulses of passions and produce human laws. However, the corollary of this naturalistic philosophy was not the 'preservation of natural liberty,' as with Physiocrats[135] and German 'passionate lawyers' from Göttingen,[136] but the subjection of some people as serfs. This is a philosophy which he started in his theoretical tracts on the foundation of natural law (of 1740 and 1744), and which he continued in his polemical *Lettres russiennes* of 1760. The only guarantee of justice in this system was belief in a trick of Nature which linked selfish personal interests to each other in such a way that individuals who would follow their '*amour propre*' would thereby do something for the common benefit.

His theories made an immediate impact in Germany and France. In Germany, Strube attracted the interest of the Göttingen school of passionate law, which saw itself as continuing the legacy of Christian Thomasius, just as Strube himself did. Johann Christian Claproth included Strube in the short history of natural law which he placed at the beginning of *Grundriss des Rechts der Natur* of 1749. Claproth's work had actually a similar title to that of Strube's work. In the historical survey at the beginning of the book, Claproth refers to Strube as 'one of the most important contemporary authors,' and places him on an equal footing with Johann Jakob Schmauss.[137] This eccentric author himself refers to Strube in the historical passage in his *Neues Systema des Rechts der Natur*[138] where he shows interest only in the theoretical part of Strube's work, but not in his defence of serfdom and in his contribution to Russian codification projects. Both Claproth and Schmauss remained silent on Strube's defence of serfdom, which had already been expounded in his theoretical tracts. This may explain why the Göttingen 'school of passionate law' evaluated Strube positively, even though he drew completely different conclusions from theirs.

In France, Strube's quest for the roots of justice that precede law attracted the interest of Denis Diderot who utilized Strube's results in the important

135 Dan Edelstein, *On the Spirit of Rights* (Chicago: Chicago UP, 2019); Thérence Carvalho, 'The Role of Physiocracy in the Birth of Human Rights,' *Opera historica* 21 (2020), 61–71.

136 Ere Nokkala, *From Natural Law to Political Economy: J. H. G. von Justi on State, Commerce and International Order* (Vienna: LIT Verlag, 2019), 66–71.

137 Johann Jakob Claproth, *Grundriss des Rechts der Natur* (Göttingen: Johann Wilhelm Schmidt, 1749), 15, § 27; Johann Jakob Claproth, *Principes du droit naturel, traduit de l'allemand* (Lausanne: J. Pierre Heubach, 1771), 25, § 27. Claproth also refers to Strube in several other places in his book.

138 Johann Jakob Schmauss, *Neues Systema des Rechts der Natur* (Göttingen: Van den Hoecks Witwe, 1754), 356, § 37.

entry 'Juste/injuste' of the *Encyclopédie*.[139] Here Diderot discusses Pufendorf's famous contention that if we need a rule to judge what is good or bad, then there is no difference between good or bad '*ante legem*.'[140] However, Pufendorf also contended that this 'law' must be issued by a superior, which might be either God or a human sovereign. Diderot was looking for a deeper source of justice that would be really natural. For this reason, he opted for a solution similar to Strube and argued that the real law of nature does not need to comply with a rule, but with the 'true essence' of human nature.[141] What is only puzzling from the point of view of the history of ideas is the fact that adhering to Strube's anti-Cartesian conception would require a return to a belief in innate principles.

Russia did not appreciate Strube's theory of passionate natural law, but his collections of Russian laws constituted a legacy. As it seems, his short compendium was used by the Legislative Commission of 1767 which was summoned by Catherine II. Strube's passionate defence of Russia against Montesquieu was not followed by the Russian intelligentsia either. While Strube maintained that Russia had all the institutions necessary for a limited monarchy, Count Mikhail Mikhailovich Shcherbatov, in his private reflections on the famous *Nakaz* (*Instruction*), which Catherine II issued for the Legislative Commission of 1767, expressed a more critical stance than the German scholar. Shcherbatov agreed that Russia had the Senate and other institutions, but he saw that these did not use their powers to limit despotism. In the eyes of the self-critical Russian thinker, Russia was still a despotic monarchy.[142]

139 Denis Diderot, 'Juste/injuste,' in: *Encyclopédie ou Dictionnaire raisonné des sciences, des arts et des métiers* (Paris, 1765), vol. 9, 86–87 (online: https://encyclopedie.uchicago.edu/, accessed on 10/11/2020). See Leland Thielemann, 'Diderot's Encyclopedic article on Justice: Its Sources and Significance,' *Diderot Studies* 4 (1963): 261–283; Anthony Burns, 'The Sources of the Encylopedia Article on Justice: A Reply to Prof. Thielemann,' *Diderot Studies* 16 (1986): 28–39.

140 Diderot made an error in his reference, the passage is in Pufendorf, *Jus Naturae et Gentium*, book I, ch. 2, § 6: 'non adparet, quo modo honestas aut turpitudo intelligi possit ante legem.'

141 Diderot, 'Juste/injuste,' 87. 'Concluons donc qu'une action qui convient ou ne convient pas à la nature de l'être qui la produit, est moralement bonne ou mauvaise.'

142 Mikhail Mikhailovich Shcherbatov, 'Замечания Щербатова на Болъшой Наказ Екатерины [Shcherbatov's Reflection on the Great Nakaz of Catherine],' in: Mikhail Mikhailovich Shcherbatov, *Избранные труды* [Selected Works] (Moscow: Rossiiskaya politicheskaya encyklopedia, 2011), 51–95. See Bugrov – Kiselev, *Естественное право*, 223–224.

Bibliography

Primary Sources

Bibliothèque française 30, Article II, 22–45, Amsterdam, 1740.

Bibliothèque française 31, Article I, 185–200, Amsterdam 1740.

Bibliothèque germanique 99, Article VI, 113–133, Amsterdam, 1740.

Bibliothèque raisonnée des ouvrages des savans de l'Europe, 28, janvier-mars 1742, Article IV, 75–91, Paris, 1742.

Claproth, Johann Jakob, *Grundriss des Rechts der Natur*, Göttingen: Johann Wilhelm Schmidt, 1749.

Claproth, Johann Jakob, *Principes du droit naturel, traduit de l'allemand*, Lausanne: J. Pierre Heubach, 1771.

Couplet, Philippe, *Confucius Sinarum philosophus, sive scientia sinensis latine exposita*, Paris: Daniel Horthemel, 1687.

Diderot, Denis, 'Juste/injuste,' in: *Encyclopédie ou Dictionnaire raisonné des sciences, des arts et des métiers*, vol. 9, 86–87, Paris, 1765 (online: https://encyclopedie.uchicago.edu/).

Glafey, Adam Friedrich, *Vernunft- und Völckerrecht*, Frankfurt am Main and Leipzig: Christoph Riegel, 1723.

Grotius, Hugo, *De jure belli ac pacis* (1625), ed. P.C. Molhuysen, Leiden: A.W. Sejthof, 1919.

Hobbes, Thomas, *Leviathan*, ed. Richard Tuck, Cambridge: Cambridge University Press, 2005.

Huet, Pierre-Daniel, *Traité philosophique de la foiblesse de l'Esprit humain*, Amsterdam: Pierre du Sauzet, 1723.

'Lettre aux éditeurs à l'occasion du nouveau Traité du Mr. de Piermont sur le droit naturel,' in *Journal helvétique* (Juin 1741, Neuchâtel), 536–547.

Locke, John, *An Essay Concerning Human Understanding*, ed. Pauline Phemister, Oxford: Oxford University Press, 2008.

Martini, Carl Anton, *De lege naturali positiones*, Wien: Joseph Kurzböck, 1762.

Martini, Carl Anton, *Lehrbegriff des Natur-, Staats und Völkerrechts*, vol. 1, Wien: Sonnleithnerische Buchhandlung, 1784.

Nöthiger Beitrag zu den Neuen Zeitungen von den gelehrten Sachen. Siebenter Theil, Leipzig 1742.

Perrault, Claude, 'Des sens extérieurs,' in: *Oeuvres diverses de physique et de méchanique de M. C. P. Perrault*, 517–683, Leiden: Pierre van der Aa, 1721.

Perry, John, *État présent de la Grande Russie ou Moscovite*, Paris: André Cailleau, 1718.

Perry, John, *The State of Russia under the present Tsar*, London: Benjamin Tooke, 1716.

Pufendorf, Samuel, *De jure naturae et gentium libri octo. Editio secunda*, Frankfurt am Main: Johann Philip Andreae, 1684.

Pufendorf, Samuel, *Le droit de la nature et des gens*, ed. Jean Barbeyrac, Amsterdam and Paris: Briasson, 1734.

Pufendorf, Samuel, *О должности человека и гражданина по закону естественному* (1726), ed. Viktor Makarovich Kruglov, Saint Petersburg: Nestor Istoria, 2011.

[Rochefort, Charles de], *Histoire naturelle et morale des iles Antilles de l'Amerique*, Rotterdam: Arnould Leers, 1658.

Schmauss, Johann Jakob, *Neues Systema des Rechts der Natur*, Göttingen: Van den Hoecks Witwe, 1754.

Strube de Piermont, Frédéric Henri, *Catéchisme de la nature, ou l'on a taché de mettre dans un plus grand jour les fondemens de la jurisprudence naturelle, de la morale strictement due et de la politique privée*, Saint Petersburg, 1774?.

Strube de Piermont, Frédéric Henri, *Discours sur l'origine et les changements des lois russiennes*, Saint Petersburg: Imprimérie de l'académie impériale, 1756.

Strube de Piermont, Frédéric Henri, 'Dissertation sur le droit de bienséance (1734),' in Frédéric Henri Strube de Piermont, *Ebauche des lois naturelles et du droit primitif*, [Supplement], 1–58, Amsterdam: J. Ryckhoff, 1744.

Strube de Piermont, Frédéric Henri, *Dissertation sur les anciens Russes par F. H. S. D. P.*, Saint Petersburg, 1785.

Strube de Piermont, Frédéric Henri, *Ebauche des lois naturelles et du droit primitif*, Amsterdam: J. Ryckhoff, 1744.

Strube de Piermont, Frédéric Henri, *Elégie sur la mort de l'illustrissime Nicolas Jerome Gundling*, Halle: Hendel, 1729.

[Strube de Piermont, Frédéric Henri], 'Examen des réflections d'un patriote allemand,' in *Les intérêts présens et les prétensions des puissances de l'Europe*, ed. Jean Rousset de Missy, vol. 1, 247–292, The Hague, Adrien Moutjens, 1734.

Strube de Piermont, Frédéric Henri, 'Exercitatio philosophica de actionibus et passionibus animae,' in Frédéric Henri Strube de Piermont, *Recherche nouvelle de l'origine et des fondemens du droit de nature*, [Supplements], 59–121, Saint Petersburg: Imprimerie de l'académie des sciences, 1740.

Strube de Piermont, Frédéric Henri, 'Краткое руководство к Российским правам [1755]. Избранные фрагменты,' in Konstantin Dimitriyevich Bugrov and Mikhail Aleksandrovich Kiselev, *Естественное право и добродетель*, 321–341, Ekaterinburg: Ural University Press, 2016.

[Strube de Piermont, Frédéric Henri], *Lettres russiennes*, [Saint Petersburg], 1760.

Strube de Piermont, Frédéric Henri, *Observata diplomatico-historica de servis servorum*, Helmstedt: Paul Dietrich Schnorr, 1727.

[Strube de Piermont, Frédéric Henri], *Программа, в которой равную пользу военной и судебной науки показывает; и купно желающих упражняться в основательнейшем учении на свои лекции призывает Фридрих Генрих Штрубе*, Saint Petersburg: Imperatorskaya akademia nauk, 1748.

Strube de Piermont, Frédéric Henri, *Рассуждениео древнихъ Россиынахъ учиненное Ф. Г. С. Д. П.* Transl. Lev Pavlovskiy, Moscow: Universitatskaya typographia, 1791.

Strube de Piermont, Frédéric Henri, *Recherche de l'origine et des fondemens du droit de la nature*, Amsterdam, 1732.

Strube de Piermont, Frédéric Henri, *Recherche nouvelle de l'origine et des fondemens du droit de nature*, Saint Petersburg: Imprimerie de l'académie des sciences, 1740.

[Strube de Piermont, Frédéric Henri], 'Réflections d'un patriote allemand et impartial sur la demande de la garantie de la pragmatique sanction impériale,' in *Les intérêts présens et les prétensions des puissances de l'Europe*, ed. Jean Rousset de Missy, vol. 1, 210–246, The Hague, Adrien Moutjens, 1734.

Tatishchev, Vasily Nikitich, *История Российская с самых древнейших времен*, Moscow: Imperatorskiy moskovskiy universitet, 1768.

Tatishchev, Vasily Nikitich, *Разговор о пользе наук и училищ*, at http://pedagogic.ru/books/item/f00.

Wolff, Christian, *Jus naturae methodo scientifica pertractatum*, Frankfurt am Main and Leipzig: Renger, 1740.

Secondary Sources

Biondi, Carminella, *Ces esclaves sont des hommes. La lotta abolizionista e la letteratura negrofilia nella Francia del Settecento*, Pisa: Goliardica, 1979.

Bugrov, Konstantin Dimitriyevich and Mikhail Aleksandrovich Kiselev, *Естественное право и добродетель*, Ekaterinburg: Ural University Press, 2016.

Burns, Anthony, 'The Sources of the Encylopedia Article on Justice: A Reply to Prof. Thielemann,' *Diderot Studies* 16 (1986): 28–39.

Butler, William E., 'F.G. Strube de Piermont and the Origins of Russian Legal History,' in *Russia in the Age of Enlightenment. Essays for Isabel de Madariaga*, ed. Roger Bartlett and Janet M. Hartley, 125–141, London: Palgrave Macmillan, 1990.

Buzin, Vladimir Seraphimovich, *Етнография восточных Славян*, Petersburg: Nestor-Istoria, 2012.

Cerman, Ivo, '"Universal Human Rights" and Social Compact in Christian Wolff,' *Jahrbuch der österreichischen Gesellschaft zur Erforschung des 18. Jahrhunderts* 31 (2016): 123–146.

Conley, John J., 'Deshouières, Antoinette Ligier de la Garde,' in *Internet Encyclopedia of Philosophy*, at iep.utm.edu/deshouli/.

Crocker, Lester G., *Nature and Culture. Ethical Thought of the French Enlightenment*, Baltimore: John Hopkins Press, 1963.

Dulac, Georges, 'Strube de Piermont,' at http://dictionnaire-journalistes.gazettes18e.fr/journaliste/758-frederic-strube-de-piermont.

Feldstein, Grigoriy Samuilovich, *Главные течения в истории науки уголовного права в России*, Yaroslav: Typographia gubernskogo pravlenya, 1909.

Grabar, Vladimir Emanuilovich, *Материалы к истории литературы международного права в России 1647–1917*, Moscow: Zercalo, 2003; 1st edition Moscow: Akademia nauk SSSR, 1958.

Haakonssen, Knud, *Natural Law and Moral Philosophy. From Grotius to the Scottish Enlightenment*, Cambridge: Cambridge University Press, 1996.

Jensen, Mads Langballe, *A Humanist in Reformation Politics. Philipp Melanchthon on Political Philosphy and Natural Law*, Leiden: Brill, 2020.

Kiselev, Mikhail Aleksandrovich, 'Montesquieu's Treatise De l'esprit des lois and fundamental Laws in Russia in the Early 1760s,' *Quaestio rossica* 5 (2017/4): 1131–1148. DOI 10.15826/qr.2017.4.271.

Kolchin, Peter, 'In defense of servitude. American proslavery arguments and Russian proserfdom arguments 1760–1860,' *American Historical Review* 85 (1980): 809–827.

Kolchin, Peter, *Unfree Labor. American Slavery and Russian Serfdom*, Cambridge, MA: Harvard University Press, 1987.

Lappo-Danilevskiy, Aleksander Sergeyevich, *Собрание и свод законов Российской империи, составленные в царствование императрицы Екатерины II.*, Moscow: Librokom, 2011, 1st edition 1897.

Материалы для истории академии наук (1725–1743), vol. VI, Saint Petersburg: Imperatorskaya akademia nauk, 1890.

Naumovich Berkov, Pavel, *История русской журналистики XVIII. веку*, Moscow: Izdatelstvo akademiy nauk SSSR, 1958.

Nikolaev, Sergei Ivanovich, *Литературная култьтура Петровской Епохы*, Saint Petersburg: Dmitriy Bulanin, 1996.

Nikolaev, Sergei Ivanovich, 'Об атрибуции переводных памятников Петровской эпохи,' *Русская литература* 30 (1988/1): 162–172.

Omelchenko, Oleg Anatolevich, *Кодификация права в России в период абсольютной монархии* (*сторая половина XVIII. века*), Moscow: Redaktsyonno-izdatelskiy sovet VYUZI, 1989.

Pekarskiy, Peter, *История императорской Академии наук в Петербурге*, Saint Petersburg: Imperatorskaya akademia nauk, 1870.

Pekarskiy, Peter, *Наука и литература в России при Ретри Великом*, Saint Petersburg: Obshchestvennaya polza, 1862.

Riley, Patrick, *The General Will before Rousseau. The Transformation of the Divine into the Civic*, Princeton, NJ: Princeton University Press, 1986.

Röd, Wolfgang, *Geometrischer Geist und Naturrecht. Methodengeschichtliche Untersuchungen zur Staatsphilosophie im 17. und 18. Jahrhundert*, München: Verlag der Bayerischen Akademie der Wissenschaften, 1970.

Scattola, Merio, *Das Naturrecht vor dem Naturrecht. Zur Geschichte des 'ius naturae' im 16. Jahrhundert*, Tübingen: Max Niemeyer Verlag, 1999.

Schneewind, Jerome, *The Invention of Moral Autonomy. A History of Modern Moral Philosophy*, Cambridge: Cambridge University Press, 1998.

Silnizki, Michael, *Geschichte des gelehrten Rechts in Rußland. Jurisprudencija an den Universitäten des Russischen Reiches 1700–1835*, Frankfurt am Main: Vittorio Klostermann, 1997.

Soboul, Albert, Guy Lemarchand, and Michèle Fogel, *Le siècle des Lumières. L'essor (1715–1750)*, Paris: Presses universitiares de France, 1977.

Thielemann, Leland, 'Diderot's Encyclopedic article on Justice: Its Sources and Significance,' *Diderot Studies* 4 (1963): 261–283.

Voisine, Jacques, 'Amour de soi/amour propre,' in *Dictionnaire de Jean-Jacques Rousseau*, ed. Raymond Trousson and Frédéric S. Eigeldinger, 32–33, Paris: Honoré Champion, 2006.

Index of Persons

Index of Places

Index of Subjects